Destination Tibet

Shangri-la, the Land of Snows, the roof of the world: for centuries the mysterious Buddhist kingdom of Tibet, locked away in its mountain fastness of the Himalaya, has exercised a unique hold on the imagination of the West. For explorers, imperialists and traders it was a forbidden land of treasure and riches. Dreamers on a spiritual quest have long whispered of a lost land steeped in magic and mystery.

When the doors were finally flung open in the mid-1980s, Tibet was in ruins. Between 1950 and 1970, the Chinese 'liberated' the Tibetans of their independence, drove their spiritual leader and some 100,000 of Tibet's finest into exile and destroyed most of the Tibetan cultural and historical heritage.

Today Tibetan pilgrims across the country are once again mumbling mantras and thumbing their prayer beads in chapels heavy with the acrid smell of incense and yak butter. A walk around Lhasa's lively Barkhor pilgrimage circuit is proof enough that the efforts of the communist Chinese to build a Brave New (Roof of the) World have foundered on the remarkable and inspiring faith of the Tibetan people. Tibet can truly claim to be on a higher plain.

For travellers, Tibet is without doubt one of the most remarkable places to visit in Asia. It offers fabulous monastery sights, breathtaking high-altitude treks, stunning views of the world's highest mountains and one of the most likeable peoples you will ever meet. But you are never far from the reality of politics. For anyone who travels with their eyes open, a visit to Tibet will be memorable, fascinating and even life-changing, but also a sobering and at times even saddening experience.

JANE SWEENEY

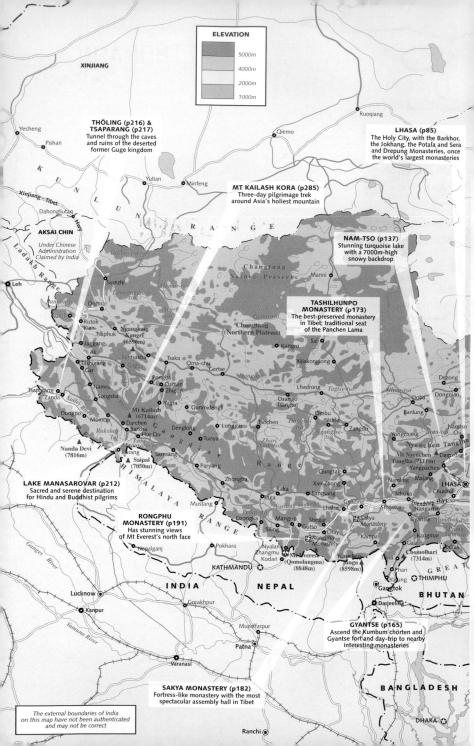

ELEVATION

5000m
4000m
2000m
1000m

XINJIANG

Ruoqiang

Yecheng
Pishan
Qiemo

THÖLING (p216) & TSAPARANG (p217)
Tunnel through the caves and ruins of the deserted former Guge kingdom

LHASA (p85)
The Holy City, with the Barkhor, the Jokhang, the Potala and Sera and Drepung Monasteries, once the world's largest monasteries

Yutian
Minfeng

MT KAILASH KORA (p285)
Three-day pilgrimage trek around Asia's holiest mountain

Xinjiang–Tibet Hwy
Dahongliutao

K U N L U N

R A N G E

NAM-TSO (p137)
Stunning turquoise lake with a 7000m-high snowy backdrop

AKSAI CHIN
Under Chinese Administration Claimed by India

Gozha tso

Ladakh Range

Leh

Sumzhi

Changtang Nature Preserve

Manni

Ishmaindong-tso

TASHILHUNPO MONASTERY (p173)
The best-preserved monastery in Tibet; traditional seat of the Panchen Lama

Memar-tso

Dormar

Dezong

Dongqiao

Rutok Xian

Tsaphuk

Nganglong Kangri (6596m)

Chibtsakha

Tsaka

Oma-chu

Gertse

Changtang (Northern Plateau)

Kangro

Sali

Xijiakonglong

Jaggang

Jaggang

Tsishigang
Gar

Pongba

Daman

Zhigon

Yagra

Dongba

Lhadrong

Dzango Tiangon

Ombu
Jaldo

Zangdo

Banlung

Doba

Dongqiao

Nam-tso

Namtso Qu

Nyenchen Tanglha

Namru

Songsha

Gunmidengli

Lunggar

Tsochen

Zhari Namtso

Dangra tso

Ngangtse-tso

Yongchang

Mt Nyenchen Tanglha (7111m)

Damping

Yangpachen

Tsaparang
Zanda

Dongpo

Moincer

Mt Kailash (6714m)

Darchen

Denglong

Tuoya

Qungtag

Namling

Majang

LHASA

Chushul

Nanda Devi (7816m)

Barkha
Hor Qu

Samsang

Paryang

Xier Zhong

Sangsang

Gyading

Tadruka

Friendship Hwy

Shigatse

Gyantse

Yamdrok-tso

Gala

Pedrak

LAKE MANASAROVAR (p212)
Sacred and serene destination for Hindu and Buddhist pilgrims

Saipal (7050m)

Zhongba

Raka

Jaga

Thatse

Kampa

Yangpachen

Chomolhari (7314m)

Mustang

Yarlung Tsangpo

Mangup

Shegar

Sakya Monastery

Kangmar

Phari

RONGPHU MONASTERY (p191)
Has stunning views of Mt Everest's north face

Dzongka

Siling

Gutso

Chay

Rongphu Monastery

Yatung

THIMPHU

Nepalganj

Pokhara

Nyalam
Zhangmu
Kodari

Mt Everest (Qomolangma) (8848m)

Junga
Kanchen (8598m)

Gangtok

Darjeeling

GREAT

BHUTAN

Ganges River

KATHMANDU

Lucknow

INDIA

NEPAL

Gorakhpur

Muzaffarpur

Kanpur

Yamuna River

Varanasi

Patna

GYANTSE (p165)
Ascend the Kumbum chörten and Gyantse fort and day-trip to nearby interesting monasteries

The external boundaries of India on this map have not been authenticated and may not be correct

SAKYA MONASTERY (p182)
Fortress-like monastery with the most spectacular assembly hall in Tibet

BANGLADESH

Ranchi

DHAKA

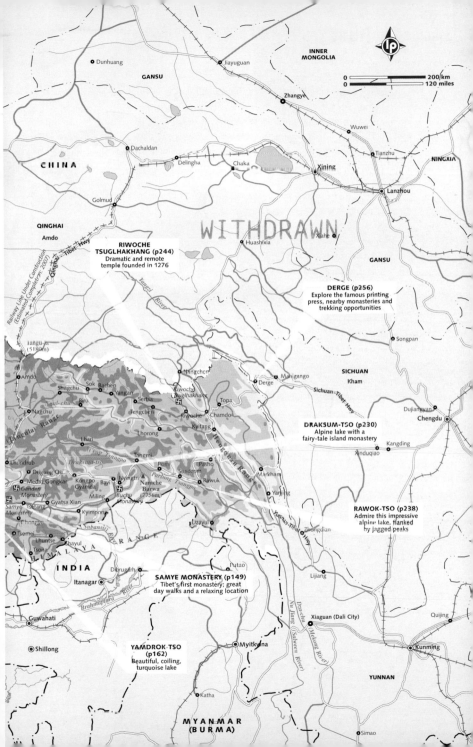

INNER MONGOLIA

GANSU

Dunhuang

Jiayuguan

Zhangye

Wuwei

CHINA

Dachaldan

Delingha

Chaka

Tianzhu

NINGXIA

Xining

Lanzhou

Golmud

QINGHAI

Amdo

WITHDRAWN

Huashixia

Xiahe

GANSU

RIWOCHE TSUGLHAKHANG (p244)
Dramatic and remote temple founded in 1276

Qinghai–Tibet Hwy

Railway Line Under Construction (Estimated Completion 2007)

Yangzi River

DERGE (p256)
Explore the famous printing press, nearby monasteries and trekking opportunities

Songpan

Tangu-la (5180m)

Amdo

Shagchu

Sok Bachen

Yangan

Nangchen

Riwoche Tsuglhakhang

Topa

Mangango

Derge

SICHUAN

Kham

Biru

Nagchu

Sertsa

Riwoche

Chamdo

Sichuan–Tibet Hwy

Dujiangyan

Chengdu

Nenl-chu

Tengchen

Kyitang

(Tanglha) Range

Lhari

Lhorong

Hengduan Range

DRAKSUM-TSO (p230)
Alpine lake with a fairy-tale island monastery

Kangding

Thundrub

Drigung Qu

Medro Gongkar

Yarlung Tsangpo

Draksun-tso

Tangmi

Pomi

Pasho

Sundzim

Parlung Tsangpo

Rawok

Markham

Xinduqiao

Ganden Monastery

Kongpo Gyamda

Bayi

Nyingtri

Namche Burwa (7756m)

Yanjing

Gyatsa Xian

Miling

Buchu Monastery

Samye Monastery

Tsetang

Chongye

Kyimpong

Uzayul

RAWOK-TSO (p238)
Admire this impressive alpine lake, flanked by jagged peaks

Tsomei

Lhuntse

Subansiri River

Zhongdian

Tsona

Chayul

HIMALAYA RANGE

INDIA

Dibrugarh

Putao

Yarlung–Tibet Hwy

Lijiang

Itanagar

SAMYE MONASTERY (p149)
Tibet's first monastery; great day walks and a relaxing location

Brahmaputra River

Guwahati

Dza-chu (Mekong River)

Nu Jiang (Salween River)

Xiaguan (Dali City)

Quijing

Shillong

YAMDROK-TSO (p162)
Beautiful, coiling, turquoise lake

Myitkyina

Kunming

YUNNAN

Katha

MYANMAR (BURMA)

Simao

0 — 200 km
0 — 120 miles

For many, the highlights of Tibet will be of a spiritual nature – magnificent monasteries, remote retreats and pilgrim paths; for others it will be the inspiring and raw high-altitude valleys, lakes and mountains of this unique plateau. Almost everyone, though, comes away with admiration and affinity for the Tibetan people, whose openness of heart makes travelling in Tibet such a joy.

Have a laugh with the monks at Sera Monastery (p122)

RICHARD I'ANSON

GRANT DIXON

Journey across the fields to Samye Monastery (p149), a great place to relax

Stand in awe of Mt Everest (p189)

GARRY WEARE

RICHARD I'ANSON

Gaze up at the impressive Potala (p98), the palace of the Dalai Lamas

WITHDRAWN

Follow the murmuring, shuffling pilgrims into the Jokhang (p94), the spiritual heart of Tibet

BERNARD NAPTHINE

JANE SWEENEY

Spiral up the multistorey stupa of Gyantse Kumbum (p167)

Trek all the way around magnificent
Mt Kailash (p285)

STAN ARMINGTON

Look out for the yak horns at sacred
Lake Manasarovar (p212)

MONIQUE CHOY

BRADLEY MAYHEW

Experience Tibet's awesome sense of space at
Nam-tso (p137), a stunning turquoise lake set
below a range of 7000m peaks

Admire the religious artwork at Tashilhunpo Monastery (p173), one of Tibet's best-
preserved monasteries

RICHARD I'ANSON

Preface

THE DALAI LAMA

The issue of Tibet is not nearly as simple as is sometimes made out. I believe that there are still widespread misunderstandings about Tibetan culture and what is happening inside and outside Tibet. Therefore, I welcome every opportunity for open-minded people to discover what is the reality in Tibet for themselves.

In the context of the growing tourist industry in Tibet, the Lonely Planet travel guide has an invaluable contribution to make in providing reliable and authoritative background information about places to visit, how to get there, where to stay, where to eat and so forth. Presenting the basic facts allows visitors to prepare themselves for what they will encounter and enables individuals to use their own intelligence to evaluate the evidence before them.

We live in times of rapid change throughout the world, but particularly at present in Asia and China. I remain confident that not very far in the future some mutually agreeable solution may be found to the Tibetan problem. I believe that my strictly non-violent approach, entailing constructive dialogue and negotiation, will ultimately attract effective support and sympathy from within the Chinese community. In the meantime, I am also convinced that as more people visit Tibet, the numbers of those who support the justice of a peaceful solution will grow.

I am grateful to everyone involved in the preparation of this sixth edition of the Lonely Planet guide to Tibet for the care and concern they have put into it. I trust that those who rely on it as a companion to their travels in Tibet will enjoy themselves in what, despite all that has happened, remains for me one of the most beautiful places on earth.

HH signed

September 15, 2004

Getting Started

Tibet is a fairly easy place to visit, once you've worked your way around the latest permit situation (see p304). Most travellers hire Land Cruisers to explore the country these days but that's not strictly necessary. A combination of buses, hitching and hiking will get you to most places and travel this way is cheap.

On a practical level, Chinese modernisation has hit the Tibetan plateau big time and you'll find all the associated conveniences from Internet connections to cans of Budweiser in most towns across the plateau. Out in the countryside traditional Tibetan life continues without much interruption.

In this book we cover the Tibet Autonomous Region (TAR) and the routes that lead to it through the ethnically and historically Tibetan areas of western Sichuan.

WHEN TO GO

See Climate Charts (p297) for more information

Climate is not such a major consideration when visiting Tibet as many people might imagine. Winter is very cold, many restaurants are shut and snowfalls can sometimes make travel difficult, but some travellers swear by the winter months. There are few travellers about at this time and Lhasa, for example, is crowded with nomads and at its most colourful. The average temperature in January is -2°C.

Spring, early summer and late autumn are probably the best times to be visiting Tibet. March is a politically sensitive month in the country (see p301) and there is occasional tightening of restrictions on travellers heading into Tibet at this time, but the weather's pretty good. April brings reliable weather in eastern Tibet and discounts on accommodation and vehicle rental in Lhasa. Everest is particularly clear during April and May.

From mid-July through to the end of September, the monsoon starts to affect parts of Tibet (the months of July and August bring half of Tibet's annual rainfall). Travel to western Tibet becomes more difficult, the roads to the east are temporarily washed out and the Friendship Hwy sometimes becomes impassable on the Nepal side or on the border itself.

Trips to Mt Kailash can be undertaken from April to October, although September and October are considered the best months. October is also the best time to make a trip out to the east. Lhasa and its environs don't get *really* cold until the end of November.

It's worth trying to make your trip coincide with one of Tibet's main festivals. New Year (Losar) is an excellent (although cold) time to be in Lhasa. Saga Dawa (April or May) is also a good time to be in Lhasa or Mt Kailash (see p300).

COSTS & MONEY

Accommodation and food are both very economical in Tibet. The major expense – unless you have plenty of time and enjoy rough travelling – is getting around. If you really want to see a lot in a short space of time you will probably have to consider hiring a vehicle (plus driver). Shared hired transport tends to work out at around US$20 to US$30 per person per day. The per-person cost for a group of six travelling with stops from Lhasa to the Nepali border is around US$120.

Getting into Tibet is also relatively expensive. Even the bus fare from Golmud has risen to around US$200, while the cheapest package by air costs around US$230.

If you don't hire transport (and it is still perfectly possible to see most of the places covered in this guide if you don't) costs are very reasonable. If you are staying in Lhasa and visiting the surrounding sights you can do it comfortably on US$20 per day. Outside the main cities of Lhasa, Shigatse and Tsetang, daily costs can drop drastically, especially if you're hitching or hiking out to remote monasteries and living on instant noodles.

TRAVEL LITERATURE

Literature on Tibet is abundant. Quite a bit of it is of the woolly 'how to find enlightenment in the mysterious Land of Snows' variety, but there is still a lot of very good stuff about.

Seven Years in Tibet by Heinrich Harrer, translated from the German in 1952 and made into a film in 1997, is an engaging account of Harrer's sojourn in Tibet in the final years before the Chinese takeover.

Magic and Mystery in Tibet by Alexandra David-Neel has the lot for the starry-eyed dreamer – flying nuns, enchanted daggers, ghosts and demons, and also some interesting background information on the mystic side of Tibet. Another good David-Neel title to look out for is *My Journey to Lhasa*.

A Mountain in Tibet by Charles Allen is a superbly crafted book that takes a look at the holy Mt Kailash and the attempts of early European explorers to reach it and to determine its geographical significance. It's a must for anyone heading out to western Tibet. Allen builds on this work with his *Search for Shangri-La* in which he returns to western Tibet to examine the region's pre-Buddhist history and mythology, focusing on Bön. For other books on Mt Kailash, see p211.

The Siege of Shangri-La by Michael McRae takes a look at current and former explorations of the Tsangpo gorges in the Pemako region of eastern Tibet.

Travelers' Tales Tibet is a compendium of travel writing on Tibet by such authors as Pico Iyer, Jeff Greenwald and Alexandra David-Kneel.

LONELY PLANET INDEX

Litre of bottled water Y4

Bottle of Lhasa beer Y4-8

Street snack (bowl of noodles) Y4

Taxi ride around town Y10

Postcard Y2

HOW MUCH?

Land Cruiser hire per day, split between four US$30

Chinese meat dish Y15-25

Monastery entry fee Y20-50

Internet connection Y5 per hour

Prayer flags from Y4 for a small string

DON'T LEAVE HOME WITHOUT...

- A good pair of sunglasses, high-factor sunscreen lotion and lip balm, to block out the strong high-altitude light.

- A sleeping bag, if heading off the beaten track or travelling outside of high summer (see p295).

- A water bottle for cooling boiled water (thus doubling as a hot-water bottle!), an alarm clock for early morning transport and a strong torch (flashlight) for viewing the inside of monasteries.

- Warm clothing – in the summer months a good sweater or fleece will do the trick unless you are planning to be trekking at high altitudes or heading out to western Tibet. A waterproof jacket is useful if you are heading out to eastern Tibet in summer.

- Hard-to-find toiletries like shaving cream, razor blades, deodorant, dental floss and tampons. Cold medicines and throat pastilles are useful as many travellers develop a cold and cough as a result of altitude.

- The latest word on permit regulations from the Lonely Planet Thorn Tree (www.lonelyplanet .com). Also, read the information on p304 and throughout the Transport chapter (p310).

TOP FIVES
GREAT READS

Stuff your rucksack with a couple of these insightful looks into the Tibetan experience:

- *Tears of Blood: A Cry for Tibet* by Mary Craig is a riveting and distressing account of the Tibetan experience since the Chinese takeover and should be read by every visitor to Tibet.
- *A Stranger in Tibet* by Scott Berry tells the fascinating story of Ekai Kawaguchi, a young Japanese monk who was one of the first foreigners to reach Lhasa in 1900 and who managed to stay over a year in the capital before his identity was discovered and he was forced to flee the country.
- *Trespassers on the Roof of the World* by Peter Hopkirk is primarily concerned with European explorers' early attempts to enter forbidden Tibet and it makes superb reading.
- *Fire Under the Snow: Testimony of a Tibetan Prisoner* by Palden Gyatso is a moving autobiography that recounts Gyatso's life as a Buddhist monk imprisoned for 33 years for refusing to denounce the Dalai Lama.
- *Tibet Tibet* by Patrick French is a recent worthy attempt to look beyond the propaganda and myth surrounding Tibet (what he terms 'the mind's Tibet') to portray a more complex and unsettling reality.

MUST-SEE FILMS

Get inspired down at the video shop with these big- and low-budget flicks:

- *Kundun* (Martin Scorsese) tells the story of the Dalai Lama ('Kundun'), through an all-Tibetan and Chinese cast, many of them descendants of the figures they portray (the Dalai Lama's mother, for example, is played by the Dalai Lama's niece). The cinematography in particular is gorgeous.
- *Himalaya* (Eric Valli) tells the epic story of succession of Tibetan herders on the salt caravan from Nepal to Tibet. The cinematography is also gorgeous (it was filmed largely in Dolpo in Nepal) and the cast is all Tibetan.
- *Seven Years in Tibet* (Jean-Jacques Annaud) is a US$70-million film that tells the story of the daring escape of Heinrich Harrer (Brad Pitt) and Peter Aufschnaiter (David Thewlis) from a prisoner-of-war camp in northern India, their epic trek across Tibet and their seven-year sojourn in Lhasa as aides to the young Dalai Lama.
- *Windhorse* (Paul Wagner) is a drama set in Lhasa. It follows a Tibetan singer (played by singer Dadon Dawa Dolma) popular with the Chinese who faces a crisis of conscience when her cousin, a nun, is imprisoned and tortured for her religious beliefs. Parts of the film were shot illegally in Tibet.
- *Tibet: Cry of the Snow Lion* (Tom Peosay) is a powerful pro-Tibetan documentary with narration by Martin Sheen and voiceovers by Ed Harris, Tim Robbins and Susan Sarandon.

OUR FAVOURITE TIBETAN CULTURAL EXPERIENCES

Don't overlook these simple joys of being in Tibet when planning your itinerary:

- The smell of juniper incense, the low murmur of Tibetan chanting and the warmth of butter lamps in monasteries everywhere.
- Following a kora with a band of happy pilgrims or scoring a lift in the back of a pilgrim truck.
- Overnighting in a small monastery such as Mindroling (p148) or Drigung Til (p144).
- Repeatedly wandering the Barkhor (p91), different every time.
- A post-hike thermos of sweet milky tea in a crowded Tibetan teahouse.

INTERNET RESOURCES

Australia Tibet Council (www.atc.org.au) Includes excellent information on travel to Tibet, including the latest travel restrictions.

Canada Tibet Committee (www.tibet.ca) Click on World Tibet Archive for a useful, free news-gathering service on issues relating to Tibet.

China Tibet Information (www.tibetinfor.com/en) News, background and tourism information from the Chinese perspective.

Office of the Dalai Lama in London (www.tibet.com) Provides lots of background information on Tibet.

Tibet Information Network (www.tibetinfo.net) Another news-gathering service with a good but dated rundown of tourist regulations in Tibet.

Tibet Map Institute (www.tibetmap.com) Highly detailed downloadable maps of almost every region of Tibet, with an overview of other commercial map sources.

Itineraries

CLASSIC ITINERARIES

LHASA & AROUND   Two weeks

The area around
Lhasa offers an
excellent range
of monasteries,
both popular and
remote, and no
travel permits are
required. Nam-tso
offers a glimpse
of the nomad life
of the north. This
route gives a good
look at Tibet in a
short time. Then
fly out of Lhasa or
travel overland to
Nepal.

The chief goal of travellers is Lhasa itself, focal point and spiritual heart of Tibet. There's enough to see in and around the city to occupy at least a week. Highlights include the World Heritage Sites of the **Potala** (p98) and **Jokhang Temple** (p94) and the **Barkhor** pilgrimage circuit (p91). The huge monastic institutions of **Drepung** (p118) and **Sera** (p122) lie on the edge of town, and **Ganden Monastery** (p126) is a fantastic day trip away.

There are plenty of excursions to be made from Lhasa and no permits are required for these trips. A three-day return trip can take you to the stunning lake **Nam-tso** (p137), giving you a break from peering at Buddhist deities, though you should allow at least a few days in Lhasa to acclimatise before heading out here. Add a day and return via the splendidly isolated **Reting Monastery** (p142) to avoid backtracking.

With another couple of days, visit atmospheric **Drigung Til Monastery** (p144) and **Tidrum Nunnery** (p145), both east of Lhasa. You can visit these directly from Reting or on an two- or three-day excursion from Lhasa.

You could spend a third or alternative second week travelling on public transport to **Shigatse** (p172) and **Gyantse** (p165). Gyantse deserves a couple of days to visit the famous stupa and fort. Hire a Land Cruiser (p321) and you can do a loop via Yamdrok-tso, following the first couple of days of the Lhasa to Kathmandu itinerary (p15). With a Land Cruiser you could probably also squeeze an overnight stay at Samye into your week.

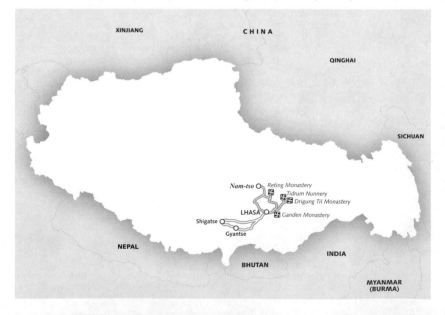

LHASA TO KATHMANDU

One to two Weeks

The Friendship Hwy between Lhasa and Kathmandu in Nepal is the main travellers' route through Tibet and allows a number of excellent detours. Most travellers take Land Cruiser tours (p321) to the border but there is much to be gained by the slower pace of an independent trip by bussing, hiking and hitching.

Land Cruiser trips generally head straight from Lhasa to the coiling scorpion-lake of **Yamdrok-tso** (p162) and take in the views from **Samding Monastery** (p164) before heading over the glacier-draped Karo-la pass to Gyantse. The town of **Gyantse** (p165) is well worth a day or two: the *kum-bum* (literally '100,000 images') stupa is a must-see and there are several adventurous excursions from town. A 90-minute drive away is Shigatse, with its impressive **Tashilhunpo Monastery** (p173). **Shalu Monastery** (p179) is a worthwhile half-day trip from Shigatse, especially if you have an interest in Tibetan art.

A popular side trip en route to Kathmandu is to **Sakya** (p182), a small monastery town located just 25km off the Friendship Hwy. Stay here the night and investigate the northern ruins or stay in the nearby town of Lhatse.

Closer to the border, and emerging as the most popular trekking destination in Tibet, is the **Everest region** (p189). Many people drive right up to Everest Base Camp and leave the next day, but it's much better to fit in an extra day to acclimatise and enjoy the extraordinary views. If you are hitching (p322), allow at least three days to get to Rongphu (Rongbuk) and back from the Friendship Hwy.

After Everest most people take the opportunity to stay the night in old **Tingri** (p192), with its wonderful views of Cho Oyu, before the straight and scenic rollercoaster ride to **Nyalam** (p193), Zhangmu and the Nepali border.

A classic overland route of around 1300km that can be done in a week on an organised Land Cruiser trip or in two to three weeks by bus and hitching. It's also a classic mountain-biking route. It takes in central Tibet's most import-ant monasteries, plus views of the world's highest peak.

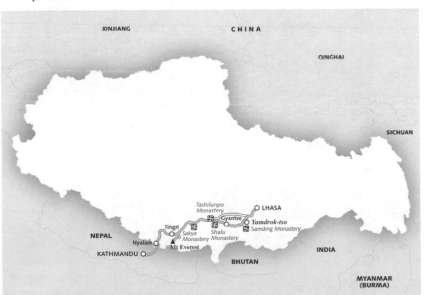

ROADS LESS TRAVELLED

MT KAILASH PILGRIMAGE

15 to 23 days

Much talked about, but little visited, is **Mt Kailash** (p210) out in western Tibet. The easiest way to get here is by rented Land Cruiser (p202). If you just want to visit Mt Kailash and Lake Manasarovar, the most direct route is the southern one (870km), a four-day drive from Lhasa along the northern spine of the Himalaya. A kora (pilgrimage circuit) of the mountain will take three or four days and you should allow at least a day afterwards to relax at **Lake Manasarovar** (p212), probably at Chiu Monastery. Pilgrims traditionally then visit the sacred hot springs at **Tirthapuri** (p213).

An ambitious but rewarding alternative is to travel out from Lhasa along the longer (1700km) northern route to **Ali** (p207) and back along the southern route, a loop that will take 21 or, preferably, 24 days. The six-day drive from Lhasa to Ali is superbly scenic but the towns en route are soulless so consider camping somewhere such as **Tagyel-tso** (p205). From Ali you can make an overnight visit to **Pangong-tso** (p220) and **Rutok Monastery** (p220), before heading down to Zanda and **Thöling Monastery** (p216). Allow at least two days here, with a day to explore the amazing Guge kingdom ruins at **Tsaparang** (p217). From Thöling it's a day's drive to Mt Kailash, though most groups stop overnight at Tirthapuri en route.

If you are heading to Nepal from Mt Kailash, it's well worth taking the short cut south via stunning **Peiku-tso** (p203) and its views of Mt Shishapangma, to join the Friendship Hwy near Nyalam.

It's possible to cover many of these sights by public transport or hitching (p322) but for this you'll need a month or more.

> A rugged mini-expedition to one of the remotest and most sacred corners of Asia. Mt Kailash, Lake Manasarovar and the ruins of the Guge kingdom are the highlights here. Land Cruiser hire will cost US$600 to S$700 per person.

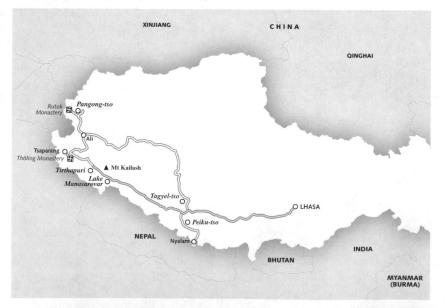

EASTERN TIBET LOOP   18 to 21 days

Equally remote are the stunningly scenic routes through eastern Tibet. Road conditions make the trip best attempted from late March to late April, or late September to early November. It's possible to travel the northern or southern routes into or out of Tibet but, to visit both, a loop route (described here) makes best sense.

From Lhasa the southern route heads eastwards over a high pass to the forested **Draksum-tso** (p230) and then proceeds to the fascinating Kongpo region and the lovingly restored **Lamaling Temple** (p234). From here the road climbs to afford excellent views of 7756m **Namche Barwa** (p235) and then drops down into the dramatic misty gorges that lie north of the Yarlung Tsangpo. Make an overnight stay in the county capital of Pomi before taking some time to visit the turquoise lake of **Rawok-tso** (p238), then swinging north over high passes and down into the deep parallel gorges of the Salween and Mekong Rivers. Reach the modern town of **Chamdo** (p240) after five or six days and rest for a day, visiting the fine Jampaling Monastery.

From Chamdo the northern route continues three days westwards to Nagqu, slowly climbing to high-altitude pasturelands. The route passes the very impressive and remote **Riwoche Temple** (p244) and several other smaller but absolutely charming Buddhist and Bön monasteries. **Sok Monastery** (p246) is a highlight in this area but you'll have to secure permission in advance.

From Nagqu it's a good idea to visit **Nam-tso** (p137) and **Reting Monastery** (p142) en route to Lhasa (allow three to four days), though the road can be completed in a day.

A shorter and cheaper five- to seven-day loop itinerary from Lhasa to Kongpo could take in Draksum-tso and Lamaling Temple before returning via Tsetang, Samye and possibly the remote oracle lake of **Lhamo La-tso** (p158).

This three-week Land Cruiser loop takes you through dramatic scenery to some rarely visited corners of Tibet. It's perhaps best suited to a second trip to Tibet. Land Cruiser hire will cost around US$600 per person; hitching without permits is difficult.

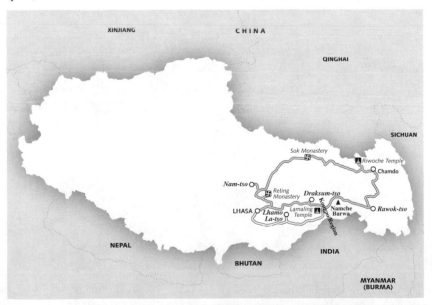

YUNNAN/SICHUAN TO LHASA   Two to three weeks

There are two main routes through Sichuan, a **northern route** (p253) and a **southern route** (p257). The Tibetan areas of western Sichuan and north-western Yunnan do not require permits; the eastern Tibetan Autonomous Region does.

Both routes take in superlative scenery. The northern route offers a range of scenery from forested alpine country to the high plateau of the Changtang and passes many large monasteries; the southern route is lower, wilder and more alpine, passing fewer towns and monasteries.

The northern route through Sichuan starts from Kangding and passes the grasslands and monastery of **Tagong** (p253) and several large monasteries around **Ganzi** (p254). The timeless printing press of **Derge** (p256) is a day's bus ride further but there are plenty of exciting excursions en route, including to remote **Dzogchen Monastery** (p256) and pretty **Yilhun La-tso** (p256). From Derge you cross into Tibet proper over some wild passes to **Chamdo** (p240), the biggest town in eastern Tibet. For the route west of Chamdo see the second half of the Eastern Tibet loop (p17); alternatively travel south to join the southern route.

The southern route through Sichuan runs west from Kangding past the Khampa town and monastery of **Litang** (p257) and then low-lying **Batang** (p260) before climbing up into Tibet at Markham and continuing over concertina passes to Pomda. For the route west, reverse the first half of the Eastern Tibet loop itinerary (p17).

A popular alternative option is to start in Yunnan at the Tibetan town of Zhongdian (Gyalthang), from where it's a day's bus ride to Deqin. From here you cross the Tibetan border (and checkpoint) near Yanjing; then it's 111km to Markham on the Sichuan southern route.

From Zhongdian to Lhasa, allow a week in a Land Cruiser. From Chengdu it takes two weeks along either the northern or southern route.

A wild overland adventure through spectacular alpine scenery. Officially open only to organised Land Cruiser tours which can be arranged in Zhongdian, Lijiang or Kunming, though increasing numbers of hitchhikers are making their way through.

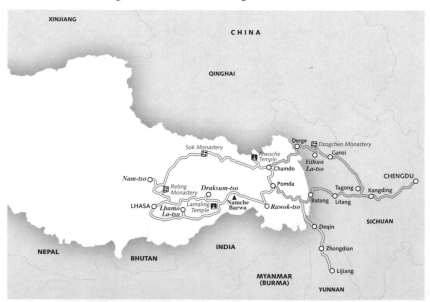

TAILORED TRIPS

MONASTERIES OFF THE BEATEN TRACK

A visit to one of Tibet's smaller monasteries could well be a highlight of your trip. The monasteries are more intimate, the monks tend to be friendlier and it's often possible to spend the night and attend prayer meetings after all the tourists have melted away.

Between Lhasa and Samye, **Mindroling Monastery** (p148) is a friendly place that's easily accessible. The surroundings offer some enjoyable walks and it's possible to stay the night.

Just a short ferry ride across the Yarlung Tsangpo is **Dorje Drak Monastery** (p147). Getting here on the ferry can be a bit of an adventure but once you're here you'll feel a million miles away from modern Tibet. There's a monastery guesthouse and a dramatic kora.

En route between Shigatse and Lhatse is the remote and little-visited **Phuntsoling Monastery** (p187). The monastery has a superb location and there are lots of ruins to explore, both at the site and a couple of hours' walk away at the ruined Jonang chörten. Permits are required here.

Along the Friendship Hwy, **Shegar** (p187) is just 7km off the main road, not far from the turn-off to Mt Everest, and has a charming monastery at the base of the impressive ruined 'Crystal Fort'.

NATURAL HIGHS

Almost everywhere in Tibet offers superb scenery but let's start at the top: **Mt Everest** (p189). Views of the north face from Rongphu Monastery are unsurpassed.

Nam-tso (p137) offers a very different landscape, more characteristic of the northern Changtang than of central Tibet. The huge salt lake is framed by the jagged white peaks of the Nyenchen Tanghla range.

The scenery of the east is different again. **Rawok-tso** (p238) is possibly the prettiest lake in Tibet, fringed by both sandy beaches and mountain peaks. **Draksum-tso** (p230), further west, is another gorgeous lake, with a superbly photogenic island monastery.

Tagyel-tso (p205) and **Dawa-tso** (p206) are two of the most impressive of the lakes in the west, with great camping en route to Mt Kailash.

Yading Nature Reserve (p259) near Daocheng in western Sichuan offers sublime mountain scenery without any of the pesky permit hassles that dog travel to the TAR. You can stay in tourist tents and hike up to meadows and glacial lakes.

Peiku-tso (p203), near the border with Nepal, is another of Tibet's awesome mountain lakes, this time with impressive views of 8012m Mt Shishapangma to the south. The deep blues of **Lake Manasarovar** (p212) are another natural highlight.

PILGRIM PATHS

Mt Kailash (p285) is the most sacred pilgrimage path in Tibet. The 53km trek is generally done in three days by foreign trekkers and takes you past several monasteries and sacred sights and over the 5600m Drölma-la.

Lake Manasarovar (p212, p292) is another sacred kora but is less popular with foreigners. Still, it's possible to just walk a section, as in the day hike from Chiu Monastery to Hor Qu.

Ganden Monastery (p126) has one of Tibet's most interesting koras and the views of the Kyi-chu Valley below are just wonderful.

The easy and pleasant **Pelri kora** (p232), near Bayi, has many links to Guru Rinpoche and is a chance to stretch the legs on a Land Cruiser trip, but it's hard to visit independently.

Tashilhunpo Kora (p173) in Shigatse is always full of pilgrims. The trail passes chörtens and rock paintings, and offers the best views of the old town and Shigatse *dzong* (fort). **Sakya Monastery** (p182) also has an interesting kora around the ruins of its northern monastery complex.

Tirthapuri kora (p213) is another short kora, but is full of interesting medicinal sites, hot springs and pilgrim action.

Perhaps shortest of all is the **Barkhor** (p91), the fascinating circuit that surrounds the Jokhang in Lhasa.

TREKKING & HIKING

There are some great day hikes around Lhasa, which will help you get acclimatised before attempting anything too adventurous. The hills surrounding **Pabonka Monastery** (p125) offer great scope for ridge hiking. The day hike to **Shugsheb Nunnery** (p129), 20km south of Lhasa, is another good warm-up trip. The retreat caves of **Drak Yerpa** (p139) offer an excellent overnight hike from Lhasa (take a sleeping bag).

The most popular trek in Tibet is probably the four- or five-day **Ganden-Samye trek** (p271). Even if you don't want to do the whole thing, there are some fine day hikes from Samye Monastery, primarily to the Chim-puk meditation caves.

A close second in popularity is the **Everest region** (p189), and specifically the trek in from Tingri (p281). The short hike between Rongphu and Everest Base Camp is a great walk, though many miss its sights by rushing up to Base Camp in their Land Cruisers. The dusty road route into Everest from Shegar is probably best done with a combination of hiking and hitching, and there are some lovely villages en route.

Hiking and hitching is also the most adventurous way to get to the sights around the **Yarlung Valley** (p155), though you'll have to keep an eye out for the PSB.

The little-visited **Riche Ganden retreat** (p170) makes for a fine half-day hike from Gyantse.

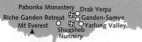

The Authors

BRADLEY MAYHEW   Coordinating Author

Bradley's first excuse to venture to Tibet came when he raced three Oxford classmates to Lhasa on a summer break, and won a crate of Lhasa Beer for his endeavours. That trip, followed closely by a reading of Peter Mattheissen's *The Snow Leopard,* cemented a long-term love affair with the Tibetan world.

Since then Bradley has been back to Tibet half a dozen times, covering the breadth of the region from Mt Kailash in the west to Kham in the east for the last three editions of Lonely Planet's *Tibet* and *China* guides, along with extended visits to the Tibetan areas of Ladakh and Spiti in northern India. A graduate of Oriental Studies from Oxford University, he speaks Chinese but would always rather try out his stumbling Tibetan.

Life on the Road

Tibet's main sights are without doubt amazing, but for me it's always the smaller places and the changing pace of travel that these trips demand that shine the brightest. Hitching and hiking out to an obscure monastery with little more than a day pack and a sleeping bag offers an intoxicating sense of freedom.

Added to this is the rare sense of calm and space that pervades Tibet, whether it's from the epic scale of the land or the occasional moments of clarity inspired by the Tibetan faith. The joy of hitching on an open-air truck or following a kora with a happy band of pilgrims also rate highly. But perhaps the memories that remain the longest are those of the Tibetan people: drinking *chang* (Tibetan barley beer) with strangers by the side of the road, or seeing the veneration and dedication of pilgrims at a religious site. It's an inspiring, humbling combination, one with which many travellers fall in love.

MICHAEL KOHN   Ü & Eastern Tibet (Kham)

After his first overland trip through Tibet in 1994, Michael returned to his native California and established a Free Tibet campaign at the University of California, Santa Barbara. An interest in the Tibetan world later led him to Dharamsala, Ladakh, Amdo and, finally, Mongolia, where he spent three years writing for the Associated Press, BBC and the local English-language press. His articles on the resurgence of Tibetan Buddhism in Mongolia have featured in the *New York Times* and the *Baltimore Sun* while his first book, *Lord of the Gobi,* captures the life of a renowned 19th-century Buddhist monk. Michael has written guidebooks to India, the USA and Mongolia, and updated Lonely Planet's *Central Asia* and *Mongolia.*

CONTRIBUTING AUTHOR

John Vincent Bellezza wrote the Trekking chapter. Raised in Europe and America, John disappeared off into the wilds of High Asia more than two decades ago, only to occasionally re-emerge over the years. Well known in the field of Tibetan studies, he has published several treatises on the Bön religion and early Tibetan culture. His books include *Divine Dyads: Ancient Civilization in Tibet, Antiquities of Northern Tibet, Antiquities of Upper Tibet* and *Sacred Mountains and the Bön Tradition in Upper Tibet.* Largely credited with the discovery of the fabled Zhang Zhung kingdom, he has charted more than 600 archaeological sites hidden away on the highest reaches of the Tibetan plateau.

23

Snapshot

The Dalai Lama continues to be vocal in the Tibetan struggle for independence in some form. He has abandoned any hope of nationhood, but continues to strive for a system of Tibetan cultural, religious and linguistic autonomy within the Chinese state. In Western political circles covert sympathy rarely translates into active support, and foreign governments continue to be careful not to receive the Dalai Lama in any way that recognises his political status as the head of an exiled government.

China's policy in Tibet has switched from ruthless persecution to a subtler policy of consolidation and economic development, but traditional life in Tibet continues to be eroded. Religious institutions are repeatedly the focus of 'patriotic education' and 'civilising atheism' campaigns, and strict quotas are imposed on the numbers of resident monks and nuns. Tibetan guides who have been educated in India have been banned from working in Tibet.

The Chinese officially deny any policy of Han immigration to Tibet, but for visitors who have made repeated trips to Tibet the increased numbers of Han Chinese people are staggering. The extent of immigration poses the grave danger that the Tibetans will become a minority in their own country, a situation the Dalai Lama has described as 'cultural genocide'.

Not all Chinese are in Tibet to earn money, though. Wealthy urban Chinese tourists from Beijing, Shanghai and Guangzhou are starting to flock to Tibet in droves, already outnumbering foreign tourists ten to one. 'Tibet chic' is increasingly utilised as a marketable commodity in China.

China's epic drive to develop its western hinterland has also had a considerable impact on Tibet. China has invested US$1.6 billion in Tibet in recent years, more than in any other province: expenditure on road building alone trebled between 2001 and 2005. In 2007 the railway line from China will finally arrive in Lhasa, doubtless bringing many changes in its wake. Pro-Tibetan groups fear that the railway will bring added migration, environmental damage and mineral exploitation (Chinese scientists announced the discovery of five billion tons of oil and gas in the Changtang region in 2001). The Chinese argue that this is just part of their efforts to raise living standards in Tibet and bring it economic prosperity.

China has recently moved to resolve its border disputes with India. In return for an Indian acceptance that Tibet is part of China, China offered a tacit agreement that Sikkim is part of India, easing a border dispute that led to a war in 1962 between the world's two most populous nations.

There are occasional signs that Beijing and the Dalai Lama are inching towards talks. Summer 2002 saw the first visit to Tibet by a delegation of the Dalai Lama's envoys for a decade. Disputes between Dharamsala and Beijing over the selection of various lamas, most notably the Panchen Lama, have spotlighted the tricky politics of reincarnation, an increasingly hot topic as the Dalai Lama heads towards his 70th birthday.

FAST FACTS

Tibetan Autonomous Region (TAR) population: 2.7 million

Global Tibetan population: 5.5 million

Area of TAR: 1.23 million sq km, or ⅛ of China's landmass

Local drink: yak-butter tea

Average number of cups of tea drunk by a nomad per day: 40

Funeral custom: sky burial

The sign for hitching: the thumbs up

To show respect: stick out your tongue

History

MYTHOLOGICAL BEGINNINGS

Little is known of the beginnings of the Tibetan people. They originated from the nomadic, warlike tribes known as the Qiang. Chinese records of these tribes, which harried the borders of the great Chinese empire, date back as far as the 2nd century BC. However, the people of Tibet were not to emerge as a politically united force until the 7th century AD.

According to myth, the Tibetan people owe their existence to the union of an ogress and a monkey on Gangpo Ri (p155) at Tsetang (prefiguring Darwin by over a millennium!). Another legend tells of how the first Tibetan king descended from heaven on a sky cord. These early myths are no doubt Bön (p61) in origin but have been appropriated by Buddhism, so that the monkey is seen as a manifestation of Chenresig (Avalokiteshvara), the Bodhisattva of Compassion. The ogress and the monkey had six children, who are seen as the ancestors of the six main tribes of Tibet.

YARLUNG VALLEY DYNASTY

As early myths of the origin of the Tibetan people suggest, the Yarlung Valley was the cradle of the civilisation of central Tibet. The early Yarlung kings, although glorified in legend, were probably no more than chieftains whose domains extended not much further than the Yarlung Valley itself (p155). A reconstruction of Tibet's first fortress, Yumbulagang, can still be seen in the Yarlung Valley, and it is here that the 28th king of Tibet is said to have received Tibet's first Buddhist scriptures in the 5th century AD. According to legend, they fell on the roof of Yumbulagang.

Credible historical records regarding the Yarlung Valley dynasty date only from the time when the fledgling kingdom entered the international arena in the 6th century. By this time the Yarlung kings, through conquest and alliances, had made significant headway in unifying much of central Tibet. Namri Songtsen (c 570–619), the 32nd Tibetan king, continued this trend and extended Tibetan influence into inner Asia, defeating the Qiang tribes on China's borders. But the true flowering of Tibet as an important regional power came about with the accession to rule of Namri Songtsen's son, Songtsen Gampo (r 630–49).

Under Songtsen Gampo, central Tibet entered a new era. Tibetan expansion continued unabated. The armies of Tibet ranged as far afield as northern India and emerged as a threat to the Tang dynasty in China. Both Nepal and China reacted to the Tibetan incursions by reluctantly agreeing to alliances through marriage. Princess Wencheng, Songtsen Gampo's Chinese bride, and Princess Bhrikuti, his Nepali bride, became important historical figures for the Tibetans, as it was through their influence that Buddhism first gained royal patronage and a foothold on the Tibetan plateau. The king went as far as passing a law making it illegal *not* to be a Buddhist.

Contact with the Chinese led to the introduction of the sciences of astronomy and medicine, and a Tibetan script was developed from Indian

'The Yarlung Valley was the cradle of the civilisation of central Tibet'

7th century	630–49
Tibetan script created by Thonmi Sambhota, based on the Sanskrit script	Rule of King Songtsen Gampo sees founding of Jokhang, Ramoche Temple and a fort on the Potala site

sources. It was used in the first translations of Buddhist scriptures, in drafting a code of law and in writing the first histories of Tibet.

For two centuries after the reign of Songtsen Gampo, Tibet continued to grow in power and influence. By the time of King Trisong Detsen's reign (755–97), Tibetan influence extended over Turkestan, northern Pakistan, Nepal and India. In China, Tibetan armies conquered Gansu and Sichuan, and controlled the great Buddhist cave complex of Dunhuang.

A Sino-Tibetan treaty was signed in 822 during the reign of King Tritsug Detsen Ralpachen (r 817–36). It was immortalised in stone on three steles: one in Lhasa, outside the Jokhang; one in the Chinese capital of Chang'an; and one on the border of Tibet and China. Only the Lhasa stele still stands (see p93). Signatories to the treaty swore that '…the whole region to the east…being the country of Great China and the whole region to the west being assuredly that of the country of Great Tibet, from either side of that frontier there shall be no warfare, no hostile invasions, and no seizure of territory…'. The treaty went on to herald a new era in which 'Tibetans shall be happy in Tibet and Chinese shall be happy in China'.

> 'there shall be no warfare, no hostile invasions, and no seizure of territory…'

INTRODUCTION OF BUDDHISM

By the time Buddhism first arrived in Tibet during the reign of Songtsen Gampo, it had already flourished for around 1100 years and had become the principal faith of all Tibet's neighbouring countries. But it was slow to take hold in Tibet.

Early missionaries, such as Shantarakshita from the Indian Buddhist centre of Nalanda (in modern-day Bihar), faced great hostility from the Bön-dominated court. The influence of Songtsen Gampo's Chinese and Nepali wives was almost certainly limited to the royal court, and priests of the time were probably Indian and Chinese, not Tibetan.

It was not until King Trisong Detsen's reign that Buddhism began to take root. Trisong Detsen was responsible for founding Samye Monastery (p149), the first institution to carry out the systematic translation of Buddhist scriptures and the training of Tibetan monks.

Contention over the path that Buddhism was to take in Tibet culminated in the Great Debate of Samye, in which King Trisong Detsen is said to have adjudicated in favour of Indian teachers who advocated a gradual approach to enlightenment, founded in scholastic study and moral precepts. There was, however, much opposition to this institutionalised, clerical Buddhism, largely from supporters of the Bön faith. The next Tibetan king, Tritsug Detsen Ralpachen, fell victim to this opposition and was assassinated by his brother, Langdharma, who launched an attack on Buddhism. In 842, Langdharma was himself assassinated – by a Buddhist monk disguised as a Black Hat dancer, during a festival – and the Tibetan state soon collapsed into a number of warring principalities. In the confusion that followed, support for Buddhism dwindled and clerical monastic Buddhism experienced a 150-year hiatus.

SECOND DIFFUSION OF BUDDHISM

The collapse of the Tibetan state in 842 put a stop to Tibetan expansion in Asia; Tibet was never again to rise to arms. Overwhelmed initially by local

755–97	763
Rule of Trisong Detsen	Tibetan armies overrun Chang'an (present Xian) and force new border treaty

> **TANGTONG GYELPO**
>
> Tangtong Gyelpo (1385–1464) was Tibet's Renaissance man *par excellence*. Nyingmapa yogi, treasure finder, engineer, medic and inventor of Tibetan opera, Tangtong formed a song-and-dance troupe of seven sisters to raise money for his other passion, bridge building. He eventually built 108 bridges in Tibet, the most famous of which was over the Yarlung Tsangpo near modern-day Chushul. Tangtong is often depicted in monastery murals with long white hair and a beard, and is usually holding a section of chain links from one of his bridges.

power struggles, Buddhism gradually began to exert its influence again, giving the Tibetan mind a spiritual bent and turning it inward on itself. As the tide of Buddhist faith receded in India, Nepal and China, Tibet slowly emerged as the most devoutly Buddhist nation in the world.

The so-called second diffusion of Buddhism corresponded with two developments. First, Tibetan teachers who had taken refuge in Kham, to the east, returned to central Tibet in the late 10th century and established new monasteries. Second, the kingdom of Guge in western Tibet invited the Bengali scholar Atisha (Jowo-je; 982–1054) to Tibet in the mid-11th century. Disciples of Atisha (Jowo-je), chiefly Dromtönpa, were instrumental in establishing the Kadampa order and monasteries such as Reting (see p142).

'Tibetan Buddhism became the state religion of the Mongol empire in east Asia'

SAKYAPA ORDER ASCENDANCY & MONGOL OVERLORDSHIP

With the collapse of a central Tibetan state, Tibet's contacts with China dwindled. By the time the Tang dynasty reached the end of its days in 907, China had already recovered almost all the territory it had previously lost to the Tibetans. Throughout the Song dynasty (960–1276) the two nations had virtually no contact with each other, and Tibet's sole foreign contacts were with its southern Buddhist neighbours.

This was all to change when Genghis Khan launched a series of conquests in 1206 that led to a vast Mongol empire that straddled Central Asia and China. Preoccupied with other matters, the Mongols did not give Tibet serious attention until 1239, when they sent a number of raiding parties into the country. Numerous monasteries were razed and the Mongols almost reached Lhasa before turning back.

Tibetan accounts have it that returning Mongol troops related the spiritual eminence of the Tibetan lamas to Godan Khan, grandson of Genghis Khan and ruler of the Kokonor region (modern-day Qinghai). In response Godan summoned Sakya Pandita, the head of Sakya Monastery, to his court. The outcome of this meeting was the beginning of a priest-patron relationship between the deeply religious Tibetans and the militarily adventurous Mongols. Tibetan Buddhism became the state religion of the Mongol empire in east Asia, and the head Sakya lama became its spiritual leader, a position that also entailed temporal authority over Tibet. Many monasteries converted (or were converted) to the Sakya school. For more on the Sakyapa reign, see p184.

The Sakyapa ascendancy lasted less than 100 years. It was strife-torn from the start. The Sakyapa relationship with the Mongol court and its rule of Tibet aroused the jealousy of other religious orders. Political intrigue,

Samye, the first monastery in Tibet, is built

Great Debate at Samye

power struggles and violence were the order of the day. By 1350, Changchub Gyaltsen, a monk who had first trained in Sakya and then returned to his home district in the Yarlung Valley as a local official, contrived, through alliances and outright confrontation, to overturn the Sakya hegemony. Just 18 years later, the Mongol Yuan dynasty in China lost its grip on power and the Chinese Ming dynasty was established.

TIBETAN INDEPENDENCE

Certain Chinese claims on Tibet have looked to the Mongol Yuan dynasty overlordship of the high plateau, and the priest-patron relationship existing at the time, as setting a precedent for Chinese sovereignty over Tibet. Pro-independence supporters state that this is like India claiming sovereignty over Myanmar (Burma) because both were ruled by the British.

In fact, Tibetan submission was offered to the Mongols before they conquered China and it ended when the Mongols fell from power in that country. When the Mongol empire disintegrated, both China and Tibet regained their independence. Sino-Tibetan relations took on the form of exchanges of diplomatic courtesies by two independent governments.

After defeating the Sakyapas, Changchub Gyaltsen undertook to remove all traces of the Mongol administration. In doing this, he drew on the tradition of the former Yarlung kings: officials were required to dress in the manner of the former royal court, a revised version of King Songtsen Gampo's code of law was enacted, a new taxation system was enforced, and scrolls depicting the glories of the Yarlung dynasty were commissioned (although Changchub Gyaltsen claimed they were 'discovered'). The movement was a declaration of Tibet's independence from foreign interference and a search for national identity.

Changchub Gyaltsen and his successors ruled Tibet from Nedong, near the Yarlung Valley, until 1435. Their rule was succeeded by the princes of Rinphug, an area southwest of Lhasa. In 1565, the kings of Tsang became secular rulers of Tibet from Shigatse. Spiritual authority at this time was vested in the Karmapa, head of a Kagyupa suborder at Tsurphu Monastery (p134).

Tibet and its History (1962) by Hugh Richardson offers an excellent, non-politicised view of Tibetan history, concentrating on the years from the Gelugpa ascendancy to the Chinese takeover. Richardson headed Britain's trade missions in Gyantse and Lhasa in the 1930s and 1940s.

RISE OF THE GELUGPA & THE DALAI LAMAS

In 1374, a young man named Tsongkhapa set out from his home near Kokonor in eastern Tibet to central Tibet, where he undertook training with all the major schools of Tibetan Buddhism. By the time he was 25, he had already gained a reputation as a teacher and a writer, although he continued to study under eminent lamas of the day.

Tsongkhapa established a monastery at Ganden, near Lhasa, and it was here that he had a vision of Atisha (Jowo-je), the 11th-century Bengali scholar who had been instrumental in the second diffusion of Buddhism in Tibet. At Ganden, Tsongkhapa maintained a course of expounding his thinking, steering clear of political intrigue, and espousing doctrinal purity and monastic discipline. Although it seems unlikely that Tsongkhapa intended to found another school of Buddhism, his teachings attracted many disciples, who found his return to the original teachings of Atisha (Jowo-je) an exciting alternative to the politically tainted Sakyapa and Kagyupa orders.

821	1040–1123
Sino-Tibetan treaty signed during the reign of King Tritsug Detsen Ralpachen (r 817–36)	Life of Milarepa

Disciples of Tsongkhapa, determined to propagate their master's teachings, established monasteries at Drepung, Sera and Tashilhunpo, and the movement came to be known as the Gelugpa (Virtuous) order.

By the time of the third reincarnated head of the Gelugpa, Sonam Gyatso (1543–88), the Mongols began to take an interest in Tibet's new and increasingly powerful order. In a move that mirrored the 13th-century Sakyapa entrance into the political arena, Sonam Gyatso accepted an invitation to meet with Altyn Khan near Kokonor in 1578. At the meeting, Sonam Gyatso received the title of *dalai*, meaning 'ocean', and implying 'ocean of wisdom'. The title was retrospectively bestowed on his previous two reincarnations, and Sonam Gyatso became the third Dalai Lama.

The Dalai Lamas are depicted in wall paintings holding the Wheel of Law (Wheel of Dharma) as a symbol of the political power gained under the Great Fifth Dalai Lama.

The Gelugpa-Mongol relationship marked the Gelugpa's entry into the turbulent waters of worldly affairs. Ties with the Mongols deepened when, at the third Dalai Lama's death in 1588, his next reincarnation was found in a great-grandson of the Mongolian Altyn Khan. The boy was brought to Lhasa with great ceremony under the escort of armed Mongol troops.

It is no surprise that the Tsang kings and the Karmapa of Tsurphu Monastery saw this Gelugpa-Mongol alliance as a direct threat to their power. Bickering ensued, and in 1611 the Tsang king attacked Drepung and Sera Monasteries. The fourth Dalai Lama fled central Tibet and died at the age of 25 (he was probably poisoned) in 1616.

THE GREAT FIFTH DALAI LAMA

A successor to the fourth Dalai Lama was soon discovered, and the boy was brought to Lhasa, again under Mongol escort. In the meantime, Mongol intervention in Tibetan affairs continued in the guise of support for the embattled Gelugpa order.

In 1640, Mongol forces intervened on behalf of the Gelugpas, defeating the Tsang forces. The Tsang king was taken captive and later executed, probably at the instigation of Tashilhunpo monks.

Unlike the Sakya-Mongol domination of Tibet, under which the head Sakya lama was required to reside in the Mongol court, the fifth Dalai Lama was able to rule from within Tibet. With Mongol backing, all of Tibet was pacified by 1656, and the Dalai Lama's control ranged from Mt Kailash in the west, to Kham in the east. The fifth Dalai Lama had become both the spiritual and temporal sovereign of a unified Tibet.

The fifth Dalai Lama is remembered as having ushered in a great new age for Tibet. He made a tour of Tibet's monasteries, and although he stripped most Kadampa monasteries – his chief rivals for power – of their riches, he allowed them to re-establish. A new flurry of monastic construction began, the major achievement being Labrang Monastery (in what is now Gansu province). In Lhasa, work began on a fitting residence for the head of the Tibetan state: the Potala. The Dalai Lama also invited Indian scholars to Tibet, and with Mongol financial support saw to the renovation and expansion of many temples and monasteries.

MANCHUS, MONGOLS & MURDER

Reincarnation lineages were probably first adopted as a means of maintaining the illusion of a continuous spiritual authority within the various monastic orders of Tibet. With the death of the fifth Dalai Lama in 1682,

1073

Sakya Monastery founded	Sakya capital of Tibet

1268–1364

REINCARNATION LINEAGES

It is not unusual for an important Tibetan lama to be a *trulku* (also spelt *tulku*), or 'incarnate lama'. There are thought to be several thousand of these lamas in contemporary Tibet. The abbots of many monasteries are *trulku*, and thus abbotship can be traced back through a lineage of rebirths to the original founder of a monastery, or at least to an important figure associated with the founding of the monastery.

Strictly speaking, however, this investiture of power through rebirth is known as *yangsid*, and a *trulku* is a manifestation of a Tantric deity that repeatedly expresses itself through a series of rebirths. The honorific title *rinpoche*, meaning 'very precious', is a mark of respect and does not necessarily imply that the holder is a *trulku*.

The most famous manifestation of a deity is, of course, the Dalai Lama lineage. The Dalai Lamas are manifestations of Chenresig (Avalokiteshvara), the Bodhisattva of Compassion. The Panchen Lama is a manifestation of Jampelyang (Manjushri), the Bodhisattva of Insight. There is no exclusivity in such a manifestation: Tsongkhapa, founder of the Gelugpa order, was also a manifestation of Jampelyang (Manjushri), as traditionally were the abbots of the Sakya Monastery.

As a general rule, the reincarnations of high-status lamas tend to be found in aristocratic families (as in the early Dalai Lamas) or in families where *trulkus* have already been identified. The family of the present Dalai Lama, for example, was by no means aristocratic but his elder brother had already been identified as a *trulku* and his younger brother was also later recognised as a *trulku*.

Lamas approaching death often leave behind clues pointing to the location of their reincarnation. The Panchen Lamas have their reincarnation confirmed by lots drawn from a golden urn. Potential candidates are tested by being required to pick out the former lama's possessions from a collection of objects. Disputes over *trulku* status are not uncommon (see The Karmapa Connection, p135). A family's fortunes are likely to improve if an incarnate lama is discovered among the children; this creates an incentive for fraud.

It is possible to see in the *trulku* system a substitute for the system of hereditary power (as in Western royal lineages) in a society where, historically, many of the major players were celibate and unable to produce their own heirs. Not that celibacy was overwhelmingly the case. The abbots of Sakya took wives to produce their own *trulku* reincarnations, and it is not uncommon for rural *trulkus* to do the same.

The major flaw with the system is the time needed for the reincarnation to reach adulthood. Regents have traditionally been appointed to run the country but this tradition takes on an added dimension under modern political circumstances. The Dalai Lama has made it clear that he will not be reincarnated in Chinese-occupied Tibet and may even be the last Dalai Lama.

however, the weakness of such a system became apparent. The Tibetan government was confronted with the prospect of finding his reincarnation and then waiting 18 years until the boy came of age. The great personal prestige and authority of the fifth Dalai Lama had played no small part in holding together a newly unified Tibet. The Dalai Lama's regent decided to shroud the Dalai Lama's death in secrecy, announcing that the fifth lama had entered a long period of meditation (over 10 years!).

In 1695 the secret was leaked and the regent was forced to hastily enthrone the sixth Dalai Lama, a boy of his own choosing. The choice was an unfortunate one (see p30) and could not have come at a worse time.

In China, the Ming dynasty had fallen in 1644 and the Manchus from the north had swiftly moved in to fill the power vacuum, establishing the

1409	1578
Ganden Monastery established by Tsongkhapa; Gelugpa monasteries founded at Drepung (1416), Sera (1419) and Tashilhunpo (1447)	Head of the Gelugpa receives the title Dalai Lama from the Mongols

---

THE SIXTH DALAI LAMA

Tsangyang Gyatso was, shall we say, an unconventional Dalai Lama. A sensual youth with long hair and a penchant for erotic verse, he soon proved himself to be far more interested in wine and women than meditation and study. He refused to take his final vows as a monk and he would often sneak out of the Potala at night to raise hell in the bawdy brothels of Shöl. A resident Jesuit monk described him as a 'dissolute youth' and 'quite depraved', noting that 'no good-looking person of either sex was safe from his unbridled licentiousness'.

Manchu Qing dynasty (1644–1912). The events that followed were complicated. Basically, Tibet's ineffectual head of state, the Qing perception of the threat of Tibetan relations with the Mongols, disunity within the ranks of Tibet's Mongol allies and Qing ambitions to extend its power into Tibet led to a Qing intervention that was to have lasting consequences for Tibet.

Tibet's dealings with the new Qing government went awry from the start. Kangxi, the second Qing emperor, took offence when the death of the fifth Dalai Lama was concealed from him. At the same time, an ambitious Mongol prince named Lhabzang Khan came to the conclusion that earlier Mongol leaders had taken too much of a back-seat position in their relations with the Tibetans and appealed to Emperor Kangxi for support. It was granted and, in 1705, Mongol forces descended on Lhasa, killing the Tibetan regent and capturing the sixth Dalai Lama with the intention of delivering him to Kangxi in Beijing. He died en route at Litang (he was probably murdered) and Lhabzang Khan installed a new Dalai Lama in Lhasa.

DID YOU KNOW?

The concept of reincarnation was first introduced by the Karmapa and later adopted by the Dalai Lamas.

Lhabzang Khan's machinations backfired. The Mongol removal, possible murder and replacement of the sixth Dalai Lama aroused intense hostility in Tibet. Worse still, it created enemies among other Mongol tribes, who saw the Dalai Lama as their spiritual leader.

In 1717 the Dzungar Mongols from Central Asia attacked Lhasa, killing Lhabzang Khan and deposing the new Dalai Lama. The resulting confusion in Tibet was the opportunity for which Emperor Kangxi had been waiting. He responded by sending a military expedition to Lhasa in 1720. The Chinese troops drove out the Dzungar Mongols and were received by the Tibetans as liberators. They were unlikely to have been received any other way: with them, they brought the seventh Dalai Lama, who had been languishing in Kumbum Monastery under Chinese 'protection'.

Emperor Kangxi wasted no time in declaring Tibet a protectorate of China. Two Chinese representatives, known as Ambans, were installed at Lhasa, along with a garrison of Chinese troops. It was just a beginning, leading to two centuries of Manchu overlordship and serving as a convenient historical precedent for the communist takeover nearly 250 years later.

MANCHU OVERLORDSHIP

The seventh Dalai Lama ruled until his death in 1757. However, at this point it became clear that another ruler would have to be appointed until the next Dalai Lama reached adulthood. The post of regent was created, and it was decided that it should be held by a lama.

It is perhaps a poor reflection on the spiritual attainment of the lamas appointed as regents that few were willing to relinquish the reins once they were in the saddle. In the 120 years between the death of the seventh Dalai Lama and the adulthood of the 13th, actual power was wielded by the Dalai Lamas for only seven years. Three of them died very young and under suspicious circumstances. Only the eighth Dalai Lama survived into his adulthood, living a quiet, contemplative life until the age of 45.

DID YOU KNOW?

In the 120 years between the death of the seventh Dalai Lama and the majority of the 13th, actual power was wielded by the Dalai Lamas for only seven years.

BARBARIANS AT THE DOORSTEP

Early contact between Britain and Tibet commenced with a mission to Shigatse headed by a Scotsman, George Bogle, in 1774. Bogle soon ingratiated himself with the Panchen Lama – to the extent of marrying one of his sisters. With the death of the third Panchen Lama in 1780 and the ban on foreign contact that came after the Gurkha invasion of Tibet in 1788, Britain lost all official contact with Tibet.

Meanwhile, Britain watched nervously as the Russian empire swallowed up Central Asia, pushing its borders 1000km further towards India. The reported arrival of Russian 'adviser' Agvan Dorjieff in Lhasa exacerbated fears that Russia had military designs on Britain's 'jewel in the crown'.

Dorjieff was a Buryat Buddhist monk from near Lake Baikal who had studied at Drepung Monastery for 15 years before finally becoming one of the spiritual advisers of the 13th Dalai Lama. Dorjieff seems to have convinced both himself and the Dalai Lama that the Russian empire was the home of Shambhala, the mythical kingdom from the north whose king (or tsar) would come to save Tibet from its enemies.

When Dorjieff led an envoy from the Dalai Lama to Tsar Nicholas II in 1898, 1900 and 1901, and when British intelligence confirmed that Lhasa had received Russian missions (while similar British advances had been refused), the Raj broke into a cold sweat. There was even wild conjecture that the tsar was poised to convert to Buddhism.

It was against this background that Lord Curzon, viceroy of India, decided to nip Russian designs in the bud. In late 1903, an expedition led by Colonel Francis Younghusband entered Tibet via Sikkim. After several months waiting for a Tibetan delegation, the British expedition moved on to Lhasa, where it was discovered that the Dalai Lama had fled to Mongolia with Dorjieff. However, an Anglo-Tibetan convention was signed following negotiations with Tri Rinpoche, a lama from Ganden whom the Dalai Lama had appointed as regent in his absence. British forces withdrew after spending just two months in Lhasa. For more on the story of the British invasion, see p170.

The missing link in the Anglo-Tibetan accord was a Manchu signature. In effect, the accord implied that Tibet was a sovereign power and therefore had the right to make treaties of its own. The Manchus objected and, in 1906, the British signed a second accord with the Manchus, one that recognised China's suzerainty over Tibet. In 1910, with the Manchu Qing dynasty teetering on collapse, the Manchus made good on the accord and invaded Tibet, forcing the Dalai Lama once again into flight – this time into the arms of the British in India.

1642	1645
Lhasa becomes capital of Tibet	Work starts on Potala Palace

TIBETAN INDEPENDENCE REVISITED

In 1911 a revolution finally toppled the decadent Qing dynasty in China, and by the end of 1912 the last of the occupying Manchu forces were escorted out of Tibet. In January 1913 the 13th Dalai Lama returned to Lhasa from Sikkim.

The government of the new Chinese republic, anxious to maintain control of former Qing territories, sent a telegram to the Dalai Lama expressing regret at the actions of the Manchu oppressors and announcing that the Dalai Lama was being formally restored to his former rank. The Dalai Lama replied that he was uninterested in ranks bestowed by the Chinese and that he was assuming temporal and spiritual leadership of his country.

Tibetans have since read this reply as a formal declaration of independence. It certainly was in spirit if not quite in letter. As for the Chinese, they chose to ignore it, reporting that the Dalai Lama had responded with a letter expressing his great love for the motherland. Whatever the case, Tibet was to enjoy 30 years free of interference from China. What is more, Tibet was suddenly presented with an opportunity to create a state that was ready to rise to the challenge of the modern world and, if needs be, protect itself from the territorial ambitions of China. The opportunity foundered on Tibet's entrenched theocratic institutions, and Tibetan independence was a short-lived affair.

ATTEMPTS TO MODERNISE

During the period of his flight to India, the 13th Dalai Lama had become intimate friends with Sir Charles Bell, a Tibetan scholar and political officer in Sikkim. The relationship was to initiate a warming in Anglo-Tibetan affairs and to see the British playing an increasingly important role as mediators in problems between Tibet and China.

The Snow Lion and the Dragon by Melvyn Goldstein is worth wading through if you want an unsentimental analysis of the historically complex issue of China's claims to Tibet, and the Dalai Lama's options in dealing with the current Chinese leadership.

In 1920 Bell was dispatched on a mission to Lhasa, where he renewed his friendship with the Dalai Lama. It was agreed that the British would supply the Tibetans with modern arms, providing they agreed to use them only for self-defence. Tibetan military officers were trained in Gyantse and India, and a telegraph line was set up linking Lhasa and Shigatse. Other developments included the construction of a small hydroelectric station near Lhasa and the establishment of an English school at Gyantse. Four Tibetan boys were even sent to public school at Rugby in England. At the invitation of the Dalai Lama, British experts conducted geological surveys of parts of Tibet with a view to gauging mining potential.

It is highly likely that the 13th Dalai Lama's trips away from his country had made him realise that it was imperative that Tibet begin to modernise. At the same time he must also have been aware that the road to modernisation was fraught with difficulties. The biggest problem was the Tibetan social system.

Since the rise of the Gelugpa order, Tibet had been ruled as a theocracy. Monks, particularly those in the huge monastic complexes of Drepung and Sera in Lhasa, were accustomed to a high degree of influence in the Tibetan government. And for the monks of Tibet, the principal focus of government was the maintenance of the religious state. Attempts to modernise were seen as inimical to this aim, and they began to meet intense opposition.

1720	1903–04
Chinese invasion, marking beginning of Chinese suzerainty over Tibet	British invasion of Tibet, Dalai Lama flees to Mongolia

Before too long, the 13th Dalai Lama's innovations fell victim to a conservative backlash. Newly trained Tibetan officers were reassigned to nonmilitary jobs, causing a rapid deterioration of military discipline; a newly established police force was left to its own devices and soon became ineffective; the English school at Gyantse was closed down; and a mail service set up by the British was stopped.

However, Tibet's brief period of independence was troubled by more than just an inability to modernise. Conflict sprang up between the Panchen Lama and the Dalai Lama over the autonomy of Tashilhunpo Monastery and its estates. The Panchen Lama, after appealing to the British to mediate, fled to China, where he was kept for 14 years until his death.

The definitive (but weighty) account of Tibetan history since 1947 is *The Dragon in the Land of Snows* by Tsering Shakya.

In 1933 the 13th Dalai Lama died, leaving the running of the country to the regent of Reting. The present (14th) Dalai Lama was discovered at the village of Pari Takster, near Xining in Amdo, but was brought to Lhasa only after the local Chinese commander had been paid off with a huge 'fee' of 300,000 Chinese dollars. The boy was renamed Tenzin Gyatso and he was installed as the Dalai Lama on 22 February 1940, aged 4½.

In 1947 an attempted coup d'état, known as the Reting Conspiracy, rocked Lhasa. And in 1949 the Chinese Nationalist government, against all odds, fell to Mao Zedong and his communist 'bandits'.

LIBERATION

Unknown to the Tibetans, the communist takeover of China was to open what is probably the saddest chapter in Tibetan history. The Chinese 'liberation' of Tibet was eventually to lead to 1.2 million Tibetan deaths, a full-on assault on the Tibetan traditional way of life, the flight of the Dalai Lama to India and the large-scale destruction of almost every historical structure on the plateau. The chief culprits were Chinese ethnic chauvinism and an epidemic of social madness known as the Cultural Revolution.

'When the iron bird flies and horses run on wheels, the Tibetan people will be scattered throughout the world and the Dharma will come to the land of red men.'
GURU RINPOCHE

On 7 October 1950, just a year after the communist takeover of China, 30,000 battle-hardened Chinese troops attacked central Tibet from six different directions. The Tibetan army, a poorly equipped force of around 4000 men, stood little chance of resisting, and any attempt at defence soon collapsed before the onslaught. In Lhasa, the Tibetan government reacted by enthroning the 15-year-old 14th Dalai Lama, an action that brought jubilation and dancing on the streets but did little to protect Tibet from advancing Chinese troops.

An appeal to the UN was equally ineffective. To the shame of all involved, only El Salvador sponsored a motion to condemn Chinese aggression, and Britain and India, traditional friends of Tibet, actually managed to convince the UN not to debate the issue for fear of Chinese disapproval.

Presented with this seemingly hopeless situation, the Dalai Lama dispatched a mission to Beijing with orders that it refer all decisions to Lhasa. As it turned out, there were no decisions to be made. The Chinese had already drafted an agreement. The Tibetans had two choices: sign on the dotted line or face further Chinese aggression.

The 17-point *Agreement on Measures for the Peaceful Liberation of Tibet* promised a one-country-two-systems structure much like that offered

1910	1940
Chinese invasion of Tibet, Dalai Lama flees to British India	Fourteenth Dalai Lama installed, aged 4½

later to Hong Kong and Macau, but provided little in the way of guarantees that such a promise would be honoured. The Tibetan delegates protested that they were unauthorised to sign such an agreement and anyway lacked the seal of the Dalai Lama. Thoughtfully, the Chinese had already prepared a forged Dalai Lama seal, and the agreement was ratified.

Initially, the Chinese occupation of central Tibet was carried out in an orderly way, but tensions inevitably mounted. The presence of large numbers of Chinese troops in the Lhasa region soon depleted food stores and gave rise to massive inflation. Rumours of massacres and forced political indoctrination in Kham (eastern Tibet) began to filter through to Lhasa.

In 1956 uprisings broke out in eastern Tibet (see p227) and in 1957 and 1958 protests and armed revolt spread to central Tibet (with covert CIA assistance). With a heavy heart, the Dalai Lama returned to Lhasa in March 1957 from a trip to India to celebrate the 2500th anniversary of the birth of the Buddha. It seemed inevitable that Tibet would explode in revolt and equally inevitable that it would be ruthlessly suppressed by the Chinese.

1959 UPRISING

The Tibetan New Year of 1959, like all the New Year celebrations before it, attracted huge crowds to Lhasa, doubling the city's usual population. In addition to the usual festival activities, the Chinese had added a highlight of their own – a performance by a Chinese dance group at the Lhasa military base. The invitation to the Dalai Lama came in the form of a thinly veiled command. The Dalai Lama, wishing to avoid offence, accepted.

As preparations for the performance drew near, however, the Dalai Lama's security chief was surprised to hear that the Dalai Lama was expected to attend in secrecy and without his customary contingent of 25 bodyguards. Despite the Dalai Lama's agreement to these conditions, news of them soon leaked, and in no time simmering frustration at Chinese rule came to the boil among the crowds on the streets. It seemed obvious to the Tibetans that the Chinese were about to kidnap the Dalai Lama. Large numbers of people gathered around the Norbulingka (the Dalai Lama's summer palace) and swore to protect him with their lives.

The Dalai Lama had no choice but to cancel his appointment at the military base. In the meantime, the crowds on the streets were swollen by Tibetan soldiers, who changed out of their People's Liberation Army (PLA) uniforms and started to hand out weapons. A group of government ministers announced that the 17-point agreement was null and void, and that Tibet renounced the authority of China.

The Dalai Lama was powerless to intervene, managing only to pen some conciliatory letters to the Chinese as his people prepared for battle on Lhasa's streets. In a last-ditch effort to prevent bloodshed, the Dalai Lama even offered himself to the Chinese. The reply came in the sound of two mortar shells exploding in the gardens of the Norbulingka. The attack made it obvious that the only option remaining to the Dalai Lama was flight. On 17 March, he left the Norbulingka disguised as a soldier. Fourteen days later he was in India.

An excellent scholarly account of modern Tibet is Melvyn Goldstein's *A History of Modern Tibet 1913–1959: The Demise of the Lamaist State*, which pulls no punches in showing the intrigues, superstitions and governmental ineptitude that led to the demise of the Lhasa government.

John Avedon's *In Exile from the Land of Snows* is largely an account of the Tibetan community in Dharamsala, but is an excellent and informative read.

1950	1956
Chinese communist invasion of Tibet; signing of 17-point agreement	Litang Monastery bombed by Chinese

TIBET IN EXILE

Modern political boundaries and history have led to the fracture of the Tibetan nation. Large areas of historical and ethnic Tibet are now incorporated into the Chinese provinces of Qinghai and Gansu (traditionally known as Amdo), and Sichuan and Yunnan (traditionally known as Kham). More Tibetans now live outside the Tibetan Autonomous Region than inside it.

Then figure on the 120,000 Tibetans in exile. Refugees continue to brave high passes and rapacious border guards to get to Kathmandu, paying as much as Y800 for a guide to help them across. The trek can take up to 25 days, with no supplies other than all the dried yak meat and *tsampa* (roasted barley flour) they can carry, and no equipment except canvas shoes to help them get over the 6000m passes. Dharamsala and McLeod Ganj (see www.tibet.net) in India's Himachal Pradesh have become de facto Tibetan towns, although the Dalai Lama, after personally meeting each refugee, actively encourages many of them to return to Tibet.

The great monasteries of Tibet have also relocated, many to the sweltering heat of South India, where you can find replicas of Sera, Ganden and Drepung Monasteries. There are also large communities of Tibetans in mountainous Switzerland and the USA.

With exile has come an unexpected flowering of Tibetan Buddhism abroad; you can now find prayer flags gracing the Scottish glens of Samye Ling Monastery in Dumfrieshire and huge chörtens decorating the countryside of California.

BLOODSHED IN LHASA

With both the Chinese and the Tibetans unaware of the Dalai Lama's departure, tensions continued to mount in Lhasa. Early on the morning of 20 March, Chinese troops began to shell the Norbulingka and the crowds surrounding it, killing hundreds of people. Later, as the corpses were searched, it became obvious that the Dalai Lama had escaped – 'abducted by a reactionary clique' went the Chinese reports.

Still the bloodshed continued. Artillery bombed the Potala, Sera Monastery and the medical college on Chagpo Ri. Tibetans armed with petrol bombs were picked off by Chinese snipers, and when a crowd of 10,000 Tibetans retreated into the sacred precincts of the Jokhang, that too was bombed. It is thought that after three days of violence, 10,000 to 15,000 Tibetans lay dead in Lhasa's streets.

SOCIALIST PARADISE ON THE ROOF OF THE WORLD

The Chinese quickly consolidated their quelling of the Lhasa uprising by taking control of all the high passes between Tibet and India. Freedom fighters were disarmed by superior Chinese troops, and able-bodied young men were rounded up, shot, incarcerated or put to work on Chinese work teams. As the Chinese themselves put it, they were liberating Tibet from reactionary forces and ushering in a new socialist society, whether the Tibetans liked it or not.

The Chinese abolished the Tibetan government and set about reordering Tibetan society in accordance with their Marxist principles. The educated and the aristocratic were put to work on menial jobs and subjected to struggle sessions, known as *thamzing*, which sometimes resulted in death. A ferment of class struggle was whipped up and former feudal exploiters – some of whom Tibet's poor may have harboured genuine resentment towards – were subjected to punishments of awful cruelty.

In 1954 the Dalai Lama was invited to Beijing, where, amid cordial discussions with Mao Zedong, he was told that religion was 'poison'.

1959	1965
Tibetan uprising; Dalai Lama goes into exile	Tibetan Autonomous Region declared

The Chinese also turned their attention to Tibet's 6000-plus 'feudal' monasteries. Tibetans were refused permission to donate food to the monasteries, and monks were compelled to join struggle sessions, discard their robes and marry. Monasteries were stripped of their riches, Buddhist scriptures were burnt and used as toilet paper, and the wholesale destruction of Tibet's monastic heritage began in earnest.

Notable in this litany of disasters was the Chinese decision to alter Tibetan farming practices. Instead of barley, the Tibetan staple, farmers were instructed to grow wheat and rice. Tibetans protested that these crops were unsuited to Tibet's high altitude. They were right, and mass starvation resulted. It is estimated that by late 1961, 70,000 Tibetans had died or were dying of starvation.

By September 1961, even the Chinese-groomed Panchen Lama began to have a change of heart. He presented Mao Zedong with a 70,000-character report on the hardships his people were suffering and also requested, among other things, religious freedom and an end to the sacking of Tibetan monasteries. Four years later he was to disappear into a high-security prison for a 10-year stay. More would soon join him.

THE CULTURAL REVOLUTION

Among the writings of Mao Zedong is a piece entitled 'On Going Too Far'. It is a subject on which he was particularly well qualified to write. What started as a power struggle between Mao and Liu Shaoqi in 1965 had become by August 1966 the Great Proletarian Cultural Revolution, a movement that was to shake China to its core, trample its traditions under foot, cause countless deaths and give the running of the country over to mobs of Red Guards. All of China suffered in Mao's bold experiment in creating a new socialist paradise, but it was Tibet that suffered most.

The first Red Guards arrived in Lhasa in July 1966. Two months later, the first rally was organised and Chinese-educated Tibetan youths raided the Jokhang, desecrating whatever religious objects they could get their hands on. It was the beginning of the large-scale destruction of virtually every religious monument in Tibet, and was carried out in the spirit of destroying the 'Four Olds': old thinking, old culture, old habits and old customs. The Buddhist *'om mani padme hum'* ('hail to the jewel in the lotus') was replaced by the communist mantra, 'long live Chairman Mao'. The Buddha himself was accused of being a 'reactionary'.

For more than three years the Cultural Revolution went about its destructive business of turning the Tibetan world on its head. Tibetan farmers were forced to collectivise into communes and were told what to grow and when to grow it. Anyone who objected was arrested and subjected to *thamzing*. The Dalai Lama became public enemy number one and Tibetans were forced to denounce him as a parasite and traitor. The list goes on, a harrowing catalogue of crimes against a people whose only fault was to hold aspirations that differed from those of their Chinese masters.

By late 1969 the PLA had the Red Guards under control but Tibet continued to be the site of outbreaks of violence. Tibetan uprisings were brief and subdued brutally. In 1972 restrictions on Tibetans' freedom of worship were lifted with much fanfare but little in the way of results.

On 1 September 1965 the Tibetan Autonomous Region was formally brought into being with much fanfare and Chinese talk of happy Tibetans fighting back tears of gratitude at becoming one with the great motherland.

1966–69

Height of Cultural Revolution

1973

CIA-funded Khampa resistance formally ended

In 1975 a group of foreign journalists sympathetic to the Chinese cause were invited to Tibet. The reports they filed gave a sad picture of a land whose people had been battered by Chinese-imposed policies and atrocities that amounted to nothing less than cultural genocide. In the same year the last CIA-funded Tibetan guerrilla bases, in Mustang, northern Nepal, were closed down.

THE POST-MAO YEARS

By the time of Mao's death in 1976 even the Chinese must have begun to realise that their rule in Tibet had taken a wrong turn. Mao's chosen successor, Hua Guofeng, decided to soften the government's line on Tibet and called for a revival of Tibetan customs. In mid-1977 China announced that it would welcome the return of the Dalai Lama and other Tibetan refugees, and shortly afterwards the Panchen Lama was released from more than 10 years of imprisonment.

Sorrow Mountain: The Journey of a Tibetan Warrior Nun by Ani Pachen and Adelaide Donnelly is the story of a nun who became a resistance leader and was imprisoned by the Chinese for 21 years before escaping to India.

The Tibetan government-in-exile received cautiously the invitation to return to Tibet, and the Dalai Lama suggested that he be allowed to send a fact-finding mission to Tibet first. To the surprise of all involved, the Chinese agreed. As the Dalai Lama remarked in his autobiography, *Freedom in Exile*, it seemed that the Chinese were of the opinion that the mission members would find such happiness in their homeland that 'they would see no point in remaining in exile'. In fact, the results of the mission were so damning that the Dalai Lama decided not to publish them.

Nevertheless, two more missions followed. Their conclusions were despairing. The missions catalogued up to 1.2 million deaths, the destruction of 6254 monasteries and nunneries, the absorption of two thirds of Tibet into China, 100,000 Tibetans in labour camps and extensive deforestation. In a mere 30 years, the Chinese had turned Tibet into a land of nearly unrecognisable desolation.

In China, Hua Guofeng's short-lived political ascendancy had been eclipsed by Deng Xiaoping's rise to power. In 1980 Deng sent Hu Yaobang on a Chinese fact-finding mission that coincided with the visits of those sent by the Tibetan government-in-exile.

Hu's conclusions, while not as damning as those of the Tibetans, painted a grim picture of life on the roof of the world. A six-point plan to improve the living conditions and freedoms of the Tibetans was drawn up, taxes were dropped for two years and limited private enterprise was allowed. The Jokhang was reopened for two days a month in 1978; the Potala opened in 1980. As in the rest of China, the government embarked on a program of extended personal freedoms in concert with authoritarian one-party rule.

The journalist Harrison Salisbury referred to Tibet in the mid-1980s as a 'dark and sorrowing land'.

THE DENG YEARS

The early 1980s saw the return of limited religious freedoms. Monasteries that had not been reduced to piles of rubble began to reopen and some religious artefacts were returned to Tibet from China.

Importantly, there was also a relaxation of the Chinese proscription on pilgrimage. Pictures of the Dalai Lama began to reappear on the streets of Lhasa. Not that any of this pointed to a significant reversal in Chinese thinking on the question of religion, which remained an 'opiate

early 1980s	1989
Limited religious freedoms restored	Panchen Lama dies

of the masses'. Those who exercised their religious freedoms did so at considerable risk.

Talks aimed at bringing the Dalai Lama back into the ambit of Chinese influence continued, but with little result. A three-person team sent to Beijing from Dharamsala in 1982 heard lectures on how Tibet was part of China, and was told in no uncertain terms that the Dalai Lama would be given a desk job in Beijing if he were to return. By 1983 talks had broken down and the Chinese had decided that they did not want the Dalai Lama to return after all. Tibet, according to the Chinese government, became the 'front line of the struggle against splittism'.

Perhaps most dismaying for Tibetans, however, was the emergence of a Chinese policy of Han immigration to the high plateau. Sinicisation had already been successfully carried out in Xinjiang, Inner Mongolia and Qinghai, and now Tibet was targeted for mass immigration. Attractive salaries and interest-free loans were made available to Chinese willing to emigrate to Tibet, and, in 1984 alone, more than 100,000 Han Chinese took advantage of the incentives to 'modernise' the backward province of Tibet.

In 1986 a new influx of foreigners arrived in Tibet, with the Chinese beginning to loosen restrictions on tourism. The trickle of tour groups and individual travellers soon became a flood. For the first time since the Chinese takeover, visitors from the West were given the opportunity to see the results of Chinese rule in Tibet.

For the Chinese, the foreigners were a mixed blessing. The tourist dollars were appreciated, but foreigners had an annoying habit of sympathising with the Tibetans. They also got to see things that the Chinese would rather they did not see.

When in September 1987 a group of 30 monks from Sera Monastery began circumambulating the Jokhang and crying out 'Independence for Tibet' and 'Long live his Holiness the Dalai Lama', their ranks were swollen by bystanders and arrests followed. Four days later, another group of monks repeated their actions, this time brandishing Tibetan flags.

The monks were beaten and arrested. With Western tourists looking on, a crowd of 2000 to 3000 angry Tibetans gathered. Police vehicles were overturned and Chinese police began firing on the crowd.

The Chinese response was swift. Communications with the outside world were broken and foreigners were evicted from Lhasa. It was still too late, however, to prevent eyewitness accounts from reaching newspapers around the world. A crackdown followed in Lhasa, but it failed to prevent further protests in the following months.

The Mönlam festival of March 1988 saw shooting in the streets of Lhasa, and that December a Dutch traveller was shot in the shoulder; 18 Tibetans died and 150 were wounded in the disturbances.

THE DALAI LAMA & THE SEARCH FOR SETTLEMENT

By the mid-1970s, the Dalai Lama had become a prominent international figure, working tirelessly from his government-in-exile in Dharamsala to make the world more aware of his people's plight. His visits to the USA led to official condemnation of the Chinese occupation of Tibet. In 1987 he addressed the US Congress and outlined a five-point peace plan.

Education was once under the exclusive control of the monasteries, and the introduction of a secular education system has been a major goal of the communist government.

An illuminating glimpse of the Tibetan experience is provided by *Freedom in Exile: The Autobiography of the Dalai Lama*. With great humility the Dalai Lama outlines his personal philosophy, his hope to be reunited with his homeland and the story of his life. *Kundun* by Mary Craig is a biography of the Dalai Lama's family.

1989	1999
Dalai Lama awarded Nobel Peace Prize	Karmapa flees Tibet

The plan called for Tibet to be established as a 'zone of peace'; for the policy of Han immigration to Tibet to be abandoned; for a return to basic human rights and democratic freedoms; for the protection of Tibet's natural heritage and an end to the dumping of nuclear waste on the high plateau; and for joint discussions between the Chinese and the Tibetans on the future of Tibet. The Chinese denounced the plan as an example of 'splittism'. They gave the same response when, a year later, the Dalai Lama elaborated on the speech before the European parliament at Strasbourg in France, conceding any demands for full independence and offering the Chinese the right to govern Tibet's foreign and military affairs.

In 2003 the economy of the Tibetan Autonomous Region grew by 12%.

Protests and crackdowns continued in Tibet through 1989, and despairing elements in the exiled Tibetan community began to talk of the need to take up arms. It was an option that the Dalai Lama had consistently opposed. His efforts to achieve peace and freedom for his people were recognised on 4 October 1989, when he was awarded the Nobel peace prize. It must have seemed a small consolation for the civilised world's notable failure to put any real pressure on China for its activities in Tibet.

The 50th anniversary of the 'liberation' of Tibet in 2001 offered a sobering moment of reflection on half a century of tragedy for the Tibetan people.

2002	2007
First visit to Tibet by a delegation of the Dalai Lama for a decade	Railway line to link Tibet and China for the first time

The Culture

THE NATIONAL PSYCHE

Tibetans are such a deeply religious people that a basic knowledge of Buddhism is essential in understanding their world. Buddhism permeates most facets of Tibetan daily life and shapes aspirations in ways that are often quite alien to the Western frame of mind. The ideas of accumulating merit, of sending sons to be monks, of undertaking pilgrimages and of devotion to the sanctity and power of natural places are all elements of the unique fusion between Buddhism and the older shamanistic Bön faith.

For travellers, the easy smile of most Tibetans is infectious and it is rare for major cultural differences to get in the way of communication. Tibetans are among the easiest people in Asia to get along with – all the more remarkable in view of the considerable anger and long-harboured resentment that must lie under the surface in Tibet.

For a look at another side of Tibet, track down *We're No Monks,* directed by Pema Dhondup (www .clearmirrorpictures.com), an iconoclastic film that moves beyond clichés to show the sometimes violent frustrations of younger Tibetans in exile.

TRADITIONAL LIFESTYLE

Traditionally there have been at least three distinct segments of Tibetan society: the nomads *(drokpa;* p138*);* the farmers of the Tibetan valleys *(rongpa);* and the community of monks and nuns *(sangha;* p41*).* Each led very different lives, although all shared a deep faith in Buddhism.

Besides Buddhism, over the centuries these communities have shared a remarkable resistance to change. Until the early 20th century it was a land in which virtually the only use for the wheel was as a device for activating mantras. Traditional Tibet has changed more in the past 50 years than it did in the previous 500 years, although many traditional social structures have endured Chinese attempts at iconoclasm.

Farming communities usually comprise a cluster of homes surrounded by agricultural lands once owned by the nearest large monastery. Most strategic agricultural valleys are protected by the ruins of a *dzong* (fort), perched on a high outcrop. The farming itself is carried out with the assistance of a *dzo,* a breed of cattle where bulls have been crossbred with yaks. Some wealthier farmers own a small 'walking tractor'. Harvested grain is carried by donkeys to a threshing ground where it is trampled by cattle or threshed with poles. The grain is then cast into the air from a basket and the task of winnowing carried out by the breeze. Animal husbandry was, and still is, extremely important in Tibet, and there are around 21 million head of livestock in the country.

One Chinese film worth watching out for is acclaimed director Tian Zhuangzhuang's *The Horse Thief,* a documentary-style look at the nomads of eastern Tibet.

Until recently such communities were effectively self-sufficient in their needs and, although theirs was a hard life, it could not be described as abject poverty. Village families pulled together in times of need. Plots of land were usually graded in terms of quality and then distributed so that the land of any one family included both good- and poorer-quality land. This is changing rapidly as many regions become economically more developed and immersed in a cash economy.

Imports such as tea, porcelain, copper and iron from China were traditionally compensated by exports of wool and skins. Trading was usually carried out in combination with pilgrimage or by nomads. Most villages now have at least one entrepreneur who has set up a shop and begun to ship in Chinese goods from the nearest urban centre.

Individual households normally have a shrine in the home or in a small building in the family compound. There might also be several religious texts, held in a place of honour, which are reserved for occasions when

---

THE WORLD OF A MONK

The Western term 'monk' is slightly misleading when it is used in the context of Tibetan Buddhism. The Tibetan equivalent would probably be *trapa*, which means literally 'scholar' or 'student', and is an inclusive term that covers the three main categories of monastic inmates. Monks in these categories should also be distinguished from lamas, who as spiritual luminaries have a privileged position in the monastic hierarchy, may have considerable wealth and, outside the Gelugpa order, are not necessarily celibate.

The first step for a monk, usually after completing some prior study, is to take one of two lesser vows, the *genyen* or *getsul* ordination – a renunciation of secular life that includes a vow of celibacy. This marks the beginning of a long course of study that is expected to lead to the full *gelong* vows of ordination. While most major monasteries have a number of *gelong* monks, not all monks achieve *gelong* status.

These three categories do not encompass all the monks in a monastery. There are usually specific monastic posts associated with administrative duties, with ritual and with teaching. *Gelong* vows are also supplemented by higher courses of study, which are rewarded in the Gelugpa order by the title *geshe*. In premodern Tibet the larger monasteries also had divisions of so-called 'fighting monks', or monastic militias. To a large extent they served as a kind of police force within a particular monastery, but there were also times when their services were used to hammer home a doctrinal dispute with a rival monastery.

---

a monk or holy man visits the village. Ceremonies for blessing yaks and other livestock to ensure a productive year are also held. One of the highlights of the year for rural Tibetans is visiting nearby monasteries at festival times or making a pilgrimage to a holy site. Before the Chinese invasion, entertainment included the occasional arrival of *lhamo* (Tibetan opera) troupes or wandering bands of musicians. As traditional life reasserts itself, many of these traditions are slowly making a comeback.

Marriage

Marriages were traditionally arranged by the families involved, in consultation with a lama or shaman. Up until the Chinese invasion many Tibetan farming villages practised polyandry. When a woman married the eldest son of a family she also married his younger brothers (providing they did not become monks). The children of such marriages referred to all the brothers as their father. The practice was aimed at easing the inheritance of family property (mainly the farming land) and avoiding the break-up of small plots.

Death

Although the early kings of Tibet were buried with complex funerary rites, ordinary Tibetans have not traditionally been buried. The bodies of the very poor were usually dumped in a river when they died and the bodies of the very holy were cremated and their ashes enshrined in a chörten. But in a land where soil is at a premium and wood for cremation is scarcer still, most bodies were, and still are, disposed of by sky burial.

After death, the body is kept for 24 hours in a sitting position while a lama recites prayers from *The Tibetan Book of the Dead* to help the soul on its journey through the 49 levels of Bardo, the state between death and rebirth. Three days after death, the body is blessed and early-morning prayers and offerings are made to the monastery. The body is folded up and carried on the back of a close friend to the *dürtro* (burial site). Here, special body-breakers known as *rogyapas* cut off the deceased's hair, chop up the body and pound the bones together with

DID YOU KNOW?

Tibetans still use the lunar calendar for traditional events. Years are calculated on a 60-year cycle and divided into five elements and 12 zodiac animals. Thus 2005 is the year of the wood rooster

There are now around 1400 functioning monasteries in Tibet

SKY BURIAL

Sky burials are funeral services and, naturally, Tibetans are often very unhappy about camera-toting foreigners heading up to sky-burial sites. The Chinese authorities do not like it either and may fine foreigners who attend a burial. You should never pay to see a sky burial and you should *never* take photos. Even if Tibetans offer to take you up to a sky-burial site, it is unlikely that other Tibetans present will be very happy about it. If nobody invited you, don't go.

---

tsampa (roasted-barley flour) for vultures to eat, although as often as not the devouring might be done by wild dogs.

There is little overt sadness at a sky burial as the soul is considered to have already departed – the burial itself is considered to be mere disposal. Sky burial is, however, very much a time to reflect on the impermanence of life. Death is seen as a powerful agent of transformation and spiritual progress. Tibetans are encouraged to witness the disposal of the body and to confront death openly and without fear, one reason why Tantric ritual objects such as trumpets and bowls are often made from human bone.

Dress

Many Tibetans in Lhasa are beginning to wear Western (or rather Chinese) clothes, but in the countryside traditional dress is still the norm. The Tibetan national dress is a *chuba* (long-sleeved sheepskin cloak), tied around the waist with a sash and often worn off the shoulder with great bravado by nomads and Khampas (those from the region of Kham). *Chubas* from eastern Tibet in particular have super-long sleeves, which are tied around the waist. An inner pouch is often used to store money belts, amulets, lunch and even small livestock. Most women wear a long dress, topped with a colourful striped apron. Traditional boots are made of leather strips and have turned-up toes, so as, it is said, to kill fewer bugs when walking.

Women generally set great store in jewellery, and their personal wealth and dowry are often invested in it. Coral is particularly valued (as Tibet is so far from the sea), as are amber, turquoise and silver. The Tibetan *zee*, a unique elongated agate stone with black and white markings, is also highly prized. Earrings are common in both men and women and they are normally tied on with a piece of cord. You can see all these goodies for sale around the Barkhor in Lhasa.

Tibetan women, especially those from Amdo (northeastern Tibet and Qinghai), wear their hair in 108 braids, an auspicious number in Buddhism. Khampa men plait their hair with red or black tassels and wind the lot around their head. Cowboy hats are popular in summer and fur hats are common in winter. Most pilgrims carry a *gau* (amulet), with perhaps a picture of the owner's personal deity or the Dalai Lama inside.

Dos & Don'ts

In general negotiations it is a good idea to ensure that the person you are dealing with does not lose face, does not appear to be wrong and is not forced to back down in front of others. A negotiated settlement is always preferable and outright confrontation is a last resort. It is best to try to sort out problems with smiling persistence – when one tack fails, try another.

Be aware that Tibetans often gesture with their lips to indicate a particular direction, so if a member of the opposite sex pouts at you, they are just showing you where to go. Older country folk may stick out their tongue when they meet you, a very traditional form of respect that greeted the very first travellers to Tibet centuries ago. Some sources say that this was done to prove that the person was not a devil, because devils have green tongues – even when they take human form.

Shorts are not a very suitable option in Tibet. The days can get pretty hot but wearing shorts in Tibet is akin to walking around with 'TOUR-IST!' tattooed on your forehead.

TRADITIONAL CULTURE UNDER THREAT

The greatest threat to cultural life comes from development and Chinese migration, as government subsidies and huge infrastructure projects change the face and ethnic make-up of cities across the breadth of Tibet.

Investment from Beijing has brought with it a surge in Han immigrants hungry for jobs. Although no figures are available, it is obvious that many Chinese people, attracted by preferential loans and tax rates, a less strictly enforced one-child policy, stipends for a hardship posting and easy business opportunities, are setting up shop in urban centres all over Tibet. An education system that exclusively uses the (Mandarin) Chinese language at higher levels reinforces the fact that only Sinicised Tibetans will be able to actively participate in Tibet's economic advances.

DID YOU KNOW?

Tibetans show respect to an honoured guest or a lama by placing a *kathak* (prayer scarf) around their neck. When reciprocating, hold the scarf out in both hands with palms turned upwards.

RESPONSIBLE TOURISM

Tourism has already affected many areas in Tibet. Most children will automatically stick their hand out for a sweet, a pen or anything. Tibetans in some regions, eg around Mt Everest, have become frustrated at seeing a stream of rich tourist groups but few tangible economic results. Please try to bear the following in mind as you travel through Tibet:

- Try to patronise as many small local Tibetan businesses, restaurants and guesthouses as possible. Revenues created by organised group tourism go largely into the pockets of the Chinese authorities.

- Doling out medicines can encourage people not to seek proper medical advice. And don't hand out sweets or pens to children – you'll turn them into beggars. If you wish to contribute something constructive, it's better to give pens directly to schools and medicines to rural clinics, or make a donation to an established charity.

- Monastery admission fees go largely to local authorities, so if you want to donate to the monastery, leave your offering on the altar.

- Don't buy skins or hats made from endangered animals such as snow leopards.

- Don't pay to take a photograph of someone, and don't photograph someone if they don't want you to. If you agree to send a photograph of someone please follow through on this.

- If you have any pro-Tibetan sympathies be very careful with whom you discuss them. Don't put Tibetans in a difficult or even potentially dangerous situation. This includes handing out pictures of the Dalai Lama and politically sensitive materials.

- Always offer to pay for accommodation if it is provided. At monasteries leave a donation even if no payment is required.

- Never disturb a collection of prayer flags or rock carvings. Similarly never buy artwork or relics belonging to a monastery or chapel, even if offered by a monk.

- Act respectfully when visiting temples and monasteries. Always circle a monastery building, statue or *chörten* (stupa) in a clockwise direction (unless it is a Bön monastery).

For more on the etiquette of visiting monasteries see p91. For information on responsible trekking see p269.

MISSION IMPOSSIBLE

Since 1958 there have been repeated investigations into building a train line from Golmud to Lhasa. Finally, in 1979, it was declared impossible.

Then in February 2001 the Chinese government announced it had approved construction of a 1142km train line from Golmud to Lhasa, the world's highest (reaching 5070m), connecting China's last province to the rail network. The US$3 billion project is part of China's huge campaign to boost economic development in its western hinterland.

While China touts its 'gift' to Tibet, Tibetan support groups fear the line will prove disastrous for local Tibetans, opening the demographic and economic floodgates to Han Chinese immigrants and troops (much like the recent line to Kashgar in troubled Xinjiang province), and leading to increased exploitation of Tibet's mineral resources. The Dalai Lama has condemned the plan and called for international corporations to boycott the venture.

Nonetheless, work is proceeding at a rapid rate and is slated to be finished by 2007, when several passenger trains daily will run to Lhasa.

Religious freedoms have increased in recent years, though any form of political disobedience is quickly crushed. Monks and nuns, who are often the focus of protests and Tibetan aspirations for independence, are regarded suspiciously by the authorities and are often subject to arrest and beatings. Nuns, in particular considering their small numbers, have been very active and accounted for 55 of the 126 independence protests in the mid-1990s. Regulations make it impossible for nuns, once arrested and imprisoned, to return to their nunneries.

A Cultural History of Tibet by David Snellgrove & Hugh Richardson is a good introduction to the history and culture of Tibet, but is marred by the use of a scholarly and at times indecipherable transliteration system of Tibetan; eg Samye Monastery is rendered 'bSam-yas'.

And yet for all the new roads, karaoke joints, Chinese TV, Internet bars and mobile phones that have swept across Tibet, traditional and particularly religious life is at the core of most Tibetans' identities. Pepsi and Budweiser may now rival Buddhist deities as the most popular Tibetan icons, but the quintessence of Tibet remains remarkably intact.

POPULATION

China's 1996 population survey put the population of the Tibet Autonomous Region (TAR) at 2.44 million, with a natural growth rate of 16.2%, the highest in China. Figures are likely to be higher than this if Han immigrants and People's Liberation Army (PLA) troops stationed in Tibet (perhaps up to 200,000) are included, but the Chinese government is very coy about releasing figures that would make it clear just how many Chinese there are in Tibet.

Official statistics claim 95% of the TAR's population is Tibetan, a figure that is hotly contested by almost everyone except the government. Chinese figures for the population of Lhasa, for example, indicate it is just over 87% Tibetan and just under 12% Han Chinese, a ratio that stretches the credulity of anyone who has visited the city in recent years. It is more likely that somewhere in the vicinity of 50% of Lhasa's population is Han Chinese. The recent flood of Chinese immigrants into Tibet has been termed China's 'second invasion'.

A census conducted in 1990 indicated that there were another 2.5 million ethnic Tibetans in Qinghai, Sichuan and Gansu provinces. There are also thought to be around 120,000 Tibetans in exile, mainly in India but also in the USA, Canada and Europe (especially Switzerland).

Population Control

Population control is a cornerstone of Chinese government policy but the regulations are generally less strictly enforced in Tibet. 'Minority nationalities', as the Tibetans are classified, are allowed two children before they lose certain stipends and housing allowances. Ironically, the most effective form of birth control in modern Tibet still seems to be to join a monastery.

Ethnic Groups

Like the Han Chinese (and almost all ethnic minorities of China), the Tibetans are classified as belonging to the Mongoloid family of peoples. They probably descended from nomadic tribes who migrated from the north and settled to sedentary cultivation of Tibet's river valleys. About a quarter of Tibetans are still nomadic. There are considerable variations between regional groups of Tibetans. The most recognisable are the Khampas of eastern Tibet, who are generally larger and a bit more rough-and-ready than other Tibetans and who wear red or black tassels in their long hair. Women from Amdo are especially conspicuous because of their elaborate braided hairstyles and jewellery.

There are pockets of other minority groups, such as the Lhopa (Lhoba) and Monpa, in the southeast of Tibet, who make up less than 1% of the total population. A more visible ethnic group are the Hui Muslims. Tibet's original Muslim inhabitants were largely traders or butchers (a profession that most Buddhists abhor), although the majority of recent migrants are traders and restaurant owners from southern Gansu province. The Tibetans' closest ethnic cousins are the Qiang, who now live mostly in northern Sichuan province. Tibetans are also closely related to the Sherpas of Nepal and the Ladakhis of India.

DID YOU KNOW?

Tibetan babies are considered to be one year old at the time of birth, since reincarnation took place nine months previously upon conception.

FINDING OUT MORE

The following organisations do excellent work to help the people of the Tibetan plateau and foster greater awareness of all aspects of Tibetan culture.

- Kham Aid Foundation – www.khamaid.org
- The Tibet Fund – www.tibetfund.org
- Braille Without Borders – www.braillewithoutborders.org
- Tibet Foundation – www.tibet-foundation.org
- Tibet Poverty Alleviation Fund – www.tpaf.org
- Tendol Gyalzur Orphanage – www.tendol-gyalzur-tibet.ch

Pro-Tibetan organisations abroad have good news services and often cultural coverage. The **Tibet Support Group** (www.tibet.org) offers online links to most pro-Tibet organisations.

- Australia Tibet Council – www.atc.org.au
- Canada Tibet Committee – www.tibet.ca
- Free Tibet Campaign (UK) – www.freetibet.org
- International Campaign for Tibet – www.savetibet.org
- Students for a Free Tibet – www.studentsforafreetibet.org
- Tibet Foundation (UK) – www.tibet-foundation.org
- Tibet House Cultural Centre – www.tibethouse.org
- Tibet Information Network – www.tibetinfo.net
- Tibet Society – www.tibet-society.org.uk

ARTS

Almost all Tibetan art, with perhaps the exception of some folk crafts, is inspired by Buddhism. Wall hangings, paintings, architecture, literature, even dance, all in some way or another attest to the influence of the Indian religion that found its most secure resting place in Tibet.

At the same time, the arts of Tibet represent the synthesis of many influences. The Buddhist art and architecture of the Pala and Newari kingdoms of India and Nepal were an important early influence, as were the Buddhist cultures of Khotan and Kashmir. Newari influence is clearly visible in the early woodcarvings of the Jokhang, and Kashmiri influence is particularly strong in the murals of Tsaparang in western Tibet. As China came to play an increasingly major role in Tibetan affairs, Chinese influences too were assimilated, as is clear at Shalu Monastery near Shigatse and in the Karma Gadri style prevalent in eastern Kham. A later, clearly Tibetan style known as Menri was perfected in the monasteries of Drepung, Ganden and Sera.

Tibetan art is deeply conservative and conventional. Personal expression and innovation are not valued and indeed individual interpretation can actually become an obstacle to art's main purpose, which is to represent the path to enlightenment. Artists generally remain anonymous in Tibet. The use of colour in art is decided purely by convention and rigid symbolism.

Much of Tibet's artistic heritage fell victim to the Cultural Revolution. What was not destroyed was, in many cases, ferreted away to China or onto the Hong Kong art market. In recent years over 13,500 images have been returned to Tibet, a fraction of the number stolen. Worse still, many of Tibet's traditional artisans were persecuted or fled Tibet. It is only in recent years that remaining artists have again been able to return to their work and start to train young Tibetans in skills that faced the threat of extinction.

The Art of Tibet by Robert Fisher is a portable colour guide to all the arts of Tibet, from the iconograpy of *thangkas* (Tibetan religious paintings usually framed by silk brocade) to statuary.

TIBET CHIC

Hollywood's flirtation with Tibet started way back in 1937 with the film version of James Hilton's classic *Lost Horizon*. The pseudo-Tibet theme continued with such films as *The Golden Child* (1986), apparently inspired by the young Karmapa of Tsurphu Monastery, and Bernardo Bertolucci's *Little Buddha* (1993), merging the life story of the Buddha (Keanu Reeves!) with the tale of a young Seattle boy who is discovered to be a reincarnated lama. But it was the release in 1997 of *Seven Years in Tibet* and *Kundun*, two films detailing the Chinese invasion of Tibet, that really made Tibet chic.

Richard Gere remains the most outspoken advocate of Tibetan independence in Tinseltown, using the Academy Awards ceremony in 1992 as a platform to publicise the cause. But the Hollywood connection doesn't end with him. Robert Thurman, the father of actress Uma Thurman, is the Tsongkhapa Professor of Indo-Tibetan Studies at Columbia University. Other celebrities with an active interest in Tibetan Buddhism include Harrison Ford, Goldie Hawn and Oliver Stone. Harrison Ford's ex-wife Melissa Matheson wrote the screenplay for *Kundun* and Ford apparently spent several days reading the script to the Dalai Lama to gauge his Holiness' reaction. The Beastie Boys' Adam Yauch, a confirmed Tibetan Buddhist, organised several Tibet Freedom Concerts. Perhaps most surprising of all was the announcement that Steven Seagal, the ponytailed, kick-boxing movie star, has been discovered to be a reincarnated *trulku* (incarnate lama) of the Nyingma order of Tibetan Buddhism.

Whether all this media fuss has actually helped the Tibetan cause is up for debate. Some argue that the hype has merely helped to perpetuate a media myth of Tibet that doesn't serve the Tibetan people. Back in Hollywood they grin knowingly: 'There's no such thing as bad press'.

Dance & Drama

Anyone who is lucky enough to attend a Tibetan festival should have the opportunity to see performances of *cham,* a ritual dance performed over several days by monks and lamas. Although every movement and gesture of *cham* has significance, it is no doubt the spectacle of the colourful masked dancers that awes the average pilgrim.

Cham is about the suppression of malevolent spirits and is a throwback to the pre-Buddhist Bön faith. It is a solemn masked dance accompanied by long trumpets, drums and cymbals. The chief officiant is an unmasked Black Hat lama who is surrounded by a mandalic grouping of masked monks who represent manifestations of various protective deities. The act of exorcism – it might be considered as such – is focused on a human effigy made of dough or perhaps wax or paper in which the evil spirits are thought to reside.

The proceedings of *cham* can be interpreted on a number of levels. The Black Hat lama is sometimes identified with the monk who slew Langdharma, the anti-Buddhist king of the Yarlung era, and the dance is seen as echoing the suppression of malevolent forces inimical to the establishment of Buddhism in Tibet. Some anthropologists, on the other hand, have seen in *cham* a metaphor for the gradual conquering of the ego, which is the aim of Buddhism. The ultimate destruction of the effigy that ends the dance might represent the destruction of the ego itself. Whatever the case, *cham* is a splendid, dramatic performance and it well worth going out of your way to see it.

Performances of *cham* are most of the time accompanied by other, less significant performances that seem to have evolved as entertainment in festivals. *Lhamo,* not to be confused with *cham,* is Tibetan opera. A largely secular art form, it portrays the heroics of kings and the villainy of demons, and recounts events in the lives of historical figures. Lhamo was invented in the 14th century by Tangtong Gyelpo, known as 'Tibet's Leonardo da Vinci' because he was also an engineer, a major bridge-builder and physician. Authentic performances still include a statue of Tangtong on the otherwise bare stage. Performances were traditionally performed by travelling troupes and would last the entire day. After the stage has been purified, the narrator gives a plot summary in verse and the performers enter, each with his or her distinct step and dressed in the bright and colourful silks of the aristocracy.

Other festival dances might depict the slaying of Langdharma or the arrival of the Indian teachers in Tibet at the time of the second diffusion of Buddhism. Light relief is provided by masked clowns or children.

Music

Music is one aspect of Tibetan cultural life in which there is a strong secular heritage. In the urban centres, songs were an important vent for social criticism, news and official lampooning. In Tibetan social life, both work and play are seen as occasions for singing. Even today it is not uncommon to see the monastery reconstruction squads pounding on the roofs of buildings and singing in unison. Where there are groups of men and women, the singing alternates between the two groups in the form of rhythmic refrains. Festivals and picnics are also opportunities for singing.

Tibet also has a secular tradition of wandering minstrels. It's still possible to see minstrels performing in Lhasa and Shigatse, where they play on the streets and occasionally (when they are not chased out by the owners) in restaurants.

www.tibetart.org has online examples of Tibetan art from dozens of collections.

www.asianart.com is an online journal with articles and galleries of Tibetan art.

For examples of contemporary Tibetan art visit www.mechakgallery.com.

Generally, groups of two or three singers perform heroic epics and short songs to the accompaniment of a Tibetan four-stringed guitar and a nifty little shuffle. In times past, groups of such performers travelled around Tibet, providing entertainment for villagers who had few distractions from the constant round of daily chores. These performers were sometimes accompanied by dancers and acrobats.

While the secular music of Tibet has an instant appeal for foreign listeners, the liturgical chants of Buddhist monks and the music that accompanies *cham* dances is a lot less accessible. Buddhist chanting creates an eerie haunting effect, but soon becomes very monotonous. The music of *cham* is a discordant cacophony of trumpet blasts and boom-crash drums – atmospheric as an accompaniment to the dancing but not exactly the kind of thing you would want to slip into the CD player.

Tibetan religious rituals use *rolmo* and *silnyen* (cymbals), *nga* (suspended drums), *damaru* (hand drums) and *drilbu* (bells), *dungchen* (long trumpets), *kangling* (conical oboes; formerly made from human thigh-bones) and *dungkar* (conch shells). Secular instruments include a *dranyen* (a six-stringed lute), a *piwang* (two-stringed fiddle) and a *gyumang* (Chinese-style zither).

Most recordings of traditional Tibetan music have been made in Dharamsala or Dalhousie in India. The country's biggest musical export (or rather exile) is Yungchen Lhamo, who sings traditional Tibetans songs, normally a cappella. She also appeared on Natalie Merchant's *Ophelia*. Other Tibetan singers based abroad include Dadon Dawa Dolma and Kelsang Chukie Tethong (whose recent CD *Voice from Tara* is worth checking out).

Literature

The development of a Tibetan written script is credited to a monk by the name of Tonmi Sambhota and corresponded with the early introduction of Buddhism during the reign of King Songtsen Gampo. Accordingly, pre-Buddhist traditions were passed down as oral histories that told of the exploits of early kings and the origins of the Tibetan people. Some of these oral traditions were later recorded using the Tibetan script.

But for the most part, literature in Tibet was dominated by Buddhism; first as a means of translating Buddhist scriptures from Sanskrit into Tibetan; and second, as time went by, in association with the development of Tibetan Buddhist thought. There is nothing in the nature of a secular literary tradition – least of all novels – such as can be found in China or Japan.

One of the great achievements of Tibetan culture was the development of a literary language that could, with remarkable faithfulness, reproduce the concepts of Sanskrit Buddhist texts. The compilation of Tibetan-Sanskrit dictionaries in the early 9th century ensured consistency in all subsequent translations.

Alongside Buddhist scriptures exists an ancient tradition of storytelling, usually concerning the taming of Tibet's malevolent spirits to allow the introduction of Buddhism. Many of these stories were passed from generation to generation orally, but some were recorded. Examples include the epic of *King Gesar of Ling* and the story of Guru Rinpoche, who is said to have been born in a lotus in the ancient kingdom of Swat before coming to Tibet and performing countless miracles to prepare the land for the diffusion of Buddhism. The oral poetry of the Gesar epic is particularly popular in eastern Tibet, where a tiny number of ageing bards just about keep alive a tradition that dates back to the 10th century.

Chö by Choying Drolma & Steve Tibbets (Hannibal Music Label) is a deeply beautiful and highly recommended recording of chants and songs by Tibetan nuns, with subtle modern production.

For world music with modern production try *Coming Home* (Real World, 1998) by Yungchen Lhamo.

MANDALAS

The mandala (*kyilkhor*, literally 'circle') is a fascinating concept, as well as often being quite a beautiful artistic creation. In a sense you might think of a mandala as being like a three-dimensional picture. What on the surface appears to be a plain two-dimensional design emerges, with the right visual approach, as a three-dimensional picture. Mandalas can take the form of paintings, patterns of sand, three-dimensional models or even whole monasteries, as at Samye.

In the case of the two-dimensional mandala, the correct visual approach can be achieved only through meditation. The mandala is associated with Tantric Buddhism and is chiefly used in a ritual known as *sadhana* (means for attainment). According to this ritual, the adept meditates on, invokes and identifies with a specific deity, before dissolving into emptiness and re-emerging as the deity itself. The process, in so far as it uses the mandala as an aid, involves a remarkable feat of imaginative concentration.

A typical mandala features a central deity surrounded by four or eight other deities who are aspects of the central figure. These surrounding deities are often accompanied by a consort. There may be several circles of these deities, totalling several hundred deities. These deities and all other elements of the mandala have to be visualised as the three-dimensional world of the central deity and even as a representation of the universe. One ritual calls for the adept to visualise 722 deities with enough clarity to be able to see the whites of their eyes and hold this visualisation for four hours.

Through the 12th and 13th centuries, Tibetan literary endeavour was almost entirely consumed by the monumental task of translating the complete Buddhist canon into Tibetan. The result was the 108 volumes of canonical texts (Kangyur), which record the words of the Historical Buddha, Sakyamuni (Sakya Thukpa), and 208 volumes of commentary (Tengyur) on the Kangyur by Indian masters that make up the basic Buddhist scriptures shared by all Tibetan religious orders. What time remained was used in the compilation of biographies and the collection of songs of revered lamas. Perhaps most famous among these is the *Hundred Thousand Songs of Milarepa*; Milarepa was an ascetic to whom many songs and poems concerning the quest for buddhahood are attributed.

Wood-block printing has been in use for centuries and is still the most common form of printing in monasteries. Blocks are carved in mirror image; printers then work in pairs putting strips of paper over the inky block and shuttling an ink roll over it. The pages of the text are kept loose, wrapped in cloth and stored along the walls of monasteries. Tibet's most famous printing presses were in Derge in modern-day Sichuan, at Nartang Monastery and at the Potala.

Very little of the Tibetan literary tradition has been translated into English. Translations that may be of interest include *The Tibetan Book of the Dead*, a mysterious but fascinating account of the stages and visions that occur between death and rebirth; *The Jewel Ornament of Liberation*, which describes the path to enlightenment as seen by the chief disciple of Milarepa and founder of the Kagyupa order; and *The Life of Milarepa*, the autobiography of the country's most famous ascetic.

DID YOU KNOW

The epic *Gesar of Ling* ('Tibet's *Lord of the Rings*') is the world's longest epic poem and takes years to recite in full!

Architecture

Most early religious architecture – the Jokhang in Lhasa for example – owed much to Pala (Indian) and especially Newari (Nepali) influences. Still, a distinctively Tibetan style of architectural design emerged, and found its greatest expression in the Kumbum of Gyantse, the monasteries of Samye and Tashilhunpo, and the Potala. The great American architect Frank Lloyd Wright is said to have had a picture of the Potala on the wall of his office.

CHÖRTENS

Probably the most prominent Tibetan architectural motif is the chörten (stupa). Chörtens were originally built to house the cremated relics of the Historical Buddha, Sakyamuni (Sakya Thukpa), and as such have become a powerful symbol of the Buddha and his teachings. Later, chörtens also served as reliquaries for lamas and holy men. Monumental versions would often encase whole mummified bodies, as is the case with the tombs of the Dalai Lamas in the Potala. And the tradition is very much alive: a stunning gold reliquary chörten was constructed in 1989 at Tashilhunpo Monastery to hold the body of the 10th Panchen Lama.

In the early stages of Buddhism, images of the Buddha did not exist and chörtens became the major symbol of the new faith. Over the next two millennia, chörtens took many different forms across the Buddhist world, from the sensuous stupas of Burma to the pagodas of China and Japan. Most elaborate of all are the *kumbums* (100,000 Buddha images), of which the best remaining example in Tibet is at Gyantse. Many chörtens were built to hold ancient relics and sacred texts and so have been plundered over the years by treasure seekers and vandals.

Buddhist Stupas in Asia: The Shape of Perfection by Joe Cummings & Bill Wasseman is an accessible and lavishly illustrated exploration of the spread of Buddhism and stupa building across India and Asia, with a chapter devoted to Tibet.

MONASTERY LAYOUT

Tibetan monasteries are based on a conservative design and share a remarkable continuity of layout. Many are built in spectacular high locations above villages. Most were originally surrounded by an outer wall, built to defend the treasures of the monastery from bands of brigands, Mongolian hordes or even rival monasteries. Most monasteries have a kora (pilgrimage path), around the complex, replete with holy rocks and meditation retreats high on the hillside behind.

Inside the gates there is usually a central courtyard used for special ceremonies and festivals and a *darchen* (flag pole). Surrounding buildings usually include a *dukhang* (main assembly or prayer hall) with *gönkhang* or *sumkhang* (side protector chapels) and *lhakhang* (subsidiary chapels), as well as monks' quarters, a library and, in the case of larger monasteries, *tratsang* (colleges), *kangtsang* (halls of residence), kitchens and a *barkhang* (printing press).

The main prayer hall consists of rows of low seats and tables, often strewn with cloaks, hats, ritual instruments, drums and huge telescopic horns. There is a small altar with seven bowls of water, butter lamps, and offerings of mandalas made from seeds. The main altar houses the main statues, often Sakyamuni (Sakya Thukpa), Jampa (Maitreya) or a trinity of the Past, Present and Future Buddhas and perhaps the founder of the monastery or past lamas. There may be an inner room behind the main hall, whose entrance is flanked by protector gods, one often blue, Chana Dorje (Vajrapani), the other red, Tamdrin (Hayagriva). There may well be an inner kora of prayer wheels. At the entrance to most buildings are murals of the Four Guardian Kings and perhaps a Wheel of Life or a mandala mural. Side stairs lead up from here to higher floors.

Protector chapels are dark and spooky halls that hold wrathful manifestations of deities, frequently covered with a cloth because of their terrible appearance. Murals are often traced against a black background and walls are decorated with Tantric deities or skeletons. Pillars are decorated with festival masks, weapons and sometimes stuffed animals such as snakes and wolves.

The monastery roof usually has excellent views as well as vases of immortality, victory banners, dragons and copper symbols of the Wheel of Law flanked by two deer.

Chörtens are highly symbolic. The five levels represent the four elements and eternal space: the square base symbolises earth, the dome is water, the spire is fire, and the top moon and sun are air and space. The 13 discs of the ceremonial umbrella can represent the branches of the tree of life or the 10 powers and three mindfulnesses of the Buddha. The top seed-shaped pinnacle symbolises enlightenment – the chörten as a whole can be seen as a representation of the path to enlightenment. The construction can also physically represent the Buddha, with the base as his seat and the dome as his body.

SECULAR ARCHITECTURE
Typical features of Tibetan secular architecture, which are also used to a certain extent in religious architecture, are buildings with inward-sloping walls made of large tightly fitting stones or sun-baked bricks. Below the roof is a layer of twigs, squashed tight by the roof and painted to give Tibetan houses their characteristic brown band. Roofs are flat, as there is little rain or snow, made from pounded earth and edged with walls. You may well see singing bands of men and women pounding a new roof with sticks weighted with large stones. In the larger structures, the roof is supported inside by wooden pillars. The exteriors are generally whitewashed brick, although in some areas, such as Sakya in Tsang, other colours may be used. In rural Tibet, homes are often surrounded by walled compounds, and in some areas entrances are protected by painted scorpions and swastikas.

Nomads, who take their homes with them, live in *bar* (yak-hair tents), which are normally roomy and can accommodate a whole family. An opening at the top of the tent lets out smoke from the fire.

For an in-depth look at Lhasa's traditional Tibetan architecture see www.tibetheritage fund.org

Painting
As with other types of Tibetan art, painting is very symbolic and can be seen on many different levels. It is almost exclusively devotional in nature.

STYLES
The strongest influence came from India. Paintings usually followed stereotyped forms with a central Buddhist deity surrounded by smaller, lesser deities. Poised above the central figure was often a supreme buddha figure of which the one below it was an emanation. Later came depictions of revered Tibetan lamas or Indian spiritual teachers, often surrounded by incidents from the lama's life or lineage lines.

Chinese influence began to manifest itself more frequently in Tibetan painting from around the 15th century. The freer approach of Chinese landscape painting allowed some Tibetan artists to break free from some of the more formalised aspects of Tibetan religious art and employ landscape as a decorative motif in the context of a painting that celebrated a particular religious figure. This is not to say that Chinese art initiated a new movement in Tibetan art. The new, Chinese-influenced forms coexisted with older forms, largely because painting in Tibet was passed on from artisan to apprentice in much the same way that monastic communities maintained lineages of teaching.

If you are interested in actually creating, not just understanding, Tibetan art, look for the master work on the subject, *Tibetan Thangka Painting: Methods & Materials* by David P Jackson & Janice A Jackson.

THANGKAS
Religious paintings mounted on brocade and rolled up between two sticks are called *thangkas*. Their eminent portability was essential in a land of nomads, and they were often used by mendicant preachers and

doctors as a visual learning aid. Not so portable are the huge *thangkas*, the size of large buildings, that are unfurled every year during festivals. Traditionally, *thangkas* were never bought or sold.

The production of a *thangka* is an act of devotion and the process is carefully formalised. Linen (or now more commonly cotton) is stretched on a wooden frame, stiffened with glue and coated with a mix of chalk and lime called gesso. Iconography is bound by strict mathematical measurements. A grid is drawn onto the *thangka* before outlines are sketched in charcoal, starting with the main central deity and moving outwards.

Colours are added one at a time, starting with the background and ending with shading. Pigments were traditionally natural: blue from lapis, red from cinnabar and yellow from sulphur. Most *thangkas* are burnished with at least a little gold. The last part of the *thangka* to be painted is the eyes, which are filled in during a special 'opening the eyes' celebration. Finally a brocade backing of three colours and a 'curtain' are added, the latter to protect the *thangka*.

www.tibetanculture.org (Conservancy for Tibetan Art & Culture) offers bite-sized overviews of many aspects of Tibetan culture.

Statuary & Sculpture

Tibetan statuary, like Tibetan painting, is religious in nature. Ranging in height from several centimetres to several metres, statues usually depict deities and revered lamas. Most of the smaller statues are hollow and are stuffed with paper prayers and relics when consecrated.

Metal statues are traditionally sculpted in wax and then covered in clay. When the clay is dry it is heated. The wax melts and is removed, leaving a mould that can be filled with molten metal. Statues are then often gilded and painted.

Sculptures are most commonly made from bronze or stucco mixed with straw, but can even be made out of butter and *tsampa* (roasted-barley flour). Butter sculptures are normally made on wooden frames and symbolise the impermanence of all things.

Handicrafts

Tibet has a 1000-year history of carpet making; the carpets are mostly used as seat covers, bed covers and saddle blankets. Knots are double tied (the best carpets have 100 knots per square inch) which results in a particularly thick pile. Tibet's secret carpet ingredient is its particularly high-quality sheep wool, which is hand spun and coloured with natural dyes such as indigo, walnut, madder and rhubarb. Gyantse and Shigatse were the traditional centres of carpet production, although the modern industry is based almost exclusively in Tibetan exile communities in Nepal.

Inlaid handicrafts are common, particularly in the form of prayer wheels, daggers, temple horns, butter lamps and bowls, although most of what you see these days in Lhasa is made by Tibetan communities in Nepal. Nomads in particular wear stunning silver jewellery; you may also see silver flints, amulets known as *gau,* and ornate chopstick and knife sets.

Tibetan singing bowls, made from a secret mix of seven different metals, are a meditation device that originated from pre-Buddhist Bön practices. The bowls produce a 'disassociated' mystic hum when a playing stick is rotated around the outer edge of the bowl.

Woodcarving is another valued handicraft, used in the production of brightly coloured Tibetan furniture and window panels, not to mention wood blocks.

Tibetan Buddhism

A basic understanding of Buddhism is essential to getting beneath the skin of things in Tibet. Buddhism's values and goals permeate almost everything Tibetan. Exploring the monasteries and temples of Tibet and mixing with its people, yet knowing nothing of Buddhism, is like visiting the Vatican and knowing nothing of Roman Catholicism. To be sure, it might still seem an awe-inspiring experience, but much will remain hidden and indecipherable.

For those who already do know something of Buddhism, who have read something of Zen, for example, Tibet can be baffling on another level. The grandeur of the temples, the worship of images and the fierce protective deities that stand in doorways all seem to belie the basic tenets of an ascetic faith that is basically about renouncing the self and following a path of moderation.

On a purely superficial level, Buddhism has historically encompassed the moral precepts and devotional practices of lay followers, the scholastic tradition of the Indian Buddhist universities and a body of mystic Tantric teachings that had a particular appeal to followers of the shamanistic Bön faith.

Tibetan Buddhism's reaction with existing Bön spirit worship and the Hindu pantheon created a huge range of deities, both wrathful and benign (although these are all merely aspects of the human ego). Apart from a whole range of different buddha aspects there are also general protector gods called *dharmapalas* and personal meditational deities called *yidams* (either male *herukas* or female *dakinis*), which Tantric students adopt early in their spiritual training. Yet for all its confusing iconography the basic tenets of Buddhism are very much rooted in daily experience. Even high lamas and monks come across as surprisingly down-to-earth.

Buddhism is perhaps the most tolerant of the world's religions. Wherever it has gone it has adapted to local conditions, like a dividing cell, creating countless new schools of thought. Its basic tenets have remained very much the same and all schools are bound together in their faith in the value of the original teachings of Sakyamuni (Sakya Thukpa), the Historical Buddha. The Chinese invasion has ironically caused a flowering of Tibetan Buddhism abroad and you can now find Tibetan monasteries around the world.

Closely linked to both Bön and Buddhism is the folk religion of Tibet, known as *mi chös* (the dharma of man), which is primarily concerned with spirits. These spirits include *nyen*, which reside in rocks and trees; *lu* or *naga*, snake-bodied spirits which live at the bottom of lakes, rivers and wells; *sadok,* lords of the earth, which are connected with agriculture; *tsen*, air spirits which shoot arrows of illness and death at humans; and *dud*, demons linked to the Buddhist demon Mara. The religious beliefs of the average Tibetan are a fascinating melange of Buddhism, Bön and folk religion.

HISTORY

Buddhism originated in the northeast of India around the 5th century BC, at a time when the local religion was Brahmanism. Some Brahmin, in preparation for presiding over offerings to their gods, partook of an asceticism that took them to remote places where they fasted, meditated and practiced yogic techniques.

For a modern overview of Tibetan Buddhism, try *Introduction to Tibetan Buddhism* by John Powers or *Essential Tibetan Buddhism* by Robert Thurman.

www.buddhanet.net is a good resource if you are interested in Buddhism.

Tibetan rosary beads are made of 108 dried seeds. Prayers are marked off by each bead; a second string marks off higher multiples. Spies working for the British adapted rosaries to record distances as they secretly mapped large areas of Tibet during the 19th century.

Many of the fundamental concepts of Buddhism find their origin in the Brahmin society of this time. The Buddha (c 480–400 BC), born Siddhartha Gautama, was one of many wandering ascetics whose teachings led to the establishment of rival religious schools. Jainism was one of these schools, Buddhism was another.

Little is known about the life of Siddhartha. It was probably not until some 200 years after his death that biographies were compiled, and by that time many of the circumstances of his life had merged with legend. It is known that he was born of a noble family and that he married and had a son before renouncing a life of privilege on a quest to make sense of the suffering in the world.

After studying with many of the masters of his day he embarked on a course of intense asceticism, before concluding that such a path was too extreme. Finally, in the place that is now known as Bodhgaya in India, Siddhartha meditated beneath a *bo* (pipal) tree. At the break of dawn at the end of his third night of meditation he became a buddha (awakened one).

Full moon days see an intensification of prayers and activity in most monasteries. The 10th day of the lunar month sees prayers dedicated to Guru Rinpoche, the 15th day to Öpagme (Amitayus), the eighth day to the medicine Buddha and the new moon to Sakyamuni (Sakya Thukpa).

BUDDHIST CONCEPTS

Buddhism's early teachings are based on the insights of the Buddha, known in Mahayana tradition as Sakyamuni (Sakya Thukpa in Tibetan), and form the basis of all further Buddhist thought. The later Mahayana school (to which Tibetan Buddhism belongs) diverged from these early teachings in some respects, but not in its fundamentals.

The Buddha commenced his teachings by explaining that there was a Middle Way that steered a course between sensual indulgence and ascetic self-torment – a way of moderation not renunciation. This Middle Way

WHEEL OF LIFE

The Wheel of Life (Sipa Khorlo), depicted in the entryway to most monasteries, is an aid to realising the delusion of the mind; a complex pictorial representation of how desire chains us to samsara, the endless cycle of birth, death and rebirth.

The wheel is held in the mouth of Yama, the Lord of Death. The inner circle of interdependent desire shows a cockerel (representing desire or attachment) biting a pig (ignorance or delusion) biting a snake (hatred or anger). A second ring is divided into figures ascending through the realms on the left and descending on the right.

The six inner sectors of the wheel symbolise the six realms of rebirth – gods, battling demigods, and humans (the upper realms), and hungry ghosts, hell and animals (the lower realms). All beings are reborn through this cycle dependent upon their karma. The Buddha is depicted outside the wheel, symbolising his release into a state of nirvana.

At the bottom of the wheel are hot and cold hells, where Yama holds a mirror that reflects one's lifetime. A demon to the side holds a scale with black and white pebbles, weighing up the good and bad deeds of one's lifetime.

The hungry spirits are recognisable by their huge stomachs, thin needle-like necks and tiny mouths, which cause them insatiable hunger and thirst. In each realm the Buddha attempts to convey his teachings (the dharma), offering hope to each realm.

The 12 outer segments depict the so-called '12 links of dependent origination', and the 12 interlinked, co-dependent and causal experiences of life that perpetuate the cycle of samsara. The 12 images (whose order may vary) are of a blind woman (representing ignorance), a potter (unconscious will), a monkey (consciousness), men in a boat (self-consciousness), a house (the five senses), lovers (contact), a man with an arrow in his eye (feeling), a drinking scene (desire), a figure grasping fruit from a tree (greed), pregnancy, birth and death (a man carrying a corpse to a sky burial).

could be followed by taking the Noble Eightfold Path. The philosophical underpinnings of this path were the Four Noble Truths, which addressed the problems of karma and rebirth. These basic concepts are the kernel of early Buddhist thought.

Rebirth

Life is a cycle of rebirths. The common assumption is that there are many rebirths, but in Buddhist thought they are innumerable. The Sanskrit word 'samsara' (Tibetan: *khorwa*), literally 'wandering on', is used to describe this cycle, and life is seen as wandering on limitlessly through time, and through the birth, extinction and rebirth of galaxies and worlds. There are six levels of rebirth or realms of existence. It is important to accumulate enough merit to avoid the three lower realms, although in the long cycle of rebirth, all beings pass through them at some point. These six levels are depicted on the Wheel of Life (p54). All beings are fated to tread this wheel continuously until they make a commitment to enlightenment.

Karma

All beings pass through the same cycle of rebirths. Their enemy may once have been their mother, and like all beings they have lived as an insect and as a god, and suffered in one of the hell realms. Movement within this cycle, though, is not haphazard. It is governed by karma.

Karma is a slippery concept. It is sometimes translated simply as 'action', but it also implies the consequences of action. Karma might be thought of as an overarching condition of life. Every action in life leaves a psychic trace that carries over into the next rebirth. It should not be thought of as a reward or punishment, but simply as a result. In Buddhist thought karma is frequently likened to a seed that ripens into a fruit: thus a human reborn as an insect is harvesting the fruits of a previous immoral existence.

Merit

Given that karma is a kind of accumulated psychic baggage that we must lug through countless rebirths, it is the aim of all practising Buddhists to try to accumulate as much 'good karma' – merit – as possible. Merit is best achieved through the act of rejoicing in giving, although merit can even be achieved through giving that is purely motivated by a desire for merit. The giving of alms to the needy and to monks, the relinquishing of a son to monkhood, acts of compassion and understanding are all meritorious and have a positive karmic outcome.

The Four Noble Truths

If belief in rebirth, karma and merit are the basis of lay-followers' faith in Buddhism, the Four Noble Truths might be thought of as the deep structure of the faith, or its philosophical underpinning. The Buddha systematised the truths in the manner of the medical practice of his time: (1) diagnose the illness, (2) identify its cause, (3) establish a cure and (4) map a course for the cure. Their equivalents in Buddhism's diagnosis of the human condition are: (1) *dukkha* (suffering), caused by (2) *tanha* (desire), which may be cured by (3) *nibbana*, nirvana (cessation of desire), which can be achieved by means of (4) the Noble Eightfold Path, or the Middle Way.

The first of the Four Noble Truths, then, is that life is suffering. This suffering extends through all the countless rebirths of beings, and finds its origin in the imperfection of life. Every rebirth brings with it the pain

There are many modern guides to practising Tibetan Buddhism – Western authors such as Lama Surya Das and Pema Chodron have written a selection of books dealing with Tibetan Buddhist concepts in a modern context.

The Dalai Lama is a one-man publishing empire! Many books attributed to the Dalai Lama are actually transcripts of public lectures. The most popular titles are *The Art of Happiness, Ethics for the New Millennium, The Meaning of Life* and *The Power of Compassion*.

The Tibetan Book of Living and Dying by Sogyal Rinpoche is an excellent background to *The Tibetan Book of the Dead* and Dzogchen tradition. Sogyal has had contact with Western students, and several travellers recommend the book for beginners and advanced practitioners.

The swastika is an ancient symbol of Buddhism and is often found painted on houses to bring good luck. Swastikas that point clockwise are Buddhist; those that point anti-clockwise are Bön.

of birth, the pain of ageing, the pain of death, the pain of association with unpleasant things, the loss of things we are attached to, and the failure to achieve the things we desire.

The reason for this suffering is the second Noble Truth, and lies in our dissatisfaction with imperfection, in our desire for things to be other than they are. What is more, this dissatisfaction leads to actions and karmic consequences that prolong the cycle of rebirths and may lead to even more suffering, much like a mouse running endlessly in a wheel.

The third Noble Truth was indicated by the Buddha as nibbana (namtrol), which is known in English as nirvana. It is the cessation of all desire, an end to attachment. With the cessation of desire comes an end to suffering, the achievement of complete non-attachment and an end to the cycle of rebirth – nirvana, the ultimate goal of Buddhism. Nitpickers might point out that the will to achieve nirvana is a desire in itself. Buddhists answer that this desire is tolerated as a useful means to an end, but it is only when this desire too is extinguished that nirvana is truly achieved.

The Noble Eightfold Path

Prayer wheels are filled with up to a mile of prayers; the prayers are 'recited' with each revolution of the wheel. Pilgrims spin the wheels to gain merit and to concentrate the mind on the mantras and prayers they are reciting.

The Noble Eightfold Path is the fourth of the Noble Truths. It prescribes a course that for the lay practitioner will lead to the accumulation of merit and for the serious devotee may lead to nirvana. The components of this path are (1) right understanding, (2) right thought, (3) right speech, (4) right action, (5) right livelihood, (6) right effort, (7) right mindfulness and (8) right concentration. Needless to say, each of these has a 'wrong' corollary.

The Ten Meritorious Deeds

The 10 deeds are: do not kill, do not steal, and refrain from inappropriate sexual activity, lying, gossiping, cursing, sowing discord, envy, malice and opinionatedness.

SCHOOLS OF BUDDHISM

Not long after the death of Sakyamuni (Sakya Thukpa), disagreements began to arise among his followers – as they tend to in all religious movements – over whose interpretations best captured the true spirit of his teachings. The result was the development of numerous schools of thought and eventually a schism that saw the emergence of two principal schools: Hinayana and Mahayana.

Prayer flags are strung up to purify the air and pacify the gods. When the flags flutter, prayers are thought to be released to the heavens. The colours are highly symbolic – red, green, yellow, blue and white represent fire, wood, earth, water and iron.

Hinayana, also known as Theravada, might be seen as the more conservative of the two, a school that encouraged scholasticism and close attention to what were considered the original teachings of Sakyamuni (Sakya Thukpa). Mahayana, on the other hand, with its elevation of compassion as an all-important idea, took Buddhism in a new direction. It was the Mahayana school that made its way up to the high plateau and took root there, at the same time travelling to China, Korea and Japan. Hinayana retreated into southern India and took root in Sri Lanka and Thailand.

Mahayana

The claims that Mahayanists made for their faith were many, but the central issue was a change in orientation from individual pursuit of enlightenment to bodhisattvahood. The bodhisattva, rather than striving for complete non-attachment, aims, through compassion and self-sacrifice, to achieve enlightenment for the sake of all beings.

In another development, Sakyamuni (Sakya Thukpa) began to take on another form altogether. Mahayanists maintained that Sakyamuni (Sakya Thukpa) had already attained buddhahood many aeons ago and that he was a manifestation of a long-enlightened transcendent being who sent such manifestations to many worlds to assist all beings on the road to enlightenment. There were many such transcendent beings, the Mahayanists argued, living in heavens or 'pure lands', and all were able to project themselves into the innumerable worlds of the cosmos for the sake of sentient life there.

The philosophical reasoning behind the Mahayana transformation of Buddhism is extremely complex, but it had the effect of allowing Mahayanists to produce newly revealed texts that recorded the words of Sakyamuni (Sakya Thukpa) as they appeared in dreams and visions. It also had the effect of producing a pantheon of bodhisattvas, a feature that made Mahayana more palatable to cultures that already had gods of their own. In Tibet, China, Korea and Japan, the Mahayana pantheon came to be identified with local gods as their Mahayana equivalents vanquished or replaced them.

Mani (prayer) stones are carved with sutras as an act of merit and placed in long walls, often hundreds of metres long, at holy sites.

Tantrism (Vajrayana)

A further Mahayana development that is particularly relevant is Tantrism (Vajrayana). The words of Sakyamuni (Sakya Thukpa) were recorded in sutras and studied by students of both Hinayana and Mahayana, but according to the followers of Tantrism, a school that emerged from around AD 600, Sakyamuni (Sakya Thukpa) left a corpus of esoteric instructions to a select few of his disciples. These were known as Tantra (Gyü).

Tantric adepts claimed that through the use of unconventional techniques they could jolt themselves towards enlightenment, and shorten the long road to bodhisattvahood. The process involved identification with a tutelary deity invoked through deep meditation and recitation of the deity's mantra. The most famous of these mantras is the '*om mani padme hum*' ('hail to the jewel in the lotus') mantra of Chenresig (Avalokiteshvara). Tantric practice employs Indian yogic techniques to channel energy towards the transformation to enlightenment. Such yogic techniques might even include sexual practices. Tantric techniques are rarely written down, but rather are passed down verbally from tutor to student.

Most of the ritual objects and images of deities in Tibetan monasteries and temples are Tantric in nature. Together they show the many facets of enlightenment – at times kindly, at times wrathful. Sometimes these deities are pictured at the centre of a mandala, which is a representation of the world they inhabit. The Tantric adept who identifies with a particular deity will visualise the mandala as a three-dimensional world, a feat of meditational concentration that takes many years of training to achieve (p49).

The mantra '*om mani padme hum*' is the most commonly carved on *mani* stones. The six syllables mean 'hail to the jewel in the lotus' and form the mantra of Chenresig (Avalokiteshvara), the Bodhisattva of Compassion.

The *dorje* (thunderbolt) and *drilbu* (bell) are ritual objects symbolising male and female aspects used in Tantric rites. They are held in the right and left hands respectively. The indestructible thunderbolt cuts through ignorance.

BUDDHISM IN TIBET

The story of the introduction of Buddhism to Tibet is attended by legends of the taming of local gods and spirits and their conversion to Buddhism as protective deities. This magnificent array of buddhas, bodhisattvas and sages occupies a mythical world in the Tibetan imagination. Chenresig (Avalokiteshvara) is perhaps chief among them, manifesting himself in early Tibetan kings and later the Dalai Lamas. Guru Rinpoche (Padmasambhava), the Indian sage who bound the native spirits and gods of

Tibet into the service of Buddhism, is another. And there are countless others worshipped in images throughout the land: Drölma (Tara), Jampelyang (Manjushri), Milarepa, Marpa and Tsongkhapa, among others. While the clerical side of Buddhism concerns itself largely with textual study and analysis, the Tantric shamanistic-based side seeks revelation through identification with these deified beings and through their *terma* ('revealed' words or writings).

A spirit trap is a series of interlocking threads, often placed on a tree, which are supposed to ensnare evil spirits and which are burnt after their job is done.

It is useful to consider the various schools of Tibetan Buddhism as revealing something of a struggle between these two orientations: shamanism and clericalism. Each school finds its own resolution to the problem. In the case of the last major school to arise, the Gelugpa order, there was a search for a return to the doctrinal purity of clerical Buddhism. But even here, the Tantric forms were not completely discarded; it was merely felt that many years of scholarly work and preparation should precede the more esoteric Tantric practices.

The clerical and shamanistic orientations can also be explained as the difference between state-sponsored and popular Buddhism respectively. There was always a tendency for the state to emphasise monastic Buddhism, with its communities of rule-abiding monks. Popular Buddhism, on the other hand, with its long-haired, wild-eyed ascetic recluses capable of performing great feats of magic, had a great appeal to the ordinary people of Tibet, for whom ghosts and demons and sorcerers were a daily reality.

The Eight Auspicious Symbols *(tashi targyel)* are associated with gifts made to Sakyamuni upon his enlightenment and appear as protective motifs across Tibet. They include the knot of eternity, wheel of law, lotus flower, pair of golden fishes and white conch shell.

Nyingmapa Order

The Nyingmapa order is the Old School, and traces its origins back to the teachings and practices of Guru Rinpoche, who came to Tibet from India and lived in the country in the 8th and 9th centuries. As Buddhism fell into decline until the second diffusion of the faith in the 11th century, the Nyingmapa failed to develop as a powerful, centralised school, and for the most part prospered in villages throughout rural Tibet, where it was administered by local shamanlike figures.

With the second diffusion of Buddhism in Tibet and the emergence of rival schools, the Nyingmapa order experienced something of a revival through the 'discovery' of hidden texts in the 'power places' of Tibet visited by Guru Rinpoche. In many cases these *terma* (revealed texts), were discovered through yogic-inspired visions by spiritually advanced Nyingmapa practitioners, rather than found under a pile of rocks or in a cave. Whatever their origins, these *terma* gave the Nyingmapa a new lease of life.

Butter lamps, or *chömay*, are kept lit continuously in all monasteries and many private homes, and are topped up continuously by visiting pilgrims equipped with a tub of butter and a spoon.

The *terma* gave rise to the Dzogchen (Great Perfection) teachings. Much maligned by other Tibetan schools, Dzogchen postulates a primordial state of purity that pre-existed the duality of enlightenment and samsara, and offered a Tantric short cut to nirvana. Dzogchen teaches that enlightenment can come in one lifetime. Such ideas were to influence other orders of Buddhism in the 19th century.

The Nyingmapa never had the centralised power of other major Tibetan schools of Buddhism, and can be considered to represent an extreme of the shamanistic orientation.

Its fortunes improved somewhat with the accession of the fifth Dalai Lama, who was born into a Nyingmapa family. He personally saw to the expansion of Mindroling and Dorje Drak Monasteries, which became the head Nyingmapa monasteries of Ü and all Tibet. In particular, he is supposed to have overcome and taught mountain goddesses with the use of Tantric sexual techniques.

This resurgence of Buddhist influence in the 11th century led to many Tibetans travelling to India to study. The new ideas they brought back with them had a revitalising effect on Tibetan thought and produced other new schools of Tibetan Buddhism. Among them was the Kagyupa order, established by Milarepa (1040–1123) who was the disciple of Marpa the translator (1012–93).

The influence of one of Milarepa's disciples, Gampopa (1079–1153), led to the establishment of numerous monasteries that became major teaching centres, eventually overshadowing the ascetic-yogi origins of the Kagyupa. The yogi tradition did not die out completely, however, and Kagyupa monasteries also became important centres for synthesising the clerical and shamanistic orientations of Tibetan Buddhism.

For more on the Dzogchen school see www.dzogchen.org.

Several suborders of the Kagyupa sprung up with time, the most prominent of which was the Karma Kagyupa, also known as the Karmapa. The practice of renowned lamas reincarnating after death probably originated with this suborder, when the abbot of Tsurphu Monastery, Dusum Khyenpa (1110–93), announced that he would be reincarnated as his own successor. The 16th Karmapa died in 1981, and his disputed successor fled to India in 1999 (see The Karmapa Connection, p135). Other Kagyupa schools, the Drigungpa and Taglungpa, are based at Drigung Til and Talung Monasteries in Ü.

Sakyapa Order

With the second diffusion of Buddhism in the 11th and 12th centuries, many Tibetan monasteries became centres for the textual study and translation of Indian Buddhist texts. One of the earliest major figures in this movement was Kunga Gyaltsen (1182–1251), known as Sakya Pandita (literally 'scholar from Sakya').

Found on all altars and replenished twice a day, the seven bowls of water refer to the 'Seven Examined Men' – the first seven monks in Tibet.

Sakya Pandita's renown as a scholar led to him, and subsequent abbots of Sakya, being recognised as a manifestation of Jampelyang (Manjushri), the Bodhisattva of Insight. Sakya Pandita travelled to the Mongolian court in China, with the result that his heir became the spiritual tutor of Khublai Khan. In the 13th and 14th centuries, the Sakyapa order became embroiled in politics and implicated in the Mongol overlordship of Tibet. Nevertheless, at the same time Sakya emerged as a major centre for the scholastic study of Buddhism, and attracted students such as Tsongkhapa, who initiated the Gelugpa order.

Many Sakyapa monasteries contain images of the Sakyapa protector deity Gompo Gur and photographs of the school's four head lamas: the Sakya Trizin (in exile in the US), Ngawang Kunga (head of the Sakyapa order), Chogye Trichen Rinpoche (head of the Tsarpa subschool) and Ludhing Khenpo Rinpoche (head of the Ngorpa subschool).

Gelugpa Order

It may not have been his intention, but Tsongkhapa (1357–1419), a monk who left his home in Kokonor at the age of 17 to study in central Tibet, is regarded as the founder of the Gelugpa (Virtuous School) order, which came to dominate political and religious affairs in Tibet.

The Buddhist parable of the Four Harmonious Brothers is painted on walls at the entrance to many monasteries. The image is of a bird atop a hare, atop a monkey, atop an elephant. On its most basic level the image symbolises cooperation and harmony with the environment.

Tsongkhapa studied with all the major schools of his day, but was particularly influenced by the Sakyapa and the Kadampa orders. The Kadampa order had its head monastery at Netang, near Lhasa, and it was here that the 11th-century Bengali sage Atisha (Jowo-je) spent his last days. The Kadampa had sustained the teachings of Atisha, which are a sophisticated synthesis of conventional Mahayana doctrine with the more arcane practices of Tantric Buddhism, and emerged as a major school,

Keith Dowman's *Sacred Life of Tibet* builds on his earlier *Power Places of Central Tibet* to provide an excellent insight into how Tibetans see the spiritual landscape of their land. It also offers a pilgrim's perspective on travelling in Tibet.

emphasising scholastic study. It may never have matched the eminence of the Kagyupa and Sakyapa orders, but in the hands of Tsongkhapa the teachings of the Kadampa order established a renewal in Tibetan Buddhism.

After experiencing a vision of Atisha (Jowo-je), Tsongkhapa elaborated on the Bengali sage's clerical-Tantric synthesis in a doctrine that is known as *lamrim* (the graduated path). Tsongkhapa basically advocated a return to doctrinal purity and monastic discipline as prerequisites to advanced Tantric studies. He did not, as is sometimes maintained, advocate a purely clerical approach to Buddhism, but he did reassert the monastic body as the basis of the Buddhist community, and he maintained that Tantric practices should be reserved only for advanced students.

Tsongkhapa established a monastery at Ganden, which was to become the head of the Gelugpa order. Other monasteries were also established at Drepung, Sera and Shigatse. Although the abbot of Drepung was the titular head of the order (and is to this day), it was the Dalai Lamas who came to be increasingly identified with the order's growing political and spiritual prestige.

PILGRIMAGE

Pilgrimage is practised throughout the world, although as a devotional exercise it has been raised to a level of particular importance in Tibet. This may be because of the nomadic element in Tibetan society; it may also be that in a mountainous country with no roads and no wheeled vehicles, walking long distances became a fact of life, and by visiting sacred places en route pilgrims could combine walking with accumulating merit. To most Tibetans their natural landscape is imbued with a series of sacred visions and holy 'power places'; mountains can be perceived as mandala images, rocks assume spiritual dimensions, and the earth is imbued with healing powers.

The motivations for pilgrimage are many, but for the ordinary Tibetan it amounts to a means of accumulating merit *(sonam)* or good luck *(tashi)*. The lay practitioner might go on pilgrimage in the hope of winning a better rebirth, to cure an illness, end a spate of bad luck or simply because of a vow to take a pilgrimage if a bodhisattva granted a wish.

In Tibet there are countless sacred destinations, ranging from lakes and mountains to monasteries and caves that once served as meditational retreats for important yogis. Specific pilgrimages are often prescribed for specific ills; certain mountains, for example, expiate certain sins. A circumambulation of Mt Kailash offers the possibility of liberation within three lifetimes, while a circuit of Lake Manasarovar can result in spontaneous buddhahood. A circuit of Tsari in southeastern Tibet can improve a pilgrim's chances of being reborn with special powers such as the ability to fly.

Pilgrimage is more powerful in certain auspicious months; at certain times, circumambulations of Bönri are reckoned to be 700 million times more auspicious than those of other mountains.

The three foremost pilgrimage destinations of Tibet are all mountains: Mt Kailash, in western Tibet; Tapka Shelri and the Tsari Valley in southeastern Tibet; and Mt Labchi, east of Nyalam, in Tsang. Lakes such as Manasarovar, Yamdrok-tso, Nam-tso and Lhamo La-tso attract pilgrims partly because their sacred water is thought to hold great healing qualities. The cave hermitages of Drak Yerpa, Chim-puk and Sheldrak are particularly venerated by pilgrims for their associations with Guru Rinpoche.

Pilgrims often organise themselves into large groups, hire a truck and travel around the country visiting all the major sacred places in one go. Pilgrim guidebooks have existed for centuries to help travellers interpret the 24 'power places' of Tibet. Such guides even specify locations where you can urinate or fart without offending local spirits (and probably your fellow pilgrims).

Bön

In Tibet the establishment of Buddhism was marked by its interaction with the native religion Bön. This shamanistic faith, which encompassed gods and spirits, exorcism, talismans and the cult of dead kings among other things, almost certainly had a major influence on the direction Buddhism took in Tibet.

Many popular Buddhist symbols and practices, such as prayer flags, sky burial, the rubbing of holy rocks, the tying of bits of cloth to trees and the construction of spirit traps, all have their roots deep in Bön tradition. The traditional blessing of dipping a finger in water or milk and flicking it to the sky derives from Bön and can still be seen today in the shamanistic folk practices of Mongolia.

But it was Bön that was transformed and tamed to the ends of Buddhism and not vice versa. The Bön order, as it survives today, is to all intents and purposes the fifth school of Tibetan Buddhism. Major Bön monasteries include Menri and Yungdrungling in central Tibet, and Tengchen in eastern Tibet. Other pockets of Bön exist in the Changtang region of northern Tibet and the Aba region of northern Sichuan. The main centre of Bön in exile is at Dolanji, near Solan, in India's Himachal Pradesh.

Torma are small offerings made of yak butter and *tsampa* (roasted-barley flour) adorned with medallions of butter, which are often coloured. Most are made during the Shötun festival and remain on display throughout the year.

Pilgrimage is not just a matter of walking to a sacred place and then going home. There are a number of activities that focus the concentration of the pilgrim. The act of kora (circumambulating the object of devotion) is chief among these. Circuits of three, 13 or 108 koras are especially auspicious, with sunrise and sunset the most auspicious hours. *Chaktsal* (prostration) is a powerful way to show devotion and follows a sequence: place your hands in a *namaste* (prayer-like) position, touch your forehead, throat and heart, get down into a half-prostration (as for Muslim prayer) and then lie full on the ground with the hands stretched out. The particularly devout carry out whole pilgrimages like this, stepping forward the length of their body after each prostration (often marking the spot with a small conch shell) and starting all over again. The hard-core even do their koras sideways, advancing one side step at a time!

Most pilgrims make offerings during the course of a pilgrimage. *Kathaks,* white ceremonial scarves, are given to lamas or holy statues as a token of respect. Offerings of yak butter or oil, fruit, *tsampa* (dough made with roasted-barley flour), seeds and money are all left at altars, and bowls of water and *chang* (barley beer) are replenished. Monks often act as moneychangers, converting Y10 notes into wads of one-mao notes, which makes limited funds go further.

Outside chapels, at holy mountain peaks, passes and bridges, you will see pilgrims throwing offerings of *tsampa* or printed prayers into the air (often with the cry 'sou, sou, sou!'). Pilgrims also collect sacred rocks, herbs, earth and water from a holy site to take back home to those who couldn't make the pilgrimage, and leave behind personal items as a break from the past, often leaving them hanging in a tree. Other activities in this spiritual assault course include adding stones to cairns, rubbing special healing rocks, and squeezing through narrow gaps in rocks as a method of sin detection. Many of these actions are accompanied by the visualisation of various deities and practices.

Koras usually include stops of particular spiritual significance, such as rock-carved syllables or painted buddha images. Many of these carvings are said to be 'self-arising'; ie not having been carved by a human hand. The Mt Kailash kora, for example, is a treasure trove of these, encompassing sky-burial sites, stones that have 'flown' from India, monasteries, bodhisattva footprints, and even at one point a lingam (phallic image).

Other pilgrimages are carried out to visit a renowned holy man or teacher. Blessings from lamas, *trulkus* (reincarnated lamas) or *rinpoches* (highly esteemed lamas) are particularly valued, as are the possessions of famous holy men. According to Keith Dowman in his book *The Sacred Life of Tibet,* the underpants of one revered lama were cut up and then distributed among his eager followers!

IMPORTANT FIGURES OF TIBETAN BUDDHISM

This is a brief iconographical guide to some of the gods and goddesses of the vast Tibetan Buddhist pantheon, as well as to important historical figures. It is neither exhaustive nor scholarly, but it may help you to recognise a few of the statues you encounter during your trip. Tibetan names are given first, with Sanskrit names provided in parentheses. (The exception is Sakya Thukpa, who is often known in Tibet by his Sanskrit name, Sakyamuni.)

Buddhas

SAKYAMUNI (SAKYA THUKPA)

Sakyamuni (Sakya Thukpa)

Sakyamuni (Sakya Thukpa) is the Historical Buddha (the Buddha of the Present Age), whose teachings set in motion the Buddhist faith. In Tibetan-style representations he is always pictured sitting cross-legged on a lotus-flower throne. His hair is dark blue and there is a halo of enlightenment around his head. The Buddha is recognised by 32 marks on his body, including a dot between his eyes, a bump on the top of his head and the Wheel of Law on the soles of his feet. In his left hand he holds a begging bowl; and his right hand touches the earth in the 'witness' *mudra* (hand gesture). He is often flanked by two disciples or bodhisattvas.

THE HISTORY OF BÖN

As a result of the historical predominance of Buddhism in Tibet, the Bön religion has been suppressed for centuries and has only recently started to attract the attention of scholars. Many Tibetans remain quite ignorant of Bön beliefs and your guide might refuse to even set foot in a Bön monastery. Yet Bön and Buddhism have influenced and interacted with each other for centuries, exchanging texts, traditions and rituals. In the words of Tibet scholar David Snellgrove, 'every Tibetan is a Bönpo at heart'.

The word 'Bön' has three main connotations. The first relates to the pre-Buddhist religion of Tibet, suppressed and supplanted by Buddhism in the 8th and 9th centuries. The second is the form of 'organised' Bön (Gyur Bön) systematised along Buddhist lines, which arose in the 11th century. Third, and linked to this, is a body of popular beliefs that involve the worship of local deities and spirit protectors.

Bön has its deepest roots in the earliest religious beliefs of the Tibetan people. Centred on an animist faith shared by all central Asian peoples, religious expression took the form of spells, talismans, oaths, incantations, ritual drumming and sacrifices. Rituals often revolved around an individual who mediated between humans and the spirit world.

The earliest form of Bön, sometimes referred to as Black Bön, also Dud Bön (the Bön of Devils) or Tsan Bön (the Bön of Spirits), was concerned with counteracting the effects of evil spirits through magical practices. Bönpo priests were entrusted with the wellbeing and fertility of the living, with curing sicknesses and affecting the weather. A core component was control of the spirits, to ensure the safe passage of the soul into the next world. For centuries Bönpo priests controlled the complex burial rites of the Yarlung kings. Bön was the state religion of Tibet until the reign of Songtsen Gampo.

Bön is thought to have its geographical roots in the kingdom of Shang-Shung, which is located in western Tibet, and its capital at Kyunglung (Valley of the Garuda). Bön's founding father was Shenrab Miwoche, who is also known as Tonpa Shenrab, the Teacher of Knowledge, who was born in the second millennium BC in the mystical land of Olma Lungring in Tajik (thought to be possibly the Mt Kailash area or even Persia). Buddhists often claim that Shenrab is merely a carbon copy of Sakyamuni (Sakya Thukpa), and certainly there are similarities to be found. Biographies state that he was born a royal prince and ruled for 30 years before becoming an ascetic. His 10 wives bore him 10 children who formed the core of his religious disciples.

MARMEDZE (DIPAMKARA)
The Past Buddha, Marmedze came immediately before Sakyamuni (Sakya Thukpa) and spent 100,000 years on earth. His hands are shown in the 'protection' *mudra* and he is often depicted in a trinity with the Present and Future Buddhas.

ÖPAGME (AMITABHA)
The Buddha of Infinite Light resides in the 'pure land of the west'. The Panchen Lama is considered a reincarnation of this buddha. He is red, his hands are held together in his lap in a 'meditation' *mudra* and he holds a begging bowl.

TSEPAME (AMITAYUS)
The Buddha of Longevity, like Öpagme (Amitabha), is red and holds his hands in a meditation gesture, but he holds a vase containing the nectar of immortality.

Tsepame (Amitayus)

MEDICINE BUDDHAS (MENLHA)
A medicine buddha holds a medicine bowl in his left hand and herbs in his right. He is often depicted in a group of eight buddhas.

Many of the tales of Shenrab Miwoche deal with his protracted struggles with the demon king Khyabpa Lagring.

Bön was first suppressed by the eighth Yarlung king, Drigum Tsenpo, and subsequently by King Trisong Detsen. The Bön master Gyerpung Drenpa Namkha (a *gyerpung* is the Bön equivalent of a lama or guru) struggled with Trisong Detsen to protect the Bön faith until the king finally broke Shang-Shung's political power. Following the founding of the Samye Monastery, many Bön priests went into exile or converted to Buddhism, and many of the Bön texts were hidden.

The modern Bön religion is known as Yungdrung (Eternal Bön). A *yungdrung* is a swastika, Bön's most important symbol. ('Yungdrungling' means 'swastika park' and is a common name for Bön monasteries). *The Nine Ways of Bön* is the religion's major text. Bönpos still refer to Mt Kailash as Yungdrung Gutseg (Nine-Stacked-Swastika Mountain).

To the casual observer it's often hard to differentiate between Bönpo and Buddhist practice. It can be said that in many ways Bön shares the same goals as Buddhism but takes a different path. The word 'Bön' has come to carry the same connotation as the Buddhist term 'dharma' (*chö*). Shared concepts include those of samsara, karma and rebirth in the six states of existence. Even Bön monasteries, rituals and meditation practice are almost identical to Buddhist versions. Still, there are obvious differences: Bön has its own Kangyur, a canon made up of texts translated from the Shang-Shung language, and Bönpos turn prayer wheels and circumambulate monasteries anticlockwise. The main difference comes down to the source of religious authority: Bönpos see the arrival of Buddhism as a catastrophe, the supplanting of the truth by a false religion.

Bönpo iconography is unique. Tonpa Shenrab is the most common central image, an is depicted as either a monk or a deity. He shares Sakyamuni's *mudra* (hand gesture) of 'enlightenment', but holds the Bön sceptre, which consists of two swastikas joined together by a column. Other gods of Bönpo include Satrid Ergang, who holds a swastika and mirror; Shenrab Wokar and his main emanation, Kuntu Zangpo, with a hooklike wand; and Sangpo Bumptri.

Complementing these gods is a large number of local deities – these are potentially harmful male spirits known as *gekho* (the protectors of Bön) and their female counterparts, *drapla*. Welchen Gekho is the king of the harmful *gekho*, and his consort Logbar Tsame is the queen of the *dralpa*.

Jampa (Maitreya)

DHYANI BUDDHAS (GYAWA RI GNA)
Each of the five Dhyani buddhas is a different colour, and each of them has different *mudras*, symbols and attributes. Öpagme (Amitabha) is one of the Dhyani buddhas.

JAMPA (MAITREYA)
Jampa, the Future Buddha, is passing the life of a bodhisattva until it is time to return to earth in human form 4000 years after the disappearance of Sakyamuni (Sakya Thukpa). He is normally seated, with a scarf around his waist, his legs hanging down and his hands by his chest in the *mudra* of turning the Wheel of Law.

Bodhisattvas
These are beings who have reached the state of enlightenment but vow to save everyone else in the world before they themselves enter nirvana. Unlike buddhas, they are often shown decorated with crowns and jewels.

Chenresig (Avalokiteshvara)

CHENRESIG (AVALOKITESHVARA)
The glorious gentle one, Chenresig is the Bodhisattva of Compassion; his name means 'he who gazes upon the world with suffering in his eyes'. The Dalai Lama is considered a reincarnation of Chenresig (as is King Songtsen Gampo), and pictures of the Dalai Lama and Chenresig are interchangeable, depending on the political climate. The current Dalai Lama is the 14th manifestation of Chenresig.

In the four-armed version (known more specifically in Tibetan as Tonje Chenpo), his body is white and he sits on a lotus blossom. He holds crystal rosary beads and a lotus and clutches to his heart a jewel that fulfils all wishes. A deer skin is draped over his left shoulder.

There is also a powerful 11-headed, 1000-armed version. The head of this version is said to have exploded when confronted with myriad problems to solve. One of his heads is that of wrathful Chana Dorje (Vajrapani), and another (the top one) is that of Öpagme (Amitabha), who is said to have reassembled Chenresig's body after it exploded. Each of the 1000 arms has an eye in the palm. His eight main arms hold a bow and arrow, lotus, rosary, vase, wheel and staff.

Jampelyang (Manjushri)

JAMPELYANG (MANJUSHRI)
The Bodhisattva of Wisdom, Jampelyang is regarded as the first divine teacher of Buddhist doctrine. School children often offer prayers to him. His right hand holds the flaming sword of awareness, which cuts through ignorance. His left arm cradles a scripture on a half-opened lotus blossom and his left hand is in the 'teaching' *mudra*. He is often yellow and may have blue hair or an elaborate crown.

Drölma (Tara)

DRÖLMA (TARA)
A female bodhisattva with 21 different manifestations or aspects, Drölma is also known as the saviouress. She was born from a tear of compassion that fell from the eyes of Chenresig (Avalokiteshvara) and is thus considered the female version of Chenresig and a protectress of the Tibetan people. She also symbolises purity and fertility and is believed to be able to fulfil wishes. Images usually represent Green Tara, who is associated with night, or Drölkar (White Tara), who is associated with day. The green version sits in a half-lotus position with her right leg down, resting on a lotus flower.

The white version sits in the full lotus position and has seven eyes, including ones in her forehead, both palms and both soles of her feet. She is often seen as part of a longevity triad, along with red Tsepame (Amitayus) and three-faced, eight-armed female Namgyelma (Vijaya).

Protector Deities

CHÖKYONG (LOKPALAS)

The Chökyong (or the Four Guardian Kings), are normally seen at the entrance hallway of monasteries and are possibly of Mongol origin. They are the protectors of the four cardinal directions: the eastern chief is white with a lute; the southern is blue and holds a sword; the western is red and holds a thunderbolt. Namtöse (Vaishravana), the protector of the north, doubles as the god of wealth and can be seen with a yellow body, riding a snow lion, and holding a banner of victory and a jewel-spitting mongoose.

Nagpo Chenpo (Mahakala)

DORJE JIGJE (YAMANTAKA)

Dorje Jigje is a favourite protector of the Gelugpa order. A wrathful form of Jampelyang (Manjushri), he is also known as the destroyer of Yama (the Lord of Death). He is blue with eight heads, the main one of which is the head of a bull. He wears a garland of skulls around his neck and a belt of skulls around his waist, and holds a skull cup and a flaying knife in his 34 arms. He tramples on eight Hindu gods, eight mammals and eight birds with his 16 feet.

NAGPO CHENPO (MAHAKALA)

A wrathful Tantric deity and manifestation of Chenresig (Avalokiteshvara), Nagpo Chenpo (Great Black One), has connections to the Hindu god Shiva. There are many varieties with anything from two to six arms. He is blue with fanged teeth and a tiara of skulls, and carries a trident and a skull cup. In a form known as Gompo, he is believed by nomads to be the guardian of the tent.

Tamdrin (Hayagriva)

TAMDRIN (HAYAGRIVA)

Another wrathful manifestation of Chenresig (Avalokiteshvara), Tamdrin has a red body. His right face is white, his left face is green, and he has a horse's head in his hair. He wears a tiara of skulls, a garland of 52 severed heads and a tiger skin around his waist. His six hands hold a skull cup, a lotus, a sword, a snare, an axe and a club, and his four legs stand on a sun disc trampling corpses. On his back are the outspread wings of Garuda and the skins of a human and an elephant. He is sometimes shown embracing a blue consort. He has close connections to the Hindu god Vishnu.

Chana Dorje (Vajrapani)

CHANA DORJE (VAJRAPANI)

The name of the wrathful Bodhisattva of Energy means 'thunderbolt in hand'. In his right hand he holds a thunderbolt (dorje or vajra), which represents power and is a fundamental symbol of Tantric faith. He is blue with a tiger skin around his waist and a snake around his neck. He also has a peaceful, standing aspect.

PALDEN LHAMO (SHRI DEVI)

The special protector of Lhasa, the Dalai Lama and the Gelugpa order, Palden Lhamo is a female counterpart of Nagpo Chenpo (Mahakala). Her origins probably lie in the Hindu goddess Kali. She is blue, wears clothes of tiger skin and human skin, and has earrings made of a snake and a

Palden Lhamo (Shri Devi)

lion. She carries a club in her right hand and a skull cup full of blood in the left. She holds the moon in her hair, the sun in her belly and a corpse in her mouth, and rides a mule with an eye in its rump.

DEMCHOK (CHAKRASAMVARA)

This meditational deity has a blue body with 12 arms, four faces and a crescent moon in his top knot. His main hands hold a thunderbolt and bell, and others hold an elephant skin, an axe, a hooked knife, a trident, a skull, a hand drum, a skull cup, a lasso and the head of Brahma. He also wears a garland of 52 heads and clothes made from tiger skin.

Guru Rinpoche

Historical Figures

GURU RINPOCHE

The 'lotus-born' 8th-century master from modern-day Swat in Pakistan, Guru Rinpoche subdued Tibet's evil spirits and helped to establish Buddhism in Tibet. Known in Sanskrit as Padmasambhava, he is regarded by followers of Nyingmapa Buddhism as the second Buddha and wears a red Nyingmapa-style hat. His domain is the copper-coloured mountain called Zangdok Pelri. He has a curly moustache, and holds a thunderbolt in his right hand, a skull cup in his left hand, and a staff topped with three heads – one shrunken, one severed and one skull – in the crook of his left arm. He has a *phurbu* (ritual dagger) in his belt. Guru Rinpoche has eight manifestations, known collectively as the Guru Tsengye.

TSONGKHAPA

Tsongkhapa

Founder of the Gelugpa order and a manifestation of Jampelyang (Manjushri), Tsongkhapa (1357–1419) wears the yellow hat of the Gelugpas. He is normally portrayed in a triad with his two main disciples, Kedrub Je and Gyatsab Je. His hands are in the 'teaching' *mudra* and he holds two lotuses. He was the founder and first abbot of Ganden Monastery and many images of him are found there.

FIFTH DALAI LAMA

Fifth Dalai Lama

The greatest of all the Dalai Lamas, the fifth (Ngawang Lobsang Gyatso; 1617–82) unified Tibet and built the bulk of the Potala. He was born at Chongye (in the Yarlung Valley) and was the first Dalai Lama to exercise temporal power. He wears the Gelugpa yellow hat and holds a thunderbolt in his right hand and a bell *(drilbu)* in his left. He may also be depicted holding the Wheel of Law (symbolising the beginning of political control of the Dalai Lamas) and a lotus flower or other sacred objects.

KING SONGTSEN GAMPO

Tibet was unified under Songtsen Gampo, who introduced Buddhism to the country early in the 7th century. He has a moustache and wears a white turban with a tiny red Öpagme (Amitabha) poking out of the top. He is flanked by Princess Wencheng, his Chinese wife, on the left, and Princess Bhrikuti, his Nepali wife, on his right.

KING TRISONG DETSEN

King Songtsen Gampo

The founder of Samye Monastery reigned from 755 to 797. He is normally seen in a trio of kings with Songtsen Gampo and King Ralpachen (r 817–36). He is regarded as a manifestation of Jampelyang (Manjushri) and so holds a scripture on a lotus in the crook of his left arm and a sword of wisdom in his right. Images show him with features similar to Songtsen Gampo's but without the buddha in his turban.

MILAREPA

A great 11th-century Tibetan magician and poet, Milarepa is believed to have attained the supreme enlightenment of buddhahood in the course of one lifetime. He became an alchemist in order to poison an uncle who had stolen his family's lands and then spent six years meditating in a cave in repentance. During this time he wore nothing but a cotton robe and so became known as Milarepa (Cotton-Clad Repa). The most images of Milarepa depict him smiling, holding his hand to his ear as he sings. He may also be depicted as green because he lived for many years on a diet of nettles.

Milarepa

Environment

The Tibetan plateau is of global ecological significance, not only as the earth's highest ecosystem and one of its last remaining great wildernesses but also as the source of Asia's greatest rivers. Furthermore, it is thought that the high plateau affects global jet streams and even influences the Indian monsoon. The Dalai Lama would like to see Tibet turned into a 'zone of peace' and perhaps even the world's largest national park.

The Tibetan Buddhist view of the environment has long stressed the intricate and interconnected relationship between the natural world and human beings, a viewpoint closely linked to the concept of death and rebirth. Buddhist practice in general stands for moderation and against overconsumption, and forbids hunting, fishing and the taking of animal life. Tibet's nomads, in particular, live in a fine balance with their harsh environment.

THE LAND

The Tibetan plateau is one of the most isolated regions in the world, bound to the south by the 2500km-long Himalaya, to the west by the Karakoram and to the north by the Kunlun and Altyn Tagh ranges. Four of the world's 10 highest mountains straddle Tibet's southern border with Nepal. The northwest in particular is bound by the most remote and least explored wilderness left on earth, outside the polar regions. With an average altitude of 4000m and large swathes of the country well above 5000m, the Tibetan plateau (nearly the size of Western Europe) aptly deserves the title 'the roof of the world'.

The Tibetan Autonomous Region (TAR), with an area of 1.23 million sq km, covers only part of this geographical plateau (the rest is parcelled off into Qinghai and Sichuan provinces). It encompasses the traditional Tibetan provinces of Ü (capital, Lhasa), Tsang (capital, Shigatse), and Ngari, or western Tibet, as well as parts of Kham (eastern Tibet). The TAR shares a 3482km international border with India, Bhutan, Nepal and Myanmar (Burma), and is bordered to the north and east by the Chinese provinces of Xinjiang, Qinghai, Sichuan and Yunnan.

Much of Tibet is a harsh and uncompromising landscape, best described as a high-altitude desert. Little of the Indian monsoon makes it over the Himalayan watershed. Shifting sand dunes are a common sight along the Samye Valley and the road to Mt Kailash.

Ütsang (the combined provinces of Ü and Tsang, which constitute central Tibet) is the political, historical and agricultural heartland of Tibet. Its relatively fertile valleys enjoy a mild climate and are irrigated by wide rivers such as the Yarlung Tsangpo and the Kyi Chu.

Towards the north of Ütsang are the harsh, high-altitude plains of the Changtang (northern plateau), the highest and largest plateau in the world, occupying an area of more than one million square kilometres. This area has no river systems and supports very little in the way of life. The dead lakes of the Changtang are the brackish remnants of the Tethys Sea that found no run off when the plateau started its skyward ascent.

Ngari, or western Tibet, is similarly barren, although here river valleys provide grassy tracts that support nomads and their grazing animals. Indeed, the Kailash range in the far west of Tibet is the source of the

The TAR is made up of the municipality of Lhasa and six prefectures – Ali, Shigatse, Nagchu, Shannan, Nyingtri and Chamdo – divided into 70 counties.

The dry, high altitudes of the Tibetan plateau make for climatic extremes – temperatures on the Changtang have been known to drop 27°C (80°F) in a single day!

subcontinent's four greatest rivers: the Ganges, Indus, Sutlej and Brahmaputra. The Ganges, Indus and Sutlej Rivers all cascade out of Tibet in its far west, not far from Mt Kailash itself. The Brahmaputra (known in Tibet as Yarlung Tsangpo), however, meanders along the northern spine of the Himalaya for 2000km searching for a way south, before coiling back on itself in a dramatic U-turn and draining into India not far from the Myanmar border.

Kham, which encompasses the eastern TAR, western Sichuan and northwest Yunnan, marks a tempestuous drop in elevation down to the Sichuan plain. The concertina landscape produces some of the most spectacular roller-coaster roads in Asia as Himalayan extensions such as the Hengduan Mountains are sliced by the deep gorges of the Yangzi (Jinsha), Salween (Nu Jiang) and Mekong (Lancang) headwaters. The Yarlung Tsangpo itself crashes through a 5km-deep gorge here as it swings around 7756m Namche Barwa, creating the world's deepest gorge. Many parts of this alpine region are lushly forested and support abundant wildlife, largely thanks to the lower altitudes and effects of the Indian monsoon.

Tibet has several thousand lakes (tso in Tibetan), of which the largest are Nam-tso, Yamdrok-tso, Manasarovar (Mapham yum-tso), Siling-tso and Pangong-tso, the last crossing the Indian border into Ladakh.

The high plateau of Tibet is the result of prodigious geological upheaval. The time scale is subject to much debate, but at some point in the last 100 million years the entire region lay beneath the Tethys Sea. And that is where it would have stayed had the mass of land now known as India not broken free from the protocontinent Gondwana and drifted off in a collision course with another protocontinent known as Laurasia. The impact of the two land masses sent the Indian plate burrowing under the Laurasian landmass, and two vast parallel ridges, over 3000km in length and in places almost 9km high, piled up. These ridges, the Himalaya and associated ranges, are still rising at around 10cm a year.

WILDLIFE

The vast differences in altitude in Tibet give rise to a spread of ecosystems from alpine to subtropical.

Animals

If you are not trekking in Tibet and your travels are restricted to sights off the Friendship Hwy, you are unlikely to see much in the way of wildlife. On the road out to Mt Kailash, however, it is not unusual to see herds of Tibetan gazelles (gowa), antelope (tso) and wild asses (kyang), particularly along the northern route.

Marmots (chiwa or piya) are very common and can often be seen perched up on their hind legs sniffing the air curiously outside their burrows – they make a strange bird-like sound when distressed. The pika (chipi), or Himalayan mouse-hare, a relative of the rabbit, is also common. Pikas have been observed at 5250m on Mt Everest, thus earning the distinction of having the highest habitat of any mammal.

A surprising number of migratory birds make their way up to the lakes of the Tibetan plateau through spring and summer. Tibet has over 30 endemic birds; 480 species have been recorded on the plateau. Birds include the black-necked crane, bar-headed goose and lammergeier, as well as grebes, pheasants, snow cocks and partridges. Flocks of huge vultures can often be seen circling monasteries looking for a sky burial.

DID YOU KNOW?

You may well find locals near Shegar selling fossils of marine animals – at an altitude of more than 4000m above sea level!

DID YOU KNOW?

As early as 1642 the fifth Dalai Lama issued an edict protecting animals and the environment.

Two of the best places to go bird-watching in summer are the lakes Yamdrok-tso and Nam-tso; a section of the latter has been designated a bird preserve, at least on paper.

YAKETY-YAK

Fifty years ago an estimated one million wild yaks roamed the Tibetan plateau. Now it is a rare treat to catch a glimpse of these impressive black bovines, which weigh up to a tonne, whose shoulder heights reach over 1.8m and whose sharp, slender horns span 1m. Wild yaks have diminished in number to 15,000 as a result of the increased demand for yak meat and a rise in hunting. Although eating yak meat is not sacrilegious in Tibetan culture, hunting wild yaks is illegal.

Few, if any, of the yaks that travellers see are *drong* (wild yaks). In fact, most are not even yaks at all but rather dzo, a cross between a yak and a cow. A domestic yak rarely exceeds 1.5m in height. Unlike its wild relative, it varies in shade from black to grey and, primarily around Kokonor in Qinghai, white. Seeing only one yak of a certain colour in a herd is considered a bad omen, while seeing two or more yaks of the same colour is considered a sign of luck.

Despite their massive size, yaks are surprisingly sure-footed and graceful on steep, narrow trails, while burdened by loads of up to 70kg. Yaks panic easily and will struggle to stay close together. This gregarious instinct allows herders to drive packs of animals through snow-blocked passes, and thus to create a natural snowplough.

Most impressive is the yak's ability to thrive in high altitudes. In fact, a descent below 3000m may impair the reproductive cycle and even expose the yak to parasites and disease. Cloaked in layers of shaggy, coarse hair and blanketed by a soft undercoat, the yak uses its square tongue and broad muzzle to forage close to the soil in temperatures that frequently drop to minus 40°C. With three times more red blood cells than the average cow, the yak thrives in the oxygen-depleted high altitudes. Its curious lung formation, surrounded by 14 or 15 pairs of ribs rather than the 13 typical of cattle, allows a large capacity for inhaling and expelling air; thus the Latin name *Bos grunniens*, which translates literally as 'grunting ox'.

Tibetans rely on yak milk for cheese, as well as for butter for the ubiquitous butter tea and offerings to butter lamps in monasteries. The outer hair of the yak is woven into tent fabric and rope and the soft inner wool is spun into *chara* (a type of felt) and is used to make bags, blankets and tents. Tails are used in both Buddhist and Hindu religious practices. Yak hide is used for the soles of boots and the yak's heart is used in Tibetan medicine. In the nomadic tradition, no part of the animal is wasted and even yak dung is required as a fundamental fuel, left to dry in little cakes on the walls of most Tibetan houses. So important are yaks to the Tibetans that the animals are individually named, like children.

Herders take great care to ensure the health and safety of their animals. Relocation three to eight times a year provides adequate grazing. Every spring the yaks' thick coats are carefully trimmed. Nomads rely on unique veterinarian skills, which they use to lance abscesses, set broken bones and sear cuts.

The yak, with its extraordinary composition and might, has been perhaps the sole enabler of the harsh life of Tibet's *drokpas*, or nomads, and the two coexist in admirable harmony.

ENDANGERED SPECIES

About 80 species of animal that are threatened with extinction have been listed as protected by the Chinese government. These include the snow leopard *(gang-zig)*, ibex *(king)*, white-lipped deer *(shawa chukar)*, musk deer *(lawa)*, Tibetan antelope *(chiru)*, Tibetan wild ass *(kyang)*, bharal, or blue sheep *(nawa na)*, black-necked crane and wild yak. Omitted from the list is the very rare Tibetan brown bear *(dom gyamuk)*, which stands up to 2m tall and can only be found in the forests of southern Tibet and the remote Changtang plateau.

The Tibetan red deer was recently 'discovered' only 75km from Lhasa after a 50-year hiatus, as was a hitherto unknown breed of ancient wild horse in the Riwoche region of eastern Tibet. The horses bear a striking resemblance to those shown in Stone Age paintings.

The *chiru*, a rare breed of antelope, was recently placed on the Red List (www.redlist.org), a list of threatened species maintained by the World Conservation Union. Numbers in Tibet have dropped from over a million 50 years ago to as few as 65,000 today. Poachers kill the animal for its *shatoosh* wool (wool from the animal's undercoat).

The illegal trade in antelope cashmere, musk, bear paws and gall bladders, deer antlers and other body parts and bones remains a problem. You can often see Tibetan traders huddled on street corners in major Chinese cities selling these and other medicinal cures.

Plants

Juniper trees and willows are common in the valleys of central Tibet and it is possible to come across wildflowers such as the pansy and the oleander, as well as unique indigenous flowers such as the *tsi-tog* (a light-pink, high-altitude bloom).

The east of Tibet, which sees higher rainfall than the rest of the region, has an amazing range of flora, from oak, elm and birch forests to subtropical plants and flowers, including rhododendrons, azaleas and magnolias. It was from here that the intrepid plant hunters of the 19th century took seeds and cuttings of species that would eventually become staples in English gardening.

NATURE PRESERVES

Nature preserves officially protect over 20% of the TAR, although many exist on paper only. The reserve with the highest profile is the Qomolangma Nature Preserve (p284), a 34,000-sq-km protected area straddling the 'third pole' of the Everest region. The park promotes the involvement of the local population, which is essential as around 67,000 people live within the park.

Tibet's newest preserve is the Changtang Nature Preserve, set up in 1993 with the assistance of famous animal behaviourist George Schaller. At 247,120 sq km (larger than Arizona), this is the largest nature reserve in the world after Greenland National Park. Endangered species in the park include bharal, argali sheep, wolves, lynxes, gazelles, snow leopards, wild yaks, antelopes, brown bears and wild asses.

Other reserves include the Medog (Metok) Nature Reserve to the south of Namche Barwa, the Dzayul (Zayu) Reserve along the far southeast border with Assam, and the Kyirong and Nyalam Reserves near the Nepali border. Unfortunately, these reserves enjoy little protection or policing.

ENVIRONMENTAL ISSUES

Modern communist experiments, such as collectivisation and the switching of century-old farming patterns (for example, from barley to wheat and rice), upset the fragile balance in Tibet and resulted in a series of great disasters and famines in the 1960s (as, indeed, they did in the rest of China). By the mid-1970s, the failure of collectivisation was widely recognised and Tibetans have since been allowed to return to traditional methods of working the land.

Other natural resources are less easily renewed. When the Tibetan government-in-exile sent three investigative delegations to Tibet in the early 1980s, among the shocking news they returned with was that Tibet had been denuded of its wildlife. Stories of Chinese troops machine-gunning herds of wild gazelles circulated with convincing frequency. Commercial trophy hunting, often by foreigners paying tens of thousands

DID YOU KNOW?

Yak-tail hair was the main material used to produce Father Christmas (Santa Claus) beards in 1950s America!

For more on environmental issues in Tibet, visit Tibet Environmental Watch at www.tew.org.

of US dollars, has had an effect on the numbers of antelope and argali sheep, in particular.

Rapid modernisation threatens to bring industrial pollution, a hitherto almost unknown problem, onto the high plateau. Several cement factories at Lhasa's edge create huge clouds of noxious smoke, which regularly blankets parts of western Lhasa.

Tibet has enormous potential for hydroelectricity, although current projects at Yamdrok-tso and elsewhere have come in for criticism both from Tibetans and foreign environmental groups. For more information see Down the Drain (p164). Reports of a planned 'super-dam' on the Yarlung Tsangpo (Brahmaputra) in the remote southeast of Tibet has the Indian government downstream deeply concerned.

The region also has abundant supplies of geothermal energy thanks to its turbulent geological history. The Yangpachen Geothermal Plant already supplies Lhasa with much of its electricity. Portable solar panelling has also enjoyed some success; the plateau enjoys some of the longest and strongest sunlight outside the Saharan region. Experimental wind-power stations have been set up in northern Tibet.

Deforestation has long been a pressing problem in eastern Tibet as Chinese logging teams continue their relentless advance from Sichuan province. It has been estimated that US$54 billion worth of timber has been felled in the Tibetan region since 1959. The effect on sediment and run-off levels for rivers downstream, especially in flood-prone China, has slowly sunk in (almost half the world's population lives downstream of Tibet) and logging activity has eased off considerably in recent years.

DID YOU KNOW?

Over 47% of the world's population (85% of Asia) gets its water from the rivers flowing off the Tibetan plateau: the Ganges, Yarlung Tsangpo (Brahmaputra), Indus, Karnali, Sutlej, Yangzi, Huanghe (Yellow River), Mekong, Salween and Irrawady Rivers all have their source in Tibet.

Food & Drink

Tibetan cuisine is not going to win any prizes and food is unlikely to be a highlight of your trip to Tibet. In Lhasa there are a few restaurants that have elevated a subsistence diet into the beginnings of a cuisine but outside the urban centres, Tibetan food is more survival than pleasure. On the plus side, fresh vegetables and packaged goods are more widely available than they once were, and there are now a lot more (mainly Chinese) restaurants around.

STAPLES & SPECIALITIES
Tibetan

Tellingly, the basic Tibetan meal is *tsampa*, a kind of dough made with roasted-barley flour and yak butter (if available) mixed with water, tea or beer – something wet. Tibetans skilfully knead and mix the paste by hand into dough-like balls – not as easy as it looks! *Tsampa* with milk powder and sugar makes a pretty good porridge and is a fine trekking staple, but only a Tibetan can eat it every day and still look forward to the next meal.

Outside of Lhasa, Tibetan food is limited to greasy *momos* and *thugpa*. *Momos* are small dumplings filled with meat or vegetables or both. They are normally steamed but can be fried and are actually pretty good.

More common is *thugpa*, a noodle soup with meat or vegetables or both. Variations on the theme include *hipthuk* (squares of noodles and yak meat in a soup) and *thenthuk* (more noodles). More ambitious and harder to find are *shemdre* (potatoes and yak meat on a bed of rice), *damje* or *shomday* (varieties of fried rice with yak meat, raisins and yoghurt) and *shya vale* (pancake-style pasties, fried, with a yak-meat filling).

Also popular among nomads is dried yak *(yaksha)* or lamb meat. It is normally cut into strips and left to dry on tent lines and is pretty chewy stuff. Sometimes you will see bowls of little white lumps drying in the sun that even the flies leave alone – it is dried yak cheese and it's eaten as a sweet. For the first half-hour it is like having a small rock in your mouth, but eventually it starts to soften up and taste like old, dried yak cheese.

Chinese

Han immigration into Tibet may be a tragic threat to the very essence of Tibetan culture…but it's done wonders for the restaurant scene (!). Even most Tibetans admit that Chinese food is better than *tsampa*, *momos* and *thugpa*. Chinese restaurants can be found in almost every settlement in Tibet these days but are around 50% more expensive than Chinese restaurants elsewhere in China.

Chinese food in Tibet is almost exclusively Sichuanese, the hottest of China's regional cuisines. Sichuanese dishes are usually stir-fried quickly over a high flame and so tend to be very hygienic.

Chinese snacks are excellent and make for a fine light meal. The most common are ravioli-style dumplings called *shuijiao*, ordered by the bowl or weight (half a *jin*, or 250g, is enough for one person), and steamed dumplings called *baozi*, which are similar to *momos* and are normally ordered by the steamer. Both are dipped in soy sauce, vinegar or chilli (or a mix of all). You can normally get a bowl of noodles anywhere for around Y5; *shaguo mixian* is a particularly tasty form of rice noodles cooked in a clay pot. Fried noodles *(chaomian)* and egg fried rice *(dan*

In most restaurants you can simply wander out into the kitchen and point to the vegetables and meats that you want fried up. The main snag with this method is that you'll miss out on many of the most interesting sauces and styles and be stuck with the same dishes over and over.

One popular Sichuanese sauce is *yuxiang*, a spicy, piquant sauce of garlic, vinegar and chilli that is supposed to resemble the taste of fish (probably the closest thing you'll get to fish in Tibet).

chao fan) are not as popular as in the West but you can get them in many Chinese and backpacker restaurants.

Muslim

The Muslim restaurants found in almost all urban centres in Tibet are an interesting alternative to Chinese or Tibetan food. These are normally recognisable by a green flag hanging outside or Arabic script on the restaurant sign. Most chefs come from the Linxia area of Gansu. The food is based on noodles, and of course there's no pork.

Dishes worth trying include *ganbanmian,* a kind of stir-fried spaghetti bolognaise made with beef (or yak) and sometimes green peppers, and *chaomianpian,* fried noodle squares with meat and vegetables. Xinjiang noodles are similar but the sauce comes in a separate bowl, to be poured over the noodles. You can often go into the kitchen and see your noodles being handmade on the spot.

Muslim restaurants also offer good breads and excellent Eight Treasure Tea *(babaocha* or *babao wanzi),* which is made with dried raisins, plums and rock sugar and only releases its true flavour after several cups.

Breakfasts

Few Chinese restaurants have menus in English and when they do the prices are often marked up by as much as 50%.

You can get decent breakfasts of yogurt, muesli and toast at backpacker hotels in Lhasa, Gyantse and Shigatse, but elsewhere you are more likely to be confronted by Chinese-style dumplings, fried bread sticks *(youtiao)* and tasteless rice porridge *(xifan)*. One good breakfast-type food that is widely available is scrambled eggs and tomato *(fanqie chaojidan)*.

Self-Catering

There will be a time when you'll need to be self-sufficient, whether you're staying overnight at a monastery, arriving at a town late at night, or on a long-distance trip to Mt Kailash. Unless you have a stove, your main saviour will be instant noodles. After a long trip to Mt Kailash and back you will know the relative tastes of every kind of packet noodle sold in Tibet. Your body will also likely be deeply addicted to MSG. Even the faintest smell of noodles will leave you nauseaus.

Fortunately the range of foods available in most towns has improved greatly in the last couple of years. Chinese supermarkets stock all kinds of dried fruit and nuts, cans of tuna, soup mixes, chocolate, sausages, biscuits, instant coffee and even Pringles.

It's a good idea to stock up on instant coffee and soups as flasks of boiling water are offered in every hotel and restaurant.

Vegetables such as onions, carrots and bok choy (even seaweed and pickled vegetables) can save even the cheapest pack of noodles from culinary oblivion, as can a packet of mixed spices brought from home.

DRINKS
Nonalcoholic Drinks

The local beverage that every traveller ends up trying at least once is yak-butter tea (see opposite).

The more palatable alternative to yak-butter tea is sweet, milky tea, or *cha ngamo*. It is similar to the tea drunk in neighbouring Pakistan. Chinese green tea, soft drinks and mineral water are available everywhere. The most popular Chinese soft drink is Jianlibao, a honey-and-orange drink (sometimes translated on restaurant menus as 'Jellybowl'!).

Alcoholic Drinks

The Tibetan brew is known as *chang,* a fermented barley beer. It has a rich, fruity taste, and ranges from disgusting to pretty good. Connoisseurs

YAK-BUTTER TEA

Bö cha, literally Tibetan tea, is unlikely to be a highlight of your trip to Tibet. Made from yak butter mixed with salt, milk, soda, tea leaves and hot water all churned up in a wooden tube, the soupy mixture has more the consistency of bouillon than of tea (one traveller described it as 'a cross between brewed old socks and sump oil'!). When mixed with *tsampa* (roasted-barley flour) and yak butter it becomes the staple meal of most Tibetans and you may well be offered it at monasteries, people's houses and even while waiting for a bus by the side of the road.

At most restaurants you mercifully have the option of drinking *cha ngamo* (sweet, milky tea) but there will be times when you just have to be polite and down a cupful of *bö cha* (without gagging). Most nomads think nothing of drinking up to 40 cups of the stuff a day. At least it stops your lips from cracking.

Most distressing for those not sold on the delights of yak-butter tea is the fact that your cup will be refilled every time you take even the smallest sip, as a mark of the host's respect. There's a pragmatic reason for this as well; there's only one thing worse than hot yak-butter tea: cold yak-butter tea.

serve it out of a jerry can. Those trekking in the Everest region should try the local variety, which is served in a big pot. Hot water is poured into the fermenting barley and the liquid is drunk through a wooden straw – it is very good. Sharing *chang* is a good way to get to know local people, if drunk in small quantities.

The main brands of beer available in Tibet are Wuquan, Snow and Huanghe (Yellow River). Lhasa Beer is brewed in Lhasa, originally under German supervision and now in a joint venture with Carlsberg. Pabst Blue Ribbon *(landai)* is a US beer brewed in Sichuan under franchise; no-one admits to drinking Pabst in the US, but out in Tibet it tastes pretty good. Domestic beer costs around Y4 in a shop, Y8 in most restaurants and Y12 in swanky bars.

Supermarkets in Lhasa stock several types of Chinese red wine, including Shangri-La, produced in the Tibetan areas of northeast Yunnan using methods handed down by French missionaries at the beginning of the 19th century. A bottle costs around Y50.

On our research trips we have never suffered any adverse effects from drinking *chang*. However, you should be aware that it is often made with contaminated water, and there Is always some risk in drinking it.

EAT YOUR WORDS – TIBETAN
Useful Phrases

I'm vegetarian.	*nga sha mi-sa-ken yin*	ང་ཤ་མི་ཟ་མཁན་ཡིན།
I don't eat meat.	*nga sha sa-gi may*	ང་ཤ་ཟ་གྱི་མེད།
I'll have what they're having.	*khong-tsö chö-ya-te na-shin nga-la gö*	ཁོང་ཚོས་མཆོད་ཡག་དེ་ན་བཞིན་ང་ལ་དགོས།
Not too spicy, please.	*men-na shay-ta ma-gyâ-ro-nâng*	སྨན་སྣ་ཤེད་ཏ་དགགས་མ་རྒྱག་རོགས་གནང་།
The meal was delicious!	*kha-la shim-bu shay-ta choong!*	ཁ་ལག་ཞིམ་པོ་ཞེ་དྲགས་བྱུང་།

Food Glossary

dumplings	*momo*	མོག་མོག
fried noodles	*gyâ-thuk*	རྒྱ་ཐུག
noodles	*thuk-pa*	ཐུག་པ
omelette	*gong-dre ngö-pâ; om-let*	སྒོང་འབྲས་བཟོས་པ་/ཨོམ་ལེཊ་
roasted-barley flour	*tsâmpa*	རྩམ་པ
stir-fried vegetable dishes	*tsay*	ཚལ་
yak meat	*yâk-sha*	གཡག་ཤ
salt	*tsha*	ཚ་
sugar	*chay-ma ka-ra; chi-ni*	བྱེ་མ་ཀ་ར་/ཅི་ནི་

Drinks

beer (bottled)	*bee-yar*	བྱི་འར་ཤེལ་ཚ
beer (home-brew)	*châng*	ཆང་
boiled water	*chu khö-ma*	ཆུ་འཁོལ་མ
mineral water	*bu-tog-chu*	བུའི་ཏོག་ཚ
butter tea	*bö-ja; cha sü-ma*	བོད་ཇ/ཇ་སྲུབ་མ

EAT YOUR WORDS – CHINESE
Useful Phrases

I don't want MSG.	*wǒ bú yào wèijīng*	我不要味精
I'm vegetarian.	*wǒ chī sù*	我吃素
not too spicy	*bú yào tài là*	不要太辣
(cooked) together	*yíkuàir*	一块儿

Many Sichuanese dishes include *huajiao* (flower pepper), a curious mouth-numbing spice.

Food Glossary

egg soup	*dànhuā tāng*	蛋花汤
wonton (soup)	*húntún (tāng)*	馄饨（汤）
steamed meat buns	*bāozi*	包子
boiled dumplings	*shuǐjiǎo*	水饺
fried rice with beef	*niúròusī chǎofàn*	牛肉丝炒饭
fried rice with egg	*jīdàn chǎofàn*	鸡蛋炒饭
fried rice with vegetables	*shūcài chǎofàn*	蔬菜炒饭
steamed white rice	*mǐfàn*	米饭
beef noodles in a soup	*niúròu miàn*	牛肉面
fried Muslim noodles and beef	*gànbàn miàn*	干拌面
fried noodle squares	*chǎomiànpiàn*	炒面片
fried noodles with vegetables	*shūcài chǎomiàn*	蔬菜炒面
Muslim noodles	*lāmiàn*	拉面
vermicelli noodles in casserole pot	*shāguō mǐxiàn*	沙锅米线
Xinjiang noodles	*xīnjiāng lāmiàn*	新疆拉面
crispy chicken	*xiāngzhá jīkuài*	香炸鸡块
double-cooked fatty pork	*huíguō ròu*	回锅肉
egg and tomato	*fānqié chǎodàn*	番茄炒蛋
'fish-resembling' eggplant	*yúxiāng qiézi*	鱼香茄子
fried green beans	*sùchǎo biǎndòu*	素炒扁豆
fried vegetables	*sùchǎo sùcài*	素炒素菜
red-cooked eggplant	*hóngshāo qiézi*	红烧茄子
spicy tofu	*málà dòufu*	麻辣豆腐
tomatoes and onions	*fānqié chǎo yángcōng*	鱼香炒洋葱
pork and green peppers	*qīngjiāo ròupiàn*	青椒肉片
pork and sizzling rice crust	*guōbā ròupiàn*	锅巴肉片
pork in soy sauce	*jīngjiàng ròusī*	京酱肉丝
spicy chicken with peanuts	*gōngbào jīdīng*	宫爆鸡丁
sweet and sour pork fillets	*tángcù lǐjǐ*	糖醋里脊
'wooden ear' mushrooms & pork	*mùěr ròu*	木耳肉

Drinks

beer	*píjiǔ*	啤酒
boiled water	*kāi shuǐ*	开水
mineral water	*kuàng quán shuǐ*	矿泉水
Muslim tea	*bābǎo wǎnzi*	八宝豌子
tea	*chá*	茶
hot	*rède*	热的
ice cold	*bīngde*	冰的

Gateway Cities

CONTENTS

Many visitors to Tibet will transit through either Chengdu or Kathmandu, or both, en route so this chapter offers basic information on these two cities. For more detail on these cities see Lonely Planet's *China* or *Nepal* guides.

KATHMANDU

☎ 01 / pop 500,000 / elev 1300m

Kathmandu has long been a popular destination for travellers, but there are a couple of drawbacks to entering Tibet from here, namely the uncertainty of getting a Chinese visa and the potential hassles involved in arranging a group tour. For detailed information, see p309 and p313.

The Thamel district of Kathmandu is a travellers' mecca and the place to get a yak steak, repair a sleeping bag, buy a backpack or a 'Free Tibet' T-shirt (don't take it into China!), shop for souvenirs or purchase hard-to-find books on Tibet (including Indian reprints of some very rare editions).

During the June to August monsoon season (when most visitors travel to or from Tibet) it is usually humid and rainy in Kathmandu.

INFORMATION
Bookshops

Pilgrims Book House (www.pilgrimsbooks.com), north of the Kathmandu Guest House in Thamel, and **New Tibet Book Store** (Tridevi Marg), east of Thamel, have the best selections.

Money

Check exchange and commission rates at both banks and licensed moneychangers as they do vary. The US dollar is worth around Rs 75 (75 rupees).

Himalaya Bank (Tridevi Marg; ☎ 8am-8pm Mon-Fri) Changes travellers cheques and gives cash advances on Visa cards.

Standard Chartered Bank (☎ 9.30am-7pm Mon-Fri, 9.30am-12.30pm Sat & Sun) Has two ATMs in Thamel and around the corner from Himalaya Bank on Kantipath.

Travel Agencies

Wayfarers (☎ 426 6010; www.wayfarers.com.np; Thamel) Excellent and reliable agency for air tickets and local tours.

DANGERS & ANNOYANCES

Nepal has been affected by political unrest for several years now. Strikes *(bandh)* and even commercial blockades regularly shut down the city's shops and transport. Getting to the airport can be difficult at these times. There have been infrequent bombings in Kathmandu, including a couple in 2004 at tourist hotels. Check news reports and your own country's travel warnings for the current situation.

TOURS TO TIBET

Many agencies in Thamel offer budget tours to Tibet and these are currently the only way to get into Tibet. See p315 for more details about tour operators. The following agencies are the most reliable, although none is especially recommended.

Eco Trek (☎ 4424112; www.ecotrek.np, www.kailashtour.com; PO Box 6438, Thamel) Tours often run in conjunction with Indian groups.

Green Hill Tours (☎ 4700803; PO Box 5072, Thamel)

Royal Mt Trekking (☎ 4241452; www.royal-mt-trek.com; PO Box 10798, Durbar Marg)

Tashi Delek Nepal Treks & Expeditions (☎ 4410746; tashidele@mail.com.np; Thamel) Often the cheapest.

Ying Yang Travels (☎ 4230485; yingyang@wlink.com.np; Kantipath)

Other travel companies in Thamel offering tours to Tibet include **Tibet Travels** (www.tibettravels.com), **Earthbound Expeditions** (www.trektibet.com), **Adventure Silk Road** (www.silkroadgroup.com) and **Dharma Adventures** (www.dharmaadventures.com), although there are many more.

SIGHTS

Kathmandu's **Durbar Square** (admission Rs 200) is the premier sight and can take up half a day. Exploring the backstreets north and south of here is a joy.

To the west of central Kathmandu, a short taxi ride or 30-minute walk, is the great stupa of **Swayambhunath** (admission Rs 50), also known as the Monkey Temple.

East of Kathmandu is the huge Tibetan chörten at **Bodhnath** (Boudha), which serves as a focus for the exiled Tibetan community. Here you'll find Tibetan hotels, restaurants, shops and half a dozen monasteries. It's a 6km taxi ride (Rs 100) from Thamel.

Pashupatinath (admission Rs 250) is the most sacred Hindu site in Kathmandu, set along the *ghats* (steps) of the Bagmati River, and is a major cremation site. A taxi will cost around Rs 100.

SLEEPING
There are dozens of places to stay in the tourist ghetto of Thamel. Listed here are just a few to get you started. Discounts are available everywhere these days, especially during the low season (May to September) – just ask.

Pilgrims Guest House (☎ 4440565; pilgrimsguest house@yahoo.com; s without bathroom $5, s with bathroom $6-10, d with bathroom $8-15) There's a good range of rooms here, from the top-floor rooms with a sofa, balcony and lots of light, to the cheapest singles, which are little more than a box. The place has a nice outdoor garden restaurant.

Hotel Ganesh Himal (☎ 4263598; htlganesh@wlink .com.np; Chhetrapati; s US$14-20, d US$18-25) Rooms here are some of the best-value available in Kathmandu, with endless hot water, satellite TV and lots of balcony and garden seating. Deluxe rooms are more spacious, with discounts of up to 50%. It's five to 10 minutes' walk southwest of Thamel.

Kathmandu Guest House (☎ 4413632; www .ktmgh.com; s with/without washbasin US$10/2, d with/ without washbasin US$14/4, s with bathroom US$17-50, d with bathroom US$20-60 plus 12% tax; 🔀) This was the first hotel to open in the area and is still one of the most popular – everything in Thamel it seems is 'near the KGH'. Reservations are strongly recommended.

Hotel Potala (☎ 4419159; s/d without bathroom Rs 125/250) Close to the heart of Thamel, almost opposite KC's Restaurant, this small and friendly Tibetan-run place is cheap and cheerful.

Siddhartha Garden Hotel (☎ 4227119; www .sidhartagardenhotel.com; s US$10-15, d US$12-25) This French-run hotel not far from Hotel Utse has stylish rooms, Tibetan staff and a pleasant fruit garden that doubles as a restaurant. Reservations are recommended. There are small discounts in the low season.

Hotel Utse (☎ 4226946; utse@wlink.com.np; s US$15-24 d US$21-30, 20% discount) The Utse is a well-run Tibetan hotel in Jyatha, with spotlessly clean and very comfortable rooms. It has a good rooftop area.

Hotel Tibet (☎ 4429085; hotel@tibet.mos.com.np; s/d US$70/80, discounted to US$35/40; 🔀) Just in front of the Radisson Hotel, this is a great mid-

range choice for Tibetophiles. The hotel is run by a friendly Tibetan family and there's a nice rooftop terrace as well as a meditation chapel.

Kantipur Temple House (☎ 4250131; kantipur@ tmplhouse.wlink.com.np; s/d US$50/60) Along a short alley at the southern end of Jyatha, this interesting hotel has been built in the style of an old Newari temple, has tastefully decorated rooms and is ecofriendly.

EATING
Thamel is rich in backpacker-friendly cafés, bakeries and restaurants in Thamel, so it is possible to get something to eat any time of day. All restaurants are open for lunch and dinner.

Yin Yang Restaurant (mains Rs 250) Just south of the intersection, this is one of Thamel's most highly regarded restaurants. It serves authentic Thai food.

Third Eye Restaurant (mains Rs 200-230) Next door and also highly regarded, this place has good Indian cuisine.

Nargila Restaurant (mains Rs 60-110; 🕑 breakfast, lunch & dinner) North of the central *chowk* (intersection) on the 1st floor, this is one of the very few places to offer good Middle Eastern food and is a fine place to just take a break from the bustle outside.

Dechenling Restaurant (mains Rs 85-150) Probably the best Tibetan restaurant in Thamel, with some interesting Bhutanese dishes.

Utse Restaurant (Tibetan dishes Rs 60-80) In the hotel of the same name in Jyatha, this is one of the longest-running restaurants in Thamel and it also turns out excellent Tibetan dishes.

GETTING THERE & AWAY
For details on flying to Kathmandu see p311.

Air China (☎ 4440650; ktmddca@wlink.com.np; Dhobi-dhara) is a 10-minute walk east of Thamel, but it won't sell you a ticket to Lhasa without a Tibet Tourism Bureau (TTB) permit (see p304).

Other international airlines that operate out of Kathmandu:

Aeroflot (☎ 422 7399; Kamaladi)
Air India (☎ 441 5637; Hattisar)
British Airways (☎ 422 2266; Durbar Marg)
Gulf Air (☎ 443 0456; Hattisar)
Indian Airlines (☎ 441 0906; Hattisar)
Japan Airlines (☎ 422 4854; Durbar Marg)

CENTRAL KATHMANDU

0 ——————— 400 m
0 ——————— 0.2 miles

To Kathmandu Bus
Station (3km)

Naya Bazar

Galko Patna

British
Embassy

Lazimpat

13

French
Embassy

Lekhnath Marg

Lainchhaur

Paknajol

Lainchhaur

17

Bhagwan
Bahal

New
Royal
Palace

23

Thamel

Kaldhara

20

16 3
34
35

Paknajol

21 12
32
7

33

2

Trisevi Marg
Post
Office

Three
Goddesses
Temple

36

4

6
10

27

Lal
Durbar

Dhalko

8

14

To Pashupatinath (2km);
Tribhuvan Airport (6km);
Bodhnath (6km)

Dhobichaur

Chhetrapati
Chowk

18

Jyatha

Chhetrapati

Ikha
Pokhari

11

To Swayambhunath
(2.5km)

Thahiti
Tole

Jyatha

15

28

31
24

26

25

To Swayambhunath
(2.5km)

Nyokha

Bangemudha

Asan
Tole

Jamal

Tukucha Khola

Yatkha
Tole

Kilagal

Kilagal
Tole

Kathmandu

Bangemuda

Rani Pokhari
(Queen's Pond)

30 22

Kamaladi

Yitum
Bahal

Bhedsingh

Asan Tole

Kel
Tole

Bhotahiti

Kot
Square

Indra
Chowk

Nasal
Chowk

9

Sanga Path

Basantapur
Square

5

New Road

Ratna
Park

Bag Bazar

Basantapur

Dharma
Path

29

City Bus
Station

Adwait Marg

Khicha
Pokhari

Vegetable
Market

Yengal

Main Post
Office

Khicha
Pokhari

Tundikhel
(Parade Ground)

Pradarshani Marg

Central Immigration Office;
Tourist Service Centre

Bhrikuti Mandap
(Exhibition
Ground)

Jaisi Deval

Taha Galli

Sundhara

Shahid Gate
(Martyrs' Memorial)

Lagankhel

Brahma
Tole

Bhadrakali
Temple

Prithvi Path

To Bhaktapur
(10.5km)

INFORMATION		Hotel Utse	14 B3	Gulf Air	(see 27)
Himalaya Bank	1 C3	Kantipur Temple House	15 B3	Indian Airlines	25 D3
New Tibet Book Store	2 B2	Kathmandu Guest House	16 B2	Japan Airlines	26 C3
Pilgrims Book House	3 B2	Pilgrims Guest House	17 B2	Lufthansa Airlines	(see 24)
Standard Chartered Bank	4 C3	Siddhartha Garden Hotel	18 B3	Pakistan International Airlines	27 D3
Standard Chartered Bank (ATM only)	5 A5			Qatar Airlines	28 C3
Standard Chartered Bank (ATM only)	(see 16)	EATING 🍴	(p79)	Royal Nepal Airlines	29 B5
Standard Chartered Bank (ATM only)	6 C3	Dechenling Restaurant	19 B3	Singapore Airlines	30 C4
Standard Chartered Bank (ATM only)	7 C3	Nargila Restaurant	20 B2	Thai Airways International	31 C3
Wayfarers	8 B3	Third Eye Restaurant	(see 21)	Tibet Air	(see 23)
		Utse Restaurant	(see 14)		
SIGHTS & ACTIVITIES	(pp78–9)	Yin Yang Restaurant	21 D2	OTHER	
Durbar Square	9 A5			Adventure Silk Road	32 B2
Royal Mount Trekking	10 C3	TRANSPORT	(pp79–81)	Eco Trek	33 B2
		Aeroflot	22 C4	Green Hill Tours	34 B2
SLEEPING 🛏	(p79)	Air China	23 D2	Tashi Delek Nepal Treks &	
Hotel Ganesh Himal	11 A4	Air India	(see 25)	Expeditions	35 B2
Hotel Potala	12 B2	British Airways	24 C3	Ying Yang Travels	36 C3
Hotel Tibet	13 D1	Budda Air	(see 27)		

Lufthansa (☎ 422 3052; Durbar Marg)
Pakistan International Airlines (☎ 443 9234; Hattisar)
Qatar Airlines (☎ 425 6579; Kantipath)
Royal Nepal Airlines (☎ 422 0757; Kantipath)
Singapore Airlines (☎ 422 0759; Kamaladi)
Thai International (☎ 422 3565; Durbar Marg)

There are three important rules concerning flights out of Kathmandu: reconfirm, reconfirm and reconfirm! This applies particularly to Royal Nepal Airlines. Make sure you get to the airport early as people at the end of the queue can be left behind.

GETTING AROUND

Taxis are reasonably priced and most of the drivers will use the meter for short trips around town, which rarely come to more than Rs 50. In the evening you may have to negotiate a fare.

Three-wheeled autorickshaws are common and cost as little as half the taxi fare. Cycle rickshaws cost Rs 30 to 50 for most rides around town. Always agree on a price before you get in.

To/From the Airport

Kathmandu's Tribhuvan International Airport is about 2km east of town. You will find an organised taxi service in the ground-floor foyer area immediately after you leave the baggage collection and customs section. The taxis from the airport have a fixed fare of Rs 250 to Thamel or Rs 200 to the Durbar Marg.

Hotel touts outside the international terminal will offer you a free lift to their hotel, but you are less likely to get a discounted room rate this way as touts receive a hefty commission.

You should be able to get a taxi from Thamel to the airport for Rs 150. The international airport departure tax is Rs 1500, or Rs 770 to neighbouring countries of India, Pakistan, Bhutan and Bangladesh).

CHENGDU 成都

☎ 028 / pop 4.1 million / elev 126m
Chengdu is the main gateway to Tibet and is the largest and most important city in southwest China. Most travellers end up spending at least a day or two here while they are arranging a flight and permit necessary for Lhasa. Temperatures can hit an uncomfortable 35°C during muggy July and August.

INFORMATION

The best source for up to the minute restaurant, bar and entertainment listings in Chengdu is the free monthly magazine *Go West*. *That's National* is a similar publication that has some interesting articles about travel.

Bank of China (Renmin Nanlu; ⏲ 8.30am-6pm Mon-Fri, 8.30am-5pm Sat & Sun) Can change money and travellers cheques and offers cash advances on credit cards. There is another branch on Renmin Donglu and a strategically placed ATM outside the Xinnanmen bus station.

Global Doctor Chengdu Clinic (☎ 8522 6058, 139 8225 6966; Ground fl, Kelan Bldg, Bangkok Garden Apts, Section 4, 21 Renmin Nanlu) Available 24 hours.

Public Security Bureau (PSB; ☎ 8640 7067; 136 Wenwu Lu; ⏲ 9am-noon & 1-5pm Mon-Fri) The foreign affairs entrance is on Tianzuo Jie; this is where you can get visa extensions.

US consulate (☎ 8558 3992; 4 Linshiguan Lu) In the south of town.

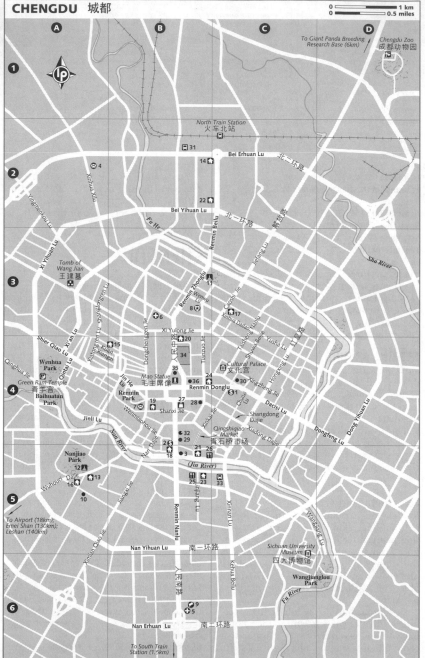

CHENGDU 城都

0 _____ 1 km
0 _____ 0.5 miles

To Giant Panda Breeding
Research Base (6km)

Chengdu Zoo
成都动物园

North Train Station
火车北站

31

14

Bei Erhuan Lu
北一环路

4

Xinhua Xilu

22

Bei Yihuan Lu
北一环路

Renmin Beilu

Jiefang Lu

Fu He

Sha River

Tomb of
Wang Jian
王建墓

Renmin Zhonglu

Renmin Wenwu

11

8

17

Xinhua Dadao

Caoshi Jie

Shier Qiao Lu

Xi'an Lu

Shangxingren Jie

6

Xi Yulong Jie

20

Taisheng Nanlu

Shuwa Beijie

Yusha Lu

Dongchengen Jie

Tianzuo Jie

Wenhua
Park

Green Ram Temple
青羊宫

Baihuatan
Park

15

Xuan
Xiang

Jin He

34

Mao Statue
毛主席像

36

35

24

30

Cultural Palace
文化宫

Xingzheng Jie

Hongxing Lu

Renmin
Park

7

19

Shanxi Jie

27

28

Renmin Donglu

1

Chunxi
Lu

Dacisi Lu

Dong Yihuan Lu

Jinli Lu

Wenmiaohou Jie

Nan Dajie

Xunan Jie

Shangdong
Dajie

Shangdong Xiadong Dajie

Qingshiqiao
Market
青石桥市场

Dongfeng Lu

Nanjiao
Park
南郊

12

16

13

32

29

2

18

3

21   26

Nan River

10

Jiangxi Jie

(Jin River)

25   23

33

5

To Airport (18km);
Emei Shan (130km);
Leshan (140km)

Renmin Nanlu

Xinnan Lu

Wangjianglou Lu

Wuhou Dajie

Xinnan Qiao Lu

Nan Yihuan Lu   南一环路

Kehua Beilu

Sichuan University
Museum
四大博物馆

Wangjianglou
Park

Fu River

9

5

Nan Erhuan Lu   南二环路

To South Train
Station (1.5km)

TOURS TO TIBET

You can only buy an air ticket to Lhasa in conjunction with a tour. For this, most travellers use the budget travel agencies at the Traffic Hotel, such as **Tibet Budget Tour** (☎ 8545 4978).

Contact Gao Liqiang at **Tibetan Trekking** (☎ 8675 1783; www.tibetantrekking.com; Rm 1614, Zhufeng Hotel, 288 Shuncheng Lu) for treks and 4WD trips in western Sichuan.

SIGHTS

To fill in the time while you wait for your ticket and permit to Lhasa you could take a taxi or bus out to the **Giant Panda Breeding Research Base** (admission Y30; ☺ 8am-6pm), 12km northeast of the city. It's easiest to take one of the tours that is run by the Dragon Town Youth Hostel or Sam's Guesthouse; they cost around Y50, which includes the entrance fee.

For a distinctly Sichuanese experience visit the teahouses in **Renmin Park** (admission Y2, tea Y5-20; ☺ 6am-8pm) or **Wenshu Temple** (Renmin Zhonglu; admission Y1; ☺ 8am-5.30pm). The monastery itself and the surrounding alleys are also worth a visit.

South of the river, on a street across from the entrance of the **Wuhou Temple** (Wuhou Si; admission Y30; ☺ 6.30am-8pm), is a small **Tibetan neighbourhood**.

SLEEPING

Traffic Hotel (Jiaotong Fandian; ☎ 8545 1017; fax 8544 0977; 6 Linjiang Zhonglu; dm Y30-40, d with bathroom Y200; ☒) Conveniently located next to the Xinnanmen bus station, the Traffic used to be the first choice for accommodation in

Chengdu but it's facing some stiff competition these days. Rooms are comfortable and air-conditioned and the shared bathrooms are super clean. The location is perfect if you are bussing to Kangding and beyond.

Dragon Town Youth Hostel (Longtang Kezhan; ☎ 8664 8408; www.dragontown.com.cn; 27 Kuan Xiangzi, dm Y15-30, d/tr per bed without bathroom Y60/40, s/d with bathroom Y80/140) Down a narrow alley in a beautiful four-storey building that dates back to the Qing dynasty, this has to be one of Chengdu's best budget options. The higher-end doubles feature antique Chinese furniture.

Chengdu Dreams Travel International Youth Hostel (Chengdu Mengzhilu Guoji Qingnian Lüshe; ☎ 8557 0315; www.dreams-travel.com/youthhostel; 242 Wuhouci Dajie; dm Y25-60) Situated in the Tibetan area of town, the dorm rooms here are good value and the roof terrace has fantastic views of the neighbouring park.

Holly's Hostel (Jiulongding Qingniang Kezhan; ☎ 8554 8131; hollyhotelcn@yahoo.com; 246 Wuhouci Dajie; dm Y15-30) This charming guesthouse can be found in the heart of the Tibetan quarter. The rooms look a bit old but they're large and clean and the staff are friendly.

Sam's Guesthouse (☎ 8615 4179; samtour@yahoo .com; 130 Shanxi Jie; dm/d Y40/100) Sam's place is in a wing of the Rongcheng Hotel. Dorms are good value but the doubles look a bit tired. Facilities include left luggage, café, email, travel service, laundry, bike rental and book exchange.

Jindi Hotel (Jindi Fandian; ☎ 8691 5339; 89 Xinhua Dadao; s/d Y220/280; ☒) If a private bathroom is top of your wish list then you won't go wrong with this decent-value hotel.

Chengdu Hotel (Chengdu Dajiudian; ☎ 8317 3888; fax 8317 6818; 29 Renmin Beilu; d Y150-280) The permanent discounts offered here make this a good choice, although you might find the location a bit inconvenient.

Tibet Hotel (☎ 8318 3388; fax 8319 3838; 10 Renmin Beilu; s/d Y598/1180) The location is not the most convenient but the rooms here are decorated in Tibetan style. This hotel has received a number of good reviews from travellers.

Jinjiang Hotel (Jinjiang Binguan; ☎ 8550 6666; www .jjhotel.com; 80, Section 2, Renmin Nanlu; d Y880-1380) The rooms here are somewhat overpriced but they do offer nonsmoking rooms, with some good views from the rooftop Chinese restaurant.

Yinhe Dynasty Hotel (☎ 8661 8888; 99 Xiaxi Shuncheng Jie; d Y1120-1440) These luxurious rooms are a good choice if you're looking for that top-end option.

Several top-end international chains are represented, including the plush **Sheraton Chengdu Lido Hotel** (☎ 8676 8999; www.sheraton .com/chengdu; Section 1, 15 Renmin Zhonglu; d Y1280-1920; 🏊 ❄ 🍴) and **Sofitel Wangda Chengdu** (☎ 6666 9999; www.sofitel.com; 15 Binjiang Zhonglu; d US$138, discounted to US$95; 🏊 ❄ 🍴).

EATING
Wenshu Temple (Renmin Zhonglu; dishes Y6-10) The excellent vegetarian restaurant here has an English menu and is a special treat for vegetarians.

Highfly Cafe (☎ 8544 2820; 18 Linjiang Zhonglu; dishes from Y12; 🕙 9am-late) An old-timer, this place still serves great breakfast, pizzas and delicious calorie-laden fudge brownies.

Paul & Dave's Oasis (☎ 8950 0646; 21/1 Binjiang Zhonglu; meals Y15-40; 🕙 6pm-late) This is one of the original backpacker cafés and its still remains popular. The large comfy sofas make it an easy place to kick back for the evening and enjoy a cheap beer or five. On weekends this place keeps going until the early hours.

Sofitel Wangda Chengdu (☎ 6666 9999; 15 Binjiang Zhonglu; breakfast & lunch buffets Y80, dinner

A TOUCH OF SILK
A silk lining for your sleeping bag will keep it clean and add extra warmth that you'll appreciate on the plateau. If you are passing through Chengdu you can buy silk in the Chengdu Department Store for about Y20 per metre (get four metres) and get a tailor to make you a liner for less than US$1.

buffet Y98, plus 15%) This place has excellent-value, all-you-can-eat buffets if you crave a final blowout before or after your trip to Tibet.

SHOPPING
For a last-minute Chinese-made tent or Gore-tex jacket, there are several gear shops on Linjiang Lu, near the Traffic Hotel.

GETTING THERE & AWAY
For details on flying to Chengdu see p311.

Air China (☎ 8666 1100; 41, Section 2, Renmin Nanlu 🕙 8am-7.30pm) Will not sell air tickets to Lhasa; tickets have to be bought through an agency as part of a tour.

Dragonair (☎ 675 5555 ext 6105; Sichuan Hotel; 31 Zongfu Lu)

Sichuan Airlines (☎ 8665 7163, 8665 4858; 31, Section 2, Renmin Nanlu)

GETTING AROUND
The most useful bus is No 16, which runs from Chengdu's north train station to the south train station along Renmin Nanlu. Regular buses cost Y1, while the double-deckers cost Y2. Taxis have a flag fall of Y5 (Y6 at night), plus Y1.4 per kilometre. Most budget accommodation rents bikes for about Y10 per day.

To/From the Airport
Shuangliu Airport is 18km west of the city. Airport bus No 303 runs every half-hour from the Air China office on Renmin Nanlu (Y8). A taxi costs around Y40.

Lhasa ལྷ་ས

Lhasa, the heart and soul of Tibet, for centuries the abode of the Dalai Lamas, and object of devout pilgrimage, is still a city of wonders, despite the large-scale encroachments of modern Chinese influence.

Your first hint that Lhasa is close at hand is the sight of the Potala, a vast white-and-ochre fortress soaring over this, one of the world's highest cities. It is a sight that has heralded the marvels of the Holy City to travellers for close to four centuries and it still gets the goose bumps going.

While the Potala dominates the Lhasa skyline and, as the residence of the Dalai Lamas, serves as a symbolic focus for Tibetan hopes of self-government, it is the Jokhang, some 2km to the east of the Potala, that holds the spiritual heart of the city. An otherworldly mix of sombre darkness, wafting incense and prostrating pilgrims, the Jokhang is the most sacred and active of Tibet's temples. Encircling it is the Barkhor, the holiest of Lhasa's devotional koras, and it is here that most visitors first fall in love with Tibet. The crowding pilgrims, the stall-holders hawking everything from prayer flags to jewel-encrusted yak skulls and the devout tapping their foreheads to the ground at every step is an exotic brew that few newcomers can resist.

However, the Potala and the Jokhang, though prominent, are just two of the sights that Lhasa has to offer. Close to the Jokhang are a number of smaller active temples little visited by foreign travellers. The white-walled alleys running off the Barkhor circuit in particular are fascinating to explore, and in Lhasa's low-lying surrounding hills are the important Gelugpa monasteries of Sera and Drepung. Allow at least a week to take in the sights.

And just a word of warning: it's not uncommon to feel breathless, suffer from headaches and sleep poorly because of acute mountain sickness (AMS; p329) if you fly straight into Lhasa. Take things easy for the first few days and try to drink lots of fluids.

HIGHLIGHTS

- Let yourself be swept around the **Barkhor** (p91), Lhasa's fascinating medieval pilgrim circuit
- Join the shuffling, murmuring pilgrims around the shrines of the **Jokhang** (p94), the spiritual heart of Tibet
- Wind your way up through the **Potala** (p98), the deserted but impressive citadel of the Dalai Lamas
- Explore **Sera** (p122) and **Drepung** (p118), two of the largest and most intact of Tibet's great monasteries
- Make an easy day trip from Lhasa to **Ganden Monastery** (p126) and walk its interesting kora
- Walk Lhasa's **koras** (p90) and rub shoulders with Tibetan pilgrims
- Visit one of Lhasa's small **off-the-beaten-track temples**

▪ TELEPHONE CODE: 0891	▪ POPULATION: 240,000	▪ ELEVATION: 3595M

HISTORY

Lhasa rose to prominence as an important administrative centre in the 7th century AD, when Songtsen Gampo (c 618–49), a local ruler in the Yarlung Valley, continued the task initiated by his father of unifying Tibet. Songtsen Gampo moved his capital to Lhasa and built a palace on the site now occupied by the Potala. At this time the temples of Ramoche and the Jokhang were established to house Buddha images brought as the dowries of Songtsen Gampo's Chinese and Nepali wives.

The rule of the Yarlung kings from their new capital, Lhasa, lasted some 250 years. Chinese records from Dunhuang state that the capital of Lhasa was a walled city with flat-roofed houses and refer to the 'king and his nobles' as living 'in felt tents'. The same records refer to an aversion to washing, the eating of *tsampa* (roasted-barley flour) and the plaited hair of Tibetan women – customs that persist to the present day.

With the break-up of the Yarlung empire, Buddhism enjoyed a gradual resurgence at monastic centres outside Lhasa and the centre of power shifted to Sakya, Nedong (Ü) and then Shigatse (Tsang). No longer the capital, Lhasa now languished in the backwaters of Tibetan history until the fifth Dalai Lama (1617–82) defeated the Shigatse kings with Mongol support.

The fifth Dalai Lama moved his capital to Lhasa. He built his palace, the Potala, on the site of the ruins of Songtsen Gampo's 7th-century palace. Lhasa has remained Tibet's capital since 1642, and most of the city's historical sights date from this second stage of the city's development. Very little remains of Lhasa's 7th-century origins.

Modern Lhasa in many ways provides the visitor with both the best and the worst of contemporary Tibet. After all, despite the city's rich historical associations and colourful Tibetan population, it is here that Chinese control is at its most trigger-happy, and much of the city's charm has fallen prey to Chinese 'modernisation'.

Photographs of the city taken before October 1950 reveal a small town nestled at the foot of the Potala and linked by an avenue to another cluster of residences in the area of the Jokhang. The population of the city before the Chinese takeover is thought to have been between 20,000 and 30,000. Today the city has a population of around 240,000, and Chinese residents outnumber Tibetans.

Shöl, the village at the foot of the Potala, has all but disappeared, and the old West Gate, through which most people entered the Holy City, was torn down during the Cultural Revolution to be replaced by a smaller, modern version in 1995. The area in front of the Potala has been made into a Tiananmen-style public square, complete with a 35m-tall monument to the 'liberation' of Tibet (under constant guard to prevent vandalism). What used to be known as Gumolingka Island, and once a traditional Tibetan picnic spot, is now a Chinese-style shopping and karaoke complex.

The Tibetan quarter is now an isolated enclave in the eastern end of town, comprising only around 4% of the total area of contemporary Lhasa. Even these lingering enclaves of tradition are under threat despite official protection. Lhasa has probably changed more in the last twenty years than in the thousand years before.

ORIENTATION

While Lhasa has emerged as a surprisingly sprawling city in recent years, orienting yourself is still a relatively simple affair. The city divides clearly into a western (Chinese) section and an eastern (Tibetan) section. The Chinese section holds most of Lhasa's upmarket accommodation options, along with Chinese restaurants, bars and the Nepali consulate. The Tibetan eastern end of town is more colourful and has all the budget and mid-range accommodation popular with independent travellers.

The principal thoroughfare is the east to west-running Dekyi Nub Lam, which then becomes Dekyi Shar Lam in the east of town (in Tibetan, *nub* means west and *shar* means east). The road is known in Chinese as Beijing Zhonglu and Beijing Donglu. The eastern end holds several of the best budget hotels, including the Yak Hotel.

The Jokhang and Barkhor Square are in between Dekyi Shar Lam and Chingdröl Shar Lam (Jiangsu Lu) and are connected to these two main roads by the Tibetan quarter, a web of winding alleyways lined with the white-washed façades of traditional Tibetan homes. This Tibetan area is not particularly extensive. Rather than worry about orientation it is more fun to simply

LHASA

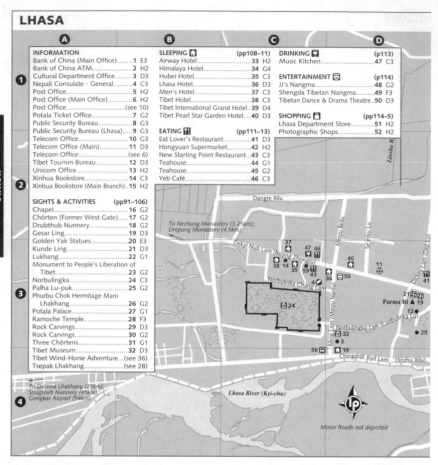

LHASA

INFORMATION	
Bank of China (Main Office)	1 E3
Bank of China ATM	2 H2
Cultural Department Office	3 D3
Nepali Consulate - General	4 C3
Post Office	5 H2
Post Office (Main Office)	6 H2
Post Office	(see 10)
Potala Ticket Office	7 G2
Public Security Bureau	8 G3
Public Security Bureau (Lhasa)	9 G3
Telecom Office	10 G3
Telecom Office (Main)	11 D3
Telecom Office	(see 6)
Tibet Tourism Bureau	12 D3
Unicom Office	13 H2
Xinhua Bookstore	14 C3
Xinhua Bookstore (Main Branch)	15 H2

SIGHTS & ACTIVITIES	(pp91–106)
Chapel	16 G2
Chörten (Former West Gate)	17 G2
Drubthub Nunnery	18 G2
Gesar Ling	19 D3
Golden Yak Statues	20 E3
Kunde Ling	21 D3
Lukhang	22 G1
Monument to People's Liberation of Tibet	23 G2
Norbulingka	24 C3
Palha Lu-puk	25 G2
Phurbu Chok Hermitage Mani Lhakhang	26 G2
Potala Palace	27 G1
Ramoche Temple	28 F3
Rock Carvings	29 D3
Rock Carvings	30 G2
Three Chörtens	31 G1
Tibet Museum	32 D3
Tibet Wind-Horse Adventure	(see 36)
Tsepak Lhakhang	(see 28)

SLEEPING	(pp108–11)
Airway Hotel	33 H2
Himalaya Hotel	34 G4
Hubei Hotel	35 C3
Lhasa Hotel	36 D3
Men's Hotel	37 C3
Tibet Hotel	38 C3
Tibet International Grand Hotel	39 D4
Tibet Pearl Star Garden Hotel	40 D3

EATING	(pp111–13)
Eat Lover's Restaurant	41 D3
Hongyuan Supermarket	42 H2
New Starting Point Restaurant	43 C3
Teahouse	44 G1
Teahouse	45 G2
Yeti Café	46 C3

DRINKING	(p113)
Music Kitchen	47 C3

ENTERTAINMENT	(p114)
JJ's Nangma	48 G2
Shengda Tibetan Nangma	49 F3
Tibetan Dance & Drama Theatre	50 D3

SHOPPING	(pp114–5)
Lhasa Department Store	51 H2
Photographic Shops	52 H2

slip away from the Barkhor circuit at some point and aimlessly wander the alleys. You won't stay lost for long.

Maps

The *Lhasa Tour Map* is a relatively useful English-language map of the city, produced by the Mapping Bureau of Tibet Autonomous Region. This and other local maps are available at the Xinhua bookstores, branches of China Post and the gift shops of most hotels. Other maps of Lhasa are available outside Tibet (p302).

INFORMATION

Useful information is scarce in Lhasa. Most travellers find out more about what is going on and how things work by sitting around chatting in the courtyards of the backpacker hotels or at the Tashi restaurants than they do by calling in to travel agencies. The information boards at the Pentoc Guesthouse and the Yak, Banak Shol, Snowlands and Kirey hotels can be very useful if you are looking for travel partners, a ride in a Land Cruiser, or even a second-hand Lonely Planet guidebook.

Bookshops

There is very little in the way of decent mapping or non-Chinese reading material available in Lhasa. The gift shops at the Lhasa Hotel, the Himalaya Hotel, the Potala and the Norbulingka stock a few glossy coffee-table souvenir books.

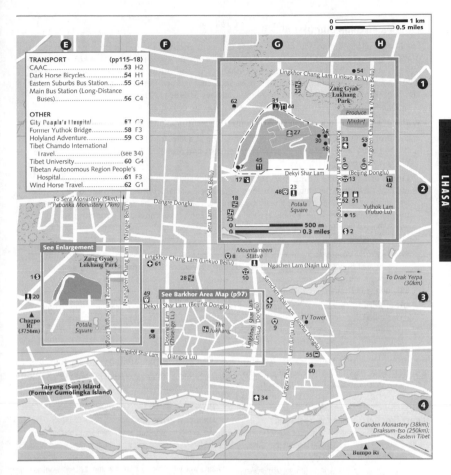

LHASA

Xinhua Bookstore Yuthok Lam (Map pp88–9); Dekyi Nub Lam (Map pp88–9) The main branch, on Yuthok Lam, about 10 minutes' walk west of Barkhor Square, has some maps, postcards and photo books.

Consulates
Nepali Consulate-General (Map pp88–9; ☎ 681 5744; rncglx@public.ls.x.cn; Norbulingka Chang Lam (Luobulinka Beilu) 🕙 10am-12.30pm Mon-Fri) On a side street between the Lhasa Hotel and the Norbulingka. Visas can be obtained here (p300).

Internet Access
There are dozens of places in Lhasa offering Internet access for around Y5 per hour. Most popular with travellers are those at the Snowlands Hotel and Yak Hotel.

Khangli Internet Bar (Map p92; Dekyi Shar Lam (Beijing Donglu) 🕙 9am-midnight) Opposite the Banak Shol Hotel.
Xinhua Bookstore (Map pp88–9; 3rd floor; Yuthok Lam; per hr Y3; 🕙 24 hr)

Laundry
The Banak Shol and Kirey hotels both offer a free laundry service to guests. The Pentoc charges Y20 for a bagful.
Snowlands Laundry (Map p92; Mentsikhang Lam; per piece Y3)

Medical Services
Several hotels around the town sell Tibetan herbal medicine recommended by locals for easing symptoms of altitude sickness,

LHASA'S PILGRIM CIRCUITS

For Tibetan pilgrims, who approach the Holy City with priorities somewhat different from those of the average Western visitor, the principal points of orientation are Lhasa's three koras (pilgrimage circuits): the Nangkhor, Barkhor and Lingkhor. For the visitor, all the koras are well worth following, especially during festivals such as Saga Dawa, when the distinction between tourist and pilgrim can become very fine. Remember always to proceed clockwise.

- **Nangkhor** – This kora encircles the inner precincts of the Jokhang.
- **Barkhor** – This traces the outskirts of the Jokhang in a circuit (p93) of approximately 800m. It is the most famous of Lhasa's pilgrimage circuits and probably the best introduction to the old town for newcomers.
- **Lingkhor** – This is the devotional route that traditionally encompassed the entirety of the old city. Nowadays the Lingkhor includes a great deal of scenery that is of a decidedly secular and modern nature, but it is still used by pilgrims. You can join the circuit (Map pp88–9, Map p92) anywhere. The whole kora is around 8km long and takes most of the morning, longer if you make many interesting stops en route, such as the rock paintings of Chagpo Ri and the Kunde Ling temple.
- **Potala Kora** – Another popular kora encircles the holy Potala passing by an almost continuous circuit of prayer wheels. The route leads past teahouses, chörtens (stupas), stone carvers, rock paintings and often buskers, and is worth a visit, especially if you want to visit the Lukhang (p103).
- **Other koras** – There are excellent koras at Drepung (p122), Ganden (p128) and Sera (p124) monasteries.

also known as AMS, which stands for acute mountain sickness). The medicine is known as *solomano* in Tibetan and *hongjingtian* in Chinese. A box of vials will cost you around Y25.

Military Hospital (Xizang Junqu Zongyiyuan; 西藏军区总医院; Map p119; Nangre Beilu) Travellers who have received medical attention confirm that this place offers the best treatment in Tibet.

Money

Bank of China branch (Zhongguo Yinhang; Map p92; Dekyi Shar Lam; 9.30am-1pm & 3.30-6.30pm Mon-Fri) The most conveniently located option changes cash and travellers cheques without fuss though it can't change money on the weekends or give a cash advance on a credit card. Between the Banak Shol and Kirey hotels. The ATM is by the Xiaofan Guesthouse, on the east side of Potala Square.

Bank of China main office (Map pp88-9; Linkuo Beiju; 9am-6.30pm Mon-Fri, 10am-5pm Sat & Sun, opening and closing half an hour later in winter). West of the Potala. For credit-card advances and foreign exchange during the weekend. Visa, MasterCard, Diners Club and American Express cards are accepted; there's a 3% commission and the minimum withdrawal is Y1200. This is also the place to arrange a bank transfer (p304). It has two ATMS: one in and one outside the building (the latter 24 hours).

Top-end hotels all have an exchange service, but this is normally available only to hotel guests.

Post

Main post office (Map pp88-9; Dekyi Shar Lam; 9am-8pm Mon-Sat, 10am-6pm Sun) The counter in the far left corner as you walk through the main doors sells stamp and packaging for parcels. Leave parcels unsealed until you get to the post office as the staff will want to check the contents for customs clearance.

Post office (Map pp88-9; 9am-7pm daily) Five minutes' walk northeast of the Banak Shol Hotel.

Public Security Bureau (PSB)

Lhasa PSB (Gonganju; Map pp88-9; 4 Dekyi Shar Lam; 9am-noon, 3.30-6pm Mon-Sat) Not a good place for visa extensions. Extensions of up to a week are sometimes given if you can conjure up some evidence of planned departure, such as an air ticket out of Tibet. If you're looking for a longer extension then it's wiser to inquire at one of the private travel agencies before revealing your plans to the PSB.

Travel permits are rarely given to individual travellers in Lhasa and you're better off trying in Shigatse (p172).

Telephone

The cheapest way to make international calls is through **private telephone booths** (☼ 8.30am-11pm) around town, often go under the name 'China Railcom'.

Telephone rates are Y2.6 to the US, Y3.8 to Europe and Australia or Y4.8 to other countries. A local city call costs Y0.4 for three minutes.

Unicom (Map pp88-9; Dekyi Shar Lam; ☼ 9am-8pm), across from the post office, offers similarly cheap rates.

Rates are a little higher at the **main telecom office** (Map pp88-9; 59 Dekyi Nub Lam; ☼ 8.30am-8pm), east of the Tibet Pearl Star Garden. The most convenient **telecom branch** (Map pp88-9; Dekyi Shar Lam (Beijing Donglu); ☼ 8.30am-10pm) is next to the main post office, a five minute walk west of the Yak Hotel. There is a smaller **telecom branch** (Map pp88-9; ☼ 8am-midnight) at the northern end of Lingkhor Shar Lam in the east of town.

Travel Agencies

At the time of research, independent travel agencies in Tibet had been outlawed by the Chinese government and all independent travellers had to arrange travel with one of two Family (or Foreign) and Independent Traveller (FIT) offices run by the Tibet Tourism Bureau (TTB).

FIT (☼ 10am-12.30pm & 3.30-5.30pm) Snowlands Hotel (Map p92; ☎ 634 9239; fax 634 3854; 4 Mentsikhang Lam) Banak Shol Hotel (Map p92; ☎ 634 4397, 696 0784; Dekyi Shar Lam) The two branches operate independently and offer different prices. Contact Sonam at Snowlands or Xiaojiang at Banak Shol. The latter is often cheaper.

Policies change like the wind in Tibet so you may find that private agencies have reappeared. They offer cheaper prices but have problems obtaining travel permits so are probably best used for trips around Lhasa and along the Friendship Hwy.

SIGHTS
The Barkhor བར་འཁོར་   Map p92

The first stop for most newcomers to Lhasa is the Jokhang in the heart of the old Tibetan part of town. But before you even venture into the Jokhang it is worth taking a stroll around the **Barkhor**, Lhasa's most interesting kora (pilgrimage circuit), a quadrangle of streets that surrounds the Jokhang and some of the old buildings adjoining it. It is an area unrivalled in Tibet for its fascinating combination of deep religiosity and push-and-shove market economics. This is both the spiritual heart of the Holy City and the main commercial district for Tibetans.

As you follow the crowds into the Barkhor circuit, there's a curious sensation of having

---

VISITING MONASTERIES & TEMPLES

Most monasteries and temples extend a warm welcome to foreign guests and in remote areas will often offer a place to stay for the night. Please maintain this good faith by observing the following courtesies:

- Always circumambulate Buddhist monasteries and other religious objects clockwise, thus keeping shrines and chörtens (stupas) to your right.
- Don't touch or remove anything on an altar.
- Don't take prayer flags or *mani* (prayer) stones.
- Don't take photos during a prayer meeting. At other times always ask permission to take photos, especially when using a flash. The larger monasteries charge photography fees, though some monks will allow you to take a quick picture for free. If they won't, there's no point getting angry; you don't know what pressures they may be under.
- Don't wear shorts or short skirts in a monastery.
- Take your hat off when you go into a chapel.
- Don't smoke in a monastery.
- If you have a guide, try to ensure that he or she is a Tibetan, as Chinese guides invariably know little about Tibetan Buddhism or monastery history.

LHASA

BARKHOR AREA

0 —————— 100 m
0 —————— 0.1 miles

Ⓐ **Ⓑ** **Ⓒ** **Ⓓ**

INFORMATION
Bank of China.............................1 C4
Family & Independent Traveller
  Office (FIT)...........................(see 27)
Family & Independent Traveller
  Office (FIT)...........................(see 36)
Khangli Internet Bar.....................2 D4
Police Station...........................(see 3)
PSB.......................................3 B5
Snowlands Laundry.......................(see 36)

SIGHTS & ACTIVITIES   (pp91–4)
Ani Sangkhung Nunnery....................4 C6
Blind Massage Centre.....................5 A4
Darchen Pole.............................6 C6
Gedun Cheophel Artists' Guild........7 C5
Gongkar Chöde Chapel.....................8 B5
Gyüme (Lower Tantric College).....9 C4
Jambhala Lhakhang.......................(see 8)
Jampa Lhakhang...........................10 B5
Karmashar Temple.........................11 C5
Lho Rigsum Lhakhang......................12 B6
Main City Mosque.........................13 D6
Mani Lhakhang............................14 B5
Meru Nyingba Monastery...................15 B5
Meru Sarpa Monastery.....................16 C4
Mosque...................................17 B6
Pode Kangtsang...........................18 B6
Rabtse Temple............................19 C6
Rigsum Lhakhang..........................20 A6
Shide Tratsang...........................21 A4
Shrine...................................22 C6
Tengye Ling..............................23 A5
Thangka Workshop.........................24 C6
Tibetan Traditional Hospital
  (Mentsikhang)..........................25 A5
Tsome Ling...............................26 A4

SLEEPING   (pp108–11)
Banak Shol...............................27 D5
Dhood Gu Hotel...........................28 B4
Flora Hotel..............................29 D6
Hotel Kyichu.............................30 A4
Kirey Hotel..............................31 C4
Mandala Hotel............................32 B6
Pata Hotel...............................33 D5
Pentoc Guesthouse........................34 A5
Shangbala Hotel..........................35 A5
Snowlands................................36 A5
Tashi Targyel Hotel......................37 B5
Tibet Gorkha Hotel.......................38 B6
Tibet Xiongbala Hotel....................39 C6
Yak Hotel................................40 B4

EATING   (pp111–13)
Axiya Restaurant.........................(see 47)
Dunya Restaurant.........................41 B4
Islam Restaurant.........................42 D6
Lucky Horse Restauarant..................43 A5
Mandala Restaurant.......................44 B6
Muslim Restaurant........................45 C4
Naga Restaurant..........................46 A5
Nam-tso Restaurant.......................(see 27)
New Mandala Restaurant...................47 A5
Pentoc Café..............................(see 34)
Pentoc Tibetan Restaurant................48 A4
Shangrila Restaurant.....................(see 31)
Snowlands Restaurant.....................49 A5
Tashi I..................................50 A5
Tashi II Restaurant......................(see 31)
Teahouse.................................(see 37)
Tibet Café...............................(see 37)
Tromsikhang Market.......................51 B5
Turquoise Dragon Teahouse................52 B4
Wholesale Food Shops.....................53 C4

Xinhua Supermarket.......................54 A4
Yuyi Restaurant..........................55 D4

DRINKING   (p113)
Another Place............................56 B4
Dunya....................................(see 41)

SHOPPING   (pp114–15)
Dorje Antique Shop.......................57 B4
Dropenling...............................58 D5
Eizhi Exquisite Thangka Shop.......59 C5
Kyichu Art Gallery.......................(see 30)
Mani Thangka Arts........................60 A5
Nirvana Tibetan Handicrafts.........61 A5
Nuoling Tsongkhang Shop..................62 D6
Outlook Outdoor Equipment.........63 C4
Snow Leopard Carpet Industries.....64 A5
Thangka Workshops........................65 B6
Yaks 'n' Nomads Gift Shop........(see 34)

TRANSPORT   (pp115–18)
Bus No 302 to Lhasa Hotel & Drepung
  Monastery...............................66 A4
Bus No 503 to Sera Monastery.........67 A4
Buses to Ganden Monastery,
  Samye & Tsetang.......................(see 74)
Land Cruiser Parking.....................68 A5
Land Cruisers & Minibuses to
  Nepal Border...........................69 C4
Lugu Bus Station.........................70 A6
Minibuses to Dagtse......................71 A6
Minibuses to Drepung Monastery...72 A5
Minibuses to Shigatse, Samye &
  Nagchu.................................73 B4
Minibuses to Tsurphu Monastery...74 B4
Ticket Office for Bus to Ganden
  Monastery..............................75 B5

OTHER
Tibet Yungdru Adventure...........76 A4

slipped back through time to a medieval carnival. This is one part of Lhasa that has resisted most invasions of the modern world. Pilgrims from Kham, Amdo and further afield step blithely around a prostrating monk and stop briefly to finger a jewel-encrusted dagger at a street stall; children dressed almost medievally in tiny robes tug at the legs of a foreign visitor; a line of monks sit cross-legged on the paving stones before their alms bowls muttering mantras. It's a place you'll want to come back to time after time.

BARKHOR SQUARE

For your first visit to the Barkhor, enter from Barkhor Square (at the eastern end of Yuthok Lam), a large plaza that was cleared in 1985 and renovated in 2000. No doubt the clearing of a plaza in the centre of Lhasa makes it easier for the Chinese to keep an eye on the activities of locals (watch out for the video cameras on the roofs above the square), but the square has still become a focus for protest and has been the scene of pitched battles between Chinese and Tibetans on several occasions, most noticeably in 1998 when several Tibetans were killed and a Dutch tourist was shot in the shoulder. At least the Chinese resisted the temptation to plunk a Mao statue in the middle of it all.

Close to the entrance to the Jokhang is a constant stream of Tibetans following the Barkhor circumambulation route in a clockwise direction. Look for the two pot-bellied, stone *sangkang* (incense burners) in front of the Jokhang. There are four altogether, marking the four extremities of the Barkhor circuit; the other two are at the rear of the Jokhang. Behind the first two *sangkang* are two joined enclosures. The northern **stele** is inscribed with the terms of the Sino-Tibetan treaty of 822. The inscription guarantees mutual respect of the borders of the two nations – an irony seemingly lost on the Chinese authorities. The southern one harbours the stump of an ancient willow tree, known as the hair of the Jowo, allegedly planted by Songtsen Gampo's Chinese wife, Princess Wencheng, and a stele erected in 1793 commemorating smallpox victims.

For your first few visits to the Barkhor circuit, it's best to let yourself be dragged along by the pilgrims, but there are also several small, fascinating temples to pop into en route.

BARKHOR CIRCUIT

As you follow the flow of pilgrims past sellers of religious photos, fake antiques and horse tackle, you'll soon see a small building on the right, set off from the main path but very much part of the pilgrim circuit. This is the **Mani Lhakhang**, a small chapel that houses a huge prayer wheel set almost continuously in motion. To the right of the building is the grandiose entrance of the former city jail and dungeons, known as the Nangtse Shar.

If you head south from here, after about 10m you will see the entrance to the **Jampa Lhakhang** (also Jamkhang or Water Blessing Temple) on the right. The ground floor of this small temple has a two-storey statue of Miwang Jampa, the Future Buddha, flanked by rows of various protector gods and the meditation cave of the chapel's founder. Pilgrims ascend to the upper floor to be blessed with a sprinkling of holy water and the touch of a holy *dorje* (thunderbolt).

Continue down the alley following the prayer wheels, then pass through a doorway into the old **Meru Nyingba Monastery**. This small but active monastery is a delight. The main attraction is less the chapel than the courtyard area, which is invariably crowded with Tibetans thumbing prayer beads or lazily swinging prayer wheels and chanting under their breath. The chapel itself is administered by Nechung Monastery and so has several images of the Nechung oracle inside. The building, like the adjoining Jokhang, dates back to the 7th century but most of what you see today is very recently constructed.

On the west side of the courtyard up some narrow stairs is the small Sakyapa-school **Gongkar Chöde** chapel. Below is the **Jambhala Lhakhang**, with a central image of Marmedze (Dipamkara), the Past Buddha, and a small inner kora path.

From here you can return north or head east to join up with the Barkhor circuit.

On the northeast corner of the Barkhor is the **Gedun Cheophel Artists' Guild** (☎ 632 3825; ⊙ 10am-9pm), an exhibition hall for a dozen modern Tibetan artists. It's a rare opportunity to view Tibetan modern art free from religious conventions (and there are good views from the roof).

The eastern side of the circuit has more shops and even a couple of small department stores on the right-hand side specialising in turquoise. In the southeast corner is a wall shrine and a *darchen* (prayer pole), which mark the spot where Tsongkhapa planted his walking stick in 1409. The southern stretch has a couple of *thangka* (religious painting) workshops, where you can watch the artists at work. The empty southern square of the Jokhang used to host annual teachings by the Dalai Lama during the Mönlam festival. The circuit finally swings north by a PSB (public security bureau) station back to Barkhor Square.

The Jokhang ཇོ་ཁང་། Map p95

The **Jokhang** (admission Y70; ☯ inner chapels 8am-noon, sometimes 3-5.30pm, outer complex open until 8pm), also known in Tibetan as the Tsuglhakhang, is the most revered religious structure in Tibet. Although little remains of its 7th-century origins and most of the sculptures that adorn its interior postdate the Cultural Revolution, the Jokhang, thick with the smell of yak butter and the murmur of mantras and bustling with awed pilgrims, is an unrivalled Tibetan experience.

HISTORY

Estimated dates for the Jokhang's founding range from 639 to 647 AD. Construction was initiated by King Songtsen Gampo to house an image of Mikyöba (Akshobhya) brought to Tibet as part of the dowry of his Nepali wife Princess Bhrikuti. The Ramoche Temple was constructed at the same time to house another Buddha image, Jowo Sakyamuni (Sakya Thukpa), brought to Tibet by his Chinese wife Princess Wencheng. It is thought that after the death of Songtsen Gampo, Jowo Sakyamuni was moved from Ramoche for its protection and hidden in the Jokhang by Princess Wencheng. The image has remained in the Jokhang ever since (Jokhang, or Jowokhang, means 'chapel of the Jowo'), and is the most revered Buddha image in all of Tibet.

It is said that Princess Wencheng chose the site of the Jokhang (p96), and that just to be difficult she chose Lake Wothang. The lake had to be filled in, but it is said that a well in the precincts of the Jokhang still draws its waters from those of the old lake. Over the years, many legends have emerged around the task of filling in Lake Wothang. The most prominent of these is the story of how the lake was filled by a sacred goat (the Tibetan word for goat, *ra*, is etymologically

connected with the original name for Lhasa – Rasa). A small carving of the goat can be seen in the Chapel of Jampa on the south wall of the Jokhang's ground-floor inner sanctum.

Over the centuries, the Jokhang has undergone many renovations, but the basic layout is ancient and differs from that of many other Tibetan religious structures. One crucial difference is the building's east–west orientation; it is said to face towards Nepal to honour Princess Bhrikuti. Alterations were undoubtedly undertaken during the centuries when Lhasa played second fiddle to other centres of power, but the most drastic renovations took place during the reign of the fifth Dalai Lama in the 17th century. A few interior carved pillars and entrance arches remain from the original 7th-century work of Newari artisans brought from the Kathmandu Valley in Nepal.

In the early days of the Cultural Revolution, much of the interior of the Jokhang was desecrated by Red Guards and many objects are thought to have been removed. At one stage the monks' quarters were also renamed Guesthouse No 5 and it is claimed that part of the Jokhang was utilised as a pigsty. Since 1980 the Jokhang has been restored, and without the aid of an expert eye, you will see few signs of the misfortunes that have befallen the temple in recent years.

GROUND FLOOR

In front of the entrance to the Jokhang is a forecourt that is perpetually crowded with pilgrims polishing the flagstones with their prostrations. Monuments stand in front of the Jokhang (p93).

Just inside the entrance to the Jokhang are the **Four Guardian Kings** (Chökyong), two on either side. Beyond this is the **main assembly hall** or *dukhang,* a paved courtyard that is open to the sky. During festivals the hall is often the focus of ceremonies. Just before the entrance to the interior of the Jokhang itself is a long row of flickering butter lamps.

Entry to the Jokhang proper is through a short, dark corridor punctuated midway by a chapel on either side. The chapel to the right houses several *naga* goddesses (*naga* being water spirits); the chapel to the left houses fierce, red-faced *nojin,* benign subterranean dragon-like creatures. Together they serve as protective deities.

THE JOKHANG

Approximate Scale
0 ___ 50 m

1 Sino-Tibetan Treaty Stele
2 Smallpox Stele and Ancient Willow Tree

GROUND FLOOR (pp94–7)
3 Guardian Kings
4 Ticket Office
5 Main Assembly Hall
6 Naga Chapel
7 Nojin Chapel
8 Jampa Statue
9 Jampa Statue
10 Jampa Statue
11 Guru Rinpoche Statue
12 Chenresig Statue
13 Guru Rinpoche Statue
14 Chapel of Tsongkhapa & His Disciples
15 Chapel of the Buddha of Infinite Light (Öpagme)
16 Chörten
17 Chapel of the Eight Medicine Buddhas

18 Chapel of Chenresig (Avalokiteshvara)
19 Chapel of Jampa
20 Chapel of Tsongkhapa
21 Chapel of the Buddha of Infinite Light
22 Chapel of Jowo Sakyamuni
23 Chapel of Jampa
24 Chapel of Chenresig (Riding a Lion)
25 Guru Rinpoche Shrine and Rock Painting
26 Chapel of Tsepame
27 Chapel of Jampa
28 Chapel of the Hidden Jowo
29 Chapel of the Seven Buddhas
30 Chapel of the Nine Buddhas of Longevity (Tsepame)
31 Chapel of the Kings
49 Drölma Chapel
50 Guru Rinpoche Chapel

FIRST FLOOR (p98)
32 Chapel of Lhobdrak Namka Gyaltsen
33 Chapel of Sakyamuni
34 Chapel of Eight Medicine Buddhas
35 Chapel of Sakyamuni
36 Chapel of Five Protectors
37 Anteroom
38 Chapel of the Three Kings
39 Chapel of Songtsen Gompo
40 Chapel of Chenresig
41 Chapel of Sakyamuni
42 Prayer Wheel
43 Chapel of Guru Rinpoche & Sakyamuni
44 Chapel of Songtsen Gompo
45 Zhelre Lakhang (Inaccessible)
46 Chapel of Guru Rinpoche
47 Chapel of Samvara
48 Palden Lhamo Statues

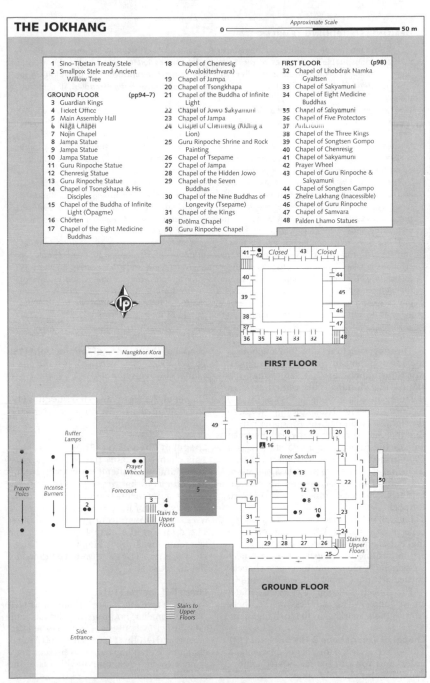

FIRST FLOOR

GROUND FLOOR

DEMONESS-SUBDUING TEMPLES

Buddhism's interaction with Bön – a shamanistic folk religion of ghosts and demons – combined with the inhospitable high places of the Tibetan plateau has led to many fables about Buddhism's taming and domestication of Tibet. The story of the early introduction of Buddhism to Tibet is attended by the story of a vast, supine demoness whose body straddled all the high plateau.

It was Princess Wencheng, the Chinese wife of King Songtsen Gampo, who divined the presence of this demoness. Through Chinese geomantic calculations she established that the heart of the demoness lay beneath a lake in the centre of Lhasa, while her torso and limbs lay far away in the outer dominions of the high plateau. As in all such fables, the demoness can be seen as symbolic of the inhospitableness of Tibet and its need to be tamed before Buddhism could take root there. It was decided that the demoness would have to be pinned down.

The first task was to drain the lake in Lhasa of its water (read life-blood of the demoness) and build a central temple that would replace the heart of the demoness with a Buddhist heart. The temple built there was the Jokhang. A stake through the heart was not enough to put a demoness of this size out of action, however, and a series of lesser temples, in three concentric rings, were conceived to pin the extremities of the demoness.

There were four temples in each of these rings. The first are known as the *runo* temples and form a protective circle around Lhasa, pinning down the demoness' hips and shoulders. Two of these are Trandruk Monastery in the Yarlung Valley and Katsel Monastery on the way to Drigung. The second group, known as the *tandrul* temples, pin the knees and elbows of the demoness. Buchu Monastery near Bayi in eastern Tibet is one of these. And the final group, known as *yandrul* temples, pin the hands and feet. These last temples are found as far away as Bhutan and Sichuan, though the location of two of them is unknown.

The inner sanctum of the Jokhang houses the most important images and chapels. Most prominent are six larger-than-life statues that dominate the central area. In the foreground and to the left is a 6m statue of Guru Rinpoche. The statue opposite it, to the right, is of Jampa (Maitreya), the Future Buddha. At the centre of the hall, between and to the rear of these two statues, is a 1000-armed Chenresig (Avalokiteshvara). At the far right are two more Jampa statues, one behind the other, and to the far rear, behind Chenresig, is another statue of Guru Rinpoche, encased in a cabinet.

Encircling this enclosed area of statues is a collection of chapels. Tibetan pilgrims circle the central area of statuary in a clockwise direction, visiting the chapels en route. There are generally queues for the holiest chapels, particularly the Chapel of Jowo Sakyamuni.

The chapels, following a clockwise route, are as follows. The numbers marked here refer to those marked on the Jokhang map.

Chapel of Tsongkhapa & His Disciples (14)

Tsongkhapa was the founder of the Gelugpa order, and you can see him seated centre, flanked by his eight disciples.

Chapel of the Buddha of Infinite Light (15)

This chapel is usually closed. Just outside is a large chörten (stupa).

Chapel of the Eight Medicine Buddhas (17)

The eight medicine buddhas are recent and not of special interest.

Chapel of Chenresig (18)

This chapel contains the Jokhang's most important image after the Jowo Sakyamuni. Legend has it that the statue of Chenresig sprang spontaneously into being and combines aspects of King Songtsen Gampo, his wives and two wrathful protective deities. The doors of the chapel are among the few remnants still visible of the Jokhang's 7th-century origins and were fashioned by Nepali artisans.

Chapel of Jampa (19)

In this chapel are statues of Jampa as well as four smaller bodhisattvas: Jampelyang (Manjushri), Chenresig, Chana Dorje (Vajrapani) and Drölma (Tara). Öpagme (Amitabha) and Tsongkhapa are also present here, as are two chörtens, one of which is of the original sculptor.

Chapel of Tsongkhapa (20)

This chapel's image of Tsongkhapa, founder of the Gelugpa order, was commissioned by the subject himself and is said to be a precise resemblance. It is the central image on the left of the raised chapel.

Chapel of the Buddha of Infinite Light (21)

This is the second of the chapels consecrated to Öpagme (Amitabha), the Buddha of Infinite Light. The outer entrance, with its wonderful carved doors, is protected by two fierce deities, red Tamdrin (Hayagriva; right) and blue Chana Dorje (Vajrapani; left). There are also statues of the eight bodhisattvas. Pilgrims generally pray here for the elimination of impediments to viewing the most sacred image of the Jokhang, that of Jowo Sakyamuni, which waits in the next chapel.

Outside the chapel are statues of King Songtsen Gampo with his two queens and also Guru Rinpoche (with a big nose).

Chapel of Jowo Sakyamuni (22)

The most important shrine in Tibet, this chapel houses an image of Sakyamuni at the age of 12 years. You enter via an anteroom containing the Four Guardian Kings and two protector statues: Miyowa (Achala) and Chana Dorje (Vajrapani). There are several large bells on the anteroom's roof. The 1.5m statue of Sakyamuni is covered in silks and jewellery and surrounded by silver pillars with dragon motifs. Pilgrims touch their forehead to the statue's left leg before being tapped on the back by a monk bouncer when it's time to move on.

To the rear of Sakyamuni are statues of the seventh and 13th Dalai Lamas, Tsongkhapa and 12 standing bodhisattvas. Look for the seventh-century pillars on the way out.

Chapel of Jampa (23)

The Jampa enshrined here is a replica of a statue that came to Tibet as a part of the dowry of Princess Bhrikuti, King Songtsen Gampo's Nepali wife. Around the statue are eight images of Drölma, a goddess seen as an embodiment of the enlightened mind of Buddha-hood and who protects against the eight fears – hence the eight statues.

Chapel of Chenresig Riding a Lion (24)

The statue of Chenresig on the back of a lion is second from the left (it's not the largest of

the icons within). The other eight statues of the chapel are all aspects of Chenresig.

Some pilgrims exit this chapel and then follow a flight of stairs up to the next floor, while others complete the circuit on the ground floor. If you're chapelled out (you've seen the important ones already), continue on upstairs, but look out first for a small hole in the wall on the left as you exit the chapel, against which pilgrims place their ear to hear the beating wings of a mythical bird that lives under the Jokhang.

Guru Rinpoche Shrine (25)

Two statues of Guru Rinpoche and one of King Trisong Detsen are next to the stairs. Beside the shrine is a gold painting of the Medicine Buddha protected by an iron grill.

Chapel of Tsepame (26)

Inside are nine statues of Tsepame (Amitayus), the red Buddha of Longevity, in *yabyum* (sexual and spiritual union) pose.

Chapel of Jampa (27)

This, another Jampa chapel, holds the Jampa statue that is borne around the Barkhor on the 25th day of the first lunar month for the Mönlam festival. Jampa's yearly excursion is designed to hasten the arrival of the Future Buddha. Jampelyang and Chenresig flank the Buddha.

Chapel of the Hidden Jowo (28)

This is the chapel where Princess Wencheng is said to have hidden Jowo Sakyamuni for safekeeping after the death of her husband. Inside is a statue of Öpagme (Amitabha) and the eight medicine buddhas.

Other Chapels

From here there are several chapels of limited interest to non-Tibetologists. The **Chapel of the Seven Buddhas (29)** is followed by the **Chapel of the Nine Buddhas of Longevity (30)**. The last of the ground-floor chapels is the **Chapel of the Kings (31)**, with some original statues of Tibet's earliest kings. The central figure is Songtsen Gampo, flanked by images of King Trisong Detsen (left) and King Ralpachen (right). Pilgrims touch their head to the central pillar. On the wall outside the chapel is an mural depicting the original construction of the Jokhang and the Potala, with musicians, dancers, wrestlers and horse races.

FIRST FLOOR

At this point you should return clockwise to the rear of the ground floor (if you did not do so earlier) and climb the stairs to the upper floor of the Jokhang. The upper floor of the Jokhang's inner sanctum is also ringed with chapels, though some of them are closed.

As you begin the circuit, you will pass by several new rooms that feature **Sakyamuni (33, 35)** accompanied by his two main disciples, and one featuring the **eight medicine buddhas (34)**. The **Chapel of Lhobdrak Namka Gyaltsen (32)** near the southeast corner features Pabonka Rinpoche, Sakyamuni, Tsongkhapa and Atisha (Jowo-je). The chapel in the southwest corner is the **Chapel of Five Protectors (36)** and has some fearsome statues of Tamdrin (Hayagriva), Palden Lhamo (Shri Devi) and other protector deities. Next is the **Chapel of the Three Kings (38)**, dedicated to Songtsen Gampo (recognisable by the tiny head projecting from his turban), Trisong Detsen and Ralpachen. Also featured in the room are Songtsen Gampo's two wives, various ministers, and symbols of royalty such as an elephant and a horse.

Also worth a look is the **Chapel of Songtsen Gampo (39)**, the principal Songtsen Gampo chapel in the Jokhang. It is positioned in the centre of the west wall (directly above the entry to the ground-floor inner sanctum). The bejewelled king, with a tiny buddha protruding from his head, is accompanied by his two consorts, his Nepali wife to the left and his Chinese wife to the right. His embossed animal-headed container for *chang* (barley beer) is placed opposite him behind a grill.

Most of the other rooms have been closed for years, the main exception being the meditation cell or **Chapel of Songtsen Gampo (44)** near the floor's northeastern corner, which has an incredible carved doorway smeared with decades' worth of yak butter. As you walk back to the stairs look at the unusual row of carved beams which look like half-lion, half-monkey creatures.

Back by the stairs, notice the doorframes of the **Chapel of Samvara (47)**, showing Samvara with consort, and the **Chapel of Guru Rinpoche (46)**, which date back to the 7th century.

Before you leave the 1st floor by the stairs in the southeast corner, ascend half a floor up to two statues of the protectress **Palden Lhamo (48)**, one wrathful, the other benign. You can sometimes gain access to a Tantric chapel up on the 2nd floor.

OTHER CHAPELS

After you've explored the interior of the Jokhang, the best part is arguably spending some time on the **roof**, with its stunning views. Monks often debate up here in the late afternoon. There is also a small teahouse. The orange building on the north side holds the private quarters of the Dalai Lama. The outer halls and the roof are effectively open daily from sunrise to sundown if you enter by the side door to the right of the main entrance.

It's worth finishing off a visit with a walk around the **Nangkhor kora**, which encircles the Jokhang's inner sanctum. If you're not utterly exhausted you could have a brief look at the **Drölma Chapel (49)**, featuring Drölma flanked by her green and white manifestations and others of her 21 manifestations. Pilgrims sometimes pop into the **Guru Rinpoche Chapel (50)**, a series of three interconnected shrines stuffed with images of Guru Rinpoche, at the back of the kora.

The Potala པོ་ཏ་ལ།   Map pp88–9

Lhasa's cardinal landmark, the **Potala** (admission Y100; 9.30am-3pm before 1 May, 9am-3.30pm after 1 May, interior chapels close 4.30pm) is one of the wonders of Eastern architecture. Your first sight of the Potala will be a magical moment that you will remember for a long time. It's hard to take your eyes off the place.

The Potala is a structure of massive proportions, an awe-inspiring place to explore, but still many visitors come away slightly disappointed. Unlike the Jokhang, which hums with activity, the Potala lies dormant like a huge museum, and the lifelessness of the highly symbolic building constantly reminds visitors that the Dalai Lama has been forced to take his government elsewhere. It's a modern irony that the Potala now hums with large numbers of chattering Chinese tourists staring with wonder at the building the generation before them tried so hard to destroy.

Pilgrims get free access to the Potala on Monday, Wednesday and Friday so crowds for many of the chapels are bigger then, though the presence of pilgrims adds interest to a visit. It's worth getting there early as there's a lot to see but beware that the big tour groups flood in around 9.30am so if you get there a bit later you'll have more space. There are extra charges for access to the roof and the exhibition room, both Y10.

An audio guide is available (Y15) but currently in Chinese only. During peak season (July and August) and holidays it's worth buying your ticket a day in advance.

Photography of the interior of the Potala is forbidden and all rooms are wired with motion sensors and video cameras.

Access to the Potala is now via the west gate and the back road that winds up to the top of the Potala. Corridors wind up through the labyrinthine bowels of the Potala, before exiting onto the roof of the White Palace. Unfortunately this new system means that visitors now have to visit the chapels in an anti-clockwise direction, in a characteristic Chinese disregard for Tibetan religious sensibilities. Pilgrims still visit clockwise by starting on the 3rd floor and descending.

The exit is via two steep access ramps to Shöl village, nestled at the southern foot of Marpo Ri. Shöl was once Lhasa's red-light district as well as housing a prison, a printing press and some ancillary government buildings.

A morning visit to the Potala can very easily be combined with an afternoon excursion to some of the sights nearby, such as Drubthub Nunnery and Palha Lu-puk (p102), Chagpo Ri (p103), Parma Ri (p103), Lukhang Temple (p103), or a circuit of the Potala kora (p102).

HISTORY
Marpo Ri, the 130m-high 'Red Hill', which commands a view of all Lhasa, was the site of King Songtsen Gampo's palace during the mid-7th century, long before the construction of the present-day Potala. There is little to indicate what this palace looked like, but it is clear that royal precedent was a major factor in the fifth Dalai Lama's choice of this site when he decided to move the seat of his Gelugpa government here from Drepung Monastery.

Work began first on the White Palace, or Karpo Potrang, in 1645. The nine-storey structure was completed three years later, and in 1649 the fifth Dalai Lama moved from Drepung Monastery to his new residence. However, the circumstances surrounding the construction of the larger Red Palace, or Marpo Potrang, are subject to some dispute. It is agreed that the fifth Dalai Lama died in 1682 and that his death was concealed

until the completion of the Red Palace 12 years later. In some accounts, the work was initiated by the regent who governed Tibet from 1679 to 1703 and foundations were laid in 1690 (after the fifth Dalai Lama's death). In other accounts, the Red Palace was conceived by the fifth Dalai Lama as a funerary chörten and work was well under way at the time of his death. In any event, the death of the fifth Dalai Lama was not announced until he was put to rest in the newly completed Red Palace.

There is also some scholarly debate concerning the Potala's name. The most probable explanation is that it derives from the Tibetan name for Chenresig's 'pure land', or paradise, also known as Potala. Given that Songtsen Gampo and the Dalai Lamas are believed to be reincarnations of Chenresig, this connection is compelling.

Since its construction, the Potala has been the home of each of the successive Dalai Lamas, although since construction of the Norbulingka summer palace in the late 18th century, it has served only as a winter residence. It was also the seat of the Tibetan government, and with chapels, cells, schools for religious training and even tombs for the Dalai Lamas, it was virtually a self-contained world.

The Potala was shelled briefly during the 1959 popular uprising against the Chinese but the damage was not extensive. The Potala was spared again during the Cultural Revolution, reportedly at the insistence of Zhou Enlai, the Chinese premier, who is said to have deployed his own troops to protect it. The Potala was reopened to the public in 1980 and final touches to the US$4-million renovations were completed in 1995.

RED PALACE   Map p100
Ground Floor
The first chapel is the **Chapel of the Holy Born** (Trungrab Lhakhang). There are statues of Guru Rinpoche, the first four Dalai Lamas, Sakyamuni, the fifth Dalai Lama and the eight medicine buddhas. Lastly, in the corner, is the statue and chörten of the 11th Dalai Lama, who died at the age of 17.

At the end of the hall, enter the beautiful **assembly hall**, which is the largest hall in the Potala and is its physical centre. Note the fine carved pillar heads. The large throne that dominates one end of the hall was the

LHASA

RED PALACE OF THE POTALA

Approximate Scale
0 _____ 50 m

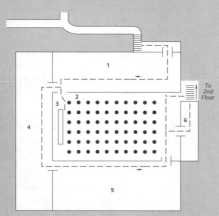

GROUND FLOOR

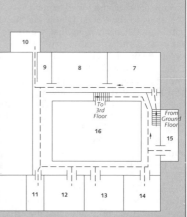

SECOND FLOOR

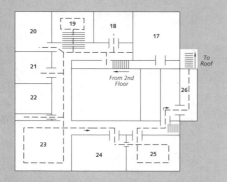

THIRD FLOOR

GROUND FLOOR
1 Chapel of the Holy Born (Trungrab Lhakhang)
2 Assembly Hall
3 Throne
4 Chapel of the Dalai Lamas' Tombs (Serdung
   Zamling Gyenjikhang)
5 Rigsum Lhakhang
6 Chapel of Lamrim

SECOND FLOOR
7 Lima Lhakhang
8 Lima Lhakhang
9 Lima Lhakhang
10 King Songsten Gampo's Meditation Chamber
   (Chogyal Druphuk)
11 Chapel of Sakyamuni (Zegya Lhakhang)
12 Treasures of the Potala Exhibition
13 Chapel of the Nine Buddhas of Longevity
   (Tsephak Lhakhang)
14 Chapel of Sakyamuni (Thuburang Lhakhang)
15 Chapel of Kalachakra (Dukhor Lhakhang)
16 Rest Area

THIRD FLOOR
17 Tomb of the 9th Dalai Lama
18 Tomb of the 8th Dalai Lama
19 Chapel of Arya Lokeshvara (Pakpa Lhakhang)
20 Tomb of the 7th Dalai Lama (Serdung Tashi
   Woibai Khang)
21 Lhama Lhakhang
22 Tomb of the 13th Dalai Lama
23 Chapel of Immortal Happiness
24 Chapel of the Victory over the Three Worlds
   (Sasum Namgyal)
25 Chapel of the Three-Dimensional Mandalas
   (Loilang Khang)
26 Chapel of Jampa (Jamkhang)

- - - Suggested Route

throne of the sixth Dalai Lama. The four important chapels frame the hall.

In the west wing of the assembly hall is one of the highlights of the Potala, the awe-inspiring **Chapel of the Dalai Lamas' Tombs** (Serdung Zamling Gyenjikhang). The hall is dominated by the huge 12.6m-high chörten of the fifth Dalai Lama, gilded with some 3700kg of gold. Flanking it are two smaller chörtens containing the 10th (right) and 12th (left) Dalai Lamas, who both died as children. Eight other chörtens represent the eight major events in the life of the Buddha. Before proceeding to the next chapel, take a look at the murals of the assembly hall.

The next chapel, the long **Rigsum Lhakhang**, is dedicated to eight Indian teachers who brought various Tantric practices and rituals to Tibet. The central figure is a silver statue of Guru Rinpoche (one of the eight), who is flanked by his consorts, as well as statues of the eight teachers on his left and a further eight statues of him in different manifestations on the right.

The last chapel on this floor is the **Chapel of Lamrim**. *Lamrim* means literally 'the graduated path', and refers to the graduated stages that mark the path to enlightenment. The central figure in the chapel is Tsongkhapa, the founder of the Gelugpa order, with whom *lamrim* texts are usually associated.

First Floor
This floor was closed to visitors at the time of research and is unlikely to reopen soon.

Second Floor
The first three rooms are all linked and are chock-a-block full of 3000 pieces of Chinese statuary. Continue to the northwestern corner where you'll find a small corridor that leads to **King Songtsen Gampo's meditation chamber** (Chogyal Druphuk), which, along with the Chapel of Arya Lokeshvara on the 3rd floor, is one of the oldest rooms in the Potala. The most important statue is of Songtsen Gampo himself, to the left of the pillar. To his left is his minister Tonmi Sambhota and to the right are his Chinese and Nepali wives. The king's Tibetan wife (the only one to bear a son) is in a cabinet by the door. The fifth Dalai Lama lurks behind (and also on) the central pillar.

Passing the **Chapel of Sakyamuni** (Zegya Lhakhang), the next room on the south side

houses a **Treasures of the Potala exhibition**. The collection is small but of a very high quality and includes such famous items as a three-dimensional mandala made of over 200,000 pearls, a crystal Sakyamuni Buddha, and a bronze statue of a lotus whose leaves open out to reveal miniature statues inside. Other items include antique armour, festival costumes and *thangkas*. Entry to this room costs an additional Y10.

In the **Chapel of the Nine Buddhas of Longevity** (Tsephak Lhakhang), look for the murals by the window – the left side depicts Tangtong Gyelpo and his celebrated bridge (now destroyed) over the Yarlung Tsangpo near Chushul. There are nine statues of Tsepame.

The **Chapel of Sakyamuni** (Thurburang Lhakhang) has a library, the throne of the seventh Dalai Lama and some fine examples of calligraphy.

The last of the chapels you come to on the 2nd floor is the **Chapel of Kalachakra** (Dukhor Lhakhang). It is noted for its stunning three-dimensional mandala, which is over 6m in diameter and finely detailed with over 170 statues. A statue of the Tantric deity Dukhor (Kalachakra) stands in the far right corner, after a variant of Jampelyang riding a snow lion, and Guru Rinpoche in the corner.

If you're exhausted already (only halfway!), you can rest your legs at a reception area in the middle of the floor.

Third Floor
The first two rooms on this floor are the jewel-encrusted **tombs of the Eighth and Ninth Dalai Lamas**, though you may have to visit the latter on the way out.

In the northwest corner, steps lead up into the small but important **Chapel of Arya Lokeshvara** (Pakpa Lhakhang). Allegedly this is one of the few corners of the Potala that dates from the time of Songtsen Gampo's 7th-century palace. It is the most sacred of the Potala's chapels, and the image of Arya Lokeshvara inside is the most revered image housed in the Potala. The statue is accompanied on the left by the seventh Dalai Lama and Tsongkhapa, and on the right by the fifth, eighth and ninth Dalai Lamas and Chana Dorje (Vajrapani). The left cabinet holds the stone footprints of Guru Rinpoche and Tsongkhapa and a huge Wheel of Law.

Also in the northwest corner is the golden **tomb of the Seventh Dalai Lama** (Serdung Tashi

Woibai Khang), constructed in 1805, and the **Lhama Lhakhang**.

From here a long corridor leads off the main circuit to a gallery that overlooks the **tomb of the 13th Dalai Lama**. You could at one time look down on the chörten from above and then descend to look at it at ground level, but the room was closed at the time of research.

Next, the **Chapel of Immortal Happiness** was once the residence of the sixth Dalai Lama, whose throne remains; it is now dedicated to Tsepame, the Buddha of Longevity, who is opposite the throne. Next to him is the Dzogchen deity Ekajati (Tsechigma), with an ostrich-feather hat and a single fang.

The **Chapel of the Victory over the Three Worlds** houses a library and displays examples of Manchu texts. The main statue is a golden Chenresig, while the *thangka* by the exit is of the Manchu Chinese emperor Qianlong in Mongol dress.

The **Chapel of Three-Dimensional Mandalas** (Loilang Khang) houses spectacular jewel-encrusted mandalas of the three principal Tantric deities of the Gelugpa order (Chana Dorje, Demchok and Yamantaka). There are some fine blackened murals near the throne of the seventh Dalai Lama.

Finally, the **Chapel of Jampa** (Jamkhang) contains an exquisite image of Jampa commissioned by the eighth Dalai Lama; it stands opposite the throne of the successive Dalai Lamas. To the right of the throne is a wooden Kalachakra mandala. The walls are stacked with the collected works of the fifth Dalai Lama. The chapel was unfortunately damaged in a fire in 1984 (caused by an electrical fault) and many valuable *thangkas* were lost. From here you can ascend onto the roof of the Red Palace for an extra Y10 before continuing onto the roof of the White Palace.

ROOF OF THE WHITE PALACE

As you arrive on the roof, take in the fine views and then head for the private quarters of the 13th and 14th Dalai Lamas. The first room you come to is the **throne room** (Simchung Nyiwoi Shar), where the Dalai Lamas would receive official guests. The large picture on the left is of the 13th Dalai Lama; the matching photo of the present Dalai Lama has been removed. There are some fine murals here, including a description of Bodhgaya, where the Buddha achieved enlightenment.

The trail continues clockwise into the **reception hall** (Dhaklen Paldseg), with a fine collection of bronze statues and fine views from the balcony. Next comes the **meditation room**, which still displays the ritual implements of the present Dalai Lama on a small table to the side of the room. Protector gods here include Nagpo Chenpo (Mahakala), the Nechung oracle and Palden Lhamo. The final room, the **bedroom of the Dalai Lama**, has some personal effects of the Dalai Lama on show, such as his bedside clock. The mural above the bed is of Tsongkhapa, the founder of the Gelugpa order of which the Dalai Lama is the head. The locked door leads into the Dalai Lama's private bathroom.

From here, a triple flight of steps leads down to the **Deyang Shar**, the external courtyard of the White Palace. (At the top of the triple stairs, look out for the golden handprints of the 13th Dalai Lama on the wall to the left.) From here, paths snake down to Shöl.

POTALA KORA

The pilgrim path that encircles the foot of the Potala makes for a nice walk before or after a visit to the main event. The kora is most active in the mornings. From the western chörten (formerly the western gate to the city), follow the alley of prayer wheels, past stalls selling everything from silk *kathaks* (votive scarves) to parts for prayer-wheels. The northwest corner is marked by three chörtens and a bustling Tibetan teahouse.

The northeast corner is marked by a large prayer wheel of the Phurbu Chok Hermitage Mani Lhakhang and then a small prayer hall occupied by nuns. Swing past the Chinese-style square, where pilgrims often prostrate in front of the Potala, and continue for a reviving cup of sweet tea in the humid cave teahouse built into the rock face. Several smaller chörtens have been rebuilt around the western chörten and you can get some good shots of the Potala from here. You can also visit the chapels of Palha Lu-puk.

Around The Potala

DRUBTHUB NUNNERY & PALHA LU-PUK

On the south side of Dekyi Nub Lam, an unmarked road leads around the eastern side of Chagpo Ri, the hill that faces Marpo Ri, site of the Potala. Take this road past stone carvers, rock paintings and prayer flags to

Drubthub Nunnery (Map pp88–9). The nunnery is dedicated to Tangtong Gyelpo, the 15th-century bridge maker, medic and inventor of Tibetan opera, whose white-haired statue graces the nunnery's main hall.

After the nunnery, head next door to the **Palha Lu-puk** (Map pp88-9; admission Y15; ☉ 9.30am-7pm), where stairs lead up to a cave temple said to have been the 7th-century meditational retreat of King Songtsen Gampo.

The main attraction of the cave is its relief rock carvings, some of which are over 1000 years old. Altogether there are over 70 carvings of bodhisattvas in the cave and on the cave's central column. Work on the carvings was probably undertaken during three different historical periods, but the oldest are generally the ones lowest on the cave walls. Many of the carvings were damaged in the Cultural Revolution and have since been repaired.

The yellow building above the Palha Lu-puk is a chapel that gives access to the less interesting meditation cave (puk) of King Songtsen Gampo's Chinese wife, Princess Wencheng.

LUKHANG

The **Lukhang** (Map pp88-9; admission Y10; ☉ 9am-5pm) is a little-visited temple on a small island in a lake, behind the Potala. The lake is in the **Zang Gyab Lukhang Park** (Map pp88-9; admission Y3; ☉ 9am-8pm), formerly known as Chingdröl Chiling (Liberation) Park, which is entered from north of the Civil Aviation Authority of China (CAAC) building or from directly behind the Potala.

The lake was created during the construction of the Potala. Earth used for mortar was excavated from here, leaving a depression that was later filled with water. *Lu* (also known as *naga*) are subterranean dragon-like spirits that were thought to inhabit the area, and the Lukhang, or Chapel of the Dragon King, was built by the sixth Dalai Lama to propitiate them. You can see Luyi Gyalpo, the *naga* king, at the rear of the ground floor of the Lukhang. He is riding an elephant, and protective snakes rise from behind his head. The *naga* spirits were finally imprisoned in the Palha Lu-puk.

The Lukhang is celebrated for its 2nd- and 3rd-floor murals, which date from the 18th century. Bring a torch. The 2nd-floor murals tell a story made famous by a Tibetan opera, while the murals on the 3rd floor depict different themes on each of the walls – Indian yogis demonstrating yogic positions (west), 84 *mahisaddhas* or masters of Buddhism (east), and the life cycle as perceived by Tibetan Buddhists (north), with the gods of Bardo, the Tibetan underworld, occupying its centre. Look for the wonderful attention to detail, down to the hairy legs of the sadhus and the patterns on the clothes. The 3rd floor also contains a statue of an 11-headed Chenresig as well as a meditation room used by the Dalai Lamas. To reach it you go up to the 3rd floor, then walk around the outside of the building and enter from the back where there is a flight of stairs.

CHAGPO RI

Apart from the Palha Lu-puk, there are a couple of other points of interest on **Chagpo Ri** (Iron Mountain; Map pp88-9), although the steel telecom mast that graces the mountain's summit is probably not one of them. The hill was once the site of Lhasa's principal Tibetan medical college, known as the Mentsikhang. Founded in 1413, the college was destroyed in the 1959 popular uprising. (The hospital, on the north side of Yuthok Lam, was set up by the 13th Dalai Lama in 1916 and Tibetan doctors still train here.)

Today, the hill's main point of interest is a series of **rock carvings** on cliff walls at three different places. Altogether there are over 5000 carvings, some of them dating back to the 7th century. The first carvings are thought to have been commissioned by King Songtsen Gampo and executed by Nepali artists. The tradition of carving images on the cliffs of Chagpo Ri continued for another 1000 years.

The best place to see the collection of carvings, prayer flags and shrines is on the southwest end of the hill (accessible from the south or west), where there is a large painting of a blue Tsepame, among others. It costs Y5 to take photos in this area. Get here by following part of the Lingkhor kora (p90) from Chingdröl Shar Lam (Jiangsu Lu).

PARMA RI

Several hundred metres west of Chagpo Ri, **Parma Ri** (Map pp88–9) is a much smaller hill with a couple of interesting sights. At the foot of the hill, close to Dekyi Nub Lam, is one of Lhasa's four former royal temples,

LHASA

Kunde Ling (Map pp88-9; admission Y10; 🕙 9am-7pm). The *ling* (royal) temples were appointed by the fifth Dalai Lama, and it was from one of them that regents of Tibet were generally appointed. There are only a couple of restored chapels open, but it is worth a visit. Look for the painting of the original Kunde Ling, 80% of which has been destroyed.

From here head north and then east along the Lingkhor path, past some holy 'rubbing stones' which pilgrims rub their backs and legs against.

At the top of Parma Ri is the **Gesar Ling** (Map pp88-9; admission Y7), a Chinese construction that dates back to 1793. It is the only Chinese-style temple in Lhasa and is a quiet place for an afternoon walk. The main temple has a statue of Gesar (linked to Guanyu, the Chinese God of War) along with Guru Rinpoche on the left and Ekajati, the Dzogchen deity, on the right. A separate yellow chapel on the kora has a statue of an orange Jampelyang with Sakyamuni, Chana Dorje (Vajrapani) and Chenresig.

Ramoche Temple ར་མོ་ཆེ་

The **Ramoche** (Map pp88-9; Ramoche Lam; admission Y20; 🕙 8am-1pm) is the sister temple to the Jokhang. It was originally built to house the Jowo Sakyamuni image that is now in the Jokhang. The principal image in Ramoche is Mikyöba (Akshobhya), brought to Tibet in the 7th century as part of the dowry of King Songtsen Gampo's Nepali wife, Princess Bhrikuti. The image represents Sakyamuni at the age of eight years. It is said to have been badly damaged by Red Guards during the Cultural Revolution.

Ramoche was built at the same time as the Jokhang, but it is thought that unlike the Jokhang, it was originally built in Chinese style. By the mid-15th century it had become Lhasa's Upper Tantric College.

The Mikyöba (Akshobhya) image can be seen in the **Tsangkhang**, a small chapel at the far rear of the temple. There is a circumambulation circuit lined with prayer wheels around the perimeter of the temple and there's an interesting kitchen to the right. Many people consider that the temple's Y20 entry fee isn't worth it.

As you exit Ramoche, look for a doorway just to the right. Pass a row of prayer wheels to reach a delightful chapel, **Tsepak Lhakhang**, with three large statues. The central image

is Tsepame, the buddha associated with longevity, flanked by Jampa and Sakyamuni. There are smaller statues of Dorje Chang (Vajradhara) and Marmedze (Dipamkara). The young monks tending this place are very friendly and the chapel is popular with pilgrims.

Gyüme རྒྱུད་སྨད་གྲྭ་ཚང་

The **Gyüme** (Map p92; 15 Dekyi Shar Lam), or the Lower Tantric College, is across from the Kirey Hotel. It is easy to miss this working temple; look for an imposing entrance set back from the road. It's a surprisingly impressive place and little visited by foreigners.

Gyüme was founded in the mid-15th century and in its time was one of Tibet's foremost Tantric training colleges. In Lhasa, its importance was second only to the monasteries of Sera and Drepung. More than 500 monks were once in residence, and students of the college underwent a physically and intellectually gruelling course of study. The college was thoroughly desecrated during the Cultural Revolution, but a growing number of monks are now in residence.

The main *dukhang* (assembly hall) has statues of Tsongkhapa, the 13th Dalai Lama and Sakyamuni. Look for the monks' alms bowls encased in crafted leather, hanging from the pillars. Behind are statues of Tsongkhapa and his two main disciples, and next door is a fearsome statue of Dorje Jigje (Yamantaka). The 2nd- and 3rd-floor chapels are sometimes open.

Other Temples   Map p92

Down the alleys off Dekyi Shar Lam are three obscure temples which can be visited if you've seen everything else.

Tsome Ling is the most interesting of the three. One of the four *ling* (royal) temples of Lhasa (along with Kunde Ling and Tengye Ling), this small site consists of two temples. To the east is the Karpo Potrang (White Palace), built in 1777, and to the west is the Marpo Potrang (Red Palace), built at the beginning of the 19th century. Both buildings have fine murals. The Karpo Potrang has statues of Öpagme (Amitabha), Jampa, and a famous tutor of the Dalai Lama. The Marpo Potrang has statues of Tsongkhapa, Atisha and the eighth Dalai Lama. There are two smaller chapels behind the central hall.

BRADLEY MAYHEW

Sand mandala (p49), Lhasa

FRANK CARTER

Monks in ceremonial costume, the Jokhang (p94), Lhasa

KEREN SU

Monks, the Jokhang (p94), Lhasa

Pilgrims swinging prayer wheels, the Barkhor (p91), Lhasa

ANTHONY PLUMMER

JULIET COOM

Yak butter for sale, the Barkhor (p91), Lhasa

Prayer flags and prayer wheels for sale, Barkhor Square (p93), Lhasa

CRAIG PERSHOUSE

RICHARD I'ANSON

Detail of restored woodwork, the Potala (p98), Lhasa

BILL WASSME

The Potala (p98), Lhasa

The obscure and rarely visited **Tengye Ling** chapel is a Nyingmapa sect temple dedicated to the red-faced deity Tseumar (whose statue is next to those of Guru Rinpoche), Pehar (a protector linked to Samye) and Tamdrin (Hayagriva). It's hidden in the backstreets west of Snowlands hotel and hard to find. To enter, look for the red walls, enter the adjacent apartment block and head to the roof.

The badly ruined temple of **Shide Tratsang** is connected to Reting Monastery and was once one of the six principal temples encircling the Jokhang. It's in a housing courtyard, down a back alley near Tashi I restaurant and remains a rare example of what was left of Lhasa before renovation teams moved in.

Rigsum Lhakhang is a small chapel hidden in an alley in a housing courtyard southwest of Barkhor Square. It's dedicated to the Rigsum Gonpo trinity of Jampelyang, Chenresig and Chana Dorje (Vajrapani). Look for the line of prayer wheels disappearing down the alley.

Die-hards can track down the hard-to-find **Pode Kangtsang**, in the south of the old town, with its old upper-floor murals and large *thangkas*. It's accessible from the south.

The Norbulingka ནོར་བུ་གླིང་ཁ Map p105

The **Norbulingka** (Mirig Lam; admission Y60; ☯ 9am-1pm & 2.30-6pm), the summer palace of the Dalai Lamas, is about 10 minutes' walk south of the Lhasa Hotel in the western part of town. It ranks well behind the other points of interest in and around Lhasa. The gardens are poorly tended and the palaces themselves are something of an anticlimax, especially as most rooms are closed to the public. Avoid the **zoo** (Y10) at all costs – it is a thoroughly depressing place.

This said, the Norbulingka is still worth a visit if you don't mind the high entry fee, and the park is a great place to be during festival times and public holidays. In the seventh lunar month of every year, the Norbulingka is crowded with picnickers for the Shötun festival. Traditional Tibetan opera performances are also held then.

HISTORY

The first summer palace to be constructed in the Norbulingka (whose name literally means 'jewel park') was founded by the seventh Dalai Lama in 1755. Rather than use

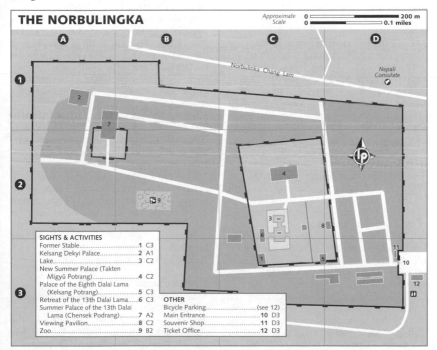

THE NORBULINGKA

Approximate Scale   0 — 200 m   0 — 0.1 miles

Norbulinka Chang Lam

Nepali Consulate

SIGHTS & ACTIVITIES	
Former Stable.....................1 C3	
Kelsang Dekyi Palace.....................2 A1	
Lake.....................3 C2	
New Summer Palace (Takten Migyü Potrang).....................4 C2	
Palace of the Eighth Dalai Lama (Kelsang Potrang).....................5 C3	
Retreat of the 13th Dalai Lama......6 C3	
Summer Palace of the 13th Dalai Lama (Chensek Podrang)..........7 A2	
Viewing Pavilion.....................8 C2	
Zoo.....................9 B2	

OTHER	
Bicycle Parking.....................(see 12)	
Main Entrance.....................10 D3	
Souvenir Shop.....................11 D3	
Ticket Office.....................12 D3	

the palace as a retreat, he decided to use the wooded environs as a summer base from which to administer the country, a practice that was to be followed by each of the succeeding Dalai Lamas. The grand procession of the Dalai Lama's entourage relocating from the Potala to the Norbulingka became one of the highlights of the Lhasa year.

The eighth Dalai Lama (1758–1804) initiated more work on the Norbulingka, expanding the gardens and digging a lake which can be found south of the New Summer Palace. The 13th Dalai Lama (1876–1933) was responsible for the three palaces in the northwest corner of the park, and the 14th (present) Dalai Lama built the New Summer Palace in 1956.

In 1959, the 14th Dalai Lama made his escape from the Norbulingka disguised as a Tibetan soldier. Unfortunately, all the palaces of the Norbulingka were damaged by Chinese artillery fire in the popular uprising that followed the Dalai Lama's flight. At the time, the compound was surrounded by some 30,000 Tibetans determined to defend the life of their spiritual leader. Repairs have been undertaken but have failed to restore the palaces to their full former glory.

PALACE OF THE EIGHTH DALAI LAMA

This palace (also known as Kelsang Potrang) is the first you come to. It was used as a summer palace by the eighth Dalai Lama and by every succeeding Dalai Lama up to the 13th. Only the main audience hall is open; it features 65 hanging *thangkas* and a throne backed by statues of the eight medicine buddhas.

NEW SUMMER PALACE

The New Summer Palace (Takten Migyü Potrang) in the centre of the park was built by the present (14th) Dalai Lama between 1954 and 1956 and is the most interesting of the Norbulingka palaces.

The first of the rooms you visit is the **Dalai Lama's audience chamber**. Note the murals on the chamber's walls. They depict the history of Tibet in 301 scenes. As you stand with your back to the window, the murals start on the left wall with Sakyamuni and show the mythical beginnings of the Tibetan people and the first agricultural field in Tibet. The wall in front of you depicts the building of the circular monastery of Samye, as well as Ganden, Drepung and other monasteries. The right wall contains the histories of the Dalai Lamas, concluding with the reincarnation of the current Dalai Lama and the building of the Norbulingka.

Next come the **Dalai Lama's private quarters**, which consist of a meditation chamber and a bedroom. The rooms have been maintained almost exactly as the Dalai Lama left them, and apart from the usual Buddhist images they contain the occasional surprise: a Soviet radio and a stylish European bed, among other things.

The **assembly hall**, where the Dalai Lama would address heads of state, is home to a gold throne backed by wonderful cartoon-style murals of the Dalai Lama's court (left, at the back) and all 14 Dalai Lamas (right). Look out for British representative Hugh Richardson in a trilby hat, and several Mongolian ambassadors. The first five of the Dalai Lamas on the right wall lack the Wheel of Law; this symbolises their lack of governmental authority. There are also murals depicting the lives of Sakyamuni (at the top) and Tsongkhapa (below). Last is the meeting room of the Dalai Lama's mother.

South of the New Summer Palace is the artificial lake commissioned by the eighth Dalai Lama. The only pavilion open here at the time of research was the personal **retreat of the 13th Dalai Lama** in the southwestern corner, featuring a library, a 1000-armed Chenresig statue, and a stuffed tiger in the corner!

SUMMER PALACE OF THE 13TH DALAI LAMA

The summer palace of the 13th Dalai Lama (Chensek Potrang) is in the western section of the Norbulingka, northwest of the awful zoo.

The ground-floor assembly hall holds the throne of the 13th Dalai Lama and is stuffed full of various buggies, palanquins and bicycles. The 2nd-floor living quarters are closed.

Nearby is a smaller building, the **Kelsang Dekyi Palace**, which was also built by the 13th Dalai Lama, but this too is closed.

Tibet Museum འགྲེམས་སྟོན་ཁང་

This grand-looking new **museum** (Map pp88-9; ☎ 681 2210; admission adult/student Y30/5; 🕐 9am-6pm), in the west of town just opposite the Norbulingka, isn't too bad as long as you can see through the offensive propaganda.

The adult ticket includes a useful audio tour (student ticket holders pay an extra Y10 for this) but the commentary suffers from terrible Americanised pronunciation (Da-*lai* La-*maaarr!*).

The halls start logically with prehistory, which highlight the Neolithic sites around Chamdo and rock paintings at Rutok and Nam tso. The 'Tibet is Inalienable in History' hall is full of boring seals and misleading Chinese political spin but it's worth seeking out the hat belonging to Songtsen Gampo, the shields from the Guge kingdom and the gold urn and ivory slips which were used to recognise reincarnations. The more interesting third hall covers Tibetan script, masks, musical instruments, medical *thangkas* and statuary. The next hall concentrates on *thangkas*, many of which are new or have been shipped in from China. The final hall has a good display of folk handicrafts, ranging from coracle boats to nomad tents and leatherware.

The top floor has a totally out-of-place collection of Chinese ceramics and a hall of stuffed Tibetan wildlife. There are toilets and a shop.

ACTIVITIES

Braille Without Borders Blind Massage Centre
(Map p92; contact Kyla ☎ 698 2715 or Digi ☎ 699 2070; 4th fl, rm 59, Dekyi Shar Lam) Offers hour-long traditional massages (Y50). The centre is in a courtyard, down an alley across from the Tashi I Restaurant. Call in advance.

Tibet Wind Horse Adventure (Map pp88–9; ☎ 683 3009; www.tibetwindhorse.com; 1 Minzu Beilu) Offers half- and full-day river rafting trips in the Lhasa area (US$100/75 per person) and a three-day trip (US$240) in the Drigung Valley, among others. The service is run by Nepal-based operator Chris Jones.

WALKING TOUR
The fragile Tibetan **old town** shelters the soul of Lhasa, far from Chinese influence. This walk (see map, right) takes in craft workshops, backstreet chapels, and pilgrim paths, offering a glimpse into family courtyards.

At the first turn of the **Barkhor Circuit** (1; p93) take a left and then quick right, past dried meat and yellow bags of yak butter and several antique stalls to the bustling **Tromsikhang Market (2)** – the original Tibetan-style building was destroyed in 1997. After

a quick look around, head north to the main road and then right into the **Gyüme Lower Tantric College (3**; p104).

About 30m further down the road is the small but active **Meru Sarpa Monastery (4**; admission free), opposite the Kirey Hotel. The building in the middle of the central compound houses a traditional wood-block printing press. In the northwest corner is an atmospheric chapel with a statue of 1000-armed Chenresig.

Take the alley down the side of the Kirey Hotel that disappears into the old town and follow the winding branch to the right. As you continue south you'll see various craftspeople making statues, cabinets and Tibetan banners. At the junction there's the **Eizhi Exquisite Tangka Shop (5)** to the left; you want to take a left here but first look down the alleyway to the right to a brassware shop, a Tibetan tailor and a noodle-making workshop.

As you head southeast past a small market, curve right to the quiet but interesting **Karmashar Temple (6)**, once the home of the Karmashar, Lhasa's main oracle. Look for the spooky icon painted on a pigskin bag and for the Karmashar statue on the far right. There are also some nice original murals of Atisha, Tsongkhapa and Tsepame on the upper walls. Enter from the south side.

Continue east to a T-junction, past outdoor pool tables where Khampas from the east of Tibet huddle over weathered felts and rarely pot a ball. At the T-junction take a left turn to visit the stylish **Dropenling crafts centre (7**; p114).

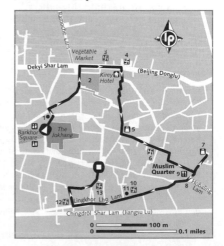

After visiting the craftsmen, head south towards the **Muslim quarter (8)**, the focus of Lhasa's 2000-strong Muslim population. Friday lunch is a great time to be here, when weekly prayers are held and the quarter is full of men with wispy beards and skullcaps (non-Muslims are denied entry to the mosque itself). Many women here wear black velvet headscarfs, characteristic of the Linxia area in China's Gansu province. Try a bowl of Muslim noodles at the **Islam Restaurant (9**; p112) if you're feeling peckish.

As you face the mosque, turn right and head southwest along part of the Lingkhor pilgrim circuit to the yellow walls of the **Ani Sanghkhung Nunnery (10**; 29 Lingkhor Lho Lam; admission Y10). This small, friendly and active nunnery is the only one within the precincts of the old Tibetan quarter. The site of the nunnery probably dates back to the 7th century, but it housed a monastery until at least the 15th century. The principal image, upstairs on the 2nd floor, is a 1000-armed Chenresig. A small alley to the side of the main chapel leads down to the former meditation chamber of Songtsen Gampo, the 7th-century king of Tibet. Just next to the entrance is an excellent and very friendly **thangka workshop (11)**.

Continue past a second mosque to the **Lho Rigsum Lhakhang (12)**, one of four chapels surrounding the Jokhang at cardinal points. A lovely chapel, almost completely ignored by tourists, with a central statue of Tsepame, flanked by the four main bodhisattvas, and its own inner kora. The chapel is looked after by monks from Ganden Monastery.

Take a right here north and then a right, then a left. At the junction you can see the **Rabtse Temple (13)**, run by Sera Monastery.

The alley north takes you to the southeast corner of the Barkhor Circuit, where you can continue clockwise to Barkhor Square.

FESTIVALS & EVENTS

If it is at all possible, try to time your visit to Lhasa with one of the city's festivals (p300). Winter and the New Year festivals see thousands of pilgrims flood into town, and the city's pilgrim circuits take on a colourful, party atmosphere. The day of the Saga Dawa festival sees huge numbers of pilgrims making pilgrim circuits around Lhasa late into the night. Many Lhasa residents trek up to the summit of Gephel Ri, the peak behind Drepung Monastery.

SLEEPING

Accommodation in Lhasa can be divided into inexpensive Tibetan-style accommodation in the central Barkhor area and less conveniently located upmarket digs on the outskirts of town. Almost all independent travellers head straight for the Barkhor area, where five Tibetan-style hotels (the first five reviewed here) dominate the market. This is simply because the Barkhor area is the most interesting part of town, the service in these hotels is friendly (if basic), and the five are the best places to meet other travellers and get the current lowdown on travel in Tibet.

The past couple of years have seen a rise in the number of mid-range options. Most of these are in shiny, faceless Chinese hotels, but the aforementioned hotels offer excellent mid-range rooms with private bathroom, carpet, TV and so on, and remain the best places to stay.

AUTHOR'S CHOICE

Pentoc Guesthouse (Panduo Luguan; Map p92; ☎ 632 6686; www.pentoc.com; 5 Mentsikhang Lam; dm Y25, s/d Y40/65; 🖳) The Pentoc is in a great location near the Snowlands, 50m north of Barkhor Square. It's a stylish place with nice touches such as a coffee shop, free videos every night at 8pm, print-outs of festival dates, and individual bed lights in the three-bed dormitories. Rooms overlooking the street can be noisy during the day. There are only two singles so it's worth making a reservation for your first night, though the booking system is chaotic at best.

Hotel Kyichu (Jiqu Fandian; Map p92; ☎ 633 8824; jqfd@public.ls.xz.cn; 18 Dekyi Shar Lam/Beijing Donglu); s/d Y200/280, deluxe d Y320) The two-star Kyichu is a friendly and well-run choice west of Tashi I restaurant, and a welcome exception to the usual Chinese-style mid-range hotels. All 52 rooms come with private bathroom and the location and service are excellent. There's also a nice garden restaurant and sitting area. A 20% winter discount is given from November to April inclusive.

Prices given here (and throughout this book) apply in the high season. Rates can be a little lower in April, May and October and lower still in winter.

Budget

Yak Hotel (Yake Binguan; Map p92; ☎ 632 3496; 100 Dekyi Shar Lam; dm/d/tr Y20/80/100, d with bathroom Y260; ☐) This is possibly the most popular place with individual travellers. The rooms that front onto the rear courtyard are quietest but can be dark. The excellent pricier doubles with Tibetan-style décor are often occupied by tour groups so book ahead. The dorms can be somewhat gloomy but the toilets are clean. Hot showers, in the far corner of the rear courtyard, are available morning and evening. There's good Internet access and bicycle hire (Y3 per hour or Y25 per day). Note that recent renovations may bring a change in prices and room options.

Banak Shol (Balangxue Luguan; Map p92; ☎ 632 3829; 8 Dekyi Shar Lam; dm/s/d Y20/30/60, d with bathroom Y100-120) Once *the* place to stay back in the early days of independent travel, this is the second most popular hotel among individual travellers and it's often full by mid-afternoon. It is not as clean or as efficiently run as the Yak, but it does have a charm that the larger Yak doesn't. Guests can titillate themselves with the thought they have checked into a medieval monastic retreat (well, almost) as they enjoy the cosy Tibetan-style rooms fronted by verandas that face the inner courtyard. The main downside is that the walls are paper thin and most look onto the noisy main road. The doubles in the new block come with carpet, bathroom and 24-hour hot water, making them among the best-value rooms in Lhasa. The cheaper doubles in the block below the Nam-tso Restaurant are poorer value, although the restaurant itself has taken off as one of Lhasa's most popular places to eat and socialise. Laundry is free, though you won't get your crusty socks washed after a week's trekking.

Snowlands (Xueyu Binguan; Map p92; ☎ 632 3687; 4 Mentsikhang Lam; dm/d/tr Y25/60-80/90, d/deluxe d with bathroom Y260/360; ☐) Snowlands is another of Lhasa's old-timers. It was a favourite with backpackers back in the 1980s, but the mood has changed a bit since then. Snowlands is quieter than the Yak or the Banak Shol, though you pay for your solitude with lower service standards. Doubles/deluxe doubles

with bathroom are sometimes discounted to Y150/250. The shower block in the corner of the courtyard has unreliable water and there's a frustrating lack of wash basins elsewhere. The rooms in the plush block at the back of the central quadrangle are clean and spacious, but not quite such good value as those at the Yak or the Banak Shol.

Kirey Hotel (Jiri Binguan; Map p92; ☎ 632 3462; 105 Dekyi Shar Lam; dm Y20, d Y50, d with bathroom Y100) The fourth and least popular of the Barkhor area's Tibetan-run hotels, the Kirey deserves more custom than it gets. It is friendly and clean, and has reliable hot water (9am to 9pm) in the shower block around the back. The doubles with private bathroom at the back of the courtyard are looking a bit tired these days. The Y50 doubles offer good value. The Tashi II restaurant are on the premises and there's lots of balcony sitting space. Laundry service is free – put your washing in the bags provided and hand it in to reception before 9am. The only grumbles we have are the scarcity of sinks and the dodgy plumbing in the toilets.

Pata Hotel (Map p92; ☎ 633 8419; 63 Lingkhor Donglu/ Shar Lam; dm/d Y20/40, tr per bed Y40, d with bathroom Y150) This new place is a bit out of the way and attracts far fewer tourists than the other budget options, but it's therefore quieter and not a bad choice if you want to be out of the action. Rooms are arranged around a large courtyard and there's plenty of common seating. The corner rooms come with a tiled Western bathroom and hot water.

Tashi Targyel Hotel (Zaxi Dajie Binguan; Map p92; 8 Mentsikhang Lam; s Y40, d & tr per bed Y20, d with bathroom Y100-150) Further up from the Pentoc and Snowlands, the grim corridors of the Tashi Targyel are probably only worth checking out if everything else is full. The cheapest doubles are actually not bad value. If you want your own bathroom it's worth spending the extra on the pricier of the en suite rooms. There are shared hot showers and squat toilets

Mandala Hotel (Manzhai Jiudian; Map p92; ☎ 632 4783; fax 632 4787; 31 South Barkhor; s/d/tr with bathroom Y180/260/360) This hotel has a great location just off the Barkhor. The rooms are clean and comfortable and there's a rooftop teahouse with great views of the Jokhang, plus a Nepali-style restaurant. Some rooms overlook the Barkhor; this is the only place with such views. Lights can be dim.

Flora Hotel (Map p92; ☎ 632 4491; flora@public.ls.xz.cn; Hobaling Lam; d Y35, d/tr with bathroom Y180/228) The Flora is a well-run hotel in the interesting Muslim quarter (it's run by a Nepali Muslim). There are some nice touches such as a minibar at local-shop prices, a stock of foreign magazines and a laundry service. The decent but slightly cramped three-bed dorms out the back (with attached toilet and shared hot shower) offer a quiet alternative to the backpacker hotels of Lhasa. There's also a decent Nepali restaurant here. Prices include breakfast.

Tibet Gorkha Hotel (Map p92; ☎ 627 2222, tibetgorkhahotel@hotmail.com; South Lingkhor; d Y180-328, ste Y568) This new hotel in the southern part of the old town has been recommended by expats for its friendly service and great atmosphere. The rooms are set around a grassy courtyard.

Meiduo Hotel (☎ 681 2798; 23 Lingkhor Chang Lam/ Linkuo Beilu; d Y120) With spacious and clean rooms, and 24-hour hot water, the Meiduo has views of the back of the Potala. Away from the Tibetan quarter, but there's a Nepali restaurant and an ice-cream store on the grounds.

Mid-Range

See also the Yak, Banak Shol and Snowlands hotels in the Budget listings for good value mid-range rooms.

Dhood Gu Hotel (Dungu Binguan; Map p92; ☎ 632 2555; dhoodgu@public.ls.xz.cn; near the Tromsikhang market; s/d Y320/480) If you are looking for a dash of style, this Nepali-run mid-range hotel is another good choice, with excellent Tibetan-style decoration and a superb location in the old town. Breakfast is included and rooms come with modern bathrooms and kettles, though the singles are cramped. The rooftop has fine Potala views.

Himalaya Hotel (Ximalaya Fandian; Map pp88-9; ☎ 632 1111; fax 623 2675; 6 Lingkhor Shar Lam; old block d/tr Y373/439, new block s/d Y456/648, deluxe d Y747) The choice here at the Himalaya is between the tatty and

overpriced old block and much better superior rooms in the new block. The rates include breakfast and discounts of 20% are normally available. Credit cards are accepted.

Airway Hotel (Hangkong Jiudian; Map pp88-9; ☎ 683 4444; fax 683 3438; 12 Kangang Donglu; d with/without Potala view Y320/280) Just east of the Potala, the Airway has excellent views of it from the larger and better-value west-facing rooms, if you can see through the dirty windows. These rooms are normally discounted to Y180. Rooms are pretty good, though the hotel lacks charm. Hot water runs from 7.30am to 10am, noon to 3pm and 6pm to midnight.

Tibet Xiongbala Hotel (Xiongbala Dajiudian; Map p92; ☎ 633 8888; fax 633 1777; 28 Chingdröl Shar Lam; s/d with bathroom Y368/518) This is a relatively new and well-run three-star Chinese hotel. Facilities include coffee bar, sauna, business centre and several restaurants. Upper floors have views of the Potala. The bathrooms are particularly nice; singles/doubles with bathrooms are normally discounted to Y295/415.

Shangbala Hotel (Map p92; ☎ 632 3888; fax 632 3577; Mentsikhang Lam; s/d Y480/580) Next to the Pentoc (and not to be confused with the Xiongbala Hotel listed earlier), this new Chinese blockhouse is totally out of place in its Tibetan surroundings. It has a decent restaurant and useful location, and is popular with American groups. Rooms are standard, with good views from the 4th floor; normally rooms are discounted to Y350.

Men's Hotel (Mingshi Jiudian; Map pp88-9; ☎ 681 6800; 92 Dekyi Nub Lam; s & d Y460) If for some reason you want to be situated in the western part of town, this is a cheap option. Spacious, clean and bright doubles with en suite hot shower make this a good deal, though the singles are much smaller for the same price, which is often discounted to Y180 for both kinds of rooms.

Top End

All the following hotels offer a minimum 20% discount in the winter months (November to March inclusive). Prices quoted are for the high season.

Lhasa Hotel (Lasa Fandian; Map pp88-9; ☎ 683 2221; sales@public.ls.xz.cn; 1 Minzu Nanlu; d Y1020-1328, tr Y980, Tibetan ste Y1555; ✗ 🖳 🖳) In 1997, Holiday Inn pulled out of Tibet under increasing pressure from pro-Tibetan groups, and handed this hotel back to the government who renamed

---

PRESSURE SITUATION

Take particular care when reopening things such as tubes of sunscreen and shampoo after a flight to or from Lhasa, as the change in pressure can cause messy explosions of volcanic proportions.

AUTHOR'S CHOICE

Nam-tso Restaurant (Map p92; Banak Shol hotel; mains Y20, set breakfast Y20) This is definitely one of the top hotel restaurants. The chicken sizzler (Y20) could well be the best meal in Lhasa. Prices are a little higher than at the Tashi restaurants but dishes on offer include vegetarian lasagne, Japanese sets and yak burgers (as good as those at the Lhasa Hotel and much cheaper). Friday and Saturday bring good Israeli dishes (though the felafel is a little wide of the mark). The outdoor roof seating is a great place for a beer in summer. The restaurant's breakfasts (muesli brought in from Kathmandu, among other things) have also achieved a devoted following. The restaurant used to be called the Kailash Restaurant until another restaurant stole the name.

it the Lhasa Hotel. Standards have certainly slid since then (the staff can be particularly clueless) but there is still a decent selection of restaurants (breakfast buffet Y80), Chang's Bar (named after the character in James Hilton's *Lost Horizon*), international satellite TV, in-house movies, a clinic with both Western and Tibetan doctors, a dirty pool and a small fitness centre. Discounts of 30% normally apply.

Tibet Hotel (Map pp88-9; ☎ 683 9999; fax 683 6787; 64 Dekyi Nub Lam; old block d/tr Y880/980) In keeping with its name, it strives to create a Tibetan ambience, but the results are a bit surreal. Service tends to dodder somewhere between apathy and incompetence. It's worth spending the extra Y100 for the brighter rooms in the new four-star block, which come with nice touches such as a hair dryer and shaving mirror. Discounts of around 30% normally apply.

Tibet Pearl Star Garden (Minzhu Huayuan Jiudian; Map pp88-9; ☎ 681 6666; fax 683 2195; 196 67 Dekyi Nub Lam; s Y120, d/deluxe Y280/460) This hotel, formerly known as the Grand, used to serve as the government guesthouse but now operates as a three-star option. It's not as plush as the lobby would like us to believe and the cheaper rooms, in particular, are quite rundown. Doubles/deluxe doubles are normally discounted to Y180/210.

Hubei Hotel (Map pp88-9; Hubei Dasha; ☎ 682 0999; 54 Dekyi Nub Lam; s/d Y260/580) A new, but standard, modern Chinese hotel west of the Lhasa Hotel. Singles/doubles are often discounted to Y220/384.

Tibet International Grand Hotel (Guoji Dajiudian; Map pp88-9; ☎ 683 2888; fax 682 0888; 1 Minzu Nanlu; d Y800) One of the better places in town, this four-star hotel opened in 2003. Rooms are comfortable but there are no direct window views and it's far from the Tibetan quarter. Doubles should be discounted to Y640.

EATING

The best places for breakfast are probably the Dunya, Nam-tso and Pentoc restaurants. All the eateries listed serve lunch and dinner, but you will struggle to find a meal after about 9.30pm.

Tibetan Quarter   Map p92

Most individual travellers eat in the Tibetan quarter around the Barkhor Square area and there are plenty of great restaurants to try.

WESTERN

Tashi I (cnr Mentsikhang Lam & Dekyi Shar Lam; dishes Y8-15) This place deserves a special mention because it has been running for a while now and, despite increased competition, continues to be a favourite. The service is friendly, the prices are cheap and everything on the menu is good. Special praise is reserved for the *bobis* (chapatti-like unleavened bread), which most people order with seasoned cream cheese and fried vegetables or meat. The Western dishes are less impressive. Tashi's cheesecakes (Y6) are still a treat.

Tashi II (☎ 632 3462; Dekyi Shar Lam) Located in the Kirey Hotel, Tashi II offers the same menu as Tashi I but is a little quieter and has charming staff.

Snowlands Restaurant (☎ 632 3687; Mentsikhang Lam; dishes Y25-35) Attached to the Snowlands hotel, this is a slightly more upmarket place that serves a mix of Tibetan and good Nepali food in very civilised surroundings. There's a 50% discount on the excellent cakes after 9pm and discounts on all food between October and May.

Dunya Restaurant (☎ 633 3374; 100 Dekyi Shar Lam; dishes Y25-40) With sophisticated décor, excellent and wide-ranging food (from yak enchiladas to Indonesian noodles) and interesting specials, this foreign-run place feels like a 'real' restaurant. It's pricier than most other places in town but it's popular with groups and travellers who aren't on a shoestring budget. The homemade sandwiches and soups are good and the Saturday brunch (Y25, 11am to 2pm) is popular with local expats. The locally made Tibetan yak cheese is worth trying.

Pentoc Café (Pentoc Hotel; breakfasts & mains Y16-26, coffee Y7) The Pentoc has a growing following for its breakfasts. Other times see light fare such as sandwiches, baked potatoes, Swiss *rosti* and salads, and there's also good coffee, cakes and ice cream. We recommend the Saturday night pizza (Y34 with salad) and Thursday night specials. The hotel lobby sells excellent homemade granola for a DIY breakfast.

Naga Restaurant (☎ 632 7509; Mentsikhang Lam; mains Y15-25, desserts Y10-15) You'd be right to be a more than a little sceptical about French food in Tibet but, thanks to a French culinary advisor, this place serves up pretty authentic crepes, pâté with homemade bread (Y15) and yak bourguignon. Vegetarians will like the eight-dish Naga Treasure salad (Y25) and the stuffed peppers and tomatoes. Top it off with a decadent glass of wine (Y12) and the superb chocolate mousse (Y12).

TIBETAN, CHINESE AND MUSLIM

Pentoc Tibetan Restaurant (dishes Y10) For something a little more authentically Tibetan, charming English-speaking Pentoc now runs this local teahouse restaurant after working in Tashi I for many years. The food runs to breakfast (eggs, Tibetan bread, pancake, curd) and it's a good place to try Tibetan standards like *momos, thugpa, shemdre* (rice, potato and meat) and fried rice/noodles, plus milk and butter tea. Pentoc is 20m down an alleyway off Dekyi Shar Lam, on the left.

The **Yuyi Restaurant** across from the Banak Shol hotel offers good, cheap Chinese dishes with an overpriced English menu of sorts.

Along Dekyi Shar Lam between the Kirey and Banak Shol hotels are a number of Muslim restaurants. One such restaurant with an English menu can be found opposite the Bank of China. There are some excellent and cheap noodle dishes on offer, including *chao mianpian* (fried noodle squares) and *ganban* (a kind of stir-fried spaghetti bolognaise). A good choice is **Axiya Restaurant** (noodles Y5-6; Chinese-language menu only), just off the Barkhor, offering good-value Lanzhou- and Xinjiang-style noodles, as well as Muslim and Chinese dishes.

Islam Restaurant (Isilan Fanzhuang; ☎ 633 9258) Muslim food flourishes in the Muslim district, and especially at Islam Restaurant. Invest in a cup of Muslim tea (*babao wanzi*; Y3) and a bowl of Xinjiang noodles (Y10).

Lucky Horse Restaurant (Yuthok Lam; mains Y6-20) This traditional Tibetan-style restaurant is a great place to soak up the local flavour or take a Tibetan friend without feeling overwhelmed (there's a picture menu for easy ordering). It has a good range of Tibetan and Chinese dishes.

NEPALI

With the arrival of half a dozen Nepali restaurants, Lhasa now rivals Kathmandu in its range of foreign foods (though prices are a bit higher). All offer a mix of Indian, pseudo-Chinese and Western dishes for about Y25, with Indian veggie dishes cheaper at Y10-12. If you are hankering for enchiladas, chocolate pudding, peach lassis and other Thamel favourites, make a beeline for these places.

Tibet Café (Mentsikhang Lam; dishes Y18-25) This restaurant is probably the pick of the bunch. Prices are lowest, service is impeccable and the food is good. The well-priced Chinese and Western dishes are joined by a good range of Tibetan, Thai and Korean dishes (the latter heavy on the *kimchi*). The warm and quiet orange interior makes it a good place to chill out over a beer or a *tonba* (Tibetan hot millet beer; Y15).

New Mandala Restaurant (☎ 634 2235; west of Barkhor Sq; dishes Y10-25) This Nepali-run restaurant is definitely a winner for its fine views over the Barkhor, either from the 2nd floor or the rooftop. The inside features some lovely Tibetan murals. The food is a mixture of Tibetan, Chinese and Nepali and good value. There's a branch at the Tashi Restaurant in Shigatse.

Mandala Restaurant (☎ 632 9645; Mandala Hotel, South Barkhor; dishes Y12-25) Perfect for a post-kora meal, this cosy place on the Barkhor circuit offers a wide range of dishes from Indian curries to pizza, plus a few special-occasion Tibetan dishes such as 'Khampa roast leg of lamb' (Y98, order 45 minutes in advance). The Indian dishes can be a bit bland so ask for the 'real' spices if that's how you like it.

Western Lhasa
Map pp88-9

The tastiest Chinese food is in Lhasa's Han-Chinese dominated west. This area is such a long hike from the Tibetan quarter that few travellers make the effort.

The Lhasa Hotel has several upmarket dining options: the **Zampu** serves Chinese food, the **Everest** has an international buffet (Y170), and the **Himalaya** prepares Tibetan dishes. The **Yak Café** (mains Y60-90) offers Continental dishes including the famous yak burger with French fries (Y68). The 'seafood in a basket' (Y88) beggars belief.

Yeti Café (Xueren Jiudian; ☎ 681 5755; 188 Dekyi Nub Lam; dishes Y15-35) This café opposite the Lhasa Hotel has nice Tibetan-style seating and a good range of reasonably priced, hard-to-find Tibetan dishes and so is popular with groups from across the road, desperate to break out of their hotel. The meaty menu (plenty of yak tongue and sheep's lungs) has little for vegetarians.

New Starting Point (Xin Qidian Canba; ☎ 6831 388; Dekyi Nub Lam; mains Y17-38) A new Nepali-run place with Western and Indian food, Nepali set meals (Y25 to Y35) and good sandwiches (Y15 to Y25), using their own bread. Desserts and breakfasts include vanilla waffles with maple syrup (Y18), lassis and strawberry yogurt. It's also a popular bar.

Eat Lover's Bakery & Restaurant (☎ 681 8933; 60-62 Deji Lu; mains Y28-50, salads Y15-30) A Chinese-run place with a good range of Western and Nepali dishes, including the famed white chocolate mousse (Y18). It's a notch up from the Barkhor restaurant, both in quality and price.

Teahouses

There are several Tibetan teahouses around town where you can grab a cheap cup of *cha ngamo* (sweet tea). Most of them are grungy Tibetan-only places, blasted by high-decibel kung fu videos, but there are a few exceptions. **Turquoise Dragon Teahouse** (Map p92) is a Tibetan-style place with a fine balcony overlooking Dekyi Shar Lam, the bustling local **teahouse** (Map p92) underneath the Tashi Targyel Hotel and the **teahouse** (Map pp88-9) on the north side of the Potala kora, on two levels with upper floor balconies.

Self-Catering & Trekking Supplies

Lhasa is the best place to stock up on food supplies for trips to Mt Kailash and the Nepali border. The town has many supermarkets, mostly Chinese-run, which sell everything from sachets of shampoo to bottles of red wine. One of the largest is the **Hongyuan Supermarket** (Map pp88-9; Dekyi Shar Lam). The nearby **Xinhua Supermarket** (Map p92; cnr Dekyi Shar Lam & Dosenge Lam) is also good. **Lhasa Department Store** (Lasa Baihuo Dalou; Map pp88-9; east of Potala Sq) also has a good supermarket.

In the Tibetan quarter, the **wholesale shops** (Map p92) near the Kirey Hotel offer the lowest prices for basic food supplies and are the places to stock up for a long trip.

The **Tromsikhang Market** area just south of here has a small selection of fresh vegetables, puffed rice and yogurt as well as Tibet's widest selection of dried fruits and nuts. Roasted peanuts are good trekking food and are available for about Y5 per *jin* (500g) from the various Chinese mobile stalls that sell duck and other dubious cuts of roast meat.

The old town has a couple of Tibetan-run Nepali supermarkets selling everything from imported muesli and chocolate spread to Indian spices and rolling tobacco, though at prices far higher than in Nepal. Try the **Nuoling Tsongkhang Shop** (Map p92), 300m south of the junction of Dekyi Shar Lam and Lingkhor Shar Lam.

The best **produce market** lies in a covered lane just east of the Potala.

DRINKING

There is not a great deal in the way of entertainment options in Lhasa. In the evening most travellers head to one of the restaurants in the Tibetan quarter and then retire to the Yak or Banak Shol hotels, which sometimes become the scene of an impromptu party.

Dunya (Map p92; Dekyi Shar Lam) The upstairs bar is popular with both local expats and tour groups. A beer will costs Y12; Friday's happy hour means a Y2 discount between 7pm and 9.30pm.

Another Place (Map p92; ☎ 627 3793) This cool Chinese-managed hangout has an underground feel, plays DVDs and has free Internet. It's just down the alley on the east side of the Yak Hotel.

Music Kitchen (Map pp88-9; Dekyi Nub Lam; beer Y12) Part of a string of bars and restaurants near the Lhasa Hotel, this one boasts some of the best Western music in Lhasa.

ENTERTAINMENT

Unfortunately there is little in the way of cultural entertainment in Lhasa. Restaurants like the Crazy Yak in the courtyard of the Kirey Hotel have song-and-dance performances for diners. For authentic performances of Tibetan opera and dancing you will probably have to wait for one of Lhasa's festivals (p300).

Tibetan Dance & Drama Theatre (Map pp88-9; cnr Mirig Lam & Dekyi Nub Lam) Opposite the Lhasa Hotel, the theatre is mostly a lost cause. It might be worth inquiring at the Lhasa Hotel whether there will be any performances that coincide with your visit, but it is unlikely.

For something a bit earthier there are several Tibetan Nangma dance halls around town, which offer a mildly nationalistic mix of disco, traditional Tibetan dance, lots of beer and a bit of Chinese karaoke thrown in for good measure. Locations change regularly so try to go with a Tibetan friend. Established places to try include **Shengda Tibetan Nangma** (Map pp88–9) on Dekyi Shar Lam or the flashy **JJ's Nangma** (Map pp88–9) on Potala Square.

The **Pentoc Guesthouse** (Map p92) shows free videos in its lobby most nights at 8pm.

SHOPPING

Lhasa is no longer the backwater it once was, and it is now a good place to stock up on basic supplies and food for trekking (p113). Items such as medical supplies, books, water-purifying tablets and deodorant are still not easy to find.

Lhasa Department Store (Lasa Baihuo Dalou; Map pp88-9) is a good one-stop shop for most supplies, especially clothes, though it's a little more expensive than elsewhere.

Photography

It is still a good idea to bring your own film supplies, but slide film is now relatively easy to find in Lhasa (although slide processing is impossible). A profusion of **photographic shops** (Map pp88–9) are clustered around the entrance to the Workers' Cultural Palace, east of the Potala Square. Prices for 100ASA Sensia can normally be haggled down to about Y45 for 36 exposures, less if you buy in bulk; Elitechrome is a little cheaper. Print film is available everywhere for between Y20 and Y25 (36 exposures). Advantix film costs around Y65. Camera batteries (2CRS) cost about Y60.

Chinese black-and-white film is cheap to buy but expensive to process in Lhasa so you won't save much over colour film.

Travel & Trekking Equipment

For basic items such as thermoses and water canisters, the best places to shop are the lanes that run from the Tromsikhang Market down to the Barkhor circuit. Cheap pots and pans (ideal for instant noodles) are available at the stalls on the east side of the Potala, near the Airway Hotel. You can also get hard-to-find items such as sunscreen, deodorant and lip cream here; otherwise dig around in the Nepali-stocked shops around the Barkhor.

Outlook Outdoor Equipment (Map p92; ☎ /fax 634 5589; 11 Dekyi Shar Lam) This great trekking shop is across from the Kirey Hotel. Apart from Western-quality sleeping bags, Gore-Tex jackets and tents, it's also full of hard-to-find travel knick-knacks such as altimeters, trekking socks and gloves. Prices are almost as high as abroad but quality is high. If you buy one of the trekking gas canisters (Y60 to Y70) you can rent the burner for free. Also available for rent are Primus multifuel stoves (Y40 per day), mats (Y10 to Y20), sleeping bags (Y15 to Y25) and tents (Y35 to Y70). Prices and deposits for equipment rental are negotiable.

Souvenirs

The **Barkhor circuit** (p93) is lined with stalls selling everything a visiting Tibetan or tourist could possibly need. Expect to be asked outrageous prices for anything you are interested in and then settle down for some serious and persistent haggling. There is an awful lot of junk for sale in this part of town, but even some of the junky items have a certain charm. Popular purchases include prayer wheels, rings, daggers, prayer scarves and prayer flags, all of which are fairly portable. Items of Tibetan clothing such as *chubas* (long-sleeved sheepskin cloaks), Tibetan dresses, cowboy hats, Chinese silk jackets, Tibetan brocade and fur hats are good buys.

The majority of shops in the Barkhor sell jewellery, most of it turquoise and coral and almost all of it fake (p307).

Dropenling (Map p92; ☎ 636 0558; www.tibetcraft .com) Run by the Tibetan Artisans Initiative, this non-profit enterprise aims to bolster traditional Tibetan handicrafts in the face of increasing Chinese and Nepalese imports. Visitors can watch local craftsmen at work in the block across the courtyard, as they grind up mineral paints for *thangka* painting. A café is planned for the roof. Products are of high quality and use traditional methods (ie natural dyes, wool not acrylic cloth etc) updated with contemporary design. Prices are fixed, with proceeds going back to artisans in the form of wages and social funds. Artefacts for sale include carpets, *thangkas*, UNDP-supported weavings and silverware, Tibetan aprons, bags, table runners, horse blankets and wood carvings.

Snow Leopard Carpet Industries (Map p92; ☎ 632 1481; fax 633 3249; 2 Mentsikhang Lam/Zangyi Lu), next to the Snowlands Restaurant, sells a collection of high-quality carpets and interesting souvenirs and can arrange delivery abroad.

There are a couple of **thangka workshops** (Map p92) just south of the Barkhor circuit and several others in the surrounding backstreets. **Mani Thangka Arts** (Map p92; ☎ 632 0818; Mentsikhang Lam), opposite the Pentoc Guesthouse, features *thangkas* made with mineral paints by local artist Phurbu Tsering. Most of the other *thangka* shops are owned by Chinese traders who sell Nepali imports.

Nirvana Tibetan Handicrafts (Map p92; ☎ 636 1027; Mentsikhang Lam) sells jewellery, bags and carpets made in Nepal according to Tibetan designs.

For better-quality souvenir items at marked-up prices, look out for the antique shops tucked away behind the stalls on the Barkhor circuit. Shops like the **Dorje Antique Shop** (Map p92; Dekyi Shar Lam) opposite the Yak Hotel and the **Kyichu Art Gallery** (Map p92) in the Hotel Kyichu offer excellent-quality items at high prices.

Yaks 'n' Nomads Gift Shop (Map p92), in the Pentoc Guesthouse, has some interesting items such as yak tails, knucklebone games, hand-made Tibetan paper, and fabulous kitsch such as *'om mani padme hum'* ('hail to the jewel in the lotus') fridge magnets! It has the best postcards in town, as well as Tibetan calendars.

There are several Tibetan dress shops on Dekyi Shar Lam where you can get a formal Tibetan dress made or buy off the rack. One good place is opposite the Kyichu Hotel.

Most tourist sites and top-end hotels have souvenir shops. Those around the Potala

and the Norbulingka offer a selection of oil paintings by local artists, *thangkas,* antiques, souvenir books and the widest selection of T-shirts in town, although prices have been pushed up by the tour groups. Most shops of this kind are run by Han Chinese from other provinces. Tibetans sell trinkets from blankets outside the Potala and the Lhasa Hotel.

If you need to get customs clearance for an antique you will need to visit the **Cultural Department office** (Wenhua Ju; Map p88-9; Mirig Lam/Minzu Nanlu), just south of the Tibet Museum.

GETTING THERE & AWAY
While there are theoretically a number of ways to get to Lhasa, the main routes (p310) are by air from Chengdu (in Sichuan), by bus from Golmud (in Qinghai), and overland or by air from Kathmandu.

Air
Flying *out* of Lhasa is considerably easier and cheaper than flying in. No permits are necessary – just turn up to the **Civil Aviation Authority of China office** (CAAC; Map pp88-9; ☎ 683 3446; 88 Nyangdren Chang Lam; ⏰ 9.30am-7pm) and buy a ticket. In August and around national holidays (p301), you'd be wise to book your ticket at least a week in advance.

To book a ticket you need to complete a form, get a reservation and then pay the cashier (in cash only). Fares discounted by up to 25% are sometimes available on flights between Kathmandu and Lhasa. You can buy onward tickets from Chengdu here, but not at discounted prices.

If you cancel a ticket, the penalty will depend on how far in advance of travel you cancel. More than 24 hours before departure, the penalty is 5% of the ticket cost (ie you get a 95% refund); two to 24 hours before is 10%; less than two hours before is 20%; and after the flight has departed the penalty is 50%.

There is no TTB permit check on arrival or departure, though you should hold on to your luggage stub as officials check these zealously on arrival.

Bus & Minibus
TO/FROM GOLMUD
The only bus service between Lhasa and the outside world is to Golmud in Qinghai province.

Tickets for sleeper buses from Lhasa to Golmud (p315) can be bought at the main bus station south of the Lhasa Hotel (Y210 to Y250, 24 hours). Buses depart at 8.30am. Check that you don't end up with a nonsleeper bus (Y180). There are also sleeper buses that continue all the way to Xining, the capital of Qinghai province (Y340, 2½ days), and even a 3287km epic ride to Chengdu (Y500, three days and four nights, via Golmud).

TO/FROM NEPAL

There are no longer direct buses to the Nepali border (at Zhangmu), though there are occasional advertisements around in the Tibetan quarter for seats in minibuses or Land Cruisers to Zhangmu. Check with FIT at Snowlands Hotel. These are vehicles that are travelling to pick up groups, so beware: if a tour is cancelled, so is the vehicle (and your booking). Seats cost around Y350 for the two-day trip, normally with an overnight stop at Shigatse.

It's worth checking the empty block of land next to the Gang Gyan Hotel for Land Cruisers and minibuses headed to the Nepali border. Vehicles normally wait here the day before departure. A seat costs around Y250 to Y300.

AROUND TIBET

Buses to popular pilgrim destinations leave early in the morning from the west side of Barkhor Square. Buses leave around 6.30am for Ganden Monastery (Y20 return, 1½ hours), 7am for Samye (Y40, 3½ hours), 7am for Tsurphu Monastery (Y25 return, 2½ hours), and 7.30am for Tsetang (advertised as Shannan, the Chinese name of the county; Y30) and Dranang. Buses depart when full so expect some hanging around.

Services operating from the **main bus station** (Map pp88–9) include those to Shigatse (Y38, 8.30am), Tsetang (Y30, every 30 minutes) and Nagchu (Y63 to Y100, eight hours, 8.30am). It's also possible to buy seats in a Santana car or Land Cruiser to most destinations. Buses to Bayi (Y50 to Y80, 8.30am) and Chamdo (Y230, every five days) are off-limits to foreign travellers. At the time of research, the ticket office was reluctant to sell tickets to foreigners but policies change like the wind. Private buses depart from the front of the main bus station for Samye, Tsetang and Shigatse.

Private buses also leave the city for Shigatse (Y38) from between the Yak and Kirey hotels on Dekyi Shar Lam at around 7am and these are the most popular ways to get to Shigatse. Some are reluctant to take foreigners as the drivers don't have the requisite permits so may charge you a higher fare.

The government bus to Shigatse (Y50) waits west of the Kirey Hotel to pick up passengers at around 8.30am, before heading to the bus station. Buses also depart at the same time for Nagchu (Naqu) and Damxiong from here or in front of the Kirey Hotel. Expect lots of sitting around before the bus leaves.

For Gyantse, you may find a direct bus from the main bus station but you'll most probably have to take a bus to Shigatse and change there. There are buses to Nangartse twice a week (Y35).

The **Eastern Suburbs Bus Station** (Dongjiao Qike Keyunzhan; Map pp88-9) has frequent minibuses to Lhundrub (Linzhou; Y10), for the road to Reting Monastery, and to Meldro Gongkar (Mozhu Gongka; Y10), for visits to Drigung Til Monastery. There are lots of minibuses to Bayi (Y80 to Y100), but at the time of research they were off limits to foreigners. There are also daily buses to Yangpachen (Y15), Damxiong (Y25), Ritok (Y25, 10am), Nyima Jangre (for Drigung, 8am) and Zashu (for Drigung, 9am).

Lhasa's chaotic **Lugu Bus Station** (Map p92) is located southwest of the Barkhor Square and has several departures daily to Medro Gungkar, Lhundrub, Chushul and Nyemo but timings are awkward and information hard to find.

Tibetan Antelope Travel and Transportation Co Ltd (Zanglingyang Luyun Youxian Gongsi; Map p208; ☎ 688 8929, 682 1333; 37 Nyangdren Chang Lam) operates buses between Lhasa and Ali in western Tibet. Buses run every other day at around 7pm and take anywhere from 50 to 60 hours nonstop. Berths cost Y650, Y750 or Y800, depending on the location in the bus (the cheaper berths are at the back and in the upper tier).

The official status of the Antelope bus is quite shaky – the company has permission to operate in Ali prefecture, but not Shigatse prefecture (though it expects to get permission soon). The company claims that passengers don't need travel permits for Ali but that foreigners have to get off at Lhatse and walk around the checkpoint! You can also arrange in advance to board the bus in Shigatse or Lhatse but the fare is the same and you must pay a deposit on your ticket in Lhasa.

The office is four doors to the right of the Ali Prefectural Office (Ali Banshi Chu), which most taxi drivers know. Minibus No 503 goes past here en route to Sera Monastery.

Rental Vehicles
Rental vehicles have emerged as the most popular way to get away from Lhasa in recent years, even though you can still travel along most of the main routes by public transport. The most popular route (p162) is a leisurely and slightly circuitous journey down to Zhangmu on the Tibet–Nepal border, taking in Yamdrok-tso, Gyantse, Shigatse, Sakya, Everest Base Camp and Tingri along the way. Mt Kailash and Nam-tso are also popular destinations.

At the time of research, all Land Cruiser trips were supposed to be organised through FIT (p91), though for trips around the Lhasa region (which require no permits) there is nothing to stop you negotiating with a driver or other travel agency. If you are organising a long trip, then read the advice given on p321.

Prices for Land Cruiser hire (with driver) fluctuate throughout the year depending upon the season, the number of available vehicles and the number of tourists. August and September tend to be the most expensive months in which to hire a vehicle.

A seven-day trip to the Nepali border via Yamdrok-tso, Gyantse, Shigatse, Sakya and Everest Base Camp will cost between Y4500 and Y6000. The price includes permits and guide but doesn't generally include the Y400 vehicle fee to enter the Qomolangma Nature Preserve. A return six-day trip to Everest Base Camp costs around Y4000 to Y4800, or Y3600 one way.

If you are heading to the Yarlung Valley then a three- or four-day trip to Samye, Mindroling Monastery, Tsetang and back again costs Y2500 to Y2800, including a guide and permits.

If independent travel agencies return to the scene, you'll have to talk to other travellers and get the latest on which are most reliable. Remember, it's often worth spending a few hundred yuan extra (it's not much spread between six people) to hire a vehicle from a bigger and more reliable agency.

GETTING AROUND
For those travellers based in the Tibetan quarter of Lhasa, most of the major inner-Lhasa sights are within fairly easy walking distance. Sights such as the Norbulingka over in the west of town, however, mean a long trudge and it's better to take a minibus or hire a bicycle.

To/From Gongkar Airport
Recently renovated Gongkar airport is an inconvenient 95km from Lhasa, though a new US$78 million tunnel and bridge will cut down that distance to 55km by 2005.

CHINESE CHARACTERS
The following Chinese characters may be useful when taking a taxi, as few Chinese drivers know the Tibetan names for even the major sites.

Jokhang	Dazhao Si	大昭寺
Barkhor	Bajiao	八角
Potala	Budala Gong	布达拉宫
Norbulingka	Luobulinka	罗布林卡
Sera Monastery	Sela Si	色拉寺
Drepung Monastery	Zhebang Sì	哲蚌寺
CAAC	Zhongguo Minhang	中国民航
Bank of China	Zhonguo Yinhang	中国银行
Banak Shol Hotel	Balangxue Luguan	八郎学旅馆
Yak Hotel	Yake Binguan	亚客宾馆
Lhasa Hotel	Lasa Fandian	拉萨饭店
Bus Station	Keyun Zhan	客运站

Airport buses (Y35, 90 minutes) leave throughout the day from the courtyard in front of the CAAC building. Staff can tell you which bus to catch if you show them your ticket. There are also buses from Gongkar airport to Shigatse (Y50). From the airport, buses wait for flights outside the terminal building.

A taxi costs around Y200 and can fit three comfortably. Shared taxis sometimes run to and from Gongkar airport for Y25 per person (for four people) but they can be tricky to track down in Lhasa. Try around the CAAC office.

Minibus

Privately run minibuses (Y2) are frequent on Dekyi Shar Lam and if you need to get up to the area around the Lhasa Hotel or the bus station this is the quickest and cheapest way to do it.

Taxi

Taxis are plentiful and charge a standard fare of Y10 to anywhere within the city.

Pedicab

There is no shortage of pedicabs plying the streets of Lhasa, but they are slow and only really useful for short trips (around Y4). If you are heading to the Potala, bear in mind that pedicabs are not allowed to proceed further west than Nyangdren Chang Lam so you'll have to walk half the distance anyway. You'd be better off hiring a bicycle and pedalling yourself around.

Bicycle

Bicycle is without a doubt the most convenient and enjoyable way to get around once you have acclimatised to the altitude. You can hire bicycles at the Banak Shol/ Snowlands hotels for Y2/3 per hour or Y20 per day. No deposit is required if you are a guest of the hotel. Otherwise, you'll have to hand over Y200 to Y400 or your passport.

Bicycle theft is a problem in Lhasa, so be sure to park your bike in the designated areas patrolled by matronly bicycle attendants (Y1). A lock and chain is a good idea.

It is possible to buy mountain bikes in Lhasa. Prices for a Chinese-made bike fluctuate around Y500. Don't expect the quality to be up to international standards, but

some travellers manage to do long trips without having the bikes fall apart.

Good quality bikes, with full suspension, from Thailand cost around Y2400 at **Dark Horse Bicycles** (Map pp88-9; Heima Zixingche; ☎ 683 2483; www.darkhorsebike.com; Lingkhor Chang Lam). It stocks hard-to-find mountain bike parts.

AROUND LHASA

Within easy cycling distance of central Lhasa are the major Gelugpa monasteries of Sera and Drepung. Both are must-sees, even if you have only a brief stay in Lhasa.

DREPUNG MONASTERY འབྲས་སྤུངས

About 8km west of central Lhasa, **Drepung** (Map p120; admission Y55/45, ☼ 9am-5pm) was at one time the world's largest monasteries (see Monasteries in Tibet, p121). The word Drepung literally translates as 'rice heap', a reference to the huge numbers of white monastic buildings that once piled up on the hillside. It suffered through the ages with assaults by the kings of Tsang and the Mongols, but was left relatively unscathed during the Cultural Revolution and there is still much of interest intact. Rebuilding and resettlement continue at a pace unmatched elsewhere in Tibet and the site once again resembles a small village. There is a far greater sense of community here than at Lhasa's other great monasteries.

Interior photography will cost Y20 per chapel. A **restaurant** near the bus stop serves reviving tea for three mao a glass and *momos* (dumplings) for two mao each.

History

Drepung was founded in 1416 by a charismatic monk and disciple of Tsongkhapa called Jamyang Chöje. He was able to raise funds for the project quickly and within a year of completion, the monastery already hosted a population of some 2000 monks.

In 1530 the second Dalai Lama established the Ganden Palace, the palace that was home to the Dalai Lamas until the fifth built the Potala. It was from here that the early Dalai Lamas exercised their control over central Tibet, and the second, third and fourth Dalai Lamas are all entombed here. Today there are around 800 monks in residence.

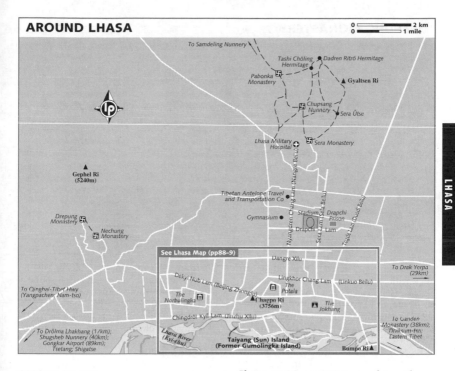

AROUND LHASA

To Samdeling Nunnery

Tashi Chöling Hermitage
Dadren Ritrö Hermitage

Pabonka Monastery

Gyaltsen Ri

Chupsang Nunnery

Sera Ütse

Lhasa Military Hospital

Sera Monastery

▲ Gephel Ri (5240m)

Tibetan Antelope Travel and Transportation Co

Drepung Monastery

Nechung Monastery

Gymnasium ●

Stadium ●

Drapchi Prison

Drapchi Lam

See Lhasa Map (pp88–9)

Dangre Xilu

To Drak Yerpa (29km)

Dekyi Nub Lam (Beijing Zhonglu)

Lingkhor Chang Lam (Linkuo Beilu)

The Potala

The Norbulingka

▲ Chagpo Ri (3756m)

Chingdröl Kyil Lam (Jiezhu Xilu)

The Jokhang

To Ganden Monastery (38km); Drak-um-tso; Eastern Tibet

To Qinghai-Tibet Hwy (Yangpachen; Nam-tso)

To Drölma Lhakhang (1 /km); Shugsheb Nunnery (40km); Gongkar Airport (89km); Tsetang; Shigatse

Lhasa River (Kyi-chu)

Taiyang (Sun) Island (Former Gumolingka Island)

Bumpa Ri ▲

0 — 2 km
0 — 1 mile

GANDEN PALACE

From the car park, follow the kora clockwise around the outside of the monastery until you reach the steps up to the Ganden Palace.

The first hall on the left is the **Sanga Tratsang**, a recently renovated chapel housing statues of the protectors Namse (Vairocana), Nagpo Chenpo, Dorje Jigje, Chögyel (Dharmaraja), Palden Lhamo (on a horse) and the Nechung oracle, all arranged around a central statue of the fifth Dalai Lama.

Head up across the main courtyard, where performances of *cham* (a ritual dance) are still held during the Shötun festival. There is a single chapel on the 1st floor of the main building and above here are three chapels making up the apartments of the early Dalai Lamas. The second of the three chapels has wonderfully detailed **murals** and the throne of the fifth Dalai Lama next to a 1000-armed statue of Chenresig. The third is a bare meditation room.

From here, descend and cross over to a final chapel whose entrance is defaced by a partially removed Cultural Revolution-era

Chairman Mao painting complete with political slogans. Signs lead past a teahouse to the exit to the north.

Main Assembly Hall

The main assembly hall, or *tsogchen,* is the principal structure in the Drepung complex. The hall is reached through an entrance on the west side.

The huge interior is very atmospheric, draped with *thangkas* and supported by over 180 columns, some of which are adorned with ancient armour used for festival dances. **Sculptures** of some interest include a two-storey Jampelyang, accompanied by the 13th Dalai Lama; Sakyamuni; Tsongkhapa; Jamyang Chöje, Drepung's founder, in a cabinet to the right; and Sakyamuni, flanked by five of the Dalai Lamas. At either end of the altar is a group of eight *arhats* (literally 'worthy ones').

The back-room chapel features the protector deities Chana Dorje (Vajrapani, blue) and Tamdrin (Hayagriva, red) and contains statues of Sakyamuni with his two disciples; the Buddhas of the Three Ages; and nine

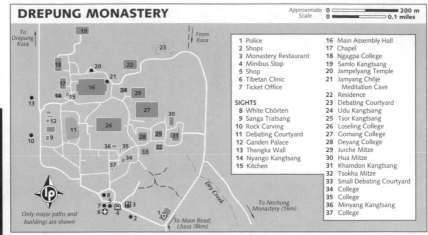

DREPUNG MONASTERY

Approximate Scale 0 — 200 m / 0 — 0.1 miles

To Drepung Kora

From Kora

1 Police
2 Shops
3 Monastery Restaurant
4 Minibus Stop
5 Shop
6 Tibetan Clinic
7 Ticket Office

SIGHTS
8 White Chörten
9 Sanga Tratsang
10 Rock Carving
11 Debating Courtyard
12 Ganden Palace
13 Thangka Wall
14 Nyango Kangtsang
15 Kitchen

16 Main Assembly Hall
17 Chapel
18 Ngagpa College
19 Samlo Kangtsang
20 Jampelyang Temple
21 Jamyang Chöje
       Meditation Cave
22 Residence
23 Debating Courtyard
24 Udu Kangtsang
25 Tsor Kangtsang
26 Loseling College
27 Gomang College
28 Deyang College
29 Jurche Mitze
30 Hua Mitze
31 Khamdon Kangtsang
32 Tsokha Mitze
33 Small Debating Courtyard
34 College
35 College
36 Minyang Kangtsang
37 College

Dry Creek

To Nechung Monastery (1km)

Only major paths and buildings are shown

To Main Road; Lhasa (8km)

LHASA

chörtens above. The walls and pillars are lined with statues of the eight bodhisattvas. To the east is Tsongkhapa. To the left there is also a statue of Lamdrin Rinpoche (a former abbot of Drepung whose photo is one of the most commonly seen in Tibet); next to it is his chörten.

Back by the main entrance, steps lead up to the 1st and 2nd floors. At the top of the stairs to the right is the **Hall of the Kings of Tibet**, featuring the fifth Dalai Lama, and to the left is a chapel containing the head of a two-storey Jampa statue. Pilgrims prostrate themselves here and drink from a sacred conch shell.

Continue moving clockwise through the **Sakyamuni Chapel**, which is stuffed with chörtens, and then descend to the **Chapel of Jampa**. This chapel contains the assembly hall's most revered image, a massive **statue of Jampa**, the Future Buddha, at the age of 12. The statue rises through three floors of the building from a ground-floor chapel that is usually closed, and is joined by Tsongkhapa and by Jamyang Chöje. The chörtens, behind, contain the remains of the second Dalai Lama (at the back) and Jamyang Chöje (at the front). At the front right are statues of seven of the Dalai Lamas.

To the right of the Sakyamuni Chapel is a **Drölma chapel**. Drölma is a protective deity, and in this case the three Drölma images in the chapel (to the immediate right) are responsible for protecting Drepung's drinking water, wealth and authority respectively.

There are also some fine examples of Tibetan Kangyur **scriptures** here. The central statue is a form of Sakyamuni whose amulet is said to contain one of Tsongkhapa's teeth.

Exit the building from the western side of the 2nd floor.

Ngagpa College

Ngagpa is one of Drepung's four colleges, and was devoted to Tantric study. The chapel is dedicated to Dorje Jigje, a Tantric meditational deity who serves as an opponent to the forces of impermanence. The cartoon-style Dorje Jigje image is said to have been fashioned by Tsongkhapa himself. Working clockwise, other statues include Palden Lhamo (second clockwise), Nagpo Chenpo (fourth), Drölma (fifth), Tsongkhapa (sixth), the fifth Dalai Lama (eighth), the Nechung oracle in the corner and, by the door, a small Dorje Drakden (p122). Look for Chögyel to the right with his hand thrusting out of the glass cabinet.

As you follow the pilgrim path (clockwise) around the back of the assembly hall you will pass the small **Jampelyang Temple** where pilgrims peer in to see a holy rock painting and get hit on the back with a holy iron rod. Just a little further tucked in on the right is the tiny **meditation cave** of Jamyang Chöje, with some fine rock paintings.

Loseling College

Loseling is the largest of Drepung's colleges, and studies here were devoted to logic.

The **main hall** houses a throne used by the Dalai Lamas, an extensive library and a long altar decorated with statues of the fifth, seventh and eighth Dalai Lamas, Tsongkhapa and former Drepung abbots. The chörten of Loseling's first abbot is covered with financial offerings. There are three chapels to the rear of the hall. The one to the left houses 16 *arhats* which pilgrims walk under in a circuit. The central chapel has a large image of Jampa and interesting photos of the new and old Nechung oracle; the chapel to the right has a small statue of Sakyamuni.

On the 2nd floor you'll come to a small chapel full of angry deities and then you pass under the body of a stuffed goat draped with one mao notes before entering the *gönkhang* (protector chapel). There are more protective deities here, including Nagpo Chenpo, Dorje Drakden and Dorje Jigje.

Gomang College

Gomang is the second largest of Drepung's colleges and follows the same layout as Loseling. The **main hall** has a whole row of images, including Jampa, red Tsepame, and

the seventh Dalai Lama. Again, there are three chapels to the rear: the one to the left houses three deities of longevity, but more important is the **central chapel**, chock-a-block with images. As at Loseling, there is a single protector chapel on the upper floor. Women are sometimes not allowed into this chapel.

Deyang College

The smallest of Drepung's colleges, this one can safely be missed if you have had enough. The principal image in the main hall is Jampa, flanked by Jampelyang, Drölma, the fifth Dalai Lama and others.

East of here is a cluster of friendly colleges, including the **Jurche Mitze**, once home to students from Inner Mongolia, and the **Khamdon Kangtsang**, the upstairs of which is defaced with faded Mao slogans and images. More buildings sport English signs saying that visitors are welcome.

Before you leave the monastery, pop into the **debating courtyard** west of Loseling College, as the monks sometimes do their music practice here, blowing huge horns and crashing cymbals in the garden (photos Y10).

MONASTERIES IN TIBET

The great Gelugpa monasteries of Drepung, Sera and Ganden were once like self-contained worlds. Drepung, the largest of these monasteries, was home to around 10,000 monks at the time of the Chinese takeover in 1951. Like the other major Gelugpa institutions, Drepung operated less as a single unit than as an assembly of colleges, each with its own interests, resources and administration.

The colleges, known as *dratsang*, were in turn made up of residences, or *kangtsang*. A monk joining a monastic college was assigned to a *kangtsang* according to the region he was born in. For example, it is thought that 60% of monks at Drepung's Loseling College were from Kham, while Gomang college was dominated by monks from Amdo and Mongolia. In total, Loseling had 23 *kangtsang*, but the three most powerful *kangtsang* were all Kham controlled. This gave the monastic colleges a distinctive regional flavour, and meant that loyalties were generally grounded much deeper in the colleges than in the monastery itself.

At the head of a college was the abbot or *khenpo*, a position that was filled by contenders who had completed the highest degrees of monastic studies. The successful applicant was chosen by the Dalai Lama. Beneath the abbot was a group of religious leaders who supervised prayer meetings and festivals, and a group of economic managers who controlled the various *kangtsang* estates and funds. There was also a squad of huge monks known as *dob-dobs*, who were in charge of discipline and administering punishments.

In the case of the larger colleges, estates and funds were often extensive. Loseling College had over 180 estates and 20,000 serfs who worked the land and paid taxes to the monastery. Monasteries were involved in many forms of trade. For the most part, these holdings were not used to support monks – who were often forced to do private business to sustain themselves – but to maintain an endless cycle of prayer meetings and festivals that were deemed necessary for the spiritual good of the nation.

LHASA

Drepung Kora

This lovely kora climbs up to around 3900m and probably should not be attempted until you have had four or five days to acclimatise in Lhasa. The walk takes about an hour at a leisurely pace (it is possible to do it more quickly at hiking speed). Look for the path that continues uphill from the turn-off to the Ganden Palace. The path passes several rock paintings, climbs up past a high wall used to hang a giant *thangka* during the Shötun festival, peaks at a valley of prayer flags and then descends to the east via an encased Drölma statue and several more rock carvings. There are excellent views to be had along the way.

Getting There & Away

The easy way to get out to Drepung is by minibus. Minibuses (Y3) run all day from in front of Barkhor Square (though there aren't many between 11am and 3pm) and cost Y3 to the parking area in front of Drepung. Minibus Nos 301-3 also go there from a block west of Tashi I restaurant, but may just drop you off at the foot of the hill; from there it's a 20-minute walk or a tractor ride. A taxi from the Barkhor is around Y20.

NECHUNG MONASTERY གནས་ཆུང་གྲྭ་ཚང་

Nechung (admission Y5 sometimes; ☎ 9am-4pm) is only 10 minutes' walk downhill from Drepung Monastery. Until 1959, it was the seat of the State Oracle. The oracle at Nechung was the medium of Dorje Drakden, an aspect of Pehar, the Gelugpa protector of the Buddhist state. The Dalai Lamas would make no important decision without first consulting him. In 1959 the State Oracle fled with the Dalai Lama to India, and Nechung is now cared for by a small number of monks.

Nechung Monastery is an eerie place associated with possession, exorcism and other pre-Buddhist rites. Note the blood-red **doors** at the entrance painted with flayed human skins and the scenes of torture along the top of the outer courtyard. For images of Dorje Drakden, the protective spirit manifested in the State Oracle, see the back-room chapel to the left of the main hall. The statue on the left shows Dorje Drakden in his wrathful aspect; the one on the right has him in a more conciliatory frame of mind. In between the two is a sacred tree.

The far right chapel has an amazing **spirit trap** and an image of Ekajati, recognisable by his single fang.

On the 1st floor is an audience chamber (closed at the time of research) with a throne used by the Dalai Lamas when they consulted with the State Oracle. The 2nd floor features a huge new statue of a wrathful Guru Rinpoche. There are fine murals in the exterior courtyard

Nechung is easily visited as a day trip along with Drepung. Bring some lunch.

SERA MONASTERY སེ་ར་དགོན་པ་

Sera Monastery (admission Y55/35; ☯ 9am-5pm), approximately 5km north of central Lhasa, was, along with Drepung, one of Lhasa's two great Gelugpa monasteries. Its once huge monastic population of around 5000 monks has now been reduced to several hundred, and building repairs are still continuing. Nevertheless the monastery is worth a visit, particularly between 3pm and 5pm (not Sundays), when debating is usually held in the monastery's **debating courtyard.** (Chapels start to close at 4pm so it makes sense to see the monastery and then enjoy the debating.)

THE NECHUNG ORACLE

Every New Year in Lhasa until 1959, the Dalai Lama would consult the Nechung oracle on important matters of state. In preparation for the ordeal, the oracle strapped on bracelets in the shape of a human eye and an elaborate headdress of feathers, so heavy that it had to be lifted onto his head by two men.

The oracle then whipped himself into a trance in an attempt to dislodge the spirit from his body. Eyewitness accounts describe how his eyeballs swelled and rolled up into his sockets, and how his mouth opened wide, his tongue curling upward as his face reddened. As he began to discern the future in a steel mirror the oracle would answer questions in an anguished, tortured, hissing voice, which would then be translated for the court by a clerk. After the trance the oracle would faint and have to be carried away.

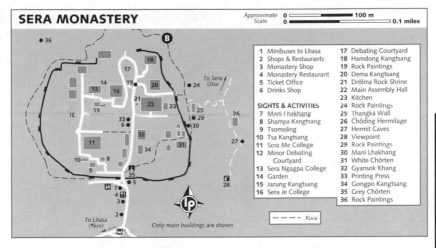

SERA MONASTERY

Approximate Scale   0 — 100 m   0 — 0.1 miles

1 Minibuses to Lhasa
2 Shops & Restaurants
3 Monastery Shop
4 Monastery Restaurant
5 Ticket Office
6 Drinks Shop

SIGHTS & ACTIVITIES
7 Mani Lhakhang
8 Shampa Kangtsang
9 Tsomoling
10 Tsa Kangtsang
11 Sera Me College
12 Minor Debating Courtyard
13 Sera Ngagpa College
14 Garden
15 Jarung Kangtsang
16 Sera Je College

17 Debating Courtyard
18 Hamdong Kangtsang
19 Rock Paintings
20 Dema Kangtsang
21 Drölma Rock Shrine
22 Main Assembly Hall
23 Kitchen
24 Rock Paintings
25 Thangka Wall
26 Chöding Hermitage
27 Hermit Caves
28 Viewpoint
29 Rock Paintings
30 Mani Lhakhang
31 White Chörten
32 Gyansok Khang
33 Printing Press
34 Gongpo Kangtsang
35 Grey Chörten
36 Rock Paintings

To Sera Ütse
To Lhasa (5km)

Only main buildings are shown

- - - - - Kora

LHASA

Interior photography will cost Y30 per chapel; video fees are an outrageous Y850. Once you're inside the monastery walls there are no ticket checks. Near the monastery entrance there is a basic **restaurant**.

History

Sera was founded in 1419 by Sakya Yeshe, a disciple of Tsongkhapa also known by the honorific title Jamchen Chöje. In its heyday, Sera hosted five colleges of instruction, but at the time of the Chinese invasion in 1959 there were just three: Sera Me specialised in the fundamental precepts of Buddhism; Sera Je in the instruction of itinerant monks from outside central Tibet; and Sera Ngagpa in Tantric studies.

Sera survived the ravages of the Cultural Revolution with light damage, although many of the colleges were destroyed.

Sera Me College

Follow the pilgrims clockwise, past the Shampa Kangtsang and Tsa Kangtsang residential halls and several minor buildings, to the Sera Me College. This college dates back to the original founding of the monastery.

The central image of the **main hall** is a copper Sakyamuni, flanked by Jampa and Jampelyang. To the rear of the hall are four chapels. To the far left is a dark chapel dedicated to Ta-og, dharma protector of the east, and Dorje Jigje. Don't miss the **masks** hanging from the ceiling. Women may be refused entry to this chapel.

Continue to the central chapel, which contains statues of the Present, Future and Past Buddhas, as well as 16 *arhats* depicted in their mountain grottos.

The next chapel is home to Miwang Jowo, a Sakyamuni statue that dates from the 15th century and is the most sacred of the college's statues. At the back are Tsepame and eight bodhisattvas. The entrance to the chapel is guarded by the protectors Tamdrin (Hayagriva; red) and Achala (blue). The last chapel is dedicated to Tsongkhapa and there are also images of several Dalai Lamas as well as of Sakya Yeshe, Sera's founder and first abbot.

There are also two chapels on the upper floor. The first, after you mount the stairs, is dedicated to Sakyamuni. The second, approached over a walkway, is a Drölma chapel and has 1000 statues of this protective deity. The third has 1000 statues of Chenresig.

Sera Ngagpa College

A Tantric college, Ngagpa is also the oldest structure at Sera. The **main hall** is dominated by a statue of Sakya Yeshe (wearing a black hat), surrounded by other famous Sera lamas. There are two chapels to the rear of the hall, one with 16 *arhats* and a large Sakyamuni statue and one with a statue of the protective deity Dorje Jigje, as well as Namtöse (Vaishravana), the guardian of the north, to the right, who rides a snow lion and holds a mongoose that vomits jewels. There are also a couple of rooms upstairs featuring Tsepame and the eight medicine buddhas (Menlha).

After exiting, most pilgrims pay a visit to the **Jarung Kangtsang** residential college.

Sera Je College

This is the largest of Sera's colleges. It has a breathtaking **main hall**, hung with *thangkas* and lit by shafts of light from high windows. Several chörtens hold the remains of Sera's most famous lamas.

To the left of the hall is a passage leading, via a chapel dedicated to the Present, Future and Past Buddhas, to the most sacred of Sera Monastery's chapels, the **Chapel of Tamdrin**. Tamdrin (Hayagriva) is a wrathful meditational deity whose name means 'horse headed'. He is the chief protective deity of Sera, and there is often a line of pilgrims waiting to touch their forehead to his feet in respect. Take a look at the weapons hanging from the ceiling. There is a second chapel for him on the upper floor, but here he is in another aspect with nine heads.

The three chapels to the rear of the hall are of less interest. One is devoted to Jampa and the 16 *arhats*, who are depicted in lovely sandalwood statues; the second is dedicated to Tsongkhapa, standing with Sakyamuni and Öpagme (Amitabha); and the third to Jampelyang, who is depicted in the *mudra* (hand position) of turning the Wheel of Law, flanked by Jampa and another Jampelyang.

To the northeast of Sera Je is Sera's **debating courtyard**. There is usually debating practice here in the afternoons from around 3pm to 5pm, which provides a welcome relief from peering at Buddhist iconography. You will hear it (with much clapping of hands to emphasise points) as you approach Sera Je. Foreign photographers circle the site like vultures at a sky burial.

Hamdong Kangtsang

Hamdong served as a residence for monks studying at Sera Je College. The back left chapel contains a bearded image of a Sera lama who died in 1962; in a case to the right is an image of Drölma, who is said to protect Sera's water supply. Look for three **photos of Ekai Kawaguchi**, the Japanese monk who studied here in disguise (p12) in 1901.

As you walk downhill, note the wonderful **rock paintings** of Jampelyang, Chenresig, Chana Dorje (Vajrapani) and Green Tara.

Main Assembly Hall

The main assembly hall is the largest of Sera's buildings and dates back to 1710. The main hall is particularly impressive and is noted for its wall-length *thangkas*. A statue of Jampa is the centrepiece. He is surrounded by other figures including Dalai Lamas on the right, while to the left is the large throne of the 13th Dalai Lama. Behind the throne is a figure of Sakyamuni accompanied by the 13th Dalai Lama and Sakya Yeshe, the founder of Sera.

Of the three chapels to the rear of the hall, the central is the most important, with its 6m-high Jampa statue. The statue rises up to the upper floor, where it can also be viewed from the central chapel. Also on the upper floor (to the far left of the central chapel) is a highly revered statue of a 1000-armed Chenresig. Pilgrims put their forehead to a pole that connects them directly to the heart of the Bodhisattva of Compassion. The pilgrim path enters the building from the back so this may be the first chapel you come across.

Printing press

Before leaving the monastery it's worth having a look at the printing blocks in this new hall. Photos are Y5. Prints made on site are for sale.

Sera Kora

The Sera kora takes less than an hour and is well worth the time. It starts outside the entrance and heads west, following an arc around the monastery walls. On the eastern descent, look out for several brightly coloured **rock paintings**. The largest ones on the eastern side of the monastery are of Dorje Jigje, Tsongkhapa and others. You can cut directly through to here by heading east from the Hamdong Kangtsang. Next to the rock paintings is a support wall used to hang a giant *thangka* during festivals.

A path leads up the side steps of this wall to the **Chöding hermitage**. The hermitage was a retreat of Tsongkhapa, and predates Sera. There is not a great deal to see, but it is a short walk and the views from the hermitage are worthwhile. A path continues south around the hillside past a holy spring to a point that has fine views of Sera and Lhasa beyond.

The kora continues into the monastery complex past two large chörtens.

Sera Ütse

Sera Ütse was another retreat used by Tsong-khapa (his retreat cave can be visited) and is currently home to two monks. It is of more interest than Chöding, but it is also more of a climb. From Sera the walk takes around 1½ hours. To get there, take the path towards Chöding hermitage and branch off to the left before you got there, climbing the ridge via a switchback path until you reach the yellow building perched high above the valley. You can also reach the retreat from Tashi Chöling hermitage (below). These walks should not really be attempted until you have had at least a few days in Lhasa to acclimatise to the altitude. The white granite rock faces of the hills around Sera give off a lot of glare and can make for hot walking, particularly in the summer months, so get an early start and take lots of water.

Getting There & Away

Sera is only a half-hour bicycle ride from the Barkhor area of Lhasa. Leave your bicycle next to the monastery restaurant.

Alternatively, head down to the intersection of Dosenge Lam and Dekyi Shar Lam and catch the No 503 minibuses (Y2, every 10 minutes) from just north of the intersection. Minibus No 502 also runs to Sera.

PABONKA MONASTERY ཕ་བོང་ཁ་དགོན་པ་

Pabonka Monastery (admission free; ☼ dawn-dusk) is one of the most ancient Buddhist sites in the Lhasa region. It is infrequently visited, but is only a one-hour walk from the Sera Monastery turn-off and is well worth the effort.

Built on a flat-topped granite boulder, Pabonka may even predate the Jokhang and Ramoche. It was built in the 7th century by King Songtsen Detsen. The Tibetan king Trisong Detsen, Guru Rinpoche and Tibet's first seven monks all meditated here at various times, and it was also here that a monk named Thonmi Sambhota reputedly invented the Tibetan alphabet. It was destroyed in 841 by the anti-Buddhist King Langdharma and rebuilt in the 11th century. It was restored again by the fifth Dalai Lama, who added an extra floor to the two-storey building. It suffered more damage in the Cultural Revolution and has undergone repairs in recent years.

The first building you come across is the Rigsum Gonpo Temple, whose most famous relic is the carved mantra 'om mani padme hum'. Inside is a fine statue and mural of an 11-headed Chenresig. The inner chapel contains 'self-manifesting' carvings depicting the trinity of Chenresig, Jampelyang and Chana Dorje (Vajrapani), after which the chapel is named.

Continue uphill past the kitchen and a row of chörtens, up to the Pabonka rock (said to represent a female tortoise) to the Palden Lhamo Cave on the west side, where King Songtsen Gampo once meditated. Images inside are of Songtsen Gampo, his two wives, Guru Rinpoche, Trisong Detsen and the protector Palden Lhamo.

Pabonka Potrang is placed on top of the ancient rock. There is nothing to see on the ground floor, but the upper floor has an intimate assembly hall with a picture of the current Pabonka Lama and a 'self-manifesting' Sakyamuni statue hidden behind a pillar to the right. The inner protector chapel holds an ancient conch shell. The four-pillared Kashima Lhakhang next door is lined with various lamas, kings and their wives. The rooftop quarters of the Dalai Lama have a fine statue of the meditational deity Demchok (Chakrasamvara) and offer fine views.

Further above the Pabonka Potrang are the remains of 108 chörtens and the yellow Jasa Podrang, or temple of Princess Wencheng. The two ground-floor rooms are dedicated to five manifestations of Tsongkhapa and the medicine buddhas, and an upper-floor chapel has a small statue of Wencheng herself in the far right. Songtsen Gampo's Nepali wife Bhrikuti is here also, as are images of Green and White Drölma, of whom the two wives are thought to be emanations.

Walks Around the Monastery

A few intrepid (and fit) travellers use Pabonka as a base for walks further afield. The half-day kora around Pabonka, Tashi Chöling hermitage and Chupsang Nunnery makes a nice addition to a visit to Sera Monastery. Midday can be hot here so bring enough water.

For those who aren't so fit, an easier, 20-minute walk from Pabonka leads up to Tashi Chöling hermitage. There's not a lot left to see at the hermitage, but again it has good views. Pilgrims drink holy spring water from the upper chapel before making a kora of the hermitage. To get here from the back of the Pabonka kora, follow the path diagonally up the hillside, following the electricity poles.

From Tashi Chöling, the trail drops down into a ravine and follows this down for 30 minutes to **Chupsang Nunnery**. There are some 80 nuns resident at Chupsang and it's a very friendly place. It's about 40 minutes' walk from the nunnery to the main road into Lhasa.

An alternative route from Tashi Chöling is to hike for 40 minutes northeast up the ravine to the cliffside hermitage of **Dadren Ritrö**. You can see the hermitage from the trail. From here, hikers can follow trails across the ridge for an hour or two to Sera monastery or Sera Ütse.

Keru (or Samdeling) Nunnery is a tough four-hour hike from Tashi Chöling or Pabonka (allow around two hours for the descent). This is a serious day hike and should not be attempted until you are well adjusted to the altitude. Take water with you, though you will probably receive some butter tea from the nuns if you make it to the top. The faint trail heads to the northwest from Tashi Chöling and follows a steep ridge. The nunnery, home to more than 80 nuns, is at an altitude of over 4200m.

Getting There & Away

To get to Pabonka, take a minibus No 503 or 502 to the Sera Monastery turn-off. Rather than take the turn right to Sera, look for a left turn a little up the road before the military hospital. The walk from here is fairly straightforward. You need to make a right turn at a T-junction, but you will see Pabonka up ahead to the left, perched on its granite boulder. The 'monastery' to the right is actually Chupsang Nunnery.

GANDEN MONASTERY དགའ་ལྡན
elev 4500m

Ganden (admission Y25; ⏰ dawn-dusk), just 40km northeast of Lhasa, was the first Gelugpa monastery and has been the main seat of this major Buddhist order ever since. If you only have time for one monastery excursion outside Lhasa, Ganden would probably be the best choice. With its stupendous views of the surrounding Kyi-chu Valley and fascinating kora, Ganden is an experience unlike the other major Gelugpa monasteries in the Lhasa area. It is possible to trek from Ganden to Samye (p271).

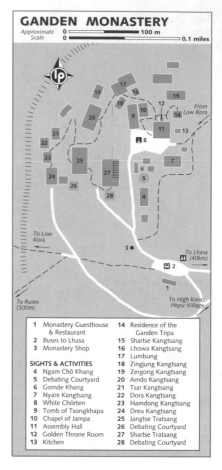

GANDEN MONASTERY

1	Monastery Guesthouse & Restaurant	14	Residence of the Ganden Tripa
2	Buses to Lhasa	15	Shartse Kangtsang
3	Monastery Shop	16	Lhowa Kangtsang
		17	Lumbung
	SIGHTS & ACTIVITIES	18	Zingjung Kangtsang
4	Ngam Chö Khang	19	Zergong Kangtsang
5	Debating Courtyard	20	Amdo Kangtsang
6	Gomde Khang	21	Tsar Kangtsang
7	Nyare Kangtsang	22	Dora Kangtsang
8	White Chörten	23	Hamdong Kangtsang
9	Tomb of Tsongkhapa	24	Dreu Kangtsang
10	Chapel of Jampa	25	Jangtse Tratsang
11	Assembly Hall	26	Debating Courtyard
12	Golden Throne Room	27	Shartse Tratsang
13	Kitchen	28	Debating Courtyard

The monastery was founded in 1409 by Tsongkhapa, who was the revered reformer of the Gelugpa order, after the first Mönlam festival was performed here. Images of Tsongkhapa and his first two disciples, Kedrub Je and Gyatsab Je, are found throughout the monastery. When Tsongkhapa died in 1411, the abbotship of the monastery passed to these disciples. The post came to be known as the Ganden Tripa and was earned through scholarly merit, not reincarnation. It is the Ganden Tripa, not, as one might expect, the Dalai Lama, who is the head of the Gelugpa order.

Ganden means 'joyous' in Tibetan and is the name of the Western Paradise (also known as Tushita) that is home to Jampa, the Future Buddha. There is a certain irony in this because, of all the great monasteries of Tibet, it was Ganden that suffered most at the hands of the Red Guards, possibly because of its political influence. In 1959 there were 2000 monks at Ganden.

Today it is the scene of extensive rebuilding, but this does not disguise the ruin that surrounds the new. The destruction was caused by artillery fire and bombing in 1959 and 1966. New chapels and residences are being opened all the time, so even pilgrims are sometimes unsure in which order to visit the chapels.

Ganden was temporarily closed to tourists in 1996 after violent demonstrations against the government's banning of Dalai Lama photos. The number of monks in Ganden seems to have dropped since then. Interior photography fees are Y20 per chapel; video fees are an amazing Y1500.

Ngam Chö Khang

The first chapel you reach from the parking area is Ngam Chö Khang. It is built on the site of Tsongkhapa's original assembly hall, or *dukhang*, and has a small shrine with images of Tsongkhapa. On the left is a protector chapel, or *gönkhang*, that houses four protective deities. The largest image is of Dorje Jigje.

Debating Courtyard

Southeast of the Gomde Khang residence is the debating courtyard. You should be able to hear the clapping of hands as you pass if there is a debate in progress.

Tomb of Tsongkhapa

The red fortress-like structure of Tsongkhapa's mausoleum, also known as the Serkhang, is probably the most impressive of the reconstructed buildings at Ganden. It's above the prominent white chörten.

The main entrance leads to an ad hoc printing press selling wood blocks. A small chapel is dedicated to Sakyamuni. The protector chapel ahead and to the right is the domain of the protective deity Chögyel (to the far right). Women are not allowed into this chapel.

Exit this building, turn to the left and take the stairs leading to the upper floors. Up the metal stairs is the throne of the Dalai Lamas.

Next to the hall is the Yangchen Khang chapel, which houses Tsongkhapa's tomb. The chapel is named after the stone in the back left, which is said to have flown from India. Both the original tomb and the preserved body of Tsongkhapa inside it were destroyed by Red Guards. The new silver and gold chörten was built to house salvaged fragments of Tsongkhapa's skull. The images seated in front of the chörten are of Tsongkhapa flanked by his two principal disciples. The room also holds several holy relics attributed to Tsongkhapa. Pilgrims line up to buy votive inscriptions written in gold ink by the monks. Hundreds of one-mao notes are stuffed in the grill outside as offerings.

Chapel of Jampa

This small chapel (Jampa Lhakhang), just across from the exit of the Tomb of Tsongkhapa, holds two large images of the Future Buddha, plus the eight bodhisattvas.

Assembly Hall

The recently renovated assembly hall has statues of the 16 *arhats* and two huge statues of Tsongkhapa. Stairs lead up to the inner sanctum, the **Golden Throne Room (Ser Trikhang)**, which houses the throne of Tsongkhapa, where pilgrims get thumped on the back by the yellow hat of the Dalai Lama.

There are two entrances on the north side of the building. The west one gives access to a 2nd-floor view of the Tsongkhapa statue, and the east one houses a library.

Residence of the Ganden Tripa

To the east of the Golden Throne Room and slightly uphill, this residence (also known as Zimchung Tridok Khang) contains another, lesser throne, this time used by the Ganden Tripa. Other rooms include a protector chapel, with statues of Demchok, Dorje Jigje and Gompo; a Tsongkhapa chapel; and the 'Nirvana Room', in which Tsongkhapa died. The upper-floor chapel has a round platform used for creating sand mandalas.

Other Buildings

From here, the pilgrim trail winds through various renovated *kangtsangs,* which offer some good opportunities to meet the local monks away from the tourist trail.

Lumbang Kangtsang is also known as the Amdo Kangtsang. Tsongkhapa himself was from Amdo (modern-day Qinghai), and several monks came from the province to study here. There are some interesting chapels to the rear of the building. To the left of the main chapel you'll find paintings of the 35 confession buddhas.

The other main buildings are the **Jangtse Tratsang**, an active college with an impressive main prayer hall, and the **Shartse Tratsang**, entered from the side, where reconstruction continues.

Ganden Kora

The Ganden kora is a simply stunning walk and should not be missed. There are superb views over strands of the braided Kyi-chu Valley along the way and there are usually large numbers of pilgrims and monks offering prayers, rubbing holy rocks and prostrating themselves along the path.

There are actually two parts to the walk: the high kora and the low kora. The high kora climbs Angkor Ri south of Ganden and then drops down the ridge to join up with the lower kora.

To walk the **high kora**, follow the path southeast of the car park, away from the monastery. After a while the track splits – the left path leads to Hepu village on the Ganden–Samye trek; the right path zigzags up the ridge to a collection of prayer flags. Try to follow other pilgrims up. It's a tough 40-minute climb up to the top of the ridge, so don't try this one unless you're well acclimatised. Here, at two peaks, pilgrims burn juniper incense and give offerings of *tsampa* before heading west down the ridge in the direction of the monastery, stopping at several other shrines en route.

The **low kora** is an easier walk of around 45 minutes. From the car park the trail heads west up and then around the back of the ridge behind the monastery. The trail winds past several isolated shrines and rocks that are rubbed for their healing properties or squeezed through as a karmic test. At one point, pilgrims all peer at a rock through a clenched fist in order to see visions. There are also several rock carvings and a **sky-burial site** along the route.

The sky-burial site is reached shortly before the high point of the trail. Some pilgrims undertake a ritual simulated death and rebirth at this point, rolling around on the ground.

Towards the end of the kora, on the eastern side of the ridge, is **Tsongkhapa's hermitage**, a small building with relief images of Atisha, Sakyamuni, Tsepame and Palden Lhamo. These images are believed to have the power of speech. Above the hermitage is a brilliantly coloured rock painting that is reached by a narrow, precipitous path. From the hermitage, the kora drops down to rejoin the monastery.

Sleeping & Eating

Accommodation at the **Monastery Guesthouse** (dm Y20) is basic but OK and used mostly by trekkers headed to Samye. Toilets are being built out the back. The **restaurant** below has low-grade *thugpa* (Tibetan noodles, Y3) and occasional fried rice.

Just up the road from the car park is a well-stocked **shop** but you're better off bringing some of your own food if staying overnight.

Getting There & Away

Ganden (1¼ hrs, Y20 return) is one of the few sights in Ü that is connected to Lhasa by public transport. At least one bus leaves from in front of the Barkhor Square some time between 6.30am and 7am (a second bus often leaves between 7am and 7.45am), returning around 2pm. Pilgrims usually buy tickets the day before from a **tin shack** (⊙ 3-6pm) near the southeast corner of Barkhor Square, but foreigners can buy tickets on the bus.

On the way back to Lhasa, the public bus normally stops at **Sanga Monastery**, set at the foot of the ruined **Dagtse Dzong** (or Dechen Dzong; *dzong* means 'fort'). There's a fine collection of *cham* masks in the building to the left of the main hall and to the far left is the atmospheric old monastery building. There are some excellent murals but you'll need a torch.

A Land Cruiser for a day trip to Ganden costs around Y400; guides and permits are not required.

DRÖLMA LHAKHANG སྒྲོལ་མ་ལྷ་ཁང་

This small but significant **monastery** (admission free; ⊙ dawn-dusk) is full of ancient relics and hidden treasures. It's only 30 minutes by bus southwest of Lhasa and is worth a stop for those interested in Tibetan Buddhism.

As you take the Lhasa–Tsetang road out of Lhasa, you will pass a blue **rock carving** of the

Medicine Buddha at the base of a cliff about 11km southwest of town. Netang village and the monastery are about 6km further on.

Drölma Lhakhang is associated with the Bengali scholar Atisha (982–1054). Atisha came to Tibet at the age of 53 at the invitation of the king of the Guge kingdom in western Tibet and subsequently travelled extensively in Tibet. His teachings were instrumental in the so-called second diffusion of Buddhism in the 11th century. Drölma Lhakhang was established at this time by one of Atisha's foremost disciples, Drömtonpa, who also founded the Kadampa order, to which the monastery belongs. Atisha died at Netang aged 72.

The monastery was spared desecration by the Red Guards during the Cultural Revolution after a direct request from Bangladesh (which now encompasses Atisha's homeland). Apparently, Chinese premier Zhou Enlai intervened on its behalf.

The entrance and exit of the monastery are both protected by two ancient guardian deities, which may even date back to the 11th-century founding of the monastery.

From the entry, pass into the first chapel, the **Namgyel Lhakhang**, which contains a number of chörtens. The black metal Kadampa-style chörten to the right reputedly holds the staff of Atisha and the skull of Naropa, Atisha's teacher. Statuary includes Atisha and the eight medicine buddhas.

The middle chapel houses a number of relics purported to be associated with Atisha. The statues at the top include an 11th-century statue of Sakyamuni and statues of the 13th Dalai Lama (left), Green Tara, and Serlingpa (right), another teacher of Atisha. A 13th-century statue of Chenresig was allegedly stolen from here recently by art thieves. The central statue behind the grill is an image of Jampa that was reputedly saved from Mongol destruction when it shouted 'Ouch!'. There are also 21 statues of Drölma, after whom the monastery and the chapel are named.

The final Tsepame Chapel has original statues of Tsepame, made with the ashes of Atisha, flanked by Marmedze (Dipamkara), the Past Buddha, the Future Buddha (Jampa), and the eight bodhisattvas. The small central statue of Atisha is backed by his original throne. As you leave the chapel, look out for two sunken white chörtens, which hold Atisha's robes.

Upstairs is the throne room of the Dalai Lama as well as a living room in the far left featuring a fine tree-of-life *thangka* depicting the Gelugpa lineages. To the right is a library.

Really keen *gompa* stompers can plod out a further hour west from Drölma Lhakhang to **Ratö Monastery**. This Gelugpa institution is renowned for its fine wall murals. It is reached via a track that heads west from the main road, south of Drölma Lhakhang.

Getting There & Away

Any bus heading south from Lhasa (eg to Shigatse, Samye Monastery, Tsetang) will take you past the entrance to Drölma Lhakhang. You could also take a minibus from the Lugu Bus Station to Chushul (Y10), but these run mostly in the afternoon so it might be easier to take a city minibus to the traffic roundabout in the western suburbs of Lhasa and then catch the first minibus headed south. Alternatively, visit on the way back from Shigatse or the Yarlung Valley, since you can get back to Lhasa by flagging down anything that comes by.

SHUGSHEB NUNNERY ལྒུག་གཤོངས་ཨ་ནེ་དགོན་པ་

Explorers and hikers will like this adventurous day trip from Lhasa. Getting here involves a bus ride or hitch 30km south of Lhasa and then a seven-hour return hike, though you can probably get a lift in a tractor for part of that.

The nunnery is set in the bowl of the surrounding hills and is home to a small village of 280 nuns. To the left of the main assembly hall is a protector chapel with a stupa-shaped spirit trap. The central hall contains a three-dimensional mandala of Drölma and some statues of Dorje Tsemba, White Tara and several old lamas. Both Nyingma and Dzogchen schools are represented here so you'll see photos of the famed exiled (and deceased) lama Dilgo Khentse. Stairs to the right lead upstairs to a chapel with a statue of Machik Labdronma (holding a double drum), the famous early adept that discovered the valley. There is also a B&W photo of one of her reincarnations.

You can hike up the hill, following the electric poles to the Gangri Tokar shrine (Trubkhang), where Longchenpa, an important 14th-century Dzogchen lama, once meditated.

Getting There & Away

Ten kilometres south of Drölma Lhakhang is a bridge across the Kyi-chu. To get to Shugsheb, cross the bridge and hike or hitch to Nyentha village (which has several shops and a restaurant) and take a right turn, soon branching left up a desert-like side valley.

Continue to the village of Ratö, past a ruined dam and then steeply uphill for 40 minutes to the nunnery, 3½ hours from the main road.

There's a daily bus from Shugsheb to Lhasa but it's of limited use to visitors as it leaves Shugsheb in the morning, returning that afternoon.

Ü དབུས་

CONTENTS

Jewel of ancient kingdoms, stage for would-be conquerors and home of the Dalai Lamas, the province known in Tibetan as Ü has long been the centrepiece of Tibetan culture. Ü is the more easterly of the two central provinces (the other being Tsang) and in modern Chinese terms, Ü consists mainly of Lhasa and Shannan prefecture.

Relic strewn Ü is the historic heartland of all Tibet. Ancient retreats such as Drak Yerpa and the Monkey Cave at Tsetang date to a time of legend and lore. Ganden, Tsurphu and Samye monasteries are some the oldest and most important in the country. Yumbulagang, Tibet's oldest building, sits atop a rocky crag in the Yarlung Valley.

With a gorgeous turquoise hue, Nam-tso, an immense saltwater lake is far and away the region's most popular natural attraction. Large-scale road-building projects have made these sites more accessible to Lhasa and most are visited on two- or three-day trips. Mysterious Lhamo La-tso, a hard-to-reach lake southeast of the capital is the only real challenge for independent travellers.

Travel in the Lhasa region and northern Ü does not require a permit, but if you are headed for Samye and beyond you'll need to get one from the Public Security Bureau (PSB).

For those wanting to bypass the tourist hot spots there's plenty of scope for independent exploration. The wide valley of the Yarlung Tsangpo has numerous side valleys sheltering a wealth of monasteries and settlements that are rarely visited by foreigners. Closer to Lhasa, the Lhundrub Valley has good trails for mountain bikers or hikers with a tent. Travellers with limited time have discovered a gem of a destination in Drigung Til Monastery and the hot springs at nearby Tidrum.

HIGHLIGHTS

- Hire a Land Cruiser to visit the stunning, turquoise, high-altitude lake of **Nam-tso** (p137), ringed with 7000m snowy peaks
- Take a relaxing ferry ride across the Yarlung Tsangpo to **Samye Monastery** (p149), Tibet's first monastery
- Day-trip from Lhasa to **Drak Yerpa** (p139), a cliff-top hermitage of holy caves and chapels
- Trek to and around the holy lake **Lhamo La-tso** (p158), beyond the remote Chökorgye Monastery
- Hike out to **Yumbulagang** (p156), the first building in Tibet, set in the stunning Yarlung Valley

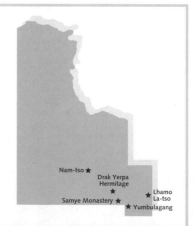

Nam-tso ★
Drak Yerpa
Hermitage
★
Lhamo
La-tso
Samye Monastery ★   ★
★ Yumbulagang

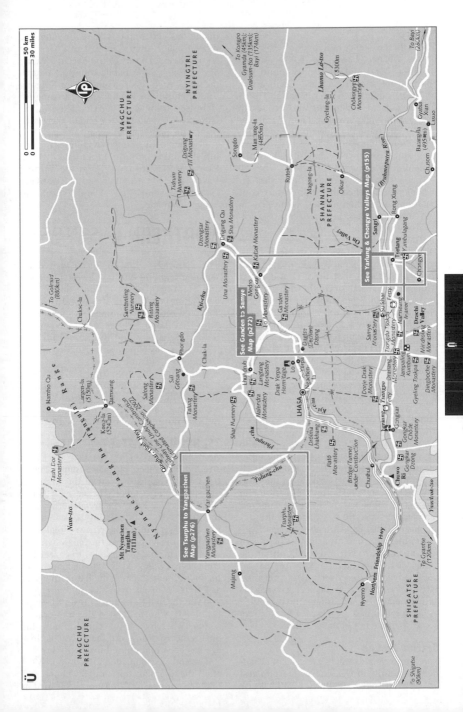

History

The earliest evidence of mankind's existence on the Tibetan plateau are 20,000-year-old fossilised hand and footprints found just 85km from modern Lhasa. Civilization, however, came much later. Central Tibet's first permanent settlements were erected in the Yarlung Valley near Tsetang. Yumbulagang is said to be the oldest building in this area, though there must have been others, long since destroyed, constructed at the same time or earlier.

It was from this valley that the earliest Tibetan kings launched their 6th-century conquest and unification of the Tibetan plateau and ruled from Lhasa for three centuries. Political power later shifted to Sakya and Shigatse in Tsang, but returned to Ü when the fifth Dalai Lama reunited the country with Mongol support in 1642, and again made Lhasa the capital. From that time, Ü and Lhasa witnessed the march of continual aggressors, as described in Peter Hopkirk's book *Tresspassers on the Roof of the World*. The region remained virtually locked out of sight, except for a few hardy explorers, until the Chinese moved in with full force in the 1950s. Because of its proximity to the capital, sacred sites in Ü were the first to be demolished during the Cultural Revolution and likewise the first to be restored in its aftermath.

Climate

The Kyi-chu and Yarlung Tsangpo Valleys, the most populated in Ü, are both prone to high winds and sand storms, but do not suffer the extreme temperature fluctuations experienced in their tributary valleys. In the dead of winter, mean temperatures in the Kyi-chu rarely fall below -10°C. Daytime summer temperatures rise to 20°C, though the dry air means that nights are always cool. Even in summer, cold and overcast weather down low can equate to blizzard conditions at the higher elevations. June through August can see flooding of some river valleys after rain. High-elevation destinations such as Nam-tso and Lhamo La-tso are particularly susceptible to bad weather and are always a few degrees cooler than the rest of the province.

Getting Around

Public transport, except to a few major attractions, is a rarity in Ü. Ganden, Tsurphu and Samye Monasteries are linked with Lhasa by public bus and minibus, as is Tsetang, the nearest major town southeast of Lhasa and a good base for visits to the Yarlung Valley. Several sights have public transport part of the way – eg to Medro Gungkar for Drigung Til, Lhundrub for Reting and Damxung for Nam-tso – from where you can hike or hitch. Otherwise, rented vehicles, hiking and hitching are the only ways to get around.

Ü offers many hiking possibilities including day hikes around Lhundrub (p141), Samye Monastery (p149) and the Yarlung Valley (p155). Two other popular treks are Ganden to Samye (p271) and Tsurphu to Yangpachen (p275).

NORTHERN Ü དབུས་བྱང་

The featured sights are often visited on separate trips: to the northwest (Tsurphu and Nam-tso), north (Lhundrub, Talung and Reting) and east (Tidrum and Drigung Til). You can also combine destinations for a five-day Land Cruiser trip to Nam-tso, Reting Monastery and the Lhundrub Valley, or a six-day trip to Nam-tso, Reting and Drigung Til/Tidrum.

Although you'll need to be self-sufficient in food and have some time, it's possible to get to all the sights in this section through a combination of hitching and hiking. Permits are not required for these sights.

TSURPHU MONASTERY མཚུར་ཕུ་དགོན་པ
elev 4480m

Around 65km west of Lhasa, **Tsurphu Monastery** (admission Y40) is the seat of the Karmapa branch of the Kagyupa order of Tibetan Buddhism. The Karmapa are also known as the Black Hats, a title dating back to 1256, when the second Karmapa was invited to China by the emperor of the Yuan dynasty, Kublai Khan, and presented with a black hat embellished with gold. Said to be made from the hair of holy women, the hat is now kept at Rumtek Monastery in Sikkim, India.

It was the first Karmapa, Dusum Khyenpa (1110–93), who instigated the tradition of *trulku* (whereby a lama could choose his next reincarnation), and the Karmapa lineage has been maintained until this day.

The 16th Karmapa fled to Sikkim in 1959 after the popular uprising in Lhasa and founded a monastery in Rumtek. He died in

THE KARMAPA CONNECTION

Anyone who thinks of the Tibetans as a lofty, spiritually absorbed people should think again. Tibetan history has been dogged by factional intrigue, continuing into the 21st century.

In 1981 the 16th Karmapa died in Chicago. Administration of the Karmapa sect in Sikkim was passed down to four regents, two of whom, Situ Rinpoche and Shamar Rinpoche, have become embroiled in a dispute that has caused a painful rift in the exiled Tibetan community.

At the centre of the dispute is Ogyen Trinley Dorje, the young man who, until late 1999, resided at Tsurphu Monastery – the 17th Karmapa. In early 1992 the four regents announced the discovery of a letter written by the 16th Karmapa that provided critical clues as to the whereabouts of his reincarnation. Curiously, just a month later, one of the regents was killed in a car crash in Sikkim. The local press declared 'suspicious circumstances', but these allegations were never investigated, apparently at the request of figures close to the regent.

Two weeks after the accident, Shamar Rinpoche announced that the mystery letter was a fraud, but it was too late. By early June clues from the letter had been deciphered, Ogyen Trinley Dorje had been found in eastern Tibet and the Dalai Lama had made a formal announcement supporting the boy's candidature.

Shamar Rinpoche opposed the Dalai Lama's decision and began a letter-writing campaign. Meanwhile, the Chinese authorities formally enthroned the 17th Karmapa at Tsurphu, using the occasion to announce that they had a 'historical and legal right to appoint religious leaders in Tibet'. In March 1994, Shamar Rinpoche announced that he had discovered the rightful reincarnation, a boy named Tenzin Chentse (also known as Thaye Dorje) who had been spirited out of China to Delhi. In December 1999, the then 14-year-old 17th Karmapa dramatically fled Tibet into India. In a letter left behind at Tsurphu he told the Chinese he was going to collect the Black Hat of the Karmapa (taken to India by the 16th Karmapa when he fled Tibet in 1959), as well as several relics, including a human skull encased in silver.

The stakes are high. The Karmapa sect has assets estimated to be worth US$1.2 billion and up to one million followers, including many in the USA. Both Karmapas have received death threats. Sikkim's Rumtek Monastery (now the head Karmapa monastery) was briefly occupied in 1993 by Indian troops to break up brawling by monks divided over the issue.

The flight of the Karmapa was a particular blow for the Chinese. The Karmapa ranks as the third-most important lama in Tibet after the Panchen Lama and the Dalai Lama. Moreover, with the recognition of the Chinese-backed Reting Rinpoche disputed by Dharamsala, the Karmapa is the only high-level reincarnation recognised by both the Chinese and Tibetan authorities. China's fury over the escape was levelled at the Karmapa's tutor Yongzin Nyima who spent 15 months in jail for his alleged involvement.

For the moment, at least, there is a stalemate. The Karmapa has been granted refugee status and residence at the Gyuto Monastery in Dharamsala, but the Indian authorities, in an attempt to avoid a political dispute with China, have not allowed him to travel to Rumtek (China does not recognise India's claim to Sikkim).

For more on the starkly differing viewpoints, see the pro-Karmapa website at www.rumtek .org and the pro-Shamar Rinpoche sites at www.karmapa.org and www.karmapa-issue.org.

1981 and his reincarnation, Ogyen Trinley Dorje, an eight-year-old Tibetan boy from Kham, was announced amid great controversy by the Dalai Lama and other religious leaders in 1992. In December 1999, the 17th Karmapa undertook a dramatic escape from Tibet into India (see above). The departure of the Karmapa slowed pilgrim traffic (and also pilgrim donations) to a near halt, leaving the place unkempt and with an air of desolation.

Tsurphu has an annual festival around the time of the Saga Dawa festival in the fourth lunar month of the Tibetan calendar. There is plenty of free-flowing *chang* (Tibetan barley beer), as well as ritual *cham* dancing by monks and lamas.

History

Tsurphu was founded in the 1180s by Dusum Khyenpa, some 40 years after he established the Karmapa order in Kham, his birthplace.

It was the third Karmapa monastery to be built, and after the death of the first Karmapa, it became the head monastery for the order.

The Karmapa order traditionally enjoyed strong ties with the kings and monasteries of Tsang, a legacy that proved a liability when conflict broke out between the kings of Tsang and the Gelugpa order. When the fifth Dalai Lama invited the Mongolian army of Gushri Khan to do away with his opponents in Tsang, Tsurphu was sacked (in 1642) and the Karmapa's political clout effectively came to an end. Shorn of its political influence, Tsurphu nevertheless bounced back as an important spiritual centre and is one of the few Kagyupa institutions still functioning in the Ü region. When Chinese forces invaded in 1950, around 1000 monks were in residence. Now there are about 300 monks.

Viewing the Monastery

The large **assembly hall** in the main courtyard houses a chörten (stupa) containing relics of the 16th Karmapa, as well as statues of Öpagme (Amitabha) and Sakyamuni (Sakya Thukpa), the Historical Buddha.

Walking west (clockwise) around the monastery complex you come to the **protector chapel** (*gönkhang*) of the main hall. There are five main rooms, all stuffed to the brim with wrathful deities.

The first room is dedicated to Tsurphu's protector deity, an aspect of blue Nagpo Chenpo (Mahakala) called Bernakchen. There are also statues of Palden Lhamo (Shri Devi) and Tamdrin (Hayagriva).

The third room features a wrathful form of Guru Rinpoche and the fourth room the Kagyu protector Dorje Phurba holding a ritual dagger. The fifth room contains a statue of Tseringma, a protectress associated with Mt Everest, on a snow lion.

The large building behind the *gönkhang* is the **Serdung Chanpo**, which served as the residence of the Karmapa. It is sometimes possible to go into the upper chapels featuring new statues of all 16 previous Karmapas.

The **Lhakhang Chenmo**, which is to the right of the Serdung Chanpo, houses a new – and remarkably ugly – 20m-high statue of Sakyamuni (Sakya Thukpa); this replaced a celebrated 13th-century image destroyed during the Cultural Revolution.

Behind the Serdung Chanpo and Lhakhang Chenmo is the sprawling **Chökang Gang Monastery**, the residence of the regent of Tsurphu.

An assembly hall accessed from a side entrance just by the main western entrance, has statues of Sakyamuni, flanked by Jampa (Maitreya) and Guru Rinpoche, and protected by blue Nagpo Chenpo (Mahakala) and red Tamdrin (Hayagriva).

Tsurphu Kora

The Tsurphu kora, a walk of two or three hours, is quite taxing if you are not acclimatised to the altitude. It winds up some 150m, providing splendid views of Tsurphu below. Above the monastery are some meditation retreats and traces of rock paintings. You may not have time for the kora if you have to return to Lhasa on the public minibus.

To follow this kora take the road west of Tsurphu and bear left. Ahead is a turn-off that snakes uphill, eventually to the top of the ridge overlooking the monastery. From here the trail is fairly obvious, descending eastward down the ridge into a gully before returning to the entrance of Tsurphu.

Sleeping

The small **Monastery Guesthouse** (dm Y25), opposite the main assembly hall and overlooking the polluted stream, has damp and dark dorm rooms with four or six beds on concrete floors.

Getting There & Away

About 40km outside of Lhasa, the road to Tsurphu crosses the Tolung-chu at the incomplete railroad bridge. From here it's another 25km up a rough dirt track to the monastery.

A minibus goes to Tsurphu (Y15/25 one way/return, 2½ hours) from Barkhor Square in Lhasa around 7am, leaving when full. It heads back to Lhasa at around 2pm, but you'll need to confirm this with the driver.

If you can't find a bus at the Barkhor, another possibility is the nearby Lugu Bus Stand.

You could hire a Land Cruiser for Y400 to Y600 return, or even tag a visit here onto a trip to Nam-tso. You should organise this in advance with your travel agency. Some will let you detour to Tsurphu for free, others will add up to Y150 to the price of the tour.

CRAIG PERSHOUSE

Sera Monastery (p122)

Monks, Drepung Monastery (p118)

CRAIG PERSHOUSE

RICHARD I'ANSON

Pilgrims, Sera Monastery
(p122)

ALISON WRIGHT

Monk making tea, Drepung Monastery
(p118)

RICHARD I'ANSON

Monk standing by prayer wheels, Ganden Monastery (p126)

CRAIG PERSHOUSE

Statue of Chenresig
(Avalokiteshvara; p96), Lhasa

Jewellery seller, Drepung
Monastery (p118)

RICHARD I'ANSON

Ganden Monastery (p126)

RICHARD I'ANSON

NAM-TSO གནམ་མཚོ

elev 4718m

Nam-tso, approximately 240km northwest of Lhasa, is the second-largest saltwater lake in China, the largest is Koko Nor (Qinghai Lake) in Qinghai province. It is over 70km long, reaches a width of 30km and is 35m at its deepest point. The Nyenchen Tanglha (Tangula) range, with peaks of more than 7000m, towers over the lake to the south – it was these mountains that Heinrich Harrer and Peter Aufschnaiter crossed on their incredible journey to Lhasa.

When the ice melts in late April, the lake is a miraculous shade of turquoise and there are magnificent views of the nearby mountains. The wide open spaces, dotted with the tents of local *drokpas* (nomads), are intoxicating.

Whatever you do, however, do not sign up for a lift out here until you have been in Lhasa for at least a week. It is not unusual for visitors to get altitude sickness on an overnight stay out at the lake. The sudden altitude gain of 1100m is not to be treated lightly. It's also a good idea to ensure that your driver has a snow shovel and tow rope, as sudden storms can block the mountain passes into Nam-tso.

Travellers heading into the area have to pay an entry fee of Y40 per person. Hang onto your ticket for the drive out or you may have to pay twice.

Those seeking detailed information on Nam-tso should refer to *Divine Dyads: Ancient Civilization in Tibet* by John Vincent Bellezza.

Tashi Dor Monastery བཀྲ་ཤིས་མདོ་དགོན་པ

Most travellers head for Tashi Dor, situated on a hammerhead of land that juts into the southeastern corner of the lake. Here at the foot of two wedge-shaped hills are a couple of small chapels, with views back across the clear turquoise waters to the huge snowy Nyenchen Tanglha massif (7111m).

This 'monastery' is really just a small chapel to the east of the accommodation area. Inside is an image of the local deity, Nyenchen Tanglha, which has its roots in Bön belief and resides in the nearby mountain of the same name. (It is also the protector of Marpo Ri, on which the Potala is built.) There are several other chapels and retreats honeycombed into the rock face.

There are some fine walks in this area. The short **kora** takes less than an hour. It leads off west from the accommodation area to a chapel hidden behind a large splinter of rock. The trail continues round to a rocky promontory of cairns and prayer flags, where pilgrims undertake a ritual washing, and then continues past several caves and a *chaktsal gang* (prostration point). The twin rock towers here look like two hands in the *namaste* greeting and are connected to the male and female attributes of the meditational deity Demchok (Chakrasamvara). Pilgrims squeeze into the deep slices of the nearby cliff face as a means of sin detection. They also drink water dripping from cave roofs, and some ingest 'holy dirt'.

From here the path curves around the shoreline and passes a group of ancient rock paintings, where pilgrims test their merit by attempting to place a finger in a small hole with their eyes closed. Nearby is a footprint of Guru Rinpoche. At the northeastern corner of the hill is the Mani Ringmo, a large *mani* (prayer) wall at whose end is a crumbling chörten with a *chakje* (handprint) of the third Karmapa. From here you can hike up to the top of the hill for good views.

If you have enough time it's well worth walking around the larger of the two hills. There are superb views to the northeast of the Nyenchen Tanglha (Tangula) range, which marks the modern border between Tibet and Amdo.

Another main attraction of a trip to Nam-tso is the opportunity to get a peek at the otherwise inaccessible nomadic life of the Changtang, Tibet's vast northern plateau. You may get the opportunity to stop at the brown or black spider-like tents of nomads. Make sure you are not forcing anyone's hospitality, and watch out for vicious dogs.

Trekking to Nam-tso

You can also reach Nam-tso from Damxung via the Kong-la (5240m). This is a demanding and remote route and is best done with a guide. It takes about two days to reach the southern shore of the lake at Tashi Dor. There are many good camping places here but the only water comes from the lake, which is slightly brackish.

Cyclists heading to Nam-tso would be better off travelling on the main road via Largen-la (5150m), following the road up

NOMADS

The *drokpas* (nomads) of Tibet travel in groups of up to 20 or more families. Traditionally at home on the inhospitable Changtang plateau, most travellers come into contact with *drokpas* on the fringe of this barren landscape, at Nam-tso. *Drokpas* live in four-sided yak-hair tents, which are usually shared by one family, though a smaller subsidiary tent may be used when a son marries and has children of his own.

The interior of a nomad tent holds all the family's possessions. There will be a stove for cooking and boiling water. The principal diet of the nomad people is *tsampa* (roasted-barley flour) and yak butter (mixed together with tea), dried yak cheese and sometimes yak meat. The tent will also house a family altar dedicated to Buddhist deities and various local protectors, including those of the livestock, tent pole and hearth.

Tending the herds of yaks and sheep is carried out by the men during the day. Women and children stay together in the camp, where they are guarded by one of the men and the ferocious Tibetan mastiffs that are the constant companions of Tibet's nomads. The women and children usually spend the day weaving blankets and tanning sheep skins.

Nomads graze their herds through the summer months and into late autumn. By this time the herds should be strong and healthy, and with the onset of winter it is time to go to the markets of an urban centre. The farmers of Tibet do the same, and trade between nomads and farmers provides the former with *tsampa* and the latter with meat and butter. Most nomads these days have a winter home base and only make established moves to distant pastures during the rest of the year.

Nomads' marriage customs differ from those of farming communities. When a child reaches a marriageable age, inquiries are made, and when a suitable match is found the two people meet and exchange gifts. If they like each other, these informal meetings may go on for some time. The date for a marriage is decided by an astrologer, and when the date arrives the family of the son rides to the camp of the prospective daughter-in-law to collect her. On arrival there is a custom of feigned mutual abuse that appears to verge on giving way to violence at any moment. This may continue for several days before the son's family finally carry off the daughter to their camp and she enters a new life.

The nomads of Tibet have also traditionally traded in salt, which is collected from the Changtang (northern plateau) and transported south in bricks, often to the border with Nepal, where it is traded for grain. These annual caravans are fast dying out. Traditional life suffered its greatest setback during the Cultural Revolution when nomads were collectivised and forcibly settled by the government. In 1981 the communes were dissolved and the collectivised livestock divided equally, with everyone getting five yaks, 25 sheep and seven goats.

Drokpas now number around 2 million, half of their pre-1950 population. Government incentives and increased fenced areas for Chinese-owned ranches are forcing the settlement of nomads, further reducing their numbers and grazing grounds. The scarcity of land has caused infighting with several instances of shooting deaths. Pressure also comes in the form of enforced migration dates and winter housing, as well as attitude changes within the *drokpa* themselves as young people are fleeing the grasslands in search of a 'better life' in urban centres. How far into the 21st century their way of life will persist is a matter for debate among Tibetologists.

from Damxung. The dirt road is raised and easy to follow, those tempted to take a short cut across the plains to Tashi Dor invariably get mired in the muck.

Keep in mind that trekking on the vast northern plains of the Changtang demands special preparation, as this is the coldest, most windswept and most unpredictable part of Tibet. Blizzards can hit even in the middle of summer.

Sleeping & Eating

The good news is that there are now at least two places to stay at Tashi Dor. The bad news is that development has brought generators, motorbikes and rising levels of rubbish – all of which are beginning to take their toll. Carry out whatever you bring in. There is still no toilet at Tashi Dor, so bury faecal waste and burn your toilet paper. Bedding is provided at all places but nights can get very cold, so it's a good idea to bring a sleeping bag and warm clothes.

Tashi (dm Y25, tent Y160) Offering the best accommodation near the lake, Tashi has white cotton tents decked out in traditional Tibetan furnishings. The four-bed dorms housed in concrete and tin boxes are, however, nothing to write home about. In summer, it might be able to rent horses and yaks for a negotiable Y50 per hour.

Byama (dm Y25, tent Y100) Guesthouse offering similar services to the next-door neighbour Tashi, with less elaborate tent accommodation. During the low season, this might be the only option.

There is good camping 100m west of the monastery at the foot of the cliffs. You can get boiled lake water (there's no taste of salt) at the canteen for Y2 a flask. Some travellers have been invited to sleep at Tashi Dor itself – a donation of Y10 is appropriate for the bed and hospitality. Others have stayed with local families who charge about Y20 per day for meals and tent accommodation.

A **canteen** (dishes Y10-15) to the left of the two guesthouses offers *thugpa* (a traditional noodle dish) and veggie dishes at slightly inflated prices.

If it's late, there are two decent hotels in Damxung, the dumpy roadhouse town that serves as a gateway to Nam-tso.

Tianhu Hotel (☎ 0891-611 2171; Nam-tso Rd; dm/d Y35/80) Unmistakeable lime-green tile building by the turn-off from the highway to the old Nam-tso bridge with reasonably clean rooms with TV. You can write off the electric heaters (in the double rooms) as useless. The bathroom at the end of the hall offers little scope for washing but you can hose yourself off at an outside bathhouse (Y5) 50m south on the main road.

Jin Zhu Hotel (☎ 0891-611 2788; main hwy; dm/d/tr/ste Y30/180/120/480) Located 100m north of the Tianhu Hotel, this is the best place to stay in Damxung, with clean rooms heated by radiator. Individual bathrooms have bathtub and sporadic hot water, while the three-bed dorms use a bathroom down the hall. Purified water coolers in each room are a rare bonus.

Tianhu Restaurant (☎ 0891-611 2083; Nam-tso Rd; dishes Y20) Below the Tianhu Hotel, this place doles out filling Chinese meals.

There are several Muslim noodle joints as you enter the town from the south.

Namtso Qu, the local government centre 25km east of Tashi Dor, also has a basic guesthouse with cheap rooms.

Getting There & Away

There is no public transport to Nam-tso. Most travellers get a group together and hire a Land Cruiser for the five- or six-hour drive from Lhasa. The price for a two-day return trip is around Y1500 (Y300 to Y400 per person). Many groups also stop off at the concrete hot-spring pools at Yangpachen (entry Y40) or Tsurphu Monastery or both, often for no extra charge. It's possible to return to Lhasa via Reting Monastery and either Drigung Til or the Lhundrub Valley, making for an interesting and adventurous loop, for around Y2800.

The nearest town to Nam-tso that is linked to Lhasa by public transport is Damxung (Dangxiong) on the Qinghai–Tibet Hwy. One daily bus departs for Damxung from the Lhasa main bus station at 8.30am (Y35, 2¾ hours). A second bus may be available in the high season. You could also ask for a Nagchu-bound bus as far as Damxung; one of these will depart at 7.30am from a curb-side bus stop 100m west of the Yak Hotel.

From Damxung, you have the option of hitching or trekking out to the village of Namtso Qu or to Tashi Dor Monastery, 66km away. By road it's 11km to the check post where you pay the entry fee, a further 17km to Largen-la and then a circuitous 38km to Tashi Dor. Some travellers have been lucky and hitched lifts with trucks or even jeeps, but it seems that most end up walking at least half the way since most traffic heads for Namtso Qu, not Tashi Dor. The gravel road is bumpy but easy to follow and navigable even in poor weather.

From Damxung, private minibuses (Y25) depart for Lhasa from the Tianhu restaurant half-hourly until noon. You can get a seat in a taxi (Y40) from the same place until around 6pm.

Some intrepid travellers have made it out to Nam-tso on a mountain bike, though the shiny wheels seem to drive most nomads' dogs even more berserk than normal.

DRAK YERPA བྲག་ཡེར་པ

For those with a particular interest in Tibetan Buddhism, Drak Yerpa hermitage, about 30km northeast of Lhasa, is one of the holiest cave retreats in Ü. Among the many ascetics who have sojourned here are Guru Rinpoche and Atisha (Jowo-je), the Bengali Buddhist who spent 12 years proselytising in Tibet. King Songtsen Gampo also meditated in a cave here, after his Tibetan wife established the first of Yerpa's chapels. The site is deeply peaceful and has stunning views.

At one time the hill at the base of the cave-dotted cliffs was home to Yerpa Drubde Monastery, the summer residence of Lhasa's Gyutö College at the Ramoche Temple. The monastery was destroyed in 1959, and more destruction occurred during the Cultural Revolution.

Monks have begun to return to Yerpa (there are currently 14) but numbers are strictly controlled by the government, which tore down several 'unauthorised' chapels as recently as 1998.

The Caves

The first building most people come to is the kitchen. Next door is the **Lhalung-puk**, the cave where the monk Lhalung meditated after assassinating the anti-Buddhist king Langdharma.

Above this and to the right is the **Dawa-puk** (Moon Cave), where Guru Rinpoche (which is the main statue) is said to have spent seven years. Watch out for the painting of Ekajati (Tsechigma) to the left and the footprints of Guru Rinpoche and Lhalung to the right.

Heading west, climb to the **Chögyal-puk**, the Cave of Songtsen Gampo. The interior chapel has a central 1000-armed Chenresig (Avalokiteshvara) statue known as Chaktong Chentong. As you start to walk around the central pillar look for the eyes of a 'self-arising' lion face. A small cave and statue of Songtsen Gampo are in the right-hand corner.

The yellow **Jampa Lhakhang** has a two-storey statue of Jampa flanked by Chana Dorje (Vajrapani) to the left and Namse (Vairocana) and Tamdrin (Hayagriva) to the right. Other statues are of Atisha (Jowo-je) flanked by the fifth Dalai Lama and Tsongkhapa.

The upper cave is the **Drubthub-puk**, recognisable by its black overhang. Continue to the **Atisha Zim-puk**, the cave where Atisha meditated. Around here are several caves dedicated to Chana Dorje, which were the first in the complex to be rebuilt.

Below the main caves and to the east is the **Neten Lhakhang**, where the practice of worshipping the 16 *arhats* (worthy ones) was first introduced. Below here is where Atisha is said to have taught. Further east is the holy mountain of Yerpa Lhari, topped by prayer flags and encircled by a kora.

There are several caves and retreats higher up the cliff face to explore if you have time.

Sleeping

It is often possible to stay in one of the caves (normally the Dawa-puk). You can sleep on the cushions provided, but you'll need a sleeping bag and preferably a mat. The caretaker is very kind and can provide boiling water and tea. If you are allowed to stay make an offering of Y10 to Y15 per person. Drinks and instant noodles may be available, but it's best to bring your own supplies and a little extra to offer to the monks. Water comes from a spring below the caves.

Getting There & Away

The caves are accessed via the village of Yerpa, 20km east of Lhasa on a good road that climbs above the hydroelectric power station before crossing the low Ngachen-la.

From Yerpa, a rough dirt road cuts up the valley for 6km to the village of Lo, passing two ruined *dzongs* (forts) and a large disused dam. The walking path above the village heads northwest for 4km up a steep hillside to a large white chörten, beyond which the caves and chapels are in clear view. It takes 1½ hours to reach the caves from Lo and about ¾ hour to come down. Drivers charge Y250 for a round trip from Lhasa to Lo, including four hours' waiting time.

Without a Land Cruiser, it's possible to hitch out of Lhasa on Ngachen Lam to the village of Yerpa, or squeeze into a Lhundrub-bound bus from the Eastern Suburbs Bus Station in Lhasa. From Yerpa traffic is sparse and you will probably have to hike for 1½ hours to Lo village.

An alternative onward route from Yerpa is to walk three hours east to Dagtse bridge, over the Kyi-chu. From the northern shore you could hitch to Lhundrub and Reting Monastery. From the southern shore you can take a minibus back to Lhasa from Dagtse or continue on to Ganden Monastery or Drigung Til.

LHUNDRUB VALLEY སྦྲུན་གྲུབ་གླུང་

☎ 0894 / elev 3800m

Few travellers get here, although it would be a great destination for mountain bikers. This lovely valley, also known in Tibetan as Phenpo, is around 65km from Lhasa, linked by public transport and dotted with interesting monasteries, so it offers plenty of scope for adventurous do-it-yourself exploration. Nalendra and Langtang Monasteries are two of the easiest to visit in the valley.

Lhundrub ལྷུན་གྲུབ་

The main town in the valley is Lhundrub (Chinese: Linzhou), which serves as a useful base. The northwestern section of town has the main shops, the centre has the Ganden Chökhorling Monastery, and the southeast has a couple of Muslim restaurants and the bus station.

There are no luxuries at **Bus Station Hotel** (☎ 612 2354; d Y30), but it's a passable place to stay in the southeast of town. The outside toilets are in the bus yard below the hotel.

Buses to Lhundrub (Y12, 75km, one hour 10 minutes) run from Lhasa's Lugu and Eastern Suburbs Bus Stations, departing when full. The last bus back to Lhasa returns in the early afternoon but you might still find a ride after that.

Nalendra Monastery ན་ལེན་ཏྲ་དགོན་པ་

Ruins still dwarf the rebuilding work at Nalendra Monastery founded in 1435 by Rongtongpa, a contemporary of Tsongkhapa, the 14th-century founder of the Gelugpa order and Ganden Monastery. It was largely destroyed in 1959.

To get an idea of the original layout, look closely at the mural on the immediate left as you enter the **main assembly hall**. The *gönkhang* (women are forbidden to enter) has a central Gompo Kur, a form of Nagpo Chenpo (Mahakala) and protector of the Sakyapa school, as well as statues of Pehar and Namse (Vairocana; in the left corner on a snow lion). Look for the three huge wild yak heads in varying states of decay. The main hall has a statue of Rongtongpa in a glass case. The inner sanctum features Rongtongpa, flanked by two Sakyapa lamas, and an inner kora.

Nalendra and Langtang Monasteries are an excellent half-day trip by tractor (Y50 to Y100) or by motorbike (Y80 per bike); both

are available for hire if you ask around in Lhundrub. A Land Cruiser connects Lhundrub and Nalendra in 25 bone-crunching minutes.

Alternatively, you can walk to Nalendra from Lhundrub in a day, stopping at Langtang en route. From Lhundrub bus station head south over the bridge and follow the tracks as they swing west parallel to the mountain ridge, or head due west out of town from the Bus Station Hotel. You can see the former road to Lhasa snaking up the mountainside to the south.

Langtang Monastery གླང་ཐང་དགོན་

On the way back from Nalendra it's worth stopping off at Langtang Monastery, visible from afar because of its huge Kadampa-style chörten. The monastery was founded in 1093 and once had 200 monks. Today only two chapels and the ruins of the main assembly hall remain, served by 33 monks. Like Nalendra, Langtang was built as a Kadampa monastery but was subsumed into the Sakyapa school. The main hall has a central statue of Jampa (Maitreya) the future Buddha with Sakya Pandita (Kunga Gyaltsen 1182–1251) to the left, plus, to the right, a small statue of Drölma (Tara) that is said to have the power of speech. The building to the left is a protector chapel which has a central image of Langtangpa, who was the 11th century founder of the monastery. To the far right are some lovely old texts in gold leaf, recovered from the nearby chörtens when they were dynamited by the Chinese.

For information on reaching Langtang Monastery, see directions to the Nalendra Monastery (left).

Other Monasteries

From Nalendra it's also possible to hike half a day to **Shar Nunnery** on the northwestern side of the valley, sleep the night there and return the next day to Lhundrub via **Nakar Monastery**. You will need a sleeping bag and food. A tent would be a sensible backup.

Other monasteries worth exploring at the northern end of the valley include **Lhundrub Dzong** and **Nisu Monastery**, the latter visible from the main road and recognisable by its row of eight chörtens. At the head of the valley the road switchbacks up to Chakla and then drops down towards Talung Monastery.

TALUNG MONASTERY སྟག་ལུང་དགོན་པ་
elev 4150m

Dynamited by Red Guards and now in ruins in the green fields of the Pak-chu Valley, the sprawling monastic complex of Talung (Taglung), is around 119km north of Lhasa by road. Rebuilding is being undertaken, but not on the scale of other more important monasteries in the area.

Talung was founded in 1228 as the seat of the Talung school of the Kagyupa order. At one time it may have housed some 7000 monks (it currently has 118), but was eventually eclipsed in importance and grandeur by the Riwoche Monastery in eastern Tibet.

The site's most important structure was its **Tsuglhakhang** (grand temple), also known as the Red Palace of Talung. The building was reduced to rubble but its thick stone walls remain. To the south in the main monastery building are the Jagi Lhakhang and the Choning Lhakhang, which has some fine *cham* masks and a statue of a bearded Tashipel, one of the structure is the rebuilt Targye Lhakhang. Look out for the destroyed set of three chörtens, one of which was the funeral chörten of Dromtonpa, the founder of Reting Monastery.

Down in the centre of the village is the renovated Tashikang Tsar, the residence of the local *rinpoche*.

A half-hour walk north of the turn-off to Talung brings you to **Sili Götsang**, an amazing eagle's-nest hermitage perched high above the valley. At the base of the cliff face are several long *mani* (prayer) walls and *drokpa* tents.

If you need to spend the night, there is a small **guesthouse** (dm Y20) at Talung, though you will need to supply your own food. The monastery is 2km west of the main road to Phongdo. For information on reaching the monastery, see p143.

RETING MONASTERY རྭ་སྒྲེང་དགོན་པ་
elev 4100m

Pre-1950 photographs show **Reting Monastery** (admission Y20) sprawled gracefully across the flank of a juniper-clad hill in the Rong-chu Valley. Like Ganden Monastery, it was devastated by Red Guards and its present remains hammer home the tragic waste caused by the ideological zeal of the Cultural Revolution. Still, the site is one of the most beautiful in the region. The Dalai Lama has stated that

should he ever return to Tibet it is at Reting, not Lhasa, that he would like to reside.

The monastery dates back to 1073. It was initially associated with Atisha (Jowo-je) but in its later years had an important connection with the Gelugpa order and the Dalai Lamas. Two regents – the de facto rulers of Tibet for the interregnum between the death of a Dalai Lama and the majority of his next reincarnation – were chosen from the Reting abbots. The fifth Reting Rinpoche was regent from 1933 to 1947. He played a key role in the search for the current Dalai Lama and served as his senior tutor. He was later accused of collusion with the Chinese and died in a Tibetan prison.

The sixth Reting Rinpoche died in 1997. In January 2001 the Chinese announced that a boy named Sonam Phuntsog had been identified out of 700 candidates as the seventh Reting Rinpoche. Significantly, the announcement came just two days after the Karmapa set off on his flight from Tibet to India (p135). The Dalai Lama refuses to recognise the choice, and denounces it as part of a long-term strategy by the Chinese government to control religious leadership in Tibet.

The young *rinpoche* currently resides under PSB surveillance at his official residence, 2km below the monastery by the riverside. While locals might be granted an audience with the young *rinpoche*, foreigners are strictly prohibited from visiting the compound.

Viewing the Monastery

The slow and arduous process of rebuilding Reting has begun by monks. The current main assembly hall, or **Tsogchen**, occupies only one side of the original hall. Enter the hall to the right to get to the main inner shrine, the Ütse. The central statue of Jampai Dorje is an unusual amalgam of the gods Jampelyang (Manjushri), Chana Dorje (Vajrapani) and Chenresig (Avalokiteshvara). To the left is a Drölma (Tara) statue credited with the power of speech; to the right is Tsongkhapa.

To the left of the Ütse entrance is a rare mural of the 14th (current) Dalai Lama; to the right of the entrance is a picture of the current Reting Rinpoche and a footprint and photo of the fifth Reting Rinpoche.

As you leave the chapel look for a second hall to your right. The hall contains a gold chörten with the remains of the sixth Reting Rinpoche, Tenzin Jigne. Lining the back wall are statues of the six previous Reting Rinpoches.

The monastery is still graced by surrounding juniper forest, said to have sprouted from the hairs of its founder. A 40-minute **kora** leads around the monastery, passing several stone carvings, a series of eight chörtens and an active *dürtro* (sky-burial site). Further up the hillside is the retreat where Tsongkhapa composed the Lamrim Chenmo (Graduated Path), a key Gelugpa text. The large escarpment to the right is the Sengye Drak (Lion's Rock), where there are several more retreats.

Reting is about 28km from Phongdo village, which has a ruined *dzong* and is overlooked by a mountain of near perfect conical proportions.

A pleasant hour-long walk northeast of Reting leads to **Samtenling Nunnery**, home to over 100 nuns. The main chapel houses the meditation cave of Tsongkhapa. The trail leads off from the sky-burial site to the northeast of the monastery.

Getting There & Away

Talung and Reting Monasteries are probably best visited together in a rented vehicle. The cost of a two-day Land Cruiser trip should be Y1000 to Y1300. A guide and permits are not necessary. You could de-tour to Drigung Til Monastery and make a nice loop for a few hundred yuan more.

A public bus departs for Reting (Y35, 168km, four hours) on Monday, Thursday, Friday and Sunday from the Lhasa Eastern Suburbs Bus Station, passing near Talung, and returning the following day. More frequent transport goes to Lhundrub, after this you'd have to rely on hitching, though if you have food and enough time you shouldn't have any major problems.

ROAD TO DRIGUNG TIL MONASTERY

Increasingly popular destinations for independent travellers are the Drigung Til and Tidrum Monasteries, around 120km northeast of Lhasa. They can only be reached by rented transport or by hitching. There are few sights here, although the valleys have an untouched and timeless quality that makes them seem much further from Lhasa than they actually are.

Medro Gungkar and Drigung Qu don't have many attractions in their own right, but they can be useful as places to break the journey.

Medro Gungkar   མལ་གྲོ་གུང་དཀར

☎ 0891 / pop 2000 / elev 3600m

On the wide banks of the Kyi-chu, 75km northeast of Lhasa, Medro Gungkar is the first pit stop en route to Drigung. If you have time it's worth stopping at **Katsel Monastery**, 3km from town on the road to Drigung. Legend has it that this Kagyupa order monastery was founded by the 7th-century King Songtsen Gampo who was led here by the Buddha disguised as a doe with antlers. The antlers are displayed in the inner sanctum, along with a hoof print. The temple is also significant as one of the original demoness-subduing temples (p96).

In case you get stuck without transport there are a couple of places to stay in Medro Gungkar, as well as a number of Chinese restaurants.

Southern Hotel (Nantong Binguan; ☎ 613 2629; Nanjing Lu; dm Y40) has clean, comfortable triples with TV and shared toilet, about 100m off the main crossroad. If you need a hot scrub, the management can direct you to a nearby bathhouse.

Grain Hotel (Liangshiju Binguan; ☎ 613 2148; cnr main rd & Nanjing Lu; per bed Y25) is the gritty underbelly of Medro Gungkar, with piggy outdoor toilets and rooms that could use a good dusting. It's on the main road at the first cross street.

Four Seasons (Tuushi; Nanjing Lu; meals Y8-15), while not quite living up to its prestigious New York namesake, can still dish up a piping hot noodle soup.

Three minibuses every day travel from Lhasa's Eastern Suburbs Bus Station to Medro Gungkar, departing when full from around 9am.

Drigung Qu འབྲི་གུང་ཆུས

☎ 0891 / pop 1500

As you continue up the valley from Katsel Monastery you pass two enormous ruined chörtens on the right. Halfway up the valley you come to Drigung Qu village (Nyima Jiangre), set at the auspicious confluence of three rivers.

A 20-minute walk northwest of town is the Drigungpa-school **Dzongsar Monastery**. Apart from the usual statues of Guru Rinpoche and Sakyamuni (Sakya Thukpa) inside the main chapel, there are also icons of Abchi, the white female protector of the region, and a two-armed standing Chenresig (Avalokiteshvara), as well as the founder of the Drigung school, Jikten Gonpo (and his golden footprints). Behind the monastery two chörtens stand sentinel over the beautiful upper Kyichu Valley.

Also nearby is **Sha Monastery**, 2km southeast of Drigung Qu and dedicated to the Dzogchen suborder. As you go in past two inscribed pillars, look up at the stuffed snow leopard. To the right is a side protector chapel with the Dzogchen trinity Dorje Lekpa, Rahulla and Ekajati. The chapel also contains the footprint of the deity who carried the pillars here. Continue on through an unusual courtyard encircling a huge chörten, to the upstairs chapel above the entrance.

Up a side valley from Sha Monastery is the Nyingmapa-sect **Shalung Nunnery**. Across the river valley from Dzongsar Monastery is **Una Monastery**. There is also a **ruined dzong** 3km south of town.

If you need to stay here, the **Monastery Guesthouse** (☎ 613 2432; dm Y10), in the centre of Drigung Qu, is an atmospheric, if not basic, hovel. One large dorm room is available for pilgrims. **Congratulations Restaurant** (☎ 650 3419) has *momos* (dumplings), *thugpa* (traditional noodle dishes), beer, tea and basic fried dishes.

Public transport for Drigung Qu includes a daily bus (Y20) departing at 8.30am from Lhasa's Eastern Suburbs Bus Station. It's approximately 35km to Drigung Til from Drigung Qu.

DRIGUNG TIL MONASTERY འབྲི་གུང་མཐིལ་
elev 4150m

Drigung Til Monastery (admission Y25) is the head monastery of the Drigungpa school of the Kagyupa order. Although it suffered some damage in the Cultural Revolution, the monastery is in better shape than most of the other monastic centres in this part of Ü. It was first established in 1167. By 1250 it was already vying with Sakya for political power – as it happened, not a particularly good move. The Sakya forces joined with the Mongol army to sack Drigung Til in 1290. Thus chastened, the monastery subsequently devoted itself to the instruction

of contemplative meditation. There are 270 monks at Drigung Til.

Drigung Til sprouts from a high, steep ridge overlooking the Drigung Valley. A steep thread of a path makes its way up into the monastic complex, although there is also vehicle access from the eastern end of the valley. The 180-degree views from the main courtyard are impressive and a serene stillness pervades the site.

The **main assembly hall** is probably the most impressive of the buildings. The central figure inside is Jigten Sumgon, the founder of the monastery. Guru Rinpoche and Sakyamuni (Sakya Thukpa) are to the left. Upstairs on the 1st floor you can see statues of Jigten Sumgon and his two successors, all wearing red hats. Jigten's footprint is set in a slab of rock at the foot of the statue. From the 1st floor you can go upstairs to a balcony and a circuit of prayer wheels. Steps lead up from here to the chörtens of two previous abbots.

The monastery **kora** then heads up the hill to the main *dürtro*. This is the holiest sky-burial site in the Lhasa region – people travel hundreds of kilometres to bring their deceased relatives here. It is sometimes possible to observe a sky burial (held on auspicious days), but it is absolutely essential that you gain permission from both the family of the deceased and the senior lama who conducts the ceremony. The lama requests that you do not take photos. Please do not abuse his and the deceased family's hospitality by sneaking any shots. If they do not want you to attend then just let it go. (For more on sky burials, see p42)

As you follow the kora along the ridge and down to the monastery, ask the monks for the path to the *gönkhang*. This **protector chapel** is dedicated to Abchi, the protectress of Drigung, who can be seen to the left of the main statue of Jigten Sumgon. To the right of the chapel there is another statue of Abchi riding a horse, which is next to Tseringma, the goddess of Mt Everest, riding a snow lion. Also look out for the pair of yak horns on the left wall of the chapel, after which Drigung is said to be named (a *dri* is a female yak and *gung* means 'camp'), and the stuffed snow leopard on the right.

It's possible to stay in the comfortable **Monastery Guesthouse** (dm Y20), which is in the main courtyard. Expect a poor sleep if you are not acclimatised. A small monastery shop here sells packaged food and you can get fresh meals at the monastery kitchen, including fried rice (Y6) and noodles (Y5).

For information on reaching Drigung Til see the directions for Tidrum Nunnery (below).

TIDRUM NUNNERY གཏི་རུམ་སློན་བཙུན་དགོན་
elev 4325m

Around three hours' walk (or a half-hour drive) from the main valley, northwest of Drigung Til and 16km up a side valley, is Tidrum Nunnery. Tidrum, with its **medicinal hot springs** (admission Y5), has a great location in a narrow gorge at the confluence of two streams. The small nunnery has strong connections to Yeshe Tsogyel, the wife of King Trisong Detsen. The Kandro-la, the resident spiritual leader of the nunnery, is considered a reincarnation of Yeshe Tsogyel.

The hot springs are delightful and are in a mercifully concrete-free zone. There are separate men's and women's bathrooms. Bring a towel and flip-flops.

If you have a day to spare you could do a tough day-hike around the caves of Yeshe Tsogyel. Take a guide from the nunnery as the trail can be hard to find.

For a short walk, head north up the gorge behind the nunnery for about 1½ hours until you get to Dranang Monastery, where the valley divides.

Sleeping & Eating

There are two guesthouses built up around the springs – both share a sordid outdoor toilet.

The more expensive 3rd-floor rooms at the **Government blocks** (d Y30-120) are clean, if overpriced. If you'd rather see your money go to the nuns instead of the Chinese government, stay at the shabby **Nunnery Guesthouse** (d Y30) next door. There is a shop selling biscuits and beer and a restaurant that serves hearty bowls of *thugpa* (Y6).

Getting There & Away

The best way to get to Drigung Til and Tidrum is by rented vehicle. The trip takes around four hours from Lhasa. It's worth spending at least one night in Tidrum or Drigung, more if you want to do any hikes. A two- or three-day trip will cost around Y1500. It is also possible to visit Drigung as part of a loop taking in Reting (around Y1500), or as a longer five-day trip taking in Nam-tso and Reting (around Y2500).

Alternatively, a public daily bus (Y30) runs from the Lhasa Eastern Suburbs Bus Station to Drigung Til, departing at 8am. Getting to Tidrum requires some hitchhiking. There's very little traffic on this last section so you may need to wait a day for a lift to arrive.

If you are hitching, it's easiest to first get a minibus to Medro Gungkar (p143) and flag down a vehicle at the road junction that heads towards Drigung Til.

YARLUNG TSANGPO VALLEY
ཡར་ཀླུང་གཙང་པོའི་གླུང་

The waters of the wide Yarlung Tsangpo meanders through a swath of land rich in Tibetan history and littered with historical sights before becoming the Brahmaputra River to the east. Although it's only a couple of hours by bus or taxi from Lhasa, the river valley offers plenty of opportunities to get off the beaten track without launching a major expedition. The ease of travel means you can jump on and off public transport to visit any combination of sights near the roadside, while with more time you could spend days exploring the various side valleys on foot or by mountain bike.

The road through the valley is sealed all the way to Tsetang and beyond, check the kilometre marker features (p146) to keep track of what is coming up. Note that the new short-cut road to the airport from Lhasa was due for completion by the end of 2005, by-passing Gongkar Dzong and Gongkar Chöde Monastery. This US$78 million road, which includes a 2437m-long tunnel, will shave off 34km from the old route.

Permits are theoretically needed for all places in this section. In reality, only the Yarlung Valley and Samye require permits.

GONGKAR གོང་དཀར་
☎ 0891 / elev 3600m

Gongkar's main claim to fame is its airport. A further 13km along the road to Lhasa are the ruins of **Gongkar Dzong** and neighbouring

KILOMETRE MARKERS ALONG THE YARLUNG TSANGPO

Chushul to Tsetang marker	Feature
72	Chuwo Ri, one of Ü's four holy mountains
73	Monastery on side of Chuwo Ri
80-81	Ruins of Gongkar Dzong & Shedruling Monastery
84	Gongkar Chöde Monastery
93-94	Gongkar airport
102-103	Gongkar Xian town
112	Ferry to Dorje Drak Monastery
117	Dongphu Chukhor Monastery
140	Ferry to Drak Valley
142	Turn-off to Dranang Monastery (signposted as 'Zhatong')
147	Road to Mindroling Monastery
148-149	Tsongdu Tsokpa Monastery
155	Samye ferry
161	Namseling Manor turn-off
190	Tsetang town

Sundruling Monastery. Nearby, by the roadside, you can normally see small coracle boats, which ferry passengers across the Yarlung Tsangpo to Sinpo Ri. All this will change with the completion of the new bridge and tunnel: the boats will become history and the ruins will then be along the 'old road' to Lhasa.

Gongkar Chöde Monastery
གོང་དཀར་ཆོས་སྡེ་དགོན།

Surprisingly large, Sakyapa **Gongkar Chöde Monastery** (admission Y15), founded in 1464 is famous for its 16th-century Kyenri-style murals. Around 10km back along the road to Lhasa, it lies 400m south of the highway – the turn-off is marked by a blue sign and a brown shrine.

The **assembly hall** has statues of founder Dorje Denpa (1432–96), Guru Rinpoche and Sakya Pandita. To the left of the hall is the *gönkhang* (women are forbidden to enter), whose outer rooms have black murals depicting sky burial. The inner hall has a statue of the Sakyapa protector Gonpo Gur and some amazing spirit traps (to the right). The inner sanctum has fine Kyenri-style murals of the Sakyapa founders by the entrance, and a kora.

The upper floor has lovely old murals, including some showing the original monastery layout. On either side of the roof is the Kyedhor Lhakhang, which has fine protector murals in *yabyum* (Tantric sexual union)

pose, and the Kangyur Lhakhang. The top floor has three new chapels to the left, as well as the Lama Lhakhang, and the Neten Lhakhang, dedicated to the 16 *arhats*.

Die-hards can hike a further 5km up the side valley to visit the **Dechen Chokhor Monastery** on the hillside.

Sleeping & Eating
There are a couple of decent places to stay near the airport if you can't face an early bus trip or you want to use Gongkar as a base from which to explore the valley.

Airport Hotel (☎ 624 6608; Gongkar Airport; d/ste Y140-200/380) Renovated main block has comfortable standard rooms but unreliable hot water, though breakfast is included. The old block has some cheaper double rooms, which also come with a bathroom, but no breakfast. The hotel is right by the terminal building.

Wujin Hotel (Army; ☎ 618 2454; Gongkar Airport; dm/d Y30/140) PLA-owned hotel has a welcoming staff and box-like doubles and dorm rooms. The management says some rooms have 24-hour hot water, though this may be optimistic. All in all, the Airport Hotel is a better bet.

Zhuhangkong Binguan (☎ 618 2109; 2nd fl, cnr main & airport rds; d Y30) Budget travellers not keen on funding the PLA may opt for this grittier option above the main road. Each of the dusty rooms has a grim attached bathroom with cold water. The public shower (Y6) is out back.

Gongkar has several Chinese restaurants, all overpriced but with decent food. A teahouse next to the airport hotel attracts off-duty soldiers to its mah-jong tables.

Getting There & Away

Airport buses run daily from the office of the Civil Aviation Authority of China (CAAC) in Lhasa to Gongkar at 6.30am, 10am, noon and 5pm (minibus Y25 or large air-con bus Y35, depending on demand). Return buses to Lhasa (and less-frequent buses to Shigatse and Bayi) are timed to coincide with the arrival of flights.

There are plenty of minibuses and shared taxis running from Tsetang to Gongkar, particularly in the afternoon.

Taxis take passengers to Lhasa for Y30 per person (Y120 per taxi), though you may get the entire taxi for less if it's returning anyway. Otherwise, you should not have to wait too long to find a bus returning to Lhasa from Samye or Tsetang.

DORJE DRAK MONASTERY རྡོ་རྗེ་བྲག་དགོན་པ་

Dorje Drak, along with Mindroling, is one of the two most important Nyingmapa monasteries in Ü. It is less accessible than Mindroling, and not as well restored, and consequently gets few Western visitors.

Dorje Drak was forcibly relocated to its present site in 1632 by the kings in Tsang and then sacked by the Dzungar Mongols in 1717. The monastery is headed by a line of hereditary lamas known as the Rigdzin, named after the first Rigdzin Godemachen, who are thought to be reincarnations of Guru Rinpoche. The 10th Rigdzin Lama currently resides in Lhasa.

A demanding **kora** leads around the back of the rock behind the monastery on to a ruined retreat atop the rock. The path passes a pleasant wooded sandy bay and the views from the retreat are stunning.

Tibetan-style beds are available at the **Monastery Guesthouse** (dm Y10). Bring a sleeping bag and food.

The monastery, on the northern bank of the Yarlung Tsangpo, can be reached via a ferry from kilometre marker 112 on the Lhasa–Tsetang road. Boats run in the morning and late afternoon (Y5, 30 minutes) or you can charter a boat for Y60. Some trekkers approach Dorje Drak from Lhasa, which means a hike of around four days.

DRANANG MONASTERY & VALLEY གྲྭ་ནང་གཙུག

A further 48km from Gongkar airport is the turn-off to **Dranang (Dratang) Monastery** (admission Y25), south of the highway. This small Sakyapa monastery of only 18 monks is of interest mainly to art specialists for its rare murals, which combine Indian and central Asian styles. Bring a torch to see the murals.

The assembly hall has central statues of Dorje Chang (Vajradhara) and the monastery's founder, Drapa Ngonshe. Look for the interesting oracle costume and mirror, in which the oracle would discern his visions. The inner sanctum holds all that remains of the murals, the best of which are on the back (western) wall.

A side protector chapel is accessed by steps outside and to the left of the main entrance. The chapel (whose central image is that of a yak's head) has a passage at the back that leads to a rooftop chapel and kora.

To get to the monastery, walk 2km south from the highway, through the modern town of Dranang into the old town, until the road curves to the right. If you need to spend the night, try the **Zhengfu (Government) Guesthouse** (☎ 13989935008; d Y40). Clean rooms here have TV and attached bathroom; running water comes at night. It's next to the PSB office at the southern end of town.

Also worth visiting if you have a particular interest are the ruins of the **Jampaling Kumbum**, a half-hour walk southeast of Dranang. The 13-storey chörten, built in 1472, was one of the largest in Tibet, with an attendant monastery of 200 monks, before it was dynamited by the Chinese in 1963. A climb up the hillside above the ruins gives an overview of the scale of the site, which includes a ruined assembly hall east of the chörten.

To get to the Jampaling, walk south out of Dranang Monastery and after a couple of minutes turn left, following a path to the base of the ruins visible on the hillside above.

Explorers with a tent and supplies could easily spend a couple of days in the Dranang Valley, hiking up the valley past the village and monastery of **Gyeling Tsokpa**, 8km from Dranang, to **Dingboche Monastery**, 14km from Dranang.

A direct minibus (Y25) comes to Dranang from Barkhor Square in Lhasa every day at 7am. Otherwise, it's a 20-minute walk from the main highway.

MINDROLING MONASTERY

 སྨིན་གྲོལ་གླིང་དགོན་པ་

A worthwhile detour from the Lhasa–Tsetang road, between the Dranang turn-off and the Samye ferry crossing, is **Mindroling Monastery** (admission Y25). It is the largest and, along with Dorje Drak, is one of the most important Nyingmapa monasteries in Ü.

Although a small monastery was founded at the present site of Mindroling as early as the 10th century, the date usually given for the founding of Mindroling is the mid-1670s. The founding lama, Terdak Lingpa (1646–1714), was highly esteemed as a scholar and counted among his students the fifth Dalai Lama. Subsequent heads of the monastery were given the title Minling Trichen. The monastery was razed in the Mongol invasion of 1718 and later restored.

Mindroling has *cham* dancing on the 10th day of the fifth Tibetan lunar month and the fourth day of the fourth lunar month. The latter festival features the creation of a sand mandala.

The central **Tsuglhakhang** is an elegant brown stone structure on the west side of the courtyard. As you walk clockwise the first chapel is the **Zhelre Lhakhang**, with statues of Guru Rinpoche and Terdak Lingpa. The main hall itself has another statue of Terdak Lingpa, along with Dorje Chang (Vajradhara) and a row of Kadam-style chörtens. The inner chapel has a large Sakyamuni (Sakya Thukpa) statue surrounded by eight ornaments. Only the statue's head is original; the body was smashed by the Chinese for its relics.

Upstairs, the Tresor Lhakhang houses a famed old *thangka* with the gold footprints and handprints of Terdak Lingpa, which was given to the fifth Dalai Lama.

The top floor holds the Lama Lhakhang, with some fine ancient murals of the Dzogchen lineages, plus a central statue of Gundu Sangba (Samanthabadri). The Dalai Lama's quarters remain empty.

The other main building, to the right, is the **Sangok Potrang**, used for Tantric practices. As you enter the hall to the right look for a famous mural of Guru Rinpoche. Several photos are on display in the hall: those of Namcai Norbu, the famous Nyingmapa teacher based in Italy; the current Minling Trichen (in exile); and the current abbot of Mindroling.

A new white **chörten** has recently been built with Taiwanese funds just outside the monastery to replace an original 13-storey chörten destroyed in the Cultural Revolution. It's possible to climb past the ground-floor statue of Jampa to upper floors and sometimes the roof.

Nice walks lead off from the kora around the Tsuglhakhang, west up the valley through the village to the ruins of what used to be a nunnery.

On the main road 1.5km towards Tsetang is the small **Tsongdu Tsokpa Monastery**. The original monastery across the road has been converted into a housing block.

Sleeping & Eating

It's possible to stay the night at the **Monastery Guesthouse** (dm Y15). A small shop outside the south gate sells noodles, Pepsi and the like.

Getting There & Away

There is no direct transport to Mindroling. One possibility is to take the Lhasa–Tsetang bus and get off at kilometre marker 147 by the English sign to the monastery. The monastery is around 8km south of the road, up the Drachi Valley, and the last section involves a climb (it's not too punishing). You won't see the monastery until you round a ridge and are below it. You should be able to hitch a lift pretty easily from the highway turn-off, where there is a shop.

Mindroling is easily slotted into a Yarlung Valley excursion if you have a rented vehicle. It should add very little to the cost of your trip as it is a detour of only 16km all up.

SAMYE VALLEY

Samye is deservedly the most popular destination for travellers in the Ü region. The monastery, in the middle of the sandy Samye Valley and approached via a beautiful river crossing, has a magic about it that causes many travellers to stay longer than they had intended. No journey in Ü is complete without a visit to Samye. (For details of the trek between here and Ganden, see p271.)

Permits

A travel permit is theoretically needed to visit Samye and it's difficult to get one without organising a tour and guide. At the time of research there were only occasional permit checks, at the ferry point on the Tsetang side and at the Monastery Guesthouse. No-one is checked for weeks and then suddenly a bunch of travellers are fined. You'll have to ask other travellers or just give it a try. Don't rely on travel agencies in Lhasa to tell you about the current situation.

If you are stopped without a permit you may be subject to a fine of up to Y500, but you can usually plead stupidity and negotiate down to Y100 or less.

Sights

SAMYE MONASTERY བསམ་ཡས་དགོན་པ་

Samye Monastery is designed to represent the Buddhist universe, and many of the buildings in the courtyard are cosmological symbols. The square in front of the Monastery Guesthouse has some interesting bits and pieces. The stubby isolated building to the north constitutes the remains of a nine-storey tower used to display festival *thangkas*.

History

Samye was Tibet's very first monastery and has a long history that spans more than 1200 years. It was founded in the reign of King Trisong Detsen (who was born close by), though the exact date is subject to some debate – probably between 765 and 780. Whatever the case, Samye represents the Tibetan state's first efforts to allow the Buddhist faith to set down roots in the country. The Bön majority at court, whose religion prevailed in Tibet prior to Buddhism, were not at all pleased with this development.

The victory of Buddhism over the Bön-dominated establishment was symbolised by Guru Rinpoche's triumph over the massed demons of Tibet at Hepo Ri, just to the east of Samye. It was this act that paved the way for the introduction of Buddhism to Tibet.

Shortly after the founding of the monastery, Tibet's first seven monks (the 'seven examined men') were ordained here by the monastery's Indian abbot, Shantarakshita, and Indian and Chinese scholars were invited to assist in the translation of Buddhist texts into Tibetan.

Before long, disputes broke out between followers of Indian and Chinese scholarship. The disputes culminated in the Great Debate of Samye, an event that is regarded by

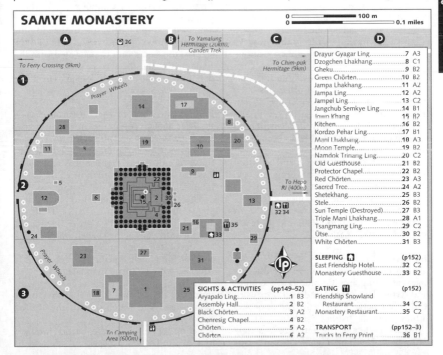

SAMYE MONASTERY

| 0 | 100 m |
| 0 | 0.1 miles |

To Ferry Crossing (9km)

Prayer Wheels

To Yamalung Hermitage (20km), Ganden Trek

To Chim-puk Hermitage (9km)

To Hepo Ri (400m)

Prayer Wheels

To Camping Area (600m)

Drayur Gyagar Ling	7 A3
Dzogchen Lhakhang	8 C1
Gheku	9 B2
Green Chörten	10 B2
Jampa Lhakhang	11 A2
Jampa Ling	12 A2
Jampel Ling	13 C2
Jangchub Semkye Ling	14 B1
Jowo Khang	15 B2
Kitchen	16 B2
Kordzo Pehar Ling	17 B1
Mani Lhakhang	18 A3
Moon Temple	19 B2
Namdok Trinang Ling	20 C2
Old Guesthouse	21 B2
Protector Chapel	22 B2
Red Chörten	23 A3
Sacred Tree	24 A2
Shetekhang	25 B3
Stele	26 B2
Sun Temple (Destroyed)	27 B3
Triple Mani Lhakhang	28 A1
Tsangmang Ling	29 C2
Ütse	30 B2
White Chörten	31 B3

SLEEPING	(p152)
East Friendship Hotel	32 C2
Monastery Guesthouse	33 B2

EATING	(p152)
Friendship Snowland Restaurant	34 C2
Monastery Restaurant	35 C2

SIGHTS & ACTIVITIES	(pp149–52)
Aryapalo Ling	1 B3
Assembly Hall	2 B2
Black Chörten	3 A2
Chenresig Chapel	4 B2
Chörten	5 A2
Chörten	6 A2

TRANSPORT	(pp152–3)
Trucks to Ferry Point	36 B1

THE SAMYE MANDALA

Samye's overall design was based on that of the Odantapuri Temple of Bihar, in India, and is a mandalic representation of the universe. The central temple represents Mt Meru (Sumeru), and the temples around it in two concentric circles represent the oceans, the continents and the subcontinents that ring the mountain in Buddhist cosmology.

At the centre of the monastery grounds is the Ütse, the most impressive of the monastery buildings, and at the centre of this is a pole that represents the core of the universe. Directly to the north is a Moon Temple and to the south a Sun Temple (now destroyed). Ringing the Ütse are four large chörtens (stupas), which are named after their colours: red, black, green and white. These were destroyed in the Cultural Revolution but were rebuilt recently – they look decidedly concrete and slightly out of place. Surrounding the chörtens are 12 *ling* chapels (lesser, outlying chapels), four major and eight minor ones. The four major *ling* chapels represent the four continents; the minor *ling* chapels are subcontinents. The complex originally had 108 buildings (an auspicious number to Tibetans) and there were 1008 chörtens on the circular wall that rings the monastery.

Tibetan historians as a crucial juncture in the course of Tibetan Buddhism. The debate, which probably took place in the early 790s, was essentially an argument between the Indian approach to bodhisattvahood via textual study and scholarship, and the more immediate Chan- (Zen) influenced approach of the Chinese masters, who decried scholarly study in favour of contemplation on the absolute nature of buddhahood. The debates came out on the side of the Indian scholars.

Samye has never been truly the preserve of any one of Tibetan Buddhism's different orders. However, the influence of Guru Rinpoche in establishing the monastery has meant that the Nyingmapa order has been most closely associated with Samye. When the Sakyapa order came to power in the 15th century it took control of Samye, and Nyingmapa influence declined, though not completely.

Samye has been damaged and restored many times throughout its long history. The most recent assault on its antiquity was by the Chinese during the Cultural Revolution. Extensive renovation work has been going on since the mid-1980s and there are now 135 monks at Samye.

The Ütse

The central building of Samye, the **Ütse** (admission Y40), comprises a synthesis of architectural styles. The ground and 1st floors were originally Tibetan in style; the 2nd floor was Chinese and the 3rd floor Indian.

Just to the left of the entrance is a **stele** dating from 779. The elegant Tibetan script carved on its surface proclaims Buddhism as the state religion of Tibet by order of King Trisong Detsen.

From here the entrance leads into the first of the ground-floor chambers: the **assembly hall**. As you enter the hall a row of figures greet you straight ahead: Namse (Vairocana); Shantarakshita, Samye's first abbot; Guru Rinpoche (a copy of a famous statue whose photo lies to the left); Trisong Detsen; and Songtsen Gampo (with an extra head in his turban). On the right are two groups of three statues: the first group is associated with the Kadampa order; the second group is multi-denominational, and includes lamas from the Nyingmapa, Sakyapa and Gelugpa orders.

To the rear of the assembly hall are steps leading into Samye's most revered chapel, the **Jowo Khang**. You enter the inner chapel via three doors – an unusual feature. They symbolise the Three Doors of Liberation: those of emptiness, signlessness and wishlessness. A circumambulation route of the inner chapel follows at this point.

The centrepiece of the inner chapel is a 4m statue of Sakyamuni (Sakya Thukpa). Ten bodhisattvas and two protective deities line the side walls of the chapel, and the walls are decorated with ancient murals. Look also for the panelled ceiling – each panel is adorned with a Tantric mandala.

To the right of the hall is a *gönkhang* with statues of deities so terrible that they must be masked. And watch out for the stuffed snake over the exit.

Before ascending to the 1st floor, take a look at the **Chenresig Chapel**, outside and to the left of the main assembly hall, which features a dramatic 1000-armed statue of Chenresig (Avalokiteshvara) and ancient bas-relief plates.

The main feature of the 2nd floor is an upper extension of the inner chapel. This houses an image of Guru Rinpoche in a semiwrathful aspect, plus Shantarakshita, Trisong Detsen and Sakyamuni. There is an inner kora around the hall.

Some of the murals outside this hall are very impressive; those on the southern wall depict Guru Rinpoche, while those to the left of the main door show the fifth Dalai Lama with the Mongol Khan Gushri and various ambassadors displaying obeisance. Also on this floor are the Dalai Lama's quarters (left) and another protector chapel and Tsepame (Amitayus) chapel (right).

The 3rd floor is a recent addition to the Ütse. It holds a mandala base as well as four statues of Namse.

Walk around the back to a ladder leading up to the 4th floor. This is a sacred chapel of great significance. The main image is of Dukhor (Kalachakra), a Tantric deity. The pillars around the central core symbolise the Four Guardian Kings, the 16 *arhats* and the 21 manifestations of Drölma (Tara).

Back on the ground floor you can follow the prayer wheel circuit of the Ütse, and look at the interesting murals showing the founding of the monastery.

Ling Chapels & Chörtens
དགོན་ཁང་དང་མཆོད་རྟེན

As renovation work continues at Samye, the original *ling* chapels (the lesser, outlying chapels) and coloured chörtens are gradually being restored. Wander around and see which are open. Following is a clockwise tour of those open at the time of research.

Look for the sacred stone in the centre of the **Tsemang Ling**, which was once the monastery printing press. The **Shetekhang** is a residential college for monks. The restored **Aryapalo Ling** was Samye's first building and is now looked after by a couple of charming monks. The **Drayur Gyagar Ling** was originally the centre for the translation of texts, as depicted on the wall murals. The main statue on the upper floor is of Sakyamuni, flanked by his Indian and Chinese translators.

The **Jampa Ling** on the west side is where Samye's Great Debate was held. On the right

as you go in, look out for the mural depicting the original design of Samye with zigzagging walls. There is an unusual semicircular inner kora here that is decorated with images of Jampa. Just north of here is a chörten that pilgrims circumambulate; south is a **sacred tree** to which pilgrims tie stones. The triple **Mani Lhakhang** to the north has lovely murals.

The green roofed **Jangchub Semkye Ling** houses a host of bodhisattvas around a 3-D wooden mandala. East of here is the **Kordzo Pehar Ling**, the home of the oracle Pehar until he moved to Nechung Monastery outside Lhasa. There are several protector chapels here, including an upper-floor chapel with unusual gods including Dorje Phurba, whose lower half is a dagger, sitting astride fantastic beasts such as a nine-headed boar.

It is also possible to enter the four reconstructed concrete chörtens, though there is little of interest inside.

HEPO RI ཧད་པོ་རི་

Hepo Ri is the hill some 400m east of Samye where Guru Rinpoche vanquished the demons of Tibet. King Trisong Detsen later established a palace here. Paths wind up the side of the hill from the road leading from Samye's east gate. A 30-minute climb up the side ridge takes you to an incense burner, festooned with prayer flags and with great views of Samye below. Early morning is the best time for photography.

CHIM-PUK HERMITAGE མཆིམས་ཕུ་སྒྲུབ་ཁང་
Chim-puk hermitage is a warren of caves that was once a retreat for Guru Rinpoche. It is a popular day hike for travellers spending a few days at Samye. The walk takes around four or five hours up and three hours down. Take some water with you. If you are lucky you might find a pilgrim truck heading up there, or you could hire a tractor in Samye (Y50). Ask at reception in the Monastery Guesthouse.

Chim-puk is northeast of Samye. If you head out of the monastery in this direction you should be able to find a path leading east through some fields. Keep following this track, bearing left. The path crosses through desert-like territory for a couple of hours before ascending into the U-shaped valley in which the caves are found.

There is a small monastery built around Guru Rinpoche's original **meditation cave** halfway up the hill. Follow the pilgrims around the various other shrines. It might be possible to stay the night here if you have a sleeping bag and food. Otherwise, there is a small **guesthouse** (dm Y10) and shop at the nunnery at the base of the hill.

If you are feeling fit and acclimatised it is possible to climb to the top of the peak above Chim-puk. You'll probably only have enough time to do this if you get a lift to Chim-puk or stay the night there. To make this climb from the Guru Rinpoche cave follow the left-hand valley behind the caves and slog it uphill for 1½ hours to the top of the ridge, where there are several clumps of prayer flags. From here you can drag yourself up along a path for another 1½ hours to the top of the conical peak, where there are a couple of meditation retreats and fine views of the Yarlung Tsangpo Valley. On clear days you can see several massive Himalayan peaks to the southeast.

If you managed to get a lift up to Chim-puk it is possible to take another route back to Samye in around four hours. From the peak descend back down to the ridge line above Chim-puk, but instead of heading straight down the way you came up, cut down the other (western) side of the ridge that divides Chim-puk from the Samye Valley. Follow paths along the western side of this ridge, slowly descending in the direction of Samye. After three hours you reach the valley floor, from where it is an easy one-hour walk to Samye.

YAMALUNG HERMITAGE གཡའ་མ་ལུང་

It is possible to head up the valley directly behind Samye to the Yamalung hermitage, around 20km from Samye. It's really too far to hike there and back in a day but you could probably hire a tractor to take you there for around Y50 return. For details of this valley see the final stages of the Ganden to Samye trek (p271).

Sleeping & Eating

Monastery Guesthouse (☎ 0893-736 2761; dm/d/tr Y30-40/100/150) Most travellers end up at this guesthouse, just in front of the Ütse compound. It lacks the intimacy of the old guesthouse next door (now used by monks) but it's still pretty good.

East Friendship Hotel (☎ 0893-736 2590; Gegushar; d Y40) Cosy and basic family guesthouse just outside Samye's east gate. Note that the gate is closed at 6pm, after which you can get there from the south or north gates.

There is fine camping in an orchard 10 minutes' walk south of the Ütse. Take your own water.

Monastery Restaurant (dishes Y7-15) Prices are cheap, the food is average and there's an English menu. This place, attached to the guesthouse, offers basic food such as *thugpa* and fried noodles.

Friendship Snowland Restaurant (☎ 0893-736 2760; Gegushar; meals Y8-18) Backpacker-inspired banana pancakes are on offer at this private restaurant outside the eastern gate of the monastery – the only other place to eat. Decent Chinese dishes are available, as well as *thugpa*, mugs of milk and tea.

The shops on either side of the guesthouse are well stocked with snacks, soft drinks, beer (essential for any monastic sojourn) and religious knick-knacks.

Getting There & Away

While it appears that Samye is easily reached by road from Lhasa, keep in mind that the main highway is south of the river, so coming from Lhasa you need to cross over to the north bank by ferry or bridge.

The only regular bus service from Lhasa to Samye via the bridge at Tsetang is a daily pilgrim bus (Y35) that departs from Barkhor Square at 6.30am. Buy your ticket the day before from Tengye Ling Temple (p105), 80m behind the Pentoc Guesthouse.

Most travellers opt for the ferry across the Yarlung Tsangpo, which saves time and a bumpy road journey. All buses from Lhasa to Tsetang pass by the Samye ferry departure point.

A bus service runs from just west of Barkhor Square to the Samye ferry, departing around 8am (Y30). Morning buses also depart from here to Tsetang (sometimes called Shannan). Seven buses reach Tsetang (Y30, 183km, three hours, hourly from 8.30am) from Lhasa's main bus station.

The ferry crossing compound has a basic restaurant and guesthouse if you arrive late (and have a permit). River crossings (one hour, per person Y10) are irregular, operating whenever there are enough people. You can charter the whole boat for Y90.

It is 9km from the ferry drop-off point to Samye and almost everyone – Tibetans included – jumps on a truck or tractor for the ride (Y3, 30 minutes).

Trucks (and occasionally the monastery minibuses) leave Samye for the ferry terminal at around 8am and 2pm, though it's worth checking these times with the guesthouse manager.

Buses to Tsetang and Lhasa wait for their passengers on the other side of the river, as does the PSB. There is occasional transport direct to Tsetang (48km) via the northern shore of the Yarlung Tsangpo and the bridge over to Tsetang, but it's a hot and bumpy drive.

NAMSELING MANOR རྣམ་སྲས་གླིང

Perhaps the only building of its type still standing in Tibet, this ruined multistorey family mansion is a minor site. You might find it worth a visit if you have your own transport.

There are a few murals left but the ruins are unstable in places so you should take care when exploring. The building is 3km south of the main highway near kilometre marker 161.

TSETANG རྩེད་ཐང

☎ 0893 / pop 52,000 / elev 3100m

An important Chinese administrative centre and army base, Tsetang is 183km southeast of Lhasa. It is the second-largest town in the Ü region, the capital of Shannan prefecture. For travellers, Tsetang is of interest mainly as a jumping board for exploration of the Yarlung Valley. The major obstacles are a lack of budget accommodation, permit hassles (see p155) and a concerted effort on the part of the Chinese to charge foreigners double for everything.

Tsetang is divided into a new, characterless Chinese town and an old Tibetan quarter. The Tibetan quarter is in the east of town, clustered around Gangpo Ri, one of Ü's four sacred mountains. The former *dzong* and village of Nedong has been subsumed into Tsetang's southern suburbs.

Information

CITS (☎ 782 5666; fax 782 1855; Tsedang Hotel; ⏰ 9.30am-12.30pm & 3.30-6.30pm) Really only interested in large groups but can organise overpriced independent day trips to the sights of the Yarlung Valley. Charges are

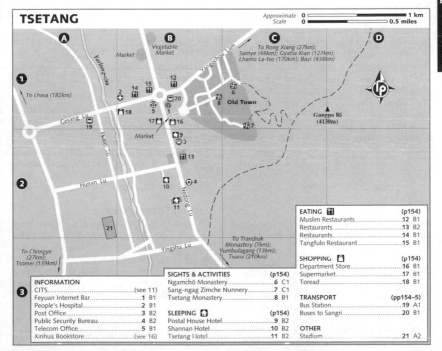

Y500 per day for a car, plus Y250 per person. The only catch is CITS requires the original travel permit you received for entry into Tibet, a piece of paper unlikely to be in your possession.

Feyuan Internet Bar (☎ 783 1965; Gesang Lu; per hr Y3) Located up a dingy stairwell on the 3rd floor of a building on the southeast side of the roundabout. Web surfing is slow.

Post office (☎ 782 1550; Nedong Lu 12; �’ 9.30am-7pm)

Telecom office (☎ 782 0405; Gesang Lu 1; �’ 9.30am-6.30pm) Calls to USA and Europe are Y8.2 per minute.

Tsetang Hotel (Zedang Fandian; ☎ 782 5666; fax 782 1855; 21 Nedong Lu) The only place to change money, a service for hotel guests only. English-speaking staff.

Sights & Activities
MONASTERY KORA
There are a couple of small monasteries in the Tibetan quarter that are worth a brief visit. Most pilgrims visit them in a clockwise circuit.

From the market head east to a small square and continue down the street to the right of the bank. After 200m you'll come to **Tsetang Monastery** (Ganden Chökhorling). This 14th-century monastery was originally a Kagyupa institution, but by the 18th century the Gelugpas had taken it over. The Chinese smashed the place up but the three storeys have been well restored.

From here head north and then east to **Ngamchö Monastery**, a somewhat livelier place. On the top floor are the bed and throne of the Dalai Lama. A side chapel is devoted to medicine, with images of the eight medicine buddhas.

A kora leads down from the monastery, follows the base of Gangpo Ri to a small shrine and then heads up to a bundle of prayer flags. From here one kora ascends the hill to hermitage caves, the other descends to **Sang-ngag Zimche Nunnery**. The principal image here is of a 1000-armed Chenresig (Avalokiteshvara), dating back to the time of King Songtsen Gampo. According to some accounts, the statue was fashioned by the king himself.

Sleeping & Eating
Finding good budget accommodation is a real problem in Tsetang. Many of the town's cheaper hotels are prevented from accepting foreigners by a strong PSB presence.

Shannan Hotel (☎ 782 6168; Hunan Lu; d Y280-480, ste Y880; ℗) This mid-range hotel isn't bad but

the less expensive doubles are small, stained and overpriced. There are triple rooms for Y120 but foreigners aren't allowed to stay in these. Rates include breakfast.

Tsetang Hotel (Zedang Fandian; ☎ 782 5666; fax 782 1855; 21 Nedong Lu; s/d/tr/ste Y888/1680/1320/2200, extra bed Y300; ℗ ⌨) This is Tsetang's premier lodging, with money exchange, Internet café (per hour Y30), a decent restaurant and overpriced rooms. The souvenir shop sells maps and slide film and the compound also includes a gym (per day Y30) and bowling alley (per game Y20).

Postal House Hotel (Youdian Gongyu; ☎ 782 1888; Nedong Lu; d Y188-318, ste Y666, extra bed Y88; ℗) While overpriced, the cheaper doubles are probably the best deal you'll get in Tsetang. You may be able to bargain the price down if you arrive late. Breakfast is included in summer only.

Tangfulo Restaurant (☎ 782 0087; Gesan Lu; dishes Y6-20; �’ 24hr) On the 2nd floor on the northwest side of the roundabout, this clean cafeteria-style restaurant offers a good variety of Chinese dishes and hot pots.

More Chinese restaurants are to be found north of the Tsetang Hotel all the way to the roundabout. A couple of good (if noisy) Muslim restaurants east of the roundabout serve up tasty noodles.

There are several well-stocked supermarkets on the main road that are good for hiking supplies.

Shopping
Outdoor equipment store **Toread** (☎ 782 4216; Gesang Lu) sells modern tents, sleeping bags and other camping gear.

For more general goods such as snacks, toiletries and maps, there is a supermarket, department store and Xinhua Bookstore on Nedong Lu, 100m south of the roundabout.

Getting There & Away
At least seven buses per day depart from Lhasa's long-distance bus station for Tsetang, almost hourly from 8.30am. You might be able to catch a bus earlier from Barkhor Square. Most travellers make their way first to Samye, spend a day or so at the monastery, and then travel on to Tsetang.

Buses and minibuses heading back to Lhasa (Y27, via the Samye ferry) depart from the bus station every hour from 8.30am. The 8.30am bus (as well as a Friday/Saturday

6.30pm bus) makes the run without stopping. Afternoon minibuses to Gongkar operate until about 5.30pm. Daily buses also depart for Nangartse (Y45, on the shore of Yamdrok-tso), Tsomei (Y40, via Chongye), Nang Dzong (Y80, via Gyantsa Xian) and Tsona (Y80, 210km, via Yumbulagang) at 8.30am, but you'll need permits for Tsona, Gyantsa Xian and Nang Dzong. Some buses do not operate on Sunday.

Morning buses to Sangri (Y8, 30km) depart from near the main roundabout. Three buses per day (11.30am, 2.30pm, 4pm) depart for Chongye town (Y5, 27km).

GANGPO RI གང་པོ་རི་

Gangpo Ri (4130m) is of special significance for Tibetans as it is the legendary birthplace of the Tibetan people. The Gangpo Ri **Monkey Cave**, where the monkey meditated, can be visited near the summit of the mountain. The walk there and back will take close to a full day. Do it in the spirit of a day walk in the hills, rather than as a trip specifically to see the Monkey Cave, as the cave itself is rather disappointing.

The most direct trail leads up from the Sang-ngag Zimche Nunnery, climbing about 550m to the cave. If in doubt, head for the collection of prayer flags.

There is a kora around Gangpo Ri, but the 10-hour walk would probably require two days. The walk starts a few kilometres east of town, along the road to Bayi, and heads south up a dry valley to the Gangpo-la and the Monkey Cave. You could probably sleep here if you had a sense of adventure, a sleeping bag and some food, before descending the next day to the main road south of Tsetang.

YARLUNG VALLEY ཡར་ཀླུང་གཞུང་

Yarlung is considered the cradle of Tibetan civilisation and it was from Yarlung that the early Tibetan kings unified Tibet in the 7th century. The massive burial mounds of these kings can be seen in Chongye. Yumbulagang, another major attraction of the area, is perched on a crag like a medieval European castle and is reputed to be Tibet's oldest building.

The major attractions of the Yarlung Valley can just about be seen in a day, but this is a beautiful part of Tibet for extended hiking and day walks. The main problem is the permit situation.

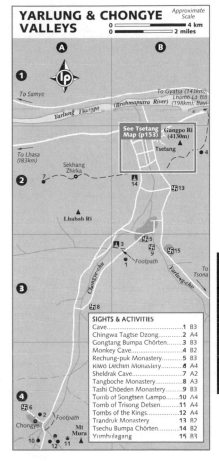

YARLUNG & CHONGYE VALLEYS

Approximate Scale

0 — 4 km
0 — 2 miles

SIGHTS & ACTIVITIES

Cave	1 B3
Chingwa Tagtse Dzong	2 A4
Gongtang Bumpa Chörten	3 B3
Monkey Cave	4 B2
Rechung-puk Monastery	5 B3
Riwo Dechen Monastery	6 A2
Sheldrak Cave	7 A2
Tangboche Monastery	8 A3
Tashi Chöeden Monastery	9 B3
Tomb of Songtsen Gampo	10 A4
Tomb of Trisong Detsen	11 A4
Tombs of the Kings	12 A4
Trandruk Monastery	13 B2
Tsechu Bumpa Chörten	14 B2
Yumbulagang	15 B3

Some travellers band together in Lhasa for a three- or four-day trip out to the Yarlung Valley by way of Tsetang, taking in Samye and Mindroling en route. The total cost (including permits and guide) for a Land Cruiser for such a trip is around Y2800. It's more cost-effective to add a Yarlung extension onto a trip to the Nepali border if you are heading that way.

Permits

Permits are needed to visit anywhere outside Tsetang town, though there weren't any formal permit checks in the valley during our research visit. It's best to leave Tsetang at the crack of dawn if you don't have a permit, but the only place you are likely to be checked is in Chongye, especially if you stay the night.

Permits are easier to arrange in Lhasa compared to Tsetang. CITS in Tsetang says it needs your original travel permit for Tibet before it can arrange permits for Chongye, though they may be able to grapple around this – for a price.

Sheldrak Cave ཤེལ་བྲག

Sheldrak Cave is the preserve of hardy hikers and Tibetan pilgrims. It is a tough six-hour climb to the west of Tsetang with an altitude gain of around 1000m.

For Tibetans, Sheldrak is one of Tibet's holiest pilgrimage destinations. It is the site of Guru Rinpoche's first meditation cave. King Trisong Detsen invited Guru Rinpoche to Tibet to exorcise the land of demons and the influence of Tibet's indigenous Bön faith. According to legend, it was here in the Crystal Cave that he got the job done. Unless you have a keen interest in Tibetan pilgrimage sites, it would be best to treat this as a strenuous hike rather than as a serious attraction.

The cave is reached from the road that heads out to Chongye from Tsetang. About 4km from the centre of Tsetang there is a large chörten known as the Tsechu Bumpa. It's worth trying to hitch a ride along this section. From the chörten a trail heads west from the Chongye road up the Sheldrak Valley to Sekhang Zhirka village, a sky-burial site and then a small monastery. From here it is a tough climb of less than an hour to Sheldrak. The cave has a small chapel and provides great views of the surrounding countryside.

Trandruk Monastery ཁྲ་འབྲུག་དགོན་པ

Around 7km south of the Tsetang Hotel, **Trandruk** (admission Y30) is one of the earliest Buddhist monasteries in Tibet, having been founded at the same time as the Jokhang and Ramoche in Lhasa. Dating back to the 7th-century reign of Songtsen Gampo, it is one of the demoness-subduing temples of Tibet. Trandruk's location corresponds to the demoness's left shoulder.

Trandruk was significantly enlarged in the 14th century and again under the auspices of the fifth and seventh Dalai Lamas. The monastery was badly desecrated by Red Guards during the Cultural Revolution and extensive restoration work has been carried out since 1988.

The entrance of the monastery opens into a courtyard area ringed by cloisters. The building to the rear of the courtyard has a ground plan similar to that of the Jokhang, and indeed shares the same Tibetan name, Tsuglhakhang.

The principal chapel, to the rear centre, holds a statue of Tara known as Drölma Sheshema (under a parasol), next to the five Dhyani buddhas. The Tuje Lhakhang to the right has Chenresig (Avalokiteshvara), Jampelyang (Manjushri) and Chana Dorje (Vajrapani), who form the Tibetan trinity known as the Rigsum Gonpo. Note the stove to the right, said to have belonged to Princess Wencheng, the Chinese consort of Songtsen Gampo.

Upstairs and to the rear is a central chapel containing a famous *thangka* of Drölma (Tara) made up of 29,000 pearls, as well as an ancient appliqué *thangka* showing Sakyamuni (Sakya Thukpa).

It is possible to walk here from Tsetung in 1½ hours, but there is also a steady stream of tractors plying the road between Trandruk and Tsetang. Bus No 2 from opposite the main roundabout comes here at least twice an hour.

Yumbulagang ཡུམ་བུ་བླ་སྒང

A fine, tapering finger of a structure that sprouts from a craggy ridge overlooking the patchwork fields of the Yarlung Valley, **Yumbulagang** (admission Y15), is considered the oldest building in Tibet. At least that is the claim for the original structure. Most of what can be seen today dates from 1982. It is still a remarkably impressive sight, with a lovely setting, and should not be missed.

The founding of Yumbulagang stretches back to a time of legend, and myths converge on the structure in bewildering profusion. The standard line is that it was built for King Nyentri Tsenpo, a historical figure who has been swallowed up in the mythology of Tibet. Legend has him descending from the heavens and being received as a king by the people of the Yarlung Valley. More than 400 Buddhist holy texts (known collectively as the 'Awesome Secret') are said to have fallen from the heavens at Yumbulagang in the 5th century. Murals at Yumbulagang depict the magical arrival of the texts.

There has been no conclusive dating of the original Yumbulagang, although some accounts indicate that the foundations may have been laid more than 2000 years ago. It is more likely that it dates from the 7th century, when Tibet first came under the rule of Songtsen Gampo.

The plan of Yumbulagang indicates that it was originally a fortress and probably much larger than the present structure. Today it serves as a chapel and is inhabited by around eight monks who double as guards – in 1999 some 30 statues were stolen from the main chapel. Its most impressive feature is its **tower**, and the prominence of Yumbulagang on the Yarlung skyline belies the fact that this tower is only some 11m tall.

The ground-floor **chapel** is consecrated to the ancient kings of Tibet. A central buddha image is flanked by Nyentri Tsenpo on the left and Songtsen Gampo on the right. Other kings and ministers line the side walls. There is another chapel on the upper floor with an image of Chenresig (Avalokiteshvara), similar to the one found in the Potala. There are some excellent murals by the door which depict, among other things, Nyentri Tsenpo descending from heaven, Trandruk Monastery, and Guru Rinpoche arriving at Sheldrak.

It does not take all that long to explore Yumbulagang. Perhaps the best part of a visit is the walk up along the ridge above the building. There are fabulous views of Yumbulagang and the Yarlung Valley from a promontory topped with prayer flags. It is an easy five-minute climb.

Yumbulagang is 6km from the Trandruk Monastery and there is a fair amount of traffic if you need to hitch there. The No 2 bus, originating from the Tsetang roundabout and passing Trandruk, also comes here.

Rechung-puk Monastery རབ་ཆུང་ཕུ་

A popular pilgrimage site associated with the illustrious Milarepa (1040–1123), is the remains of Rechung-puk Monastery, set on a dramatic escarpment high above the Yarlung Valley.

Milarepa, founder of the Kagyupa order, is revered by many as Tibet's greatest songwriter and poet. It was his foremost disciple, Rechungpa (1083–1161), who founded Rechung-puk as a cave retreat. Later a monastery was established at the site; it eventually housed up to 1000 monks. For pilgrims, the draw of the monastery is the **cave of Black Heruka**, where

they are hit on the back with holy relics by the craggy-faced resident monks.

To get to Rechung-puk, follow the road between Yumbulagang and Trandruk and head west (left) at kilometre marker 132. You can see the ruins of the monastery up on the ridge that divides the two channels of the Yarlung Valley. The road enters a small village and then bends to the south (left), finally crossing a river next to a small school. A couple of kilometres from the main road is a second village, Khurmey, from where it is a steep 20-minute walk up to the monastery, passing a white chörten.

A path leads over the ridge from the Heruka cave, past some ruined chapels and down to the minor road. From here, you can head west along a dirt track towards the large Gongtang Bumpa chörten and then join the main road from Tsetang to Chongye.

Tangboche Monastery བང་པོ་ཆེ་

A minor site thought to date back to 1017, Tangboche Monastery is about 15km southwest of Tsetang on the way to Chongye. Atisha (Jowo-je), the renowned Bengali scholar, stayed here in a meditation retreat. The monastery's murals, which for most visitors with an interest in things Tibetan are the main attraction, were commissioned by the 13th Dalai Lama in 1913. They can be seen in the monastery's main hall – one of the few monastic structures in this region that was not destroyed by Red Guards.

Tangboche is easily visited if you are travelling by rented transport between Tsetang and Chongye. You should be able to see the building on the left once you're about 15km out of Tsetang. You have to look carefully, as it is partially obscured by a village. There is a short trail from the road to the village and monastery.

CHONGYE VALLEY འཕྱོངས་རྒྱས་གཤོངས་

Most visitors to Chongye Valley (Map p155) go as a day trip from Tsetang, and combine it with attractions in the Yarlung Valley. It is possible to stay in the town of Chongye but you leave yourself open to permit hassles. If you want to visit the surrounding sites and don't have a permit, it's worth detouring around the central PSB office and generally keeping a low profile. A road on the eastern side of the valley bypasses the centre of town and leads to the Chongye tombs.

Chongye is a beautiful valley enclosed by rugged peaks. The views from some of the burial mounds are superb. It is also well worth climbing up to Riwo Dechen Monastery and the ruins of the old *dzong* behind it for more views of the mounds.

Chongye Town འཕྱོངས་རྒྱས་གྲོང་རྡལ་
☎ 0893 / pop 3000
Chongye town is a dusty street lined with the occasional shop and restaurant, and culminates in a T-junction. On the main drag, 250m before the junction, is the basic **Post Hotel** (☎ 735 2783; Sonzon Lu; beds Y20). It is not a town in which you'll want to linger, but it makes a good base for hikes in the Chongye Valley area. Chongye is around 27km south of Tsetang and hitching here is not that easy, though by no means impossible.

From Tsetang, there are three buses a day to Chongye town (11.30am, 2.30pm, 4pm; Y5). From there, most of the important sights are easily accessible on foot.

Chongye Burial Mounds
འཕྱོངས་རྒྱས་སྲོང་བཙན་བང་བས་
The Tombs of the Kings at Chongye represent one of the few historical sites in the country that gives any evidence of a pre-Buddhist culture in Tibet. Most of the kings interred here are now firmly associated with the rise of Buddhism on the high plateau, but the methods of their interment point to the Bön faith. It is thought that the burials were probably officiated at by Bön priests and were accompanied by sacrificial offerings. Archaeological evidence suggests that earth burial, not sky burial, might have been quite widespread in the time of the Yarlung kings, and may not have been limited to royalty.

Accounts of the location and number of the mounds differ. Erosion of the mounds has also made some of them difficult to accurately identify. It is agreed, however, that there is a group of 10 burial mounds just south of the Chongye-chu.

The most revered of the mounds, and the closest to the main road, is the **Tomb of Songtsen Gampo**. It is the largest of the burial mounds and it has a small **Nyingmapa temple** (admission Y30) atop its 13m-high summit. The southernmost of the group of mounds, high on the slopes of Mt Mura, is the **Tomb of Trisong Detsen**. It is about a one-hour climb, but there are superb views of the Chongye Valley.

Chingwa Tagtse Dzong འཕྱིང་བ་སྟག་རྩེ་རྫོང་
The *dzong* (fort), can be seen clearly from Chongye town and from the burial mounds, its crumbling ramparts straddling a ridge of Mt Chingwa. Once one of the most powerful forts in central Tibet, it dates back to the time of the early Yarlung kings. The *dzong* is also celebrated as the birthplace of the fifth Dalai Lama. There is nothing to see in the fort itself, but again you are rewarded with some great views if you take the 40-minute or so walk up from Chongye. Paths lead up from the centre of town, from the nearby ruins of the red chapel and from the gully behind Riwo Dechen Monastery.

Riwo Dechen Monastery
འཕྱོང་རྒྱས་རི་བོ་བདེ་ཆེན་
The large, active, Gelugpa-sect Riwo Dechen Monastery sprawls across the lower slopes of Mt Chingwa below the fort. There are some nice walks up to the ridge north of the monastery and then down to the fort.

Riwo Dechen Monastery can be reached by a half-hour walk from Chongye's excellent old Tibetan quarter. Turn west at the town's T-junction and ask for the 'gompa'. Halfway up is a grand, new chörten. It is sometimes possible to stay the night at the monastery – a magical experience.

LHAMO LA-TSO ལྷ་མོའི་བླ་མཚོ་
One of Ü's most important pilgrimage destinations, Lhamo La-tso is around 115km northeast of Tsetang. The *la* of La-tso is a Tibetan word that means 'soul' or 'life spirit'. La resides in both animate and inanimate forms, including lakes, mountains and trees. The two may sometimes be connected, as in the Tibetan custom of planting a tree at the birth of a child – such a tree is known as a *la-shing*. In the case of Lhamo La-tso, 'la' is identified with the spirit of Tibet itself.

The Dalai Lamas have traditionally made pilgrimages to Lhamo La-tso to seek visions that appear on the surface of the oracle lake. The Tibetan regent journeyed to the lake in 1933 after the death of the 13th Dalai Lama and had a vision of a monastery in Amdo that led to the discovery of the present Dalai Lama. The lake is also considered the home of Palden Lhamo.

The gateway to Lhamo La-tso is the dramatic, but mostly ruined, **Chökorgye Monastery** (4500m), wedged between three mountains,

Zhidag (north), Shridevi (south) and Begtse (east), in the Tsichu Valley. Founded in 1509 by the second Dalai Lama, Gendun Gyatso (1476–1542), the monastery served later Dalai Lamas and regents as a staging post for visits to the lake. Some 500 monks were in residence until the place was flattened by the Chinese during the Cultural Revolution; a handful have returned and the main hall has been rebuilt.

On the nearby slope is a *mani* wall that consecrates a footprint stone of the second Dalai Lama.

Just short of the mountain pass that over-looks Lhamo La-tso is a ritual *shökde* (throne) built for the Dalai Lamas. It is now buried under a mound of *hadak* (silk scarves). It's a 15-minute walk from the *shökde* to the pass and another 1½ hours to get down to the lake which is encircled by a kora.

Permits

A visit to Lhamo La-tso requires four permits (three days to process), which are usually arranged with the help of a tourist company in Lhasa. The only place you are likely to be checked is at guesthouse at Chökorgye Monastery or a hotel in Gyantsa Xian. We weren't checked during our visit, but because we were without a permit we didn't hang around too long.

Sleeping & Eating

Lhamo La-tso is difficult to reach and receives few foreign visitors. You should have your own food and be prepared for rain, snow and cold weather – the lake is at an altitude of over 5000m.

The nearest accommodation to Lhamo La-tso is at **Chökorgye Monastery** (dm Y50), which has basic dorm rooms at outrageous prices. There are good camping spots behind the temple walls if you have a tent.

For those who have a permit, there are a couple of hotels in Gyatsa Xian.

Clean and bright with TV and two double beds, **Jimao Binguan** (☎ 0893-7322537; d Y80) is the best option in Gyantsa Xian. It is in a blue-tile building above some shops. The other option is the barracks-style and overpriced **Sunfu Binguan** (dm Y50), down the cross-street nearby the vegetable market. A bathhouse (Y5) is opposite the Ji Mao. Gyatsa Xian is well-endowed with food shops and Chinese restaurants.

Getting There & Away

The approach to Lhamo La-tso begins from Tsetang, usually by hired vehicle. From Tsetang it is 27km to the village of Rong Xiang where a bridge crosses the Brahmaputra to Sangri. Continuing east the road passes by **Chaga Monastery**, situated above the road next to a large purple water tank. Most of the monastery stands in ruins, but the main hall has been rebuilt and features a statue of Sakyamuni (Sakya Thukpa). Check out Songsten Gampo's sword on the pillar to the left. If the main hall is locked you can get a key from the caretaker who lives next door.

The paved road ends here and it's slow going for 32km to Chusom (3880m), where the **Mansion of Lhagyari** – a three-storey, mud-brick pile – looms above the road. You can scamper up to the 13th century ruins in about five minutes. The interior bears some painted crossbeams but is pretty unstable.

From Chusom the road climbs 36km to Batang-la (4950m) and then descends 26km to Lasuo village, where you can stay in a basic **guesthouse** (dm Y10) if it is late. Another 26km brings you to Gyatsa Xian, where a bypass leads 3km to a bridge that spans the Yarlung Tsangpo. Traffic is sparse but you might be able to ride from here up to Chökorgye Monastery, otherwise, it's a 55km walk of two days. Keep a low profile in Gyatsa Xian if you have no permit.

Altogether, it takes about six hours to drive from Tsetang to Chökorgye Monastery.

From the monastery, 4WD vehicles can drive (one hour) up a twisting mountain road to the *shökde*. Without transport, you can walk to the pass from the monastery in four hours – you have to be fit, acclimatised and well equipped to attempt it.

The most interesting way to reach the lake is to trek from Rutok (six days, via Dzingchi and Magong-la) or from Sangri, both routes via Gyelung-la. Coming from Sangri it's 42km along a driveable road to Olkhar, where you can break the journey at a hot spring pool. For detailed information on this trek see Gary McCue's *Trekking in Tibet – A Traveler's Guide*.

A three-day trip to Lhamo La-tso in a hired vehicle, including permits and guide, will cost around Y4000. Private drivers who don't mind the illegal trip will travel without permits and charge Y2100.

Tsang གཙང་

CONTENTS

TSANG

The traditional Tibetan province of Tsang lies to the west of Ü, the province with which Tsang has long shared political dominance and rivalries over the Tibetan plateau. The two major urban centres of Tsang are Shigatse and Gyantse. Both contain important historical sights and are popular destinations for travellers.

Most travellers make their way through Tsang in rented vehicles, going from Lhasa to Kathmandu via Yamdrok-tso, Gyantse, Shigatse, Sakya, Everest Base Camp, Tingri and Zhangmu. It is a convenient route along the 725km Friendship Hwy that takes in Tsang's most important attractions. By public transport it is possible to get as far as Lhatse but after that you must rely on your thumb.

Most of Tsang's sights involve detours from the highway. Sakya is 21km from the highway, close to Lhatse and well worth an overnight visit, while Everest Base Camp is 91km from Shegar by road or a three-day trek from Tingri. If you're heading to Lhatse by Land Cruiser you can detour off the Friendship Hwy to check out the scenic Phuntsoling Monastery. There's plenty of scope for travel off the beaten track, particularly from the Friendship Hwy and to smaller monasteries around Gyantse and Shigatse.

Apart from Shigatse, most areas of Tsang require a travel permit from the PSB in Shigatse. In practice we found no checks in any of the towns along the Friendship Hwy, nor in Gyantse or Shalu.

The entries in this chapter follow a southwesterly route through Tsang from Lhasa to the border with Nepal, taking in the main attractions of the area on the way.

TSANG

HIGHLIGHTS

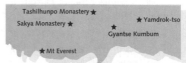

- Gaze at the turquoise waters of **Yamdrok-tso** (p162), the coiling scorpion-shaped lake
- Visit **Tashilhunpo Monastery** (p173) and the spectacular tombs of the Panchen Lamas
- Climb through the levels of the **Gyantse Kumbum** (p167), the most stunning architectural wonder in Tibet
- Tour the breathtaking assembly hall of **Sakya Monastery** (p182), one of Tibet's greatest treasures
- Take in the magnificent views of the north face of **Mt Everest** (p189)

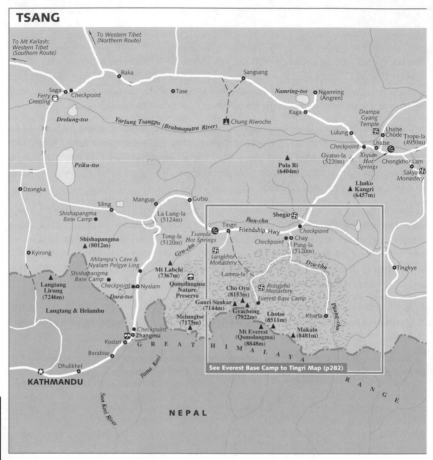

TSANG

To Mt Kailash;
Western Tibet
(Southern Route)

To Western Tibet
(Northern Route)

Raka

Saga
Ferry
Crossing
Checkpoint

Sangsang

Tase

Namring-tso
Ngamring
(Ängren)

Kaga

Drampa
Gyang
Temple

Drolung-tso
Yarlung Tsangpo (Brahmaputra River)
Chung Riwoche

Lulung
Lhatse
Chöde
Tropu-la
(4950m)

Checkpoint
Lhatse

Gyatso-la
(5220m)
Xiqian
Hot
Springs
Chongkhor Lam

Peiku-tso
Pula Ri
(6404m)
Sakya
Monastery

Dzongka

Siling
Mangup
Gutso

Lhako
Kangri
(6457m)

Shishapangma
Base Camp
La Lung-la
(5124m)

Shegar

Bun-chu
Tingri

Friendship Hwy
Checkpoint

Shishapangma
(8012m)

Tong-la
(5120m)
Tsamda
Hot Springs
Checkpoint
Chay

Pang-la
(5120m)

Kyirong

Gyu-chu

Langkhor
Monastery

Dza-chu

Tingkye

Milarepa's Cave &
Nyalam Pelgye Ling
Mt Labchi
(7367m)

Lamma-la

Shishapangma
Base Camp
Checkpoint
Nyalam
Qomolangma
Nature
Preserve

Cho Oyu
(8153m)
Rongphu
Monastery

Everest Base Camp

Langtang
Lirung
(7246m)
Dara-tso

Gauri Sankar
(7144m)

Phung-chu

Langtang & Helambu

Melungtse
(7175m)
Gyachung
(7922m)
Lhotse
(8511m)
Kharta

Checkpoint
Zhangmu
Kodari
G   R   E   A   T
H   I   M   A   L   A   Y   A

Mt Everest
(Qomolangma)
(8848m)
Makalu
(8481m)

Barabise

Dhulikhel
Tama Kosi
R   A   N   G   E

KATHMANDU

Sun Kosi River

See Everest Base Camp to Tingri Map (p282)

NEPAL

History

With the decline of the Lhasa kings in the 10th century, the epicentre of Tibetan power moved to Sakya, under Mongol patronage from around the mid-13th to the mid-14th centuries.

Following the fall of the Sakya government, the power shifted back to Ü and then again back to Tsang. However, until the rise of the Gelugpa order and the Dalai Lamas in the 17th century, neither Tsang nor Ü effectively governed the whole of central Tibet, and the two provinces were usually rivals for power. Some commentators see the rivalry between the Panchen Lama and Dalai Lama as a latter-day extension of this provincial wrestling for political dominance.

Getting Around

Most public transport runs along the middle Friendship Hwy along the Yarlung Tsangpo; the road is currently being upgraded. Land Cruiser trips (p117) generally take the interesting southern route via Yamdrok-tso but there is less public transport here. Another option is the northern route via Yangpachen, with excellent views around the Shugu-la.

Public transport runs along the Friendship Hwy as far as Shegar. After that, you're on your own.

YAMDROK-TSO ཡར་འབྲོག་མཚོ་
elev 4488m

On the old road that travels from Gyantse to Lhasa, dazzling Yamdrok-tso is normally

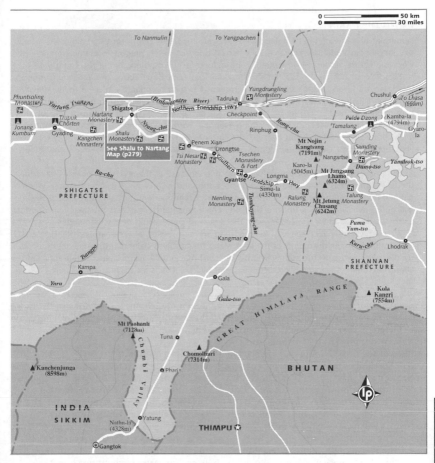

first seen from the summit of the Kamba-la (4794m). The lake lies several hundred metres below the road, and in clear weather is a fabulous shade of deep turquoise. Far in the distance is the huge massif of Mt Nojin Kangtsang (7191m).

Yamdrok-tso is a coiling, many-armed body of water shaped like a scorpion. It doubles back on itself on the western side, effectively creating a large island within its reaches. For Tibetans, it is one of the four holy lakes of Tibet (the others are Lhamo La-tso, Nam-tso and Manasarovar), home to wrathful deities, and devout Tibetan pilgrims circumambulate the lake, a walk of around seven days.

Most Western travellers are content with a glimpse of the lake from the Kamba-la and

views from the town of Nangartse, where you can stay the night. The views of the valley from Samding Monastery are another highlight.

Permits

Yamdrok-tso is in Shannan prefecture and officially you need a permit from Tsetang Public Security Bureau (PSB) to visit independently, but it's unlikely that you will be checked. If you hire a vehicle, the agency will arrange your permit for you.

Nangartse ཡ་རྣ་རྩེ།

☎ 0893 / elev 4500m

Nangartse is the largest town on the lakeside and a popular stop for the night. It's not a

---

DOWN THE DRAIN

Yamdrok-tso is one of Tibet's holiest lakes and an important centre for pilgrimage. Yet what devout Tibetan Buddhists perceive as a sacred body of water, pragmatic Chinese engineers view as a natural resource just waiting to be utilised for the development of the country.

Yamdrok-tso has an unusual location locked in a high bowl above the Yarlung Tsangpo (Brahmaputra River) and the Chinese government has long harboured a plan to utilise gravity to create a hydroelectric supply. By the mid-1980s the Chinese leadership had sanctioned a plan to build a 6km tunnel 10m below the surface of the lake that would send the waters of the lake dropping some 846m into the Yarlung Tsangpo. Work was temporarily halted after opposition by the Panchen Lama, but by 1997 the turbines had started to produce electricity for the Lhasa region. You can see the pumps from the Lhasa–Shigatse road, 15km southwest of Chushul.

The project is highly controversial, and not only because of the reverence Tibetans have for the lake. Yamdrok-tso is a dead lake with no outlet and no perennial source of water. Water drained from it can never be replenished naturally. Chinese scientists claim that excess power will pump river water back up into the lake. Environmentalists fear that the lake, an important breeding ground for the endangered black-necked crane, could be dry within 20 years.

Water levels do indeed seem to be dropping and the section of water around Nangartse is now cut off from the main body of the lake. Many Tibetans also claim that the energy produced by the lake's hydroelectric supply will be directed mainly at fuelling Chinese migration into Lhasa. The Chinese reaction is predictable: other hydroelectric sites are in the pipeline.

---

particularly attractive place but there is a small monastery in the south of town, an old Tibetan quarter and a small *dzong* (fort) to the north (famed as the birthplace of the mother of the fifth Dalai Lama). There are also opportunities for walks nearby, such as to Samding Monastery. You can't actually walk to the lakeshore as you will soon find yourself up to your knees in bog, but the views are still good and bird-watchers in particular will have a field day in Nangartse during the summer months.

All the guesthouses and the restaurants are within 200m of each other on the main road. All have pit toilets but no showers.

Post Guesthouse (Youzheng Zhaodaisuo; dm/tr/q per bed Y20/35/30) Beds in the triple rooms are probably the best bet here. Buckets of cold water are available outside rooms. Cheerful Tibetan staff and a teahouse give the place a much-appreciated touch of warmth.

Caiyuan Zhaodaisuo (d per bed Y50) This is the government-run guesthouse, and it has the best and most expensive rooms in town. It's clean and comfortable but you still only get pit toilets for your money.

Sunshine Grain Hotel (Riguang Liangshiju Zhaodaisuo; dm Y25-30) Pretty basic and a bit grubby but has a redeeming Tibetan-style veranda.

Lhasa Restaurant (dishes Y10-16; ☺ lunch & dinner) Land Cruiser tours pull into this Tibetan-style joint for lunch. Grab a seat downstairs among the friendly locals knitting and playing cards. There's an English menu.

Samding Monastery བསམ་སྡིངས་དགོན་པ

On the shores of Yamdrok-tso, **Samding** (admission Y10) sits around 10km east of Nangartse. The monastery is sited on a ridge that separates the northern arm of the lake from Dumotso, a smaller lake between the northern and southern arms of Yamdrok-tso. It provides excellent views of the Dumo plain and the mountains to the south. You can walk here from Nangartse in about two hours.

Samding is noted for the unusual fact that it is traditionally headed by a female incarnate lama named Dorje Phagmo (Diamond Sow). When the Mongolian armies invaded Samding in 1716, Dorje Phagmo changed her nuns into pigs to help them escape the terrors. Her current incarnation is working for the government in Lhasa.

It's possible to visit the main *dukhang* (assembly hall), to the right of the courtyard, which is dominated by a statue of Sakyamuni (Sakya Thukpa). There's also a footprint of the ninth Dorje Phagmo here, plus an eerie protector chapel and several chapels upstairs. There are 31 monks in residence.

To walk on to Samding, take the dirt road leading from the northern end of Nangartse across to a small village recognisable by its trees. Once you get here, take the path on the right and follow it all the way to the monastery. It's worth climbing up the ridge behind the monastery for fantastic views. It's also possible to drive here in a Land Cruiser, but the road turns to glue after it rains.

Getting There & Away

Many people travelling in rented vehicles include Yamdrok-tso in their trip to the Nepali border, en route from Lhasa to Kathmandu. It's also possible to hire a vehicle for a four-day loop from Lhasa visiting the lake, Gyantse and Shigatse. At the time of research, the road between Lhasa and Yamdrok-tso over the Kamba-la was under repair and traffic was being rerouted (though this will probably change when repairs are completed) via the Gyaro-la, which lies south of Gongkar Chöde Monastery (p146).

A bus heading to Nangartse (Y40, six hours) departs from Lhasa's main bus station at around 8.30am every second day. The bus returns at 8.30am the next day from the main street in Nangartse. Daily buses also pass through Nangartse between Lhasa and Lhodrak.

Leaving Yamdrok-tso is as spectacular as arriving, since you have to cross the 5045m Karo-la, with its awesome roadside views of the Nojin-Kangtsang Glacier. It was here that Colonel Younghusband's British troops clashed with Tibetan forces en route to Lhasa (p170).

There is no public transport between Yamdrok-tso and Gyantse, and hitching can be difficult as most of the vehicles on the road have been hired by tourists who have paid for their ride.

RALUNG MONASTERY རྭ་ལུང་དགོན་པ
elev 4550m

If you have your own transport and you want to get right off the beaten track, you could make a detour to **Ralung Monastery** (admission Y15), 5km south of the road west of the Karo-la. Ralung was founded in 1180 and gets its name from the monastery's self-manifesting image of a goat (*ra* in Tibetan).

The original Tsuglhakhang (great temple) stands in ruins, as does a chörten (stupa) visible from the roof (compare the latter with a B&W photo of the original, in the Tsepame Chapel). There are several small chapels to

visit. Look for images of the founder Tsanpa Gyare and the Drukpa Rinpoche (the monastery belongs to the Drukpa Kagyud school), who resides in India.

There are buses every four days running from Gyantse to Ralung village (Y10), but the inconvenient schedule means you'll have to spend two nights somewhere at Ralung. Two roads run to the monastery from either end of the Friendship Hwy. The 5km western road turns off at kilometre marker 196; the eastern road at kilometre marker 189 is longer at around 8km.

GYANTSE རྒྱལ་རྩེ
☎ 0892 / elev 3950m

Gyantse, located in the Nyang-chu Valley is famed for the Gyantse Kumbum, the largest chörten in Tibet. The chörten is a magnificent tiered structure that has only two ruined and remote contemporaries in the Buddhist world: Jonang Kumbum (p187), 60km northeast of Lhatse, and the even more remote Chung Riwoche in the west of Tsang. Gyantse is worth a couple of days, especially if you are interested in making day trips to little-visited monasteries in the vicinity.

Between the 14th and 15th centuries, the town emerged as the centre of a fiefdom, with powerful connections to the Sakyapa order. By 1440 Gyantse's most impressive architectural achievements – the *kumbum* and the *dzong* – had been completed. The Pelkor Chöde Monastery also dates from this period.

Gyantse's historical importance declined from the end of the 15th century, although the town continued to be a major centre for the trade of wood and wool between India and Tibet – Gyantse carpets were considered the finest in Tibet. The town's position at the crossroads of trade routes leading south to Bhutan, west to Shigatse and northeast to Lhasa turned Gyantse into the third-largest town in Tibet by the time of the Chinese takeover but it's since been eclipsed by Chamdo, Bayi and Tsetang. In 1904 it became the site of a major battle during Colonel Younghusband's advance on Lhasa (p170), and British troops spent a month in the Gyantse Dzong before continuing to Lhasa.

Gyantse has a horse-racing and archery festival in the summer, which is traditionally held in the middle of the fourth lunar

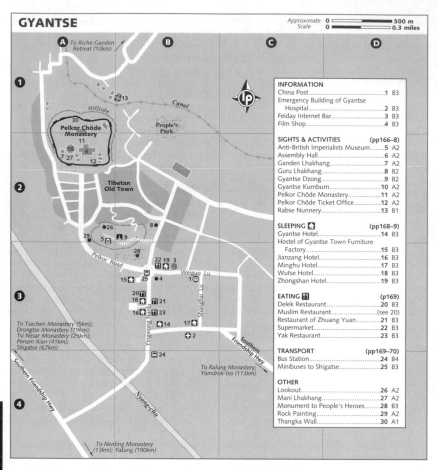

GYANTSE

Approximate Scale

0 — 500 m
0 — 0.3 miles

month, though recently dates seem to have been fixed in mid-July.

Travel permits for Gyantse are normally available from Shigatse PSB (Y50) but many travellers take the risk without one. We've never been asked for a permit.

Orientation

Buses stop at Gyantse's one major intersection. To the north and west is the old Tibetan part of town. It is concentrated around the main road leading to Pelkor Chöde Monastery past the *dzong*, which looms over the town on a high ridge, and spills north over the hill. To the south and east is an incipient Chinese quarter, with government buildings, shops, restaurants and a couple of hotels.

Information

Feiday Internet Bar (Weiguo Lu; per hr Y4) The connection is so slow that it's probably quicker to write down your message and post it.

Sights

PELKOR CHÖDE MONASTERY

The monastery compound in the far north of town houses **Pelkor Chöde Monastery** (☎ 817 2680; Pelkor Lam; admission Y40; ⏱ 8.30am-7pm, some chapels closed 1-3pm) and the Gyantse Kumbum. Founded in 1418, the Pelkor Chöde was once a complex of 15 monasteries that brought together three different orders of Tibetan Buddhism in the one compound: a rare instance of multidenominational tolerance. Nine of the monasteries were Gelugpa, three were Sakyapa and three belonged to the obscure Büton suborder whose head monastery was Shalu (p179) near Shigatse.

Today, much of the sprawling courtyard, enclosed by walls that cling to the hills backing onto the monastery, is bare. The best way to get an idea of the original extent of Pelkor Chöde is to view it from the Gyantse Dzong.

The **assembly hall** is dark and if you want a good look at the various murals and *thangkas* (Tibetan religious paintings) it is a good idea to bring a torch. The entrance is decorated with statues of the Four Guardian Kings instead of the usual paintings. Look out for the jewel-vomiting mongoose. Just by the entrance on the left is a particularly spooky protector chapel, with murals depicting sky burial. Look for the huge *tormas* (sculptures made out of *tsampa*, roasted-barley flour) in a case outside the entrance.

The main chapel is located to the rear of the assembly hall. There is an inner route around the chapel, which is lined with fine murals. The central image is of Sakyamuni (Sakya Thukpa), who is flanked by the Past and Future Buddhas. Images of bodhisattvas line the walls.

To the left of the main chapel is the Dorjeling Lhakhang, with a four-headed Namba Namse (Vairocana) and the other four Dhyani Buddhas.

The first chapel to the left on the upper floor is noted for a three-dimensional mandala that dominates the room; the paintings of the Indian-looking *mahasiddhas* (highly accomplished Tantric practitioners) that adorn the walls; and lacquered images of key figures in the Sakyapa lineage. Have a look at the 84 *mahasiddhas*, each of whom is unique and shown contorted in a yogic posture. Other chapels are dedicated to Jampa (Maitreya), Tsongkhapa and the 16 arhats (literally 'worthy ones'). It can be a hassle getting the monks to open up all the chapels. Photos cost Y10 per chapel.

A new and easily overlooked **Ganden Lhakhang** chapel to the left of the Kumbum is worth a quick look for the largest Tsongkhapa statue in Tibet.

GYANTSE KUMBUM

Commissioned by a Gyantse prince in 1427, the **Gyantse Kumbum** (admission included in entry to Pelkor Chöde) is the town's foremost attraction.

The chörten is packed with some exquisite Tibetan mural paintings and rises 35m over four floors surmounted by a gold dome. The dome rises like a crown over four sets of eyes that gaze serenely out in the directions of the cardinal points. As you climb upwards through the chapels of the *kumbum* you are drawn through progressively higher levels on the Tantric path.

A clockwise route leads murmuring pilgrims up through the six floors, taking in the 77 chapels that line the walls. There are two sets of four central chapels that extend to the floor above from the 1st and 3rd floors, and each of these is surrounded by smaller chapels in diminishing numbers and size as the floors ascend.

Much of the statuary in the chapels was damaged during the Cultural Revolution but it has now been restored. The murals, however, have weathered very well. They are of 14th-century provenance and if they were not created by Newari (Nepali) artisans they are obviously influenced by Newari forms. Experts also see evidence of Chinese influence and, in the fusion of these Newari and Chinese forms with Tibetan sensibilities, the emergence of a syncretic but distinctly Tibetan style of painting.

Whatever the case, there are an awful lot of murals to see (*kumbum* means '100,000 images'!) and, unless you have a special interest in the evolution of Tibetan Buddhist art, it is difficult not to hurry through the last two floors. Lingering in a few of the chapels and having a close look at the wall frescoes is enough to give you an idea of what is on offer in other chapels. For a superb view of the whole chörten, climb the hills behind the monastery (you can even walk along the defensive walls).

Depending on the position of the sun, certain chapels are sometimes illuminated with a warm, soft light that allows flashless photographs. There is photography charge of Y10 for interior shots.

First Floor

This floor has four main chapels, oriented according to the cardinal points. The four chapels are dedicated to Sakyamuni (along with two disciples, medicine buddhas and Guru Rinpoche) in the south; Sukhavati, the 'pure land of the west' and home of red Öpagme (Amitabha) in the west; Marmedze

(Dipamkara, the Past Buddha) in the north; and Tushita (another 'pure land' and home of Jampa) in the east. In between are some excellent murals depicting minor Tantric and protector deities. Statues of the Four Guardian Kings in the east mark the way to the upper floors.

Second Floor
The first four chapels in order clockwise from the stairs are dedicated to Jampelyang (known in Sanskrit as Manjushri), Chenresig (Avalokiteshvara), Tsepame (Amitayus) and Drölma (Green Tara). Most of the other chapels are devoted to wrathful protector deities, including to Drölma (White Tara; 12th chapel from the stairs), Chana Dorje (Vajrapani; 14th chapel) and Mikyöba (Akshobhya; 15th chapel), a blue buddha who holds a *dorje* (thunderbolt).

Third Floor
This floor is dominated by a second series of two-storey chapels at the cardinal points portraying the four Dhyani Buddhas – red Öpagme (Amitabha) in the south, yellow Rinchen Jungne (Ratnasambhava) in the west, green Donyo Drupa (Amoghasiddhi) in the north and blue Mikyöba (Akshobhya) in the east. There are several other chapels devoted to the fifth Dhyani Buddha, white Namse (Vairocana). Again, most of the other chapels are filled with wrathful deities.

Fourth Floor
The 11 chapels on this floor are dedicated to teachers, interpreters and translators of obscure orders of Tibetan Buddhism. Exceptions are the Three Kings of Tibet on the north side (eighth chapel clockwise from the steps) and Guru Rinpoche (10th chapel).

Upper Floors
The 5th floor, which is also known as the Bumpa, has four chapels and gives access to the roof of the *kumbun*. Hidden steps behind a statue on the western side lead up to the 6th floor and take you onto the veranda at the level of the eyes painted on the wall. From here there are great views of the town and monastery. There is also a series of murals painted around a central cube. The top floor portrays a Tantric manifestation of Sakyamuni (Sakya Thukpa), but you may find it locked.

GYANTSE DZONG
This 14th-century **fort** (☎ 817 2116; admission Y30; ⏱ 8.30am-8.30pm) is worth the stiff 20-minute climb to its upper limits. This is more for the amazing views of Gyantse, the monastery compound at the end of town and the surrounding Nyang-chu Valley, than for what is left of the *dzong* itself, which is not much.

Some of the *dzong*'s buildings can be entered and explored, but generally there is very little to see. About midway up through the fort complex is an **Anti-British Imperialists Museum** featuring a fabulously warped version of the 1904 British invasion. The displays start off with the predictable 'Tibet is an inalienable part of the motherland...' and the inevitable dioramas of oppressed serfs. Some of the more spurious facts quoted include references to the '10,000 British troops' (the British claim 1000 troops and 10,000 servants), the death of reporter Edmund Chandler (he actually returned home to write a bestseller) and the claim that the Tibetan troops were 'fighting to safeguard the [Chinese] motherland'.

Entry to the *dzong* is via a gate, just north of the main roundabout and the crumbling 'People's Heroes' park. You can also enter up the from Pelkor Rd via the alley marked 'Lane Castle', which is the route that Land Cruisers take.

OTHER SIGHTS
Hidden behind the hill that runs between the monastery and *dzong* is **Rabse Nunnery**, a delightful place decorated with prayer flags, chörtens, *mani lhakhangs* and a nice kora path. The 'correct' way to visit is along the clockwise pilgrim trail that leads around the back of the Pelkhor Chöde Monastery. You can also approach from the northern part of the Tibetan town. Head northwest and then turn left when you get to the group of warehouses decorated with Communist red stars.

Close to the eastern entrance to Gyantse Dzong is the welcoming **Guru Lhakhang**, a small chapel with a central statue of Guru Rinpoche.

Sleeping
BUDGET
Jianzang Hotel (☎ 817 3720; www.jzjzhotel.com; Yingxiong Nanlu; d Y180-200, tr per bed with/without bathroom Y50/40) Run by English-speaking Tibetan doctor Gyantsen, this gets our vote as the best

place in town. Rooms are clean, spacious and good value, and the upper balcony is a nice place to kick back. Some rooms have squat toilets; others are Western-style and there are shared hot showers for the cheaper rooms. Staff are friendly and there's a cosy Tibetan-style dining room (but disappointing food). Laundry is available for Y3 per piece. The best rooms are in the new block overlooking the main road. The website is entertaining.

Wutse Hotel (☎ 817 2909; fax 817 2880; Yingxiong Nanlu; dm Y40, s/d/tr with bathroom Y220/286/320) Another popular place set around a courtyard. The cheap beds are in musty quads and the shared toilets are a bit rough but there are clean showers and decent meals. Discounts of 20% sometimes apply.

Hostel of Gyantse Town Furniture Factory (☎ 817 2254; Pelkor Rd; dm Y30) This snappily named hostel on the main junction is do-able but there are better options. The double rooms are fairly clean, and basic squat toilets and scummy showers (Y5) are available.

MID-RANGE

Zhongshan Hotel (☎ 817 5555; 10 Weiguo Lu; s/d Y150/288) For that new hotel smell try this carpeted and clean Chinese-style option, with 24-hour hot water. Cheaper rooms without bathroom are planned for Y120. Discounts of 20% are standard.

Gyantse Hotel (☎ 817 2222; fax 817 2366; 8 Yingxiong Nanlu; d/tr Y460/575, ste Y768-1100) This huge place is the main group-tourist pad. It has all you would expect – a deserted gift shop, a two-week old copy of China Daily, awful coffee and clocks showing the wrong time in all major capitals. Splurge on a massage (Y160 for 45 minutes) or copy the Chinese tourists and get dressed up in traditional Tibetan clothes (Y5). Discounts of 20% apply from November to March.

Minghu Hotel (Minghu Fandian; ☎ 817 2468; 1 Shanghai Lu; d/tr Y369/380) A clean and quiet two-star Chinese-style hotel with spacious but smoky rooms. Doubles/triples are sometimes discounted to Y230/250.

Eating

Almost all restaurants in Tibet are open during meal times and will often cook at any time. There's usually no fixed opening hours.

Restaurant of Zhuang Yuan (Yingxiong Nanlu; dishes Y15-35) The owners of the Zhuang Yuan

are very keen to please and offer excellent Chinese dishes. It's not the cheapest place in town but portions are large and prices are flexible. The sweet and sour chicken (Y35) is legendary; make sure you are in the kitchen to see the pyrotechnics.

Delek Restaurant (☎ 817 2793; Yingxiong Nanlu; mains Y15-40) This decent Nepali restaurant serves all the favourites, from apple *momos* to Nepali curries. The food is fairly ordinary but the atmosphere is relaxed and the staff are competent.

Similar is the **Yak Restaurant** (Yingxiong Nanlu; mains Y15-30), offering backpacker treats like French toast (Y12), pizza, burgers, sizzlers – dishes served on a hot, sizzling plate – and breakfasts.

Wutse Restaurant (Wutse Hotel; breakfast Y20, set Nepali meal Y30, mains Y12-20) The Nepali menu here looks good, from ginger carrot soup to chicken butter *masala*, but don't expect anything too authentic. Service is lackadaisical. The rooftop would be a great place if they ever get it going.

Muslim Restaurant (Yingxiong Nanlu; noodles Y5-8) If you are after something a little cheaper, you can get a good plate of *ganbian* (homemade noodles fried with yak meat) or *chao mianpian* (fried noodle squares) at this Muslim place.

Getting There & Away

The easiest way to get to Gyantse is from Shigatse and this way you have the added opportunity of getting a permit for the trip from Shigatse PSB. Minivans depart from in front of Shigatse's main bus station between 10am and 8pm (Y25, 90 minutes). Alternatively get a seat in a taxi for around Y20 (one hour, Y80 for the taxi all to yourself). If you take an early morning bus from Lhasa you can get all the way to Gyantse the same day.

Minivans from Gyantse back to Shigatse leave every hour or so from the main intersection in Gyantse. Gyantse's bus station is derelict.

Hitching to Yamdrok-tso is not easy; you are best off walking a way along the road and trying from there. You'll probably get a lift as far as the hydroelectric engineering works, 30km east of Gyantse. From here, hitching is tricky and your best bet is to walk about 1km east and hope for a truck bound for Nangartse.

BAYONETS TO GYANTSE

The British invasion of Tibet, also known as the Younghusband expedition, drew Tibet into the 'great game' between imperial Russia and Britain. Wild speculation about Russian designs on Tibet had reached epidemic proportions in Britain by the turn of the 19th century. And when Tibet thumbed its nose at the British-drafted Sikkim-Tibet convention of 1890, which hoped to open Tibet for trade with the Raj, the British decided on more persuasive tactics. Francis Younghusband, an army officer with rich experience of Central Asia, was instructed to advance on Gyantse from Yatung with 1000 troops (plus 10,000 servants and 4000 yaks) to gain 'satisfaction' from the Tibetans.

Despite previous brushes with British firepower, the Tibetans seem to have had little idea what they were up against. About halfway between Yatung and Gyantse, a Tibetan army of 1500 troops bearing a motley assortment of arms confronted a British force carrying light artillery, Maxim machine guns and modern rifles. The Tibetans' trump card was a charm marked with the seal of the Dalai Lama which they were told would protect them from British bullets. It didn't. Firing began after a false alarm and the British slaughtered 700 Tibetans in four minutes.

The British buried the Tibetan dead (the Tibetans dug them up at night and carried them off for sky burial) and set up a field hospital, dumbfounding the wounded Tibetans, who could not understand why the British would try to kill them one day and save them the next.

The British continued their advance and found the Gyantse Dzong deserted. Curiously, rather than occupy the *dzong*, the British camped on the outskirts of Gyantse. After waiting a month for officials from Lhasa to arrive (they never came), a force of 800 Tibetan troops reoccupied the *dzong* under the cover of darkness. Meanwhile Younghusband sped off up to the Karo-la to take on 3000 Tibetans who had dug themselves in at over 5000m – the highest battle in British military history and a fine example of frozen stiff upper lip.

Getting Around

All of Gyantse's sights can be reached comfortably on foot. Guests can hire bikes from the Gyantse Hotel for a pricey Y5 per hour.

AROUND GYANTSE

There are several excellent adventurous half-day trips to sights around Gyantse that could warrant an extra day or two in town.

Tsechen Monastery & Fort རྩེ་ཆེན་དགོན་པ

The traditional village of Tsechen is about 5km northwest of Gyantse and is a nice half-day trip from town. There is a small monastery above the village but the main reason to hike out here is to climb the ruined fortress, wander along the defensive walls and enjoy great views of the (often flooded) river valley below. It's a good idea to bring a picnic.

The fortress is believed to have been built as early as the 14th century and was used by the British during their 1904 invasion, although it was already partly ruined by then. Hike up to the right side of the fortress and then cross over to the highest ramparts on the left. Across the highway and behind a hill are more monastic ruins.

To get to Tsechen you can either walk, hitch or take a taxi along the Southern Friendship Hwy to Shigatse. The village is just past the turn-off south to Yatung. On the way back it's possible to cut through fields to the river and follow this back to the Gyantse bridge. You might get a lift back on a tractor for a couple of yuan; otherwise it's an hour-long walk.

Riche Ganden Retreat རི་ཆེ་དགའ་ལྡན

Hidden in a fold of a valley north of town, this ruined and little-visited monastery is a fine 10km (two hours) hike from Gyantse. Vehicles can travel three quarters of the route as far as a water storage tank. The last section is the only steep section, as you drop into a ravine and then climb from a ruined manor house and herders' camp. Watch out for the dogs here.

There are ruins all around the site, including what was once the main Drölma Lhakhang; compare it with the B&W photos taken of the monastery before it was destroyed. Today there are eight Gelugpa monks here. The central Tsongkhapa statue has a glass plate in his chest which holds an older image of Tsongkhapa.

After nearly two months waiting for Lhasa officials, the British troops received orders to re-take the Gyantse Dzong and march on Lhasa. The assault on the Gyantse Dzong involved a diversionary attack on the northeast front while the real attack took place on the southwest. Artillery fire breached the walls, and when one of the shells destroyed the Tibetan gunpowder supply (and much of the *dzong* with it) the Tibetans were reduced to throwing rocks at their attackers. The *dzong* fell in one day, with over 300 Tibetan dead and four British casualties.

The fall of the Gyantse Dzong was the last straw. The British proceeded to the Yarlung Tsangpo (Brahmaputra River), which they finally crossed after five days of continual ferrying, and reached Lhasa without further incident.

Once in Lhasa there were some fine moments of imperial culture clash while Younghusband tried to ascertain where the bloody hell the Dalai Lama was (he had fled to Mongolia). The troops discovered that British goods were already trickling in to the bazaars – one British soldier wrote that he found a sausage machine made in Birmingham and two bottles of Bulldog stout in the Barkhor. Others tried in vain to persuade monks to sell them the statues from inside the Jokhang. Earlier that year in Tuna, the stalwart British officers had even managed to rustle up a Christmas dinner of turkey, Christmas pudding and (frozen) champagne.

After a month, Younghusband managed to get the Tibetan regent to sign an agreement allowing British trade missions at Gyantse and Gartok (near Mt Kailash), and the troops with-drew from their camp behind the Potala. A more profound agreement was signed in 1906 be-tween the British and Chinese authorities, which assigned Tibet to China's sphere of influence, effectively ending both British and Russian influence.

But for Younghusband himself, the most significant event of the campaign was yet to come. As he looked out over Lhasa on the evening before his departure he felt a great wave of emotion, insight and spiritual peace: an almost religious awakening that changed his life, later citing that 'that single hour on leaving Lhasa was worth all the rest of a lifetime'.

The road to Riche heads up from be-hind the Pelkhor Chöde Monastery; alter-natively, walk up from the town centre via Rabse Nunnery.

Nenling Monastery གནས་གླིང་དགོན་པ

This remote monastery and ruined fort, about 13km from Gyantse, is another adven-turous half-day trip. The town and walled monastery is actually in Kangmar county, which is closed to foreigners, so keep a low profile here. The monastery was founded by Jampel Sangwa, whose statue you'll see in the main hall.

Behind the monastery is the high splin-ter of **Nenling Dzong**, a ruined fort that was fought over by the British and Tibetans for three days during the British invasion of Tibet in 1904. Hike up into the valley behind the town to several ruined buildings and then search out the faint paths that lead up behind the fort to several hanging walls and look-out towers. It's a fun place to explore but the path can be very hairy so take care.

As you head back to Gyantse, after a few hundred metres look left to a ruined her-mitage on a diagonal slope.

You should be able to hitch to and from the site on a tractor. Buses run from Shigatse but rarely pick up foreigners. A return taxi should cost Y40, including waiting time.

Other Monasteries

If you have your own transport, there are several minor monasteries you can visit on the road connecting Gyantse and Shigatse.

Places to explore around Gyantse include **Drongtse Monastery** and chörten, 19km from Gyantse; **Tsi Nesar Monastery**, 25km from Gyan-tse, a **monastery** at the county capital Penam Xian, 41 km from Gyantse and another **mon-astery** 62km from Gyantse (p179; 8km before the turn-off to Shalu Monastery).

YUNGDRUNGLING MONASTERY
གཡུང་དྲུང་གླིང་

The Bönpo **Yungdrungling Monastery** (admission Y10) makes an impressive sight across the river on the road between Lhasa and Shigatse. It was once the second most influential Bönpo (p62) monastic institution in Tibet and was home to 700 monks. The number of monks occupying the monastery is now limited to 45 by the Chinese government and consists largely of different factions of Bönpos from the Aba region of northern Sichuan.

To many, Yungdrungling looks much like a Buddhist monastery – but note the swastikas swirling anticlockwise and remember to make the rounds in an anticlockwise direction as well. Foreigners can visit the large *dukhang*, with the impressive thrones of the monastery's two resident lamas. There are 1300 small iron statues of Shiromo (Sakya Thukpa) along the walls – look for the deity's characteristic swastika mace. You may be able to visit a couple of chapels behind the main hall, including the Namjya Lhakhang.

The monastery is 170km west of Lhasa on the north bank of the Yarlung Tsangpo (Brahmaputra River), just east of where the Nangung-chu meets it. Follow the road for 2km north along the Nangung-chu to a footbridge. From here it's about 1.5km up to the monastery (take the path diagonally up the hillside after crossing the stream).

SHIGATSE གཞིས་ཀ་རྩེ

☎ 0892 / elev 3900m

About 250km southwest of Lhasa, Shigatse is Tibet's second-largest town and the traditional capital of Tsang province. Since the Mongol sponsorship of the Gelugpa order, Shigatse has been the seat of the Panchen Lama, traditionally based in Tashilhunpo Monastery. Tashilhunpo is a highlight of Tibet and is Shigatse's foremost attraction.

The town, formerly known as Samdruptse, has long been an important trading and administrative centre. The Tsang kings exercised their power from the once imposing heights of the Shigatse Dzong – the present ruins only hint at its former glory – and the fort later became the residence of the governor of Tsang. The modern city is divided into a tiny old Tibetan town huddled at the foot of the fort, and a rapidly expanding modern Chinese town that has seen a huge influx of capital and Chinese settlers in recent years.

Far too many travellers speed through Shigatse on their way to the Nepali border, leaving just an afternoon to poke around Tashilhunpo and a night to rest. This is a pity because Shigatse is a good place to hang out, explore the nearby monasteries and enjoy a beer in the Tenzin Hotel while gazing across at the ruins of the fort. It's also one of the few places in Tsang with reliable and frequent public transport connections to Lhasa.

During the second week of the fifth lunar month, Tashilhunpo Monastery becomes the scene of a three-day festival and a huge *thangka* is unveiled.

Information

INTERNET ACCESS

Telecom Internet Bar (☎ 882 1266; per hr Y4; 🕙 24hr) Just south of the post office on Shandong Lu.
Kai Yuan Computer (🕙 9am-10pm; Shandong Lu; per hr Y5)

MONEY

Bank of China (Shanghai Zhonglu; 🕙 9am-1pm & 3.30-6.30pm Mon-Fri, 10am-5pm Sat & Sun, until 5pm in winter) Next door to the Shigatse Hotel, changes travellers cheques and cash and gives credit-card advances. There's a 24-hour ATM outside.

PERMITS

At the time of writing, the **PSB** (Qingdao Xilu, signposted West Qingdao Lu; 🕙 9.30am-12.30pm, 3.30-6.30pm Mon-Fri) was issuing 10- to 15-day permits for Gyantse, Shalu Monastery and all towns along the Friendship Hwy to the border (including Sakya, Rongphu and Everest Base Camp) and but not for places off the highway. The cost of any permit (no matter how many destinations it covers) is Y50 per person. The office is sometimes open on the weekend.

Be warned that the Shigatse PSB may stop issuing travel permits at any time (the permit system itself may change). Your best bet is to ask other travellers, as the rules change like the wind.

POST

Post office (cnr Shandong Lu & Zhufeng Lu; 🕙 9am-noon & 4-7pm) It is possible to send international letters and postcards from here, but not international parcels.

TELEPHONE

The cheapest places to make calls are the many private telecom booths around town.
Telecom (Zhufeng Lu; 🕙 9am-6.30pm) You can send faxes and make international phone calls here, around the corner from the post office.

TRAVEL AGENCIES

FIT (☎ 883 8068, 899 0505; Zhufeng Lu) Branch office of the Lhasa government agency, next to the carpet factory. Can arrange Land Cruiser hire but only along the Friendship Hwy. Sample prices are Y3400 per vehicle for a three-day round-trip to Rongphu, or Y3300 for a three- to four-day trip to Zhangmu.

SHIGATSE

| 0 | 500 m |
| 0 | 0.3 miles |

You could also try to hire a Land Cruiser unofficially by talking to the drivers who park outside the Tenzin Hotel. Arranging to rent vehicles in Shigatse is more difficult than in Lhasa. Expect to pay Y2500 to Y3000 for a vehicle to Rongphu and the Nepali border, but you'll have to arrange your own permits with the PSB.

Sights
TASHILHUNPO MONASTERY
The impressive monastery of **Tashilhunpo** (☎ 882 2114; Qingdao Xilu; admission Y55; ☯ 9am-noon & 3.30-6.30pm) is one of the six great Gelugpa institutions, along with Drepung, Sera and Ganden in Lhasa, and Kumbum (Ta'er Si) and Labrang in Amdo (modern Gansu and

Qinghai provinces). It was founded in 1447 by a disciple of Tsongkhapa, Genden Drup. Genden Drup was retroactively named the first Dalai Lama and he is enshrined within Tashilhunpo. Despite its association with the first Dalai Lama, Tashilhunpo was initially isolated from mainstream Gelugpa affairs, which were centred in the Lhasa region.

The monastery's standing rocketed, however, when the fifth Dalai Lama declared his teacher – then the abbot of Tashilhunpo – to be a manifestation of Öpagme (Amitabha; a deification of the Buddha's faculty of perfected cognition and perception). Thus Tashilhunpo became the seat of an important lineage: the Panchen Lamas (pp176–7).

TSANG

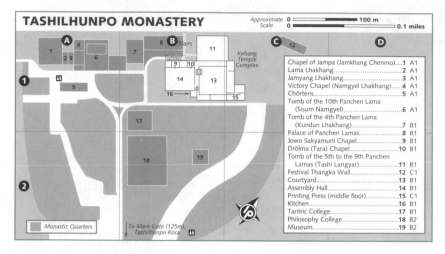

TASHILHUNPO MONASTERY

Approximate Scale 0 — 100 m / 0 — 0.1 miles

Chapel of Jampa (Jamkhang Chenmo)	1 A1
Lama Lhakhang	2 A1
Jamyang Lhakhang	3 A1
Victory Chapel (Namgyel Lhakhang)	4 A1
Chörtens	5 A1
Tomb of the 10th Panchen Lama (Sisum Namgyel)	6 A1
Tomb of the 4th Panchen Lama (Kundun Lhakhang)	7 B1
Palace of Panchen Lamas	8 B1
Jowo Sakyamuni Chapel	9 B1
Drölma (Tara) Chapel	10 B1
Tomb of the 5th to the 9th Panchen Lamas (Tashi Langyar)	11 B1
Festival Thangka Wall	12 C1
Courtyard	13 B1
Assembly Hall	14 B1
Printing Press (middle floor)	15 C1
Kitchen	16 B1
Tantric College	17 B1
Philosophy College	18 B2
Museum	19 B2

Monastic Quarters

To Main Gate (125m); Tashilhunpo Kora

Kelsang Temple Complex

Panchen means 'great scholar' and the title was traditionally bestowed on abbots of Tashilhunpo. But with the establishment of the Panchen Lama lineage of spiritual and temporal leaders – second only to the Dalai Lamas themselves – the spectre of possible rivalry was introduced to the Gelugpa order. China declared the next Panchen Lama ruler of Tsang and western Tibet, a move seen by many as part of a continuing effort by the Chinese to encourage a schism between the Panchen Lama and the Dalai Lama, though there had long been disputes between Lhasa and Shigatse over the autonomy of Tashilhunpo Monastery.

From the entrance to the monastery, visitors get a grand view. Above the white monastic quarters is a crowd of ochre buildings topped with gold – the tombs of the past Panchen Lamas. To the right, and higher still, is the great white wall that is hung with massive, colourful *thangkas* during festivals. The entire complex is surrounded by a high wall and a kora.

You'll see a lot of photos of the ninth, 10th and 11th Panchen Lamas. The ninth is recognisable by his little moustache. The 11th is the disputed Chinese-sponsored lama, a young boy.

Information

Tashilhunpo is one of the few monasteries in Tibet that weathered the stormy seas of the Cultural Revolution relatively unscathed. It is a real pleasure to explore the busy cobbled

lanes twisting around the aged buildings – the monastery is essentially a walled town in its own right. Go to Tashilhunpo several times if you can – there really is too much to see in a single visit.

On the downside, the monastery has a very high profile as the largest functioning monastic institution in Tibet, a fact that does not escape the government. The monks here are sometimes cool and there is conjecture that many of the English-speaking monks are in cahoots with the Chinese authorities. Be careful about voicing controversial opinions, and certainly don't hand out any Dalai Lama pictures.

Opening and closing hours at Tashilhunpo are fairly arbitrary. You may be told by monks at, say, 5pm (after you've already bought your ticket) that the monastery is closing in half an hour. If this happens they will usually let you in on the same ticket the next morning.

The morning is the best time to visit as more of the chapels are open. Try to catch lunchtime prayers at 12.30pm in the main assembly hall.

Severe restrictions are in place on photography inside the monastic buildings. The going cost for a photograph varies, but be prepared for a pricey Y75 fee per chapel, and as high as Y150 in the assembly hall.

Chapel of Jampa (Jamkhang Chenmo)

Walk through the monastery and bear left for the first and probably the most impressive of

Tashilhunpo's sights – the Chapel of Jampa (Maitreya). An entire building houses the world's largest gilded **statue** – a 26m image of Jampa (Maitreya), the Future Buddha. It was made in 1914 under the auspices of the ninth Panchen Lama and took some 900 artisans and labourers four years to complete.

The impressive, finely crafted and serene-looking statue looms high over the viewer. Each of Jampa's fingers is more than 1m long, and in excess of 300kg of gold went into his coating, much of which is also studded with precious stones. On the walls surrounding the image there are a thousand more gold paintings of Jampa set against a red background.

Victory Chapel (Namgyel Lhakhang)
This chapel is a centre for philosophy and houses a large statue of Tsongkhapa flanked by Jampa (Maitreya) and Jampelyang (Manjushri). If it's not open, ask one of the monks to let you in.

Tomb of the 10th Panchen Lama (Sisum Namgyel)
This impressive gold-plated funeral chörten holds the remains of the 10th Panchen Lama, who died in 1989 (pp176–7). His image is displayed in front of the tomb, surrounded by kaleidoscopic rainbow swirls. The ceiling of the chapel is painted with a Kalachakra mandala and the walls are painted with buddhas of real gold.

Tomb of the Fourth Panchen Lama (Kundun Lhakhang)
The 11m silver-and-gold funerary chörten of the fourth Panchen Lama (1570–1662) was the only tomb chörten to escape destruction during the Cultural Revolution.

From here you pass through a dark walkway that leads out to the Kelsang Temple complex.

Kelsang Temple
The centrepiece of this remarkable collection of buildings is a large **courtyard**, which is the focus of festival and monastic activities. This is a fascinating place to sit and watch the pilgrims and monks go about their business. Monks congregate here before their lunchtime service in the main assembly hall. A huge prayer pole rears up from the centre of the flagged courtyard, while the surrounding

walls are painted with buddhas. There are splendid photo opportunities here.

The **assembly hall** is one of the oldest buildings in Tashilhunpo, dating from the 15th-century founding of the monastery. The massive throne that dominates the centre of the hall is the throne of the Panchen Lamas. The hall is an atmospheric place, with rows of mounted cushions for monks, and impressive *thangkas*, depicting the various incarnations of the Panchen Lama, suspended from the ceiling. The central inner chapel holds a wonderful statue of Sakyamuni (Sakya Thukpa), while the chapel to the right holds several images of Drölma (Tara).

You can also visit the huge new **Tomb of the Fifth to the Ninth Panchen Lamas (Tashi Langyar)**, built by the 10th Panchen Lama to replace tombs destroyed in the Cultural Revolution. The central statue is of the ninth Panchen Lama. The 10th Panchen Lama returned to Shigatse from Beijing to dedicate the tomb in 1989. He fulfilled his prediction that he would die on Tibetan soil just three days after the ceremony.

There are a dozen other chapels in the complex. Follow the pilgrims on a clockwise circuit, ending up in a tangle of chapels above the assembly hall. Here in the far left (upper) corner chapel you'll find views of the two-storey Jampa statue below and, to the right, the tombs of the first and third Panchen Lamas and First Dalai Lama. Then descend to the middle floor and do another clockwise circuit taking in the interesting **printing press** and **monastic kitchen**.

Other Buildings
As you leave Tashilhunpo, it is also possible to visit the monastery's two remaining colleges. They are on the left-hand side as you walk down towards the main gate. The first is the **Tantric College** and the second is the brown **Philosophy College**. Neither is particularly interesting, but you might be lucky and find yourself in time for debating, which is held in the courtyard of the Philosophy College.

A new **museum** (admission Y5) has been opened on the eastern side of the monastery complex but it's of minor interest.

Tashilhunpo Kora
The kora around Tashilhunpo takes just an hour to walk and provides photogenic views of the monastery.

THE PANCHEN LAMAS

Traditional abbots of Tashilhunpo Monastery, frequent rivals to the central authority of Lhasa and often pawns in Chinese designs on the high plateau, the Panchen Lamas have been the focus of decidedly unspiritual squabbles. The ninth Panchen Lama (1883–1937) spent the last of his days in the clutches of a Chinese Nationalist warlord after attempting to use the Chinese as leverage to gain greater influence in Tibet during a disagreement with the 13th Dalai Lama. His reincarnation grew up in the control of the Chinese.

This Chinese connection hung over the 10th Panchen Lama like a grim cloud, and he was regarded with suspicion by his own people for much of his life. Even his authenticity was subject to doubt.

There had been at least two other candidates for the position in Tibet itself, but the Chinese had forced Tibetan delegates in Beijing in 1951 to endorse the Chinese choice. It is said that in 1949, the 11-year-old Panchen Lama had written to Mao Zedong asking him to 'liberate' Tibet, although, it is unlikely he did it of his own volition. When the Panchen Lama became joint chairperson (with the Dalai Lama) of the Preparatory Committee for the Autonomous Region of Tibet (PCART) and later vice-chairman of China's National People's Congress, it was commonly felt that he was a mere Chinese puppet.

By the time he died of a heart attack at Shigatse in 1989, however, the Panchen Lama was regarded throughout Tibet as a hero. From his triumphant arrival at Tashilhunpo Monastery as the Chinese trump card in 1951, by 1965 the Panchen Lama had become a 'big rock on the road to socialism' according to Chinese authorities. What happened?

It seems likely that the Panchen Lama had a major change of heart about his Chinese benefactors after the 1959 Lhasa uprising. In September 1961, the Panchen Lama presented Mao with a 70,000-character catalogue of the atrocities committed against Tibet, and a plea for increased freedoms. The answer was a demand that he denounce the Dalai Lama as a reactionary and take the latter's place as spiritual head of Tibet. Not only did the Panchen Lama refuse but, in 1964, with tens of thousands of Tibetans gathered in Lhasa for the Mönlam festival, he announced to the crowds that he believed Tibet would one day regain its independence and the Dalai Lama would return in glory as its leader.

It must have come as quite a shock to the Chinese to see their protégé turn on them. They responded in time-honoured fashion by throwing the Panchen Lama into jail, where he remained for 14 years, suffering abuse and torture. His crimes, according to the Chinese authorities, included

From the main gate, follow the monastery walls in a clockwise direction and look out for an alley on the right. The alley curves around the western wall past rock paintings of Guru Rinpoche and Chenresig (Avalokiteshvara) to the 13-storey white tower used to hang a giant *thangka* at festival time. The path then splits in two: down the hill to complete the circuit of the monastery, and (more interesting) along a ridge to the ruins of Shigatse Dzong (Map p173), a walk of around 20 minutes.

For those staying at the Tenzin Hotel, the kora can also be approached by turning left out of the hotel and following the road past Tibetan homes before bearing left at the walls of the monastery. This alley leads down to the main road and to the entrance of the monastery, where you can continue along the kora, finishing back on the trail

that leads back to the hotel. To avoid giving offence, try to follow the route clockwise.

SHIGATSE DZONG

Once the residence of the kings of Tsang and later the governor of Tsang, very little remains of the *dzong*. It was destroyed in the popular uprising of 1959. Pictures taken before the Chinese occupation, however, show an impressive structure that bears a remarkable resemblance to the Potala, albeit a smaller version.

The main attraction of the Shigatse Dzong today are the views it commands over Shigatse and the surrounding valleys. One approach is via the Tashilhunpo kora. The other is to turn left out of the Tenzin Hotel and after about 200m look for a paved alley heading north (right). Watch out for dogs. The walk takes around 20 minutes.

participating in orgies, 'criticising China' and raising a private insurrectionary army. A 'smash the Panchen reactionary clique' campaign was mounted, and those close to the Panchen Lama were subject to 'struggle sessions' and in some cases were imprisoned.

After emerging from prison in early 1978, the Panchen Lama rarely spoke in outright defiance of the Chinese authorities, but continued to use what influence he had to press for the preservation of Tibetan cultural traditions. (He also married and had a child). It is believed that shortly before his death he again fell out with the Chinese, arguing at a high-level meeting in Beijing that the Chinese occupation had brought nothing but misery and hardship to his people. Accordingly, many Tibetans believe that he died not of a heart attack but by poisoning. Others maintain that, exhausted and perhaps despairing, the Panchen Lama came home in 1989 to die as he always said he would on Tibetan soil.

Of course in Tibet the story doesn't just end here. In May 1995 the Dalai Lama identified Gedhun Choekyi Nyima, a six-year-old boy from Amdo, as the reincarnation of the Panchen Lama. Within a month the boy had been forcibly relocated to a government compound in Beijing and an irate Chinese government had ordered the senior lamas of Tashilhunpo to come up with a second, Chinese-approved choice. Chadrel Rinpoche, the abbot who led the search that identified Gedhun, was later imprisoned for six years for 'splitting the country' and 'colluding with separatist forces abroad' (ie consulting the Dalai Lama), and Tashilhunpo was closed to tourists for a few months.

Tashilhunpo's lamas eventually settled on Gyancain Norbu, the son of Communist Party members, who was formally approved in a carefully orchestrated ceremony.

Beijing's interest is not only to control the education of Tibet's number-two spiritual leader, but also to influence the boy who could later be influential himself in identifying the reincarnation of the Dalai Lama.

Meanwhile, the young 11th Panchen Lama remains under house arrest at an undisclosed location in China, causing him to be dubbed the 'world's youngest political prisoner'.

There are a number of groups campaigning to free the Panchen Lama. Check out the websites of the Tashilhunpo Monastery in exile (www.tashilhunpo.org/panchen.html), the Australia Tibet Council (www.atc.org.au), and the Canada Tibet Committee, which has a page designed for kids (www.tibet.ca/panchenlama).

The Search for the Panchen Lama by Isabel Hilton is a look at the political intricacies of Tibet, with an emphasis on the controversial Panchen Lama and China's abduction of his current reincarnation.

SUMMER PALACE OF THE PANCHEN LAMAS

This **complex** (admission Y15; 9am-12.30pm, 3.30-6pm) is 1km south of Tashilhunpo, hidden in a walled compound. The straggly gardens form the Panchen Lamas' version of the Norbulingka, but there's a lot less to see.

The palace was built in 1844 by the Seventh Panchen Lama, Tenpei Nyima, though only a couple of rooms are open to visitors, including two **chapels** on the ground floor, the 10th Panchen Lama's lavish **sitting rooms** on the 1st floor, and his impressive **audience chamber** on the 2nd floor. On holidays the grounds outside are a popular picnic spot.

Sleeping

BUDGET

Tenzin Hotel (☎ 882 2018; fax 883 1565; 8 Bangchelling; dm/tr per bed Y30/35, d with/without bathroom Y200/120, deluxe d Y260) With a fine location in the old town and the long-time backpacker favourite. It was rebuilt and upgraded in 2002 but remains a friendly and busy place, popular with both backpackers and Land Cruiser groups. The dorms are on the ground floor and can suffer from vehicle noise; the top floor triples are quieter for almost the same price. The shared bathrooms are excellent and have 24-hour hot water. The comfortable double rooms with en suite bathroom are often discounted to Y160. The restaurant is a bit pricey but a good place to hang out. An Internet bar is planned.

Shambhala Hotel (dm Y20-25, d with/without bathroom Y120/70) If the Tenzin is full, this is decent alternative budget choice. The dorm rooms are clean and spacious (the 4th floor is quietest). There are communal squat toilets and sinks and you can take a hot shower in one of the double rooms for Y5.

Qomolongma Friendship Hotel (Zhufeng Youyi Binguan; ☎ 882 1929; dm Y30, d Y200-258, tr Y288) This place is often used by budget tour companies from Nepal, though it's not really up to scratch. The dorm block out back is basic, with pit toilets across the courtyard. For a double room you are better off at the Tenzin. Get a shower at the 'Bathroom of Clean Water' on the main street (Y5).

MID-RANGE & TOP END

Manasarovar Hotel (☎ 883 9999; www.shigatsetravels .com/manasarovar.htm; 20 Qingdao Lu; ordinary/superior d Y280/480, tr Y320) This new three-star hotel is a bit of a hike from the action but is probably the best mid-range place in town. Rooms are spacious and spotless, and the bathrooms have 24-hour hot water. Only the superior rooms have en suite bathrooms. Discounts of 50% are usual.

Samdruptse Hotel (Sangzhuzi Fandian; ☎ 882 2280; 2 Gongjueling Lu; d & tr per bed Y90, s Y180, d with bathroom Y180-260) Just down the road and around the corner from the Tenzin is this Chinese-style hotel, an uninspiring but comfortable-enough place to stay. It's often booked out by tour groups. The cheapest doubles and triples come without bathrooms but you can pay per bed.

Shigatse Shandong Hotel (☎ 882 6138; fax 882 6124; 5 Shandong Lu; s/d with bathroom Y300/320) The tallest building in the city, this overpriced and soulless new hotel overlooks an incongruous statue of Confucius from nine ugly storeys. The hotel hopes to impress its guests with its gargantuan chandelier, Internet bar and oxygen machines, but the light fittings don't quite work and the carpets are already stained.

Shigatse Hotel (☎ 882 2525; fax 882 1900; 13 Shanghai Zhonglu; d/tr Y300/360) This is a slightly tatty three-star group place in the south of town. The Tibetan-style rooms are cosy, with a fridge and kettle, though the bathrooms are decidedly average. Doubles are often discounted to Y240.

Holyland Hotel (☎ 882 2922; 5 Shandong Lu; d Y360; 🔀) Better value than the Shandong is this clean, fresh hotel. Bathrooms are clean and have hot water from 7pm to midnight. The upper floors hold the better rooms. Doubles are often discounted to Y180.

Post Hotel (Youzheng Binguan; ☎ 882 2938; 12 Shanghai Zhonglu; s/d Y140-160 d220/360) Two-star option across from the Shigatse Hotel. The more

expensive doubles were recently upgraded. Singles/doubles are often discounted to Y120/180.

Eating

Shigatse is swarming with good restaurants, most of which are Chinese and are generally open for lunch and dinner.

There's a collection of tiny Chinese restaurants with foreign menus around the corner from the Tenzin Hotel. Names and owners change regularly but menus remain the same. All serve up Sichuanese dishes for around Y10 (vegetable dishes) to Y18 (meat dishes). Note that the English menus in these restaurants are 25% more than Chinese menus.

Gongkar Tibetan Restaurant (☎ 882 1139; Qingdao Lu; dishes Y10) West of Samdruptse Hotel, this local restaurant has an English menu. Travellers have recommended the rooftop seating.

Galgye Tibetan Restaurant (dishes Y10-15) Just round the corner from the Gongkar, this similar place has Tibetan seating and a reasonable range of Tibetan dishes, including curried potatoes and Lhasa beer (Y6).

Tashi Restaurant (☎ 883 5969; dishes Y15-28) For a break from Chinese food there are several Nepali restaurants which, though pricier than the Chinese and Tibetan options, offer a wider range of comfort food. This Nepali-run restaurant has everything from yogurt muesli to pizza and Nepali curries to choose from. It's connected to Lhasa's New Mandala Restaurant but has no connections to Lhasa's Tashi restaurants.

Songtsen Tibetan Restaurant (☎ 883 2469; mains Y20-35) A similar but brighter Tibetan-style place popular with tour groups, serving Indian and Nepali dishes (set lunch Y25-30), plus chicken sizzlers and breakfasts.

Monastery Restaurant (opposite Tashilunpo Monastery) Grab a plate of *momos,* a bowl of fried potatoes from the stalls outside and a glass of sweet tea and join the other pilgrims at this basic place.

There's also **Tianfu Restaurant** and the next door **Yuanfu Restaurant** (also known as Yingbing, and formerly known as Greasy Joe's). A little further down is the **Zhengxin Restaurant**, which is good and has some breakfast foods like pancakes and banana yogurt. You'll find a great range of fresh produce at the **fruit and vegetable market** (Qingdao Lu).

Shopping

The **Tibetan market** in front of the Tenzin Hotel is probably the best place outside Lhasa to pick up souvenirs such as prayer wheels, rosaries and *thangkas*. Bargain hard.

Tibet Gang Gyen Carpet Factory (☎ 882 2733; www .tapis-du-tibet.com; 9 Zhufeng Lu; ⌚ 9am-1pm & 3-7pm) A five-minute walk from Tashilhunpo and 100m down a dirt track (follow the enormous signs), this slick French joint venture exports carpets to America and Europe. Women work on the carpets on the premises, singing as they weave, dye, trim and spin; you are free to take photographs. Only 100% Tibetan sheep's wool is used. Around 44% of the profits go to Tashilunpo Monastery. Expect to pay around US$200 plus shipping (US$50) for a carpet measuring 185cm x 90cm. Ask for director Kelsang Nima.

Toread Outdoor Sports (☎ 882 3195; Shanghai Zhonglu) If you are headed off on a trek but totally unprepared you can pick up basic equipment here such as tents, stoves and jackets.

A **photo shop** in front of Tashilhunpo sells some slide film.

Getting There & Away

Minibuses to Lhasa (Y35) leave from around 8am from a stand on Qingdao Lu on the eastern side of Shigatse. You can also catch the similar public bus services which run from the main bus station.

Going between Lhasa and Shigatse (p116), taxis do the trip for around Y70 per person (four hours) and wait for fares near the spot where the minibuses depart. You might even be able to find a seat in a Land Cruiser here for Y100.

At the main bus station there are daily minibuses at around 8am, and possibly also minivans at 3.30pm, for Sakya (Y32 to Y43, four hours). Heading west, there are daily morning minibuses to Lhatse (Y30, five hours) and Dingri (Y65). At the time of research, foreigners were not allowed on buses to closed destinations such as Yadong and Kangbar and you may have difficulties buying tickets for anywhere other than Lhasa.

Minivans to Gyantse (Y20, one hour) run when full from outside the main bus station from 10am until 8pm daily but they can also be reluctant to take foreigners. Taxis run when full for Y20 per seat (Y80 for the taxi) and will take anyone's money.

Those aiming for the Nepali border can hunt around for the occasional minibus to Zhangmu but it may be better to inquire at the Tenzin Hotel about Land Cruisers heading out to the border to pick up a tour group. The cost for hooking up with one of these should be around Y250 per person but you will probably need to ask for three or four days in a row before you get lucky. Otherwise start hitching from Tingri or try on renting a Land Cruiser (p172).

The Civil Aviation Authority of China (CAAC) runs a daily bus direct to the airport (Y50) from the Bank of China office on Zhufeng Lu at 10am. Book your ticket in advance.

Getting Around

Shigatse is not that large and can be comfortably explored on foot. For trips out to the Shigatse Hotel or Post Hotel, you might want to use a pedicab (Y3 to Y5). A ride anywhere in town in one of the many taxis will cost Y10.

AROUND SHIGATSE

There are many sights around Shigatse, but few are visited by Western travellers. En route to Lhatse you can stop at **Nartang Monastery**, a 12th-century Kadampa monastery famed for wood-block printing the Nartang canon in the 18th century, and **Kangchen Monastery**. Both are signposted in English just off the Friendship Hwy. There is a trek from Shalu to Nartang (p278). It is even possible to visit Gyantse as a day trip from Shigatse.

Shalu Monastery ཞ་ལུ་དགོན་པ

This important **monastery** (admission Y40) is about 19km south of Shigatse, 4km off the Shigatse-Gyantse road, and is easily spotted because of its Chinese-style, green-tiled roof. The monastery, which dates back to the 11th century, rose to prominence in the 14th century when its abbot, Büton Rinchen Drup, emerged as the foremost interpreter and compiler of Sanskrit Buddhist texts of his day. A suborder, the Büton, formed around him. Shalu (or Zhalu) was also a centre for training in skills such as trance walking, made famous by the flying monks of Alexandra David-Neel's book *Magic & Mystery in Tibet*.

Shalu is divided into a Tibetan-style monastery from the 10th century and the Chinese-influenced inner Serkhang, founded in the

KILOMETRE MARKERS ALONG THE FRIENDSHIP HIGHWAY

The following towns, geographical features and points of interest along with their appropriate kilometre markers (signifying distance from Beijing) may be of help to travellers, hitchhikers and, in particular, mountain bikers. Bear in mind that the kilometre-marker system changes at some points, and in certain regions the markers have disappeared – sometimes turning up as doorsteps in new buildings.

There are enough of them left, however, for you to be able to keep a fairly accurate track of your progress and identify turn-offs to places of interest.

Lhasa to Shigatse

Marker	Feature
4646	Lhasa's eastern crossroads to Golmud or Shigatse
4656	Blue Buddha rock painting
4661	sign to Nyetang Tashigang Monastery
4662/3	Netang village and Drölma Lhakhang
4673	bridge on left to Shugsheb Nunnery (p129)
4683	new bridge and tunnel to Gongkar Airport
4695-7	Chushul
4703	bridge over the Yarlung Tsangpo to Nangartse and Tsetang; shops and restaurants.
4712	hydroelectric project on the far side of the river – the structure shaped like a golf ball atop the hill is a radar and meteorological centre
4718	ruined fortress on left and village
4724	village, ruined *dzong* and monastery
4732	jagged peaks ahead and valley begins to narrow
4758	bridge and road to Nyemo to north; restaurants
4768	suspension footbridge to left
4780	bridge over to south side
4801	checkpoint, turn-off to Rinbu and shops
4821	Traduka, ferry to Yungdrungling Monastery and Yangpachen; restaurants
4835	Drakchik Ferry
4840	Huda village
4869	Ansa Monastery on hillside to south
4874/5	bridge north to Nanmulin
4876	ferry to north bank
4900-5	Shigatse

Shigatse to Tingri

Marker	Feature
4900-5	Shigatse
4913	turn-off to Ngor Monastery
4917	Nartang Monastery
4928	Gyeli village
4932/3	very gentle mountain pass of Tso-la (4500m)
4936	Kangchen Monastery to right
4956/7	asphalt starts; turn & go 1km north to interesting ruined Trupuk Chörten
4960/1	Gyading; ruined fort, restaurants and shops
4973	Dilong village

4977/8	turn-off to Phuntsoling Monastery
4985-5005	sealed road (in bad condition in places)
4994	Daoban
4998	restaurant and bus lunch stop
5000	marker showing 5000km from Shanghai; small monastery and ruined *dzong*
5009	village and start of climb to pass
5014	Tropu-la (4950m)
5028	Sakya bridge – turn-off to Sakya; rebuilt hilltop monastery
5036	ruined *dzong*
5041	village and turn-off to Xiqian Hot Springs
5052	Lhatse
5058	checkpoint and turn-off to western Tibet
5063	start of climb to pass, with a height gain of around 1000m
5083	Gyatso-la (5220m)
5100	rough roads 5km either way
5114	views of Everest and the Himalaya
5121	hermitage across river
5124	bridge; to nunnery and fortress
5127/8	Qiabu village, fort and caves
5133-42	good sealed road
5133	Shegar and turn-off to main town
5139	Shegar checkpoint
5145	turn-off to Everest Base Camp
5155	ruined *dzong* to left
5162	village
5170	village
5193-4	Tingri

Tingri to Nyalam

Marker	Feature
5193-4	Tingri
5206	Tsamda Hot Springs
5216	two small Tibetan guesthouses
5232	Gutso village; guesthouse and restaurant
5237	village on west side of the river
5254	small guesthouse and restaurant
5258	ruins by road
5263	start climb to La Lung-la
5276	La Lung-la (5124m)
5282	bridge, Danba hostel and restaurant
5289	Tong-la (5120m) and view of Cho Oyu and Mt Everest
5292	short cut down the hillside, used by Land Cruiser drivers
5303	roadworkers' hostel and village
5311	village, with ruins behind
5334	Gangka village and track to Milarepa's Cave
5345	Nyalam
5376	approximate check point
5378	Zhangmu
5386	Nepali border

TSANG

15th century. The former was destroyed in the Cultural Revolution, but the Serkhang has survived reasonably well. The design of the monastery represents the paradise of Chenresig (Avalokiteshvara), a haven from all worldly suffering.

Shalu is noted for its 14th-century murals which fuse Chinese, Mongol and Nepali Newari styles, but it's hard for most non-specialists to discern this much. The best murals line the walls of a corridor that rings the central assembly hall; bring a powerful torch to really appreciate these.

The inner Serkhang contains a Kanjyur Lhakhang (scripture chapel), with fine 14th-century mandala murals. The west chapel has a black stone statue of Chenresig Kasrapani, the monastery's holiest relic. The northern chapel has more fine murals, including one in the left corner depicting the monastery's founder. There are a couple of upper chapels, including the Mudu Lhakhang which holds the funeral chörten of Büton.

From Shalu you can make the trek to Nartang (p278) or take an hour's walk up to **Ri-puk Hermitage**, a former meditation centre built around a spring, with nice views of the Shalu Valley. It's now popular as a weekend picnic site and there's a small **hotel** (dm Y30, ste Y100) and restaurant here.

GETTING THERE & AWAY
Shalu Monastery is one of the more accessible sights around Shigatse. If you take a Gyantse-bound minibus from Shigatse, get off at the village of Tsündu (also known as Shalu) and look out for the turn-off a couple of hundred metres past a hill covered with prayer flags. From here the hour's walk up to Shalu village passes the small Gyanggong Monastery, dedicated to the protectress Palden Lhamo (Shri Devi) and famed as the place where Sakya Pandita was ordained.

Occasionally there are direct buses to the monastery from a block south of the Shigatse Hotel. A shop in Shalu village sells soft drinks, water and noodles. Bring a hat, sunscreen and water.

SAKYA ས་སྐྱ
☎ 0892 / elev 4280m
The monastic town of Sakya is one of Tsang's most significant attractions, and occupies an important place in Tibetan history. Of Sakya's two monasteries, on either side of the Trum-chu, the brooding fortress-like southern monastery is the more interesting. Most of the original, northern monastery has been reduced to picturesque ruins, although restoration work is ongoing.

One characteristic feature of the Sakya region is the colouring of its buildings. Unlike the standard whitewashed effect that you see elsewhere in Tibet, in Sakya the buildings are ash grey with white and red vertical stripes. The colouring symbolises the Rigsum Gonpo, the trinity of bodhisattvas and stands as a mark of Sakya authority. Sakya literally means 'pale earth'.

If you are doing the grand tour of Tibet – that is Lhasa and environs, Gyantse, Shigatse, Everest and the border – you can overnight in Sakya or stay longer in a town that has suffered little from the encroachments of the modern Chinese world.

One person you'll see a lot of photos of here is the Sakya Trizin, the exiled head of the Sakyapa school, recognisable by his ponytail, glasses and round face.

Permits
Officially you need a travel permit from the PSB in Shigatse to visit Sakya, although if you turn up without one, no-one seems to care in the least.

Sights
SAKYA MONASTERY
The immense, thick-walled southern **monastery** (☎ 824 2352; admission Y45; 🕙 9.30am-1pm & 4-6pm) is Sakya's main attraction. Before the Cultural Revolution, Sakya Monastery was one of the largest monasteries in Tibet. It crouches grim and forbidding among the cluster of houses that make up Sakya township. Taking photos costs Y5 each or Y20 for a roll.

The southern monastery was established in 1268 and is designed defensively, with watchtowers on each of the corners of its high walls. It is possible to walk around the top of these outer walls.

Directly ahead of the east-wall main entrance is the entry to the central courtyard of the monastery, an impressive area with a towering prayer pole surrounded by chapels. Try to tag along with a group if possible as the monks might be convinced to open up more rooms. Morning is the best time to visit as more of the chapels are open.

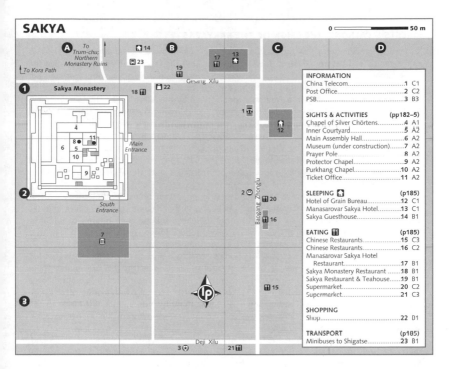

SAKYA

0 ━━━━━ 50 m

The chapel to the left (south) is the **Purkhang Chapel**. Central images are of Sakyamuni (Sakya Thukpa) and of Jampelyang (Manjushri), while wall paintings behind depict Tsepame (Amitayus) to the left, Drölma (Tara) and white Namgyelma (Vijaya) to the far left, as well as a medicine buddha, two Sakyamunis and Jampa (Maitreya). Murals on the left wall depict Tantric deities central to the Sakya school.

The **main assembly hall (Lhakhang Chenmo)** to the west of the courtyard is a huge structure with 3.5m-thick walls. It also tends to be very dark, although the morning sunshine lights the place up with a diffuse ambience. It is still a good idea to bring a torch with you. The hall's ceiling is supported by massive sacred pillars made of entire tree trunks. In the far left corner of the hall is a huge drum. Look for the maces on the pillars.

The walls of the assembly hall are lined with towering buddhas, which are unusual in that many also serve as reliquaries for former Sakya abbots. The buddha in the far left corner, contains relics of Sakya Pandita;

the one next to it houses those of the previous abbot of Sakya. The largest central buddha contains remains of the founder of the monastery. To the right of the central buddha are statues of Jampelyang (Manjushri) and a seated Jampa (Maitreya), among others. Sakya's famous **library** is accessible from this hall but hidden from sight and it is rarely opened up to tourists.

To the north of the courtyard is a chapel containing 11 silver chörtens, which are also reliquaries for former Sakya abbots. Look to the left corner for the sand mandala. A sometimes-locked door leads into another chapel with additional amazing chörtens and murals.

There are several chapels upstairs. On the right-hand side of the east-wall entrance are stairs leading up to a 2nd-floor chapel of five chörtens. Another flight of stairs in the left corner of the courtyard leads up to another couple of chapels. A long flight of stairs outside the central complex leads up to a single rooftop protector chapel.

There are a couple of chapels open outside of this central complex, although the

PRIESTS & PATRONS: THE REIGN OF THE SAKYAPAS

It's hard to imagine today how the small town of Sakya would have looked during its glory days as the capital of Tibet from 1268 to 1354. It was here that the fascinating alliance between the Sakya lamas and Mongol Khans developed to rule Tibet. The alliance saved Tibet from the annihilation met by nearby countries trying to resist Mongol advances, and converted the entire Mongolian empire in east Asia to Tibetan Buddhism, led by the Sakya lama.

The Sakya Monastery was founded in 1073 by Kön Könchog Gyelpo (1034–1102), a member of the influential Kön family. The 11th century was a dynamic period in the history of Tibetan Buddhism, largely due to renewed contact with Indian Buddhists. At this time, the Kagyupa order was founded by Marpa and his disciple Milarepa, and in Sakya, the Kön family established a school that came to be called the Sakyapa. Unlike most other schools and monasteries that were headed by a succession of incarnate lamas, the abbotship of Sakya was hereditary and restricted to the sons of the Kön family.

By the early 13th century, Sakya had emerged as an important centre of scholastic study. This was initially aided by Indian translators such as Shakyashribhada, who came to Sakya in 1204. But before long, Tibetan scholars began to make their own unique contributions to Buddhist scholarship. The most famous of these was a Sakya abbot, Kunga Gyaltsen (1182–1251), who came to be known as the Sakya Pandita, literally the 'scholar from Sakya'.

There is no doubt that it was Sakya Pandita's scholastic and spiritual eminence that led him to represent the Tibetan people to the Mongol prince Godan (the son of Genghis Khan) when the Mongols threatened to invade Tibet in the mid-13th century. Sakya Pandita made a three-year journey to Mongolia, arriving in 1247, and after meeting with Godan offered him overlordship of Tibet. Sakya Pandita defended his actions by noting that resistance to the Mongols was pointless – they had already easily conquered the Western Xia, as well as other kingdoms that had resisted their advances.

After Sakya Pandita's death in 1251, one of his nephews became the abbot of Sakya and, therefore, with the Mongol support of Kublai Khan, also the ruler of all Tibet. This was the first religious government with a lama as head of state, and set an important precedent for Tibetan government.

The association between Tibetan lamas and their Mongol masters (which Tibetans characterised as like the relationship between religious teacher and patron) set yet another important precedent. The association was one that was open to various interpretations, would trouble the Tibetan state for centuries to come and would help the Chinese justify claims over the high plateau.

As it was, Mongol overlordship and Sakya supremacy were relatively short-lived. Mongol corruption and rivalry between the Sakyapa and Kagyupa orders led to the fall of Sakya in 1354, when power fell into the hands of the Kagyupa and the seat of government moved to Nedong in Ü.

Sakya was to remain a powerful municipality, however, and like Shigatse enjoyed a high degree of autonomy from successive central governments. Even today, you can see homes across the plateau painted with the red, white and blue-black stripes associated with Sakya Monastery.

most interesting is the very spooky **protector chapel** of the Pakspa Lhakhang, where scary monsters, huge *cham* masks and stuffed wolves await you in the dark recesses. To the left is an assembly hall.

Finally, climb up onto the walls of the monastery for superb views of the surrounding valley.

A new **museum** is being built just south of the monastery.

NORTHERN MONASTERY RUINS

Very little is left of the monastery complex that once sprawled across the hills north of the Trum-chu but it is still worth climbing up through the Tibetan town and taking a wander around what remains. The northern monastery predates the southern monastery (the oldest temple at the northern monastery was built in 1073), and it is alleged to have contained 108 buildings, like Ganden. It may

Yumbulagang (p156), Yarlung Valley

Monk, Samye Monastery (p149)

Prayer flags, Nam-tso (p137)

Ferry crossing the Yarlung Tsangpo (p146)

ANTHONY PLUMM

Yamdrok-tso (p162), beside the Friendship Highway

RICHARD I'ANSON

Religious artwork (p51), Sakya Monastery

Prostrating pilgrim, Gyantse Kumbum (p167), Gyantse

BILL WASSM

BRADLEY MAYHEW

Mt Everest (p189)

once have housed some 3000 monks who concentrated on Tantric studies.

Aim for the white chörten, which is a reconstruction of a chörten that held the remains of Kunga Nyingpo, the founder of the Sakyapa order and the second Sakya abbot. There are three main complexes on this side of the river: the main **Labrang Shar**, the **Namja Choede** to the left and the **Rinche Gang nunnery** to the far left, to be visited clockwise.

The best way to get an overview is to walk the 45-minute northern **kora**. Join it by crossing the river over the western bridge and climbing up the trail and then gully to the left. The trail leads up to a couple of chörtens and an impressive ruined complex that mirrors the southern monastery. The path winds around the hillside to the Rinche Gang Nunnery before descending to town.

UJAY LHAKHANG

This small monastery linked to Sakya is located in the village of Chongkhor Lam, around 5km along the road from Sakya to the Friendship Hwy. There's nothing special here, but it's a good place to aim for if you fancy an hour's walk.

Sleeping

Sakya Guesthouse (☎ 824 2233; dm Y15-20) The rooms are basic but bearable if you have a sleeping bag, and there's a certain timeless feel about the place. Your minibus will probably pull in here; if not, look for the English sign saying 'Hotel'.

Manasarovar Sakya Hotel (☎ 824 2222; 1 Gesang Xilu; dm/d/tr Y30-40/280/220-280) En suite plumbing has finally come to Sakya, for better or worse, with this big, new, modern hotel. Rooms are carpeted, clean and comfortable, with hot showers, and there are superb views from the roof. One of the dorm rooms comes with en suite toilet and shower; the others have no access to a shower. Expect occasional karaoke blowouts when the visiting local politburo pull into town. Discounts of 33% sometimes apply.

Hotel of Grain Bureau (Liangshiju Zhaodaisuo; per bed Y35) Foreigners can pay per bed in fairly cramped triples, though the common bathrooms are a bit nasty and there's no shower.

Eating

Sakya has a lot of fairly pricey Chinese restaurants, all set up by Sichuanese immigrants.

All restaurants serve lunch and dinner, and have no fixed opening hours.

Manasarovar Sakya Hotel Restaurant (☎ 824 2222; 1 Gesang Xilu; mains Y15-25, set breakfast Y20-25) This is the best place for western food, conjured up by a Nepali-trained chef. The chicken sizzler is top notch, and there are Indian dishes, burgers and pizza. The Tibetan dishes have no English translation but the chef can explain.

Sakya Monastery Restaurant (☎ 824 2267; dishes Y7-12) This Tibetan eating place is owned by the monastery and serves up fried rice, *thugpa* and milk tea.

Sakya Restaurant and Teahouse (mains Y5-15) You can get a decent breakfast of omelette, bread and instant coffee here.

There are several **supermarkets**, where you can stock up on most supplies, as well as Tibetan teahouses which double as video halls.

Getting There & Away

There are daily minibuses from Shigatse bus station to Sakya (Y32 to Y42, four hours). Minibuses from Sakya depart from the Sakya Guesthouse at around 11am. These minibuses are guaranteed to be the slowest vehicles on the road.

Another option is to take a Lhatse-bound bus to the Sakya turn-off and then hitch the remaining 25km, although there aren't many vehicles on this road. The distance between Shigatse and the turn-off is 127km (kilometre marker 5028).

Very occasionally there are buses from Sakya to Lhatse but you'll probably have to change transport at the Sakya turn-off (Y5). If you are hitching this way it's worth heading out early to catch the morning minibuses that run from Shigatse to Lhatse.

LHATSE རྒྱ་རྩེ་
☎ 0892 / elev 4050m

Approximately 150km southwest of Shigatse and some 30km west of the Sakya turn-off, Lhatse is a spread-out town lining the Friendship Hwy. Most of the traffic here is en route to Zhangmu on the Nepali border, but some vehicles take the turn-off 6km down the road for Ali in western Tibet (p197).

Lhatse is a decent place to be stuck for a day or so. You could visit the ruined **dzongs** at each end of town, although there's not much to see except the views of the plain below. At the western end of town is the small **Changmoche Monastery**. You can also hike 10km out to the Xiqian Hot Springs (below) or visit Lhatse Chöde and Drampa Gyang Temple (p187).

Information

Sitong Internet Bar (per hr Y6; ☾ 24 hr) On the 2nd floor of a building just west of the central square, accessible by a flight of stairs at the back of the building.
Hot Showers (Haohua Yushi; Y6; ☾ 10am-11pm) On the east side of the square.

Sleeping

Lhatse Tibetan Farmers Adventure Hotel (☎ 832 2333; dm Y25-35, d Y70-90) Probably the best place to stay in town, with genial Tibetan staff, cheerful flowerbeds and a nice and cosy, sociable restaurant.

Dewang Hotel (☎ 832 2888; d/tr per bed Y40/60) A close second is this Tibetan family-run place, diagonally across the street. The rooms are clean and the doubles are even carpeted. There's a nice Tibetan-style dining area, agreeable chefs who will try anything, plus an alleged hot shower and secure parking to keep your driver happy.

Lhatse Hotel (☎ 832 2208; dm Y15-20, tr/q per bed Y35/25, d Y80) This place has gone downhill in recent years. It has a range of rooms set around a huge courtyard, but the cheaper ones are grubby and the staff are uninterested. The double rooms come with a TV and aren't bad but there's no running water.

Tianhu Hotel (☎ 832 2838; tr per bed Y30) The apathetic staff here can't spoil the modern clean rooms, good quality beds and pleasant Tibetan-style lobby here.

Another option is the **Meteorological Hotel** (☎ 832 2599; dm/d/tr/q Y15/60/75/80), with a string of rather smelly rooms off an endless green-and-white corridor.

Eating

All restaurants serve lunch and dinner and have no fixed opening hours.

Chengdu Restaurant (dishes Y16-20) This place on the main street near the central square is expensive but the food is good; try the 'fish-resembling eggplant' (Y20). It consists of eggplant cooked with *yuxiang wei*, a tasty fish-flavoured sauce that draws on vinegar, soy sauce, garlic and ginger.

Tashi No 2 Restaurant (Lhatse Hotel; dishes Y16-30) If you just want an English menu, try this average place. It has no connection to the

Tashi restaurants in Lhasa (the food is all Chinese).

Many other **Chinese and Muslim restaurants** line the south side of the street; wander in and take a look around the kitchen – no-one seems to mind.

Getting There & Away

Daily minibuses run between Shigatse and Lhatse. In Lhatse they circle for customers every morning around 9.30am, 150m east of the Lhatse Hotel, and depart when full. The cost is Y35. Through buses to Shegar pass through around noon. You can also hitch from here to Ali (p207) and Mt Kailash (p210) in western Tibet.

If you are hitching, prospective lifts who don't have permission to carry foreigners are scared off by the checkpoint 6km to the west, so it's well worth walking 1½ hours to the checkpoint and then looking for a lift a kilometre or two on the other side.

A ride from Lhatse to Zhangmu should run to around Y150, although this will probably require some determined bargaining. Those looking at hitching to Tingri or Shegar for the trek to Everest Base Camp will probably have to pay around Y40, but again this depends on how hard you bargain. It will also help if you get a travel permit in Shigatse for Lhatse, Shegar, Nyalam and Zhangmu.

AROUND LHATSE

There are lots of places to explore from Lhatse if you have time and a sense of adventure. For an idea of some little-visited regional monasteries, see the excellent map in the lobby of the Lhatse Hotel.

Xiqian Hot Springs ཕོ་རེས་པ་རྒྱ་ཚོན་

Tibetans come from far and wide to bathe in the healing waters of these **hot springs** (baths per person Y15-20), which are said to cure a multitude of ills, especially skin irritations. The largest pool is in a rectangular courtyard surrounded by veranda posts and reclining bathers so that it resembles a Roman bath. Watch out – the water is very hot and gets hotter in the middle. There are also private baths. The manager can find somewhere to stay for Y30 per person.

The hot springs are 10km east of Lhatse. Turn north off the Friendship Hwy at the town of Xiqian (or Xiqin; km marker 5041)

and continue 750m north (it's signposted). There's a small shop here selling beer and soft drinks. It's a good idea to agree beforehand about including the springs in your itinerary if you want to visit by hired Land Cruiser.

Lhatse Chöde ལྷ་རྩེ་མཆོད་སྡེ་

About 10km from Lhatse (55km from Phuntsoling), you'll pass the traditional village of Lhatse Chöde, its small monastery and a ruined *dzong*. East of town is **Drampa Gyang Temple**, one of Songtsen Gampo's demoness-subduing temples (p96), and in this case it pins the troublesome demoness' left hip. From Lhatse Chöde you hit the main road at kilometre marker 5052, just 1km east of modern Lhatse.

PHUNTSOLING MONASTERY ཕུན་ཚོགས་གླིང་ & JONANG KUMBUM ཇོ་ནང་སྐུ་འབུམ་

Situated at the bottom of a gargantuan sand dune, **Phuntsoling Monastery** (admission Y30) was once the central monastery of the Jonang-pas. This Kagyu sect is especially known for the examination of the nature of emptiness undertaken at the monastery by its greatest scholar, Dolpopa Sherab Gyaltsen (1292–1361). He was one of the first proponents of the hard-to-grasp notion of *shentong*. Roughly, this is based on the idea that the Buddha-mind (which transcends all forms) is not ultimately empty, even though all forms are empty illusions.

Shentong has been debated among Buddhist philosophers for seven centuries. The Gelugpa school did not share Dolpopa's view – to the point where in the 17th century the fifth Dalai Lama suppressed the Jonangpa school and forcibly converted Phuntsoling into a Gelugpa institution.

You can visit the large **assembly hall**, which is dominated by a statue of Chenresig (Avalokiteshvara). Other statues include those of the 10th Panchen Lama, Tsongkhapa and the fifth Dalai Lama. The **inner sanctum** of the hall contains a statue of Akshobhya (Mikyöba), while the **murals** on the roof tell the story of the life of Sakyamuni (Sakya Thukpa).

The highlight of the monastery is a walk up to the ruined red fortifications behind the monastery, which offer stunning views of the valley. Look for the ruined *dzong* on a cliff across the Yarlung Tsangpo. One

of Tangtong Gyelpo's (p26) famous iron bridges once spanned the river here.

From Phuntsoling you can head south up the valley for a two-hour walk to the ruins of the **Jonang Kumbum**. Once 20m high, the chörten was built by Dolpopa in the 14th century and was the spiritual centre of the Jonangpas. It was said to be one of the best-preserved monuments in Tibet, resembling the Gyantse Kumbum, before it was wrecked during the Cultural Revolution.

Getting There & Away

Phuntsoling Monastery can be visited on the way from Shigatse to Lhatse. Take the detour north of the Friendship Hwy, 17km west of the Gyading checkpoint at kilometre marker 4978/9. The monastery is 34km (about 1½ hours) northwest from here. It's a 61km journey on from Phuntsoling to Lhatse (2½ to three hours). The dirt road follows the Yarlung Tsangpo for much of the way and is in excellent condition, after repairs in 2003.

SHEGAR ཤེལ་དཀར་

☎ 0892 / elev 4050m

The turn-off to Shegar (also known as New Tingri, but not to be confused with Tingri) on the Friendship Hwy is where you can buy your permit for the Qomolangma Nature Preserve. Inside the preserve are Everest Base Camp, Rongphu Monastery and Cho Oyu Base Camp. The **preserve office** (☎ 826 2835; ☼ 24hr), which is in the QNP San Chen Guesthouse, is the place to get your Everest permit (p189).

Shegar itself, a 7km diversion northwest of the Friendship Hwy, is worth a visit for the ruins of **Shegar Dzong** (Crystal Fort), once the capital of the Tingri region. The remains of the *dzong*'s defensive walls snake incredibly over the abrupt pinnacle that looms over the town. A two-hour kora trail leads up from the western side of town. Morning light is best for taking photographs.

Also of interest here is the **Shegar Chöde Monastery** (admission Y10), which is a small Gelugpa institution that was built in 1269 at the foot of the mountain. A painting inside depicts the monastery at its height, when it had around 800 monks. If you climb up to the wall behind the monastery you can get a peek at the top of Everest far in the distance. Paths continue up from here around to the *dzong*.

Sleeping & Eating

Shegar is a popular place for groups to sleep the night before heading out early the next morning to catch dawn over the Himalaya at Pang-la.

Kangjong Hotel (per bed Y25) The rooms are basic but neat at this friendly Tibetan guesthouse. It's right on the highway at the turnoff to Shegar town. The real attraction of the place is the **restaurant** and sitting area which offers wall-to-wall comfy sofas arranged around a warm stove. Simple but good food is available (Y10-15 per dish) and you can kick back with a thermos of sweet tea.

Qomolangma Hotel Tingri (Zhufeng Binguan; ☎ in Lhasa 0891-682 9313; dm Y40, d Y310-350, tr Y400-460, q Y320) Over the river from the Kangjong Hotel is this ridiculously expensive attempt to capture passing tour groups. The dorms and quads come with a toilet but no shower; the other rooms have shower and toilet.

QNP San Chen Guesthouse (d/tr Y100/150) This former Chinese-American joint venture over the river is like a skier on Mt Everest – going downhill fast. The simple rooms come with outside bathroom and hot water is unreliable at best. Things may improve when new owners take over.

In Shegar centre, 7km from the main road, the decent **Xinju Binguan** (dm/s Y30/80, d Y100-120) has rooms without bathrooms as well as a restaurant. Other basic places include **Amdo Hotel** and **Zhuangyuan Guesthouse**; both charge Y25 per bed. Electricity can be dicey.

There are several overpriced Chinese restaurants by the road junction but the best

---

THE ASSAULT ON EVEREST

There had been 13 assaults on Everest before Edmund Hillary and sherpa Tenzing Norgay finally reached the summit in John Hunt's major British expedition of 1953. Some of these attempts verged on insanity.

In 1934 Edmund Wilson, an eccentric ex-British army captain, hatched a plan to fly himself from Hendon direct to the Himalaya, crash land his Gypsy Moth halfway up Everest and then climb solo to the summit, despite having no previous mountaineering experience (and marginal flying expertise). Needless to say he failed spectacularly. When his plane was impounded by the British in India he trekked to Rongphu in disguise and made a solo bid for the summit. He disappeared somewhere above Camp III, and his body was later discovered by the mountaineer Eric Shipton at 6400m. Shipton read Wilson's diary until the entries abruptly finished on 31 May. A second solo effort was later attempted by a Canadian in disguise from the Tibet side. It was abandoned at 7150m.

From 1921 to 1938, all expeditions to Everest were British and were attempted from the north (Tibetan) side, along a route reconnoitred by John Noel – disguised as a Tibetan (with blue eyes) – in 1913. In all, the mountain claimed 14 lives. Perhaps the most famous early summit bid was by George Mallory and Andrew Irvine (then aged 22), who were last seen going strong above 7800m, before clouds obscured visibility. Their deaths remained a mystery until May 1999 when an American team found Mallory's body, reigniting theories that the pair may have reached the top two decades before Norgay and Hillary. The possibility, however slight, has become one of the most enduring mysteries of mountaineering. It was Mallory who, when asked why he wanted to climb Everest, famously quipped 'because it is there'.

With the conclusion of WWII and the collapse of the British Raj, the Himalaya became inaccessible. Tibet closed its doors to outsiders and, in 1951, the Chinese invasion clamped the doors shut even more tightly. In mountaineering terms, however, the Chinese takeover had the positive effect of shocking the hermit kingdom of Nepal into looking for powerful friends. The great peaks of the Himalaya suddenly became accessible from Nepal.

Much to their dismay, the British found that the mountain was no longer theirs alone. In 1951, Eric Shipton led a British reconnaissance expedition that explored the Nepali approaches to Everest and came to the conclusion that an assault via Nepal might indeed be met with success. In 1952, however, Nepal issued only one permit to climb Everest – to the Swiss. The Swiss, who together with the British had virtually invented mountaineering as a sport, were extremely able climbers, and British climbers secretly feared that the Swiss might mount a successful ascent on their first attempt; something that eight major British expeditions value is the **Muslim Restaurant** (noodles Y8, other dishes Y15) at the eastern end of town. You can pick up noodles and biscuits for your trekking snacks in the **shops** near the Kangjong Hotel.

Getting There & Away

A slightly unreliable daily bus leaves Shegar centre for Shigatse between 8am and 9am (bus Y52, minibus Y65). If hitching, a ride from Shegar to Lhatse should cost around Y50, and from Shegar to the Nepali border around Y150. It may be possible to hitch from the Friendship Hwy to Shegar, but the chances are you'll end up walking the 7km stretch of road. It's 6km from the Shegar turn-off to the Shegar checkpoint and another 6km to the Everest turn-off.

EVEREST REGION

For foreign travellers, Everest Base Camp has become the most popular trekking destination in Tibet, offering the chance to gaze on the stunning north face of the world's tallest peak, Mt Everest (8850m). The Tibetan approach provides far better vistas than those on the Nepali side, and access is a lot easier as there is also a road all the way up.

Everest's Tibetan name is generally rendered as Qomolangma, and some 27,000 sq km of territory around Everest's Tibetan face have been designated as the Qomolangma Nature Preserve (p284). Planning for the project was cooperative and included local Tibetan organisations, the Chinese Academy of Sciences and The Mountain Institute of the USA.

had failed to achieve. As it happened, the Swiss climbed to 8595m on the southeast ridge – higher than any previous expedition – but failed to reach the summit.

The next British attempt was assigned for 1953. Preparations were particularly tense. It was generally felt that if this attempt were unsuccessful, any British hopes to be the first to reach the summit would be dashed. There was considerable backroom manoeuvring before the expedition set off. As a result, Eric Shipton, who had led three previous expeditions (including one in 1935), was dropped as team leader in favour of John Hunt, an army officer and keen Alpine mountaineer who was relatively unknown among British climbers.

Shipton's 1951 expedition had at the last minute accepted two New Zealand climbers. One of them was Edmund Hillary, a professional bee-keeper and a man of enormous determination. He was invited again to join Hunt's 1953 expedition. Also joining the 1953 expedition was Tenzing Norgay, a sherpa who had set out on his first Everest expedition at the age of 19 in 1935 and who had subsequently become infected with the dream of conquering the world's highest peak.

On 28 May 1953, Hillary and Norgay made a precarious camp at 8370m on a tiny platform on the southeast approach to the summit, while the other anxious members of the expedition waited below at various camps. The two men feasted that night on chicken noodle soup and dates. At 6.30 the next morning they set out.

Almost immediately they were in trouble, confronted with a vast, steep sweep of snow. It was the kind of obstacle that had turned back previous expeditions, but Norgay agreed with Hillary that it had to be risked. It was a gamble that paid off. The next major obstacle was a chimney-like fissure which the two men squirmed up painfully. Struggling onwards they suddenly found themselves just metres away from a snow-clad dome. At 11.30am, 29 May, they stepped up to the top of Mt Everest and stood at the closest point to the heavens it is possible to reach on foot.

By 2000, around 900 people had reached the peak of Everest (including George Mallory II, Mallory's grandson), while more than 160 climbers had died in the attempt. The first woman to reach the summit was Junko Tabei from Japan on 16 May 1975. The youngest person was 15-year-old sherpa Temba Tseri from Nepal, who reportedly reached the top in May 2001 after losing five fingers to frostbite in a previous attempt. The oldest person to make the climb was Toshio Yamamoto at 63 years and 311 days. In May 1999 a National Geographic Society expedition recorded a global positioning system (GPS) reading at the top of Everest which pegged the height at a controversial 8850m – two metres higher than the 8848m accepted since 1954. Reports on the latest attempts on Everest are available at www.everestnews.com.

The most satisfying way to get to Everest is to make the popular three- or four-day trek from the Friendship Hwy at Tingri (p281). However, most people include Everest Base Camp in their itinerary for a Land Cruiser trip to the border and drive all the way up to Base Camp. This doesn't mean that the region is exactly swarming with travellers, but it is also not realistic to expect that you will be the only one up there.

Whatever you do, don't attempt to walk to Base Camp directly after arriving in Tingri from the low altitudes of the Kathmandu Valley. Land Cruiser trips often reach Base Camp within two days of leaving Zhangmu, and the altitude gain of over 2600m in less than 30 hours leaves most people reeling from the effects of AMS (acute mountain sickness, also known as altitude sickness).

Finally, and just as importantly, do not be tempted by the enthusiasm of others to climb any higher than you feel comfortable. As Base Camp becomes more popular, many travellers are starting to set their sights on higher camps, though the Chinese have recently tried to clamp down on this. Remember that unlike on the Nepali side, there is no rescue service up here in the shadow of Everest.

Permits

You need two permits to visit Everest Base Camp. The first is the usual PSB travel permit, which is available in Shigatse for Y50 (if you've hired a Land Cruiser the travel agency will arrange this one for you). The second one is a park-entry permit for Qomolangma Nature Preserve (QNP) that you must buy at either the QNP San Chen Guesthouse at the turn-off to Shegar on the Friendship Hwy (p188) or in the Snow Leopard Guest House in old Tingri (if coming from Nepal). It costs Y405 per vehicle, plus Y65 per passenger for

---

WHAT'S IN A NAME?

In 1849 the Great Trigonometrical Survey of India mapped the heights of peaks in the Himalaya range. The calculations were carried out from the Indian foothills of the Himalaya, and three years later the computed results showed a peak, known to the West as Peak XV, to be the highest mountain in the world. This came as a surprise, as until this time a mountain called Kanchenjunga near Sikkim (now in India) was thought to be the peak whose head rose closest to the heavens. Peak XV was rather an ignominious name for the highest mountain in the world, and immediately a search began for its real name.

Western linguists working in Nepal and India reported various local names for the mountain. In Nepal, it was claimed, XV was known as Devadhunga (Abode of the Gods). German explorers, on the other hand, reported that the Tibetan name was Chingopamari. In 1862 the Royal Geographic Society opted for an alternative Nepali name for the mountain: Gaurisanka.

In the meantime, Andrew Waugh, surveyor general of India, embarked on a mission of his own: to have the mountain named after the head of the Great Trigonometrical Survey, Sir George Everest (actually pronounced eve-rest). He met with much opposition (including from Everest himself), largely because it was argued that a local name would be more appropriate. In 1865 the Royal Geographic Society decided to back the Everest contingent because of the uncertainties surrounding Gaurisanka (in 1902 it was determined that Gaurisanka was another peak, some 50km from Everest).

The Everest name stuck amid much controversy, not least due to the fact that there was probably no shortage of experts who knew the true Tibetan name for the mountain to be Chomolangma (or Qomolangma, as the Chinese have transliterated it). As early as 1733, the French produced a map on which Everest is indicated as Tschoumou Lancma.

Chomolangma can be interpreted as 'Goddess Mother of the Universe' ('Sagarmatha' in Nepali), or (more literally, if less poetically) 'Princess Cow'. According to Tibetan scriptures safeguarded at Rongphu Monastery, Chomolangma is the name of the mountain while the goddess who dwells there is called Miyo Langsangma. She is one of a group of five well-known long-lived sisters called the Tsering Che Nga, Tibetan deities who predate Buddhism.

The Tibetans and Chinese have little regard for the Westernised name of the world's loftiest peak. Trekkers who make it up to Everest Base Camp have to make do with a posed photograph in front of a sign inscribed with the words 'Mt Qomolangma Base Camp'.

a 10-day pass. A 15-day pass costs Y150 per person. Locals pay Y25. Some Lhasa agencies include the price of both personal park entry and vehicle entry in their tour costs, others include just the vehicle fee and some agencies don't include anything, so check with your agency beforehand.

Your passport (only) will be scrutinised at the checkpoint 6km west of Shegar. The park permit is checked at the Chay checkpoint, 3km after the turn-off from the Friendship Hwy. Officials don't seem to be too worried about travellers leaving the Everest region, so you probably won't have to worry about the park-entry permit if you trek in from Tingri and leave via Chay.

Shegar to Rongphu

The Everest access road turns off the Friendship Hwy around 6km west of the Shegar checkpoint shortly after kilometre marker 5145. The 91km drive takes around two or three hours.

About 3km from the Friendship Hwy you get to the village of Chay (4300m), where your entry permit is checked. From Chay, it is a winding drive up to Pang-la (5120m). The views here are stupendous on a clear day, and feature a huge sweep of the Himalaya range including Makalu, Lhotse, Everest, Gyachung and Cho Oyu. A plaque on the pass shows you what's what. You can climb up a scree slope to the left for slightly wider views.

The road descends past a couple of photogenic villages and ruins down into the fertile Dzaka Valley and the village of Tashi Dzom (also known as Peruche), where you can get lunch or a bed for the night at several places (including the Chomolongma Benba Guest House and Snow Lappy GH). Look for the extremely obtuse road signs here (the sign to Kharta says 'Apart from loud 89km in ditchma' – what!?).

The dirt road then bumps up the wide valley, passing the small villages of Lha Shing, Rephel, Pelding and Puba before reaching Pasum, which also offers accommodation, at the **Pasum Pembah Teahouse** (dm Y25-35) and Basum Yeti Family Hotel. The next main village is Chödzom (more accommodation) and from here the road turns south towards Rongphu (or Rong-puk). The first views of Everest appear half an hour before you arrive at Rongphu.

Rongphu Monastery རོང་ཕོ་ཆེ་དགོན་པ་
elev 4980m
Though there were probably monastic settlements in the area for several hundred years, **Rongphu Monastery** (admission free) is the main Buddhist centre in the valley and once co-ordinated the activities of around a dozen smaller religious institutions, all of which are now ruined. It was established in 1902 by a Nyingmapa lama. While not of great antiquity, Rongphu can at least lay claim to being the highest monastery in Tibet and thus the world. There were once 500 monks and nuns living here, but locals report that there are now only 20 nuns and 10 monks. The nuns and monks use the same prayer hall but have separate residences.

Renovation work has been ongoing at the monastery since 1983, and some of the interior murals are superb. The monastery and its large chörten make a great photograph with Everest thrusting its head skyward in the background.

Monastery Guesthouse (dm Y25) This place, arranged around a courtyard opposite the monastery, is the main traveller accommodation. Rooms are basic – avoid the ones with broken windows or you'll spend the whole night shivering. There's a cosy **restaurant** serving up egg, meat, noodle and rice dishes to order for around Y10 each.

Government Hotel (☎ 0892-858 4535; d per bed Y200) This spectacularly inappropriate new behemoth deserves to be boycotted by travellers just because it's so damned ugly. If that's not enough, the comatose staff are too busy watching DVDs in the restaurant to help, there's no hot water and US$50 for a double gets you stinky squat toilets.

Most people drive from Rongphu to Everest Base Camp but the 90-minute hike is worthwhile and straightforward if you're acclimatised (the route climbs only 220m in around 8km). The walking path cuts through meadows from Rongphu Monastery and by the photogenic ruins of **Rong Chung**, a former meditation retreat. The path drops down to the road and passes the rebuilt **Sherab Chöling Hermitage** on the left, before shortcutting over the glacial moraine to Base Camp.

Everest Base Camp ཇོ་མོ་གླང་མའི་ག་ཤམ་ཚོག
elev 5200m
Endowed with springs, Everest Base Camp was first used by the 1924 British Everest

expedition. The site has a couple of permanent structures, half a dozen tea tents, a post office and clusters of tents belonging to various expeditions. Clamber up the small hill festooned with prayer flags for great views of the star attraction, then have your photo taken at the Base Camp marker, which disappointingly does not even mention the word 'Everest'. It reads 'Mt Qomolangma Base Camp' and the Chinese below indicates that it is 5200m above sea level.

Chinese tourists can get their postcards stamped 'Everest Base Camp' for Y7 at the **post office** (🕙 10.30am-1pm & 3-6pm) kiosk, before dropping them in the highest post box on earth.

Signs warn that tourists will be fined US$200 for proceeding past Base Camp without a guide.

If you are into the mountaineering vibe, a scruffy collection of tents with names like **Hotel California**, **Sherpa Hotel**, **Summit B&B Tea Shop** and **Qomolongma Benpa Guesthouse Branch Restaurant** offer a bed for the night (Y25) and basic food (noodles Y7). Expect nights to be cold here.

Getting There & Away

There is no public transport to Everest Base Camp. Most people include Everest as part of a 'package' of sights to visit in a hired Land Cruiser travelling between Lhasa and the Nepali border. Hiring a Land Cruiser in Lhasa for a round trip will cost almost as much – about Y4000. In Shigatse, a round trip to Everest costs Y3400 for three or four days. You'll need a minimum of one night at Rongphu; two nights is much better.

It is possible to hike into or out of the Everest Region from Tingri (p281).

Not everyone wants to trek the entire distance, however, and a combination of trekking and hitching can get you to Everest Base Camp. Up to 20 vehicles a day head up to Rongphu and while it's difficult to get a lift because most of them are Land Cruisers filled with tourists, you might be able to score a ride at least part of the way. A lift from Shegar to Base Camp will probably cost somewhere between Y50 and Y100.

Coming down from Rongphu, your best bet is to befriend a tour group at the monastery guesthouse. If hitching out, try to get a lift before 3pm when transport starts to dry out.

TINGRI ར་རི་
elev 4390m

Tingri (sometimes called Old Tingri) is a photogenic huddle of Tibetan homes that overlooks a sweeping plain bordered by towering Himalayan peaks. For newcomers from Kathmandu, the discomforts of the sudden altitude gain are likely to make it an unpleasant stay. There is little in the way of sights around Tingri, although the views of Everest and the muscular-looking massif of Cho Oyu more than compensate for this.

Ruins on the hill overlooking Tingri are all that remain of the **Tingri Dzong**. This is a fort that was not blown up by Red Guards, but rather destroyed in a Nepali invasion in the late 18th century. On the plains between Shegar and Tingri, dozens more ruins that shared the same fate can be seen from the Friendship Hwy.

It is possible to trek between Everest Base Camp and Tingri (p281).

Sleeping & Eating

All accommodation is on the Friendship Hwy. Most places offer basic double rooms around a main courtyard, with squat toilets and a cosy Tibetan restaurant or teahouse.

Amdo Hotel (dm Y25) This basic truck stop is popular with Land Cruiser tours. There's nice tea and *thugpa* on the upper-floor veranda. Hot showers are available (Y10/15 for guests/nonguests).

Lhasa Guesthouse (dm Y25-45) Prices rise with the quality of mattresses here. An extra Y10 gets you a hot shower.

Everest Guest House and Eatery (dm Y15) The restaurant is the drawcard at this family-run place. It's currently being renovated so prices might go up.

Everest View Hotel (dm Y25) The 'Lao Dhengre Haho Everest Veo Hotel & Restaurant', as the sign cryptically advertises, is shabby with a basic restaurant and shop.

Snow Leopard Guest House (☎ 826 2711; d Y80-160) A short walk 400m east of town takes you to the best place in town. The cosy, all-brick rooms are spotlessly clean and some have views of Cho Oyu. There's also a nice restaurant (dishes Y25) and sitting area, which doubles as reception. The solar shower block is very clean with hot water from 7pm to midnight. Singles can pay by the bed if things aren't busy. Beware: the cheaper doubles have saggy beds.

Other places include the cheapest option, the ramshackle **Himalaya Hotel** (dm Y10) and the **Tingri Snowland Guesthouse** (☎ 892 6017; dm Y25), 800m west of the centre of town, with a bright restaurant and shower block.

Most ambitious of the restaurants is the **Everest Guest House and Eatery** (mains Y10-20) where optimists can try the pasta and Nepali dishes. The **Lhasa Restaurant** (snacks Y10-15) has curry potatoes and pancakes.

There are several **Chinese restaurants** nearby which cater largely to the local army garrison. All the English menus are the same, with dishes starting at around Y20.

Getting There & Away

Occasional buses pull through Tingri around noon en route to Zhangmu. Hitching a lift with vehicles bound for the border from Shigatse or Lhatse would be your best bet. Expect to pay around Y70 to Y100 to get to Zhangmu, or around Y50 to Nyalam. For sights along the road see p181.

AROUND TINGRI
Langkhor Monastery གནས་འཁོར་དགོན་པ

If you've got time on your hands you could head out to Langkhor Monastery, which is about 20km southwest of Tingri. The monastery is associated with Padampa Sangye, an Indian ascetic who was an important figure in the second diffusion of Buddhism on the Tibetan plateau. There's not much to see here, but it's a good chance to hire a pony and cart (Y50-70) for the bumpy ride out there. Most villagers have a cart and although it's not a comfortable 4½-hour return ride (bring some padding!), you'll get to see much more this way.

Tsamda Hot Springs མཚམས་བཟང་ཆུ་ཚན

Twelve kilometres west of Tingri, this small complex makes a pleasant stop. Baths cost Y20 per person in the slimy communal pool in the middle of the guesthouse courtyard, or Y45 in a clean, comfortable well-tended private pool. The water is a good temperature for soaking in. The springs are 1km off the Friendship Hwy, and are signposted in English near kilometre marker 5206.

Hot Spring Guesthouse (☎ 892 6030; dm Y30, d Y200-240) If you fancy a night at the springs, this place has simple dorm rooms with dirt floors (watch where you drip), damp overpriced doubles with bathroom and a basic restaurant/bar. Rooms were recently renovated by the Snow Leopard Guesthouse.

NYALAM གཉའ་ལམ

☎ 0892 / elev 3750m

Nyalam is a one-street town with a checkpoint, about 30km before the Nepali border. It's the usual overnight spot for Land Cruiser trips to or from Nepal and is a base for trekking in the southern Shishapangma region.

From Nyalam, the road drops like a stone off the Tibetan plateau into a mossy gorge of waterfalls and cascades. During the summer monsoons, the road is submerged in a sea of cloud – no doubt one of the reasons why Nyalam means 'gateway to hell' in Tibetan.

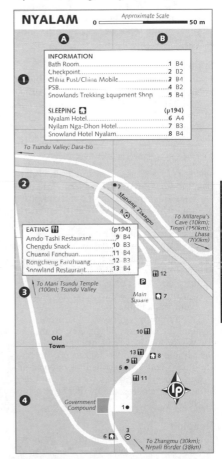

The **post office** (9.30am-1pm & 4-7pm) is at the top (southern) end of Nyalam. The China Mobile branch here has the cheapest international calls.

Snowland Hotel will change cash US dollars (up to US$300) at a reasonable rate and offers pricey Internet (Y10 per hour).

For those who want to use Nyalam as a base for treks, Gary McCue has a section on treks around Nyalam in his book *Trekking in Tibet – A Traveler's Guide*. One possible day hike takes you up the valley behind Nyalam for three hours to Dara-tso, a holy lake from which glaciers of the Langtang and Jungal Himal, and maybe even Shishapangma (the only mountain over 8000m planted squarely in Tibet), are visible on a clear day.

Snowland Hotel can help organise porters for around Y50 per day and sells basic Chinese-made trekking gear from its shop across the road.

Sights

In the old part of town is the **Mani Tsundu Temple**. It's often closed and there's not much to see, but it's a pleasant five-minute walk to the temple and there are usually a few pilgrims around. To get there, take the road that branches off from the southern end of town.

The closest cultural sight to Nyalam is **Milarepa's Cave** (admission Y10) and **Nyalam Pelgye Ling**, the small temple built over it. Milarepa was a famous Buddhist mystic and composer of songs who lived in the late 11th and early 12th centuries. During his long meditation in this cave he renounced all luxuries and survived on a diet of local weeds (famously turning green as a result). Milarepa is credited with many magical feats in Tibetan literature; one was raising the ceiling of his cave with his bare hands. You can still see his handprints in the roof.

The temple is signposted 10km north of Nyalam, at Gangka village. Ask around in the village for the key before descending to the temple as it's often locked up. It takes about two hours to hike here from Nyalam.

Other nearby features that may interest you are signposted along the Friendship Highway (p181).

Sleeping

None of the guesthouses in town has showers, but you can have one at **Chengdu Snack** (Y10; until 11pm) or the **Bath Room** (Y10; 8am-11pm), opposite the government compound.

Nyilam Nga-Dhon Hotel (827 2113; old/new block d Y30/50) The spacious, comfy doubles in the new block out the back are the best in town. The inferior old-block rooms are cramped with thin walls. The owners are friendly, and there's a clean toilet and washing block.

Snowland Hotel Nyalam (827 2111; snowland hotelnyalam@hotmail.com; d per bed Y30) Further up the road, this place has good services like Internet and a café/bar with real coffee (Y20) but the walls are paper thin and rooms can be dark. At least there are doors on the communal toilets.

Nyalam Hotel (827 2507; per bed Y30-35) Despite the alluring sign, there are no hot showers to be found here, only depressing box-like rooms with paper-thin walls and no doors on the shitters.

Eating

All restaurants serve lunch and dinner and have no fixed opening hours.

Amdo Tashi Restaurant (dishes Y15-20) The main travellers' dive is straight across the road from the Snowland Hotel. There are two rooms, one with Western tables and one with Tibetan couches. The menu makes a similar split – you can get a bowl of ice cream or good *thanthuk* (Tibetan noodles).

Snowland Restaurant (veg dishes Y15-20, meat dishes Y25-30) This is the classiest place for a final Chinese dinner blowout before the hedonistic delights of Kathmandu. There are private booths and functioning lazy Susans.

Chengdu Snack (dishes Y15-20) There are several cheap Chinese restaurants near the main square. This one has an English menu and slightly inflated prices (although they may offer to knock Y5 off the listed price).

Other cheaper Chinese places without an English menu include **Rongcheng Fanzhuang** (check out the sign!) and **Chuanxi Fanchuan**, where veggie dishes run at around Y10.

Getting There & Away

It's a stunning 30km journey from Nyalam to Zhangmu, through clouds, past waterfalls and under towering green cliffs. There's no scheduled transport so hitch a lift with a Land Cruiser or taxi heading back to Zhangmu (Y30 per seat). If headed east to Tingri (Y50), start hitching a couple of hundred meters past the PSB checkpoint.

ZHANGMU (DRAM) འགྲམ་

☎ 0892 / elev 2300m

Zhangmu, also known as Khasa in Nepali and Dram in Tibetan, is a remarkable town that hugs the rim of a what seems a never-ending succession of hairpin bends down to the customs area at the border of China and Nepal. After Tibet, it all seems incredibly green and luxurious; the smells of curry and incense in the air are smells from the subcontinent, and the babbling sound of the fast-flowing streams that cut through the town is music to the ears.

Zhangmu is a typical border town, much larger than Nyalam, and has a restless, reckless feel to it. The population is a fascinating mix of Han, Tibetan and Nepali, the shops brim with goodies from India, Nepal and China, and in the curry shops Tibetans watch videos of Indian soap operas. Chinese officials strut around town with coiffed hair, microthin socks and jackets hanging off their shoulders like parading generals. Meanwhile, Nepali traders squeeze their Tata trucks through the congested streets, sending Western tour groups running.

There are fine views of the town from behind **Mani Lhakhang**, halfway up the town.

Information

Moneychangers deal openly in front of the Zhangmu Hotel and change any combination of Chinese yuan, US dollars or Nepali rupees at better rates than on the Nepali side.

Bank of China (Zhongguo Yinhang; ☒ 9.30am-1.30pm & 3.30-6.30pm Mon-Fri, 11am-2pm Sat & Sun) Will change cash and travellers cheques into yuan and also yuan into dollars, euros or pounds, if you have an exchange receipt, but doesn't deal in Nepali rupees.

PSB (Gonganju; ☎ 874 2264; 20m north of the Gang Gyen Hotel) The officers won't give you an Alien Travel Permit to head north into Tibet unless you have a guide, a driver and the mysterious Tibetan Tourism Bureau (TTB) permit – effectively making it impossible for independent travellers to come up from Nepal without having booked a tour in Kathmandu. The checkpoint just north of town makes sure of this. The PSB cannot extend your visa.

Cheap phone calls are available at the **China Mobile** in the **post office** near the Gang Gyen Hotel. There are a couple of **Internet bars** further uphill (Y5 per hour) and a couple of **bath houses** (hot showers Y10).

You can get passport photos made in a day or on the spot next door to the Pema Hotel.

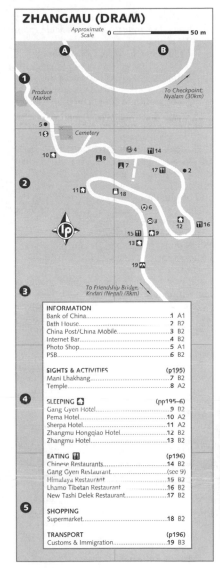

ZHANGMU (DRAM)

Approximate Scale   0 ————————— 50 m

INFORMATION	
Bank of China.............................1	A1
Bath House...............................2	B2
China Post/China Mobile...............3	B2
Internet Bar..............................4	B2
Photo Shop...............................5	A1
PSB.......................................6	B2

SIGHTS & ACTIVITIES	(p195)
Mani Lhakhang...........................7	B2
Temple....................................8	A2

SLEEPING 🏠	(pp195–6)
Gang Gyen Hotel.........................9	B2
Pema Hotel..............................10	A2
Sherpa Hotel............................11	A2
Zhangmu Hongqiao Hotel...............12	B2
Zhangmu Hotel.........................13	B2

EATING 🍴	(p196)
Chinese Restaurants....................14	B2
Gang Gyen Restaurant.............(see 9)	
Himalaya Restaurant...................15	B2
Lhamo Tibetan Restaurant.............16	B2
New Tashi Delek Restaurant...........17	B2

SHOPPING	
Supermarket............................18	B2

TRANSPORT	(p196)
Customs & Immigration................19	B3

Sleeping

Zhangmu Hotel (☎ 874 2221; fax 874 2220; dm Y50, d/tr with bathroom Y400/480) The main hotel in Zhangmu is right down in the south of town next to customs. As you might expect of the last tourist-class hotel in Tibet, it is expensive and apathetically run. It's also the only hotel in Tibet whose reception is on the top floor! While the double rooms are really very luxurious, hot water is only available from 9pm to 11pm.

Gang Gyen Hotel (☎ 874 2188; dm/d Y40-50/150) Most budget travellers sensibly give the Zhangmu Hotel a miss in favour of this place across the road. The dorms are spacious but sheets are grubby and the communal bathrooms are a little grim. Hot showers are available on the roof and are free for guests (Y10 for nonguests).

Zhangmu Hongqiao Hotel (☎ 874 2261; dm/d Y20-25/100-120) For the cheapest beds in town this local hotel is good value. There's not much English spoken. Rooms are clean and bright, though there's no privacy in the shared bathrooms. It's a five-minute walk uphill from the Gang Gyen.

Sherpa Hotel (☎ 874 2078; tr per bed Y40, d Y100-150) Rooms at this Nepali-run place are a little overpriced but clean. The triple bed dorm is too cramped for strangers. There's no shower but there is a pleasant Nepali restaurant (dishes Y15-20) on the top floor.

Pema Hotel (☎ 874 2106; fax 874 2605; dm/tr per bed Y35/50, d with/without bathroom Y388/180) Rooms here are generally way overpriced, though the triples aren't bad value. The dorms are in the dingy basement and the doubles are up a tiny spiral staircase on the top floor. Showers costs Y10 extra. It's in the north of town – look for its pedestrian overpass.

Eating
There is not a shortage of restaurants in Zhangmu. Wander up the hill for an excellent selection of Chinese, Tibetan and Nepali cuisine. All restaurants serve lunch and dinner and have no fixed opening hours.

Gang Gyen Restaurant (ground floor, Gang Gyen Hotel; dishes Y15-30) This hotel has a popular but pricey ground-floor restaurant that serves a full range of Nepali, Chinese, Tibetan and Western mains, including steaks and breakfast foods (from 7.30am).

Himalaya Restaurant (opposite Gang Gyen Hotel; mains Y15-20) A good place for Tibetan, Nepali or Chinese food or to toast Tibet goodbye with a farewell beer on the terrace.

For Tibetan food try the **Lhamo Tibetan Restaurant** or the **New Tashi Delek Restaurant**, both a short walk up the hill from the border.

Most Chinese restaurants deliver a final slap in the face with double-priced English menus and lacklustre service; head uphill for a better choice.

Getting There & Away
TO KATHMANDU
At **Chinese immigration** (⊗ 9.30am-6.30pm, sometimes closed 1.30-3.30pm) you will need to fill in an exit form and health declaration and you may be asked for your travel permit but the process is painless.

From customs, go on to Nepal via the Friendship Bridge and Kodari, around 8km below Zhangmu. Cars and pickups offer lifts across this stretch of no-man's land (Y10). Occasional landslides force travellers to scramble over debris in the places where vehicles can't pass. At the Friendship Bridge you need to show your passport one last time.

At **Nepali immigration** in Kodari it's possible to get a Nepali visa for the same price as in Lhasa (US$30 cash, plus one passport photo, or extra US$5 if no photo) although it is sensible to get one in Lhasa just in case.

If you are planning to come from Nepal into Zhangmu you won't find Chinese immigration open if you leave the Nepali side after 3.30pm

There are a couple of hotels on the Nepali side. For those looking at continuing straight on to Kathmandu, there are buses every hour or so to Barabise, around halfway, where you'll have to change to a Kathmandu bus.

The other option is to hire a vehicle from near Nepali immigration.

A ride to Kathmandu (four to five hours) costs Rs 1500 to Rs 2000 per car, or around Rs 500 per person. Due to Maoist activity there are currently around a dozen military checkpoints along the road and bus passengers have to disembark at many of these, causing the bus trip to last around seven hours.

Nepal is 2¼ hours behind Chinese time.

Western Tibet
(Ngari) མངའ་རིས

CONTENTS

Ngari, the western region of Tibet, is one of the most remote and inaccessible parts of the country. Huge, scarcely populated and at an average altitude of over 4500m, Ngari is a frontier in one of the remotest corners of Asia. The landscape is dominated by the Himalaya range to the south, the huge salt lakes of the Changtang plateau to the north and the trans-Himalayan ranges, such as the Gangdise, which separate them.

Highlights of the long trip from Lhasa are sacred Mt Kailash (Tibetan: Kang Rinpoche) and Lake Manasarovar (Mapham yum-tso), two of the most remote and legendary travel destinations in the world. You have to be a certain kind of person to make this journey – many of the pilgrims on the road have been planning it all their lives. The main attractions of what is likely to be a three-week trip are a mountain and a lake, but what a mountain and what a lake!

The otherworldly ruins of the ancient Guge kingdom at Tsaparang are one of Asia's un-known wonders. And for the truly intrepid there are countless remote monasteries, hidden valleys and sights of historical and archaeological significance to explore. For those not overly fussed by the spiritual significance of Mt Kailash, going to one of the most isolated and beautiful corners of the globe is likely to be an attraction in itself.

Until recently, Western travellers were quite rare in Ngari – the area was largely the pre-serve of tour groups and occasional intrepid travellers with a taste for adventure and lots of time. This situation, for good or bad, is changing as the engine of Chinese development chugs steadily across the plains. Travel in Ngari is still not easy or comfortable but improved roads and new bridges and telephone lines make it more accessible. There's even a bus from Lhasa to Ali (Shiquanhe), a small but growing network of public transport and a planned airport; all would have been unthinkable just a few years ago. Now is the time to explore Ngari.

HIGHLIGHTS

- Make the **pilgrimage** to one of the most mystical and remote corners of the world

- Wash away your sins on the three-day trek around holy **Mt Kailash** (p210)

- Wind down at sacred **Lake Manasarovar** (p212), a sacred body of turquoise water bordered by snowy peaks

- Camp on the shores of the stunning turquoise lakes **Tagyel-tso** (p205) or **Dawa-tso** (p206), along the northern route to Ali, or **Peiku-tso** (p203)

- Tunnel through the cliff-side ruins of the ancient Guge kingdom at **Tsaparang** (p217)

- Spot **prehistoric engravings** (p220) near Rutok before visiting timeless **Rutok Monastery** (p220)

★ Rutok

★ Tsaparang

★ Mt Kailash   ★ Dawa-tso
   ★ Lake Manasarovar

                                    ★ Tagyel-tso

              Peiku-tso ★

WESTERN TIBET (NGARI)

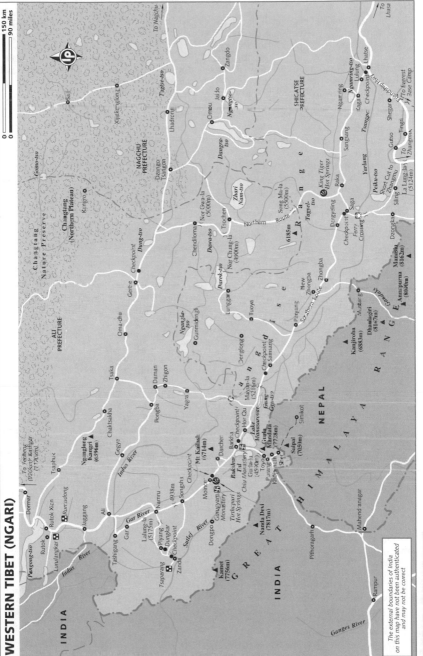

0 150 km
0 90 miles

To Yecheng
(820km)/Kashgar
(1170km)

To Nagchu

To Lhasa

Changtang
Nature Reserve

Changtang
(Northern Plateau)

NAGCHU
PREFECTURE

SHICATSE
PREFECTURE

ALI
PREFECTURE

**To Everest
Base Camp**

NEPAL

INDIA

INDIA

GREAT

HIMALAYA

RANGE

The external boundaries of India
on this map have not been authenticated
and may not be correct.

History

Most histories of Tibet begin with the kings of the Yarlung Valley region and their unification of central Tibet in the 7th century. But it is thought that the Shangshung (or Zhangzhung) kingdom of western Tibet probably ruled the Tibetan plateau for several centuries before this. According to some scholars, the Bön religion made its way into the rest of Tibet from here. The Shangshung kingdom may also have served as a conduit for Tibet's earliest contacts with Buddhism. There is little material evidence of the Shangshung kingdom in modern Tibet, though the Khyunglung Valley, on the Sutlej River near Tirthapuri Hot Springs, marks the site of the old kingdom.

The next regional power to emerge in Ngari was the Guge kingdom in the 9th century. After the assassination of the anti-Buddhist Lhasa king Langdharma, one of the king's sons, Namde Wosung, established this kingdom at Tsaparang, west of Lake Manasarovar and Mt Kailash. The Guge kingdom, through its contacts with nearby India, led a Buddhist revival on the Tibetan plateau and at its peak was home to over 100 monasteries, most of them now in ruins.

In the late 16th century, Jesuit missionaries based in the enclave in Goa took an interest in the remote kingdom of Guge, mistaking it for the long-lost Christian civilisation of Prester John (a legendary Christian priest and king who was believed to have ruled over a kingdom in the Far East). The Jesuits finally reached Tsaparang in 1624 after two failed attempts but if their leader, Father Antonio de Andrede, had expected to find Christians waiting for him, he was disappointed. Nevertheless, he did meet with surprising tolerance and respect for the Christian faith. The Guge king agreed to allow de Andrede to return and set up a Jesuit mission the following year. The foundation stone of the first Christian church in Tibet was laid by the king himself.

Ironically, the evangelical zeal of the Jesuits led not only to their own demise but also to the demise of the kingdom they sought to convert. Lamas, outraged by their king's increasing enthusiasm for an alien creed, enlisted the support of Ladakhis in laying siege to Tsaparang. Within a month the city fell, the king was overthrown and the Jesuits imprisoned. The Guge kingdom collapsed.

At this point, Ngari became so marginalised as to almost disappear from the history books – with one notable exception. In the late Victorian era, a handful of Western explorers began to take an interest in the legend of a holy mountain and a lake from which four of Asia's mightiest rivers flowed. The legend, which had percolated as far afield as Japan and Indonesia, was largely ridiculed by Western cartographers. However, in 1908 the Swedish explorer Sven Hedin returned from a journey that proved there was indeed such a mountain and such a lake, and that the remote part of Tibet they occupied was in fact the source of the Karnali (a major tributary of the Ganges), Brahmaputra (Yarlung Tsangpo), Indus (Senge Tsangpo) and Sutlej (Langchen Tsangpo) Rivers. The mountain was Kailash and the lake, Manasarovar.

Permits

Foreigners are supposed to have a fistful of permits: an Alien Travel Permit, military permit, Tibet Tourism Bureau (TTB) permit, foreign affairs permit… If you arrange a Land Cruiser trip in Lhasa the travel agency will organise all these permits for you but this means it can take up to a week for it to arrange a trip.

Those planning on doing the trip on their own will only really need an Alien Travel Permit (see p304). You'll have no luck obtaining this from either the Lhasa or Shigatse Public Security Bureau (PSB) offices, and will be better off not drawing attention to yourself by trying. The way to do it at present is to get yourself to Ali, by bus or hitching, and surrender yourself immediately to the PSB office there. In return for a Y300 fine and a slice of humble pie you should receive a travel permit for most places in the prefecture (eg Mt Kailash, Manasarovar, Purang, the Guge kingdom, Rutok, Gertse and Tsochen), making the rest of your trip delightfully legal. Be warned, however, that this could change at any time, so check with other travellers before you head off.

There are occasional checkpoints all along the road, including at Saga and Barkha, but the main danger spots for permitless travellers are Ali and Darchen, where there are a couple of English-speaking PSB officers with a special interest in foreigners.

If you want to visit the Buddhist caves of Dungkar (p219) you will need a special permit from the Cultural Affairs Bureau in Zanda (p215).

Western Tibet is a politically sensitive area and is periodically closed to foreigners, due either to political unrest on the Kailash kora or military tension along the contested borders of China, India and Pakistan.

When to Go

May, June, and from mid-September to early October are probably the best times to head out to Ngari. Rates for Land Cruiser hire are cheapest in November. Drölma-la on the Mt Kailash kora is normally blocked with snow from late October or early November until early April.

The festival of Saga Dawa (see p211) during May or June is a particularly popular time to visit Kailash and hundreds of pilgrims and tourists descend on the mountain at this time.

What to Bring

Warm clothes are essential, even in summer, and a sleeping bag is recommended. A tent is very useful if you want to camp at the most beautiful spots on your Land Cruiser trip or are hitching or trekking around the Mt Kailash area, though you can get by without one. Other items to consider are water purification, a stove and cooking pot (and hand towel), and a water bottle that can hold boiling water. If you're hitching, a face mask will help keep out some of the dust. See p321 for other ideas.

Supplies are few and far between in western Tibet and it's well worth bringing along a few treats to ease you through the bare patches. Possibilities include dried fruit and meat, peanuts, sachets of hot chocolate, boiled eggs, chocolate bars and dehydrated food from home.

The only places to change money in Ngari are banks in Ali and, less reliably, Purang – it's much easier to change US dollars as cash rather than traveller's cheques. Depending on the kind of trip you're doing, you'll need to budget for hitching costs, permits, fines and the steep entrance fees for the main attractions.

Getting There & Away

Most travellers approach Ngari from Lhasa because it's the easiest place to organise permits and find travelling companions.

Ngari can also be approached from Xinjiang and Nepal.

Four-wheel-drive trips are the most popular way to get to Mt Kailash. During the peak season (July, August and September) you'll probably find three or four trips advertised on Lhasa's noticeboards at any one time. You really need a minimum of a week to organise a trip of this sort. For tips on planning Land Cruiser trips, see p202 and p321.

There's now a nonstop bus service along the northern route between Lhasa and Ali (see p116 and p209), which costs around US$100 one way. This has been joined by a local-transport network based in Ali and reaching to regional towns.

Travellers planning on hitching to Ngari should take the bus to Lhatse first. There's a checkpoint 6km west of Lhatse, but most hitchhikers just walk straight through it and onto the bridge, which is 2km further on. This is a good place to begin hitching, because a sharp corner in the road means that traffic has to slow down before crossing the river. Truck drivers are generally reluctant to give foreigners lifts and hitchhikers sometimes do have to turn back. One traveller wrote of how he placed a stone on the roadside for every truck that passed him as he waited for a lift. After three days he gave up and headed back to Lhasa to rent a Land Cruiser, leaving behind a sizable road-side chörten.

For those hitching, the northern route probably has the most traffic but there's not much in it these days. If you are lucky enough to get a ride all the way to Ali, expect to pay from Y200 to Y500 depending on the condition of the road and the attitude at the checkpoints. You need to be very flexible with your itinerary, carry plenty of supplies and, more importantly, have sufficient time (a minimum of three weeks) remaining on your visa.

FROM LHASA

See p16 for an overview of the two routes to Kailash.

There are now bridges over all the major rivers along the shorter southern route, which has boosted traffic (though sand can still be a problem in places). For hitchhikers, it can be difficult to get a ride on the southern route (you are at the mercy of tourists who are generally not interested in freeloaders).

PLANNING A LAND CRUISER TRIP TO MT KAILASH   *Andre Ticheler*

Any pilgrimage worth its salt involves its fair share of trials and tribulations, but with careful planning it's possible to avoid many of the common pitfalls of arranging a trip to Mt Kailash.

Obviously, the first step is to draw up a detailed proposed itinerary for the trip, to give to both your agency and other prospective travellers. One point to consider carefully when drawing up an itinerary is the rate of altitude gain. Build in an extra day early on to acclimatise – after Lhatse nowhere is lower than 4500m.

Most basic itineraries take around 17 to 21 days, which allows for six days to get to Mt Kailash stopping en route at places such as Sakya Monastery, a couple of days around Lake Manasarovar to rest up and enjoy the lake, four days on the Mt Kailash kora and four to five days to get back to Lhasa. A visit to Thöling Monastery or Tsaparang will add on at least three days, probably four. An itinerary that takes in both the northern and southern routes will eat up around 21 days. A final consideration if you are heading for Nepal is whether to take the short cut from Saga to Zhangmu.

Costs depend on a number of factors but usually come to about US$650 to US$700 per person for four people on a 21-day trip with a driver and guide, their expenses, a Land Cruiser, permits and fuel. (As a comparison, a 14-day Kailash tour from Kathmandu starts at around US$1300 per person.) Usually, if you have more than four people in your party you need a truck to carry supplies, which adds another US$2000 or so to the trip. Additional days or changes in the routing (for example, getting dropped off in Zhangmu) seem to add little to the cost.

Although there are no stellar attractions on the longer northern route, the scenery of northwest Tibet is superb and this is the road taken by the Lhasa-Ali bus. The northern route is under constant repair, making it easier for trucks and buses to get through in summer. There are also better facilities at the expanding towns along this route and it has the added advantage of taking you through Ali, 330km northwest of Mt Kailash, where you can arrange a permit for Mt Kailash and Lake Manasarovar.

FROM XINJIANG

Although it's a very difficult road, the route along the Xinjiang–Tibet Hwy is increasingly popular with hitchhikers, cyclists and tour groups. It's now even possible to take a bus between Yecheng and Ali when road conditions allow. The route passes through the remote Aksai Chin region; with the unpredictability of breakdowns, it can take three days to a week or more to travel the 1100km from Yecheng to Ali. For a rundown of the route see p317.

FROM NEPAL

If you're coming from Kathmandu on the Friendship Hwy, a shortcut to Saga takes a full day's travel off your trip. It is also possible to enter Ngari on a four-day trek from Simikot in the Humla region of western Nepal to Purang on the Chinese border near Mt Kailash. This route is open only to tour groups that trek in from Humla, which is a restricted region.

SOUTHERN ROUTE

The southern route to Ngari really begins in Saga (Sajia) but there are two ways to approach Saga: you can come from Lhasa through Lhatse, or from Zhangmu on the Nepali border.

Lhatse to Saga (306km)

Both the northern and southern routes follow the same road beyond Lhatse to the northern turn-off near Raka.

Just 4km beyond Lhatse the paved road ends; from there it's dust and corrugations all the way to Ali. At the Lhatse checkpoint (6km after Lhatse), the road leaves the Friendship Hwy and bears west. From the bridge across the Yarlung Tsangpo, 2km after leaving the Friendship Hwy, the road soon enters a surprisingly lush river valley, scattered with Tibetan villages.

The road edges around the north side of a lake and climbs up to the Ngamring-la. At kilometre marker 2085, 60km from Lhatse, the road passes through the very small town of **Kaga** (Kajia), next to the very picturesque **Ngamring-tso**. A turn-off runs round the east side of the lake to the larger settlement and army base of **Ngamring** (Angren), visible on the northeast side of the lake and about 6km off the main route. Ngamring has at least one hotel and several restaurants.

Within 10km of Kaga, 70km west of Lhatse, you'll pass the last trees for many days and soon after you'll also leave behind the last agricultural fields. Just beyond kilometre marker 2060, prayer flags mark the start of a path to a dramatic hill-top **monastery** overlooking the road from the north. The road then makes a zigzag ascent past nomads' camps to the 4700m Kar-la before dropping down to Sangsang.

Sangsang, 122km west of Lhatse, is a larger town than Kaga. The decent **Hotel Sangsang** (d/q per bed Y35/25), which is on the main junction, is clean and has a good Chinese restaurant. There are a couple of other very basic truck-stop guesthouses, plus teahouses and noodle bars. The small Nyingma-school **Wösaling nunnery** overlooks the town from the north and is worth a short visit.

From Sangsang the route passes through a succession of valleys and follows a gorge into the spectacular, wide ravine of the Raka Tsangpo. Emerging from this ravine it skirts a lake and then crosses a flood plain, which is prone to flood damage during the monsoon. The route then climbs a couple of passes and goes past a small guesthouse and chörten at Padeng village, before dropping down again past the tiny settlement of **Raka** (kilometre marker 1912), about 6km before the junction of the northern and southern routes, and 120km from Sangsang. The **Lhato Hotal Teahouse Shop** (d Y20) here is pretty decent and rooms have their own fireplaces. There are a couple of restaurants and other guesthouses. If you're taking the northern route, this is pretty much the last hotel for 240km, though you are able to camp at Tagyel-tso. Confusingly, many maps show Raka (or Raga) right at the crossroads; in fact the turn-off 6km away is marked only by a weather-worn sign in Tibetan and Chinese pointing to Ali.

If you are continuing west from the northern turn-off, it's 60km to Saga.

Zhangmu to Saga (170km)

The scenic short cut from Zhangmu on the Nepali border to Saga (Sajia) on the southern route to Ngari saves 250km (at least a day of travel) and is used by Land Cruiser groups visiting Ngari directly from Nepal.

See p193 and p195 for more details on the first part of this route. Past Nyalam the road climbs to the 5120m Tong-la and then the 5124m La Lung-la. Not long after, the short cut branches west off the Friendship Hwy, rounding some hills at the entrance of a vast stony plain.

Near the **Siling** (or Scylong) village travellers must pay Y25 per person (Y40 per car) entry to the western section of the Qomolongma Nature Reserve. There is also a small but decent **guesthouse** (dm Y25) at the checkpoint. The nearby village has a fine monastery and ruined *dzong* (fort).

To the south come views of **Shisha Pangma** (8012m), known to the Nepalese as Gosainthan, the only 8000m-plus mountain planted completely inside Tibet. The road provides access to the mountain's north base camp before skirting the huge turquoise lake **Peiku-tso** (4591m). There's fine camping by the lakeshore here, with stunning views of Shisha Pangma and Nepal's Langtang range, but you need to bring your own drinking water and be well acclimatised. Try to find a sheltered camp site as winds whip up in the afternoon.

The bumpy route then follows a narrow gorge before passing the turn-off to the scenic but off-limits Kyirong Valley. After passing the small Drolung-tso you climb to a pass and then drop steeply down to the cable ferry across the Yarlung Tsangpo. From here, it's 3km to Saga, where you join the southern route.

Saga ས་དགའ་
☎ 0892 / elev 4600m

The army town of Saga is the last town of any size on the southern route and it's your last chance to eat a lavish meal. The town consists of an east–west road that connects the eastern road to Lhatse and the southwestern road to Zhangmu. A fairly lax checkpoint at the east entrance to town checks travel permits.

If you are headed to Nepal it's a good idea to cross the river on the ferry in the afternoon and get an early start the next morning as the ferry doesn't start operations until 10am.

You can get **Internet access** (☾ 11am-11pm; per hr Y5) on the 2nd floor of the cultural centre building overlooking the main square.

Yak Guesthouse (dm Y25), a Tibetan courtyard-style place with basic rooms and dirt floors.

Look for the yak's head outside the gate and the sign 'House Keepling'. Next door, **Sheru Hotel** (dm Y25-35) has higher-priced and higher-quality beds.

At the **Post Hotel** (Youzheng Zhaodaisuo; ☎ 820 3008; 5-bed dm Y25, q per bed Y30; ▣) the quads with carpet and TV in the main building are the best. The Internet bar in the courtyard is expensive. A similar government option is the **Telecom Guesthouse** (tr per bed Y30) across the road.

The new three-star **Jilin Tour Hotel** (Jilin Lüyou Dajiudian; ☎ 892 0888; d Y228-288, discounts of 20%; ✂), on the main (western) square, is the best in the region, with clean, spacious and heated rooms with hot showers.

Moon Star Hotel (Xingyue Zhaodaisuo; ☎ 820 3008; dm Y40, d without bathroom Y120, d Y180-200), above the flashy restaurant of the same name at the east end of town, has clean rooms set around an interior courtyard, meaning they can be noisy. The dorms are clean but there's no communal shower. The best doubles come with a hot shower.

Buses run to Shigatse (Y100, 16 hours) on Thursday and Sunday from opposite the Yak Guesthouse.

Saga to Zhongba (145km)

There are several ruined monasteries along this stretch, including one just 1km out of Saga. **Dargyeling Monastery**, on the right side of the highway, 42km from Saga and 15km from Dargyeling town, is the best preserved and worth a stop.

From here, you cross a river and then pass the ruins of a large monastery, 12km from Dargyeling Monastery. The road then climbs to a pass marked by hundreds of miniature chörtens, before dropping 23km to Zhongba.

Zhongba འབྲོང་པ་

'Old' Zhongba is a dusty ghost town on the main road with a couple of guesthouses and a small monastery. 'New' Zhongba, 25km northwest, is a small Chinese town with a couple of shops, hotels and restaurants. It's 10km north of the main road and has little to recommend it. Given the choice, try to stay at Saga.

Yak Hotel (☎ 0892-858 1011; dm Y30) is the pick of the bunch in old Zhongba, with rooms off an upper-storey balcony and a fireplace and kettle in each room. There's

a decent Chinese restaurant opposite the entrance.

Other places include the **Tashi Hotel** (dm Y30), at the eastern entrance to town, which also offers Tibetan food, and the friendly but chaotic **Tibet of Hostel** (dm Y20), in the centre. Both are pretty basic.

Zhongba to Paryang (110km)

From Zhongba, the road deteriorates and the kilometre markers disappear. This section is particularly prone to invasion from the sand dunes on either side of the road and many trucks get stuck briefly here – the experienced drivers carry long poles that they wedge between the twin rear wheels of their trucks for traction. You shouldn't have any real problems in a Land Cruiser.

A photogenic section of dunes, lake and mountains kicks in 60km from Zhongba. About 23km before Paryang you crest a pass and drop past more dunes to Paryang.

Paryang པར་ཡངས་
elev 4750m

Paryang is about five hours' drive from Saga. It is a surprisingly Tibetan town and the centre has a small *mani lhakhang* (a chapel with a large prayer wheel) that attracts elderly Tibetan pilgrims. Also gracing the centre of town is an enormous rubbish dump. There are wonderful views of nomads' tents and Himalayan peaks across the plains, just to the south of town.

Of the cluster of basic hotels, the **Diki Hotel** (dm Y20) and **Yak Hotel** (dm Y25) are the better choices. The Yak is set around a large compound and can be noisy, with toilets outside the main compound; the Diki is a smaller, family-run place on the southern edge of town. Other options include the basic but acceptable **Tashi Hotel** (dm Y30).

There are a few Chinese restaurants in town, such as the Silutong, Chongqing and Tianfu restaurants, and you can buy basic supplies from the nomad tents in the main square.

Paryang to Hor Qu (223km)

There is a tricky section of sandy road 12km west of Paryang where many trucks get stuck but all the major river crossings now have bridges, which makes this long stretch a much easier journey than before. There's a checkpoint at the Mazhang Bridge, 108km from Paryang. Just 3km from here is a **guest-house** (dm Y25) and tent restaurant, which is a popular lunch stop.

From here, the road runs 21km to the Mayun-la (5216m). The road improves as you cross from Shigatse to Ngari prefectures and descends to the long Gung Gyu-tso. Mt Kailash comes into view approximately 90km after the Mayun la, just before the town of Hor Qu.

Hor Qu ཧོར་ཆུས་

elev 4560m

Hor Qu is 40km from Darchen, the closest town to Mt Kailash. There are a couple of guesthouses and some limited dining options. There are good views of 7728m Gurla Mandata but Lake Manasarovar itself is a long hike away. Some trekkers walking the Lake Manasarovar kora (p292) spend the night here.

Yang-tso Guesthouse (dm Y40) is the best of the bunch, a clean and decent cooperative at the east end of town. Hot showers are planned.

There are a couple of inferior and basic guesthouses, including the **Shenhu Binguan** (dm Y25) and **Tarba Zhaodaisuo** (dm Y25). The Tarba is currently building some new rooms, which might be worth checking out.

From Hor Qu, it's 22km to the crossroads settlement of Barkha (Barga), where there's a major checkpoint, some restaurants and a decent **guesthouse** (dm Y25).

NORTHERN ROUTE

The northern route is the longer of the two routes from Lhasa to Ngari but is the more popular with hitchhikers because there's more traffic and public transport. The Chinese are developing the area, and new white-tiled buildings are being hastily constructed in the towns along the way. Although it's no freeway, the road is at least maintained by teams of sweating road workers.

The first part of the northern route, like the southern route, follows the road from Lhatse to the turn-off near Raka (see p202). From Raka, there is basically no accommodation before Tsochen, 240km away. If you're travelling by Land Cruiser, the possibilities for putting up a tent along the road are excellent and there's no shortage of grassy river-side spots with beautiful mountain views. You'll see a lot of seminomadic herders along this route.

King Tiger Hot Springs & Tagyel-tso སྟག་རྒྱལ་ཆུ་ཚན་

Only 21km north of the Raka junction are the Tagyel Chutse, or **King Tiger Hot Springs**, a small collection of gushing geysers, bubbling hot springs, puffing steam outlets and miscellaneous smoking holes in the ground. They are found on both sides of the fast-flowing river that issues from the lake, as well as along the road that leads down to the river. Yellowstone it's not, but the spurting springs, which reach heights of up to 15m, are worth a quick look.

From the hot springs, the road runs around the western side of a lake, then through a wide valley, one of the stretches of flat terrain in Ngari where every driver seems to have been intent on pioneering his own new route. As a result, myriad different tracks fan out across the plain. From a low pass, the route descends to a much larger lake, **Tagyel-tso**, the waters of which are a miraculous shade of the deepest blue imaginable and ringed with snowy peaks. This is a great place to camp if you are prepared for the cold and altitude (around 5170m).

North to Tsochen

For 25km the road runs along the eastern side of Tagyel-tso, mountain ranges closing it in on both sides, before passing two small truckers' guesthouses and climbing to the 5500m Song Ma la. A further 45km and the road crests a small pass and leads down to two joined lakes, past a small salt mine. Eventually you pop out into the wide sandy valley of the Yutra Tsangpo, where the road splits *Mad Max* style into a dozen parallel tracks. Look out for the prayer flags of the **Drubkhang Monastery** on a ridge to the left. The town of Tsochen is 8km further on.

Tsochen མཚོ་ཆེན་

Tsochen (Coqen or Cuoqin), 235km from the northern turn-off, 173km south of the northern road proper and sheltered under a ridge, doesn't look like much when you pull in but it's actually the most interesting of the route's towns.

Head to the east end of town, through the Tibetan village, to the mass of **mani stones**, **prayer poles** and **yak skulls** that local pilgrims flock to daily at dusk.

From here, you can see the desert plateau to the north and a second mass of prayer flags about 1km away; just below here is the **Mentong Monastery**, a small but friendly place with 30 monks. Visitors can enter the main prayer hall and the Kuding Lhakhang, which has an inner chapel. The monastery belongs to the Kagyud school so there are several pictures of Milarepa, Marpa and the Karmapa.

One potential excursion from Tsochen is to **Zhari (Tsari) Nam-tso**, a huge salt lake that is 50km east of town towards the town of Tseri (Tsitri). You will need to have this visit pre-arranged with your driver before leaving Lhasa or arrange extra payment for the half-day trip.

At the **Government Hotel** (Zhengfu Jiedailou; dm Y15-25, d per bed Y35-40, deluxe d per bed Y50-70), the best value rooms are the doubles, which offer bare concrete rooms but comfortable new beds. It's on the north side of Tsochen's main street, 200m left of China Telecom. It's popular, so the greenhouse-style corridor can be noisy at night.

Telecom Guesthouse (Dianxin Binguan; per bed Y40-50) is not a close runner-up, with only four rooms and grubby bedding. It's in the courtyard behind China Telecom, in the far left corner.

The main street is lined with Chinese restaurants – try the **Chengdu Kuaian** (dishes Y15-25), 100m east of China Telecom.

Tsochen to Gertse (257km)

From Tsochen to the junction of the northern road is a journey of about 180km; Gertse is another 77km, making a total drive of around nine hours. The route crosses the relatively insignificant Tsochen-la and then, 43km north of Tsochen, the more impressive 4900m **Nor Chung-la** (Small Wild Yak Pass) before descending to the dramatic turquoise waters of **Dawa-tso**, another superb camping spot. For the next 60km the route crosses from one attractive valley to another, sometimes connected by the river and gorge, at other times by minor passes.

The road crosses the **Nor Gwa-la** (Wild Yak Head Pass), another pass of nearly 5000m, 94km north of Tsochen. From the pass, the route descends to a bridge, 109km from Tsochen, at **Chendiloma**, where there is a small guesthouse and teahouse.

From about 10km before Chendiloma and for the next 50km, the road runs right beside a beautiful, snowcapped mountain

range running north–south, crossing several of its glacial outwashes. The valley narrows towards its northern end before the road suddenly pops out onto a wide plain to meet the northern road proper (the one that links Amdo with Ali). So many different roads fan out across the plain at this point that it's difficult to pinpoint exactly where the roads meet. Just north of here are the salt marshes surrounding lake **Dung-tso** (it's not possible to walk to the lakeshore). Some trucks travelling the northern road come this far to collect salt and take it back to Lhasa or Shigatse and hitching prospects are better along this road.

From the junction it's two hours west to Gertse, with the whites of the saltpans blushing into mineral purples and pinks. There's a minor checkpoint for drivers 24km before Gertse.

Gertse སྐྱེ་རྩེ་

☎ 0897

Gertse (Gaize) is a bleak and windy town – a dust mask is an essential accessory for the locals. It's the biggest of the towns along the northern route and Western civilisation has finally arrived in the shape of dry-cleaning, computer-generated bingo and prostitution. Budget an hour to visit the long wall of **chörtens**, **mani stones**, **prayer flags** and **yak horns** that stretches off to the south of town.

The PSB maintains a strong presence by the main roundabout. Grab a hot shower at the Muslim-run **bathhouse** (Y10), 100m east of the main roundabout. There is a 2nd-floor **Internet bar** (per hr Y7) on the main drag, provided the electricity holds out.

The **Government Guesthouse** (Zhengfu Zhaidaisuo; beds in q/d Y35/45, deluxe s/d Y120/160), which is unmarked, is opposite the hospital west of the roundabout. There are three blocks. The cheapest quads are smelly and cramped and come with foam mattresses. The doubles have better beds but are still a bit musty. The deluxe doubles are comfortable but the en suite bathrooms remain tantalisingly out of reach, locked up due to a lack of running water.

Zhengjisuo Zhaodaisuo (per bed Y35-40), at the west end of town, has cleaner and brighter rooms but there are only quads so you may have to pay for the extra beds if you value your privacy. It's diagonally across from the market.

Jindalai Canting (dishes Y15-25) is a recommended Chinese restaurant just west of the China Telecom office at the western end of the town.

Shigatse Tibetan Restaurant (dishes Y10) has no English menu, only friendly staff and a range of Tibetan dishes offering various combinations of meat, rice and potatoes. It's on the 2nd floor.

Guanghan Canting (dishes Y25), opposite the basketball courts of the central Culture Sq, is the fanciest place in town, with napkins and everything.

A sleepy indoor market offers such unexpected treats as bananas and pears.

Gertse to Gegye (368km)

It's a full day's drive from Gertse to Gegye, the next town of any size. Soon after leaving Gertse, you'll pass several small lakes set in a wide plain that switches between Mongolian-esque grasslands to Central Asian–style desert. Keep your eyes open for round tomb-like buildings that are actually *tsampa* (roasted barley) storage bins. **Oma-chu**, a small village huddled beneath a rocky outcrop, is 54km west of Gertse.

After about 30km the road passes large Tarab-tso (or Dara-tso), from where it's another 75km to **Tsaka** (about 4½ hours from Gertse). This is a major salt-mining community and many hitchhikers find themselves dropped off 8km before town by a salt-laden truck. The centre of town has a **guesthouse** (dm Y15-30). There's a nice stream-side picnic spot 8km up the side valley towards Pongba.

Another route continues west from the turn-off to meet the Ali-Kashgar road just north of Pangong-tso. The main road to Pongba climbs to the 4878m Gya-la, then passes nomads' tents and curves around salty Bar-tso, before crawling to another pass that has a large cave on one side. The desolate sense of space along this section is truly awesome. The road then descends to **Pongba** (Shungba or Xiongba) town, a dismal wool-trading centre for the nomads of the region, 96km from the turn-off. Here you'll find a very basic truckers' guesthouse and a few restaurants.

The last stretch of road between Pongba and Ali is fairly good. An hour or so out of Pongba the road enters a gorge and follows the Indus River past Dongba to Gegye, 105km (two hours) from Pongba.

Gegye དགེ་རྒྱས

The quiet small, town of Gegye (Geji), nestled against a ridge, is a good place to stop for lunch or the night There's nothing to see but there is an **Internet bar** (per hr Y6) just south of the main intersection (which is where the PSB is located).

The unmarked government guesthouse **Gegye Binguan** (☎ 0897-763 745; per bed Y45 or Y80) is the best in town. Bizarrely, the clean and carpeted ground-floor rooms are exactly the same as the upper-floor rooms, yet almost half the price. Both floors give access to the wonderfully useless electric shoe-shining machine. It's at the south end of town, on the left as you pull in.

The greenhouse-style **Xianhe Luguan** (per bed Y30) has clean and spacious tiled rooms. Put your feet up on the sofa and turn on the TV to feel right at home, but don't forget the squat toilets are a hike away. It's at the north end of town, on the right.

A similar, but crummier place is the **Kaifa Gongsi Zhaodaisuo** (per person Y35). It's at the south end of town, on the east side.

The main road contains a couple of good supermarkets, plenty of Chinese and Muslim **restaurants** (dishes Y20-30) and a couple of Tibetan teahouses.

Gegye to Ali

Ali is just 112km (2½ hours) from Gegye; 30km before Gegye the road reaches the infant Indus River, not far from its birthplace north of Mt Kailash, and follows it all the way to Ali. At first it's a gently looping river, spreading out in multiple channels across the valley floor, but later it straightens out and the valley narrows.

Ali emerges like a bizarre mirage. From afar it looks very large and modern and the shock is reinforced when you actually reach the town. It has clusters of modern-looking buildings, shops, neon signs, paved roads and hordes of taxis, just like Beijing. Here, you'll drive on your first bitumen road since Lhatse and it's an amazing experience to glide smoothly into town after five or six days bouncing around the northern plateau.

ALI ཨ་ལི
☎ 0897 / elev 4280m

Ali, also known as Shiquanhe in Chinese and Senge Khabab (Town of the Lion) in Tibetan, is the capital of the Ali prefecture.

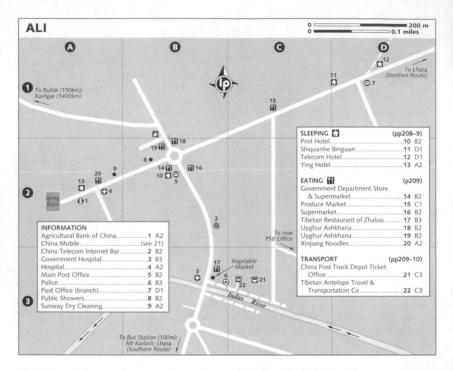

ALI

0 ————— 200 m
0 ————— 0.1 miles

To Rutok (150km);
Kashgar (1400km)

To Lhasa
(Northen Route)

To new
PSB Office

Vegetable
Market

Indus River

To Bus Station (100m);
Mt Kailash; Lhasa
(Southern Route)

INFORMATION
Agricultural Bank of China...............1 A2
China Mobile.............................(see 21)
China Telecom Internet Bar.............2 B2
Government Hospital......................3 B3
Hospital......................................4 A2
Main Post Office............................5 B2
Police...6 B3
Post Office (branch).......................7 D1
Public Showers.............................8 B2
Sunway Dry Cleaning......................9 A2

SLEEPING (pp208–9)
Post Hotel..................................10 B2
Shiquanhe Binguan.......................11 D1
Telecom Hotel.............................12 D1
Ying Hotel..................................13 A2

EATING (p209)
Government Department Store
& Supermarket..........................14 B2
Produce Market...........................15 C1
Supermarket...............................16 B2
Tibetan Restaurant of Zhaluo..........17 B3
Uyghur Ashkhana.........................18 B2
Uyghur Ashkhana.........................19 B2
Xinjiang Noodles..........................20 A2

TRANSPORT (pp209–10)
China Post Truck Depot Ticket
Office.....................................21 C3
Tibetan Antelope Travel &
Transportation Co.......................22 C3

There is nothing much to see, but it is a good place to clean up, have some decent food, top up supplies and rest up for a while, before heading off to the real attractions of Ngari.

Ali is thoroughly Chinese. There are plenty of Tibetans wandering the streets but, like you, they are probably visitors from further afield. The town is expanding rapidly, especially to the south of the river, and there's a big army presence. After the barren emptiness of the surrounding country, Ali, with its video-game parlours, department stores and karaoke bars, comes as a real shock to the system.

For views of the town, climb up to the prayer flag–strewn hills to the north of town. Don't take pictures of the army compound to the west (recognisable by the huge army symbol painted on the hillside above it).

Information

For most travellers, Ali offers the first chance to take a shower in many dusty days. Clean, hot **public showers** (Y10; ☼ until 11pm) are available around town.

Agricultural Bank of China (☼ 10am-1pm & 4.30-7pm Mon-Fri) Near the army post, west of the roundabout. Will change cash US dollars, euros and pounds only (no travellers cheques). Head to the 2nd floor, third door on the right, for an English-speaking teller.

China Mobile (☼ 9.30am-11pm) Next to China Post, with cheap international calls (Y2.80 to the US).

China Telecom Internet Bar (per hr Y3; ☼ 24hr) You'll need your passport here.

PSB (Goganju; ☎ 282 1542, 13618977294; ☼ 10am-1pm & 4.30-7pm Mon-Fri) Groups will need to register here. Individuals without permits will be fined Y300 and then given a travel permit for the region for Y50, making the rest of your journey delightfully legal. Visa extensions of 30 days are possible but only if you have just a couple of days left on your visa. The new office is way out in the southeastern suburbs; take a taxi and ask for the *xin gonganju* – 新公安局. The office is on the ground floor, at the end of the corridor to the left.

Sunway Dry Cleaning (Saiwai Ganxidian; per piece Y2-3) Will do laundry; ask for normal wash (*shuixi*; 水洗) not dry-cleaning (*ganxi*; 干洗).

Sleeping

Ying Hotel (☎ 282 1354; dm Y35, tr with bathroom per bed Y45, d with bathroom per person Y60) The somewhat decrepit Ying is the pick for many budget travellers. Rooms are stained and dirty but the bathrooms steam with hot water from 10pm until midnight.

Shiquanhe Binguan (Shanxi Binguan; ☎ 282 4977; standard d Y320, discounted to Y200, economy s/d without bathroom Y80/100, tr per bed Y30) This charmless two-star hotel offers bright Western-style rooms with small bathroom (24 hour hot water). The cheaper rooms are clean but damned ugly.

Post Hotel (Youzheng Jiudian; ☎ 282 8888; d Y320, discounted to Y200, tr Y260-280, ste Y350-500) This is a spacious, clean and good-value mid-range option, with en suite bathrooms and hot water. The lobby is behind the main China Post office.

Telecom Hotel (☎ 282 2998; d Y300, tr Y200) This posh Chinese place has pleasant rooms that open off an atrium with a central skylight. Enjoy the 24-hour hot water.

A budget hotel is planned at the new compound of Tibetan Antelope Travel and Transportation Co.

Eating

Ali has numerous Sichuanese restaurants south and west of the main junction and, given the town's remote location, they are surprisingly good value for money.

Uyghur Ashkhana (noodles Y10) North of the roundabout and across the road from each other, these two places offer great Central Asian kebabs, nan bread, *suoman* (fried noodles), *pilau* rice and green tea.

Tibetan Restaurant of Zhaluo (dishes Y10-20) Comfy Tibetan furniture makes this a good place for Tibetan food or a glass of sweet milky tea. It's south of the roundabout.

Xinjiang Noodles (noodles Y10, Chinese dishes Y15) Good noodles, Chinese dishes and an English menu, only a stone's throw from the Ying Hotel.

Ali is a good place to stock up on some supplies. The best selection are in the supermarkets by the main roundabout. For the best produce (seafood and bananas!) head to the market a couple of hundred metres east.

Getting There & Away

From Ali to Darchen, the only town in the vicinity of the Mt Kailash kora, it's a day's journey of around 330km.

A civilian airport is planned for Ali but no date has been set for its opening.

BUS

Tibetan Antelope Travel and Transportation Co (☎ 282 2226, 282 3828; ttt010406@sina.com; 3 Binghe Beilu) runs a bus service between Lhasa and Ali. The office is currently just north of the Indus River but should move in 2005 to a new compound in the far southeast of town, at the junction of Jiangsi Dajie and Wenhua Lu, not far from the new PSB building. Ask for English-speaking Mr Xiao.

The sleeper bus runs every two or three days nonstop along the northern route and takes a minimum 48 hours. The tickets are priced from Y650 to Y750 from September to November (Y500 to Y700 June to August, and cheaper still December to May). Booking tickets two or three days in advance is essential. For details of the Lhasa office and services see p116.

Tibetan Antelope also offers a service from Ali to Yecheng/Khargilik (Y280, 30 hours, twice a week), road conditions permitting. The company plans to start a Land Cruiser service from Ali to Darchen (Y236), Purang (Y400), Zanda (Y350) and Rutok (Y300), though it would be cheaper to band together and hire an entire Land Cruiser, at around Y1000 per day.

If you have a travel permit you are free to take the government buses from the **bus station** (◷ 9.30am-6.30pm) at the south end of town. Buses run to Lhasa (Y450 to Y550, every two days), Darchen/Purang (Y230 to Darchen, Y280 to Purang, every three days), Zanda (Y230, every three days), Rutok (Y50, daily) and Yecheng (Y280), though these are subject to change.

If these timings don't work for you, try the China Post trucks, running to Darchen (Y150) on Thursday, Zanda (Y150) on Sunday, Rutok (Y50) on Saturday and Gegye (Y50) on Wednesday, Friday and Sunday. Buy tickets the day before from the **China Post truck depot ticket office** (◷ 10am-3pm & 4-7pm).

Getting Around

Fleets of taxis are part of the mirage-in-the-desert shock of arriving in Ali – the town is crowded with little Daihatsu Charades, ricocheting around like birds in a cage. None of them would survive 5km beyond the city limits without falling apart on the corrugations or getting stuck in a sand drift (which raises the question of how they got here in the first place). Within the city limits there's

TO THE LAND OF SHIVA

At Mt Kailash you may well find bands of hundreds of shivering Indian pilgrims hauling themselves around the mountain. An agreement between China and India allows a limited number of Indians to make the pilgrimage to Lake Manasarovar and Mt Kailash each year. Hindus believe Mt Kailash to be the abode of Shiva and Lake Manasarovar to be a mental creation of Brahma. The trip is so important to Hindus that the quota is oversubscribed and places have to be determined by a lottery.

a standard taxi fare of Y5, but the centre of town is actually compact enough that you can walk anywhere.

MT KAILASH   གངས་རིན་པོ་ཆེ་

Throughout Asia, stories exist of a great mountain, the navel of the world, from which flow four great rivers that give life to the areas they pass through. The myth originates in the Hindu epics, which speak of Mt Meru – home of the gods – as a vast column 84,000 leagues high, its summit kissing the heavens and its flanks composed of gold, crystal, ruby and lapis lazuli. These Hindu accounts placed Mt Meru somewhere in the towering Himalaya but, with time, Meru increasingly came to be associated specifically with Mt Kailash. The confluence of the myth and the mountain is no coincidence. No-one has been to the summit to confirm whether the gods reside there (although some have come close), but Kailash does indeed lie at the centre of an area that is the key to the drainage system of the Tibetan plateau. Four of the great rivers of the Indian subcontinent originate here: the Karnali, which feeds into the Ganges (south); Indus (north); Sutlej (west); and Brahmaputra (Yarlung Tsangpo, east).

Mt Kailash, at 6714m, is not the mightiest of the mountains in the region, but with its hulking shape – like the handle of a millstone, according to Tibetans – and its year-round snowcapped peak, it stands apart from the pack. Its four sheer walls match the cardinal points of the compass, and its southern face is famously marked by a long vertical cleft punctuated halfway down by a horizontal line of rock strata. This scarring

resembles a swastika – a Buddhist symbol of spiritual strength – and is a feature that has contributed to Kailash's mythical status. The mountain is known in Tibetan as Kang Rinpoche, or 'Precious Jewel of Snow'.

Mt Kailash has long been an object of worship for four major religions. For Hindus, it is the domain of Shiva, the Destroyer and Transformer. To the Buddhist faithful, Mt Kailash is the abode of Demchok (Sanskrit: Samvara), a wrathful manifestation of Sakyamuni, thought to be the equivalent of Hinduism's Shiva. The Jains of India also revere the mountain as the site at which the first of their saints was emancipated. And in the ancient Bön religion of Tibet, Kailash was the sacred Yungdrung Gutseg (Nine-Stacked-Swastika Mountain) upon which the Bönpo founder Shenrab alighted from heaven.

Mt Kailash has been a lodestone to pilgrims and adventurous travellers for centuries but until recently very few had set their eyes on the sacred mountain. This situation has begun to change in recent years. In May 2001 Spanish climbers even gained permission to climb the peak, only to abandon their attempt in the face of international protests. (Reinhold Messner also gained permission to scale the peak in the 1980s, but abandoned his expedition in deference to the peak's sanctity when he got to the mountain.)

Rumours currently abound of potentially disastrous Chinese plans to build a road around the kora (indeed, vehicles can already navigate about a third of the route). Nepalese air companies are currently seeking permission to fly aerial sightseeing trips around Mt Kailash from Kathmandu. Perhaps the best thing for the mountain would be the protection offered by a possible Unesco World Heritage listing.

Mt Kailash is accessed via the small town of Darchen (elevation 4560m), the starting point of the kora. It is a forgettable little village, littered with various compounds and there's a Swiss-funded Tibetan medical clinic to the northwest. Most travellers linger long enough to organise their kora and then get out.

The PSB is on the west side of town, inside the Gandise Hotel. Groups will need to get their travel permit stamped here on arrival. 'Tickets' for the Mt Kailash kora (Y50) are available here. For more on Kailash and details of the kora, including details about hiring porters or yaks in Darchen, see p285.

Activities

If you've got extra time at Darchen, or you want to spend a day or two acclimatising before setting out on the Mt Kailash kora, you can find some interesting short walks in the area. The ridge to the north of the village obscures Mt Kailash, but an hour's walk to the top of the ridge offers fine views of the mountain. To the south you will be able to see the twin lakes of Manasarovar and Rakshas Tal.

You can also venture north of this ridge – walking 2½ hours along a new dirt road will take you to the **Gyangdrak Monastery**, largest of the Mt Kailash monasteries. Like other monasteries, it was rebuilt (in 1986) after the depredations of the Cultural Revolution. It is possible to drive here but not to **Selung Monastery**, a two-hour walk to the west.

Festivals & Events

The festival of **Saga Dawa** marks the enlightenment of Sakyamuni (Sakya Thukpa), and occurs on the full-moon day of the fourth Tibetan month (in May or June). Saga Dawa is a particularly popular time to visit Kailash, though you will have to share the Tarboche camping area with several hundred other foreigners, most of them on group tours. You can also expect that all the hotels in Darchen will be booked solid throughout this time. The rudeness of some tourists and their intrusive camera lenses can spoil the occasion. Other times offer a less colourful but more personally spiritual time to make your kora.

The highlight of the festival is the raising of the Tarboche prayer pole on the morning of Saga Dawa. Monks circumambulate the pole in elaborate costumes, with horns blowing. There are plenty of stalls, a fair-like atmosphere and a nonstop tidal flow of pilgrims around the pole. After the pole is raised at about 1pm everyone sets off on their kora.

How the flagpole stands when it is re-erected is of enormous importance. If the pole stands absolutely vertical all is well, but if it leans towards Kailash things are not good; if it leans away, things are even worse.

Particularly large numbers of pilgrims assemble at Mt Kailash every 12 years, in the Tibetan year of the horse. The next gathering is in 2014.

Sleeping & Eating

Darchen Guesthouse (dm Y80) You cannot miss this ramshackle place because the road into

KAILASH & MANASAROVAR BOOKS

There are numerous books about Mt Kailash, Lake Manasarovar and the surrounding area, but the gold star for Kailash enthusiasm has to go to the Indian author Swami Pranavananda. His numerous stays in the region between 1928 and 1947 included two visits that lasted a year each. Not only did he complete 23 *parikramas* (circuits of the holy mountain; the Hindu equivalent of a kora), he also did 25 circuits of Lake Manasarovar, including seven when it was completely frozen, and visited the source of all four holy rivers. He also sailed on the holy lake, made many scientific measurements and, in 1949, published his findings in *Kailas Manasarovar*. It was reprinted in India in 1983 and you should be able to find a copy in a Kathmandu bookshop.

The Kailash chapters in German-born Lama Anagarika Govinda's *The Way of the White Clouds* (1966) includes a classic account of the pilgrimage during a trip to Tibet in 1948.

Kathmandu bookshops may also have Sven Hedin's three-volume *Transhimalaya: Discoveries & Adventures in Tibet* (1909–13). Volumes II and III cover Hedin's time in the Mt Kailash region.

Charles Allen's *A Mountain in Tibet* investigates the hunt for the sources of the region's four great rivers and is perhaps the best introduction to the region.

The Sacred Mountain by John Snelling reports on early Western explorers, as well as the colourful list of characters who turned up in the early 1980s when the door to China and Tibet first creaked narrowly open. *Kailas: On Pilgrimage to the Sacred Mountain of Tibet* by Kerry Moran with photos by Russell Johnson is a beautifully photographed essay on Mt Kailash, Lake Manasarovar and the region's colourful pilgrims. *Walking to the Mountain* by Wendy Teasdill is a delightfully laid-back account of the author's lengthy pilgrimage to Mt Kailash, a far from easy task when she visited there in 1988.

the village leads straight through its central gate. Foreigners are charged an extravagant price for the grubby facilities of the guesthouse, although with determined bargaining you may be able to knock off Y20. The shower and toilet blocks (which are signposted the 'Holy Shower') were built in the compound before anyone remembered that there's no running water in Darchen. Deciding to camp doesn't help, because you must set up your tent inside the ugly guesthouse compound, and you're charged the same price as a bed for that dubious pleasure. A much better idea is to walk the 1½ hours to Tarboche on the Mt Kailash kora and camp there for free.

Gangdise Hotel (d Y240, tr Y300) The newest government place has clean and bright rooms with Western-style bathroom but an iffy water supply. The triples don't have private bathrooms.

Tibet Manasarovar Travels Guesthouse (tr per bed Y120) Rooms at this new option in the southwest corner of the compound are basic, clean and overpriced.

Darchen Poverty Alleviation Guesthouse (dm Y80) More crazy prices at this basic courtyard at the southeast corner of town. The foam mattresses in a dirt room would cost Y30 anywhere else.

Om Coffee House (dm Y25-30) Outside the east gate, the Om offers basic dormitory accommodation next to his shop and cosy teahouse, making it the only budget place in town. The owner can help arrange guides and porters.

There's a **Chinese restaurant** (dishes Y15-25) on the north side of the compound, while, in the high season, nomad traders offer a limited range of food supplies.

Getting There & Away

The town of Darchen, the starting point for the Mt Kailash kora, is 6km north of the main Ali–Paryang road and about 12km from Barkha, 107km north of Purang, 330km southeast of Ali and a lonely 1200km from Lhasa.

Tibetan Antelope Travel & Transportation Co (☎ 0897-282 3828; ttt010406@sina.com) plans set up a Land Cruiser service operating from Ali to Darchen. China Post trucks also make the run at least once a week but no-one seems to know exactly when these happen. Ask around for details.

LAKE MANASAROVAR མ་ཕམ་གཡུ་མཚོ
elev 4560m

Lake Manasarovar, or Mapham Yum-tso (Victorious Lake) in Tibetan, is the most venerated of Tibet's many lakes. According to ancient Hindu and Buddhist cosmology the four great rivers of the Indian subcontinent, the Indus, Ganges, Sutlej and Brahmaputra, arise from Manasarovar, though in reality only the Sutlej originates at the lake.

Manasarovar is linked to the smaller Rakshas Tal (known to Tibetans as Lhanag-tso) by the channel called Ganga-chu. On rare occasions, water flows through this channel from Lake Manasarovar to Rakshas Tal; this is said to augur well for the Tibetan people. The channel had long been dry, but water has indeed been flowing between the two lakes in recent years. The two bodies of water are associated with the conjoined sun and moon, a powerful symbol of Tantric Buddhism. Sadly, the sacred landscape of the lake has been disturbed by the construction of a large mine dug by bulldozers on the isthmus between the two lakes.

Manasarovar has been circumambulated by Indian pilgrims since at least 1700 years ago when it was extolled in the sacred Sanskrit literature called the *Puranas*. A Hindu interpretation has it that *manas* refers to the mind of the supreme god Brahma, the lake being its outward manifestation. Accordingly, Indian pilgrims bathe in the waters of the lake and circumambulate its circumference. Tibetans, who are not so keen on the bathing bit, generally just walk around it. It's not unusual to see naked Westerners throwing themselves into the lake to wash away the sins of a lifetime (and the dirt of the last week). Legend has it that the mother of the Buddha, Queen Maya, was bathed at Manasarovar by the gods before giving birth to her son.

The Hindi poet Kalidasa once wrote that the waters of Lake Manasarovar are 'like pearls' and that to drink them erases the 'sins of a hundred lifetimes'. Be warned, however, that the sins of a hundred lifetimes tend to make their hasty exit by way of the nearest toilet. Make sure that you thoroughly purify Manasarovar's sacred waters before you drink them, however sacrilegious that may sound.

Most groups and individuals base themselves at the picturesque Chiu Monastery (below), on the northwestern shore of the lake, and use it as a base for day walks. For detailed information on the Lake Manasarovar kora and a map of the region, see p292. These days it's possible to do the kora in a Land Cruiser, following dirt roads around the lake and stopping at monasteries en route. A less sacrilegious (and more adventurous) option is to hire horses for a three- or four-day kora.

Chiu Monastery

Thirty three kilometres south of Darchen and 14km south of Barkha, on the main highway, **Chiu Monastery** (admission free) enjoys a fabulous location atop a craggy hill overlooking the sapphire blue Lake Manasarovar. The chapel here contains images of Sakyamuni (Sakya Thukpa) and Guru Rinpoche. Climb to the roof of the monastery for stunning views of the lake and, on a clear day, Mt Kailash. The huge peak on the southern horizon is 7728m Gurla Mandata, near the border with Nepal. A new chapel is nearing completion behind the main chapel.

There are hot springs behind the monastery and a small glass-roofed **bathhouse** (admission Y20) close to the village. The water is channelled from the hot springs into individual cubicles via open ducts and it's barely lukewarm by the time you can get a few centimetres of water into the mouldy tiled tubs. Don't expect a pleasant soak but if you need a wash this is a good spot. You can also do your laundry in the warm outflow around the back.

For a hike, walk along the ridge to the southeast of the monastery or make a half-day hike along part of the lake kora to the ruined chörten and prayer wall at Cherkip, returning via the shoreline cave retreats (see p292). There are fine views and lots of nesting birds along this route but bring repellent against the annoying shoreline flies.

There are a couple of friendly, unmarked **guesthouses** (d Y25-35) near the bathhouse, but food and electricity is scarce. Tent teahouses sell basic supplies but you may have to content yourself with instant noodles. You can also camp by the lake with the tour groups. The lakeshore **Manasarovar Guesthouse** (d Y120), built for Indian pilgrims, is overpriced and normally deserted.

There is also a decent **guesthouse** (dm Y25) at the crossroads town of Barkha.

Getting There & Around

You will have made it this far either by hitching or by hiring a Land Cruiser. There is no public transport and very little in the way of truck activity on the road between Darchen and the monastery. There may occasionally be trucks on the main Ali–Purang road, which is around 6km south of Darchen – be prepared for a long wait if you are hitching.

TIRTHAPURI HOT SPRINGS & KORA
ཏེ་ཧུ་སྤུ་རི་རྐྱང་ཆོན།

On the banks of the Sutlej, only a few hours' drive northwest of Darchen, the Tirthapuri Hot Springs enjoy close associations with Guru Rinpoche. Pilgrims traditionally bathe here after completing their circuit of Mt Kailash. Tirthapuri gets its name from the Sanskrit for 'Town of the Dead'.

It takes less than an hour to walk Tirthapuri's own short kora. Starting from the hot springs the trail climbs to a cremation point, an oval of rocks covered in old clothes and rags. From this point, an alternative longer kora climbs to the very top of the ridge, rejoining the trail near the long *mani* wall. The regular kora trail continues past a hole where pilgrims dig 'sour' earth for medicinal purposes. Further along, there's a 'sweet' earth hole. The trail reaches a miniature version of Mt Kailash's Drölma-la, marked with *mani* stones and a large collection of yak horns and skulls. Below, prayer flags hang right across the gorge and a series of rocky pinnacles are revered as *ranjung*, or self-manifesting chörtens.

The trail passes the **Guru Rinpoche (Tirthapuri) Monastery**. Where the trail doubles back to enter the monastery there is a rock with a hole in it right below the solitary prayer wheel, which is a handy karma-testing station. Reach into the hole and pull out two stones. If both are white your karma is excellent; one white and one black means that it's OK; and if both are black you have serious karma problems. Perhaps another Kailash kora would help?

The monastery *dukhang* (assembly hall) has stone footprints of Guru Rinpoche and his consort Yeshe Tsogyel to the right of the altar. At one time, the monastery was connected with the important Hemis Monastery in neighbouring Ladakh.

Outside the monastery a large circle of *mani* stones marks the spot where the

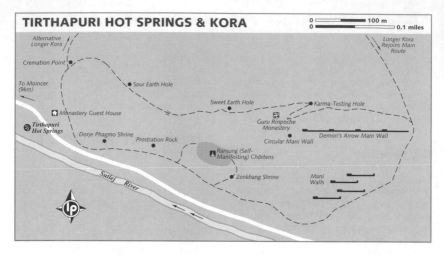

TIRTHAPURI HOT SPRINGS & KORA

0 ——— 100 m
0 ——— 0.1 miles

Alternative Longer Kora

Longer Kora Rejoins Main Route

Cremation Point

To Moincer (9km)

Sour Earth Hole

Sweet Earth Hole

Karma-Testing Hole

Monastery Guest House

Guru Rinpoche Monastery

Tirthapuri Hot Springs

Dorje Phagmo Shrine

Prostration Rock

Circular Mani Wall

Demon's Arrow Mani Wall

Ranjung (Self-Manifesting) Chörtens

Zenkhang Shrine

Mani Walls

Sutlej River

gods danced in joy when Guru Rinpoche was enshrined at Tirthapuri. Beside it is a *mani* wall (a wall made of *mani* stones) over 200m long, the end result of a demon firing an arrow at the guru. He stopped the arrow's flight and transformed it into this wall. Finally, the kora drops back down to the river, passing a large collection of *mani* walls of various sizes on the way.

There are limited facilities at the hot springs so you should be self-sufficient. The **monastery guesthouse** (d Y30) has a couple of rooms and basic food but most foreigners camp further downstream (purify all river water here). Don't plan to wash away the dust of Ngari's roads here; the springs simply gush down to the river, although pilgrims have dug a couple of very public bathing holes.

There is no public transport to Tirthapuri. The hot springs are 9km south of Moincer (Mensi), which in turn is 65km west of Darchen along the main road to Ali. There's a checkpoint at Moincer, which sometimes charges a fee to proceed to Tirthapuri. Moincer is the dormitory town for the coal mines 20km to the northeast and has a decent selection of shops, restaurants and the basic Meiman Zhaodaisuo guesthouse.

A further 14km east from Tirthapuri is the Bönpo-sect **Gurugyam Monastery**. The nearby upper Sutlej region, a further 10km, is peppered with abandoned cave settlements and forms the **Kyunglung (Garuda) Valley**, the location of the early kingdom of Shangshung (see p200). If you have a particular interest

in this archaeological site and other remote monasteries in the area, bring a copy of Victor Chan's *Tibet Handbook* and be prepared for some serious exploration.

GUGE KINGDOM གུ་གེ་རྒྱལ་རབས

Thöling and neighbouring Tsaparang are the ruined former capitals of the ancient Guge kingdom of Ngari, accessed from the modern Chinese town of Zanda (Zhada). Tsaparang, in particular, is a truly amazing sight, in part because it is so little known. The 9th-century ruins are etched into the steep sides of an imposing ridge. Cave dwellings, stunning monastic murals and a ruined palace are linked by twisting paths and secret tunnels that worm their way into the cliff.

Tsaparang is 20km east of Zanda, and the Guge monastery at Thöling is now merely an adjunct to the town. The two sights and the surrounding scenery of the Sutlej Valley are a highlight of Ngari and are well worth the three- or four-day detour from the Ali–Kailash road.

In particular, the northern road from Ali into Zanda passes through incredible desert canyons and amazing eroded mountains, cut through by the Sutlej River on its way to the subcontinent.

History

This barren landscape seems an unlikely place for a major civilisation to have developed, yet the Guge kingdom thrived as an important stop on the trade route between

India and Tibet. By the 10th century it was a wealthy centre supporting several thousand people, and the great Guge king Yeshe Ö began to nurture an exchange of ideas between India and Tibet. Yeshe Ö sent the young monk Rinchen Zangpo (958–1055) to study in India; the monk returned 17 years later to become one of Tibet's greatest translators of Sanskrit texts and a key figure in the revival of Buddhism across the Tibetan plateau. Rinchen Zangpo built 108 monasteries throughout western Tibet, Ladakh and Spiti, including the great monasteries of Tabo (Spiti) and Alchi (Ladakh). Two of the most important were those at Tsaparang and Thöling. He also invited Kashmiri artists to paint the unique murals still visible today. It was partly at Rinchen Zangpo's behest that Atisha, a renowned Bengali scholar and another pivotal character in the revival of Tibetan Buddhism, was invited to Tibet. Atisha spent three years in Thöling before travelling on to central Tibet.

The kingdom fell into ruin just 50 years after the first Europeans to enter Tibet arrived in 1624, after a siege by the Ladakhi army (see p200).

Permits

Having done their best to destroy Tholing Monastery and Tsaparang, the Chinese now charge Western visitors to see what escaped their ravages. It's worth checking the latest situation in Ali or Lhasa, as part of the fee for Tsaparang has, in the past, been paid in Lhasa and Ali. You may also need a separate permit from the Zanda PSB to visit Tholing, although this wasn't required during our recent visit.

Your guide will register you with the PSB in town. Make sure your permit is stamped in Ali or Darchen, otherwise you risk a fine here.

Getting There & Away

There is infrequent public transport to the Guge kingdom sites, so unless you have a rented Land Cruiser getting to these areas can involve some tough hitching. There are two main roads to Zanda from the Darchen to Ali road. Both are rough and go over some very high passes. In a Land Cruiser it's possible to make it to Zanda from either Ali or Mt Kailash in a single day, providing

you get an early start. Many travellers break the trip at Tirthapuri (p213).

TO/FROM DARCHEN

It is 65km between Darchen and Moincer, which is the turn-off to Tirthapuri, and then another 56km from there to the army base at Ba'er/Songsha, where there's a basic Tibetan restaurant. From there, a road leaves the main Ali route and climbs for 15km to a pass, then over the next 80km zigzags down into a series of gorges and climbs up the other side before eventually making a long, winding and very rough descent down a fantastically eroded gully. Eventually this side valley debouches into the wider Sutlej Valley and, after crossing a bridge, the road finally reaches the oasis-like town of Zanda, six or seven hours and 122km from Songsha. En route you could visit the caves of Dungkar (p219).

TO/FROM ALI

Coming from Ali, the road is equally tough going. The road is smoothly paved to the turn-off near Namru and provides excellent views of the Gar Valley. About 64km from Ali the route crosses a bridge to the western side of the valley. After a further 10km the road branches right off the main road, climbing huge switchbacks up to the 5175m Lalung-la (Laling Gutsa), then the Laochi-la before descending and climbing again to a third pass. From the plateau below there are stunning 180-degree views of the Indian Himalaya, stretching from Nanda Devi in the south to the Ladakh range in the north.

From this plateau, the route drops down into deep, eroded wadi-like gullies before finally reaching the Sutlej Valley. The road detours left to a bridge tha crosses the Sutlej, though another bridge is currently being built nearer Zanda. It's 130km from Namru to Zanda.

Zanda ཙ་མདའ་
elev 3650m

Zanda, or Tsamda, the base for visits to the ancient Guge kingdom, has an incredible location. It's perched against crumbling cliffs high above the Sutlej River– a patch of vivid green among unrelentingly barren canyons. There are even real trees, the first in hundreds of kilometres.

ZANDA & THÖLING MONASTERY

Approximate Scale

0 — 200 m
0 — 0.1 miles

Langchen Tsangpo (Sutlej River)

Thöling Monastery

Tibetan Old Town

Zanda

To Tsaparang (21km)

To Ali (204km); Darchen (241km)

INFORMATION	
China Post...1	B2
China Telecom.....................................2	B2
Cultural Affairs Bureau......................3	B3
Hot Shower..4	B2

SIGHTS & ACTIVITIES	(pp216–17)
Chörten..5	A2
Lhakhang Karpo..................................6	A1
Lines of Minature Chörtens...............7	A1
Main Assembly Hall............................8	A2
Serkhang Chörten...............................9	B1
Yeshe Ö's Mandala Chapel...............10	A2

SLEEPING	(p216)
Guge Hotel...11	A2
Hubei Hotel..12	B3
Shuili Binguan...................................13	B2

EATING	(p216)
Bei Bei Quick Meal Shop...................14	B2
Guge Restaurant................................15	B2
Happy Restaurant for Travellers........16	B2
Muslim Restaurant.............................17	B2
Supermarket.......................................18	B2

The **Cultural Affairs Bureau** (☎ 0897-062 2110), just south of the entrance on the Hubei Hotel courtyard, issues permits for the caves at Dungkar (p219). Contact Mr Jiang Lin; if he's not here, look for him at Thöling Monastery.

There's a hot **shower** (Y15) in the centre of town near the Guge Restaurant.

The government-sanctioned **Guge Hotel** (beds Y90) is poor value with beds in basic triples and quads and little going for it.

You'll still have to pay over the odds at the **Hubei Hotel** (beds Y90) but it's much better value. The double rooms are clean and tiled but the bathrooms have no water so you'll have to trek to the stinky pit toilets out back.

Shuili Binguan (beds Y45) isn't open to foreigners without special permission but it's worth asking about as it's much better value than the two main options.

The **Guge Restaurant** (mains Y25, veg Y15) is probably the best in town, plus there's the usual **Muslim restaurant** and odd supermarket. Look for cheaper dishes at places such as the **Bei Bei Quick Meal Shop** and **Happy Restaurant for Travellers**.

Thöling Monastery མཐོ་གླིང་

Founded by Rinchen Zangpo, **Thöling Monastery** (admission Y80) was once Ngari's most important monastic complex. It was still functioning in 1966 when the Red Guards shut down operations. Three main buildings survive within the monastery walls.

MAIN ASSEMBLY HALL (DUKHANG)

The *dukhang* has especially fine wall murals, showing strong Kashmiri and Nepali influences; bring a powerful torch (flashlight) to enjoy the rich detail. Scholarly opinion varies on whether the murals date from the 13th and 14th, or 15th and 16th centuries. The Kashmiri influences are noticeable in the shading on the hands and feet, the detail of the jewellery and dress, the tight stomach lines and non-Tibetan images of palm trees and *dhotis* (Indian-style loin cloths).

The main statues here are of the past, present and future buddhas, and there's also a footprint of Rinchen Zangpo. The lower walls of the inner area have murals depicting the life of the Buddha. Murals of the protectors Dorje Jigje (Yamantaka) and Namse (Vairocana) decorate the main entry.

LHAKHANG KARPO

The entry to this side chapel is marked by interesting *deodar* (cedar) columns originating in India. Inside are fine 15th- and 16th-century murals. The left wall in particular has been hit by water damage and a Swiss team is currently working on a restoration plan. Male deities line the left

KEREN SU

Thöling Monastery (p216), Guge Kingdom

KEREN SU

Khampa (p45), Nyingtri

Mt Kailash (p210)

GARRY WEARE

BILL WASSMAN

Lake Manasarovar (p212)

Ganden Kora (p128)

Tingri (p192) with Cho Oyu in the background

Trekkers enjoying the view of Mt Everest (p189)

wall; female bodhisattvas on the right. The far-right-corner murals depict sky burial.

YESHE Ö'S MANDALA CHAPEL (NAMNANG LHAKHANG)

Once the main building in the Thöling complex, Yeshe Ö's Mandala Chapel was also known as the Golden Chapel. Before its destruction in the Cultural Revolution, the square main hall had four secondary chapels at the centre of each wall. Figures of the deities were arrayed around the wall facing towards a central image atop a lotus pedestal, in the form of a huge three-dimensional Tibetan *mandala* (a circular representation of the three-dimensional world of a meditational deity). All the images have been destroyed but the four chörtens remain.

You'll enter the mandala chapel through the Gyatsa Lhakhang, now a minimuseum, and finish off a visit by walking around an interior kora of empty chapels.

OUTSIDE THE MONASTERY WALLS

A few steps east of the monastery compound, across a horrible Chinese-style square, is the recently restored **Serkhang chörten**. A similar **chörten** stands in total isolation just to the west of the town. To the north, between the monastic compound and the cliff face, that falls away to the Sutlej River below, are two long lines of miniature **chörtens**. The area is superbly photogenic at dusk.

The entrances to the valleys behind Zanda are pockmarked with ruins and **meditation caves** and offer an excellent day of exploration. The three valleys each offer ruins to explore; the more interesting collection is at the mouth of the middle valley. If you poke around, you'll discover cave trails leading up to cliff-top fortifications and more retreat caves.

Tsaparang ༪ཕྲང

The citadel of **Tsaparang** (admission Y110; ☾ dusk-dawn) has been gracefully falling into ruin ever since its slide from prominence in the 17th century. The spectacular ruins, which seem to grow organically out of the hills, make for a photogenically surreal landscape and it's great fun exploring the winding trails, walls and tunnels of this ancient anthill. The site's early Tantric-inspired murals are of particular interest to experts on early Buddhist art. See p214 for a history of the site.

The ruins climb up the ridge through three distinct areas. At the bottom of the hill is the monastic area with the four best-preserved buildings and their murals. From there the trail to the top climbs through former residential quarters, where monks' cells were tunnelled into the clay hillside. Finally, the route burrows straight into the hillside and through a tunnel before emerging in the ruins of the palace citadel at the very top of the hill. The views from the top are fantastic.

Because Tsaparang was already partially abandoned at the time of the Cultural Revolution, the Chinese did not attack it with quite the same level of vandalistic fury that they vented upon other religious complexes

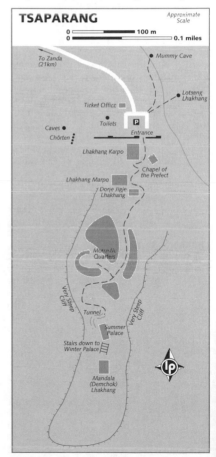

TSAPARANG

Approximate Scale

0 ————— 100 m
0 ————————— 0.1 miles

To Zanda (21km)

Mummy Cave

Lotsang Lhakhang

Ticket Office

Toilets

P

Caves
Chörten

Entrance

Lhakhang Karpo

Chapel of the Prefect

Lhakhang Marpo

Dorje Jigje Lhakhang

Monastic Quarters

Very Steep Cliff

Tunnel

Very Steep Cliff

Summer Palace

Stairs down to Winter Palace

Mandala (Demchok) Lhakhang

in Tibet. However, when a little more survives it only makes it even more sadly evident how much was destroyed.

Tsaparang is 21km west of Zanda but unless you're lucky hitching a ride, the only way to get there is with a rented vehicle or by walking. The road follows the south side of the fantastically eroded Sutlej Valley from Zanda and takes the right branch after 12km. Many maps incorrectly show both centres on the north side of the river.

Early evening (particularly around 8pm) offers the best light; during the middle of the day photos of the site will look bleached out. No photography is allowed inside the chapels. Bring a strong torch, lunch and water and expect to spend at least half a day exploring the ruins; longer if possible.

SIGHTS

Chapel of the Prefect

Just inside the entrance to the complex is a small building that was a private **shrine** for Tsaparang's prefect or regent. The caretaker has named it the 'Drölma Lhakhang' after his own sculpture of Drölma (Tara) displayed here. The wall murals date from the 16th century, by which time the style evinced in other Tsaparang murals was in decline. The exuberant murals include fantastic multicoloured images of elephants, garuda-like bird people, hermits and snow lions, among others. The main mural on the back wall shows Sakyamuni flanked by Tsongkhapa and Atisha. Small figures of the Buddha's disciples stand beside his throne.

Lhakhang Karpo

Slightly above the entrance, the large **Lhakhang Karpo**, or White Chapel, holds the oldest paintings at Tsaparang and is probably the most important chapel in Ngari. The murals of the chapel date back to the 15th or 16th century but their influences extend back to 10th-century Kashmiri Buddhist art, and for this reason are of particular interest to scholars of Buddhist art. Apart from Tsaparang, very little material evidence of early Kashmiri art remains (noticeably at Alchi Monastery in Ladakh). Lay people can spot the Kashmiri influence in the Hindu-inspired deities, with their slender torsos and thin waists, the detailed brocade of the figures' robes and the general richness of the colours.

The ceiling is beautifully painted, as are the many thin columns that support it. The carvings and paintings of Sakyamuni that top each column are particularly noteworthy and the paintings around the skylight are especially vivid. At one time, 22 life-size statues lined the walls; today only 10 remain and these are severely damaged. Even so, this chapel has fared better than most temples attacked during the Cultural Revolution. Each statue would originally have been framed by a *torana* (halo-like garland). Only partial sections of these remain (look in the far left corner and back recess) but you can still see the holes where these structures were once anchored to the walls.

The doors are flanked by two 5m-high guardian figures, red Tamdrin (Hayagriva) and blue Chana Dorje (Vajrapani). Again, both are damaged but even armless they hint at the lost marvels of the chapel.

The huge figure of Sakyamuni that once stood in the recess, the Jowo Khang, at the back of the hall has been replaced by one of the caretaker's statues. On the side walls at the back were once row after row of smaller deities, each perched on its own small shelf. A few of these figures on the higher levels have survived intact.

Lhakhang Marpo

Above the Lhakhang Karpo is the equally large **Lhakhang Marpo**, or Red Chapel, which was built around 1470, perhaps 30 years earlier than the Lhakhang Karpo. The murals in this chapel were repainted around 1630, shortly before the fall of the Guge kingdom, so they are actually younger than those in the Lhakhang Karpo.

The original chapel door, with its concentric frames and carvings of bodhisattvas, mantras and elephants, has survived and is worth close inspection. Inside, many thin columns support the chapel roof, similar to those of the neighbouring Lhakhang Karpo. By the main door are images of Chenresig (Avalokiteshvara), Green Tara and an eight-armed white Tara, with Drölma and Jampelyang (Manjushri) to the right.

The statues that once stood in the chapel were placed towards the centre of the hall, not around the edges, and although only the bases and damaged fragments remain, the crowded feel to the space, the intense colours and the eerie silence combine to create a powerful atmosphere. You almost expect Indiana Jones to come striding out from behind the wreckage.

Although the wall murals have been damaged by vandalism and water leakage they remain so remarkably brilliant it's easy to forget that they are actually over 350 years old. On the left wall are the famous murals chronicling the construction of the temple: animals haul the building's huge timber beams into place as musicians celebrate the completion of the temple. Officials stand in attendance (a Kashmir delegation wears turbans), followed by members of the royal family, the king and queen (under a parasol), Amithaba Buddha (Öpagme) and, finally, a line of chanting monks. The royal gifts frame the bottom of the scene.

Murals on the far right (northern) wall depict the life of the Buddha, showing him tempted by demons and protected by a naga serpent, among others. On the eastern wall are eight stylised chörtens, representing the eight events in Buddha's life.

The main deities in the chapel have very ornate *toranas*, decorated with birds and crocodiles and topped with flying *apsaras* (angels). At the back of the hall, statues of the 35 confessional buddhas once sat on individual shelves; a handful of them still have bodies but all the heads have gone.

Dorje Jigje Lhakhang

The murals in the smaller **chapel** a few steps above the Lhakhang Marpo are also painted red and gold, and are almost solely devoted to wrathful deities such as Demchok (Chakrasamvara), Hevajra and the buffalo-headed Dorje Jigje (Yamantaka), to whom the chapel is dedicated. On the left as you look back at the door is Namtöse, the God of Wealth, riding a snow lion and surrounded by square bands of Tibetan warriors.

Like the Chapel of the Prefect, the paintings here are of later origin, central Tibetan in style (rather than Kashmiri-influenced) and of lower quality; the golden years had passed by this point. All the statues that once stood here were destroyed.

Summer Palace

From the four chapels at the base of the hill, the path to the top climbs up through the monastic quarters and then ascends to the palace complex atop the hill via a tunnel.

The **Summer Palace**, at the northern end of the hill top, is empty, with a balcony offering wonderful views across the marvellously eroded valleys around the site. The Sutlej Valley is just to the north, while across the smaller valley to the northeast is the ruined Lotsang Lhakhang.

The most interesting of the palace buildings is the small but well-preserved Mandala (Demchok) Lhakhang, the red-painted building in the centre of the hill-top ridge. The centrepiece of this small chapel was a wonderful three-dimensional *mandala* with Tantric murals, only the base of which survived the desecrations of the Cultural Revolution. It is currently being restored and so is closed to visitors.

Winter Palace

Accessed by a steep and treacherous eroded staircase, the **Winter Palace** is an amazing ants nest of rooms tunnelled into the clay below the Summer Palace. The rooms were built 12m underground in order to conserve the warmth, and the eastern rooms have windows that open out onto the cliff-face. There are seven dusty chambers, all empty, linked by a cramped corridor. Branching off from the stairs is a dim passage that provided vital access to water during sieges and served as an emergency escape route for the royal family.

The easily missed stairs to the Winter Palace lead down from between the Summer Palace and the Mandala (Demchok) Lhakhang. Don't go down if you're prone to vertigo or claustrophobia.

Other Sights

North of the main entrance to Tsaparang a trail follows a green river valley down about 700m to a cave on the left that holds the mummified remains of several bodies.

On the way back, visit the chörten and ruined chapel of the **Lotsang Lhakhang**. Only the feet of the main statue remain. Also worth a quick visit are the **caves** and **chörtens** to the west of the main site, near the public toilet behind the caretaker's compound.

DUNGKAR & PIYANG དུང་དཀར

Caves with extensive wall paintings were discovered at remote **Dungkar** (admission Y80, plus Y10 to the caretaker), approximately 40km north of Zanda, during the early 1990s. At

WESTERN TIBET (NGARI)

around 1100 years old, the cave paintings are possibly the oldest in Ngari and have much in common stylistically with the Silk Road cave murals of Dunhuang in China (particularly in their almost cartoon style, and the flying *apsara*s, painted on a blue background). There are three main caves, of which the best preserved is the mandala cave. Photography is normally allowed (without flash) for Y10 per shot.

Getting permission to visit the caves can be tricky. The PSB in Lhasa and Ali often refuse permission. Fortunately, the Cultural Relics Bureau in Ali currently issues tickets in the form of a letter of introduction to the caretaker, Ngawang Shugyi, who you will have to find in Dungkar village, 1.5km from the caves. If he's not at home, you won't get in as no-one else has the key. You need to have an interest in early Tibetan and Silk Road art for the trip to be worthwhile. Lovely Dungkar village also has a ruined **monastery** above the town.

A couple of kilometres north, further up the side valley, the village of **Piyang** is worth the small detour. It lies at the foot of large ridge honeycombed with thousands of caves and topped with ruined monastery buildings and walls.

The two sights are best visited en route between Darchen and Zanda. From Zanda, take the road to Darchen and take a left side valley, turning left at a post, and then again at another post 17km further, before the final 8km to the village. Piyang is 2.5km further. Perhaps the best way to visit is a longer loop from Zanda, starting up the road to Ali and then turning right after 42km to climb a ridge that offers breathtaking views of the eroded Sutlej Valley and the Himalaya behind, before dropping down to Piyang and then Dungkar, 57km from Zanda.

RUTOK XIAN ར་ཐོག

The new Chinese town of Rutok Xian, which is 132km from Ali, is a modern army post but there are a couple of great sights nearby that warrant the trip.

About 8km north of Rutok Xian, the road hits the east end of lovely turquoise **Pangong-tso** (4241m), offering great views. The long lake extends 110km into Ladakh in India. Continue 5km to a deserted checkpoint, which has several fish restaurants and boats

that offer short, polluting spurts around the bay (Y40).

The old Tibetan village of Rutok lies about 10km off the main road from a turn-off about 5km south of Rutok Xian. The drive passes the pretty **chörtens** of Bankor village en route. Lovely white-painted traditional Rutok huddles at the base of a splinter of rock, atop which is **Rutok Monastery**, flanked at both ends of the hill by the crumbling, but still impressive, ruins of **Rutok Dzong**. From here, you can see the reservoir below and Pangong-tso in the distance. The surrounding villages are largely deserted in summer, as herders have moved to higher pastures.

The intensely atmospheric main chapel of the monastery has a large statue of Jampa and a bronze Garuda to the left. Clearly, at one time the whole eastern face of the hill was covered in monastic buildings. The monastery was destroyed during the Cultural Revolution and rebuilt in 1983–84; it now has just six monks.

Ancient Petroglyphs

In 1985 prehistoric rock carvings, or petroglyphs, were found at several sites in Rutok county. This was the first time such finds had been made in Tibet, although similar finds have since been made at numerous other sites.

The extensive collection of rock carvings at **Rumudong** is right beside the road, about 36km south of the old Rutok turn-off, or about 96km north of Ali. There are kilometre markers every 5km along this road. Travelling north from Ali, start looking on the east side of the road at kilometre marker 970; the petroglyphs would be at around 967. There are two distinct groups on the rock face right beside the road, just before it crosses a bridge to travel along a causeway over the marshy valley floor of the Maga Zangbu-chu.

The first, and more extensive, group also features a number of more recent Buddhist carvings, some of them carved right over their ancient predecessors. The most impressive of the rock carvings features four extravagantly antlered deer racing across the rock and looking back at three leopards in hot pursuit. Also depicted are eagles, yaks, camels, goats, tigers, wild boars and human figures.

Less often visited are the **Lurulangkar** paintings, about 12km southwest of Rutok. The relatively primitive carvings are right beside the road, up to a height of 4m above the ground, and show a variety of pre-Buddhist symbols and animals, including dogs, yaks, eagles, deer and goats. Human figures are shown standing in isolation or riding on horses. There are a number of hunting scenes showing dogs chasing deer and hunters shooting at them with bows and arrows.

Sleeping

Hebei Binguan (Rutok Xian; dm old block Y15, d/tr per bed Y30/20, new block tr without bathroom per bed Y50, d with bathroom Y120) Rooms in the new block are bright and tiled, with a bathroom but no running water. The old block is more basic but still acceptable. The **restaurant** (dishes Y30) is good and you can get a hot shower here for Y10. The hotel is in the centre of town, by the junction.

Shunfa Lüshe (Rutok Xian; tr per bed Y30) This privately run place on the southern side of the street offers foam beds and squat toilets out back. Some rooms are darker than others.

There are lots of restaurants in Rutok Xian, including several good Uyghur restaurants.

There's no accommodation or any other facilities at old Rutok, only some pleasant grassy camp sites, which can get very windy in the afternoon.

Getting There & Away

Ali bus station has minibuses (Y50) every morning to Rutok Xian but there's no public transport to old Rutok and very little traffic on the road. Hitching is the best option.

WESTERN NEPAL TO MT KAILASH

See Lonely Planet's *Trekking in the Nepal Himalaya* for details of the trek from Humla, a restricted region in the far west of Nepal, to Mt Kailash. This route is open only to tour groups that trek in from Humla and you will need a specially endorsed Chinese visa.

From the Nepali border at Sher, the road makes a long descent to a stream and then follows the Humla Karnali to the village of Khojarnath, 10km north.

Khojarnath ᠎ᢅᢇᢁᢄᢀᢅ

elev 3790m

For those travelling up from Nepal, Khojarnath, 21km south of Purang, is the first large village over the border in Tibet. It boasts the **Korjak Monastery** (admission Y30), an important monastery of the Sakya order. This monastery escaped the worst excesses of the Cultural Revolution, and the damage it sustained has been repaired with financial assistance from German and Italian sponsors. *Cham* (a ritual dance carried out by monks and lamas) dances are held here during a festival on the 15th to 20th of the first Tibetan lunar month

The atmospheric main hall is presided over by a figure of Jampa (Maitreya). Hanging from the ceiling are the stuffed carcasses of a yak, an Indian tiger, a snow leopard and a wolf. The entrance door carvings are particularly fine.

The eight-pillared Rinchen Zangpo Lhakhang adjoining the main hall is dominated by the trinity of Chenresig (Avalokiteshvara), Jampelyang (Manjushri) and Chana Dorje (Vajrapani). Look for the large mantra painted on the outside of the monastery walls as you do a final kora.

Purang ᢌᢀᢂᢆ

☎ 08060 / elev 3800m

Purang (Taklakot to the Nepalis) is a large trading centre composed of a number of distinct settlements separated by the Humla Karnali River, known in Tibetan as Mabja Tsangpo (Peacock River). Nepali traders come up from the Humla district and also the Darchula region in the extreme west of Nepal to trade a variety of goods, including rice, carried up from Nepal in huge trains of goods-carrying goats. Indian consumer goods and Nepali rice are traded for Tibetan salt and wool in the Darchula bazaar, a 15-minute walk south of Purang.

Purang is also the arrival point for the annual influx of Hindu pilgrims from India, intent on making a *parikrama* (the Hindu equivalent of a kora) of Mt Kailash, which devout Hindus consider the abode of Shiva. For tourists, the town is worth a detour from Lake Manasarovar even if you aren't headed to Nepal.

The hill northwest of town is the site of a huge army base said to extend far into the mountain in a series of caves. It's even rumoured there are missiles here, aimed at New Delhi. There are hundreds of People's Liberation Army (PLA) soldiers in baggy green uniforms in the town.

Slogans in Chinese characters on the hills above town read '10,000 years long life to

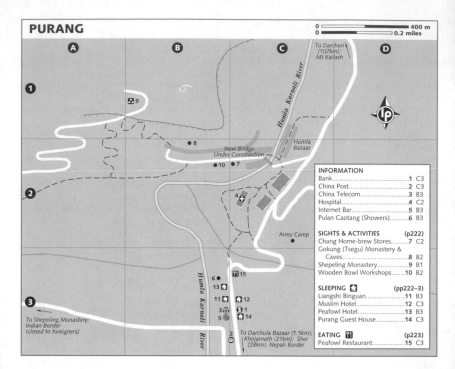

PURANG

0 ————— 400 m
0 ————— 0.2 miles

To Darchen
('107km);
Mt Kailash

Humla Bazaar

New Bridge
Under Construction

Army Camp

To Shepeling Monastery;
Indian Border
(closed to foreigners)

To Darchula Bazaar (1.5km);
Khojarnath (21km); Sher
(28km); Nepali Border

INFORMATION	
Bank.............................1	C3
China Post.....................2	C3
China Telecom................3	B3
Hospital........................4	C2
Internet Bar...................5	B3
Pulan Caotang (Showers)........6	B3

SIGHTS & ACTIVITIES	(p222)
Chang Home-brew Stores........7	C2
Gokung (Tsegu) Monastery &	
Caves........................8	B2
Shepeling Monastery.............9	B1
Wooden Bowl Workshops.......10	B2

SLEEPING	(pp222–3)
Liangshi Binguan.................11	B3
Muslim Hotel...................12	C3
Peafowl Hotel..................13	B3
Purang Guest House...............14	C3

EATING	(p223)
Peafowl Restaurant...............15	C3

Chairman Mao' and 'Twice 10,000 years long life to the Communist Party of China'.

INFORMATION

The **bank** (☼ Mon-Fri) will change cash US dollars but not Nepali rupees or traveller's cheques. Out of hours you may be able to change cash US dollars in the Peafowl Hotel, though the rate will be low. Nepali rupees are accepted in Tibetan and Nepali shops in town. Nepali traders refer to yuan as 'suka'.

Internet bar (per hr Y8) Offers pretty fast connections, by China Telecom.

Pulan Caotang (hot showers Y15; ☼ 10.30am-midnight) Behind the Peafowl Hotel.

SIGHTS

In the hills above the lacklustre Humla Bazaar are many retreat **caves** formed around the cliff-side **Gokung (Tsegu) Monastery**. Here, a ladder leads up to a couple of upper-floor cave chapels decorated with prayer flags. The dirt road from Humla Bazaar passes several **chang homebrew stores** and **bowl workshops**.

The ruined **Shepeling Monastery** towers over the town from its dramatic hill-top position.

In 1949 the Swami Pranavananda described this Kagyud monastery, which housed 170 monks, as the biggest in the region. The Chinese shelled it during the Cultural Revolution and today only the Assembly Hall is being restored. The monastery is administered by Chuku Monastery, on the Kailash kora.

There are fine views of the roads to India and Nepal but be careful not to photograph the Chinese military base to the east. Look over the back of the hill to spot the cave complex in the valley behind. Steep paths wind up from Gokung Monastery or take the longer winding road (it's possible to drive to the top).

SLEEPING & EATING

Purang Guest House (☎ 2140; q per bed Y80) This guesthouse compound on the east side of the main road is scruffy and shamelessly tries to overcharge Western visitors (you can often haggle down to Y50 per bed). There is no running water (but there are drums of water outside the rooms) and the row of pit toilets at the rear of the compound are nasty.

WESTERN TIBET (NGARI)

Peafowl Hotel (☎ 2362; beds Y100) Offering decent Western-style rooms, this place in the government compound is not bad if it's not full.

Muslim Hotel (per bed Y30) If you don't mind risking a possible brush with the PSB you could try this decent place, as it's the only good-value hotel in town. It's above a good Muslim restaurant. The rooms are clean but there are only four of them.

Liangshi Binguan (☎ 2215; d per bed Y40-50) This comfortable place is good value but would not take foreigners at the time of research.

Despite the proximity to Nepal, there's little flavour of the subcontinent in Purang's restaurants. There are the usual large number of Chinese restaurants around the guesthouses, including a good Muslim restaurant. The Peafowl Restaurant has a decent range of Chinese dishes.

GETTING THERE & AWAY

Western trekkers arriving from Nepal usually arrange to be met at the border town of Sher for the 28km drive via Khojarnath to Purang.

Buses run every four or five days to Ali (Y200) via Darchen (Y150) from the Peafowl Hotel. You should be able to find some kind of transport on other days if you wait long enough.

From Purang it's 74km north to the Chiu Monastery on the shores of Lake Manasarovar and another 33km from there to Darchen, starting point for the Mt Kailash kora. The road from Purang passes Toyo, where the Sikh invader Zorawar Singh was killed in 1841, before passing a number of small Tibetan settlements and fording several rivers en route to the Gurla-la (4590m). Coming from Tibet you'll notice the lush terraced fields and the different design of the houses and chörtens.

Just beyond the pass, Rakshas Tal and (on a clear day) Mt Kailash come into view. A few kilometres before reaching the village at Chiu Monastery you will pass by a gold mine.

Eastern Tibet (Kham) ཁམས་

CONTENTS

Kham, also called Eastern Tibet, is a land apart from the rest of Tibet. Its climate, geography, flora and fauna all lend it a unique, almost magical atmosphere. The stone villages resemble those in Bhutan and the unusually shaped chörtens (stupas) would seem at home in Mustang. The scenery often resembles more the Swiss Alps than the high Tibetan plateau. The Chinese presence remains pronounced along the strategic Sichuan–Tibet Hwy, but the countryside still belongs to windswept Khampa nomads and bands of Bönpo pilgrims.

Kham gains much of its charm from its people. Khampa men, long regarded as both the most religious and most warlike of all Tibetans, can be seen swaggering along the streets of many settlements wearing red (from Chamdo) or black (from Derge) braids in their long hair and a *chuba* (long-sleeved sheepskin cloak) hanging off the right shoulder. Many wear broad-brimmed cowboy hats, big boots and a knife by their side. The women traditionally wear elaborate coral and amber jewellery and arrange their hair into 108 braids.

Geographically the region varies from subtropical low-lying jungle, to the glaciated peaks of Namche Barwa (7756m) and the high grasslands of northeastern Tibet. At its eastern end, the headwaters of some of Asia's greatest rivers – the Mekong (Dza-chu), Salween (Nu Jiang) and Yangzi (Dri-chu) – tumble off the Tibetan plateau, carving a dramatic concertina landscape of deep gorges and remote valleys.

There are two main routes through the region. The southern road, a strategic military road paved for most of its length, ranges from snowbound passes to subtropical gorges. The largely unpaved northern road is a higher roller-coaster ride with remote villages and ramshackle towns. Travel in the region is restricted to Land Cruiser tours or illegal hitching.

The traditional Tibetan province of Kham incorporates modern-day eastern Tibet (the eastern part of the Tibetan Autonomous Region, or TAR), western Sichuan and northwest Yunnan. For information on travel in western Sichuan and Yunnan, see p249.

HIGHLIGHTS

- Hike around the gorgeous alpine lake of **Draksum-tso** (p230), with its fairy-tale island monastery

- Gaze open-mouthed at the magnificent scenery from **Nyingtri to Pomi** (p235), passing from lush subtropical forest to alpine valleys over snowy passes

- Relax by the stunning turquoise lakes of **Rawok-tso** (p237), fringed with alpine peaks

- Explore the dramatic, towering and remote **Riwoche Tsuglhakhang** (p244)

- Visit the 'mini-Potala' of **Sok Tsanden Monastery** (p246)

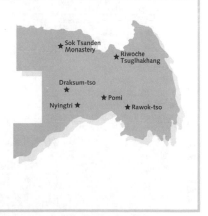

EASTERN TIBET (KHAM)

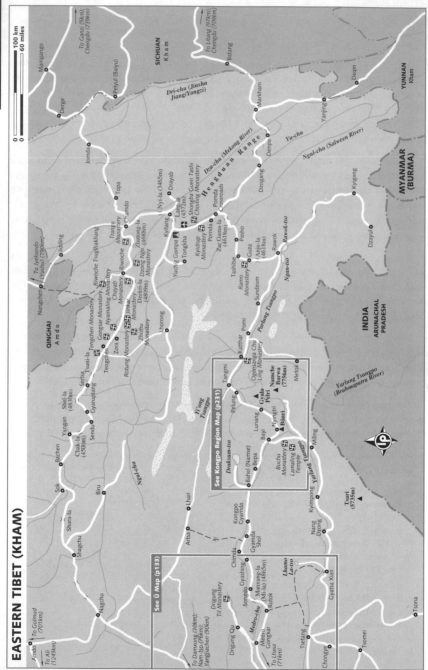

History

The area around Chamdo was one of the first settled in Tibet, as attested to by the 5000-year-old Neolithic remains at nearby Karo. Fossilised millet hints at a 5000-year tradition of agriculture in the region.

Kham was the home of many holy men including the founders of the Drigungpa and Karmapa schools. In 1070, many Buddhists fled persecution in central Tibet to Kham, where they set up influential monasteries, later returning to central Tibet to spearhead the so-called second diffusion of Buddhism in Tibet.

Lhasa's control over the region has waxed and waned over the centuries. Lhasa first gained control of Kham thanks to Mongol assistance, but the majority of the region has enjoyed political independence. Until recently, much of Kham comprised many small fiefdoms ruled by kings (Derge), lamas (Litang) or hereditary chieftains (Batang). Relations with China were mostly restricted to those involving trade caravans, which carried bricks of Chinese tea in, and pastoral products out.

Chinese warlords such as Zhao Erfeng and Liu Wenhui swept through the eastern part

FOUR RIVERS, SIX RANGES: THE KHAMPA RESISTANCE

By the late 1950s thousands of Khampa warriors had begun to rebel against Chinese rule and reforms. News of the armed rebellion filtered through to central Tibet but the Khampas' pleas for help fell on deaf ears. The Dalai Lama, keen to avoid conflict with the Chinese, asked the Khampas to disarm. Without organisation or cohesive leadership the rebellion was routed.

Yet a core of Khampa fighters managed to regroup in Lhoka, in southern Tibet, and in a rare moment of Khampa unity formed an organisation called Chizhi Gangdrung (Four Rivers, Six Ranges), the traditional local name for the Kham region. Soon 15,000 men were assembled, led by Gonbo Tashi, and a new flag was created.

The Khampas eventually attracted the attention of exiled Tibetan leaders in Kalimpong (India), as well as the Chinese Kuomintang (KMT or Nationalist Party; some Khampas were trained in Taiwan) and even the CIA, who liaised with the Tibetans through Thubten Norbu and later Gyalo Dhundup, both brothers of the Dalai Lama.

Before long, Tibetan leaders were liaising with CIA agents in Kolkata (Calcutta), arranging meetings through dead letter drops and secret messages. The first batch of six Khampa agents trekked over the border to Kalimpong, were driven to Bangladesh and then were flown to the Pacific island of Saipan, where they were trained to organise guerrilla groups. Agents were later parachuted behind enemy lines into Samye and Litang.

In 1957, guerrilla attacks were made on Chinese garrisons and road camps, and in 1958, 700 Chinese soldiers were killed by guerrillas near Nyemo. The movement met with the Dalai Lama in southern Tibet when he fled Lhasa in 1959 as the CIA readied three plane loads of arms – enough for 2000 people.

The flight of the Dalai Lama to India marked a setback for the resistance and the focus switched to a base in Mustang, an ethnically Tibetan area in Nepal, where between 1960 and 1972 the Nepalis turned a blind eye to the movement. Between 1960 and 1962 over 150 Tibetans were sent to Colorado for training.

Yet the resistance was living on borrowed time. The Americans never had much confidence in the Tibetans and by the mid-1960s CIA funding had dried up. By 1972 the international political climate had changed; US president Richard Nixon's visit to China and the coronation of Nepal's pro-Chinese king had left the Khampas out on a limb. Moreover, the resistance was riddled with feuds – most of the Khampa rebels had always been fighting more for their local valley and monastery than for any national ideal. In 1973 the Nepalis demanded the closure of the Mustang base and the Dalai Lama asked the rebels to surrender. It was the end of the Khampa rebellion and the end of Tibetan armed resistance to the Chinese.

For more on the CIA's funding of Tibetan resistance guerrillas and the diplomatic wrangling behind the scenes, read *Orphans of the Cold War: America and the Tibetan Struggle for Freedom* by John Kenneth Knaus. Knaus, a 44-year veteran of the CIA, was personally involved in training Tibetan agents in Colorado. For a Tibetan perspective, try *Warriors of Tibet* by Jamyang Norbu.

of Kham (modern-day western Sichuan) in the late 19th and early 20th centuries to set up the Chinese province of Xikang (western Kham). Khampa rebellions occurred frequently, notably in 1918, 1928 and 1932, though not all were against the Chinese; in 1933 the Khampas tried to shake off Lhasa's nominal rule.

In 1950 Chamdo fell to the People's Liberation Army (PLA; p242) and much of eastern Tibet was subsumed into China. In 1954 the eastern part of Kham was merged into Sichuan province and a program of land reforms was introduced, including the collectivisation of monasteries. Then in 1955 the Chinese tried to disarm the Khampas and settle nomads. The Kangding Rebellion erupted in the winter of 1955-6 and fighting spread to Litang, Zhongdian and Daocheng. As the PLA arrived, monasteries were bombed in Daocheng and Litang and the rebels fled into Chamdo and later to India and Nepal, to organise armed resistance from Mustang (Nepal) with CIA assistance.

Today eastern Tibet remains quite Sinicised in western Sichuan and along the Sichuan–Tibet Hwy, where there is a string of army bases, logging camps and even prisons, but off the highways Khampa life remains culturally strong.

Climate

Kham has a dramatically different climate from the rest of Tibet. The summer monsoon from Assam brings a lot of rain from early June to September. Snowfall generally starts in October. Northern areas between Sok and Nagchu receive strong winds year round and sudden blizzards even in summer. Nagchu is Tibet's coldest city, in July temperatures range between 3°C and 15°C, with January temperatures bottoming out at minus 25°C. In March, while the northern road remains dry and bleak, southern farms around Pomi are already filled with verdant crops surrounded by lush forest.

The best times to travel are from late March to early May, and from September to early November. During other times the southern route is usually out of use for weeks at a time.

Permits

Kham is officially forbidden to foreigners without a guide, private transport (normally a Land Cruiser) and a fistful of permits, including a military permit. These can only be obtained by the travel agency arranging your trip. The situation becomes more complex without permits. If you're caught you'll probably be fined and sent back. Pilgrim trucks are usually scanned at checkpoints – you'll need to disguise your backpack inside a sack and cover your face with a scarf. Heading out of the region is always easier and you are less likely to be hassled.

Even with all the requisite permits you may still encounter problems visiting Sok Tsanden Monastery. Try to get this monastery (not just the town of Sok) actually specified by name on your permits. If a particular destination is listed on your permit but local Public Security Bureau (PSB) still deny access, contact your travel agency in Lhasa which can lodge complaints with the PSB in Lhasa and Chamdo. (In some instances, such as Sok Tsanden, Chamdo may have more influence). Be persistent, it may take a few calls to get your point across. Places close to the disputed Indian border such as Namche Barwa and the Tsangpo gorges are almost impossible to get permits for; your agency will need military connections for these. Nervous guides will often want to register your group with every county-level PSB office along your route, which can be a real pain.

If you decide to hitch through eastern Tibet you will have to be extremely cautious, especially in larger towns and county capitals. The biggest problem with hitching is that you'll probably need to remain out of sight for large sections of the trip, so you may miss much of the scenery. Permits are most often checked in hotels so you'll dramatically increase your chances of not getting caught if you have a tent and are self-sufficient in food.

Getting There & Away

Lhasa is the logical place from which to launch an expedition to Kham. It's the closest gateway city and the permits are relatively hassle-free to acquire with agency support. There are daily bus connections to Bayi (Y80; seven hours) and beyond, but unless the permit situation changes you won't be allowed to buy a ticket. The most reasonable way into Kham from Lhasa is by hired Land Cruiser, arranged by the

FIT office in Lhasa (see p91). Expect to pay around Y15,000 for a two week trip, including permits, guide and driver.

The longer routes into the region set out from Chengdu (Sichuan), Litang or Kunming (Yunnan). Tours from the east usually terminate in Lhasa, making for an interesting route into Tibet proper. The trip from Chengdu to Chamdo takes 60 hours and costs Y450 on the daily bus. From Kunming you could travel to Markam (70 hours; Y500) and then proceed to Lhasa via Pasho. Travel on local transport, however, is still illegal and there's a risk of being sent back. The least travelled route is through Qinghai via the town of Yushu (Jyekundo), a rough track from here (impassable in rain) eventually leads to the fabled monastery of Riwoche Tsuglhakhang. Buses are uncommon on this route – wait for a pilgrim truck, or hitch.

Getting Around

Travel by hired Land Cruiser is the most feasible way to get around Kham and see the sights on offer. Finding others to share the cost of the car might be the hardest part of organising your trip. A 14- to 17-day loop (taking in Draksum-tso, Bayi, Pasho, Chamdo and back to Lhasa via Riwoche and Sok) in a newish Land Cruiser (4500 series) will cost around Y16,000. FIT in Lhasa (with offices at Lhasa hotels Snowlands and Banak Shol) can launch your trip in a minimum of three days, the time needed to organise the permits. Most sights listed herein are close to the main road, requiring minimal backtracking.

Both pilgrim and passenger trucks ply the main highways and are the most likely vehicles to pick up a hitchhiker. Hitching a ride from Chengdu to Lhasa takes around 10 days. Watch out for PSB check points when trucks are inspected. Take particular care at bathroom and lunch stops.

Independent travellers without a permit may have trouble buying bus tickets within Kham, although we experienced no such hassles. Getting to Kongpo Gyamda isn't too tough, after which you'll have to tread lightly.

A surprising number of cyclists without permits, but self-sufficient with tent and food, make it through the region on push bikes.

KONGPO GYAMDA ཀོང་པོ་དགའ་ལྡན་

☎ 0894 / pop 4500 / elev 3400m

There's little reason to stop in this modern town, unless you get a late start from Lhasa and need to spend the night. The nearby village of Gyamda Shol, 13km to the west of Kongpo Gyamda, was once an important stop on the Lhasa–Chamdo caravan trail, which branches north from here over the mountains into the Yi'ong Tsangpo Valley.

The **Kathok Nunnery**, located in the hills to the north of town, is home to four nuns and a small chapel housing an image of Guru Rinpoche. A path (30 minute walk) leads up to the nunnery from the eastern outskirts, weaving through a picturesque old quarter. The nunnery is backed by the forested Baripo Mountain which has a small **hermitage** marked by fluttering prayer flags; it takes 45 minutes to walk there from the nunnery. To kill time you could also walk up the hills bedecked in prayer flags to the south of town.

The PSB office is at the eastern end of town.

Rutok Hot Springs Resort (☎ 0891-6132448), also at the eastern end of town, has private hot tubs (per hour Y60), along with a new hotel catering to Chinese soldiers on leave.

Sleeping & Eating

Kongpo Gyamda is a decent place to spend the night.

Baksun Tso Hotel (☎ 541 2186; Transan Lu; d/ste Y100/150) Rooms in this hotel are comfortable and come with a Western toilet, private bathroom and TV. Running water is most reliable on the 3rd floor; hot water comes in thermoses only. There is a small teashop next door.

Grain Department Guesthouse (Liangshiju Zhaodaisuo; ☎ 541 2604; Transan Lu; d Y50) The wall-to-wall red velvet and dim hallways are a bit frightening, but the rooms are of reasonable standard and come with TV and attached bathroom.

Bank Guesthouse (Yinhang Zhaodaisuo; ☎ 541 2541; s Y15, d Y20-30) Rooms are passable but there's no shower and the share toilet at the end of the hall is rightly vile.

The main street is lined with Sichuanese restaurants. Look out for **Taihulo** (☎ 541 3228) a good Sichuanese restaurant near the main intersection.

KONGPO REGION

The Kongpo region is culturally, ecologically and linguistically quite distinct from the rest of Tibet. A former kingdom of the early Yarlung kings and rival to Lhasa, Kongpo has for centuries been vilified by central Tibetan rulers as a land of incest and poison, where strangers are routinely drugged so that the locals can steal their souls. Along the road to Draksum-tso, look out for the tall 12-sided stone towers; these are referred to locally as *dudkhang* (demons' houses).

The traditional Kongpo costume features a round hat with an upturned rim of golden brocade for men (known as a *gyasha*) and a pretty pillbox hat with winged edges (known as a *dieu*) for women. Men wear brown woollen tunics, belted around the waist.

Kongpo is now the scene of a large-scale resettlement program. In 2003 ten new villages were built in the region to settle newcomers from the eastern borderlands, moved here by the Chinese to protect fragile ecosystems at the upper reaches of the Yangzi. The plan has some precedent. Forty years ago, during the Cultural Revolution, Kongpo was home to a vast network of prisons and work camps for political prisoners. Some of these are still in use.

Getting There & Away

Kongpo Gyamda is 284km from Lhasa, over the impressive 4865m Manxung-la (also known as the Mi-la). En route, in the upper Medro-chu Valley, the road passes Rutok, which has a monastery and several Tibetan teahouses and is the trailhead for the trek to Lhamo La-tso (p158).

A bus for Kongpo Gyamda (Y60, 8am, four hours) departs daily from Lhasa's Eastern Suburbs Bus Station. You could also try a Bayi-bound bus. Most transport will stop for a meal in Songdo, 96km west of Kongpo Gyamda, which has the basic **Snowland Friendship Hotel** (☎ 0894-5413225). Buses to Lhasa (Y50 to Y60) leave at about 8am from Kongpo Gyamda's main street.

DRAKSUM-TSO བྲག་གསུམ་མཚོ་

elev 3540m

This beautiful alpine lake, also known as Bagsum-tso and Basong-tso (depending on the dialect), is a long day's drive from Lhasa and a worthy 41km detour off the Sichuan–Tibet Hwy. Apart from the sheer beauty of the lake and its surrounding 6000m peaks, the site has strong connections to Gesar of Ling, the semimythical ruler of eastern Tibet, and Guru Rinpoche, the Indian sage, both of whom are said to have resided at the lake. Many pilgrimage sites are connected to the two.

A Y50 entrance fee into the area, which includes admission to the monastery, is payable at a toll gate 33km past Bahel, and four kilometres west of the lake.

The highlight of the lake is the charming **Tsodzong Monastery** (also spelled Tsomum Monastery), a small Nyingmapa chapel sited on a photogenic island just off the southern shore. The island is an organic fusion of dozens of types of flora and a sprinkle of holy sights. The 'ferry' across the narrow straight is a plank raft that you navigate by pulling on a cable; there is usually someone around to help you across.

The monastery was founded by Sangye Lingpa in the 14th century and is now home to three Nyingmapa nuns. The main monastery building has statues of a wrathful and peaceful Guru Rinpoche and smaller statues of Sakyamuni (Sakya Thukpa), Chenresig (Avalokiteshvara) and Kongtsun Demo, a local protector. The statues were actually shot and then burned by Red Guards during the Cultural Revolution, before being restored by the famous local lama Dudjom Rinpoche and his son Chuni Rinpoche (now resident at Lamaling Monastery near Bayi). In the corner of the monastery is what is said to be a stone hoofprint of Gesar's horse. The monastery entrance is flanked by ancient-looking male and female fertility symbols.

A small *kora* (ritual circumambulation circuit) around the monastery passes many hard-to-discern holy sites, including a tree said to resemble a conch horn, a sky-burial site, a 'body print' of Gesar, an underground treasury of the Karmapa, a tiger print and a tree whose leaves bear magical symbols.

For the best short walks around the island walk west back along the road to a small pass which is decorated with prayer flags and rock paintings and ascend the hill to the north side of the road. You could also walk a couple of hours east along the south shore

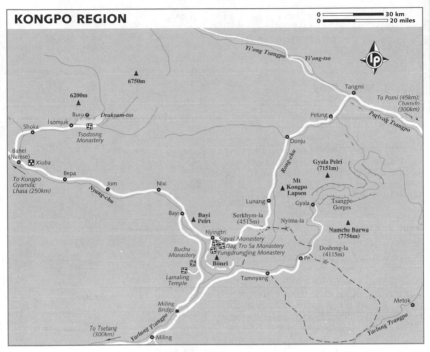

KONGPO REGION

or even further to Tsongo village for the best views of the mountains to the north.

A two-day **kora** rings the lake. The path includes the north-shore village of **Buru**, at the base of a mountain locals call the throne of Zambala (god of wealth). Buru is on the 'tea table in front of the throne.' East of the village is the 'pool of the Dakinis', a holy place that attracts barren women wanting a child.

Draksum-tso is slowly being developed for tourists and you're likely bump into a busload or two of visitors from the mainland. Blueprints have been drawn up for more hotels and tourist facilities, though for the moment all that's on offer are tours on tiny red motorboats, docked by the monastery. A turn around the island is Y10 per person or you can hire the boat for a one-hour lake tour (Y400).

PSB officers at the toll gate before the lake and any hotel at the lake will want to see your travel permits. It's hard to visit Draksum-tso if you don't have a permit.

Six kilometres east of Bahel is Xiuba, a fortress built by tribespeople in the reign of Songtsen Gampo. Five magnificent **towers** (admission Y10) and a pleasant village grace this small plateau near the highway. Look for the access road on the left.

Sleeping & Eating

Tourism officials haven't made it all that easy to visit the lake, and accommodation remains a problem.

Draksum Lake Tourism Holiday Village (Basong Hu Luyou Dujia Cun; ☎ 0894-541 3510; dm/s/d Y80/90/180) This basic resort offers beds in comfortable but overpriced rooms. Management also tries to force foreigners to pay a fee of Y100 for camping anywhere around the lake. If you are camping and without travel permits it's best to get off the beaten track as fast as possible.

There is a second government guesthouse, with similar prices, at Tsomjuk (Tsojom), at the mouth of the lake, but few people stay here. To get there take the turn off near the toll gate.

Food at both hotels is grossly overpriced, so bring your own. Foreigners are not permitted to stay overnight at the monastery.

It's possible to stay at Bahel village, on the Sichuan–Tibet Hwy near the turn-off to Draksum-tso; **Lhasa Gesar Drukhang** (☎ 0894-541 3039; dm Y10) has beds in cosy, if basic, wooden rooms above a restaurant.

Getting There & Away

The road to Draksum-tso branches off the main highway at Bahel Bridge (also known as Namse). On the right, high on the cliff, is the Pangri Jokpa hermitage. After 15km the road crosses a bridge and swings to the right, passing Shoka and Jara villages and an abandoned military radio station. The lake comes into view 35km from Bahel at Tsomjuk (Lake's Mouth). The road continues another 6km to Tsodzong island.

BAYI བྲག་ཡུལ་གཞིས་ཀ

☎ 0894 / pop 60,000 / elev 2990m

Bayi, 80km east of Bahel, is a large Han Chinese military town of minor interest, except perhaps as a base from which to visit the surrounding sights or to restock your supplies. 'Bayi' in Chinese means '1 August', the founding date of the PLA. Groups will probably need to register with the unfriendly local PSB; travellers without a permit should steer well clear of the town.

Information

Gracious Bathhouse (Ya Fung Lum Yu; ☎ 582 6121; Guangdong Lu; bath Y5; ☼ 10am-midnight) Located 200m north of the Post Hotel.

Eastern Express Internet Café (Dong Fong Fai Che; ☎ 582 3926; Macau Lu; per hr Y4) Clean and comfortable Internet café with a slow connection. It's located on the north side of the canal.

Mt Everest Internet Bar (Zhu Fong Wong Ba; ☎ 582 2621; Three Road intersection; per hr Y2) On the top floor of a blue glass building on the northwest side of the main roundabout.

Post office (Zhu Hai Lu; ☼ 9.30am-8pm)

Telecom Office (☎ 582 1048; Zhu Hai Lu; ☼ 9.30am-7.30pm) Calls to USA and Europe are Y2 per minute.

Pelri Kora

At the eastern edge of the town rises Bayi Pelri, a holy mountain that is associated with Guru Rinpoche, who fought demons on the hill and then he conjured up the surrounding farmland from a vast lake.

A delightful three-hour kora rings the peak but finding the correct path can be tricky business without the help of pilgrims.

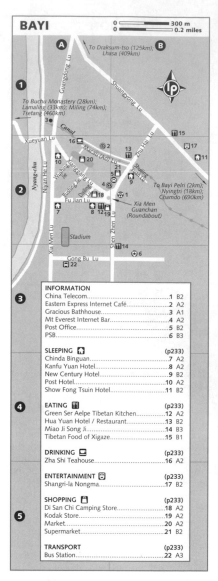

BAYI

0 ___ 300 m
0 ___ 0.2 miles

To Draksum-tso (125km);
Lhasa (409km)

To Buchu Monastery (28km);
Lamaling (33km); Miling (74km);
Tsetang (460km)

To Bayi Pelri (2km);
Nyingtri (18km);
Chamdo (690km)

Xia Men
Guanchan
(Roundabout)

Stadium

Gong Bu Lu

INFORMATION	
China Telecom	1 B2
Eastern Express Internet Café	2 A2
Gracious Bathhouse	3 A1
Mt Everest Internet Bar	4 A2
Post Office	5 B2
PSB	6 B3

SLEEPING 🏠	(p233)
Chinda Binguan	7 A2
Kanfu Yuan Hotel	8 A2
New Century Hotel	9 B2
Post Hotel	10 A2
Show Fong Tsuin Hotel	11 B2

EATING 🍴	(p233)
Green Ser Aelpe Tibetan Kitchen	12 A2
Hua Yuan Hotel / Restaurant	13 B2
Miao Ji Song Ji	14 B3
Tibetan Food of Xigaze	15 B1

DRINKING 🍸	(p233)
Zha Shi Teahouse	16 A2

ENTERTAINMENT 🎭	(p233)
Shangri-la Nongma	17 B2

SHOPPING 🛍	(p233)
Di San Chi Camping Store	18 A2
Kodak Store	19 A2
Market	20 A2
Supermarket	21 B2

TRANSPORT	(p233)
Bus Station	22 A3

If you are walking on your own, it's easiest to follow the logging road that switchbacks up the hill, keeping to the left of the peak. Hidden off the road about halfway up is the tiny Geshigong Monastery. Atop a saddle on the north side of the hill is a forest of prayer flags surrounding a white chörten. From here the kora leads clearly around the back of Pelri, past several sacred sites where pilgrims hang hats, bowls and even miniature ladders, to several rock prints associated with Guru Rinpoche. The path continues through forest and eventually descends back to the logging road.

Sleeping

Post Hotel (Youzheng Dajiudian; ☎ 588 9666; btwn Xianggang Lu & Xia Men Lu; d with/without bathroom Y388/98, ste Y598) The old block of rooms out back (ask in Chinese for the *putongjian*) might be your only budget option in town. The plush standard rooms come with hot showers and carpet and are worth a splurge, especially when discounted.

Kanfu Yuan Hotel (☎ 582 1800; 3 Fu Jian Lu; d/ste Y168/228) Rooms are large and include TV; the cheaper doubles come with Asian-style toilet. You can also inquire about the good-value doubles without toilet for Y80; these are routinely 'full', so ask your guide to scout them out before you enter the place.

Show Fong Tsuin Hotel (☎ 582 5606; 18 Shuangyong Lu; d/tr/ste Y280/300/580) Easily the classiest place in town, with a courteous staff and good value triples. Rooms are painted 'monastery crimson' and prettily decorated with photos of Tibetan scenery. There is an excellent buffet-style restaurant downstairs called Hugu Fandian.

The **Chinda Binguan** (☎ 582 6999; cnr Fu Jian Lu & Xia Men Lu; d Y368-388, ste Y688-888), along with the **New Century Hotel** (Xin Shiji Dajiudian; ☎ 588 5388; 13 Shuijingyuan Lu; d/ste Y388/618), offers modern rooms with air-con and heater.

Eating

Hua Yuan Hotel / Restaurant (☎ 582 5415; cnr Macau Lu & Zhu Hai Lu; dishes Y20-40) Somewhat pricey, but excellent Chinese cuisine. You can eat highbrow-Chinese style in a private room with TV or mix with the hoi polloi in the downstairs café.

Miao Ji Song Ji (☎ 582 5288; Shen Zhen Lu; hot pot Y58-118) A decent place for hot pot if you have a group.

Green Ser Aelpe Tibetan Kitchen (☎ 582 8618; Xia Men Guanchan; dishes Y8) Located on the southern side of the roundabout, this tarted-up Tibetan-style eatery with a nonsensical name has passable yak curries. It's best for a milk tea and a game of cards.

Tibetan Food of Xigaze (☎ 582 4786; Shuangyong Lu) is a less fashionable Tibetan place.

Drinking

Zha Shi Teahouse (☎ 588 4735; East Man Made Lake; beer Y12, tea Y6) This kitsch Chinese teahouse was built to resemble Lamaling Temple and is the most eye-catching building in town. You'll find lots of mah-jong-playing locals here in the afternoon.

Entertainment

Shangri-la Nongma (☎ 582 8878; Shuangyong Lu; 9pm-4am) Enjoy some innocent *nangma* (entertainment club) fun with comedy acts, song-and-dance routines, and stone-faced, waltzing locals.

Shopping

Xianggang Lu is the main shopping drag. There's a supermarket next to the post office and an outdoor market near the canal.

Di San Chi Camping Store (☎ 582 8835; Dailing Jie) Tents, sleeping bags, backpacks etc.

Kodak Store (☎ 582 3276; Xia Men Guanchan) For decent SLR cameras and film.

Getting There & Away

The bus to Bayi (Y80, 401km, seven hours, 8am) departs from Lhasa's East Bus Station. Other buses depart when full from here until 5pm. There is a fair amount of traffic on this route if you are trying to hitch, though without a permit you'll have to lay low beyond Medro Gongkar.

Buses back to Lhasa (Y60 to Y80, hourly until 5pm) depart from **Bayi Bus Station** (☎ 582 27714) about 500m southwest of the main roundabout. The station also has buses to Kongpo Gyamda (Y30, 127km, two hours, three daily), Pomi (Y90, 216km, 5½ hours, twice weekly), Chamdo (Y290, 715km, two days; Tuesday, Thursday, Saturday) and to Miling (Y30, 74km, 1½ hours, twice weekly). A daily bus also departs for Lang Dzong (Langxian; Y75, 8am) via Miling.

If you miss the Miling bus, there are private vehicles (Y35) that depart from the main bridge over the Nyang-chu. Frequent minibuses to Nyingtri (Y5) depart from a car park near the New Century Hotel. Private jeeps also use this car park for Pomi (Y100). Every second day there is a sleeper bus to Chengdu (Y460, six days); it travels via the Pomda crossroad and Markham.

At the time of research an airport worth US$87.5 million was being constructed near Bayi.

EASTERN TIBET (KHAM)

AROUND BAYI
Buchu Monastery བུ་ཆུ་ས་དགོན་པ་

Some 28km south of Bayi is the small but ancient Gelugpa monastery of Buchu. The original dates from the 7th century, when it was built at the command of King Songtsen Gampo as one of the demoness-subduing temples (p96); it pins the demoness' right elbow. The monastery is recognisable by its striking golden roof.

The entrance to the main chapel is flanked by unusual murals of several protector gods. The main hall has statues of a standing Guru Rinpoche (right) and Jampa (Maitreya) and there are two small statues of the protectors Dorje Lekpa and Kongtsun Demo. The inner sanctum houses statues of a 1000-armed Chenresig (Avalokiteshvara) flanked by Songtsen Gampo. Behind these are the Indian translator Shantarakshita, Guru Rinpoche and King Trisong Detsen. Upstairs is a cheesy, modern 3-D mandala. Buchu Monastery is home to three lamas and five monks.

Lamaling Temple བླ་མ་གླིང་དགོན་པ་

About 1.5km south of Buchu a dirt road (impassable after heavy rain) branches 4km west off the main road to the stunning Lamaling (Zangdrok Pelri) Temple. The monastery was until recently the seat of the exiled Dudjom Rinpoche (1904–87), the former head of the Nyingma order. It is now looked after by his son Chuni Rinpoche, along with eight monks.

The octagonal main temple has been wonderfully restored (reconstruction began in 1989) and rises through four storeys, bringing to mind the Ütse of Samye Monastery. The building is draped in long strands of wooden prayer beads. The grassy courtyard in front is home to a few doleful mountain goats brought here from Tsodzong Monastery at Draksum-tso. Don't get too close: they buck.

Above the main prayer hall is a kora with four protector chapels in each corner. The chapel above this houses statues of Öpagme (Amitabha), flanked by Chenresig (Avalokiteshvara) and by Chana Dorje (Vajrapani). The top-floor chapel contains a four-armed Chenresig as well as two statues of Jampelyang (Manjushri).

The other main building, to the right, is where most religious services are held,

on the 10th, 15th and 25th days of each lunar month. The hall is dominated by a huge statue of Sakyamuni (Sakya Thukpa). Pilgrims circumambulate both this building and the main temple.

Behind this building, trails lead right to a small chörten. Another trail leads up the hillside for about 40 minutes (follow the prayer flags) to Norbu Ri, where the original Lamaling Temple stood before it was destroyed in 1930 in an earthquake. The small chapel has a statue of Dorje Julut and an old photo of Dudjom Rinpoche. Look out for the Sakyamuni footprint above the door.

It's not possible to stay the night at Lamaling so you'll have to either visit as a day trip from Bayi or camp in the friendly village below.

Nyingtri ཉིང་ཁྲི་
☎ 0894 / pop 3100 / elev 3000m

This two-street town (which is sometimes spelled Nyangtri; Linzhi in Chinese) is much smaller than Bayi, 18km away, but is actually the county capital.

Neche Goshog Monastery (Neche Kushuk Monastery; admission Y5) is a small Bön monastery 1km southwest of Nyingtri. Turn right at the new wooden sign that says 'Classical Elegance of Nichi'. The monastery, home to ten monks, is famous for its 2000-year-old juniper tree that is sacred to Bönpos. The manicured courtyard includes a small new temple dedicated to the Bön founder Tonpa Shenrab. Remember to enter the monastery in an anticlockwise direction.

En route between Bayi and Nyingtri look out for a group of 2500-year-old cypresses just north of the highway near Pagyi (Bajie) village. There is a small fee for entry to the nature reserve.

There are a couple of basic hotels in town but you'll find higher standards in Bayi.

Post Guesthouse (Danyougou Zhaodaisuo; ☎ 589 2340; dm Y10) Unexciting and cramped concrete dorm rooms. When we asked where the bathroom was the caretaker swept her arm across the horizon. The guesthouse is on the left as you enter the main street from the west. Another option is the **Trade Company Guesthouse** (Maoyi Gongsi Zhaodaisuo), 75m further along on the left. This place has a bathhouse with hot showers (Y5) in the backyard.

Bönri བོན་རི་

Bönri is the Bön (p61) religion's most sacred mountain, a sprawling massif where Bön founder Tonpa Shenrab fought and defeated his arch-rival Khyabpa Lagring. Bönpo pilgrims come from all over Tibet to circumambulate the mountain in an anticlockwise direction.

The full 60km kora takes two or three days, climbing to the 4500m Bönri-la on the second day. The kora passes many sites connected to Tonpa Shenrab as well as an ancient burial tumulus, a 9th-century stele and a cemetery for babies.

Perhaps the easiest Bön monastery to visit on the kora is **Yungdrungling Monastery**, 6km south of Nyingtri along a motorable road (take the left fork early on) and then another 1.5km up a side valley. The main monastery has a series of gods that will be unfamiliar even to visitors who are *au fait* with Buddhist iconography. The main prayer hall has some Bön publications in English from Solan in India's Himachal Pradesh. The ruins behind the monastery offer fine views over the valley, and there are some lovely ruined chörtens and water-driven prayer wheels.

Another easily visited Bön monastery is the **Sigyal Monastery**, a two-hour hike from Nyingtri (alternatively, you can drive part of the way down the road to Yungdrungling and then hike an hour from there). Take a guide or ask villagers for directions. It's possible to hike from Nyingtri to Sigyal and then continue down to Yungdrungling, visiting both of the monasteries on a nice day trip.

NYINGTRI TO POMI

From Nyingtri the road heads east and up a river valley in shadow of Bönri. A few kilometres out of town a side road turns right into a village from where it is a 3km uphill walk (along a motorable road) to **Dag Tro Sa Monastery**, another Bön pilgrimage site. The sanctuary contains a large central stone with 'tiger paw prints' on it. Long ago, legend says, monks decided to build a temple here after seeing an auspicious tiger crouching on the rock.

The main road towards Pomi switchbacks up the hillside, past the final sections of the Bönri kora and up to the 4515m **Serkhym la**. From the pass you can scramble up 250m to the ruins of a military camp, which gives dramatic views of Namche Barwa (7756m) and Gyala Pelri (7151m). A new Chinese military camp is visible to the north, so try not to be too conspicuous.

THE TSANGPO GORGES

Hidden deep behind the mountains south and east of the Sichuan–Tibet Hwy, the swollen Yarlung Tsangpo makes some dramatic U-turns and crashes over a series of spectacular falls, through what Chinese scientists claim is the world's deepest gorge. With 7756m Namche Barwa and 7151m Gyala Pelri towering over either side of the gorge, only 27km apart, the gorge records a depth of 5382m (almost three times the depth of the Grand Canyon), with a length of 496km. At one point the river narrows to a mere 20m, before bursting out into the Assamese plain as the vast Brahmaputra River.

The region remains one of the world's least explored areas, and is home to king cobras, leopards, red pandas, musk deer, monkeys, tigers, waterfalls and virgin forests.

For a contemporary account of Tsangpo exploration, read Tom Balf's *The Last River: the Tragic Race for Shangri-la*, which details an ill-fated 1998 *National Geographic*–sponsored expedition in which kayaker Doug Gordon was killed.

You'll need plenty of time, money and luck to get into the area. This strategic border area is tightly monitored by the PLA and getting permits is difficult. In the spring of 2004 five French tourists managed to get in, with agency help, for a 25-day trek with porters costing US$5000 per person. Chinese tour groups are allowed to trek between Pe and Gyala; the other access point is via a bridge near Pelung.

You may also need to hurry. While the Chinese government publicly insists otherwise, Beijing reportedly has plans to build a huge hydroelectric station on the river, a move that would have huge environmental, social and political consequences for Tibet, China, India and Bangladesh.

Lunang ལུ་གྲོང་

☎ 0894 / pop 3000 / elev 3375

From the Serkhym-la the road descends past gorgeous alpine valleys lined with rhododendron bushes into the Rong-chu Valley and the logging town of **Lunang**. There are some lovely villages in the valley (the closest one to Lunang are on the east bank of the Rong-chu) and fine views of Mt Kongpo Lapsen to the north.

Lunang has a PSB office, a bathhouse next door to that, and several decent restaurants. The valley is perfect for camping, but fixed accommodation is also available.

Nyingtri Lunang Hotel (Linzhi Lulang Binguan; ☎ 589 9108; dm/d Y15-20/40) This place is at the northern end of the main street, opposite the PSB office. The plumbing doesn't function particularly well but the comfortable and clean rooms make it the best place to stay.

Brother & Sister Hotpot Hotel (Jia Di Tong Guo Binguan ☎ 13638949628; r Y30) At the southern end of town, look for this bright Tibetan building, which doubles as a teahouse. The upstairs rooms are boxy but clean; there is a pit toilet outside.

Lunang Hotpot Guesthouse (Lulang Sha Guo Zhaodaisuo; ☎ 589 2502; r Y30) A few doors south of the Nyingtri Lunang Hotel, this Chinese restaurant has basic rooms in a concrete annexe out back.

Lunang to Pomi

From Lunang the road passes **Pelung**, home to communities of Monpa people. Not far from here the Rong-chu and the Parlung Tsangpo meet and flow away southeast into the Yarlung Tsangpo (Brahmaputra River). This marks the lowest part of the Sichuan–Tibet Hwy (around 1700m). The next 17km to Tangmi, and the 10km after Tangmi, are loaded with treacherous bends and sheer drops. The hillsides are scarred by numerous landslides and are often hidden in subtropical fog. The plentiful hot springs around here are testament to the region's geological instability. Road washouts are common during the rainy season, so it's best to check conditions in Lunang before setting off.

At **Tangmi** the Yi'ong Tsangpo joins the valley. There is a basic **guesthouse** (☎ 0894-5423316; dm Y10) and a couple of noodle shops. As you enter town from the west look for the **monument** dedicated to a group of road

builders who were trapped in a mudslide in August 1969 – ten died trying to drag their truck from the mire.

A poor-quality side road heads about 25km northwest up to the **Yi'ong-tso** (elevation 2150m), a stunning but hard-to-reach lake. Tea is produced in this area.

As the main road heads up the Parlung Tsangpo Valley, pine trees and settlements slowly return and the scenery becomes increasingly spectacular. This area is known in Tibetan as Powo. Local lore says that Princess Wencheng stayed in this valley on her journey to the plateau in the 7th century. Some 64km from Tangmi is the 800-year-old **Ogensanga Chu Ling Monastery** (also called Bakhar), stunningly located on a grassy knoll above the river, overlooked by the spiky Kangmi mountain range. Cross the bridge, turn left and a footpath leads up to the monastery after about 20m. The site has a small community of both nuns and monks, and plenty of opportunities to stroll among the verdant fields, pine forests and the occasional *mani* (prayer) wall. There is no guesthouse, but if you have a tent the monks will point out a decent camping site.

From the monastery it's just 35km along a good condition road to Pomi, so there is no need to rush out of here. If you are on a hired Land Cruiser tour of Kham, this is one place to abandon the car for a while and explore the surrounds on foot.

POMI སྤོ་སྨད་

☎ 0894 / pop 11,000 / elev 2740m

Formerly called Tramo, this small county capital has well-stocked shops and several hotels and restaurants, making it a logical place to spend the night. While the town itself is an eyesore, the surrounding scenery is stupendous and there is plenty of scope for exploring the nearby valleys.

Information

Bathhouse (☎ 13541164511; ⏰ 9.30am-midnight; shower Y4, bath Y50, sauna Y50) Located 100m west of the Hong Hu Binguan, look for the sign that says 'Bathroom'.

Thinking Language Internet Bar (Shin Yu Wong Ba; ☎ 542 2907; ⏰ 9am-midnight; per hr Y5) This Internet café, with a slow connection, is on the 2nd floor of a building next to the Traffic Hotel.

WALK ON THE WILD SIDE

Warmer, wetter and more forested than anywhere else in Tibet, Kham's wide vertical range creates a series of biological niches that hide Tibet's largest concentration of rare animal and plant species. Takins, red pandas, musk deer, gorals, long-tailed leaf monkeys, Himalayan tahrs, tragopans, pheasants and Himalayan monals all live in the tropical and subtropical regions along Tibet's southeastern borderlands.

Eastern Tibet is also a botanical powerhouse, and attracted the attention of intrepid 19th- and 20th-century British plant hunters such as F Kingdon Ward. From May onwards the region is a riot of wildflowers, bursting with 190 species of rhododendrons, 110 types of gentians and 120 species of primula, not to mention rare flowers such as the blue poppy, which was discovered by the explorer (and spy) FM Bailey in the Rong-chu Valley in 1913. Many of the rhododendrons and azaleas found in the West do indeed descend from samples taken from eastern Tibet. Pockets of ancient cypresses up to 2500 years old continue to thrive and the first week of April brings the bloom of cherry blossom trees.

Overlogging is a serious problem in the temperate forests of eastern Tibet, though logging was formally banned in the Tibetan areas of Sichuan and Yunnan in 1998 after a series of devastating floods.

Sights

Around 4km east of Pomi, on the opposite bank of the river, is the tranquil **Dodung Monastery**, set on a pine-clad hill overlooking the valley. The main prayer hall includes, to the right, a collection of *cham* (dance) masks and a flaccid snake (it's a fake). Upstairs are murals depicting the life story of two forms of Gesar, as well as Guru Rinpoche and Tsepame (Amitayus). The monastery has 30 monks and two lamas.

To reach the monastery from Pomi, cross the road bridge over the Parlung Tsangpo, opposite the Traffic Motel, then take the right fork and continue 30 minutes or so to a smaller second bridge and a collection of prayer flags and *mani* walls. From here it's a 20-minute climb to the monastery. A quicker option is to take a three-wheel rickshaw (Y8) from the bridge to the base of the hill.

Sleeping & Eating

Hong Hu Binguan (☎ 542 2213; dm/d/tr/ste Y15/128/90/268) In the middle of the main street, just east of the PSB, this place offers affordable downstairs dorm rooms and better double rooms upstairs with private bathrooms. It is clean and welcoming and the suites are huge, but the common toilet for the dorm rooms is unpleasant and there is no hot water.

Traffic Hotel (Jiaotong Dajiudian; ☎ 542 3040; d Y60-80, tr Y60, d/ste with bathroom Y280/488) Quieter than the Hong Hu, this is a decent option, but the rooms with attached bathrooms are grossly

overpriced. It is located at the west end of town, close to the bridge.

Traffic Motel (Jiaotong Luguan; ☎ 542 2798; dm/d Y25/80) Not to be confused with the larger nearby hotel of the same name, this basic place has unexciting rooms and dorms with private bathrooms. It is above some shops opposite the bridge.

Bashu Jiulou (☎ 13989940577; dishes Y20-25) Good Chinese dishes here, although the civilian patrons are usually ignored if the PLA or PSB turn up. It is located next to the Hong Hu Binguan.

Getting There & Away

Pomi is 160km from Lunang and 127km from Rawok. Buses running between Bayi and Chamdo or Chengdu will drop off and pick up passengers at the bus station at the western end of town. There is also a twice weekly bus to Bayi (Y90, 216km, 5½ hours). Share jeeps parked on the main road are mostly bound for Bayi (per seat Y100), but can be chartered for other destinations.

POMI TO RAWOK

From Pomi the road winds through pine forests in the shadow of craggy peaks until emerging at the spectacular Sundzom Valley, surrounded by the snow-covered Nimbotore (west), Gungtoje (north) and Bande Lhamo (south) mountains. The valley's centrepiece is the small Sundzom Temple (42km east of Pomi), a 15th-century monastery that was home to 200 monks before

TIBET'S HIDDEN LANDS

The Pemako region south of Pomi is a *beyul* (or *pelyul*), one of 16 'hidden lands' scattered throughout the Himalaya that were rendered invisible by Guru Rinpoche to provide hidden retreats in times of danger. Guidebooks on how to get to the hidden lands were written by Guru Rinpoche as *terma* (concealed teachings), to be rediscovered at a suitable time (in this case it was the 17th century) by *terton* (treasure seekers).

Spiritual realisation is said to be easily attained in such places, and, in some cases, the *beyul* also act as sanctuaries providing protection in times of war or famine. Many Khampas fled to Pemako when the Chinese invaded eastern Tibet in the 1950s.

the Cultural Revolution. Four monks now oversee the slow rebuilding process. It is 100m off the highway.

The condition of the road deteriorates as it climbs from Sundzom up the Parlung Tsangpo Valley. There are several stunning side valleys on this high alpine route before you get your first magical views of the blue waters and sandy beaches of Ngan-tso (both Rawok-tso and Ngan-tso are commonly referred to as Rawok-tso). There are good camping and picnicking spots by the lake.

RAWOK ར་བོག
☎ 0895 / pop 2900 / elev 2600

Rawok – with its military presence and transient population of truckers and loggers – has all the elements of a frontier outpost, without the charm. The short main drag of concrete and white tile is strewn with guesthouses, noodle joints, mechanic shops and discarded car parts, not to mention the occasional body part (we found a human skull lying ignored in the gutter). Still, it lies amid spectacular scenery and there are opportunities for walking to the nearby lakes.

The old town is worth a look. Take a right by the antenna of the telecom office into the medieval warren. From here you can work your way through to the large chörten, *mani* wall and small temple overlooking the lake in the southeast of town. The surrounding

fields are full of wooden platforms for drying barley.

It's worth heading north of town and taking a side road southeast for around 7km to a second lake, Rawok-tso. The views here are excellent and it's a great place for a picnic. From Rawok town it's a 1½-hour hike or a short jeep trip past a small hydroelectric station.

The road from Rawok-tso continues past a check post into the border region of Dzayul (Zayu), which is just 20km from Myanmar (Burma). Foreigners are not allowed on this road and there are check posts.

Sleeping & Eating
If you plan on making stops en route, a run from Pomi to Pasho is too much for single day, making Rawok a logical place to break the journey. If the weather is clear then the best option is to camp around either of the two lakes. Otherwise there are several hotels in Rawok town.

Ping'an Guesthouse (Ping'an Zhaodaisuo; ☎ 456 2606; r Y40) The profusion of plastic plants add a homely, if tawdry, element to this old plywood dosshouse. The tiny rooms include TV and little privacy, but it's more atmospheric than the other options.

Lai San Jiu Jia Binguan (☎ 13908958112; dm Y20) This modern faux-Tibetan-style building is on the right as you enter town from the west. At the time of research they only had dorm rooms out the back, but there were plans to add double rooms upstairs.

Rawok has several **restaurants** catering to the nearby army base. You'll find the Chinese restaurants on the left-hand side of the road; the Tibetan restaurants are on the right.

Getting There & Away
There's no public transport to Rawok so if you haven't organised a tour you'll have to hitch. Traffic is meagre at best.

RAWOK TO PASHO
From Rawok the road climbs north past nomads' camps on to the Anju-la (4618m), which marks a dramatic step up from the subtropical Parlung Tsangpo Valley onto the arid high plateau. The pass also marks the watershed between the waters of the Brahmaputra, flowing into India, and the Salween, flowing into Southeast Asia.

Around 13km from the pass on the left, near Guza village, is a ruined *dzong* (fort) and Ramo Monastery. Look for the stuffed sheep hanging from the wall and watch out for dogs. This is a very friendly village and you'll need to allocate extra time for yak butter tea breaks with the locals. There is another small temple, the Sank Lhakhang, as you enter the village (again, look for the hanging, bedraggled sheep). The monastery is a 30-minute walk from the highway. It's a decent area to camp if you are self-sufficient with tent, food and water.

There is another ruined *dzong* 26km further on at Tashitse. As the road descends, the landscape changes colour from arid khakis to rocky reds, reminiscent of the southwest of the USA.

PASHO ষ্মৰ'র্ণৃ

☎ 0895 / pop 3700 / elev 2600

Pasho (Bashe), formerly known as Pema (Baima), is a pleasant town that makes for a good overnight stop.

Information

Internet Café (☎ 456 2282; ☽ 10.30am-midnight; per hr Y4) Opposite Fu Kang Hotel.

Telecom office (☎ 465 2182; ☽ 8am-10.30pm Mon-Fri) Next to the Fu Kang Hotel. Calls to the USA or Europe per minute are Y8.

Sights & Activities

On the northwestern outskirts of the town is **Neru Monastery**, a Gelugpa monastery that was destroyed during the Cultural Revolution, and is worth a quick look. The renovated central chapel holds the throne of the Pakhpala, a religious leader based in Chamdo, whose current incarnation is a government minister. It was the current Pakhpala who paid for the restoration of Neru Monastery. The back wall contains the funeral chörten of the monastery's last *trulku* (reincarnated lama) and the back room has a large seated Jampa (Maitreya) statue made by craftsmen from Chamdo. The top floor contains a *gönkhang* (protector chapel) loaded with old Khampa weaponry. The monastery is a 25-minute walk from the centre of town, reached via a motorable road and bridge west of the main street.

About 4km east of town, on the main highway, is the crumbling **Dola Monastery**. The small main chapel is surrounded by chörtens and lovely old prayer wheels. A kora leads up the mountainside to a plateau and then descends west to Pasho town, with fine views of the arid valley. The leisurely half-day kora is chock-a-block with jovial pilgrims on the 15th and 16th days of the fifth lunar month, around the time of the Saga Dawa festival (p300).

Sleeping & Eating

Fu kang Hotel (Fukang Binguan; ☎ 488 1885; dm/d Y20/50) The nicer double rooms in the main block have king-sized beds, desks, carpeting and sofas while the more basic rooms in the annexe have twin beds. All rooms use a shared toilet but there is a hot-shower block (Y5).

Transport Centre Hotel (Keyun Zhongxin Zhaodaisuo; ☎ 465 2235; dm/d Y20/50) Reasonably clean double rooms and dorms with a TV and a shared toilet. They have a rooftop clothesline for drying laundry. Showers (Y6) are made available to guests and the public here in the afternoon and evening until around midnight. It is on the western end of town and the office is on the right as you enter the compound.

Bu Yun Xuan Jin Jia (☎ 491 6248; dishes Y20) This popular restaurant is on the main street in front of the Fu Kang Hotel – one of many nondescript Chinese joints.

The morning fruit-and-vegetable market on the main street is one of the few places in Tibet where you can buy pineapples and mangoes.

PASHO TO CHAMDO

From Pasho the road east passes picturesque villages and chörtens reminiscent of those in Ladakh. There is a stretch of road 32km from Pasho that is particularly susceptible to landslides, so check on road conditions before setting off. From here the road crosses the Ngul-chu (Nu Jiang or Salween River) and then starts a series of 72 switchbacks up to the 4618m **Zar Gama-la**, marking the highest single altitude gain of any motorable pass in Tibet.

From the pass the road descends 13km to the Pomda crossroad (elevation 4390m) where the southern Sichuan–Tibet Hwy branches off to Markham (p261). There are several hole-in-the-wall restaurants here and there's very basic accommodation at a government truck stop for Y15 per bed.

The distance between Pasho and Pomda is 97km.

Six kilometres from the crossroads lies the lovely village and monastery of Pomda, set at the edge of a wide valley. The village has several grand houses that feature fine woodwork.

Pomda Monastery dates back 360 years but was destroyed in the Cultural Revolution and rebuilt in 1980. It is now home to 100 monks. The main hall has excellent murals and statues of Sakyamuni (Sakya Thukpa), flanked by Jampelyang (Manjushri), Jampa (Maitreya) and Drölma (Tara). The inner sanctum features Tsongkhapa and his two disciples. There is also a protector chapel and a debating courtyard, as well as a huge *mani* wall and a *mani lhakhang* (prayer wheel chapel).

Another 13km brings you to **Kyidrup Monastery**, home to seven monks and two nuns. A further 10km from here a bridge gives access to the yellow-painted and rather derelict **Shongba Guen Tashi Choiling Monastery**. It is visible from the highway, across a glorious grassy plain; a pleasant walk there takes about 25 minutes. The Chamdo Airport is another 20km further north, from where it's still 130km to Chamdo town. There's a hotel at the airport (see p243). At over 4300m, the airport is reckoned to be world's highest civilian airport.

Around 6km north of the airport is a turn-off onto a dirt road that heads towards the wealthy **Yuchig Gompa**, home to 50 Kargyupa monks, and three *trulkus*, one of whom is considered as a manifestation of Milarepa. The main hall contains images of Sakyamuni, Amitayus and Guru Rinpoche and the **kora** around the monastery is lined with 80 stupas. The monks here are friendly and will probably invite you inside for blended yak butter tea; leave a donation if they do. The turn-off for the monastery is difficult to spot. It's behind a collection of derelict homes and oil drums, a couple hundred metres before the bridge that takes the road to the east bank of the river.

Some 16km north of the airport is the turn-off west for Lhorong (Luolong). This road follows the former caravan trail on to Lhasa. Soon the main road descends into gorges, rises to the 4572m Lang-la and then descends dramatically 29km to **Kyitang** (Gyitang) village. **Tra'e Monastery**, on the eastern

edge of the village amid the barley fields, is worth a look. The stone and timber structure was built in 1930 and left relatively untouched during the Cultural Revolution. It's a 15-minute walk from the village crossroad and a bit tricky to find on your own, although locals are usually willing to point you in the right direction. The **Jintan Guesthouse** (Jintan Zhaodaisuo; dm Y10-20) is a barracks-style place at the north end of town with basic rooms and pit toilets. Kyitang is 65km from Chamdo.

Travelling from Kyitang, you cross a ridge over the Nya-la to be met with views of the chocolate-coloured Dza-chu (Mekong River). Just before the pass, look for a series of intriguing **hermit caves** in the cliff face across the valley.

The road now parallels the Mekong, passing villages of contrasting purple baked-mud houses and green terracing. Around 7km after the pass is a turn-off leading 34km southeast along a dirt track to **Drayab town** and **Endun Monastery**.

CHAMDO ཆབ་མདོ་

☎ 0895 / pop 80,000 / elev 3600m

Chamdo (literally meaning 'river confluence' or Changdu in Chinese), at the strategic river junction of the Dza-chu and the Ngon-chu, is a surprisingly pleasant town. It is dominated by the hilltop Jampaling Monastery, below which huddle the Tibetan old town and the Chinese new town. Over 1000km from Lhasa and 1250km from Chengdu, the town is the major transport, administrative and trade centre of the Kham region.

Chamdo has had a troubled relationship with nearby China. The Chinese warlord Zhao Erfeng (the 'Butcher of Kham') captured Chamdo in 1909 and ruled the region until the Tibetans recaptured it in 1917. Chamdo fell to communist troops in 1950 (see p242).

Information

There is nowhere to change your money in Chamdo.

Wishing You Healthy Bathhouse (Ju Kong Yusu; Changdu Xilu; ☎ 482 2435; shower Y5) Along with hot showers, this place does laundry.

Galloping Internet Bar (Bontung Wong Ba; Tsong Qing Zhong Lu; ☽ 7am-midnight; per hr Y3)

Internet Friend's Bar (Wong You Jiu Jia; ☎ 484 3581; Changdu Xilu; ☽ 24hr)

QQ Internet Café (☎ 488 2970; Pedestrian Market; ⏲ 10am-11pm; per hr Y3)

Post Office (Dekyi Lam; ☎ 424 1225; ⏲ 9.30am-6pm)

PSB (☎ 482 4794; ⏲ 9.30am-12.30pm & 3-6pm) 30-day visa extensions are available for Y100, provided you have permits to be in Chamdo.

Telecom (Changdu Xilu; ☎ 482 5560; ⏲ 10am-9pm) Calls to Europe and the USA are Y8.

Sights

GALDEN JAMPALING MONASTERY

དགའ་ལྡན་བྱམས་པ་གླིང་དགོན

This active hilltop monastery (Qiangbalin Si) of over 800 monks dominates Chamdo. The monastery was built between 1436 and 1444 by Jangsem Sherab Zangpo, a disciple of Tsongkhapa. It was destroyed in 1912 and then rebuilt in 1917, after the Tibetan army retook Chamdo.

Pilgrims continuously circumambulate the walled compound and it's worth following them on at least one circuit. Behind the monastery, to the north of town, trails lead up to a sky-burial site.

Visitors enter the monastery from the east side and a paved road leads up from the town below. The first building on the right is the impressive **Tseni Dukhang** (Dialectic College), behind which is a debating courtyard. Just to the left of the college is an entrance; go in here, take an immediate left up the stairs and then turn right at the top. This leads to a *gönkhang* (protector chapel) packed with old **Khampa weaponry**.

Back outside, the monastery's enormous **kitchen** is well worth a look, but only men can go inside.

The main **dukhang** (assembly hall) is particularly impressive, especially when it is packed with hundreds of murmuring monks. This is probably the largest assembly of monks you will see in Tibet these days, outside festival times. The inner sanctum is dominated by Sakyamuni (Sakya Thukpa) and his two disciples.

In the main courtyard is the *gönkhang*, full of the protector gods such as the bull-headed Dorje Jigje (Yamantaka), Palden Lhamo (Shri Devi) and Chögyel (Dharmaraja), plus lots of old armour.

Behind the *gönkhang* is the former residence of the Pakhpala. The south part of the building holds the Tsenkhang (earth spirit house), hidden around the back of the interior courtyard, with a fantastic collection of

INFORMATION		
China Telecom	1	A2
Galloping Internet Bar	2	B3
Home of the Web Friends	3	A3
Post Office	4	B3
PSB	5	A2
QQ Internet Café	6	B3
Wishing You Healthy Bathhouse	7	A2

SIGHTS & ACTIVITIES	(pp241–2)	
Eight Chörtens	8	B2
Galden Jampaling Monastery	9	B2
Golden Eagle Statue	10	A3
Prayer Flag	11	B2
Prayer Flag	12	B2
Prayer Flag	13	A2
Sky Burial Site	14	A1

SLEEPING 🛏	(p242)	
Chamdo Hotel	15	A2
Jindian Hotel	16	A2
Kangsheng Hotel	17	A3
Post Hotel	(see 4)	
Telecom Hotel	18	A2
Yuxin Hotel	19	B3
Zhonglu Guest House	20	A3

EATING 🍴	(pp242–3)	
Friendship Market & Friendship Happy		
Good Food City	21	B3
Tibetan Restaurant	22	B3
Vegetable Market	23	A2
Yinsinju Restaurant	24	A3

TRANSPORT	(p243)	
Bus Station	25	A3

protector masks stuck up on a series of pillars, along with a stuffed wolf and snake.

OLD TOWN རྫོང་ཚོ་རྙིང་པ་

Squeezed between the encroaching Chinese streets and piled up on the hillside around the monastery, the Tibetan old town is worth a wander. The main market street has been modernised but the surrounding warren of streets is interesting and there are lots of silver workshops around here.

Sleeping

Chamdo has lots of hotels, and the local PSB seems surprisingly relaxed about where foreigners can stay. The Kangsheng Hotel on Changdu Xilu, once the top hotel in town, was undergoing renovation at the time of research.

Zhonglu Guest House (Zhonglu Zhaodaisuo; ☎ 488 3443; d Y50) This place has a good location and TVs, but rooms are boxy and basic.

Jindian Hotel (Jindian Dajiudian; ☎ 482 4910; Changdu Xilu; d Y60-80, ste Y120; P) If you do not mind staying on the edge of town, this place has reasonably-priced budget rooms that have been renovated (though the toilets are still crumbling).

Yuxin Hotel (Yuxin Binguan; ☎ 13989054458; dm/ d/ste Y15/60/160) The large and scruffy rooms

here are par for the course. It's hidden on the upper floors of a concrete building, above a supermarket. The entrance is around the back.

Post Hotel (Youzheng Binguan; d/ste Y150/280) The rooms are comfortable and clean. They have hot-water heaters but the tap only turns on after 8pm. The hotel is opposite a car park at the north end of the pedestrian mall, smack in the centre of town.

Chamdo Hotel (Changdu Fandian; ☎ 482 5998; fax 482 1428; 22 Changdu Xilu; d Y180-200, tr/ste Y120/380; P) Clean rooms, 78 in total, with TVs and huge bathrooms, although it's a bit dim and draughty. Hot water is available from 8.30pm to 10.30pm.

Telecom Hotel (☎ 484 8888; 17 Changdu Xilu; d Y260-320, ste/deluxe ste Y580/880; P 🖳) Rooms cut to international standard, with nice bathrooms and reliable hot water. Other facilities include sauna (Y40) and bowling alley (hotel residents Y10, nonresidents Y25).

Eating

A good place to load up on vegetables and foodstuffs is the large **vegetable market** opposite the post office. Chinese restaurants are plentiful on the northern part of Changdu Xilu while there are a few Tibetan places east of the Post Hotel.

THE FALL OF CHAMDO

In spring 1950, Chamdo was in real trouble. Although there were still pockets of resistance at Derge and Markham, the communist Chinese had taken control of Kham without even a fight. Chinese armies were moving in on Tibet from Xinjiang and Xikang (now Sichuan) provinces in a strategy masterminded by, among others, Deng Xiaoping.

The first skirmish between Chinese and Tibetan troops took place in May 1950 when the People's Liberation Army (PLA) attacked Dengo on the Dri-chu (Yangzi River). Then on 7 October 1950 the PLA moved in earnest, as 40,000 troops crossed the Dri-chu and attacked Chamdo from three directions: Jyekundo to the north, Derge to the east and Markham to the south.

As panic swept through Chamdo, the city responded to the military threat in characteristic Tibetan fashion with a frenzy of prayer and religious ritual. When the local Tibetan leader radioed the Tibetan government in Lhasa to warn of the Chinese invasion, he was coolly told that the government members couldn't be disturbed because they were 'on a picnic'. To this the Chamdo radio operator is said to have replied *'skyag pa'i gling kha!'*, or 'shit the picnic!'. It was to be the last ever communication between the Chamdo and Lhasa branches of the Tibetan government.

The city was evacuated (with the Chamdo government commandeering most of the town's horses) but the PLA was one step ahead. Chinese leaders know that speed is of the essence (the Chinese described the military operation as 'like a tiger trying to catch a fly') and had already cut the Tibetans off by taking Riwoche. The Tibetans surrendered without a shot on October 19. The Tibetan troops were disarmed, given lectures on the benefits of socialism and then given money and sent home. It was the beginning of the end of an independent Tibet.

Friendship Happy Good Food City (☎ 499 3700; Friendship Market, 2nd fl) It's no McDonalds, but travellers suffering from fast-food deprivation can get their fix at this pseudo-Western-style restaurant. Set meals, such as a chicken burger, chips and drink, will cost around Y18. Beware of the 'sandwich' which is actually a cake, and an unappetising one at that. They also have a few Chinese items including fried rice and noodles, plus *zhen zhu nai chai* (pearl tea – a Hong Kong creation of sweet tea and bean curd balls).

Yin Xing Jiu Jia Restaurant (☎ 482 4787; Changdu Xilu; dishes Y25-40; ☯ 9am-midnight) This is one of the classiest joints in town, with both Sichuan and Cantonese cuisine, as well as some refreshing fruit desserts.

Getting There & Away
AIR
China Southwest Airlines operates a flight every Thursday to Lhasa (Y700) and three flights a week to Chengdu (Y750). The **ticket office** (☎ 482 1004, ☯ 9.30am-noon) is 500m south of the Dza-chu River. Staff will sell you a ticket without checking for permits but you might still be asked for them at the airport when you check in.

Bangda (Pomda) airport is 130km south of Chamdo. Airport buses (Y40) depart at 3pm the day before flights, requiring an overnight stay at the airport. Rooms at the **Airport Hotel** (☎ 0895 462 2086; dm/d/ste Y40/160/360) represent poor value for money and the staff are not up for negotiating. The share toilet for the dorm rooms is piggy and very damp, though it does have a hot-water heater. The restaurant here serves mediocre Chinese dishes for Y10 to Y15.

BUS
Purchasing bus tickets at the **Chamdo Bus Station** (☎ 482 7351) is fairly straightforward, though you'll need to keep your guard up if you have no permit. There are buses to Lhasa (Y280, 1121km, two to three days, Monday, Wednesday and Friday), via Nagchu, stopping overnight in hotels en route. Sleeper buses operate nonstop to Chengdu (Y450, 1300km, 60 hours, daily 8.30am). Other buses go to Jomda (Y70, 228km, eight hours, daily 8.30am), Riwoche (Y50, 105km, five hours, daily 8.30am), Bayi (Y220, 715km, two days, daily 8am) and Yanjing (Y135, 550km, Tuesday and Friday 8am).

Getting Around
Taxis cost a flat Y5 to anywhere in town.

CHAMDO TO RIWOCHE
The northern highway to Nagchu passes a weir 5km outside Chamdo and then crosses the river near a series of chörtens and a large *mani lhakhang*. Kiss the tarmac a fond farewell here. Soon the road leaves the Mekong River and swings south, eventually climbing past the stunningly located **Trangu Monastery** on a grassy plateau backed by a huge granite wall. If you want to get there, head up the right bank of the river before it crosses at a bridge, about 36km past Chamdo (and 4km before the monastery).

The main road continues to climb, through sections of 1500-year-old juniper forest, protected as a nature reserve since 1992. The road crosses the 4688m Zhutong-la before making a long descent into an alpine valley. About 83km past Chamdo, next to the road, is **Dzong Ngo Monastery**. The monastery houses 40 monks and is worth stopping at for its spectacular location, reminiscent of Colorado. Another 22km past the monastery (and 105km past Chamdo) is Riwoche town.

RIWOCHE རི་བོ་ཆེ་
☎ 0895 / pop 2800 / elev 3800m
It's important to realise that there are two places called Riwoche: Riwoche town (also known as Ratsaka and Leiwuqi Zhen), which is the county capital on the main highway, and the village of Riwoche 29km northwest, which is home to the *tsuglhakhang* (literally 'grand temple').

Riwoche town is of little interest but you may well have to stay here if you want to visit Riwoche Tsuglhakhang. Electricity is sporadic and only comes on after dark, rendering most facilities, such as Internet cafés, useless in the daytime. The telecom office is closed on weekends. **Feisha Internet bar** is on the main street below the Sunshine Hotel.

Sleeping
Post Hotel (Youzheng Binguan; ☎ 450 3007; dm Y30) This budget option has reasonably comfortable rooms that share a grim toilet. It is located 25m north of the Telecom office. Entry is through a courtyard off the street.

Sunshine Hotel (☎ 450 9004; d Y100, d with bathroom Y160-220, tr/ste with bathroom Y120/388) This brand new hotel on the main road offers

---

FLORA OR FAUNA?

In summer you will see nomads and entrepreneurs camped in the high passes and digging for a strange root known as a *yartse gompu (Cordiceps sinensis)* that locals say is half-vegetable, half-caterpillar. It is a fusion of a fungus and the caterpillar that lives off it as a parasite. The root is particularly valued in Tibetan and Chinese medicine and can fetch Y12 for a single root, making it one of the most expensive commodities in Tibet. The business is most lucrative in Tengchen county, accounting for more than 60% of the local GDP.

---

spotless doubles and a friendly staff. If there is no running water you're entitled to a discount and they'll bring a hot thermos. It is located opposite the City Hall and there is a decent restaurant out back.

RIWOCHE TSUGLHAKHANG

 རི་བོ་ཆེ་གཙུག་ལག་ལཁ་ཁང་

From the western edge of Riwoche town a road branches northwest off the main highway and follows the river north, west and then north again. The 'road' rapidly degenerates into a mud pie after rain so check its condition before you set off. A couple of kilometres before Riwoche village the road crests a ridge and you get your first views of the amazing *tsuglhakhang.*

Founded in 1276 by Sangye On, who relocated to Kham after the death of his master Sangye Yarjon, the third leader of the Taglung order, Riwoche started as an offshoot of Talung Monastery in Ü. Eventually, however, it grew to overshadow its parent monastery. It is still the more vibrant of the two, retains the characteristic red, white and black vertical stripes of the Taglung school and is home to 305 monks.

The Temple

The *tsuglhakhang* towers over Riwoche village, dwarfing the medieval-looking pilgrims who circumambulate the massive structure. You enter through huge doors on the eastern side into a breathtaking open inner courtyard.

The eye is immediately drawn to the huge beams and enormous statues lining

the walls. The entry is flanked on the left by Zambala, the god of wealth, and eight chörtens, and on the right by two protector masks on a pillar. The left wall has statues of Öpagme (Amitabha), Tsepame (Amitayus), Guru Rinpoche (one peaceful and one smaller wrathful variety) and Sakyamuni (Sakya Thukpa). The west wall has a Sakyamuni, a funerary chörten, a second version of Sakyamuni, two abbots, and Sakyamuni with the two early Taglung lamas – Sangye Yarjon (1203–72) on the right and Sangye On to the left. Along the right wall is a white statue of Namse (Vairocana) in front of a mandala, a gold chörten, a seated Jampa (Maitreya), Matrö Bodhisattva, a medicine buddha and finally two 1000-armed statues of Chenresig (Avalokiteshvara).

The upper floor is bare but has some fine murals of several protector deities, Milarepa and Marpa, and the Kagyud lineage. There are statues of Guru Rinpoche, a 1000-armed Chenresig (Avalokiteshvara), Sakyamuni and Guru Rinpoche.

The top floor is where the real gems are kept. The most precious items are behind a locked grill, and include some lovely statues and an old saddle said to have belonged to Gesar of Ling. The main central statues are of Sakyamuni (Sakya Thukpa) and Panchuk Rinpoche. Look out for the very old statue of Dorje Chang (Vajradhara). As the room is usually locked you'll need to get permission, and the keys, from the head monk in residence.

Monks' quarters and the grander residences of the abbot and *rinpoche* lie to the north. It's worth walking up the hillside a little to get overviews of the site. One track leads diagonally up the hillside to a high collection of prayer flags.

Sleeping & Eating

Both accommodation and food in the village are meagre at best. At the time of research there was plenty of construction going on by migrants relocated here from other parts of Kham, so facilities may improve.

The barracks-style **Government Guesthouse** (☎ 0895-450 3293; dm Y30) has unexciting dorm rooms and a staff that doesn't really know what to do with foreigners. You might be able to rustle up some food from the Chinese restaurant outside.

Getting There & Away

There's little traffic and no public transport at all between Riwoche town and the *tsuglhakhang* (29km, 1½ hours by Land Cruiser). A terrible road does lead north to Nangchen (200km) and Jyekundo (Yushu) in Qinghai province but it's far from certain that even a Land Cruiser would make it through on this route, especially after rain. It's an adventurous trip and well worth a try if you're properly prepared, but it would be wise to come with a back-up plan.

RIWOCHE TO TENGCHEN

Back at Riwoche town the main highway west swings to the south and starts to climb, reaching **Chayab Monastery** after 17km. This small, charming monastery is surrounded by around 75 chörtens, thousands of *mani* stones and a short kora. High above the monastery is a sky-burial site.

The design of the main chapel is similar to that of Lamaling Temple but on a much smaller scale. Look for a photo of the current Takzham Rinpoche, the reincarnation of Takzham Nuden Dorje, an 18th-century *terton* who founded the monastery (and whose portrait is painted in the right-hand corner of the chapel). Monks will probably invite you for delicious yogurt and yak milk fresh from the surrounding nomadic encampments – leave a donation if they do. There are lovely camping sites nearby.

A further 5km along the highway are the ruins of Sibta Dzong, above the village of Mardo. After another 4km, the road passes a striking white marble mountain before it peaks at the 4809m Dzekri-la. During the summer many nomads camp here, employed in the lucrative search for medicinal roots (see p244).

The road descends through a series of very impressive gorges until, 95km from Riwoche, you reach **Jinkar Monastery**, a small Gelugpa monastery of about 30 monks.

From the western end of the monastery a path leads for about five minutes past a chörten and through barley fields, down to the remarkable **Rotung Monastery**, which is a small Nyingmapa monastery of 40 monks surrounded by tens of thousands of votive carved *mani* stones. Pilgrims circumambulate the monastery from dawn to dusk each day and the surrounding village has a medieval atmosphere.

About 13km past Rotung, easily seen above the road to the west, is **Nyamaling Monastery**. The short walk to this Gelugpa monastery affords excellent views of the valley. The road winds another 26km through red canyonlands to **Gongsar Monastery**, a hard 45-minute climb from the road. There are some small ruins and a two-storey chapel here; further up the hillside are more ruins.

If you've got time, one of the most interesting sites to visit in the area is **Zhizhu Monastery** (Tsedrum), considered to be Tibet's largest Bön monastery. To get there, take the turn-off 5km past the village of Gyangon to the west bank of the river. After the bridge, the road to the monastery forks left and switchbacks for around 10km up to the monastery. All told, it's a 45-minute drive from the main road. There is another fine-looking monastery 3km before you arrive in Tengchen.

The distance between Riwoche town and Tengchen is 146km.

TENGCHEN སྟེང་ཆེན་

☎ 0895 / pop 8000 / elev 4200m

Tengchen (Dingqing) is a forlorn outpost with an unpaved main road lined with poorly stocked dry-goods stores and crumbling concrete blocks. Aside from the overpriced hotels averse to accepting foreigners, the main source of income is the curious 'caterpillar fungus' (p244). Both Tengchen and the surrounding area of Khyungpo are strong centres of the Bön religion.

Information

The China Telecom office is closed on weekends. If you need to make an international call, you can do so from kiosks with the orange and white 'Public Telephone' sign. There is one in the shop next to the Pengsheng Hotel and another opposite the Government Hotel. Calls to Europe and the USA are Y8 per minute. Also opposite the Government Hotel is QQ Internet Café.

Sights & Activities

The main reason to stop here is to visit the **Tengchen Monastery**, on a hillside 4km west of town. This interesting Bön monastery is actually made up of two separate institutions. The main building, founded in 1110, has an impressive assembly hall and upper-floor chapel. Bön deities here include Tonpa

Shenrab and an amazing Palpa Phurbu, whose lower half consists of a ritual dagger.

To the east is the Ritro Lhakhang, built in 1180. The main chapel, the Serdung, contains three funerary chörtens (including that of Monlam Tai, the founder of the monastery) and another many-armed Palpa Phurbu. Another chapel displays a row of six Bön gods on a variety of mounts. There are fine views from the roof.

There are said to be **hot springs** in the valley that leads north of Tengchen, between the town and monastery.

Sleeping & Eating

Pengsheng Hotel (Pengsheng Binguan; ☎ 459 2662; d Y160) This overpriced and unfriendly hotel may be your only choice if you arrive late as the cheaper places fill up quickly with truck drivers. The rooms are dim, untidy and have share bathrooms, but they do come with TV. There's a public bathhouse just west of the hotel entrance that offers hot showers for Y5 until 10pm.

Grain Department Guesthouse (Liangshiju Zhaodaisuo; ☎ 459 2141; dm Y20) Bleak barracks-style accommodation around an oily car park – look for the red and white 'Hotel' sign just to the east of the lion statues of the Grain Department. Another landmark is a tin-roofed temple-style building (Simiao Zhaodaisuo) which is actually bar and bunkhouse, where it may be possible to get a bed for Y10.

Government Guesthouse (Zhengfu Zhaodaisuo; ☎ 459 2573; d Y150) This is a local-government guesthouse with small but clean rooms with TV and electric blankets. The outdoor toilet is an abomination. To get here take the northwest branch at the town's only junction; you'll find the guesthouse about 400m along on the right. There is lower-standard government guesthouse in the west end of town on the road to Tengchen Monastery.

There are several decent Chinese restaurants in town, including the Cantonese-style **Fu Rong Jiu Lu** (☎ 459 3126; dishes Y15) located 80m east of the Telecom office.

TENGCHEN TO SOK

The 37km from Tengchen to the Tsuni-la launches you up into the highlands of northeastern Tibet, offering fabulous views of nomad camps and yak herds made tiny by the huge range of snowy peaks to the south. The pass itself gives fine views westward to the Nyenchen Tanglha (Tangula) range. The road then drops 10km to the lovely village and monastery of **Sertsa** (Kartang) which has a guesthouse just past the bridge. About 14km from Sertsa keep an eye out for the monastery across the valley perched dramatically on the face of a high ridge. Some 66km past Tengchen is the unremarkable town of Choedo which has some shops and another guesthouse.

Here the road swings north and starts to climb up to the stunning **Shel-la** (4830m, 102km past Tengchen), the highest and most dramatic pass along the northern route. Some 40km past Shel-la brings you to **Gyaruptang** (Ronpo), a small roadside village with a restaurant and a basic but atmospheric guesthouse, the **Ronpo Ji Zhaodaisuo** (☎ 0896-370 2961; dm Y15). There is a large *mani* wall at the western end of town.

The road climbs yet again to the 4500m Chak-la, where you turn a corner for a dramatic view of one of the Salween's many tributaries. The road then makes a long descent to some scattered nomad camps, a chörten and then **Yangan** village, where there is a collection of basic **Tibetan guesthouses** and **teahouses**. It's a good place to catch your breath and fill up on butter tea.

From here it's another 48km to **Bachen**, a dismal town buried under a layer of garbage. If it's late, you can stay at the **Government Guesthouse** (☎ 0896-361 2214; d Y140) which has large, clean, but overpriced rooms. There is a Bön monastery on Bachen's western fringe. From Bachen it's 33km to Sok.

SOK སོག

☎ 0896 / pop 4500

Sok's claim to fame is the impressive **Sok Tsanden Monastery**, set on an outcrop in the northwestern suburbs. The monastery, founded by the Mongol leader Gushri Khan, brings to mind a miniature Potala.

The monastery was made off limits to foreigners in 2001 after tourists smuggled out a letter from the monks of Sok to the Dalai Lama. Local authorities remain wary of foreign visitors. If you want to visit the monastery, make sure that Sok Monastery (not just the town) is specifically written on your travel permits. Even this is no guarantee of entry as police will contend that the matter is in local hands. In this case, contact your travel agent who can appeal to the Lhasa and Chamdo PSB (Chamdo may have highest authority in the matter).

There is also a nunnery on the hill to the northeast of town. If you decide to stay the night you could easily take some nice hikes in the vicinity, if you are not first pushed out of town by the PSB.

The PSB office is inside a compound in the east of town, not far from the main crossroads. There are several shops, a super-market, a Telecom office and a post office in the west of town.

Sleeping

There are a few places to stay. None has running water and electricity is sporadic.

Darjeeling Guesthouse (Darjeeling Zhaodaisuo; d Y25) On the corner of the main junction, rooms here are run down but light and airy and come with TV. The **Chengdu Hotel** (☎ 370 2591; d Y40) across the road is of similar ilk, but its Chinese manager does not take kindly to foreigners.

Electricity Hotel (Dianli Binguan; ☎ 370 2694; d/tr Y50/35) The clean and modern rooms here are a welcome sight and the friendly staff will bring buckets of water and a hot thermos. It is located in a new building just north of the main crossroad. There is a public bathhouse below the hotel.

Yali Sun Yeun Jiudian (☎ 370 3000; d with/without bathroom Y200/50) This place, located behind the Telecom office on the west side of town, has clean rooms with TV, heater and phone.

SOK TO NAGCHU

South from Sok the road passes several small villages and their small monasteries and then a large chörten by the roadside. After the No 47 *daoban* (roadwork unit), the road rises to the gentle Shara-la and then descends past the turn-off to Biru.

Shagchu, 135km from Sok, is a truck stop with a good restaurant, the **Sichuan Zigong Fan-guan**. From here it's 103km over high plateau grassland and a couple of gentle passes to Nagchu. You are now well and truly in the grasslands of northern Tibet.

NAGCHU ནག་ཆུ་

☎ 0896 / pop 70,000 / elev 4500m

Nagchu (Naqu) is one of the highest, coldest and most windswept towns in Tibet. Perched on the edge of the Changtang (northern plat-eau), it is a dismal town of mud and concrete,

but is still an important pit stop on the road between Qinghai and Tibet. It's a literally breathtaking place: oxygen levels here are only 60% of those at sea level, so be prepared for headaches and watch for the symptoms of altitude sickness. Bring extra clothes, even in summer.

Nagchu has a horse-racing festival from 10 to 16 August, when the town swells with up to 10,000 nomads and their tents from all over the Changtang. Accommodation can be very tight at this time. Unless you plan to head further east to Sok, you won't need a permit to visit Nagchu.

On the western outskirts of the town are the **Zhabten Monastery** and the **Samtenling Nun-nery**. There are also a couple of markets in town where you might see the occasional northern nomad trading fleeces for pots and pans and other goods.

Information

Lucky Orange Bathhouse (Haoyunde Juzi Yusu; cnr Middle Zheijiang Lu & Chiudan Lu, bath Y5 ☑ 10am-7pm)
Getting Healthy Internet Bar (Kang Da Wong Ba; ☎ 382 1741; per hr Y4; ☑ 10am-11pm) This clean Internet café, on the street corner opposite the Grassland Hotel, has a fast connection and serves free tea.
Post office (cnr Zheijiang Lu & Lianling Lu; ☑ 9.30am-7pm Mon-Fri, 10am-6.30pm Sat & Sun)
Telecom Office (☎ 382 3000; 14 Zheijiang Lu; ☑ 9.30am-7pm Mon-Fri, 11am-5.30pm Sat & Sun) IP cards for international calls sold here.

Sleeping

Nagchu has several decent budget hotels on the main drag, though some, like the West-ern Hotel, will not accept foreigners.

Naqu Hotel (Naqu Fandian; ☎ 382 2424; d/tr Y120/105, d/ste with bathroom Y260/300) This place is often booked out with groups (local and foreign), so you may have to call ahead. The spartan but essentially clean triples aren't a bad deal though it's clear this place has seen better days.

China Tibet Grassland Telecom Hotel (☎ 382 8888; Middle Zheijiang Lu; tr Y180, d with bathroom Y480-980, ste with bathroom Y1580) This new hotel is the best Nagchu can offer, although most of the walls are already peeling in places. The rooms are comfortable and the Tibetan-style murals in the lobby give the hotel some charm, a rare hotel commodity in this part of Tibet. The hotel is in the northeast of the town, around 400m from the Naqu Hotel.

The triple rooms, in the annexe outside, are reasonably priced.

Post Hotel (☎ 382 0999; cnr Zheijiang Lu & Lianling Lu; d/tr Y300/200) Above the post office, this place has mediocre rooms with TVs, although the 1st-floor bar is a lively hangout for the town's teen set.

Chuan Wei Tsi Fu (☎ 382 1075; Middle Zheijiang Lu) This decent Sichuanese restaurant, nearly opposite the post office, is one of several places on the main road.

Getting There & Away

The **main bus station** (☎ 382 2159) is in the south of town. A taxi from the centre costs Y10. There are buses that go to Lhasa (Y53, 326km, seven hours, 8.30am, 9.30am, 10.30am, 11.30am), Biru (Y75, 8.30am), Lhari (Y80, Monday, Wednesday, Friday, 8.30am), Chamdo (Y240, 8am). There are also four buses per morning to Sok (Y65, 237km, six hours) that depart when they are full. Two of these buses will continue to Bachen. When there is demand, minibuses may also depart in the afternoon for Lhari.

It is difficult to get a sleeper bus for Golmud (Y170) as these originate in Lhasa and are usually full. Locals will sometimes pile into a truck (Y100) or hire a Land Cruiser (Y2300).

NAGCHU TO LHASA

The road south of Nagchu is the Qinghai–Tibet Hwy (Tso-Bö Lam), the busiest and most strategic highway in Tibet. The highland scenery along the road swings from completely dismal in bad weather to breathtakingly beautiful in good light.

Past a couple of truck stops, the road crosses the Goluk Bridge, 109km from Nagchu, and climbs to Chokse-la, where Tibetans throw into the air the paper prayers they bought at Nagchu bus station. Just after the pass, 128km from Nagchu and 40km from Damxung, is the Chörten Rango, a line of eight chörtens that commemorate the eight main events in the life of Sakyamuni.

Damxung (p137) is the turn-off for Namtso and is a good place to get lunch.

About 18km south of Damxung a side road branches off to the east towards Reting Monastery (p142), while the main highway continues south on to Yangpachen, Tsurphu Monastery (p134) and Lhasa.

Roads to Tibet

Wild, mountainous and remote, the Tibetan areas of western Sichuan (and to a smaller extent northwest Yunnan) are culturally and geographically very much part of the Tibetan plateau. The area was once part of the Tibetan region of Kham, before it became part of Xikang province and was later incorporated into Sichuan province in 1951. It has long been the meeting point of the Chinese and Tibetan worlds and it was this region that first experienced the Chinese invasion and provided the stiffest resistance to it.

It is an irony that because it is part of Sichuan, Tibetan culture is in many ways better preserved here and is subject to fewer religious restrictions than in the Tibetan Autonomous Region (TAR). You'll see photos of the Dalai Lama in monasteries, though these are outlawed in Tibet 'proper'. Since they are not subject to travel restrictions in Sichuan or Yunnan, travellers enjoy more freedom to explore remote monasteries and Tibetan villages than in the TAR.

This chapter details overland routes through western Sichuan to the borders of Tibet. For other land routes to Tibet, see p314. The northern and southern roads offer the main sights, including the big monasteries of Ganzi, Derge and Litang. Off the main roads, where travel gets rougher, are several spectacularly situated and rarely visited monasteries. Hikers should head for the sublime scenery of Yading Nature Reserve, or the valleys around Derge (ideally suited to horse trekking). Gary McCue's *Trekking in Tibet* details several hikes in the region.

Western Sichuan sees few visitors, partly because travel is still rough and time-consuming, but tourism is growing and there are some real Tibetan cultural jewels to be discovered.

HIGHLIGHTS

- Take in the rollercoaster ride to Tibet, over mountain passes, down deep gorges and past remote Tibetan villages

- Watch traditional Tibetan block printing done by hand at **Bakong Scripture Printing Press** (p256) in Derge

- Jump off the bus and explore Tibetan monasteries at small towns such as **Rongbatsa** (p255), **Tagong** (p253) or **Luhuo** (Drango; p254)

- Explore the mountain valleys around remote **Dzogchen Monastery** (p256)

- Hike the kora of **Yading Nature Reserve** (p259) amid the region's most stunning scenery

- Hike and then hitch out to **Tsopu Gou** (p261), a remote monastery by a holy alpine lake surrounded by prayer flags

- Play pool with wild-looking Khampas in the high-altitude town of **Litang** (p257), before exploring the large monastery

★ Dzogchen Monastery
★ Derge
★ Rongbatsa
★ Luhuo
TIBET
★ Tsopu Gou
Tagong ★
Litang ★
CHINA
Sichuan
★ Yading Nature Reserve

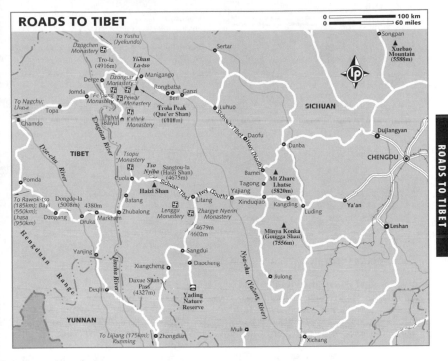

ROADS TO TIBET

KANGDING 康定

☎ 0836 / elev 2560m

Kangding (Tibetan: Dardo or Dartsedo) is nestled in a steep river valley at the confluence of the Zheduo and Yala Rivers, known in Tibetan as the Dar-chu and the Tse-chu. (The 'do' of the town's Tibetan name means 'river confluence'). The swift currents of the Zheduo provide hydroelectric power.

Arriving in Kangding, there is a tangible sense that you have reached the border of the Chinese and Tibetan worlds. The town has been a trade centre between the two cultures for centuries with the exchange of yak hides, wool, herbs and, especially, bricks of tea from Ya'an wrapped in yak hide. It also served as an important staging post on the road to Lhasa, as indeed it does today as western Sichuan's largest town.

Kangding was historically the capital of the local Tibetan kingdom of Chakla (or Chala) and later, between 1939 and 1951, the capital of the short-lived province of Xikang, when it was controlled by opium-dealing warlord Liu Wenhui. Today Kangding is largely a Chinese town.

Information

Agricultural Bank of China (Zhongguo Nongye Yinhang; Xi Dajie; ⏰ 9am-5pm Mon-Fri) Can change US dollars and UK pounds. It cannot change travellers cheques or offer cash advances on credit cards. There is no ATM in town.

China Telecom (Yanhe Xilu) Next to the Black Tent; offers cheap international phone calls.

Internet cafés (Guangming Lu; per hr Y2-3; ⏰ 8am-midnight) There is a telephone office with Internet service on Xi Dajie and you can also get online at Sally's Café (p252), which has a very speedy Internet service for Y3 per hour.

Kangding Tour Service (Kangding Lüyou Fuwu Zhongxin; ☎ 283 4000; Xi Dajie) Offers information and tours of nearby sights. The Tibetan owner speaks English and can tailor tours to suit you.

PSB (☎ 281 1415; Dong Dajie; ⏰ 8.30am-noon & 2.30-5.30pm Mon-Fri) In the southern part of town; processes visa extensions quickly and painlessly.

Sights

There are several minor monasteries in and around Kangding. Just behind the Black Tent Guesthouse, the **Ngachu Monastery** (Anjue Si) is a fairly quiet temple built in 1654. It is home to around 20 monks and a new Jampa Chapel.

The **Nanwu Monastery** in the west of town is the most active monastery in the area and has around 80 lamas in residence. To reach it, walk south along the main road and follow its bend to the left for 2km. South of town is the **Dorje Drak Monastery** (Jingang Si), which was under renovation at last look.

You can head up **Paoma Shan** for excellent views of Kangding and, if you're lucky, Mt Minya Konka (7556m). Take particular care when wandering around Paoma Shan and try to avoid hiking on your own. A British tourist was murdered here in the spring of 2000. In town, the **market** on Dong Dajie is worth a look.

Festivals & Events

The **Zhuanshanjie**, or 'walking around the mountain' festival, takes place on Paoma Shan on the eighth day of the fourth lunar month to commemorate the birthday of Sakyamuni (Sakya Thukpa). White and blue Tibetan tents cover the hillside and there's plenty of wrestling and horse racing, with visitors from all over western Sichuan.

Sleeping

If you're only staying in Kangding a night, to catch an onward bus, it's convenient to be in the east of town near the bus station, although most guesthouses and attractions are over the river on the west side of town.

Black Tent Guesthouse (Gonggashan Lüshe; ☎ 886 2107; 28 Yanhe Xilu; dm/d Y20/25) Next to Ngachu Monastery, this clean and sociable place has a teahouse on the ground floor and is the spot to meet other travellers. There are hot showers.

Sally's Café (Beibao Kezhan; ☎ 283 8377, 13060075296; dm Y20) This laid-back hostel is next to Dorje Drak Monastery. Washing facilities are basic and the hot water is temperamental (despite claims that it is 24-hour), but the rooms are good and you can sleep in colourful carved wooden beds. There is a café and restaurant on the ground floor and fast Internet access (per hour Y3). A taxi from the bus station will cost you Y5.

Changcheng Binguan (☎ 882 2956; Xinshi Qianjie; d Y40-50) Not far from the bus station, this tired hotel is a decent option for solo travellers looking for a cheap room of their own.

Mid-range places include the **Kalaka Dajiudian** (☎ 282 8688; fax 282 8777; 5 Yanhe Donglu; d Y190) and the flashy **Love Song Hotel** (Qingge Dajiudian; ☎ 281 3333; fax 281 3111; 156 Dongda Xiaojie; d Y580).

Eating

For a rousing cup of yak-butter tea, try the **teahouse** on the ground floor of the Black Tent Guesthouse.

Almost next door to the Black Tent is an upmarket **Tibetan Restaurant** (Qingkexiang; dishes from Y20) that features a staggering number of yak meat dishes on its menu. Fortunately it also does some very good *momo* filled with potato and vegetables. Walking north from the Black Tent, the restaurant is down the first alley you come to on your left on the 2nd floor.

At **Jixiang Fandian** (Dongda Xiaojie; dishes from Y7), the friendly owners offer an English menu and serve tasty local cuisine at good prices. Try the potato pancake (Y5) or the fish with black-bean sauce (Y18).

Getting There & Away

The completion of the Erlang Shan (Two-Wolf Mountain) tunnel has cut the ride to Chengdu down to a comfortable eight hours. Buses leave hourly for Chengdu from 6am to 4pm (Y101 to Y113). If you are heading to the Traffic Hotel make sure your bus is bound for the Xinnanmen bus station.

Going west from Kangding there are daily buses at 7am for Litang (Y80, eight hours), at 6am for Ganzi (Y106, 12 hours), at 6.45am for Batang (Y138, 11 hours), at 7.15am for Derge (Y166, two days) and at 7.15am for Xiangcheng (Y115, 14 hours). Local minibuses run to Yajiang, Daofu and Luhuo.

THE NORTHERN ROUTE

This is one of the two main routes of the Sichuan–Tibet Hwy, which links the Tibetan areas of western Sichuan with Tibet proper. Longer than the southern route, the northern route extends from Kangding to Chamdo, via Derge and Ganzi.

TAGONG 塔贡

In the midst of lovely grasslands dotted with Tibetan herders is the vibrant Tibetan community of Tagong, an excellent place to spend a day or so exploring.

At the north end of town, **Tagong Monastery** (admission Y10) blends Han Chinese and Tibetan styles and appears to have survived the ravages of time amazingly well, though two of the three main halls have been rebuilt recently. The holiest statue in the far right building is a replica of Lhasa's Jowo Sakyamuni Buddha, said to have been carved in situ when the original passed through en route to Lhasa in the 7th century. Note also the beautiful 1000-armed Chenresig (Avalokiteshvara) in the building to the left. Make sure you visit the stunning collection of over 100 chörtens behind the monastery; finish off your visit with a clockwise kora of the site.

The velvety hills around Tagong, topped with prayer flags and chörtens, offer views of the rolling grasslands and the stunning 5820m pyramid peak of Zhare Lhatse. Take a walk up to the hill above town, which is topped by a chörten surrounded by votive rags, amulets and beads left by pilgrims.

The grasslands are also the stage for an annual horse-racing festival, held at the beginning of the eighth lunar month (mid-July to August) and attended by thousands of local Tibetan herders.

A 20-minute walk west of town, over the river, leads to the *shedra* (Buddhist college), which has a large collection of Buddhist rock carvings in the plain below.

Sleeping & Eating

The best option is the two-storey building diagonally opposite the monastery entry – look for the English-language sign that says 'Tibetan Food and Butter Tea'. A karaoke pitstop for Chinese tourists during the day, the ornately decorated Tibetan-style room moonlights as a **guesthouse** (dm Y20) in the evening. Privacy and traffic noise can be a problem during the day, but things do quieten down at night.

The ramshackle **Tagong Hotel** (Tagong Lüshe; dm Y10) has acceptable rooms. To find it head 50m south down the main street, away from the monastery, and it's on your right in a government compound.

Along the main street you'll find a number of small restaurants and noodle shops to satisfy your hunger.

Getting There & Away

Buses to Tagong run daily from Kangding (Y23 to Y33, three hours) at 6am. If you're heading to Ganzi, you can pick up the same bus the next day at about 9am as it passes through town. A bus that is heading north to Luhuo also passes through Tagong around 9.30am.

Afternoon buses returning to Kangding can be flagged down in Tagong. You can also catch a minibus or shared taxi (Y20) to take you to the Xinduqiao crossroads, from where there are buses through to Kangding and Litang.

TAGONG TO GANZI

Several bustling but little visited towns en route from Tagong to Ganzi offer impressive monasteries and some basic accommodation. The Khampa houses in this region, built from wood and stone, are particularly elegant.

Bamei (Tibetan: Garthar) is a lunch stop about 20km north of Tagong; there's a pretty series of chörtens in the south of town. Bamei is famous as the birthplace of the 11th Dalai Lama. Just 8km northeast of town, along the road to Danba, is the **Garthar Chöde Monastery** (Chinese: Haiyuan Si), built by the seventh Dalai Lama.

A further 72km is **Daofu** (Tibetan: Tawu), home to the 450-year-old Gelugpa-school **Nyitso Monastery**, the largest monastery in the region. The **Xuecheng Binguan** (☎ 712 3373; 3/4-bed dm Y20/10, d with bathroom Y70) is right next to the bus station. There are daily buses to Kangding (Y58) at 7am, 8am and 11am. Private minibuses will do the run to Kangding for Y450. For Ganzi and Derge you need to change at Luhuo.

Luhuo (Tibetan: Drango), 70km further, has **Drango Gompa**, which once had over 1000 monks. The monastery sits on the hillside in the Tibetan-style southern part of town and has a large newly carved wooden statue of Jampa (Maitreya). The Tibetan name of Drango means 'head of the rock' and derives from Luhuo's strategic position at the confluence of two rivers.

The best place to stay in Luhuo is the **Kasa Fandian** (☎ 0836-732 2368; q Y58, tr with bathroom Y60), offering the best showers this side of Chengdu. Turn left out of the bus station and the hotel is a few metres down on your left. At the top of the hill as you turn right out of the bus station, **Luhuo Binguan** (d/tr Y60/54, d with bathroom Y100) is a second choice.

Luhuo has daily buses to Daofu (Y16 to Y21, 1½ hours, 6.30am), Ganzi (Y25, two to three hours, 6am and 3pm), Tagong (Y36 to Y53, five hours, 6.30am), Derge (Y88, nine hours, 6am), Baiyu (Y88, nine hours, 3pm), Manigango (Derge bus Y50, five to six hours) and Kangding (Y56 to Y79, eight hours, 6.30am).

About 20km before Ganzi the road rises to a high pass before dropping down past the lake and monastery of **Kasuo-tso**.

GANZI 甘孜

☎ 0836 / elev 3394

The noisy market town of Ganzi (which is also spelled Kandze and Ganze) sits in a valley at 3400m, surrounded by the sleeping giants of the Trola (Chola) range, and is a natural place to break your trip. The gorgeous surrounding countryside is peppered with Tibetan villages and resurgent monasteries. A couple of isolated bombings took place in Ganzi and Chengdu between 1998 and 2002, a sign of the growing frustrations of local Tibetan communities.

Sights

Over 540 years old, **Garze Monastery** is just north of the town's Tibetan quarter and is the region's largest monastery, with over 500 monks. Encased in the walls of the main prayer hall are hundreds of small golden Sakyamuni (Sakya Thukpa) statues. In a smaller hall just west of the main hall is an impressive statue of Jampa (Maitreya), dressed in silk.

To find the monastery, turn left out of the bus station and head north for about 10 minutes until you reach the Tibetan neighbourhood. A kora winds clockwise around and above the monastery. To follow it take one of the roads to the left when you reach the Tibetan quarter and look for a huge chörten and then a hall of prayer wheels, from where the path winds uphill.

Den Monastery in the southern part of town is smaller but older and much more atmospheric. The inner chapel is surrounded by three pilgrimage paths and houses fierce statues of the protector god Nagpo Chenpo (Mahakala). Upstairs are several Mao slogans left over from the Cultural Revolution and a small printing press.

For a nice half-day walk head south from the bus station over the Nya-chu (Yalong River). The right fork leads through barley fields for 20 minutes to **Dongtong (Dontok) Monastery** and the new but impressive **Dingkhor chörten**. The left fork leads to **Pongo Monastery** after about an hour or so.

Ganzi has the region's best antique shops and many general stores selling Tibetan goods.

Sleeping & Eating
Accommodation options in Ganzi are limited as most of the hotels do not accept foreigners.

Hongmofang Hotel (☎ 752 2676; d with bathroom Y60, tr without bathroom Y45) This hotel's policy on accepting foreigners changes frequently. The rooms are simple but comfortable and washing facilities are basic. The hotel has one double room with an en-suite but you might find that staff allow other hotel guests to use your shower when you are not in the room! To find it, turn left out of the bus station, cross the main intersection, and continue up the road until you see the red-and-white sign (no English) on your left.

Golden Yak Hotel (Jinmaoniu Jiudian; ☎ 752 2353; dm Y30, d with bathroom Y120-180) This hotel is above the bus station (there's no English sign). The cheap dorm beds can be found in the older building while the more expensive doubles are in the shiny new building opposite.

Some small restaurants are located around the main intersection, just north of the bus station. The Muslim restaurants in a row just east of here double as video bars and offer good noodles if you can stand the ear-shattering sounds of kung fu.

Getting There & Away
Buses to Ganzi (Y106, 12 hours) leave Kangding daily at 6am. From Ganzi, a bus leaves each morning at 6.30am for Kangding. A rather decrepit bus leaves every couple of days to Derge (Y60, eight hours), or try for a seat on the bus from Kangding.

To reach Beri and Dargye Monasteries (see the next section), catch anything heading west or negotiate a taxi down to Y20.

You can also head north from Ganzi to Yushu (Tibetan: Jyekundo) in Qinghai, via the town of Sêrxu.

GANZI TO DERGE
A 15km excursion from Ganzi, on the north side of the river, is the Gelugpa **Beri Monastery**. There are several other monasteries in the pretty village of Beri.

Rongbatsa
☎ 0836
Around 65km before Manigango, near the village of Rongbatsa, are the circular walls of **Dargye Monastery** (Dagei Si). The nearby hot springs, although more lukewarm than

hot, may be the only bathroom you get for some time.

A local lama named Gyalten Rinpoche operates the excellent **Gyalten Rinpoche Guesthouse** (dm Y30), a couple of kilometres west of Dargye Monastery. Set against a backdrop of white-capped mountains, this wonderful guesthouse feels completely isolated, as there are no neighbours to be seen for miles. The rooftop commands some breathtaking views of the valley and you can easily lose yourself here for a day or two. Simple meals are available. Beds are mattresses covered with Tibetan carpets; you will need a sleeping bag here. To get to the guesthouse, walk out of Dargye Gompa's west gate and head straight for around 15 minutes. If you can't find it, one of the friendly monks at the monastery will help show you the way.

From the monastery it's a two-hour walk north along the Nya-chu (Yalong River) to **Hadhi Nunnery**, home to around 60 nuns who operate a basic shop and are reportedly happy to receive short term guests.

Manigango
☎ 0836
This scruffy crossroads town halfway between Ganzi and Derge can be a useful base for visiting Yilhun La-tso or Dzogchen Monastery (see p256). There is one guesthouse, **Manigango Guesthouse** (Manigange Shisudian; dm Y10-20), where all the buses stop. The rooms are comfortable if basic but the toilets are half a mile up the road – make sure you bring a torch! The staff are very friendly and can help with travel information and can even organise a horse and guide for trekking in the surrounding areas (prices start at Y100 per day for a horse and Y100 per day for a guide).

Next door, **Yulong Shenhai Fandian** (dm Y15-30) is more modern and has it's own public toilet. Look for the large red sign with white Chinese characters

Both hotels have a restaurant attached. The restaurant at the Manigango Guesthouse has particularly tasty food and is very cheap. There is a good beef noodle shop next door to the petrol station.

From Manigango a daily bus passes through at 11am for Derge (Y35). Coming from Derge, a bus stops in Manigango at 11am and heads on to Ganzi (Y25), Luhuo (Y50) and then Kangding (Y130). The bus stops overnight in Luhuo and continues on to Kangding the next morning. A 9am bus leaves daily for Sêrxu.

Manigango to Derge

A 50km detour north from Manigango takes you to **Dzogchen Monastery** (Zhuqing Si), the home of the Dzogchen school (see p58). The monastery and *shedra* have a stunning location at the foot of a glacial valley. It's possible to stay at the college for Y15, though you'll need a sleeping bag and your own food. There are a couple of well-stocked shops in the village 1km below in the valley. Several important high Nyingmapa lamas, now exiled abroad, originally came from nearby valleys. Getting here can be tricky. Buses to Yushu and Sêrxu pass the monastery but it's probably easier to hitch. If you do hitch, make sure you set out in the morning as there is not much traffic on the roads in the afternoon. A private car from Manigango (ask at the Manigango Guesthouse; p255) with a driver costs around Y250 return.

Around 13km after Manigango is **Yilhun La-tso** (Xinlu Hai; admission Y20), a stunning, holy alpine lake bordered by chörtens and dozens of rock carvings. The lake is backed by the huge glaciers of 6018m Trola Peak (Que'er Shan) and it's possible to walk an hour or two up the left (east) side of the lakeshore for glacier views. The lake has many great places to camp, though you need to guard against the mosquitoes. To get here you'll have to hitch to the turn-off where there's a bridge and trail 1km to the lake.

From the lake the road ascends to the wild and craggy scenery of the 4916m Trola before descending through deep gorges and some pretty Tibetan villages to arrive in Derge.

DERGE 德格

☎ 0836 / elev 4000m

Resting in a valley between the Tibetan border to the west and the Trola (Chola) range to the east, Derge forms the cultural heartland of Kham. While the Chinese influence is evident and growing rapidly in the town, the old town and surrounding villages are very much Tibetan.

There are many historically important monasteries in the valleys south of Derge, namely at Pelpung (Chinese: Babang), Dzongsar, Pewar (Baiya), Kathok and Pelyul (Baiyu).

For details on these monasteries and wonderful treks in the area see Lonely Planet's *South-West China* guidebook or visit the website www.khamaid.org.

Sights

At the heart of Derge is the 18th-century **Bakong Scripture Printing Press and Monastery** (admission Y35; ☉ 8.30am-noon & 2-6.30pm). The press houses more than 217,000 engraved blocks of Tibetan scriptures from all the Tibetan Buddhist orders (including Bön); the collection makes up an estimated 70% of Tibet's literary heritage. These texts include ancient works about astronomy, geography, music, medicine and Buddhist classics, including two of the most important Tibetan sutras. A history of Indian Buddhism comprising 555 wood-block plates is the only surviving copy in the world (it is written in Hindi, Sanskrit and Tibetan).

Within the monastery, dozens of workers hand-produce over 2500 prints to order each day, as ink, paper and blocks fly through the workers' hands at lightning speed. Upstairs is an older crowd of printers who produce larger and more complex prints of Tibetan gods on paper or coloured cloth.

You can also examine storage chambers, paper-cutting rooms and the main hall of the monastery itself. Protecting the monastery from fire and earthquake is the guardian goddess Drölma (Tara). There are some nice murals in the two ground-floor chapels, so bring a torch. You can get a close-up look at the workers who carve the printing blocks (in relief) in the administrative building across from the monastery.

Admission to the monastery includes an English-language brochure and an obligatory guide. Photography is not allowed.

To reach the printing house, turn left out of the bus station and right over the bridge. Continue up this road to the southeast of town and to the monastery's front door.

Just uphill behind the printing house, the large Sakyapa **Gonchen Monastery** is well worth a look. Restored during the 1980s, the three inner sanctums are dedicated to Guru Rinpoche, Sakyamuni (Sakya Thukpa) and Jampa (Maitreya).

Also worth seeking out is the **Tangtong Gyelpo Chapel** (Tangyel Lhakhang) – as you head uphill to the printing press look out for the small alley leading to the right. For an introduction to the remarkable Tang-tong Gyelpo, see p26.

Sleeping

Derge Hotel (Dege Binguan; ☎ 822 2157; 4-bed dm Y10, d with bathroom Y180) The only place in town officially open to foreigners has clean, damp and overpriced doubles and fairly grim and musty dorm rooms.

Some travellers have managed to bag a bed in the **Wuzi Zhaodaisuo** (dm Y20), directly opposite the bus station, which has nicer dorms although they are still very basic. Look for the multicoloured bunting strung up outside.

Getting There & Away

From Derge a daily early morning bus leaves for Kangding (Y166, two days) via Mani-gango (Y35, three hours), Ganzi (Y60, eight hours) and Luhuo (Y86, 10 to 12 hours), where it stops for the night before carrying on to Kangding the following day.

If you're travelling west, note that individuals are officially forbidden from travelling into the TAR without travel permits (see p304). The occasional sleeper bus trundles through to and from Chamdo but rarely has empty berths. There is occasional transport west to the town of Jomda, just over the Tibetan border.

DERGE TO CHAMDO

From Derge it's 111km to Jomda (Jiangda), crossing the Dri-chu (Jinsha Jiang or Yangzi River) at the Tibetan border. From here it's 228km to Chamdo via Topa and several high passes. If you are hitching along this route you'll have to be careful at Jomda (where there are a guesthouse and a PSB office) and at the check post at the bridge over the Dri-chu (though checks are usually fairly cursory here).

The occasional minibus travels between Jomda, Derge and Chamdo, but you will probably have to change rides when you get to Jomda.

THE SOUTHERN ROUTE

The southern route that goes from Kangding to Pomda is shorter than the northern route and passes equally stunning scenery. It offers fewer monasteries but includes the option of detouring south to Yading Nature Reserve and continuing on the rugged back-door route to Zhongdian (Tibetan: Gyalthang) in Yunnan.

LITANG 理塘

☎ 0836 / elev 4014m

Resting on open grassland framed by snow-capped peaks, Litang is a friendly and authentically Tibetan place to hang out in for a couple of days. A horse-racing festival from 1 to 7 August sees the town swell with local Khampas and is a great time to visit, though accommodation can be hard to come by at this time.

Litang is famed as the birthplace of the seventh and 10th Dalai Lamas and also four of the Pabalas, Chamdo's religious leaders. After a visit to Litang the sixth Dalai Lama wrote a famous poem about a crane, indicating through it that his reincarnation would be born in Litang. The area around Litang also has strong connections to the epic warrior Gesar of Ling and a statue of the man, complete with plastic palm trees, decorates a square in town.

Information

China Post (◷ 9-11.30am & 2-5.30pm) On the main north–south street. Next door is a place where you can use IP telephone cards.

Cultural Travel Bureau of Litang County (☎ 532 2142) Can organise trips to Lenggu Monastery and others. Ask at the High City Hotel (p258) for the current office location. Kalsang Tsering is a good English-speaking guide.

Internet cafés (◷ until midnight; per hr Y5) One block north of the High City Hotel and diagonally opposite the same hotel, on the 3rd floor above shops.

Public showers (Yuanxisu Zhongxin; showers Y8) Hot showers are available here; south of the main crossroads.

Sights

At the northern end of town is the large **Litang Chöde Monastery**, built for the third Dalai Lama. Inside is a statue of Sakyamuni (Sakya Thukpa) that is believed to have been carried from Lhasa by foot. A collection of chörtens and *mani*-stone (prayer-stone) carvers line the main entrance. The monastery was bombed by Chinese troops in 1959 during a Khampa rebellion.

On the eastern edge of Litang is a recently erected 33m-high **chörten**, supported by snow lions, around which active worshippers seem to be perpetually circling.

A difficult-to-find 420-year-old building known as the Zenkhang marks the **birthplace of the seventh Dalai Lama**. The upper-floor sleeping room of the Dalai Lama has a statue and several relics of the man, and an interesting old Chinese army bag. It can be hard to find the lady with a key. No photos.

There are **hot springs** (admission Y6-7) at the western edge of town, 4km from the centre. A taxi here costs Y7 one way.

Sleeping & Eating

Litang has decent food and lodging, making it a fine place to break a trip for a day or more. No hotels have hot water and electricity can be dodgy.

Crane Guest House (Xianhe Binguan; ☎ 532 3850; beds Y25) Cosy double and triple rooms here are a good deal, with electric blankets and heaters. There's a single shared toilet and the washing facilities consist of basins, flasks of boiling water and a drum of cold water. It is run by two Tibetan sisters and you can store your bags here. Take a left out of the bus station and head about 350m east into town; it's on the right-hand side of the road.

High City Hotel (Gaocheng Binguan; d Y100-120, tr Y120) This government-run hotel has spacious rooms that come with heater, TV and squat toilet but no shower. The nice lobby has a killer karaoke setup loaded and ready at all times.

Former Residence of Jiamuyang (beds Y50) This place has cold and dim double rooms with lovely Tibetan murals and B&W photos of the former occupant, a prominent lama at Labrang Monastery. It seems to be aimed at groups and has squat toilets without any doors.

Good Luck Guest house (Jixiang Binguan; ☎ 532 3688; d with/without toilet Y120/60) Another option with pretty good spacious rooms. Singles will have to pay for two beds. The reception is accessed from the back.

Litang has countless small restaurants, the most popular of which are on the south side of the main road a couple of hundred metres west of the Crane Guest House. Of these, the **Lianmeixuan Restaurant** (dishes Y10-15; ☯ lunch & dinner) has an English speaker.

Getting There & Away

Litang's bus station is a chaotic place so double-check all times and prices. At the time of writing buses were leaving Litang

for Kangding (Y76, eight hours) at 7am, Batang (Y46 to Y56, 5½ hours) at 7.30am and Derong (Y110) at 7am. One or two buses pass through each day from Kangding en route to Daocheng and Xiangcheng. It's 284km to Kangding and 654km to Chengdu.

A back-door route to Yunnan runs south from Litang, through 400km of spectacular scenery to Zhongdian, from where another road leads into Tibet (see p317). Buses run to Xiangcheng (Y60, five hours) at 7am; a ride to Sangdui (for Yading Nature Reserve) costs Y35 and takes three hours.

AROUND LITANG

The **Zhargye Nyenri Monastery** (Jiage Shenshan Si), 18km from Litang along the road to Daocheng, is next to a holy outcrop of rock honeycombed with caves and covered in prayer flags, *kathaks* (prayer scarfs), sacred symbols, eagles' nests and a hard-to-make-out image of self-arising Jampa (Maitreya). Pilgrims come here to make an hour-long kora around the peak, past several caves and sin-testing spots, particularly on the second day of the eighth month. The monastery itself has images of Tsongkhapa, Drolma, Jampelyang and Marpa, plus fine murals by artists from Ganzi. To get to Zhargye Nyenri, take the morning bus to Daocheng or Xiangcheng, get off at the monastery and hitch back. It's possible to stay the night here. Sadly two bears are kept chained up in the courtyard.

Lenggu Monastery is in a remote but stunning area 70km from Litang, between 6224m Mt Gambo Gonga (Genie Feng) and 5807m Mt Xiaozha. The monastery was built by the first Kamarpa in 1164. It's an adventure to get here as there's little public transport; from Litang branch left off the main road to Batang after 15km or so to the village of Lamaya in Reke district. From here walk or hire a horse to Legando village (a short day) or the monastery (a long day). It's a minimum three-day return trip but with more time you could make day trips to Xiaozha Lake and waterfall, and to Ruogen-tso. It's possible to stay with families in Lamaya and Zhamla villages and Legando. The region is part of Genie Natural Biological Tourism Protection Zone.

The road from Litang to Batang traverses the **Maoya Grasslands** and crosses the Sangtou-la pass before dropping down to the twin lakes of **Tso Nyiba**, with a backdrop of the Haizi Shan, before continuing to Batang.

DAOCHENG 稻城
☎ 0836 / elev 3800m

The county town of Daocheng (Tibetan: Dabpa) is mainly a jumping-off point for Yading Nature Reserve (right). Peak season for Chinese tourists is the first week of May, followed by the first week of October.

There are two **Internet cafés** (per hr Y5; ☾ 24hr) on the renovated cobblestone street that leads off the main north–south drag.

The **Xiongdeng Monastery** is a large Gelugpa monastery about a two- to three-hour walk northeast of town. The monks are friendly and the views are good. Head east out of town to the bridge and then north up the hillside. You can hitch parts of the way on a passing tractor or you can hire a minivan from town for Y50.

After a trek in Yading, soak your weary limbs in the **Rapuchaka Hot Springs** (admission Y10), 4km southeast of town. A taxi here costs Y10 one way.

Sleeping

There are numerous excellent Tibetan-style B&Bs. Most offer beds from around Y20, basic pit toilets and no showers. Rates are flexible and are 30% higher in May.

Peng Song Cuo's House (☎ 572 8581; dm Y20-30, d with bathroom Y60-120) The most upmarket of the homestays, the doubles have en suite bathrooms and hot showers are available. The atmosphere can change quickly if a Chinese tour group pulls in.

B&B Bounchou (☎ 572 8093; dm Y20) Next door is run by a friendly Tibetan couple, but the rooms can be a bit dark. It's a five-minute walk north then west from the bus station.

One street to the south has the **Lucky Folk House** (dm Y15-20) and next door **Seeburay Guest House** (☎ 572 8668; dm Y30), both of which are good.

Further west from here is the **Best Tibetan Home of Ji Xin** (☎ 572 8587; dm Y30), which has dark rooms but a nice courtyard. There are several other places nearby.

Modern Chinese hotels include the three-star **Yading Hotel** (Yading Binguan; ☎ 572 7522; d/tr Y280/320), which has hot water only during the peak season, and the recently renovated **Kawa Karpo Hotel** (Kawagapu Jiudian; d with/without bathroom Y100/60).

Getting There & Away

Buses run from Daocheng at 6.30am to Kangding (Y120) via Litang (Y44), and to Zhongdian (Y101).

If you take the bus between Litang and Xiangcheng you may get dropped off at the junction of Sangdui, 28km from Daocheng. Microvans shuttle people to Daocheng (45 minutes) for Y10 per person, or Y40 for the vehicle. If you get stuck in Sangdui you can get decent food and basic accommodation at the **Happy Shop Guesthouse** (beds Y10). About 5km north of Sangdui is the recently re-built Kagyud-school **Benpo Monastery**, which is well worth a visit.

An airport is being built at Daocheng and direct flights to Chengdu should start in 2007.

YADING NATURE RESERVE 亚丁

Six hours south of Daocheng, this stunningly beautiful **reserve** (admission Y138) is the real reason to shlepp all the way out here. You'll need to time your trip well, as April and October see snowfalls and early May and October sees a flood of Chinese tourists during national holidays. September is a good time to visit.

The reserve is centred around the three peaks of Jambeyang (Yangmaiyong Shenshan; 5958m) to the south, Chana Dorje (Xiari Duoji Shenshan; 5958m) and Chenresig (Xiannairi Shenshan; 6032m). The mountains are named after the Rigsum Gompo, the Tibetan Buddhist trinity of bodhisattvas. None have ever been climbed. The reserve is a strong contender as the inspiration for James Hilton's novel *Shangri-La*.

The region was once part of the old kingdom of Muli and was visited by the fifth Dalai Lama in the 17th century. Joseph Rock, National Geographic's 'man in China', who counted the corpulent King of Muli as a close personal friend, visited in the 1930s and described the famed 'Bandit Monastery', whose 400 monks would regularly head out on plundering expeditions before returning to prayer and contemplation.

En route to the reserve you'll pass **Rewu Monastery** on the other side of the valley and then, after a high pass, **Konkaling Monastery** (Gongling Si), the largest in the region, before reaching the town of Riwa. Sixty kilometres from Daocheng, Riwa has accommodation.

ROADS TO TIBET

Just south of Riwa, where the road branches, you have to pay the hefty park entry fee. Yading village and the entrance to the park is 35km further.

At the reserve entrance you can hire horses (with an obligatory guide) for Y80 to Y100 per day. There are several inns here, including the friendly **Gedong Hotel** (☎ 0836-572 7119; dm Y30), offering basic beds and food (Y15) in a Tibetan home. It's signposted on the main road before you reach the park entrance. The owners can advise on the two-hour hike up to Qingwa Lake.

The Kora

From the entrance it's a 45-minute walk through dripping forests and past chörtens to **Tsongu Monastery** (Chonggu Si), currently under renovation, where there is a **tent hotel** (beds Y25) and basic restaurant.

Two hours' walk southeast is Luorong Pasture (Luorong Muchang; 4188m), where there is another **tent hotel** (beds Y30) and restaurant. From here it's three hours to alpine Milk Lake (Niunai Hai; 4720m). Five Colours Lake (Wuse Hai) lies just over the side ridge.

From this point most Chinese tourists return the way they came but it is possible to do a kora of the mountain. For this you'll need camping equipment for one night. From the lake the kora climbs for one hour to a wide 4400m triple pass, it then branches right and descends to meadows, a popular place to camp. There are shepherds' huts here, where guides or porters normally stay the night.

From the valley a trail leads west to the main road but the kora continues two hours northeast to Drölma-la (4375m). The trail continues four hours downhill, beneath the north face of Chenresig and past spectacular **Drölma-tso** (Tara Lake, sometimes called Pearl Lake) en route back to Tsongu Monastery. It's also possible to do a day hike to Drölma-tso from Tsongu Monastery.

Getting There & Away

In summer minibuses run from Daocheng to Riwa (Y35, four hours) and possibly to Yading (Y60, 110km, six hours). Otherwise you will have to hire a minivan (from Y200 one way). Out of season it's not a bad idea to arrange for your driver to take you back at a pre-arranged time. Snows can block the road without warning in April and October.

BATANG 八塘

☎ 0836 / elev 2700m

Lying 32km from the Tibetan border and 5½ bumpy hours down a dirt track from Litang, low-lying Batang is the closest town to Tibet that is open to foreigners. An easy-going and friendly place with lots of street-side barbeque grills and outdoor seating, the modern town is surrounded by suburbs of beautiful ochre Tibetan houses. When it's still the end of winter in Litang it's already spring in Batang. There are colourful *cham* dances outside town on the 26th of the ninth Tibetan month.

Many travellers try to sneak into Tibet from here, so – unsurprisingly – the local PSB is a little suspicious of foreigners.

Sights

Gelugpa-sect **Chöde Gaden Pendeling Monastery** in the southwest of town is well worth a visit. The monks (over 500) are friendly and active (they had just finished building a sand mandala during our visit). There are three chapels behind the main hall; up some stairs via a separate entrance is a room for the Panchen Lama, lined with photos of exiled local lamas. An old, Chinese-style hospital is now used as monk accommodation. Stop in the kitchen for some butter tea before leaving. A kora of prayer wheels surrounds the monastery.

There are some fine walks around town. Head north to a lovely Tibetan hillside village and then west to a riverside chörten and a few inevitable pilgrims. Alternatively, head south from the town centre over a bridge and then east to a hilltop covered in prayer flags and offering views of the town.

Sleeping

Jinhui Hotel (Jinhui Binguan; ☎ 562 2700; dm Y10-15, d with/without bathroom Y70/50, tr Y60) Doubles without bathroom are a good bet here, though they are quite run down. Get a room away from the street to escape the karaoke. The communal hot-water showers are pretty good and there's lots of space for washing clothes. From the bus station continue into town and take the first right after the huge, hard-to-miss golden bird; it's a block down on the left.

Bawu Binguan (☎ 562 2882; dm Y15-25, s/d per bed Y60/40, d with bathroom Y120) This central option is a decent budget bet, with communal hot showers and pleasant doubles.

Batang Binguan (☎ 562 2590; d with bathroom Y80-160) Right on the square, this one can be noisy. Cheaper doubles come with a grotty bathroom but alleged hot water. Deluxe rooms come with stains and dodgy plumbing.

Government Hotel (Ying Binglou; ☎ 562 1566; d Y266, often discounted to Y180) The top place in town offers smoky but comfortable rooms with hot-water shower, kettle and even a Western toilet.

There are plenty of Sichuanese restaurants around the town, and local supermarkets stock everything from chocolate to French red wine.

Getting There & Away

The **bus station** (☉ 6.30am-10pm) has buses at 7am to Litang (Y59, six hours), Kangding (Y135, two days via Litang) and Chengdu (Y231, two days via Yajiang). The road to Litang is under major construction work until 2006 so expect serious delays. The bus station is a 10-minute walk from the town centre.

Headed west there are buses at 2pm (Y44, four hours) and afternoon microbuses (Y50) to Markham, 138km away inside the TAR. Foreigners may have problems buying tickets to Markham as the town is officially closed.

AROUND BATANG

One excellent detour from the Litang–Batang road is to **Tsopu Gou**, a scenic valley, lake and monastery 78km from Batang, then 38km off the main road. From Litang or Batang get off the bus at Cuola (Y30 from Batang), where there is basic accommodation, and arrange a ride up the valley. The route passes the village of Chaluo, a monastery and some hot springs before entering a wide valley and village at the base of the lake.

A beautiful kora leads clockwise around the lake to the Nyingma-sect **Tsopu Monastery**, whose guesthouse offers mattresses on the floor for Y20. Bring your own food and purify the stream water. You can hike for a couple of hours up the valley behind the monastery to a glacial lake, or just get the views from the retreat chapels above the monastery.

BATANG TO POMDA

The road west from Batang crosses the Dri-chu (Jinsha Jiang) into Tibet at Zhubalong and continues to Markham, where it joins the road from Yunnan.

Markham (3900m), traditionally known as Garthog Dzong, is where permitless hitchhikers from Sichuan and Yunnan commonly get caught by the vigilant PSB. Try to avoid the town's main road. Coming from the east, head for the road to the north of town that connects with the main highway. Markham has a **County Guesthouse**. There's a checkpost about 3km west of town.

It's 158km on to **Dzogang** (3800m; Chinese: Yougong; also known as Wamda in Tibetan) over a 4380m pass, dropping to cross the Dza-chu (Mekong River) at Druka, rising again to the 3900m Joba-la, dropping to stunning scenery around Denpa, then rising again to the 5008m Dongdo-la (phew!). There is a basic **guesthouse** in Dzogang. Transport along this stretch of the road is particularly infrequent.

The road continues along the Yu-chu, a tributary of the Salween River, for 107km to the main Lhasa–Chamdo road at Pomda (see p239).

(see p239).

ROADS TO TIBET

Trekking

CONTENTS

TREKKING

A place as vast and mountainous as Tibet offers almost unlimited potential for walkers. From the frigid high northern plains to the steamy jungles of the southeast, Tibet is a land of rich cultural and ecological contrasts. The remoteness of Tibet combined with climatic extremes poses special challenges for trekkers – and unique rewards. In the higher reaches of the plateau snow squalls and blistering heat are both possible on a single day. There are few places left in the world where you can walk for days, witnessing an ancient and sophisticated culture without having the experience marred by the dross of modern civilisation.

Most trekking is in the centre of the region, around the major towns and highways. Cities such as Lhasa and Shigatse provide bases from which to equip and launch treks. The trailheads of four of the six treks covered in this chapter can be reached by public transport.

In the 17th century, Jesuit priests intent on spreading Christianity trekked over the mountains of western Tibet. In the late 19th and early 20th centuries a slew of spies, explorers and scholars, often in caravans, covered great distances on foot in their attempts to reach the Holy City, Lhasa. Most never made it, and some paid for their Tibetan adventure with their lives. One such unfortunate person was Dutreuil de Rhins, the leader of a French expedition who, in 1891, after being refused permission to enter Lhasa, was murdered by brigands. One of the greatest treks was made by George Roerich's Central Asiatic expedition in the 1920s. During its archaeological explorations it traversed a great swathe of Tibet's northern plains.

Still, there were many places that the early explorers didn't reach, and there are many new frontiers still beckoning the experienced, well-equipped trekker. Mastering the six great treks covered here will serve you well should you decide to venture further afield. There is no shortage of places to explore, and spots such as Shishapangma, west of Mt Everest, and Pasam Lake in Kongpo are becoming more popular with trekkers. For the most adventurous and time-rich, it is even possible to cross large sections of Tibet's mountain ranges on foot.

HIGHLIGHTS

- Tread the old pilgrim trail from **Ganden to Samye** (p271), a test of physical mettle as much as a spiritual feat
- Hike from **Shalu to Nartang** (p278), a great introduction to trekking in Tibet and a window on the ancient art of pilgrimage
- Circumambulate **Mt Kailash** (p285) – not just a walk around a mountain but a quest for deeper glimmerings of the self and the universe
- Stretch the imagination as well as the legs while peering into the lucid waters of sacred **Lake Manasarovar** (p292)
- Hike in the shadow of **Mt Everest** (p281), for spectacular scenery, rigorous exercise and the opportunity to come close to Tibetan culture

ENVIRONMENT
The Land
For all its attractions, Tibet is a formidable place where even day walks involve survival skills and generous portions of determination. As it's situated on the highest plateau on earth and crisscrossed by the world's highest mountains, nothing comes easily and careful preparation is all important. Even on the most popular treks, which can involve several days of travel without any outside help, high passes up to 5300m are crossed.

Eastern and much of central Tibet are laced with large mountain ranges, towering passes and deep valleys and gorges. Western and northern Tibet are even higher, but between the mountains are expansive valleys and plains that can take days to traverse.

Wildlife
The mountain slopes of Tibet are home to many dozens of plants and flowers, but you should resist the temptation to pick them. There really is no need as many of the most useful plants are readily available as medicines, incense and condiments in the city markets. If you are interested in identifying Tibetan medicinal plants, check out *Tibetan Medical Thangkas Of The Four Medical Tantras*, a lavish coffee-table book available in most Lhasa bookshops. Also see *Flowers of the Himalaya* by Oleg Polunin and Adam Stainton for some examples of Tibetan flora.

TREKKING DISCLAIMER

Although the authors and publisher have done their utmost to ensure the accuracy of all information in this guide, they cannot accept any responsibility for any loss, injury or inconvenience sustained by people using this book. They cannot guarantee that the tracks and routes described here have not become impassable for any reason in the interval between research and publication.

The fact that a trip or area is described in this guidebook does not mean that it is safe for you and your trekking party. You are ultimately responsible for judging your own capabilities in the conditions you encounter.

The more remote valleys and mountains are home to a rich variety of wildlife (see p69). If you are lucky you might see the Himalayan black bear or perhaps the giant Tibetan brown bear searching for food in the alpine meadows. Snow leopards in the craggy heights and the common spotted leopard in eastern Tibet are occasionally spotted by alert trekkers.

Less daunting, but no less spectacular, are the ungulates of Tibet, which include several species of deer, wild yaks, antelopes, gazelles, blue sheep and the argali, the largest species of wild sheep in the world. Smaller mammals, a panoply of birds and numerous reptiles and amphibians can be seen while trekking. Generally, large predatory animals are not attracted to camp sites and stay well away from humans. Still, do not court trouble by discarding food scraps near your camp – you would be extending a welcome to the local rodent population.

Environmental Issues
Trekking responsibly in Tibet is a matter for special consideration (see also p269). The beautiful but fragile alpine biomes of Tibet's upland regions deserve the utmost respect. A fire, for instance, can scar the landscape for centuries. In recent years, the environment of Tibet has suffered tremendously. Forests are being decimated, wildlife eradicated and economically important plants depleted. In such a context it is imperative that trekkers make their way lightly and leave nothing behind but the proverbial footprints. Stay off fragile slopes and try not to tread on plants. Follow the Tibetan ethos, killing not even the smallest of insects. In the long term, this approach will buy trekkers respect from Tibetans and will help guarantee that later visitors enjoy the most pristine environment possible.

In the arid climate of much of Tibet, water takes on a special significance and is highly regarded in Tibetan traditional beliefs. The *lu* (water spirits) guard the wellbeing of the community and are thought to be very dangerous if transgressed. For these reasons Tibetans tend to treat water reverently. Their traditional practices resemble those adopted by the ecotrek movement. For example, toilets are never constructed where they could contaminate water sources, and the washing of clothes in rivers and streams is restricted. In both traditional and modern terms, the aim is the same: to avoid the introduction of foreign substances into water sources.

CLIMATE

Trekkers must be prepared for extremes in climate, even in the middle of summer. A hot, sunny day can turn cold and miserable in a matter of minutes, especially at higher elevations. Night temperatures at 4500m and above routinely fall below freezing even in July and August! At other times of the year it gets colder. In midwinter in northwestern Tibet, minimum temperatures reach minus 40°C. Yet Tibet is a study in contrasts, and in summer a scorching sun and hot, blustery winds can make even the hardiest walker scurry for any available shade. Between the two extremes, the Tibetan climate – cool and dry – is ideal for walking but always be prepared for the worst.

GETTING STARTED

WHEN TO TREK

The best time to plan a trek in Tibet is during the warmer half of the year. May and June are good months without much rain or snowfall but some high alpine passes in eastern Tibet may still be closed. July and August are the hottest months of the year but they tend to be rainy and this can make walking messy and trails harder to find. September and October are excellent months for trekking but in high areas the nights are cold and early snow is always a possibility.

It is always a good idea to budget in a few extra days for your trek, especially if much road travel is needed to get to the trailhead, as roads can be blocked, especially in the wet summer months. You might also need more time hiring local guides and beasts of burden.

WHAT KIND OF TREK

The kind of trek you take will depend on your experience and the amount of time you can allot. Unless you have already hiked extensively in the Andes or Himalayas, it may be better to consider organising your walk through a travel agency. It is important to know that trekking without

---

SOCIAL TREKKING

In most out-of-the-way places trekkers can quickly become the centre of attention, and sometimes just a smile may lead to dinner invitations and offers of places to stay. If you really detest being the star of the show, don't camp in villages; if you do, don't expect Western notions of privacy to prevail.

If you ask directions be prepared to be sent in the direction you are walking no matter where you are trying to go. To avoid this age-old travellers' trap, be prepared to patiently and repeatedly explain what your travel goals are and, if in doubt, ask someone else.

If you have any religious sentiments your trek probably qualifies as a pilgrimage, in which case you will generally receive better treatment than if you are 'just going someplace'. Another helpful hint: if all else fails try a song and dance. Even the most amateur of efforts are met with great approval.

For other cultural considerations related to trekking, see p42.

---

permits and minders is still illegal in China. This hardly stops the independent traveller but should you opt to go it alone you must be willing to face the consequences. The most likely time to be apprehended by the police is when hitchhiking, so be particularly careful in towns and truck stops. The good news is that the few people who manage to get caught are usually let off with a talking down and a light fine. Still, in some extreme cases, trekkers have been held by the police for several days and large sums of money demanded from them; some have even been deported.

WHAT TO TAKE

There is a great deal to see while trekking and you will be revitalised by the natural surroundings, but you must be prepared for extremes in weather and terrain. The time of year you choose to walk will dictate the equipment you will need.

Clothing & Footwear

As a minimum, you will need basic warm clothing, including a hat, scarf, gloves, down jacket, long underwear, warm, absorbent socks, all-weather shell and sun hat, as well as comfortable well-made pants and shirts. Women may want to add a long skirt to their clothing list.

If you attempt winter trekking you will certainly need more substantial mountaineering clothing. Many people opt for synthetic-pile clothing, but also consider wool, which has proven itself in the mountains of Tibet for centuries. One of your most important assets will be a pair of strong, well-fitting hiking boots. And remember to break them in before starting the trek!

As in much of Asia, nudity and open displays of affection are frowned upon. Try to dress modestly, which is pretty easy in such a rugged environment. You are better off covering up in the intense solar radiation of Tibet with light-coloured, lightweight clothing. Be especially vigilant at monasteries – these are not places for immodest Western fashions. As a rule, don't wear shorts or short dresses, especially in villages and at religious sites.

Equipment

Three essential items are a tent, sleeping bag and backpacking stove. There are no restaurants in the remote areas of Tibet and provisions are hard to come by, so you will probably end up cooking all of your own food. Count on camping because, except in certain villages that are on the main trekking routes, it can be difficult to find places to sleep. Invest in a good tent that can handle big storms and heavy winds. A warm sleeping bag is a must. Manufacturers tend to overrate the effectiveness of their bags, so always buy a warmer one than you think you'll need – you can unzip it if you get too hot.

You will also need a strong, comfortable backpack large enough to carry all of your gear and supplies. To save a lot of misery, test the backpack on day hikes to be certain it fits and is properly adjusted.

Nonessential items include a portable stereo, journal and elaborate camera gear. Basics, however, must include water containers with at least 2L capacity, a system for water purification, a torch (flashlight), compass, pocketknife, first-aid kit, waterproof matches, sewing kit, shrill whistle and walking stick or ski pole. This last item acts as a walking aid and, even more importantly, for defence against dog attacks. Tibetan dogs can be particularly large and brutal and they roam at will in nearly every village and herders' camp. Bring your walking stick or pole from home or purchase a shovel handle in Lhasa. They can be found at any of the hardware stores on Lingkhor Chang Lam.

Petrol for camping stoves is widely available in towns and cities but is of fairly poor quality. To prevent your stove from getting gummed up you will have to clean it regularly. Kerosene (*meiyou* in Chinese) can also be obtained in cities. In Lhasa you will find kerosene vendors on Dekyi Shar Lam, opposite the road to Ramoche.

For details on buying and hiring trekking gear in Tibet, see the information on p114. Nowadays, there are scores of shops in Lhasa selling such equipment.

MAPS

There are numerous commercially available maps covering Tibet, but very few of these maps are detailed enough to be more than a general guide for trekkers. The Chinese government produces small-scale topographic and administrative maps but these are not for sale to the general public. The US-based Defense Mapping Agency Aerospace Center produces a series of charts covering Tibet at scales of 1:1,000,000, 1:500,000 and 1:250,000 (though the last can be hard to find). The most useful of the American 1:500,000 references for trekking in Tibet are H-10A (Lhasa region, Ganden to Samye, Tsurphu to Yangpachen), H-9A (Kailash and Manasarovar) and H-9B (Shigatse region, Shalu to Nartang, Everest region).

Soviet 1:200,000 topographic maps can now be consulted in many large university library map rooms. However, most libraries will not permit you to photocopy them because of international copyright laws. Buying them, however, has become easier with commercial outlets in the West stocking them. Punch 'Tibet maps' into your computer search engine to see who might carry them in your area.

The Swiss company **Karto-Atelier** (www.karto -atelier.com) produces a 1:50,000-scale Mt Kailash trekking map.

For details of places to buy maps of Tibet and Lhasa, see p302.

PHYSICAL PREPARATION

Before embarking on a trek, make sure you are up to the challenge of high-altitude walking through rugged country. Test your capabilities by going on day walks in the hills around Lhasa and Shigatse. Attempt a hike to the top of a small mountain such as Bumpa Ri, on the other side of the Kyi chu from Lhasa.

TREKKING AGENCIES

There is now a plethora of private agencies in Lhasa, some of which can arrange treks. Let the buyer beware, for the standard of service fluctuates wildly and may bear no correspondence to the amount you pay. In general, standards of service and reliability are much lower than in Kathmandu. Shop around carefully and compare the services and attitudes of at least several agencies. Kickbacks and shady dealings are part of everyday business but with some luck they won't ruin your trip.

The main advantage of going with an agency is that it takes care of all the red tape and deals with officials. Most agencies offer a full-package trek, including transport to and from the trailhead, guide, cook, yaks or burros to carry the equipment, mess tent and cooking equipment. The package may include tents, at least up to the task of trekking in Tibet. Make sure the agency spells out exactly what is included in the price it is quoting you, and be prepared to provide all your own personal equipment.

It is essential to sign a written contract with the tourist agency with which you intend to travel. However, as none of the Lhasa companies seem to have contracts at hand you may find yourself drafting one up. If so, be certain to include details of the service you are paying for and money-back guarantees should your operator fail to deliver what has been agreed. For the standard contents of tour contracts, have a look at the brochures of adventure-travel companies in your home country.

None of the Lhasa-based agencies that are listed below are unconditionally recommended, but all have run many successful treks. Trekkers are particularly at the mercy of those driving them to and from the trailheads. Drivers are usually private contractors who are sometimes known to act like rogue pirates with you being their captive.

To avoid problems, it is prudent to use the driver and guide for a day trip to somewhere such as Ganden or Tsurphu Monastery to see what you think before heading off into the wilds with them.

Prices vary according to group size and location but none are cheap. Costs per person tend to be lower in bigger groups. For treks in remote and border areas, expect to wait at least four days for the permits to be sorted out. If you feel you have been cheated by your agent, you may find help with Jigme, director of marketing and promotion for the **Tibet Tourism Bureau** (Map p88-9; ☎ 0891-683 4315; fax 683 4632) in Lhasa. This government organisation is in charge of training tour guides and monitoring the performance of all companies running treks and tours.

Tibetan Agencies

Holyland Adventure (Map pp88-9; ☎ 0891-683 6652; holyland@public.ls.xz.cn; 215 Dekyi Nub Lam; per day US$130) Two blocks west of the Lhasa Hotel and just east of the Xinhua Bookstore, this long-established company is managed by the congenial Thupten Gendun and arranges treks just about anywhere.

Tibet Chamdo International Travel (Map pp88-9; ☎ 0891-633 3871; tntc@public.ls.xz.cn; Mandala Hotel, 31 Barkhor South; per day US$100) Managed by a Tibetan named David Migmar. He and his staff have substantial trekking experience and are willing to please.

Tibet International Sports Travel (☎ 0891-633 4082; tist@public.ls.xz.cn; 4th fl, Himalaya Hotel, 6 Lingkhor Shar Lam; per day US$130) The oldest agency specialising in trekking. Now managed by Jigdrel Wangchuk.

Tibet Yungdru Adventure (Map p92; ☎ 0891-633 6642; tny@public.ls.xz.cn; 3rd fl, New Century Hotel, 155 Dekyi Lam Shar; per day US$120). A main focus of the managing director Thupten is trekking in the more remote regions of Tibet.

Wind Horse Travel (Map pp88-9; ☎ 0891-683 3009; jampa_w@hotmail.com; West Lingkhor Rd no. 48 ; per day US$120) One of the best managed agencies in town and partnered with several international travel companies. The running of treks is handled by Jampa, the deputy general manager. To date, this is the only company in Tibet to offer white-water rafting trips.

Kathmandu Agencies

If you want to organise your Tibet trek from Kathmandu, here are some of the most qualified agencies:

Arniko Travels (☎ 01-421684; www.arnikotravel.com; PO 469, Baluwatar)

Dharma Adventures (☎ 01-430499; www.dharma
adventures.com; PO Box 5385, Gairidhara)
Great Escapes (☎ 01-418951; grt@greatpc.mos.com.np;
PO 9523, Baluwatar)
Malla Treks (☎ 01-410089; www.mallatreks.com;
PO Box 5227, Lekhnath Marg)
Mountain Travel Nepal (☎ 01-411225; info@tiger
mountain.com.np; PO Box 170, Lazimpat)

Western Agencies

A few Western companies organise fixed-
departure treks in Tibet. These tours can be
joined in your home country or abroad, usually in Kathmandu. Prices are higher than
treks organised in Tibet or even Kathmandu,
but they take the hassle out of organising a
trek and are useful if you have the money but
only a couple of weeks.

A standard trek organised at home will
include a Western leader, a local leader,
porters, a cook and so on. All your practical
needs will be taken care of and you will be
free to enjoy the trekking itself.

PERMITS

Officially, individuals are not permitted to
trek independently in Tibet and thus are
required to join an organised group. Trekking, as with all travel in Tibet apart from
that around Lhasa, requires a travel permit
(see p304).

That said, a number of trekkers opt to
go it alone, in the true spirit of independent travel, and many succeed. If you are
caught by the security police without the
right documents, be friendly but firm in
your conviction that you did not know any
better. You will probably be let off with a
small fine, unless you (or the police) lose
your cool. It is unusual to be asked for any
documentation while on a trek.

Trekkers on the Ganden to Samye route
without a travel permit will face a problem
after their trek is finished when they take
the ferry over to the Tsetang side. Trekkers
in the Mt Kailash region face the same
permit regulations as other travellers. At
the time of research, there were no permit
checks anywhere on the Tsurphu to Yangpachen or Shalu to Nartang treks but the
trailhead at Tsurphu is often patrolled by
police. Travel permits are not needed for
Ganden, but at Tingri, Everest Base Camp
and Shalu the authorities are within their
rights to ask for one.

ON THE TREK

Bear in mind that the trekking trails in Tibet
are not marked and in many places there are
not people from whom to ask directions.
Paths regularly merge, divide and peter out,
making route-finding inherently difficult. If
you are not good at trail blazing, your only
alternatives are to employ a local guide or to
go through a travel agency.

HEALTH

To maintain your health in such a difficult
high-elevation environment you will need
to take some special precautions. With a
little preparation and good sense your trekking experience will be one of the highlights
of your trip to Tibet. Bring a first-aid kit (see
p325) with all the basics and perhaps some
extras as well. Tibet is not the place to wander alone – always trek with companions. If
anything goes wrong, you will need others
to depend on. In case of a real emergency
you may need medical and evacuation insurance, which should be purchased before
leaving home. For detailed information, see
Medicine for Mountaineering published by
Mountaineers Books.

The most common trekking health
problem is sunburn. In serious instances
(when accompanied by heat exhaustion)
sunburn can require hospitalisation but
fortunately it is preventable. Wear loose-
fitting clothes that cover your arms, legs
and neck and choose a wide-brimmed
hat like the ones Tibetans wear. There are
many fancy and expensive sunscreen lo-
tions on the market but the most effective
and cheapest is zinc oxide ointment. Bring
it from home because you probably won't
find it in Tibet.

Subfreezing temperatures mean there is
a risk of hypothermia, even during the summer season. Make sure you have the right
clothing and an outer shell that will protect
against rain, snow and wind. Remember
that exposed plains and ridges are prone to
extremely high winds and this significantly
adds to the cold. For example, on a 5000m
pass in central Tibet in July, the absolute
minimum temperature is roughly -4°C, but
regularly occurring 70km/h winds plunge
the wind-chill factor or apparent temperature to -20°C.

RESPONSIBLE TREKKING

Tibet is one of the great unspoiled wildernesses left on earth. Please consider the following tips when trekking and help preserve the unique ecology and beauty of this fragile region.

Fires & Cooking

Building fires is not an option. Wood is non-existent in much of Tibet and where there are trees and bushes they are often scarce resources needed by locals. Cook on a lightweight kerosene, petrol, alcohol or multifuel stove and avoid those powered by disposable butane gas canisters.

If you are trekking with a guide and porters, supply stoves for the whole team. In alpine areas, ensure that all members are outfitted with enough clothing so that fires are not needed for warmth.

Rubbish

Carry out all your rubbish. Don't overlook easily forgotten items such as silver paper, orange peel, cigarette butts and plastic wrappers. Empty packaging weighs very little and should be stored in a dedicated rubbish bag. Gain good karma by carrying out rubbish left by others.

Never bury your rubbish: digging disturbs soil and ground cover and encourages erosion. Buried rubbish will more than likely be dug up by animals, which may be injured or poisoned by it. Moreover, it may take years to decompose, especially at Tibet's high altitudes.

Minimise the waste you must carry out by taking minimal packaging and taking no more than you will need. If you can't buy in bulk, unpack small-portion packages and combine their contents in one container before your trek. Take reusable containers, zip-lock bags or stuff sacks.

In Tibet it is not a good idea to burn plastic and other garbage as this is believed to irritate mountain spirits and affronts the sensibilities of more traditional Tibetans.

Sanitary napkins, tampons and condoms should also be carried out despite the inconvenience. They burn and decompose poorly.

Toilets

Where there is a toilet, please use it. Where there is none, human waste should be left on the surface of the ground away from trails,

water and habitations to decompose. Aridity, cold and high ultraviolet exposure renders wastes into innocuous compounds relatively quickly.

If you are in a large trekking group, dig a privy pit. Be sure to build it far from any water source or marshy ground and carefully rehabilitate the area when you leave camp. Pieces of turf, rocks and soil removed from the hole can be used to cap it. Also, be certain that the latrine is not near *mani* (prayer) walls, shrines or any other sacred structures. Encourage all party members, including porters, to use the site.

Washing

Don't use detergents or toothpaste in or near watercourses, even if they are biodegradable. For personal washing, use biodegradable soap and a water container (or even a lightweight, portable basin) at least 50m away from the watercourse. Widely disperse the waste water to allow the soil to filter it fully before it finally makes it back to the watercourse.

Wash cooking utensils 50m from watercourses using a scourer, sand or snow instead of detergent.

Erosion

Hillsides and mountain slopes, especially at high altitude, are prone to erosion. It is important to stick to existing tracks and avoid short cuts that bypass a switchback. If you blaze a new trail straight down a slope it will turn into a watercourse with the next heavy rainfall and eventually cause soil loss and deep scarring.

If a well-used track passes through a mud patch, walk through the mud: walking around the edge will increase the size of the patch.

Avoid removing the plant life that keeps topsoil in place.

Camping

Seek permission to camp from landowners. They will usually be happy to grant permission if asked, but may be confrontational if not.

TREKKING

Trekkers are particularly at risk from acute mountain sickness (AMS; also known as altitude sickness). For information on this vital subject, see p329.

GUIDES & PACK ANIMALS

The rugged terrain, long distances and high elevations of Tibet make most people think twice about carrying their own gear. In villages and nomad camps along the main trekking routes it is often possible to hire yaks to do the dirty work for you. Even on less-travelled routes you might find help.

You will need to know some Tibetan to negotiate what you want and how much you are willing to pay. Be prepared for a good session of bargaining and don't set out until you and the Tibetans working for you are perfectly clear about what's been agreed. To avoid any misunderstandings, be sure to spell out the amount of time you expect from your helpers and the exact amount you intend to pay. Your mule skinner or yak driver will also serve as your guide, an important asset on the unmarked trails of Tibet. Consider just hiring a guide if you don't want or can't get pack animals – this could save you a lot of frustrating hours looking for the route.

Guides can also share their knowledge of the natural history and culture of the place, greatly adding to your experience. Even large trekking companies depend on local guides to make their trips work.

FOOD

You should be self-sufficient in food since there isn't much to eat along the trail. In most of the villages there is little or no food surplus and thus probably nothing to buy. But there is no need to worry about supplies; in Lhasa there are now thousands of stalls and stores selling a huge variety of foodstuffs, making well-balanced, tasty meals possible on the trail. Even in Shigatse and the smaller cities there are many foods suitable for trekking.

Vacuum-packed red meat and poultry, and packaged dried meat and fish are readily found in Lhasa. Plenty of varieties of packaged and bulk dried fruits are sold throughout the city. The newest and tastiest offerings are figs and pineapples, which make a great and tasty trail mix combined

with peanuts and walnuts. You can even find almonds and pistachios imported from the USA.

Soybean- and dairy-milk powders can be used with several kinds of prepackaged cereals. Pickled and dried vegetables are good for dressing up soups and stir-fries. On the Barkhor are stalls selling Indian pickles and curry powders for an added touch. Lightweight vegetables such as bok choy and dried mushrooms can do wonders for macaroni and instant noodles, both of which are readily available.

Cooking mediums include butter, margarine, vegetable oil and sesame oil. Butter can be preserved for long treks or old butter made more palatable by turning it into ghee (boil for about 20 minutes and then strain). For those with a sweet tooth, all kinds of biscuits and sweets are sold in Lhasa and the larger regional towns. Decent-quality Chinese and Western chocolate is available in Lhasa.

DRINK

As wonderfully cold and clear as much of the water in Tibet is, do not assume that it's safe to drink. Livestock contaminate many of the water sources and Tibetans do not always live up to their cultural ideals. Giardia is common in Tibet and can slow your trek to a crawl.

To protect your health, you should treat all water before drinking by using chemical or filtration methods or by boiling it for at least 10 minutes. For added protection, more than one method can be used in tandem. If you plan to rely on chemical purification, bring your supply from home so that you know how to use it. For more information see p332.

Follow Tibetan tradition and eliminate the monotony of drinking plain water by downing as much tea as you can. You can buy Chinese green tea in virtually every city and town in Tibet.

Consider staying clear of *chang* (Tibetan barley beer), which is made with untreated water, but give yak-butter tea a try. More like a soup than a tea, it helps fortify you against the cold and replenishes the body's salts. If you are offered tea, have it served in your own cup as per tradition – this eliminates the risk associated with drinking from used cups.

OVERVIEW OF TREKS

Trek	Days	Distance	Passes	Description
Ganden to Samye	4–5	80 km	Shug-la (5250m), Chitu-la (5100m)	medium to difficult – the most popular trek in Tibet, connecting two of its most important monasteries
Tsurphu to Yangpachen	3–4	55 km	Lasar-la (5300m)	medium to difficult – gives a good insight into the lives of Tibet's seminomadic herders
Shalu to Nartang	2–3	40 km	Showa-la (4200m), Char-la (4600m)	moderate – easy access and relatively low passes make this a good beginners' trek
Everest Base Camp to Tingri	3–4	60 km	Geu-la (5170m) or Pang-la (5200m)	medium to difficult – an adventurous exit route if you drive to Everest Base Camp
Mt Kailash Kora	3	52 km	Drölma-la (5630m)	medium to difficult – one of Tibet's holiest pilgrimage treks
Lake Manasarovar Kora	4–5	110 km	4680m	difficult – a most sacred and beautiful lake, with a shore dotted with monasteries.

TREKKING ROUTES

Detailed descriptions of six popular treks are given here. They offer fantastic walking, superb scenery and, with the exception of Lake Manasarovar and Mt Kailash, are close to Lhasa or the Friendship Hwy. Walking times given are just that; they don't include breaks, nature stops or any other off-your-feet activities. On average, plan to walk five or seven hours at most in a day, interspersed with frequent short rests. You will also need time to set up camp, cook and just plain enjoy yourself.

The trek stages can be used as a daily itinerary but plan ahead to avoid spending the night at the highest point reached in the day.

The directions 'right' and 'left' given in the following descriptions of the routes always correspond with the direction you are travelling.

GANDEN TO SAMYE

This trek has much to offer: lakes, beautiful alpine forests and meadows, as well as two centres of Tibetan religious culture. With so much to offer, its popularity is understandable, but you should not underestimate the trek. Only those with experience hiking and

camping in higher-elevation wildernesses should attempt this trek alone. Otherwise, it makes good sense to join with an organised tour.

The best time for the trek is from mid-May to mid-October. Summer can be wet but the mountains are at their greenest and wild flowers spangle the alpine meadows. Barring heavy snow, it is also possible for those with a lot of trekking experience and the right gear to do this trek in the colder months. If you are coming straight from

THE TREK AT A GLANCE

Duration 4–5 days
Distance 80km
Standard medium to difficult
Start Ganden Monastery
Finish Samye Monastery
Highest Point Shug-la (5250m)
Nearest Large Towns Lhasa and Tsetang
Accommodation camping
Public Transport bus
Summary This demanding trek crosses two passes over 5000m, connects two of Tibet's most important monasteries and begins less than 50km from Lhasa. It has emerged as the most popular trek in the Ü region.

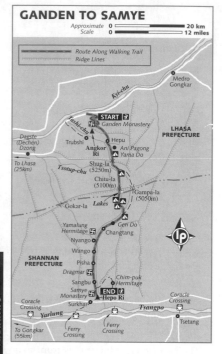

GANDEN TO SAMYE

Approximate Scale
0 —————— 20 km
0 —————— 12 miles

••••••• Route Along Walking Trail
Ridge Lines

Kyi-chu

Medro
Gongkar

START
Ganden Monastery

LHASA
PREFECTURE

Dagste
(Dechen)
Dzong

Trubshi

Hepu

Ani Pagong
Yama Do

Angkor
Ri

To Lhasa
(25km)

Tsotup-chu

Shug-la
(5250m)

Chitu-la
(5100m)

Gampa-la
(5050m)

Gokar-la

Lakes

Yamalung
Hermitage

Gen Do
Changtang

Nyango

Wango

Pisha

SHANNAN
PREFECTURE

Dragmar

Sangbu

Chim-puk
Hermitage

Samye
Monastery

END
Hepo Ri

Coracle
Crossing

Surkhar

Tsangpo

Coracle
Crossing

Yarlung

Tsetang

To Gongkar
(55km)

Ferry
Crossing

Ferry
Crossing

Lhasa you will need to spend a couple of nights at Ganden Monastery (4500m) to acclimatise.

Public buses run between Lhasa and Ganden (see p126), and between Lhasa and the Samye ferry crossing (see p149).

Stage 1: Ganden to Yama Do

5–6 hours, 17km / 300m ascent / 450m descent

The trek begins from the parking lot at the base of Ganden Monastery. Leave the parking lot and look for the well-trodden trail heading south along the side of Angkor Ri, the highest point on the Ganden kora. The trail gradually ascends for 1½ hours before reaching a saddle. Near the saddle, the trail comes close to the top of the ridge marked by cairns. The **saddle** itself is marked by a *lapse* (cairn) 2m tall and 3m in diameter.

From the saddle, look west down the Kyi-chu Valley to Lhasa. Traversing the west side of the ridge from the saddle, the trail reaches a spur surmounted by a cairn after 30 minutes. The trail now descends towards Hepu village. Twenty minutes from the spur is a

spring. From here it is a further 30 minutes to the village.

There are around 30 houses in the village of **Hepu** and it is possible for trekkers to camp or find accommodation among the friendly locals.

If carrying your gear up the pass beyond Hepu is not a pleasant thought, you might be able to rent yaks to do the work for you. Villagers charge around Y50 per yak per day, plus the salary of the yak herder, which is also approximately Y50 per day. You will also have to pay half-charges for the time it takes the yaks and herder to return home. Usually, herders feed themselves and provide their own camping gear, but make this clear before you set out. Intimately familiar with the environment, these people know how to make themselves at home on the trail. A yak can carry two or three backpacks, depending on their weight. Yak herders will load the beasts lightly to maximise their income and save wear and tear on the animals.

Finding a person willing to accompany your party all the way to Samye is not easy. You may have to settle for the summit of the first or second pass, which is a big help. If you don't get yaks all the way, you might find others at a herders' camp further along but this not a sure bet. It you have no luck in Hepu try down valley in the nearby village of Trubshi.

From Hepu, the trail climbs towards the Shug-la, 3½ hours away. Look for a red-and-yellow masonry structure and white incense hearths at the edge of the village. This is the **shrine** of Hepu's *yul lha* (local protecting deity), the Divine White Yak. Go east from here and look for the bridge crossing the Tashi-chu, which runs below the village. Outside of summer you can also easily ford this stream to the west bank. Head down the valley for a few minutes to the confluence with another stream. Round the inner side of the confluence and head upstream along the east bank. You are now following the watercourse originating from the Shug-la. Near the confluence are good camp sites.

One hour from Hepu you reach **Ani Pagong**, a narrow, craggy bottleneck in the valley. A small nunnery used to be above the trail. From Ani Pagong, the trail steadily climbs for one hour through marshy meadows to **Yama Do**.

Yama Do offers extensive camp sites suitable for larger groups. Consider spending the night here as it is still a long way to the pass.

Stage 2: Yama Do to Tsotup-chu Valley

5–7 hours / 10km / 1000m ascent / 450m descent

Above Yama Do the valley's watercourse splits into three branches. Follow the central or south branch, not the southeast or southwest branches. The route leaves the flank of the valley and follows the valley bottom. Beyond Yama Do the trail becomes indistinct but it is a straight shot up to the pass. Thirty minutes from Yama Do are two single-tent camp sites, the last good ones until the other side of the pass, at least five hours away. One hour past Yama Do leave the valley floor and ascend a shelf on the east (left) side of the valley to avoid a steep gully that forms around the stream. In another 45 minutes you enter a wet alpine basin studded with tussock grass. Because of the unsuitable terrain, you should only consider camping here in an emergency.

The Shug-la is at least 1¼ hours from the basin. Remain on the east side of the valley as it bends to the left. You have to negotiate boulders and lumpy ground along the final steep climb to the pass. The **Shug-la** (5250m) cannot be seen until you're virtually on top of it. It is marked by a large cairn covered in prayer flags and yak horns.

The route continues over the Shug-la and descends sharply through a boulder field, losing 200m of elevation. Be on the lookout for a clear trail marked by cairns on the left side of the boulder field. This trail traverses the ridge in a southeasterly direction, paralleling the valley below. Do not head directly down to the valley from the pass unless you have good reason. It is a long, steep descent and once at the bottom you would have to go back up the valley to complete the trek. Retreat down the valley for a bolt hole back to the Lhasa–Ganden Hwy, a long day of walking away. The bolt hole is a direct and relatively easy way back to civilization down a long gently inclined valley.

The trail gradually descends to reach the valley floor, 1½ hours from the pass. Cross the large Tsotup-chu, which flows through the valley. During heavy summer rains, take special care to find a safe ford. The pastures in the area support large herds of

yaks, goats and sheep, and during the trekking season herders are often camped here. This is an ideal place to camp and meet the *drokpas* (nomads). It is a two- to 2½-hour walk from the stream ford to the second pass, the Chitu-la, and at least 1¼ more hours to the first camp site from the ford.

An alternative route to Samye via the **Gampa la** (5050m) follows the main branch of the Tsotup-chu past a couple of lakes to the pass. South of the Gampa-la the trail plunges into a gorge, crisscrossing the stream that flows down from it. These fords may pose problems during summer rains or when completely frozen. See Gary McCue's *Trekking in Tibet – A Traveler's Guide* for details of this route.

Stage 3: Tsotup-chu Valley to Herders' Camps

5 hours, 14km / 300m ascent / 400m descent

From the Tsotup-chu ford, the main watercourse flows from the southeast and a minor tributary enters from the southwest. Follow this tributary (which quickly disappears underground) steeply up for about 30 minutes until you reach a large basin. Stay on the west (right) side of the basin and turn into the first side valley opening on the right. Follow this broad valley, which soon arcs south to the Chitu-la. The pass can be seen in the distance, a rocky rampart at the head of the valley. At first, stay on the west (right) side of the valley; there is a small trail. As you approach the pass, the trail switches to the east side of the valley. If you miss the trail just look for the easiest route up; the terrain is not particularly difficult.

The **Chitu-la** (5100m) is topped by several cairns. Also on the pass is a small glacial cairn. Move to the west side of the pass to find the trail down and to circumvent a sheer rock wall on its south flank. A short but steep descent will bring you into a basin with three small lakes. The trail skirts the west side of the lakes. It takes 45 minutes to reach the south end of the basin. Drop down from the basin on the west side of the stream and in 30 minutes you will hit the first place to set up camp. Herders have carved out level places for their tents here.

Below the herders' highest camp, the valley is squeezed in by vertical rock walls, forcing you to pick your way through the rock-strewn valley floor. There is no trail in this gorge and the descent is very steep. In about 20 minutes, cross over to the west (right) side of the widening valley to recover the trail. In 10 more minutes you will come to a flat and a seasonal **herders' camp** on the east side of the valley, good for camping. At the lower end of the flat, return to the west side of the valley. The trail again disappears as it enters a scrub willow and rosebush forest but there is only one way to go to get to Samye and that is downstream.

In 15 minutes, when a tributary valley enters from the right, cross to the east side of the valley. Fifteen minutes further, you will reach another seasonal **herders' camp**, inhabited for only a short time each year. Another 15 minutes beyond this camp, hop back to the west bank to avoid a cliff hugging the opposite side of the stream. Pass through a large meadow and ford the stream back to the east bank. From this point the trail remains on the east side of the valley for several hours.

Camp sites, some of which can cater for large groups, are numerous. Soon, the trail crosses the stream draining the valley coming from the Gampa-la. At times of heavy summer rain you might not be able to ford this stream. If so, you will have no alternative but to wait for the water to subside.

Stages 4 & 5: Herders' Camps to Samye Monastery

10 hours / 39km / 1200m descent

The trail is now wide and easy to follow as it traces a course down the east side of the valley. Walk through the thickening scrub forest for one hour and you will come to another stream entering from the east side of the main valley. Look for a small wood-and-stone bridge 200m above the confluence. The valley now bends to the right and the trail enters the thickest and tallest part of the scrub forest. The right combination of elevation, moisture and aspect create a verdant environment, while just a few kilometres away desert conditions prevail.

The next three-hour stretch of the trail is among the most delightful parts of the entire trek. According to local woodcutters, more than 15 types of trees and shrubs are found here, some growing to as high as 6m. Fragrant junipers grow on exposed southern slopes while rhododendrons prefer the shadier slopes. The rhododendrons start to bloom in early May and by the end of the month the forest is ablaze with pink and white blossoms.

The trail winds through a series of meadows. In one hour look for a ruined stone structure at a place known as Gen Do. Nearby is a **shrine** to the protector of the area, the ancient goddess Dorje Yudronma. Just past the shrine, cross a small tributary stream. In one hour the forest rapidly thins and **Changtang**, the first permanent village since Hepu, pops up. Named after the northern plains of Tibet, its inhabitants are predominantly engaged in animal husbandry, just like their northern counterparts. Although the villagers are friendly enough, the village is infested with fierce dogs, which fortunately are usually tied up.

Look south to the distant mountains; this is the range on the far side of the Yarlung Tsangpo Valley. Forty five minutes down the valley is the turn-off for the **Yamalung Hermitage**. Look for a field of small cairns to the right of the trail pointing towards a bridge over the valley stream. It is nearly a one-hour steep climb to the hermitage. Group members not interested in making the climb can wait near the bridge with the group's gear. Yamalung (also called Emalung) is where Guru Rinpoche is said to have meditated and received empowerment from the long-life deity Tsepame (Amitayus).

The hermitage consists of several small temples, and a few meditators live here. Below the temple complex is a sacred spring and an old relief carving in stone of Guru Rinpoche, King Trisong Detsen and the Indian scholar Shantarakshita, all of whom lived in the 8th century. The cave Guru Rinpoche meditated in is enshrined by the Drup Pug Mara Titsang Temple. Inside are the footprint and handprint of the saint, said to have been created when he magically expanded the size of the cave.

From the turn-off to Yamalung the trail becomes a motorable track and the valley much wider. In 15 minutes you will reach a bridge; the trail now remains on the west (right) side of the valley all the way to Samye, a 3½-hour walk away. Twenty minutes from the bridge you will come to the village of **Nyango** with its substantially built stone houses. A big tributary stream, entering from the northwest, joins the Samye Valley here.

The old trade route from Lhasa to Samye via the Gokar-la follows this valley. In the lower half of Nyango are four small shops selling soda, cigarettes and, maybe, basic food supplies such as instant noodles. If you are looking for a place to doss down, ask the shopkeepers; they might oblige you.

Thirty minutes past Nyango is the village of Wango and, an hour beyond it, the hamlet of Pisha. En route there are several meadows in which you can set up camp.

From the lower end of Pisha, a hill can be seen in the middle of the mouth of the Samye Valley. This is Hepo Ri (p151), one of Tibet's most sacred mountains. The entire lower Samye Valley – a tapestry of fields, woods and villages – can be seen from Pisha. Pisha is the last place that water can be conveniently drawn from the river. From here on, the trail only intersects irrigation ditches.

Fifteen minutes past Pisha a ridge spur called Dragmar meets the trail. On the summit is the partially rebuilt **palace** where King Trisong Detsen is said to have been born. Formerly a lavish temple, it now stands empty. Below, just off the road, is a small red-and-white **temple** enshrining the stump of an ancient tree. Legend has it that a red-and-white sandalwood tree grew here, nourished by the buried placenta of Trisong Detsen. During the Cultural Revolution the tree was chopped down.

Twenty minutes further down the trail is Sangbu village, from where there are good views of the golden spires of Samye. The route follows the Land Cruiser track direct to Samye along the margin of woods and desert; it takes about one hour. Use the shiny temple roof as your beacon. The closer you get to Samye the hotter the valley can become; in May and June it can even be fiery hot. If the heat gets too much, flee to the stands of willows and poplars not far from the road. The gilt roofs get ever brighter as you approach the monastery. You will reach **Samye** 10 minutes after passing inside the monastery's perimeter wall.

If you can't catch a lift you are in for about a two-hour walk from Samye to the ferry crossing. One day's walk down the Yarlung Tsangpo Valley at Tsetang, or six hours upstream from Samye, are alternative ferry crossings using traditional Tibetan leather coracles. If you don't have a travel permit for Samye, authorities can be eluded

at these other crossings but the route is through extremely harsh sand-dune country. It is probably better to give them a miss unless your party is prepared for full-blown desert conditions.

TSURPHU TO YANGPACHEN

Beginning at Tsurphu Monastery, this rugged walk crosses several alpine valleys before emerging into the broad and windswept Yangpachen Valley. This is a high-elevation trek exceeding 4400m for the duration. Combining alpine tundra and sweeping mountain panoramas with visits to monasteries and a nunnery, this trek nicely balances cultural and wilderness activities.

The best time for this walk is from mid-April to mid-October. Summer can be rainy but be prepared for snow at any time. As you will be in nomad country, beware of vicious dogs, some of which take a sadistic pride in chasing hapless foreigners. Fuel and food are not available so come prepared. There are few permanent settlements along the way and the inhabitants are often away from home, so don't count on these places to provide accommodation. Your only option on this trek is to be fully self-sufficient.

Tsurphu Monastery (4500m) is a good place to spend a couple of nights acclimatising. Two kilometres downstream from Tsurphu, beside the Karmapa's summer palace, is a small copse that is ideal for camping. Some of the area's herders spend a lot of time at the monastery so this is a good place to start looking for guides and yaks.

TREKKING

THE TREK AT A GLANCE

Duration 3–4 days
Distance 55km
Standard medium to difficult
Start Tsurphu Monastery
Finish Yangpachen Monastery
Highest Point Lasar-la (5300m)
Nearest Large Town Lhasa
Accommodation camping
Public Transport pilgrim buses
Summary An excellent choice for those who want to get a close look at the lifestyle of the *drokpas* (nomads). Although they have permanent winter homes they spend much of the year camping with their animals.

TSURPHU TO YANGPACHEN

Approximate Scale 0 — 20 km
0 — 12 miles

Route Along
Walking Trail
Ridge Lines

Nyenchen Tanglha Range

To Damshung (50km)

Hot Springs

Yangpachen Monastery **END**

To Shigatse (245km)

Nyango-chu

Yangpachen Valley

Yangpachen

Brize

Ngangkar

Dechen

Dorje Ling Nunnery

Tajung

Bartso

Lasar-la (5300m)

Damchen Nyingtri

Leten

Shupshading **START**

Tsurphu Monastery

Karmapa Lingka

Mang

Railway Line Under Construction (Estimated Completion 2007)

To Lhasa (35km)

TREKKING

However, Tsurphu is often crawling with police; if it is, you'd better head up valley before letting your plans be known.

Minibuses leave the Barkhor in Lhasa daily between 7am and 8am for Tsurphu (Y15, 2½ hours). Minibuses to Yangpachen (Y25, three hours) depart from the office of the Civil Aviation Authority of China (CAAC) in Lhasa. Lhasa–Nagchu minibuses also pass through Yangpachen.

Stage 1: Tsurphu Monastery to Leten
3½–4 hours / 11km / 500m ascent

The trek begins by heading west or up the valley. Follow the kora trail 20 minutes west to a walled copse of old trees with a brook. This garden-like wood is used by the monks in the summer so ask permission before you set up camp. The trees here are the last you will see until after finishing the trek. Just above the copse, the valley splits: follow the northwest branch and remain on the north side of the stream.

Forty five minutes of walking through a rocky chasm along a well-graded trail brings you to **Shupshading**, a herders' camp on a shelf above the trail. If you are looking for yaks to carry your equipment, ask the herders here. The valley remains narrow above Shupshading and is often engulfed with ice left from winter. After 30 minutes cross a seasonal stream coming from the northwest (right). Soon the trail switches over to the south (left) side of the valley. Forty five minutes on, the trail forks. The left branch switches

back up the ridge south of the valley and then traverses west into the *drokpa* settlement of **Leten** (5000m). Although you want to go here, take the right fork that follows the valley floor – this is a more straightforward route to Leten, about 1½ hours away.

Leten is divided by the stream running through it. Several families live here permanently, braving the severe climate with their livestock. Leten is the last chance to find yaks and a guide, both of which are highly recommended because the route to and from the Lasar-la is not easy to find.

Spend one or, preferably, two days in Leten acclimatising.

Stage 2: Leten to Bartso
5–6 hours / 15km / 300m ascent / 600m descent

It is around a three-hour walk from Leten to the Lasar-la. Head for the northern half of the settlement (assuming you aren't already there). The route climbs steeply up the north side of the Leten Valley, reaching the highest house. Bear northwest into a steep side valley. As you ascend, a reddish knob of rock looms up ahead. Angle to the north, or right, of this formation and leave the valley by climbing to the top of a spur marked by three cairns. It is a 45-minute walk to here from Leten. This spur, called **Damchen Nyingtri**, is holy to the god ruling the environs.

As per Buddhist tradition, stay to the left of the cairns crowning Damchen Nyingtri and descend sharply into a narrow valley. Once on the valley bottom, cross to the east (right) side of the stream and strike out north (up the valley). In 15 minutes the valley forks: follow the north (right) branch. Cross back to the left side of the stream as the terrain here is easier to traipse over. Walk up the widening valley through arctic-like mounds of tundra for one hour, following a minor trail. Then, as the valley turns west, look for a cairn on the opposite bank of the stream.

Using this cairn as a marker, bear northwestwars over an inclined plain. This plain parallels the valley floor before the two merge. Continue ascending as the plain opens wider in the direction of the pass. There is no clear trail to follow but favour the west side of the plain; the east side spills down into another valley system. The **Lasar-la** (5300m) is a broad gap at the highest point in the plain and is heralded by cairns lining the final approach.

From the Lasar-la there is a steep descent into a north-running valley. A trail can be found on the east (right) side of this valley. In a few minutes the grade levels out and the trail crosses the stream bed and continues down the west side of the valley. There are many possible camp sites between the Lasar la and Bartso.

As the trail descends, you peer into the expansive Yangpachen Valley, a broad plain laced with streams, that then opens up in front of the Nyenchen Tanglha (Tangula) Range to the north. This range is part of the trans-Himalaya, which circumscribes the plateau, dividing southern Tibet from the Changtang.

The Yangpachen Valley is covered with hummocks but there is a trail that avoids the ups and downs of these mounds of turf and earth. About an hour from the pass a break in the ridge running along the eastern side of the valley comes into view. The break coincides with a big westward bend in the valley. As soon as you spot this interruption in the ridge line, ford the stream and traverse up to the right into a side valley. Heading north, the valley soon gives way to a plain paved with big plates of tundra.

There are superb views of the mountains surrounding the valley along this stretch of the walk. In the north is Brize, which is a heavily glaciated peak enclosing the south side of the Yangpachen Valley, and towards the west is a distinctive pinnacle named Tarze. Brize, meaning 'female-yak herder', and Tarze, 'horse keeper', are just two of many topographical features in a mythical society ruled by the mountain god Nyenchen Tanglha. These two mountains make convenient landmarks for trekkers as you go against the grain by heading north over a series of drainage systems that run from east to west.

In one hour the trail intersects an east–west valley at the settlement of **Bartso**. This *drokpa* village of five homes with a permanent sources of water is a good place to camp. The slopes around the village are still covered in juniper. In the 1960s and '70s huge amounts of this valuable bush were extracted from the region and trucked to Lhasa to feed the hearths of the new provincial city.

Stage 3: Bartso to Dorje Ling Nunnery
3½–4 hours / 15km / 150m ascent / 150m descent

Look northwest from Bartso to the opposite side of the valley. Clearly visible, a wide trail winds up from the valley to the top of the ridge. Ford the valley stream and make for this trail, 25 minutes' walk over marshy ground from Bartso. It is another half-hour to the summit of the ridge. From the top you'll see a saddle north of an intervening valley. On the far side of this saddle is Dorje Ling Nunnery, still over 2½ hours away.

Views of Nyenchen Tanglha, the 7111m mountain that gives its name to the range, are fantastic from here. This huge massif has a quite distinctive flat summit. Nyenchen Tanglha is the holiest mountain in central Tibet and is said to be inhabited by a god of the same name. Envisioned as a regal white warrior on a white horse, his half-smile, half-grimace symbolises both the benevolent and destructive sides of his personality.

From the saddle, drop down to the valley in about 25 minutes to the village of **Tajung**. Stay to the left of the 14 whitewashed houses and ford the stream below the village. Bear northeastwards into the parting in the ridge and, after a few minutes, cross a low saddle. Continue going northeast in the direction of Brize until a large dip appears in the hills to the west, 40 minutes from Tajung. Leave the trail going towards Brize and head to the right of the dip cross-country. Traverse to the right of the low point in the ridge, remaining high enough to avoid the highest part of the east–west ridge that is looming up ahead. If you have gained enough height, you will be able to see a group of white houses at the base of a hill to the northwest. The Dorje Ling Nunnery is just downstream of here.

A 25 minute traverse will bring you to a stream at the base of the ridge, aligned east to west. A broad trail appears on the north bank of the stream. Follow it to the top of the ridge. From this point, you'll have good views of the village just upstream of Dorje Ling Nunnery. The nunnery, which is out of view, sits at the bottom of a rock outcrop visible from the ridge top.

During winter, you can strike out across a swamp that fills the valley to go directly to Dorje Ling, reaching it in just 30 minutes. Otherwise, you will have to take the long way around and skirt the north edge of the swamp to reach the north side of the Dorje Ling Valley. This longer route requires at least an hour of hiking. There's a motorable road on the far side of the valley and the nunnery is only 10 minutes from here.

The centrepiece of this friendly **nunnery** is a red *lhakhang* (chapel) in the midst of a group of little white houses. The *lhakhang* is very simply decorated, reflecting the modest means of the 52 nuns who call this place their home. A concerted effort is under way to build a house for all of them. The nuns are quite happy to show visitors around the nunnery and donations are most welcome. Without them, reconstruction and maintenance of the nunnery is not possible.

Good camping is found in the meadows around Dorje Ling.

Stage 4: Dorje Ling Nunnery to Yangpachen Monastery
3½–4½ hours / 14km / mostly level

From Dorje Ling, follow the motorable road west, or downstream. In 15 minutes the road crosses to the south bank of the stream and soon forks. Take the right fork over the small concrete bridge and continue along the track down the east bank of the stream. Forty five minutes from Dorje Ling the valley drains into the spacious Yangpachen Valley. Stay on the same track, which turns into a motorable road as it runs north, paralleling the course of the Nyango-chu, which drains the upper Yangpachen Valley. The road stays close to the east bank of the river, skirting meadows that afford fantastic camping and encompassing views of the trans-Himalaya.

Once entering the Nyango drainage area it is an easy two-hour walk to a steel bridge spanning the river. Cross over the bridge to join up with the northern road to Shigatse. Walk northwards on the road for about 15 minutes, suddenly coming to the **Yangpachen Monastery**, at the end of a line of cliffs. Perched on top of a small hill on the left side of the road, the monastery overlooks a broad sweep of trans-Himalaya peaks. There are several trails leading from the road to the monastery but beware of the pack of dogs loitering around the grounds. The monastery was home to 115 monks, but many of them have fled to Rumtek Monastery in Sikkim. Yangpachen is headed by Shamar Rinpoche, a leading lama of the Kagyupa order, who is based in India. If you're in-

terested in seeing what Nyenchen Tanglha looks like, check out the mural in the inner vestibule of the main assembly hall. It depicts the god in several of his wrathful animal manifestations. Donations are expected should you want to visit the chapels.

From Yangpachen Monastery it is a 15km road journey to Yangpachen. If your luck holds you should be able to hitch there. The **hot-springs complex** (admission Y20), 7km west of Yangpachen, is great to ease your aching limbs. From here there are many minibuses back to Lhasa (three hours).

SHALU TO NARTANG

This trek begins at the historic Shalu Monastery (p179) and traverses west over a couple of small ranges to Ngor Monastery. From Ngor it is a downhill slog to Nartang Monastery. The route passes through several villages as well as uninhabited dry canyons. It is about a 10-hour walk to Ngor from Shalu, which is best divided into two days, and another five hours from there to Nartang. Finding guides and burros (yaks are not an option) to carry your gear is not easy but you can try in Shalu. If you can get local support, go for it, because the route is not always easy to discern – in the canyons the trail tends to peter out.

The optimal walking season is from the beginning of April to the end of October. In summer the trail can be sizzling hot, and in other months, cold and windy, so be prepared. One advantage of hiking in summer is that this region gets less rainfall than the Ü region.

THE TREK AT A GLANCE

Duration 2–3 days
Distance 40km
Standard medium
Start Shalu Monastery
Finish Nartang Monastery
Highest Point Char-la (4600m)
Nearest Large Town Shigatse
Accommodation camping
Public Transport bus
Summary This walk is a good opportunity to get a feel for trekking in Tibet. The two passes, Showa-la and Char-la, are not particularly high or difficult and the trailheads are easily accessible from Shigatse.

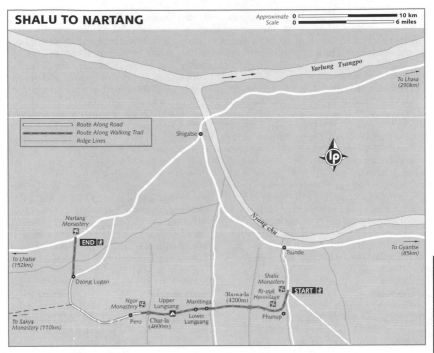

SHALU TO NARTANG

Approximate Scale

0 _____ 10 km
0 _____ 6 miles

Route Along Road
Route Along Walking Trail
Ridge Lines

Yarlung Tsangpo

To Lhasa (290km)

Shigatse

Nyang-chu

Nartang Monastery

END

To Lhatse (152km)

Tsunde

To Gyantse (85km)

Dzong Lugari

Shalu Monastery
Ri-puk Hermitage   **START**

Ngor Monastery   Upper Lungsang   Manitinga   Showa-la (4200m)

Pero   Chu-la (4600m)   Lower Lungsang   Phunup

To Sakya Monastery (110km)

For information on getting to Shalu, see p182. Lhatse–Shigatse minibuses travel the Friendship Hwy and pass near Nartang.

Stage 1: Shalu Monastery to Upper Lungsang

5½–6 hours / 14km / 250m ascent / 200m descent
From Shalu Monastery, walk the motorable road south (up the valley). Thirty minutes from Shalu you will pass by the **Ri-puk Hermitage**, set on a hillside on the west side of the valley. If you wish to visit, cut across the fields and head directly up to the hermitage – the way is not difficult and there are several trails leading up to it.

Forty five minutes from Shalu the road forks: take the south (right) fork. In the south, a conical-shaped hill and a village at its base can be made out. If you struck out in Shalu, stay on the road to this village, called Phunup, about a one-hour walk away, to look for a guide and pack animals. Otherwise, there is a short cut that saves 2km of walking. A few minutes from the fork in the road, look for the base of a long red ridge. Leave the road and skirt the base of this

ridge, going in a southerly direction. First cross a flood plain to reach a rectangular red shrine and, beyond it, enter a plain bounded in the south by the red ridge.

Gradually the trail climbs to a small white ridge blocking the route to the south. As you approach you will see white cairns marking its summit. Look for the trail that ascends to the cairns, a one-hour walk from the fork in the road. From the ridge's summit, Phunup village is to the left and the Showa la is to the west. The pass is the obvious low point in the range at least one hour away. The trail descends gradually to enter the stream bed coming from the Showa-la 30 minutes from the cairns. If you came via Phunup, your route will converge with the main trail here.

The climb up to the pass and the descent on the other side are through some heavily eroded, waterless ravines and slopes, or badlands. Bring plenty of drinking water. From the stream bed the trail soon climbs back up the right side of the valley only to drop back in and out of the stream bed in quick succession. Don't make the mistake of walking up the stream bed for you would soon encounter ledges and other difficult terrain. After twice briefly dropping into the narrow stream bed, be alert for a trail carving a route up the right slope. The trail climbs steeply to a group of ruins and then winds around to the pass in 30 minutes.

From the **Showa-la** (4200m), the second pass, Char-la, can be seen in the range of hills west of an intervening valley. It is the dip in the crest of the range. The easy-to-follow trail descends from the pass along the south (left) side of a ravine. In one hour you will reach the valley floor. Leave the trail when it crosses a small rise marked with cairns and continue west towards a distant group of trees. Cross over the sandy north–south valley, intersecting a road. Shigatse is about three hours north along this road.

The valley watercourse is dry except during summer flash floods. West of it is a **poplar and willow copse**, the only bit of shade in the area. Consider stopping here for lunch and a rest. From the copse, you enter a side valley, continuing in a westerly direction towards the Char-la. In a few minutes you will reach the village of Manitinga, on the southern margin of the valley, and pick up the main cart track going up the valley. The track passes through the village of Lower Lungsang and, one hour from the copse, crosses to the south side of the valley. You can glimpse the Char-la from here, which for most of the trek is hidden behind the folds in the mountains.

In 30 minutes you will reach **Upper Lungsang**. There is a fine old wood here ideal for camping and resting.

Stage 2: Upper Lungsang to Ngor Monastery

3½–4 hours / 8km / 550m ascent

From Upper Lungsang, then cross back to the northern side of the valley. The cart track does not extend past the village and the trail up to the pass may be difficult to find in places. If you are in doubt, try to hire a local person to show you the way. It is at least 2½ hours from Upper Lungsang to the Char-la. At first, the trail skirts the edge of a gravel wash. However, in 15 minutes a series of livestock tracks climb out of the stream bed and onto an eroded shelf that forms above it.

The terrain becomes more rugged and a gorge forms below the trail. There is a side stream and small **reservoir** 45 minutes above

Upper Lungsang. This is the last convenient place to collect water until over the pass. From the reservoir, the trail descends back to the stream bed but quickly exits the opposite side of the valley.

Look for a series of switchbacks on the southern (left) side of the gorge and then follow them up. A further fifteen minutes on, the trail crosses a gully and then another gully in 15 more minutes. The final leg to the pass is cross-country over a steep slope of raw expanses of rock. From the second gully, the Char-la can be reached in 45 minutes of steep uphill walking. At one time this trail was well maintained and formed a main trade link between Shalu and Sakya Monasteries but it has fallen into disrepair.

Eventually, cairns along the summit ridge come into focus. The pass is the obvious notch in the ridge line. From **Char-la** (4600m), mountain ranges stretch to the west across the horizon and Ngor Monastery is visible below. Ngor is a 45-minute downhill ramble from the pass. The route from the Char-la descends the south (left) side of a ravine that forms below it. Several trails cross the stream that flows from the pass and provide access to Ngor, but the first trail is the quickest route – it climbs the right side of the ravine and traverses directly to the monastery. Consider camping near Ngor (ask the monastery for permission and the best place to camp) and save the last five hours of walking for the next day, when you're rested.

Sakya master Ngorchen Kunga Sangpo founded **Ngor Monastery** in 1429, giving rise to the Ngorpa suborder, a distinctive school of Buddhist thought. Once an important centre of learning, Ngor used to boast four monastic estates and 18 residential units inhabited by about 340 monks. Only a small fraction of the monastery has been rebuilt. The most eye-catching feature has been a beautiful row of chörtens at the lower end of the complex dedicated to the eight victorious forms of the Buddha. The largest structure is the assembly hall, called the Gonshung. The outer walls of its gallery are painted in vertical red, white and blue stripes, a characteristic decorative technique used by the Sakya order. The three colours represent the Rigsum Gonpo, the three most important bodhisattvas. The present head of Ngor, Luding Khenpo, resides in northern India.

Stage 3: Ngor Monastery to Nartang Monastery

5 hours / 18km / 300m descent

From Ngor, a motorable road runs down the valley. Fifteen minutes from the monastery is the sizable village of Pero. Ninety minutes from Ngor the valley and road bend to the north while the old trade route to Sakya continues west over a saddle. Thirty minutes further, there is a copse at the edge of the flood plain that is good for fair-weather camping.

The road now swings to the west side of the wide alluvial valley and 30 minutes past the copse is the village of Dzong Lugari. The road exits the north side of the village and extends northeast for 10km before joining the Lhatse–Shigatse Hwy 10km southwest of Shigatse. The trail to Nartang Monastery, however, splits from the road on the northern outskirts of Dzong Lugari and heads north. From Dzong Lugari, it is at least a two-hour hike across a broad valley to Nartang.

The trail to Nartang crosses over a small stream and an electric utility line. The track tends to merge with a welter of agricultural trails and if you miss it, simply continue walking north. Soon the massive ramparts that surrounded the Nartang Monastery come into view. Just before arriving, cross the Lhatse–Shigatse Hwy, about 14km west of Shigatse. Donations are expected if you want to visit the chapels and famous printing presses at the **monastery**. For your physical needs, you will find several shops selling soft drinks and noodle soup on the roadside. It should be pretty easy to catch a ride from here to Shigatse.

EVEREST BASE CAMP TO TINGRI

This route passes through an isolated valley on the way up to the Nam-la and then enters a region used by herders and their livestock. Following the Ra-chu Valley, the route swings northwards to the plains of Tingri. It is also possible to do this trek in the opposite direction, one tiny advantage of which is that you may not be required to pay the fee of Y65 for entry to the Qomolangma Nature Preserve. If you get tired of trekking along the road you can always try to get a lift for part of the way. Four-wheel drives ply the route during the summer and there are also plenty of pony carts along the way if you want a brief respite from carrying your bag.

If you do decide to trek into Everest from Tingri by reversing the direction in this trek description it is usually possible to hire yaks, guides and even pony carts in Tingri, though if you want to keep a low profile it might be better to organise this in Ra Chu.

The trekking season in the Everest region extends from April to late October. This is a difficult high-elevation region with altitudes ranging between 4400m and 5300m, and the high point is at the beginning of the trek! Careful preparation and having the right gear are imperative. Subfreezing temperatures can occur even in summer at higher elevations and, conversely, hot gusty winds in May and June can make walking a sweaty experience. For well-equipped and seasoned walkers, winter treks to Everest Base Camp are often possible. Thanks to the rain shadow created by Mt Everest (Qomolangma) and its lofty neighbours, even the monsoon months are relatively dry in the region.

It is a very good idea to travel with a tent and stove despite there being a couple of restaurants and lodges on the route. These facilities are few and far between and the service rudimentary. The only way to ensure privacy and comfort is to have your home and hearth in your pack.

The trek via the Nam-la is the fastest route from Everest Base Camp to Tingri, but if you are short on supplies or not so well equipped consider one of the alternative passes covered in Gary McCue's *Trekking in Tibet – A Traveler's Guide*. The longer routes may be

---

THE TREK AT A GLANCE

Duration 3–4 days
Distance 60km
Standard medium to difficult
Start Everest Base Camp
Finish Tingri
Highest Point Nam-la (5250m)
Nearest Large Town Shigatse
Accommodation camping
Public Transport no
Summary If you drove to Everest Base Camp and are looking for an alternative exit route consider this trek to Tingri, crossing through remote country where it is essential to be self-sufficient. You may be able to buy some basic foodstuffs at the small shop at the Rongphu Monastery.

TREKKING

EVEREST BASE CAMP TO TINGRI

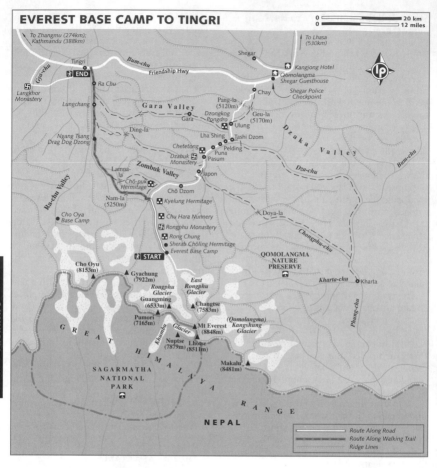

preferable because they follow more of the main road, reaching villages where supplies might be bought – but don't count on finding much. Once you leave Rongphu Monastery there are no permanent settlements until well in reach of Tingri, three days away. Such an untravelled route is great for those who are up to a wilderness experience but is best missed by everyone else. Don't chance this trip unless you are really ready.

Be aware that expeditions beyond Base Camp are only for those very experienced in trekking and mountaineering. It is all too easy, once you have reached Base Camp, to succumb to the temptation to push further up the mountains. Do not do it without adequate preparation. At the very least,

spend a couple of days acclimatising in the Rongphu area and doing day hikes to higher altitudes.

For highly fit and prepared groups it is possible to trek beyond Base Camp as far as Camp III. Including time for acclimatisation, you would need to allow at least one week for this trek. The route skirts the Rongphu Glacier until Camp I and then meets the East Rongphu Glacier at Camp II. This glacier must be crossed in order to reach Camp III (6340m). For information on reaching the advanced camps on the route, also see Gary McCue's book.

There is very little public transport in the region but it shouldn't be too difficult to get a lift along the Friendship Hwy to either the

DÉTENTE *John Vincent Bellezza*

Since the 1980s, accounts of unfriendly villagers, petty theft and stone throwing have come out of the Everest region. Such incidents have not helped relations between the local Tibetans and foreigners but the good news is that in recent years there seems to have been a drop in the number of incidents. While there are no excuses for bad behaviour, there are historical factors that have contributed to antisocial episodes.

Under the Chinese, the entire religious and civic infrastructure of the region was destroyed and never satisfactorily restored, creating many hardships in a particularly high, dry and poor area. In the early 1980s travellers and climbers started appearing in ever-greater numbers, and the majority of them spent little or no money locally. This marginalisation of the locals created ill will that continues to this day. While the locals are not antiforeigner, they are clamouring for a piece of the action. The Qomolangma Nature Preserve has begun to deliver on its promise of bettering lives, and this should give the people of the area a bigger piece of the economic pie.

With some goodwill and understanding on your part you should be able to pull off an unforgettable trip without any grief from local residents. A realisation is dawning among the Tibetans that working with tourists rather than repelling them is the best long-term strategy. Encourage this new attitude by patronising local services and businesses as much as possible and, as always, go that extra mile to make friends and gain insights into the workings of the Everest region.

turn-off to Everest (kilometre marker 5145) or Tingri. Hired Land Cruisers can go all the way to Everest Base Camp.

For additional information relating to the Everest region, including the Everest Base Camp, see p189.

Stage 1: Everest Base Camp to beyond the Nam-la

9½ hours / 27km / 450m ascent / 520m descent

Setting out downstream, the roadside meadows recede as the valley narrows between boulder-strewn slopes. A trail angles down a steep embankment from the road to the bridge. Cross the bridge and look for the trail along the west bank of the river. Soon the trail starts to ascend the embankment and emerges onto a shelf above the Dza-chu. In a few minutes the trail climbs further and traverses around the base of a slope to the mouth of a side valley. It takes 30 minutes to reach the mouth of this valley from the bridge.

While the majority of the Dzaka Valley is dry and barren, this side valley is relatively luxuriant, hosting a variety of plants and shrubs, and plenty of freshwater. This is a nice place to camp or take a long lunch break. The valley bends to the left as the trail to Nam-la leaves the valley floor and climbs past a corral onto a plain abutting the north (right) side of the val-

ley. The route to the pass now bears west all the way to the summit, paralleling the valley floor. It is at least a 3½-hour hike to reach the pass.

As you begin your ascent towards the pass there is a saddle in the ridge bounding the northern side of the valley – this is the most direct route to the Zombuk Valley. Walk close to the ridge enclosing the northern side of the valley. Past the corral there is no trail. The route clambers over rock-strewn shrubby terrain and then over big plates of tundra that fit together like a giant jigsaw puzzle. About one hour from the corral, a steep slope blocks the view to the west. It takes 10 minutes to climb over this onto another broad tundra-covered pitch. In 10 more minutes you will be able to see the head of the valley; however, the Nam-la is out of sight, tucked behind the folds in the ridge.

The route gradually levels out and in 15 minutes descends into a marshy side valley. There is a small stream in this valley, the last place you can count on for water until well beyond the pass. Look for a small corral on the far side of the side valley and bear to the left of it. Continue walking up for 10 minutes before gradually descending into the main valley floor in another 15 minutes.

Remain on the right side of the valley, taking the trail that steeply climbs towards

---

QOMOLANGMA NATURE PRESERVE

The Qomolangma Nature Preserve (QNP) was established in 1989 by the government of the Tibetan Autonomous Region to conserve the natural and cultural heritage of the Mt Everest region.

Bordering Nepal's Sagarmatha, Langtang and Makalu-Barun National Parks and their buffer zones, the 34,000-sq-km preserve is part of the only protected area to straddle both sides of the Himalaya. QNP's park managers hold regular exchanges with their counterparts in Nepal to share experiences and promote conservation cooperation across political boundaries.

More than 7000 foreign tourists visit the QNP each year, and their numbers are growing. The goal of the QNP is to encourage tourism and generate local benefits and employment while protecting the environment. Entry fees to core preserve areas are invested in maintaining access roads and controlling litter at major mountaineering and trekking camps.

Funding for various environmental and economic-development activities comes from national and regional governments. QNP also collaborates with a number of international organisations. The **Mountain Institute** (www.mountain.org; 1828 L Street NW, Suite 725, Washington DC 20036) is one such organisation; it supports QNP in conserving local environment and culture and improving village livelihoods through its multiyear Qomolangma Conservation Project (QCP).

In Tibet, you can get information on the project from **Christopher La Due** (☎ 891-636 4037; qcp@mountain.org; ste 1306, Lhasa Tashi Norbu Hotel, 24 South Tuanjie Xingcun Lane, Lhasa, TAR 850000), director of the institute's Peak Enterprise Program.

---

the pass. The trail remains clear for 40 minutes until it is absorbed by the tussock grass of the valley floor. The pass is near where the ridge south of the valley bends around to the west. It is still 40 minutes from here to the Nam-la over alpine meadows, but the terrain is now much more open and the gradient less steep.

Proceed west, looking out for the lowest point on the horizon. The **Nam-la** (5250m) is a very broad summit simply delineating the parting of drainage basins over a vast plain. There are a few small cairns on top of the pass, seen only when you are already upon them. Towards the west, and across a wide, wet, downhill slope, is a small valley and the Ra-chu Valley far beyond that. North of the Nam-la, with only a small summit in between, is the Lamna-la coming from the Zombuk Valley.

Descend from the pass in a westerly direction over tussock grasses and tundra for one hour, and cross the cart track coming from the Lamna-la. If the time is right you may see gazelles during your descent. From the cart track, descend a precipitous slope into the valley floor. There are both springs and a stream in this swampy valley of grasses and wild flowers, a tributary of the Ra-chu. Great camp sites are found on the drier margins of the valley. It is at least a five-hour trek from here to the first village, Lungchang.

Stage 2: Base of Nam-la to Lungchang
5–6 hours / 21km / 200m descent

Do not follow the valley down and northward. It is easier to walk in a westerly direction to the ridge next to the valley and pick up the cart track. You can see the cart track cutting across the ridge from a group of corrals on the west side of the valley. The track goes all the way to Tingri, making routefinding easy.

By tracing a northwest trajectory over the ridge the track avoids the swampy valley floor. Follow the cart track for 20 minutes, coming to a junction marked by a cairn. The foot trail to Lamna-la leaves the road here and goes east to intersect the valley. Leave the cart track and take the trail bearing northwest – this is a short cut that rejoins the main track in 15 minutes.

The short cut descends to cross the cart track and then merges with it after a switchback. Back on the valley floor, the track stays on the south (left) side of the valley, crossing a small stream coming in from the south. This unbridged crossing may pose some problems during heavy summer rains, in which case try to ford it during the early morning when the volume of water is lower.

The track angles across the middle of the stony valley and is very wide and straight, like a runway used by bush planes. In 30 minutes the track returns to the left side of the valley.

Fifteen minutes further, it passes through a narrow constriction in the valley formed by a series of orange cliffs. Beyond the cliffs the valley turns north (right) and retains this bearing all the way to Tingri. A few minutes after emerging through the bottleneck, look for a continuation of the track on the north bank of the stream. During summer rains it's best to carefully select a ford in the area a little downstream of the track crossing.

The view to the north is now dominated by the blue or purple Tsebu Mountains. Tingri is in front of these mountains, south of the Bum-chu. The mostly sandy track unfolds along the east (right) bank of the stream for 45 minutes. It then ascends above the bank and traverses the side of a ridge with the stream running through a narrow channel directly below. Look south to see the glittering white Cho Oyu massif. In 30 minutes descend into the widening valley floor. In 10 more minutes cross a small side valley.

The track unrolls over a level shelf above the stream for 30 minutes before climbing over a small ridge that circumvents the gorge forming below. Just upstream of the gorge, the stream you've been following from the base of the pass flows into the much higher-volume main branch of the Ra-chu, which originates from the flanks of Cho Oyu. The summit of the ridge is marked with a cairn and prayer flags and takes 10 minutes to reach from the shelf.

From the summit, the track descends to cross a side valley before ranging across a long and barren stretch of valley. In the distance you can see two rocky knobs at the end of the long east ridge line. It takes about one hour to reach the knobs. On top of them you will find the disintegrating walls of the long-abandoned fort known as **Ngang Tsang Drag Dog Dzong**. Thirty minutes after passing beneath the ramparts of the ancient fort you reach **Lungchang**, which is the first permanent settlement since Rongphu.

The cubicle two-storey houses of Lungchang are impeccably whitewashed and decorated with red, blue and white stripes near their roof lines. Blocks of dung are neatly stacked on the roofs between prayer-flag masts. At the northern end of the village, in one of the houses, is a small lodge and shop marked by a sign that reads 'Leg Jang'. Simple meals and beds are usually available here or with other families in the village.

Stage 3: Lungchang to Tingri
3½ hours / 12km / 150m descent

From Lungchang, you can see several low-lying hills in the mouth of the Ra-chu Valley: Tingri is at the foot of the northernmost of these. From Lungchang, the track moves towards the middle of the valley, following a bluff along the edge of the Ra-chu. In 1½ hours it reaches the outskirts of the village Ra Chu. Before the village, at a white shrine, the track splits: the right, or main, branch goes to Tingri via Ra Chu village, while the left fork jogs west and then north over wide pastures to Tingri. The left fork is the shorter route and is a more pleasant walk. The lower part of the Ra-chu Valley is green during the warmer half of the year; extensive meadows support flocks of goats and sheep. The homes of the shepherds dot the edges of the huge expanse of turf.

Fifteen minutes south of Ra Chu you will pass ruins on the slopes bounding the east side of the valley – look back to see Everest pop up from behind the anterior ranges. The two tracks that split near Ra Chu are reunited 45 minutes beyond the village.

Thirty minutes further on, you reach a bridge over the Ra-chu, which allows you to access the south side of Tingri. You can cross the Ra-chu here and pass through the village to the highway or remain on the right bank and cross the new highway bridge. It is only 15 minutes to the highway. If you stay on the right bank there is an irrigation ditch to cross below the shoulder of the highway.

For information on Tingri, see p192.

MT KAILASH KORA

See p210 for an introduction to Mt Kailash and the kora, as well as for further information on Darchen, the shabby little town where the walk starts and finishes.

The Kailash trekking season runs from mid-May until mid-October but trekkers should be prepared for changeable weather at any time. Snow may be encountered on the Drölma-la at any time of year and the temperature will often drop below freezing at night. The pass tends to be snowed in from early November to early April.

Darchen PSB requires all foreigners to buy a Y50 permit for the Kailash and Manasarovar region, even if you already have one from Lhasa. Some travellers have apparently

THE TREK AT A GLANCE

Duration 3 days
Distance 52km
Standard medium to difficult
Start/Finish Darchen
Highest Point Drölma-la (5630m)
Nearest Large Town Ali
Accommodation camping and monastery guesthouses
Public Transport bus
Summary The circuit, or kora, of Mt Kailash (6714m) is one of the most important pilgrimages in Asia. A religious sanctuary since pre-Buddhist times, a trek here wonderfully integrates the spiritual, cultural and physical dimensions of any trip to Tibet, which explains its growing attraction. Being able to meet pilgrims from across Tibet and other countries is one of the many allures of this walk.

been fined for spending the night at Manasarovar before heading to Darchen to buy the permit. Check with your tour agency or with the PSB at Darchen or Ali.

If you have a heavy load, or even if you don't, it is well worth considering hiring a porter or yaks; the Darchen guesthouses can help to make arrangements and store gear while you are on the kora. Porters are usually friendly young guys who know the circuit well and typically cost Y80 per day, perhaps less if you make arrangements yourself in the town. If you hire yaks and yak drivers, count on about Y120 per yak and another Y50 for each handler; yaks are skittish creatures and they require expert management. Allow a few days to organise the yaks.

Instant noodles and a very limited range of other supplies are available at the shops in Darchen. A wider range is available in Ali to the north and Purang to the south.

If you do not have a tent, the accommodation possibilities on the kora are very limited. There are primitive guesthouses associated with the Dira-puk and Zutul-puk Monasteries, but they only have a half-dozen rooms each. During the Indian pilgrimage season (June to early September), it may be possible to get a bed in the tents that are erected for the pilgrims near the two monasteries. Very limited food may

also be available at the guesthouses. If at all possible, you should bring a tent since there is no guarantee you will find a room free or a bed available in a pilgrim tent. If you are equipped for camping, however, there are wonderful grassy camp sites all around the kora and there is certainly no shortage of water. Fuel for cooking is another matter. There is no wood and even yak dung is in very short supply. In the busy Saga Dawa season a tent is a must.

Buses ply the route from Ali and Burang to Darchen; see p212 for relevant information about transport.

Stage 1: Darchen to Dira-puk Monastery
6 hours / 20km / 200m ascent
The Mt Kailash kora trail quickly leaves grubby Darchen behind, heading westward along the base of the east–west ridge, which blocks views of the holy mountain. The vast Barkha plain spreads out to the south, Gurla Mandata (7728m) rises to the southeast, Api and other peaks in Nepal to the south and the twin, sharp humps of Kamet (7756m) in India off to the southwest. Only 4km from Darchen the trail climbs up over the southwest end of the ridge to reach a **cairn** at 4730m. It's bedecked with prayer flags and marks the first views of the mountain's southern or sapphire face and a *chaktsal gang*, the first of the kora's four prostration points. From here, the more rounded profile of Nanda Devi (7816m) in India can also be seen, to the east of Kamet.

From this point the trail bends round to the north and enters the Lha-chu Valley, where the tall **Tarboche flagpole** soon comes into view. It's about an hour's walk to the flagpole, at 4750m. The flagpole is replaced each year at the major festival of Saga Dawa (p211).

Just to west of the Tarboche is the 'two-legged' **Chörten Kangnyi**. It's an auspicious act for pilgrims to walk through the small chörten's archway. The kora trail continues along the eastern bank of the Lha-chu, but a short climb above the Tarboche is the sky-burial site of the 84 *mahasiddhas* (Tantric practitioners who reached a high level of awareness), which is revered as it was once reserved for monks and lamas. This eerie site is marked by numerous small rock cairns draped with clothing, shoes and locks of hair; visitors are unlikely to be welcome

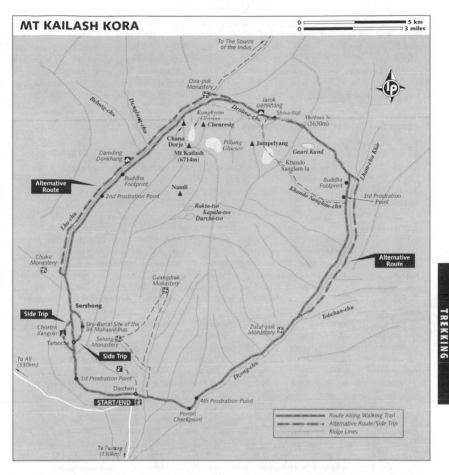

MT KAILASH KORA

if a sky burial is under way. The first of the kora's three Buddha footprints is here but it's hard to find.

You can continue across this small plateau and descend back to the kora trail and the river in the area known as Sershong. The valley narrows dramatically at Sershong, with majestic hills falling down to the swift-flowing Lha-chu and Mt Kailash appearing impressively above the eastern ridge. The trail passes a series of ruined chörtens and a number of long *mani* (prayer) walls before arriving at a small bridge across the Lha-chu at 4710m. The bridge is less than an hour's walk from Tarboche, or about three hours from Darchen, and is directly below Chuku Monastery.

Chuku Monastery (4820m) is perched high above the valley floor, on the hillside to the west, and blends secretively into its rocky background. All Kailash monasteries were wrecked during the Cultural Revolution and the Chuku (or Nyenri) Monastery was the first to be rebuilt. It takes about 20 minutes to climb from the river bank to this hillside monastery, founded in the 13th century by Götsangpa Gompo Pel, who was a Kagyupa-order master. In a glass case over the altar there's a highly revered marble statue called Chuku Opame (originally from India and reputed to talk!) and a conch shell inlaid with silver. Beside the altar there's a copper pot and elephant tusks, offering articles as found in temples in Bhutan.

From the Chuku bridge there are alternative trails along the east and west banks of the river. The trail along the eastern bank is the regular pilgrim route but the western trail offers better views of the west face of Mt Kailash. Either way it's about another three hours before reaching Dira-puk Monastery.

Trekking groups generally take the western trail since there are some fine grassy camp sites on the river banks at Damding Donkhang (4890m), about an hour before the monastery. The west or ruby face of Kailash makes a dramatic backdrop to this camp site and in the early morning Tibetan

ESSENTIAL CONSIDERATIONS FOR WALKING AROUND MT KAILASH

These are the important questions for walking the 52km circuit – a kora if your pilgrimage is a Buddhist one, a parikrama if you're on a Hindu circuit – of Asia's most holy mountain. Buddhist or Hindu, you should be walking the mountain in a clockwise direction, but if you meet walkers coming the other way (anticlockwise), don't be surprised; they're followers of Bön, the ancient pre-Buddhist religion of Tibet – a religion that still thrives in remote parts of Tibet, particularly in the east.

If you're a Tibetan Buddhist you'll probably plan to complete the circuit in one hard day's slog. Achieving this feat requires a predawn start and a late-afternoon return to Darchen. Occasionally, Westerners emulate this feat but don't expect to be faster than the average Tibetan walker, who makes it around the mountain in about 14 hours. Hindu pilgrims, with the odd ritual immersion in an icy lake to endure along the way, typically take three days, overnighting in encampments set up for them close to the Dira-puk and Zutul-puk Monasteries. Independent Western visitors usually aim for a three-day circuit as well. Western trekking groups typically do the circuit in three or four days, as a longer circuit allows time for side trips and excursions to such things as the Kailash north-face glaciers.

Eschewing the normal high-speed one-day circuit, some very enthusiastic Tibetans make the walk much more difficult by prostrating themselves the entire way. They lie down at full length with their arms stretched over their heads, then stand up, place their feet where their hands ended up and repeat the process. Count on around three weeks to complete a prostration kora.

How many times around the mountain? Well, at least once to wipe out the sins of a lifetime, although even that small achievement requires the right predeparture attitude and perhaps a couple of checks of your current sin status at the sin-testing stones on the ascent to the Drölma-la. Tibetans look upon three circuits as a much more satisfactory starting point and 13 as the real minimum. Like gold status for frequent fliers, completing 13 circuits also allows access to high-status detours, such as the short cut over the Khando Sanglam-la, or a visit to an inner kora (nangkor) on the south side of the mountain. Real walkers should aim for 108 circuits, which guarantees instant nirvana and a clean sin slate for all your lifetimes. Economisers should note that koras completed during a full moon are better than ordinary ones; ditto for koras during the Tibetan Year of the Horse.

And the rivers? Well, it's a geographic quirk that four of the subcontinent's most important rivers all have their birth close to the base of Mt Kailash. The mighty Indus flows off to the northwest through Ladakh and the Pakistani-held portion of Kashmir before turning south and flowing through the whole length of Pakistan, eventually emptying into the Arabian Sea to the east of Karachi. The Sutlej River heads off to the west, flowing through the Indian states of Himachal Pradesh and Punjab then turning southwest into Pakistan and finally joining the Indus near Multan.

The Humla Karnali heads straight off to the south, cutting its way across the Himalaya through western Nepal then turning east and, as the Ghaghara or Gogra, joining the mighty Ganges River just before Patna. Finally, the Yarlung Tsangpo flows east all the way across Tibet before bending south around the easternmost end of the Himalaya and, as the Brahmaputra River, flowing through India and down into Bangladesh. The Ganges and Brahmaputra both empty into the Bay of Bengal in an extensive delta system between Kolkata (Calcutta) and Dhaka, 2500km east of the Indus' arrival at the Arabian Sea.

pilgrims can be seen striding resolutely past on the other side of the river, already well into their one-day circuit.

At various points along the trail the west and north faces of the mountain can be seen together. The steep hillsides on both sides of the valley make this one of the most impressive stretches of the walk. Golden *piyu* (marmots) regularly pop out of their holes to peer worriedly at passing walkers. Many of the formations along this stretch have mythical connections, a number of them related to Tibet's legendary hero Gesar of Ling. The second prostration point is also encountered on the east side of the valley, followed by the second Buddha footprint and a rock carving of the god Tamdrin, next to a pair of teahouses.

Dira-puk Monastery, which was rebuilt in 1985, looks across to the north or gold face of Kailash from the hillside north of the Lha-chu. Walkers who have followed the Lha-chu's east-bank trail will have to cross the river to reach the monastery and its guesthouse, at the base of the hill below. There's a bridge here to cross over to the western side, so no need to get your feet wet. There's also an Indian guesthouse and teahouse with a half-dozen rooms on the east bank, facing the Kangkyam Glacier. From here, you can hike up to the glacier in an hour.

Further along the kora is another bridge taking you over to the main trail on the west side, meeting the trail from the monastery. Most groups camp in the vicinity of the Indian guesthouse; for something quieter try the northern valley east of the monastery (the valley that leads to the source of the Indus). West-bank walkers have to cross the Belung-chu and Dunglung chu, tributaries of the Lha-chu, before they reach the monastery.

The monastery takes its name from the words *dira* (meaning 'female-yak-horn') and *puk* ('cave') – this is where the Bön warrior god Drabla tossed boulders around with his horns. The great saint Götsangpa meditated here and Buddhists say he first discovered the kora route around Mt Kailash. He was led to Dira-puk by a yak that turned out to be the lion-faced goddess Dakini (Khadroma), who guards the Khando Sanglam-la. The main image in the *dukhang* is of Chenresig (Avalokiteshvara), flanked by images of the Buddha and a fearsome protector deity.

From the monastery, there are superb views of the impressive northern face of Mt Kailash. Three lesser mountains are arrayed in the front of Kailash: Chana Dorje (Vajrapani) to the west, Jampelyang (Manjushri) to the east and Chenresig (Avalokiteshvara) in the centre.

The Kangkyam Glacier descends from the north face of Mt Kailash, between Chenresig and Chana Dorje, and it takes a about two hours to walk up to the glacier and back. Independent walkers often overnight in the monastery's rather basic **guesthouse** (Y30), which has grubby mattresses on the dirt floor.

Stage 2: Dira-puk Monastery to Zutul-puk Monastery

6–7 hours / 18km / 550m ascent / 600m descent

The Lha-chu flows down the valley running north from Dira-puk. Swami Pranavananda followed this valley up to the source of the Indus River, a two to three-day walk. Kora walkers, on the other hand, head off to the east, crossing the Lha-chu by a bridge and starting the long ascent up the Drölma-chu Valley that will eventually lead to the Drölma-la. The route climbs on to a moraine and soon meets the trail from the east bank of the Lha-chu.

Less than an hour along this route some trekking groups set up camp on the meadow at **Jarok Donkhang** (5210m). It is not wise to camp any higher up than Jarok Donkhang because of the risk of problems related to with acclimatisation.

Nearby a trail branches off to the southeast, leading over the snow-covered Khando Sanglam-la, a short cut to the east side of Mt Kailash that bypasses the normal route over the Drölma-la. Don't be tempted to take this route – only on your auspicious 13th kora is the pass open to you and intruders are likely to find themselves face to face with the pass' protector, the fearsome lion-faced goddess Dakini (Khadroma).

Another glacier descends from the east ridge off the north face of Mt Kailash, down through the Pölung Valley between Chenresig (Avalokiteshvara) and Jampelyang (Manjushri). This glacier can be reached in a round trip of a couple of hours from Jarok Donkhang. You can follow the glacial stream that runs down the middle of the valley to merge with the Drölma-chu or

TREKKING

MILAREPA VERSUS NARO BÖNCHUNG

All around the Mt Kailash kora there are signs of the contest for supremacy that was fought between Milarepa, the Buddhist poet-saint, and Naro Bönchung, the Bön master. According to the Buddhists, in all encounters it was Milarepa who came out the victor, but despite this he still agreed to a final, winner-takes-all duel, a straightforward race to the top of the mountain. Mounting his magic drum, Naro Bönchung immediately set out to fly to the summit but, despite his acolytes' urging, Milarepa didn't bother getting out of bed. Finally, as the first rays of dawn revealed that Naro Bönchung was at the point of reaching the top, Milarepa rose from his bed and was carried by a ray of light directly to the top. Shocked by this defeat, his opponent tumbled off his drum, which skittered down the south face of the mountain, gouging the long slash marking Mt Kailash to this day. Hindu pilgrims call the slash the 'stairway to heaven'. Gracious in victory, Milarepa decreed that Bön followers could continue to make their customary anticlockwise circuits of Mt Kailash, and awarded nearby Bönri as their own holy mountain.

you can avoid losing altitude from Jarok Donkhang by terracing around the side of Jampelyang.

From this point to the Drölma-la there is a constant parade of interesting points along the trail. Only a short distance above Jarok Donkhang is **Shiva-tsal** (5330m), a rocky expanse dotted with stone cairns draped with items of clothing. Pilgrims are supposed to undergo a symbolic death at this point, leaving their old life behind along with an item of clothing to represent it. A drop of blood or a lock of hair might be even better. If you really do decide to drop dead at this point, this is a very meritorious place to die. Right by the trail at the end of the Shiva-tsal is a red **footprint of Milarepa**.

Climbing beyond Shiva-tsal the trail comes to the sin-testing stone of **Bardo Trang**. A narrow passage squeezes under the flat stone and pilgrims are supposed to measure their sinfulness by wriggling under the stone. Fat or thin, you may find yourself stuck under the rock if your sin quota is too high, and in that case the sin-washing power of a Kailash kora may not be sufficient to clean up your karma. High above the trail is a large **mirror rock**; it looks red to ordinary people, white to bodhisattvas and black to sinners. A little further along, the much more convoluted passage under the **Dikpa Karnak** awaits those in need of a second opinion. Other points of interest along this stretch include a stack of stones marking where Milarepa and Naro Bönchung engaged in one of their contests of saintly one-upmanship (see p290). The stone of the triumphant Milarepa tops the pile. Note that these stones can be hard to find on your own.

Finally the trail turns towards the east for the completion of the ascent to the 5630m **Drölma-la**. Look south for your last glimpse of the north face of Mt Kailash. A small glacial trickle halfway up the ascent presents your last sin-washing opportunity before the top. Allow around an hour for the 200m climb to the wide and rocky pass, which is festooned with an enormous number of prayer flags strung from the **Drölma Do** (Drölma's Rock). Pilgrims perform a circumambulation, pasting money onto the rock with butter, stooping to pass under the lines of prayer flags and chanting the Tibetan pass-crossing mantra, 'ki ki so so, lha gyalo' ('ki ki so so' being the empowerment and happiness invocation, 'lha gyalo' meaning 'the gods are victorious').

Naturally, there's a tale associated with this revered rock. When Götsangpa, who pioneered the kora for the Buddhists, wandered into the valley of Dakini (Khadroma), he was led back to the correct route by 21 wolves that were, of course, merely 21 emanations of Drölma (Tara), the goddess of mercy and protectress of the pass. Reaching the pass, the 21 wolves merged into one and then merged again into the great boulder. To this day Drölma helps worthy pilgrims on the difficult ascent – it did seem easier than you expected, didn't it?

Weather permitting, most pilgrims and trekkers pause at the pass for a rest and refreshments before starting the steep descent. Almost immediately, **Gauri Kund** (5608m; one of its Tibetan names translates as 'Lake of Compassion') comes into view below. Hindu pilgrims are supposed to immerse themselves in the lake's green waters, breaking the ice if necessary.

Tibetans, as is well known, really have no truck with all this bathing nonsense. It takes approximately an hour to make the long 400m descent across some generally barren and rocky ground, passing a much-revered **footprint of Milarepa**, before reaching the grassy banks of the Lham-chu Khir. There's a teahouse and the remains of a stone hut where the trail meets the river, leaning up against a huge rock topped by the kora's third **Buddha footprint**.

As with the Lha-chu Valley on the western side of Mt Kailash, there are routes that follow both sides of the river. The eastern-bank trail presents better views and there's less marshy ground but it requires a lot of boulder hopping and wading back across the river at some point. If you opt for that side, keep an eye on the river level, which may become uncomfortably deep further south during the wetter months. Not far to the south, a valley comes down from the Khando Sanglam-la to join the main trail. This valley provides the only glimpse of Mt Kailash's eastern or crystal face; the kora's third prostration point is at the valley mouth.

Trekking groups may decide to camp on the grassy western banks of the river somewhere along this stretch, but those walkers without tents will probably decide to press on to reach the guesthouse at the **Zutul-puk Monastery** (4790m). The monastery is about two hours' walk along the valley. By this point, the river has changed name to the Dzong-chu, which translates as 'Fortress River'.

The miracle *(zutul)* cave *(puk)* that gives the monastery its name is at the back of the main hall. Milarepa is said to have meditated in this cave, which was also the site of yet another confrontation between the Buddhist poet-saint and Naro Bönchung. Needing shelter from the rain, they agreed to jointly construct a cave but when Milarepa casually put the roof in place, without waiting for Naro Bönchung to make the walls, it was yet another easy victory for Buddhism. Milarepa then decided the roof was too high and went outside and pressed it down with his foot, leaving a footprint. Back inside he realised he'd pushed it too far, but some more shoving from below adjusted things to his satisfaction. His hand and head prints can be seen on the cave ceiling but the monastery roof covers the footprint atop the cave.

The monastery **guesthouse** (beds Y40) is primitive but is probably in slightly better shape than the one at Dira-puk.

Stage 3: Zutul-puk Monastery to Darchen
3–4 hours / 14km / 150m descent

The final day's walk begins with the easy stroll down to where the river emerges onto the Barkha plain. The valley narrows and at times its sides look like something from the American Southwest or the Australian outback, except for the prayer flags fluttering across the river.

Where the trail emerges onto the Barkha plain, close to the fourth prostration point (4610m), Gurla Mandata again provides

TREKKING

THE FACES & RIVERS OF MT KAILASH

It's easy to confuse the mystical Mt Kailash, the symbolic Mt Meru of legend reaching from the lowest hell to the highest heaven, with the real one. From the legendary Mt Kailash a river flows into the legendary Lake Manasarovar, from which flow four legendary rivers in the four cardinal directions. In reality, no rivers flow from Manasarovar but four real rivers do issue from the mountain in, more or less, the cardinal directions. And Kailash really does have four distinct faces – composed, according to legend, of lapis lazuli, ruby, gold and crystal.

Direction	Face	Mythical River	Real River
south	lapis lazuli	Mabja Kambab (River from the Peacock Mouth)	Karnali
west	ruby	Langchan Kambab (River from the Elephant's Mouth)	Sutlej
north	gold	Seng-ge Kambab (River from the Lion's Mouth)	Indus
east	crystal	Tamchog Kambab (River from the Horse's Mouth)	Yarlung Tsangpo (Brahmaputra)

the backdrop to Rakshas Tal (Lhanag-tso; 4573m). There's a rough road from here back to Darchen and it's less than an hour's walk, passing many *mani* walls embellished with yak skulls.

LAKE MANASAROVAR KORA

Very few Western travellers undertake the Lake Manasarovar kora. One of the main problems is the marshiness of the ground around the lake, and there are also many streams to ford, some of which become quite deep in summer. But those who do may be rewarded. The lake represents the female or wisdom aspect of enlightenment and is a symbol of good fortune and fertility. While Mt Kailash stands fully revealed, the depths of Lake Manasarovar are hidden from view to all but the greatest of adepts.

Sacrilege as it may be, increasingly tourists are driving around all or part of Lake Manasarovar. It is also possible to hire horses to make the circuit, a fine balance between whizzing around the lake in a vehicle and humping your own pack. The best place to hire horses and a guide is in Hor Qu, the town on the northeastern side of the lake.

The best place to start the Lake Manasarovar circuit is at the northwest corner, near Chiu Monastery. The road from Kailash comes within 1km of here. Chiu (Little Bird) Monastery sits astride a crag that overlooks the lake and enshrines a cave said to have been used by Guru Rinpoche at the end of his life. The fantastic view from the top of the monastery helps place the trek in perspective – there are not many treks of this duration where the entire route is visible from the starting point.

At the base of the monastery are two small shops selling basic foods. Nearby, at the edge of the Ganga-chu, are hot springs great for washing. Some of the eroded stone walls in the area are part of a pre-Buddhist archaeological site. (For more information on Chiu, see p213.)

Don't expect to find many supplies in the local area; bring everything you need. In particular be sure to stock up on high-protein foods such as canned fish, nuts and cheese to supplement the meagre ration of instant noodles available locally. May, June and September are the best months to trek. July and August are also good months but in some years they are very wet and hordes of gnats infest the shores. A tent and stove are required on this trek and be prepared for any kind of weather any time. Strong winds often hit in the afternoon so plan on doing most of your walking in the morning.

The kora, save for a spell on the north side, follows the lakeshore. The route alternates between sandy, gravelly and marshy ground. Manasarovar is often a gem-like cobalt colour but during storms it can turn into a churning black sea. High elevation lends it a radiance unmatched by lower lakes and its fresh waters are as clear as can be.

Since there is little public transport in western Tibet, you may have made it this far by either hitching or hiring a Land Cruiser. If you are hitching, you should be aware of the permit restrictions in this region (see p200 for details).

Stage 1: Chiu Monastery to Hor Qu
7½–8 hours / 30km / 120m ascent / 120m descent
As with Buddhist tradition, head off in a clockwise direction from Chiu, travelling to the east along the north shore. You will pass **mani stones** nearly 2m tall. The trail soon leaves the waterline and ascends over the top of a red escarpment for two hours. The cliffs below are sprinkled with caves that have been used by religious practitioners for centuries. Some of these caves have been converted into permanent homes. From the grass-capped, rolling top of the escarpment, the route descends into a small vale where you can see the ruins of **Cherkip Monastery**; at

---

THE TREK AT A GLANCE

Duration 4–5 days
Distance 110km
Standard medium to difficult
Start/Finish Chiu Monastery
Highest Point 4560m
Nearest Large Town Ali
Accommodation camping
Public Transport none
Summary The kora of Lake Manasarovar (4560m) is a sacred circuit following the edge of the lake which displays brilliant hues at this high elevation The journey is enlivened by a series of friendly monasteries that mark the way.

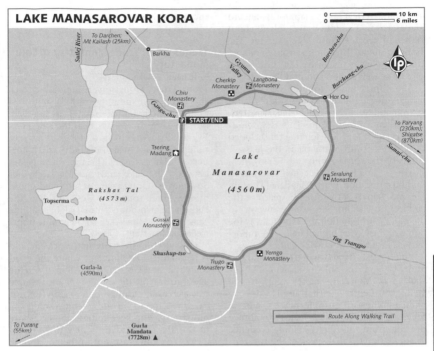

this point you're a little over two hours from Chiu Monastery.

From Cherkip, it is faster to follow the trail east over the headlands to **Langbona Monastery**, a 1½-hour walk. There is also a lakeshore route past more caves and cliffs. When the escarpment ends look, for the trail going north along the Gyuma Valley to Langbona on the west bank of the Gyuma-chu.

East of Langbona the route traverses a marshy plain to the settlement of Hor Qu, four hours away. There are camp sites along the watercourses before Hor Qu so this does not have to be a long day.

Look for a series of tracks heading towards the distant margin of the plain. Under no circumstances return to the edge of the lake from Langbona. The swamps along this part of the lakeshore give way to several lakes that flow into Manasarovar, effectively blocking the route to all but birds and fish.

Hor Qu is the administrative centre of the area and there are several shops here that sell beer, soda, instant noodles and other basics. For more information on Hor Qu, see p205.

Stage 2: Hor Qu to Seralung Monastery
3 hours / 13km / level

The trail from Hor Qu leaves the settlement in a southwesterly direction, avoiding the extensive swamps abutting the lake. A little south of Hor Qu you cross the bridge over the Samui-chu – the main road east initially follows this valley. South of the swampy tracts, the trail rejoins the lakeshore along a stone beach. Look out for white-and-black polished stones, sacred to both Buddhists and Hindus.

The route is squeezed between the water and a cliff before a side valley and **Seralung Monastery** appear. Some of the monastery's religious property thrown into Lake Manasarovar during the Cultural Revolution has been recovered. The monastery was rebuilt in the mid-1980s. The valley here is a good place to camp.

Stage 3: Seralung Monastery to Trugo Monastery
7 hours / 27km / level

At first the route south of Seralung stays near the lakeshore, but in about one hour the mountains retreat and a plain forms next to Manasarovar. The trail moves inland about 1km and crosses the bridge over the Tag Tsangpo about three hours from Seralung. Up this valley are extensive hot springs and geysers as well as Bön and Buddhist sites.

About three hours from the Tag Tsangpo bridge you will round the south side of Manasarovar and reach the ruined **Yerngo Monastery**, situated in a broad plain. This is spacious country, ideal for those looking for secluded camp sites. South of the plain, the massive flanks of the Gurla Mandata (7728m) massif rise up to a heavily glaciated summit. In Buddhist tradition, Gurla Mandata (Tibetan: Menmo Nanyi) is the dwelling place of the goddess of wisdom, Saraswati. However, in the older Bön tradition the mountain is the home of the Queen of the Dralha, an important class of ancient warrior deities.

You'll reach **Trugo Monastery** after another hour. Trugo is the only monastery at either Kailash or Manasarovar belonging to the Gelugpa order. Trugo (Bathing Head) is so named because of its importance as a place for ritual bathing. Kailash seems to embrace the lake from this angle, lending credence to ancient myths that speak of the two representing a god and goddess in union. Large by local standards, Trugo has both a shop and **hostel** (beds around Y30) and is a fine place to take a day or two off the trail to just enjoy the atmosphere. You can arrange a bed here for about Y30.

Stages 4 & 5: Trugo Monastery to Chiu Monastery
9–10 hours / 40km / level

From Trugo Monastery, a motorable track shoots off over the range of hills southwest of the lake to join the Purang–Darchen road, but the kora route stays near the lakeshore. Eventually, swampy ground gives way to sandy expanses near the southwestern corner of Manasarovar. The trail then passes between the lake and the much smaller Shushup-tso along a narrow sand-and-gravel bridge. You'll round the western side of the lake about two hours from Trugo; continue walking along the beach for two more hours to **Gossul Monastery**.

Gossul Monastery sits on top of a cliff and is best known as the place where the great Kagyupa saint Götsangpa meditated. On the lakeshore below the monastery are a couple of caves used by pilgrims to camp. Retreat caves are found on the circuit around the monastery. The kora follows the lakeshore to the Tsering Madang Valley three hours away. You can crash out in the guesthouse here unless the authorities have been coming down particularly hard on individual travellers. From here, it is two more hours back to Chiu along the beach.

Directory

CONTENTS

PRACTICALITIES

- Tibet subscribes to the PAL video standard, the same as Australia, New Zealand, the UK and most of Europe.

- Electricity is 220V, 50 cycles AC. Plugs come in at least four designs: three-pronged angled pins (like in Australia) three-pronged round pins (like in Hong Kong), two flat pins (US style but without the ground wire) or two narrow round pins (European style), and three rectangular pins (British style).

- The metric system is widely used in Tibet. Traders measure fruit and vegetables by the *jin* (500g). Smaller measurements (eg for dumplings) are measured in *liang* (50g).

ACCOMMODATION

The main urban centres of Lhasa, Gyantse, Shigatse, Tsetang, Zhangmu and Ali offer a decent range of hotels, many with hot showers and some three or four-star options. Other smaller towns and villages along the Friendship Hwy and the Tibet–Sichuan Hwy offer a limited range of basic but comfortable inns. Elsewhere in Tibet travellers will be limited to a bed in a basic, often mud-floored room.

In smaller places electricity and running water are luxuries that cannot be expected. Hot water is provided everywhere in thermoses and even in basic places a basin and drum of cold water is usually provided for washing. Bedding is provided but it's often not clean so a sleeping bag is a good idea.

In the towns, the government keeps a pretty tight lid on which places can and cannot accept foreigners. Most tourists will only come up against this problem in Tsetang and Zanda, where the bottom-end hotels are not permitted to accept foreigners.

Camping

A large proportion of the Tibetan population is nomadic, and there is a strong tradition of making your home wherever you can hammer in a tent peg. You probably run the risk of an unpleasant run-in with the Public Security Bureau (PSB) if you attempt to set up a tent in Lhasa, but get 20km or so out of town and the nearest patch of turf is yours for the picking. Always ask permission if camping near a settlement or encampment and watch out for the dogs (see p298).

Guesthouses & Hotels

In Lhasa there are several clean, well-run Tibetan-style guesthouses. Similar set-ups can be found in Shigatse, Sakya and Tingri. Tibetan-style guesthouses tend to be much more friendly and homy than Chinese guesthouses; prices are also lower.

Some monasteries, such as Samye, Ganden, Drigung Til, Dorje Drak, Mindroling,

SLEEPING BAGS

The question of whether you need a sleeping bag or not depends entirely on where you plan to go and how you plan to travel. Those who aim to spend time in Lhasa and then head down to Nepal via the sights of Tsang could do without one, although they are always a nice comfort, especially in budget hotels. Anyone planning on trekking or heading out to remoter areas such as Nam-tso, Everest or western Tibet should definitely bring one along.

Tidrum and Reting, also have their own guesthouses, normally a bank of carpeted seats that double as beds (bring a sleeping bag). Remoter monasteries often have a spare room, or even a chapel, which they may be willing to let out. Fees are around Y20 per person; if no fee is asked, leave a donation in the prayer hall.

Most of the larger hotels are anonymous Chinese-style hotels and share several traits: the plumbing is often very dodgy, the carpets are dotted with a mosaic of cigarette burns, and all offer a ratty pair of flip-flops so you don't have to touch the bathroom floor. Hotel rates range from Y60 to Y400 for a double room. Few of the top-end hotels have single room rates.

Some hotels (generally the cheaper ones) price their accommodation per bed rather than per room, which can work out well for solo travellers. To guarantee that you have the room to yourself you would theoretically have to pay for all beds (and a few hotel owners will try to force you to do so), but usually that's not necessary. If you are alone in a double room or are a couple in a triple room, staff will not normally put others in the room, although they have the right to. They may possibly put other foreigners in the room, but it is rare for a hotel to mix foreigners and Chinese or Tibetans in one room. This depends largely on your negotiations.

In some areas of Tibet, notably in Lhasa, accommodation prices vary seasonally. Throughout this book, the prices provided apply in the high season (June to September). Rates can be a little lower in April, May and October, and lower still in winter. Discounts are commonly available as the rack rate is usually more about optimism than reality. It's always worth your while to ask for a discount.

Truck Stops & Daoban

Hitchhikers and cyclists may get to sample the odd truck stop. They are basically just places to crash after a long day of travelling. The bedding is usually filthy so it's a good idea to have a sleeping bag (and even a ground sheet!). If you value your privacy it is also a good idea to pay for a whole room (usually four or five beds), because drivers turn up at all times of the night.

Cyclists might have to make use of road-maintenance camps (*daoban* in Chinese), recognisable by the steering wheel symbol. In free-market China these camps are normally open to foreigners and go under such glamorous names as the '22nd Team Road Maintenance Division Guesthouse'. Tariffs are usually around Y15 per bed and food is usually available.

ACTIVITIES

Tibet offers the type of topography to delight mountaineers, white-water rafters, horse riders and others, though the problem, as always, is the confusing travel permit system, which many authorities manipulate to their own financial advantage.

Cycling

Tibet offers some of the most extreme and exhilarating mountain biking in the world. If you are fit and well-equipped it's possible to visit most places in this book by bike, although the most popular route follows the Friendship Hwy from Shigatse down to Kathmandu. For more information see p319.

Horse Riding

There's something romantic about travelling across Tibet on horseback. The easiest place to arrange this is in the Kham region of western Sichuan, but even here it's a matter of coming to an agreement with local herdsmen. A kora of Lake Manasarovar (p121) on horseback is a great idea and a few travellers have managed to arrange this.

Foreign travel companies, such as **Hidden Trails** (www.hiddentrails.com) and **Boojum Expeditions** (www.boojum.com) offer expensive horse-riding tours in Kham.

Mountaineering

There are some huge peaks in Tibet, including the 8000m-plus the giants of Cho Oyu, Shishapangma and, of course, Everest, which are enough to send a quiver of excitement through vertically inclined explorers. Unfortunately, the Chinese government charges exorbitant fees for mountaineering permits, which puts mountaineering in Tibet out of the range of most individuals or groups devoid of commercial sponsorship.

A few individuals have succeeded in getting to Advanced Everest Base Camp and even beyond but the authorities are clamping down on this (see p189).

Foreign travel companies such as **Alpine Ascents** (www.alpineascents.com) and **Jagged Globe** (www.jagged-globe.co.uk) arrange for mountaineering trips to Tibet but these don't come cheap.

Rafting

Tibet Wind Horse Adventure offers rafting trips in Central Tibet. See p107 for details.

Trekking

One of the remarkable things about Tibet, considering the difficulties placed in the way of those heading up there by Chinese authorities, is that once you are up on the high plateau there is considerable freedom to strike off on foot and explore the Tibetan valleys and ranges. Of course no-one at CITS or any other Chinese organisation will tell you this, but nevertheless it is the case. Experienced and hardy trekkers have the opportunity to visit places that are almost impossible to reach any other way, and are unlikely to find any official obstacles. For information on trekking routes see p262.

High Asia (www.highasia.com) offers some of the most interesting treks in the region.

BUSINESS HOURS

Banks, offices, government departments and the PSB are open Monday to Friday, with perhaps a half-day on Saturday. As a rough guide only, they open from around 9am until 6pm and close for two hours in the middle of the day.

Many of Lhasa's main tourist attractions are open only in the morning. Most smaller monasteries have no set opening hours and will open up chapels for you once you've tracked someone down. Others, such as Samye, are notorious for only opening certain rooms at certain times. In general it's best to try to tag along with pilgrims or a tour group.

CHILDREN

Be especially careful with children as they won't be on the lookout for signs of altitude sickness. Children don't get on with Tibetan food or toilets any better than grown ups. They also tire more easily from an endless round of visiting monasteries. Bring along a copy of *Tintin in Tibet* for when morale flags. In Kathmandu several bookshops sell Tibetan *thangka* (religious paintings) and mandala colouring books.

On the upside children can be a great icebreaker and generally generate a lot of interest. Many hotels have family rooms, which normally have three or four beds arranged in two connected rooms.

Tibet is probably not a great place to bring a very small child. You should bring all supplies (including nappies and medicines) with you. Small spoons can be useful as most places have only chopsticks. There's plenty of boiling water to sterilise bottles etc. It's possible to make a cot from the copious numbers of duvets supplied with most hotel rooms.

CLIMATE CHARTS

Tibet has similar seasons to China, though with lower temperatures due to higher altitudes. Winters (from November to March) are very cold (the average temperature in January is -2°C) but there isn't all that much snow. Summers (May to September) have warm days with strong sunshine and cool nights. At higher elevations (ie above 4000m) even summer days can be chilly. Spring and autumn can bring anything from midday heat to snow storms and you need to be prepared for four seasons in one day at this

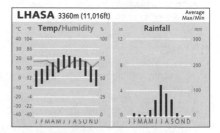

time (or anywhere in Tibet above 4000m). There are some regional variations; northern and western Tibet are generally higher and colder. The monsoon affects parts of Tibet (particularly Eastern Tibet) from mid-July to the end of September (July and August bring half of Tibet's annual rainfall). For more on Tibet's climate, see p10.

COURSES

It is possible to enrol in a Tibetan language course at the Tibet University. Tuition costs US$1000 per semester; semesters run from March to July and September to January. There are two hours of classes a day and around 70 foreign students currently attend (although some are undercover missionaries). For an application form contact the **Foreign Affairs Office** (☎ 0891-634 3254; fsd@utibet .edu.cn; Tibet University, Lhasa 850000, Tibet Autonomous Region). Once you are accepted the university will help arrange a student ('X') visa and, after three months, residency status in Lhasa. Students have to stay in campus accommodation, which costs Y40 per day for a private room with toilet, but no hot-water shower or heating in winter.

It should also be possible to hire a private tutor from the university for around Y20 per hour.

Many travellers find it more convenient to study at Dharamsala or Kathmandu, although students say that the mix of dialects and high levels of English make them less effective places to study. Courses offered there include Tibetan Buddhist philosophy, Tibetan language and Tibetan performing arts. The **Kopan Monastery** (www.kopan-monastery .com) outside Kathmandu, in Nepal, is a particularly popular place to study aspects of Tibetan Buddhism.

The various Tibetan organisations across the world offer courses and meditation retreats. The **Tibet Foundation** (☎ 020-7404 2889; www.tibet-foundation.org) in London, for example, offers a 10-week Tibetan language course for UK£130.

CUSTOMS

Chinese border crossings have gone from being severely traumatic to exceedingly easy for travellers.

You can legally bring in or take out only Y6000 in Chinese currency. There are no such restrictions on foreign currency except that you should declare any cash amount exceeding US$5000 (or its equivalent in other currencies). You are allowed to import a maximum of 72 rolls of film. It's also officially forbidden to bring more than 20 pieces of underwear into the PRC (we kid you not).

It is illegal to import any printed material, film, tapes etc 'detrimental to China's politics, economy, culture and ethics'. This is a particularly sensitive subject in Tibet, but even here it is highly unusual to have Chinese customs officials grilling travellers about their reading matter. Maps and political books printed in Dharamsala, India, could cause a problem.

It is currently illegal to bring into China pictures, books, videos or speeches of or by the Dalai Lama. Moreover, you may be placing the recipient of these in danger of a fine or jail sentence from the Chinese authorities. Pictures of the Dalai Lama with the Tibetan national flag are even 'more' illegal.

Be very circumspect if you are asked to take any packages, letters or photos out of Tibet for anyone else, including monks.

Anything made in China before 1949 is regarded as a cultural treasure and cannot be taken out of the country.

DANGERS & ANNOYANCES
Beggars

Being a devout Buddhist region, Tibet has a long tradition of begging for alms. It is unusual to sit down in a restaurant in Tibet without being pestered by women with babies in their arms, wizened old men, urchins dressed in rags, boy monks and even itinerant musicians. Generally, they will approach you with thumbs up and mumble *'guchi guchi'* – 'please, please' (not a request for Italian designer clothes). Only the monks are occasionally pushy. Often it is food that is being sought and restaurant owners seem to tolerate this – the instant you push your plate to one side (or get up to leave) anything remaining on it is likely to disappear instantly.

Tibetans with money are generally very generous with beggars and usually hand out a couple of *mao* to anyone who requests it.

If you do give (and the choice is entirely yours), give the same amount Tibetans do; do not encourage the beggars to make foreigners a special target by handing out large denominations. In this case it's worth keeping all your small change in one pocket – there's nothing worse than pulling out a Y100 note! Banks will swap a Y10 note for a wad of one-*mao* notes and these will go a long way.

Bookjacking

Tibetans are a curious and devout people and so the slightest glimpse of a photo of a monastery or a Dalai Lama picture will result in the temporary confiscation of your Lonely Planet guide. For many Tibetans this is their only chance to see other parts of their country so try to be patient, even after the 10th request in five minutes. A good deed like this can often open hitherto locked doors (literally) in the place you are visiting.

Dogs

Clean-up campaigns in Lhasa and Shigatse has largely done away with packs of rabid-looking dogs that used to make catching a predawn bus a frightening, and even a life threatening experience. Dogs can still be a problem in other towns though, and you should be especially vigilant when exploring back streets or seeking out an obscure monastery. Hurling a few rocks in their direction will let them know you are not in the mood for company, while a hefty stick is good for action at close quarters. The most dangerous dogs belong to remote homesteads or nomad encampments and should be given a very wide berth. See p327 for information on what to do if you are bitten.

Staring Squads

It is very unusual to be surrounded by staring Tibetans and Chinese in Lhasa, unlike other remote parts of China, but visiting upcountry is another matter. Trekkers will soon discover that it is not a good idea to set up camp beside Tibetan villages. The spectacle of a few foreigners putting up tents is probably the closest some villagers will ever come to TV.

Theft

Tibet is very poor and there is a small risk of theft when travelling here. Trekkers in the Everest region have reported problems with petty theft, and pickpockets work parts of Lhasa. That said, Tibet is safer than most other provinces of China.

Small padlocks are useful for backpacks and some dodgy hotel rooms. Bicycle chain locks come in handy not only for hired bikes but for attaching backpacks to railings or luggage racks.

If something of yours is stolen, you should report it immediately to the nearest foreign affairs branch of the PSB. They will ask you to fill in a loss report before investigating the case and they sometimes even recover the stolen goods.

If you have travel insurance (which is recommended), it is essential to obtain a loss report so you can claim compensation.

DISABLED TRAVELLERS

Tibet can be a hard place for disabled travellers. The high altitudes, rough roads and lack of access make travelling difficult. Monasteries in particular often involve a hike up a hillside or steep, very narrow steps. Few of the hotels offer any facilities for the disabled.

Braille Without Borders (☎ 0891-633 1763; Braille WB@qmx.net; ww.braillewithoutborders.org) Blind visitors can contact this excellent organisation based in Lhasa. They developed the first Tibetan Braille system and run a school for blind Tibetan kids. The founder is the author of the book *My Path Leads to Tibet: The Inspiring Story of How One Young Blind Woman Brought Hope to the Blind Children of Tibet.*

Navyo Nepal (☎ 01-280056; www.navyonepal.com; GPO Box 8974, PCN 329, Kathmandu, Nepal) This Nepal-based company has some experience in running tours for the disabled to Tibet and Nepal.

EMBASSIES & CONSULATES
Chinese Embassies

In major cities abroad, Chinese embassies include those in the following countries:
Australia (☎ 02-6273 4780, 6273 4781; www.china embassy.org.au; 15 Coronation Dr, Yarralumla, ACT 2600)
Canada (☎ 613-789 3509; www.chinaembassycanada .org; 515 St Patrick St, Ottawa, ON KIN 5H3)
France (☎ 01 47 36 02 58; www.amb-chine.fr; 9 Ave Victor Cresson, 921130 Issy Les Moulineaux, Paris)
Germany (☎ 0228-361095; www.china-botschaft.de; Kurfürstenallee 12, 53177 Bonn, Bad Godesberg)
India (☎ 011-611 6682; fax 688 5486; 50-D Shantipath, Chanakyapuri, New Delhi 110021)
Japan (☎ 03-3403 3380, 3403 3065; 3-4-33 Moto-Azabu, Minato-ku, Tokyo 106)
Nepal (☎ 01-411740; fax 414045; Baluwatar, Kathmandu; ⊗ 9.30-11am Mon, Wed & Fri, closed on all Chinese & Nepali holidays)

DIRECTORY

Netherlands (☎ 070-355 1515; Adriaan Goekooplaan 7, 2517 JX, The Hague)
New Zealand (☎ 04-587 0407; www.chinaembassy.org .nz; 104A Korokoro Rd, Pentone, Wellington)
UK (☎ 020-7636 8845, 24hr premium-rate visa information 0891-880808; www.chinese-embassy.org.uk; 31 Portland Place, London WIN 5AG)
USA (☎ 202-328 2500, 338 6688; www.chinaembassy.org; Room 110, 2201 Wisconsin Ave NW, Washington DC 20007) Visa US$50. No longer accepts postal applications. See also www.chinaconsulatesf.org.

For embassies not listed above consult the Chinese Foreign Ministry website at www .fmprc.gov.cn/eng/.

Consulates in Tibet

The only diplomatic representation in Tibet is the **Nepali Consulate-General** (Map pp88-9; ☎ 0891-681 5744; rncglx@public.ls.x.cn; ☻ 10am-12.30pm Mon-Fri) in Lhasa. Visas are issued within 24 hours, sometimes on the same day.

Visa fees change regularly, but at the time of research they were Y255 for a 30- to 60-day visa or Y680 for a six-month multiple entry. If this is your second trip to Nepal in the calendar year and you stayed more than 15 days on your first trip then your second visa is currently free of charge, in an effort to promote tourism. All visas are valid for six months from the date of issue. Remember to bring one visa photo. Visits of less than three days are currently visa free.

It is also possible to obtain visas for the same costs as above at Kodari, the Nepali border town, although it would be sensible to check first that this has not changed.

FESTIVALS & EVENTS

Tibetan cultural heritage took such a hammering during the Cultural Revolution that traditional festivals, once important highlights of the Tibetan year, are only now starting to revive.

Tibetan festivals are held according to the Tibetan lunar calendar, which usually lags at least a month behind our Gregorian calendar. Ask around for the exact dates of many festivals because these are often only fixed by monasteries a few months in advance. To check Tibetan lunar dates against Western Gregorian dates, try www.kalachakranet.org /ta_tibetan_calendar.html.

The following are just some of the more important festivals:

January
Shigatse New Year Festival Held in the first week of the 12th lunar month.

February/March
Year End Festival Dancing monks can be seen on the 29th of the 12th lunar month in this festival which is held to dispel the evil of the old year and auspiciously usher in the new one.
New Year Festival (Losar) Taking place in the first week of the first lunar month, Losar is a colourful week of activities; Lhasa is probably the best place to be. There are performances of Tibetan drama and pilgrims making incense offerings, and the streets are thronged with Tibetans dressed in their finest.
Lantern Festival This is held on the 15th of the first lunar month; huge yak-butter sculptures are placed around Lhasa's Barkhor circuit.
Mönlam (Great Prayer Festival) Held midway through the first lunar month (officially culminating on the 25th). Monks from Lhasa's three main monasteries assemble in the Jokhang and an image of Jampa (Maitreya) is borne around the Barkhor circuit, attracting enthusiastic crowds of locals and pilgrims. The festival was first instituted by Tsongkhapa in 1409 at Ganden Monastery.

May/June
Birth of Sakyamuni (Sakya Thukpa) This is not exactly a festival, but rather an important pilgrimage date. The seventh day of the fourth lunar month is sees large numbers of pilgrims visiting the Holy City of Lhasa and other sacred areas in Tibet. Festivals are held at this time at Tsurphu (see next entry), Ganden, Reting and Samye Monasteries.
Tsurphu Festival *Cham* dancing (ritual dancing carried out by monks) and *chang* drinking (barley beer) are the order of the day at this festival on the 10th day of the fourth lunar month. The highlight used to be the dance of the Karmapa (the spiritual leader of the Karma Kagyupa suborder, now in India) so it remains to be seen how the festival continues.
Saga Dawa (Sakyamuni's Enlightenment) The 15th day of the fourth lunar month (full moon) marks the date of Sakyamuni's (Sakya Thukpa's) conception, moment of enlightenment and entry into nirvana. It is an occasion for outdoor operas and sees large numbers of pilgrims at Lhasa's Jokhang, on the Barkhor circuit and also at Mt Kailash. Many pilgrims climb Gephel Ri, the peak behind Drepung Monastery, to burn juniper incense.

June/July
World Incense Day A day of incense burning and picnicking.
Gyantse Horse-Racing Festival A traditional festival whose date authorities are trying to fix to the middle of

July to boost the number of tourists. The fun and games include dances, picnics, archery and equestrian events.

Worship of the Buddha During the second week of the fifth lunar month, the parks of Lhasa, in particular the Norbulingka, are crowded with picnickers.

Tashilhunpo Festival During the second week of the fifth lunar month, Shigatse's Tashilhunpo Monastery becomes the scene of a three-day festival, and a huge *thangka* is hung.

Samye Festival Held from the 15th day of the fifth lunar month (full moon) for two days. Special ceremonies and *cham* dancing in front of the Ütse are the main attractions. The monastery guesthouse is normally booked out at this time so bring a tent.

August/September

Chökor Duchen Festival Held in Lhasa on the fourth day of the sixth lunar month, this festival celebrates Buddha's first sermon at Sarnath near Varanasi in India.

Guru Rinpoche's Birthday Held on the 10th day of the sixth lunar month, this festival is particularly popular in Nyingmapa monasteries.

Ganden Festival On the 15th day of the sixth lunar month, the Ganden Monastery displays its 25 holiest relics, which are normally locked away. A large offering ceremony accompanies the unveiling.

Drepung Festival The 30th day of the sixth lunar month is celebrated with the hanging of a huge *thangka* at Drepung Monastery. Lamas and monks do masked dances.

Shötun (Yogurt Festival) Held in the first week of the seventh lunar month, this festival starts at Drepung and moves down to the Norbulingka. Operas and masked dances are held, and locals take the occasion as another excuse for more picnics.

September/October

Bathing Festival The end of the seventh and beginning of the eighth lunar months sees locals washing away the grime of the previous year in an act of purification that coincides with the week-long appearance of the planet Venus in the night sky.

Horse-Racing Festival Held in the first week of the eighth lunar month, this festival featuring horse racing, archery and other traditional nomad sports takes place in Damxung and Nam-tso. A similar and even larger event is held in Nagchu a few weeks earlier, from 10–16 August.

Onkor In the first week of the eighth lunar month Tibetans in central Tibet get together and party in celebration of this traditional harvest festival.

November/December

Lhabab Düchen Commemorating Buddha's descent from heaven, the 22nd day of the ninth lunar month sees large numbers of pilgrims in Lhasa. Ladders are painted afresh on rocks around many monasteries, to symbolise the event (or Buddha's descent).

Palden Lhamo (Shri Devi) Held on the 15th day of the 10th lunar month, this festival features a procession in Lhasa around the Barkhor bearing Palden Lhamo (Shri Devi), protective deity of the Jokhang.

Tsongkhapa Festival Respect is shown to Tsongkhapa, the founder of Gelugpa order, on the anniversary of his death on the 25th of the 10th lunar month; monasteries light fires and carry images of Tsongkhapa in procession. Check for *cham* dances at the monasteries at Ganden, Sera and Drepung.

GAY & LESBIAN TRAVELLERS

Homosexuality has historical precedents in Tibet, especially in Tibetan monasteries, where male lovers were known as *trap'i kedmen*, or 'monk's wife'. The Dalai Lama has sent mixed signals about homosexuality, describing gay sex as 'sexual misconduct', 'improper' and 'inappropriate', but also by saying 'There are no acts of love between adults that one can or should condemn'.

The official attitude to gays and lesbians in China is also ambiguous, with responses ranging from Draconian penalties to tacit acceptance. Travellers are advised to act with discretion. Chinese men routinely hold hands and drape their arms around each other without anyone inferring any sexual overtones.

Canada-based company **Footprints Travel** (☎ 1-888-962 6211, 416-962 8111; www.footprintstravel .com; Ste 200, 506 Church St, Toronto, ON, Canada M4Y 2C8) organises gay and lesbian group trips to Tibet.

HOLIDAYS

The PRC has nine national holidays. These are mainly Chinese holidays and mean little to many Tibetans, but they are still a good opportunity to catch a Tibetan opera or join families picnicking in a local park.

New Year's Day 1 January
Chinese New Year Usually February
International Working Women's Day 8 March
International Labour Day 1 May
Youth Day 4 May
Children's Day 1 June
Anniversary of the founding of the Communist Party of China 1 July
Anniversary of the founding of the People's Liberation Army 1 August
National Day 1 October

Chinese New Year, otherwise known as the Spring Festival, officially lasts only three days but many people take a week off from work. Be warned: this is definitely not the time to cross borders (especially the Hong Kong one) or to be caught short of money. In general, however, Spring Festival has a minor effect in Tibet compared to the chaos engendered in the rest of China.

You should be aware that 10 March is a politically sensitive date, as it is the anniversary of the 1959 Tibetan uprising and flight of the Dalai Lama. Also, 23 May marks the signing of the *Agreement on Measures for the Peaceful Liberation of Tibet*, while 1 September marks the anniversary of the founding of the Tibetan Autonomous Region (TAR). Other politically sensitive dates marking political protests are 5 March, 27 September, 10 December and 1 October. It may be impossible for travellers to fly into Tibet for a few days before these dates.

INTERNET ACCESS

It is possible to send and receive emails in Lhasa, Shigatse, Tsetang, Ali and Chamdo, either in private Internet bars (which double as video arcades) or in the 'business centres' of China Telecom offices. Most places charge around Y5 for an hour's Internet access.

Some websites (eg those of the BBC and Dalai Lama) have been blacklisted by the Chinese government and are unavailable inside China.

LEGAL MATTERS

Most crimes are handled administratively by the PSB, which acts as police, judge and executioner.

China takes a particularly dim view of opium and all its derivatives. It's difficult to say what attitude the Chinese police will take towards foreigners caught using marijuana – they often don't care what foreigners do if it's not political and if Chinese or Tibetans aren't involved. Then again the Chinese are fond of making examples of wrong-doings and you don't want to be the example.

Public Security Bureau (PSB)

The Public Security Bureau (PSB) is the name given to China's police, both uniformed and plain clothed. The foreign affairs branch of the PSB deals with foreigners. This branch (also known as the 'entry-exit branch') is responsible for issuing visa extensions and Alien Travel Permits.

In Tibet it is fairly unusual for foreigners to have problems with the PSB, though making an obvious display of pro-Tibetan political sympathies is guaranteed to lead to problems. Photographing Tibetan protests or military sites will lead to the confiscation of your film and possibly a brief detention. Attempting to travel into or out of Tibet on any of the closed routes (mainly to Sichuan or Yunnan) is likely to end in an encounter somewhere en route. If you are caught in a closed area without a permit you face a fine of Y200 to Y500, which can often be bargained down. Some officers have been known to offer a 'student discount' on fines!

If you do have a serious run-in with the PSB, you may have to write a confession of guilt and pay a fine. In the most serious cases, you can be expelled from China (at your own expense). But in general, if you are not doing anything really nasty (like smuggling suitcases of dope through customs), the PSB will probably not throw you in prison.

MAPS

It shouldn't come as a surprise that good mapping for Tibet is not easy to come by. Stock up on maps before you leave.

MAPS OF LHASA

If you intend to explore Lhasa in detail, look out for *Lhasa City* (1:12,500) published by the Amnye Machen Institute in Dharamsala (www.amnyemachen.org). The detail of the maps is awesome and includes many unorthodox sites. It is available from **Stanfords** (☎ 020-7836 1321; www.stanfords.co.uk; 12-14 Long Acre, Covent Garden, London WC2E 9LP) for UK£10.95.

On This Spot – Lhasa, published by the International Campaign for Tibet (ICT), is a unique political map of the Lhasa region, pinpointing the location of prisons, demonstrations, human-rights abuses and more. It's a really fascinating read, but it's too politically subversive to take into Tibet. It costs US$5.95 and can be ordered from ICT (www.savetibet.org).

MAPS OF TIBET

In Lhasa three maps are available: two in Chinese (and possibly also Tibetan) and one in English. The 166-page *Xizang Zizhiqu Dituceng* (Tibet Autonomous Province Atlas) is very detailed; it shows major roads and towns and has a scale of up to 1:300,000. A fold-out version is available with a scale of 1:2,200,000. Both are of very limited use, however, if you do not read Chinese. Even if you do, most of the place names are known locally in Tibetan only, not Chinese.

The English-language map *China Tibet Tour Map*, by the Mapping Bureau of the Tibet Autonomous Region, is the best local alternative if you are just travelling around Tibet by road.

Road maps available in Kathmandu include *Tibet – South-Central* by Nepa Maps; *Latest Map of Kathmandu to Tibet* by Mandala Maps; the *Namaste Trekking Map*; and *Lhasa to Kathmandu*, which is a mountain-biking map by Himalayan Map House. They are marginally better than Chinese-produced maps but still aren't up to scratch.

Back at home, look out for the Nelles Verlag *Himalaya* map, which has excellent detail of central Tibet. Geocenter's *Tibet, Nepal, Bhutan* is also good. A good map if you are doing a lot of travelling is the *Tibet Road Map* by Berndtson & Berndtson. It has a detailed insert of central Tibet and is laminated, so it won't rip like all the others.

A specialist map, fascinating but of little practical use, is the *Terrain Map of Qinghai-Xizang Plateau*, which is coproduced by the Chinese Academy of Science & Woodlands Mountain Institute. It provides fascinating geographical information in the form of a satellite photo of the Tibetan plateau. You can find it in the gift shops of top-end hotels in Lhasa for US$15 to US$20.

For detailed online maps of Tibet, try the Tibet Map Institute at www.tibetmap.com.

MONEY

For your trip to Tibet bring a mix of travellers cheques (say, 60%), cash in US dollars (40%) and a credit card. Consult the inside front cover for a table of exchange rates and refer to p10 for information on costs.

Credit Cards

You'll get very few opportunities to splurge on the plastic in Tibet unless you spend a few nights in a top-end hotel. Flights out of Lhasa can't be paid using a credit card, although this may change in the future. The Lhasa central branch of the Bank of China is the only place in Tibet that provides credit card advances. A 3% commission is usually deducted and the minimum advance is normally Y1200.

Currency

The Chinese currency is known as Renminbi (RMB) or 'people's money'. The basic unit of this currency is the *yuan*, and is designated in this book by a 'Y'. In spoken Chinese, the word *kuai* is almost always substituted for the *yuan*. Ten *jiao* (commonly known as *mao*) make up one yuan. Ten *fen* make up one *jiao*, but *fen* are becoming rare because they are worth so little – some people will not accept them.

RMB comes in paper notes in denominations of one, two, five, 10, 20, 50 and 100 yuan; and one, two and five *jiao*. Coins are in denominations of one yuan; five *jiao*; and one, two and five *fen*.

China has a problem with counterfeit notes. Very few Tibetans or Chinese will accept a Y100 or Y50 note without first subjecting it to intense scrutiny, and many will not accept old, tattered notes or coins. Check the watermark when receiving any Y100 note.

Exchanging Money

In Tibet, the only place to change foreign currency and travellers cheques is the Bank of China. The top-end hotels in Lhasa have exchange services but only for guests. Outside of Lhasa, the only other locations to change money are in Shigatse, Zhangmu, Purang (cash only) and Ali, and at the airport on arrival. If you are travelling upcountry, try to get your cash in small denominations: Y100 and Y50 bills are sometimes difficult to get rid of in rural Tibet.

The currencies of Australia, Canada, the US, the UK, Hong Kong, Japan, the euro zone and most of the rest of Western Europe are acceptable at the Lhasa Bank of China. The official rate is given at all banks and most hotels so there is little need to shop around for the best deal. The standard commission is 0.75%.

Since the floating of the RMB, there is no problem taking the currency out of the country. However, it would be sensible to change it back into a more useful currency. There are plenty of moneychangers at Zhangmu who will change yuan into Nepali rupees and vice versa. Yuan can also easily be reconverted in Hong Kong. Keep your exchange receipts as you'll need these to change your yuan back to dollars at the Bank of China.

International Transfers

Getting money sent to you in Lhasa is possible but it can be a drag. One option is by using the Bank of China's central office in Lhasa. Staff claim it takes seven days for money to arrive. Money should be wired to the Bank of China, Lhasa branch, bank account No 148340001. Double-check wiring instructions with the bank beforehand.

The second option is via **Western Union** (www .westernunion.com), which can wire money via the Express Mail Service (EMS; see p306) at Lhasa's **main post office** (Map pp88-9; Dekyi Shar Lam; ☯ 9am-8pm Mon-Sat, 10am-6pm Sun).

Security

A moneybelt or pockets sewn inside your clothes is the safest way to carry money.

Keeping all your eggs in one basket is not advised – you should keep an emergency cash stash of small-denomination notes in US dollars apart from your main moneybelt, along with a record of your travellers cheque serial numbers, emergency contact numbers and passport number.

Taxes

Although big hotels and top-end restaurants may add a tax or 'service charge' of 10% to 15%, all other consumer taxes are included in the price tag. For information on departure tax see p311.

Tipping & Bargaining

Tibet is one of those wonderful places where tipping is not done and almost no-one asks for a tip. If you go on a long organised trip out to eastern or western Tibet, your guide and driver will probably expect a tip at the end of the trip, assuming all went well. Figure on around Y50 to Y100 per person.

Basic bargaining skills are essential for travel in Tibet. You can bargain in shops, hotels, street stalls and travel agencies, and with pedicab drivers and most people – but not everywhere. In small shops and street stalls, bargaining is expected, but there is one important rule to follow: be polite.

Tibetans are no less adept at driving a hard deal than the Chinese and, like the Chinese, aggressive bargaining will usually only serve to firm their conviction that the original asking price is the one they want. Try to keep smiling and firmly whittle away at the price. If this does not work, try walking away. They might call you back, and if they don't there is always somewhere else.

Travellers Cheques

Besides the advantage of safety, travellers cheques are useful to carry in Tibet because the exchange rate is higher (by about 3%) than it is for cash. Cheques from the major companies such as Thomas Cook, Citibank, American Express and Bank of America are accepted.

PERMITS

There are three levels of bureaucracy you need to jump through to travel in Tibet: a visa to enter China, a Tibet Tourism Bureau (TTB) permit to get into Tibet and an Alien Travel Permit to travel to certain regions of Tibet.

Beware that the permit situation is subject to rapid and unpredictable change by the Chinese government, so it's worth checking the current situation with other travellers in Lhasa or Chengdu. Don't trust travel agencies on this one, as they have a vested interest in booking you on one of their tours. Rumours are that the permit system will change radically when the railway arrives in 2007, though it could happen well before this. Central Tibet will probably be the first region to do away with permits, followed by Western Tibet and, lastly, the remoter regions of the Eastern TAR.

Tibet Tourism Bureau (TTB) Permit

The official Tibetan government line is that a TTB permit is required to visit Tibet. This is partly true. However, even if you fork out whatever local authorities are charging for the 'permit', you will probably never see anything that looks remotely like a travel permit. You are basically paying a 'fee' that will allow you to travel to Tibet independently. If you fly from Chengdu you *will* need to show this permit to buy an air ticket. Dependent on the level of restrictions one member of your 'group' may have to carry the group TTB permit on the plane and hand it over to the guide at Lhasa, though this was no longer necessary at the time of research.

See p313 for more information on buying air and bus tickets into Tibet from Kathmandu, Golmud or Chengdu. The amount of time you can stay in Tibet is normally determined by the length of time on your visa, not the TTB permit.

TTB permits are also needed by groups travelling by Land Cruiser but this will be arranged by the travel agency organising the trip.

Since 2003 Chinese residents of Hong Kong and Macau no longer require a TTB permit to enter Tibet.

Alien Travel Permit

Once you have a visa and have managed to wangle a TTB permit, you'd think you were home dry. Think again. You'll probably need to arrange an extra travel permit for much of your travel around Tibet.

Tibet is slightly more complicated when it comes to travel permits than elsewhere in China. An Alien Travel Permit (usually just called a 'travel permit') is granted by the PSB for travel (independent or group) to an area that is officially closed.

At the time of research, travel permits were *not* needed for the towns of Lhasa, Shigatse and Tsetang, or for places in the Lhasa region (not just Lhasa town), or for nonstop travel on the Friendship Hwy. The Lhasa region includes such places as Ganden, Tsurphu, Nam-tso, Drigung Til and Reting, giving you quite a lot of scope.

Gyantse, Sakya, Samye, the Yarlung Valley, the Everest region and western Tibet all require permits. At the time of research, however, the only places that were actively checking permits were Samye, the Yarlung Valley and the road to Mt Kailash, although in theory you could be checked anywhere outside these places.

Lhasa PSB will not issue travel permits to individuals and will direct you to a travel agency. Agencies can arrange a travel permit to almost anywhere but only if you book a Land Cruiser, driver and guide.

The only glimmer of light in this situation is Shigatse PSB (God bless them). For some reason that nobody can quite work out, Shigatse PSB will issue permits to individuals for most places within the Shigatse prefecture (Sakya, Everest Base Camp, Nangartse, Shalu, Gyantse and anywhere on the Friendship Hwy). Permits are issued on the spot for Y50. You may have to pay a fully refundable Y200 deposit for a permit to Gyantse. You are then free to catch a bus or hitch to these places without having to book an expensive tour. Shigatse PSB has had to cut down on the number of permits it hands out in recent years and may well soon stop the practice completely.

Travel permits for Samye and the areas around Tsetang are almost impossible to come by without booking a tour. At the time of research there were only sporadic checks at Samye and most people visit without a permit. Permits for the Yarlung Valley are only available from Tsetang PSB and you must book transport and a guide with Tsetang's China International Travel Service (CITS), though once again many travellers risk a visit without one.

Permits cost Y50 and can list any number of destinations. If you get caught by the PSB without a permit (most likely when you check into a hotel) you theoretically face a fine of between Y200 and Y500, though many travellers have paid lower fines or no fines at all by playing dumb and claiming anything from student poverty to sickness or road closures. Even if you do pay a fine, you've got away with paying less than you would on a tour. Get a receipt to make sure you don't get fined a second time during your return to Lhasa.

You should give your agency an absolute minimum of four working days to arrange your permits, longer if military or other permits are required (see below). If you are arranging a Land Cruiser trip from abroad the travel agency may ask for up to one month to arrange permits.

Other Permits

Sensitive border areas such as Mt Kailash and eastern Tibet also require a military permit and a foreign-affairs permit.

For Thöling and Tsaparang in western Tibet you may also need a permit from the local Cultural Affairs Bureau. All these will be arranged by the tour agency if you book a tour. Dungkar in western Tibet requires a permit from the Zanda Cultural Affairs Bureau (see p215).

For remote places such as the Yarlung Tsangpo gorges or the Bönri kora in eastern Tibet, or for any border area, you may not be able to get permits even if you book a tour through an ordinary travel agency. For this you will need an agency that has military connections.

PHOTOGRAPHY & VIDEO
Film & Equipment

Tibet is one of the most photogenic countries in the world and you should bring twice as much film as you think you'll need. It is fairly easy to pick up print film in Lhasa and Shigatse, even Advantix film, almost always in 100ASA. It is more difficult to find slide film, but you can buy Provia or Ektachrome film in Lhasa and Shigatse for around Y45 to Y65 for 36 exposures. A decent range of memory cards for digital cameras is available in Lhasa.

It is possible to process print film in Lhasa, and with fairly good results, for around Y20 for 24 shots. It's not possible to process slide film in Tibet. Even in Kathmandu, with the exception of a couple of professional outfits, it is a risky proposition.

Restrictions

Photographs of airports and military installations are prohibited; bridges are also a touchy subject. Don't take any photos or especially video footage of civil unrest or public demonstrations. The Chinese are paranoid about foreign TV crews filming unauthorised documentaries on Tibet.

Restrictions on photography are also imposed at most monasteries and museums. This is partly an attempt to stop the trade of antiquities out of Tibet (statues are often stolen to order from photos taken by seemingly innocuous 'tourists'). In the case of flash photography, such restrictions protect wall murals from damage. Inside the larger monasteries, a fee is often imposed in each room or building for taking a photograph. Generally this is Y50 per shot but you can often negotiate with the monks. Video fees can be up to Y800 (US$100!) in some monasteries. You are free, however, to take any photos of the exteriors of monasteries.

Be aware that these rules are generally enforced. If you want to snap a few photos where you shouldn't, then start with a new roll of film. This way, if it is ripped out of your camera, you won't lose 20 photos from some other part of Tibet as well.

See p43 for guidelines when planning to take photographs of people.

Technical Tips

Bear in mind, when taking photographs in Tibet, that special conditions prevail. For one, the dust gets into everything – make a point of carefully cleaning your lenses as often as possible. The high altitudes in Tibet mean that the best time to take photographs is when the sun is low in the sky: early in the morning and late in the afternoon. At other times getting a good exposure becomes more difficult – you are likely to end up with a shot full of dark shadows and bright points of light.

One useful accessory to cope with Tibet's harsh light conditions is a polarising filter. When using it, turn the filter until the contrast improves; if there are any clouds in the sky, they will become whiter as the sky itself becomes a deeper shade of blue.

POST

Airmail letters and postcards take seven to 10 days to reach their destinations. Writing the country of destination in Chinese should speed up the delivery.

An airmail letter of up to 20g costs Y6 to any country, plus Y1.8 per additional 10g. Postcards cost Y4.50 and aerograms Y5.20.

Rates for parcels vary depending on the country of destination and seem quite random. As a rough guide, a 1kg airmail package costs around Y144 to Y160 to most countries. A 5kg packet to the UK costs Y523 by airmail, Y368 by surface mail and Y201 by sea mail. Surface and sea mail take around two months. The maximum weight you can send or receive is 30kg. Lhasa is the only place in Tibet from where it is possible to send international parcels.

Post offices are very picky about how you pack things; do not finalise your packing until the parcel has its last customs clearance. If you have a receipt for the goods, then put it in the box when you are mailing it, since it may be opened again by customs further down the line.

Express Mail Service (EMS), a worldwide priority mail service, can courier documents to most foreign countries within a couple of days. Packages/documents up to 500g cost Y210/160 to Australia, Y280/220 to Western Europe and Y240/180 to the US, with each additional 500g costing from Y55 (Australia) to Y75 (US and Europe). There are charges of Y2.30 for recorded delivery and Y6.50 for registered mail.

There is a reliable poste restante service at the main post office in Lhasa

SHOPPING

Tibet is not a bad place for souvenir hunting, although much of the stuff you see in markets, particularly the bronzes, has been humped over the high passes from Nepal and can probably be bought cheaper in Kathmandu, where you will have a better selection of quality goods.

For an overview of possible purchases in Tibet, the best place to look is the Barkhor in Lhasa. Prayer flags, shawls, prayer wheels and daggers are all popular buys. Itinerant pilgrims may also come up to you with things to sell – proceeds will often finance their trip home.

Most of the stalls on the Barkhor circuit seem be selling jewellery and most (some would say all) of it is fake. The vast majority of the jewellery on offer is turquoise and coral; Tibetans believe that turquoise is good for the liver and coral for the heart. Locals will tell you that the turquoise comes from the mountains and the coral from the lakes of Tibet – more likely sources are Taiwan and China (if it doesn't come from a factory, that is).

It is easy to tell fake turquoise (or 'new turquoise' as the stall holders call it) from the real thing ('old turquoise'). The fake stuff is bluer and is flawless; beware of a string of identically shaped and rounded beads – nature did not intend them to be this way. The final test is to scratch the surface with a sharp metal object, the fake turquoise will leave a white line, the real stuff won't show a thing. When you've established what you're buying have a closer look at the stone to make sure it's all in one piece. Unscrupulous stall holders glue together tiny bits of turquoise with black glue to make larger pieces of stone. The same rules apply to coral – if you see a perfectly formed set of red beads the chances are they aren't real. Look for bubbles and imperfections.

You'll also see Buddha eye beads, known as *zee* – black or brown oblong beads with white eye symbols. These are replicas of fossils found in rocks in the mountains containing auspicious eye symbols thought to represent the eyes of the Buddha. The real thing is priceless; copies are more affordable. The more eyes the higher the price.

Be prepared to bargain hard for any purchase, especially in the Barkhor. You can probably reckon on at least halving the price,

but there are no hard-and-fast rules. Shop around for a while and get a feel for prices.

Other possible buys are Tibetan ceiling drapes and *thangkas*. Some ceiling drapes and door curtains are very tasteful and can be bought in Lhasa and Shigatse. Most of the *thangkas* for sale are gaudy – good ones do not come cheap. There are a couple of workshops in Lhasa where you can see *thangkas* being painted (see p107).

TELEPHONE

China's phone system has been rapidly modernised and long-distance and international direct dialling is available almost everywhere. Most hotels in Lhasa have direct-dial international telephones but levy a hefty 30% surcharge on calls.

International rates have fallen dramatically in recent years. China Unicom, private telephone booths and IP cards (see below) offer the cheapest rates: around Y2.40 per minute to the US and Y3.60 to most other countries. 'Domestic' calls cost Y1.50 per minute to Hong Kong, Macau and Taiwan, and Y0.30 elsewhere in China. China Telecom charges Y4.80 per minute for international calls, and up to Y8 in remote areas.

Lines are amazingly clear considering where you are. In fact, the biggest problem will probably be the guy yelling in the booth next door on a local call to Shigatse.

There are two main types of phone cards. IC cards can be used at any card phone and are the more expensive of the two. IP cards offer the cheapest rates but have to be used at public phones. IP cards are available in increments of Y30, Y50 and Y100. You dial in a local access number, then punch in your card number (followed by #), a password number (followed by #) and finally the number you wish to call (followed by a final #). English-language instructions are available. You cannot currently use a card purchased in Tibet in other provinces of China. In general the private telecom booths are the easiest to use (most are open until around 11pm).

It is still impossible to make collect calls (reverse-charge calls) or to use foreign telephone debit cards. The best you can do is give someone your number and get them to call you back.

Local area codes are given at the start of each town's entry within this guidebook.

TIME

Time throughout China – including Tibet – is set to Beijing time, which is eight hours ahead of GMT/UTC. When it is noon in Beijing it is also noon in far-off Lhasa, even if the sun only indicates around 9am or 10am. See also the World Time map (p335).

TOILETS

Chinese toilets might be fairly dismal, but Tibetan toilets make them look like little bowers of heaven. The standard model is a deep hole in the ground that bubbles and gives off noxious vapours. Many Tibetans (including women with long skirts) urinate and defecate in the street. On the plus side there are some fabulous 'toilets with a view'. Honours go to the Samye Monastery Guesthouse, the Sakya Guesthouse, the public toilets in the Potala, and the small village of Pasum on the way to Everest Base Camp.

With the exception of the odd hotel here and there, toilets in Tibet are of the squat variety – as the clichés go, good for the digestion and character building too. Always carry a small stash of toilet paper or tissues with you. Be warned that toilets are not secure – keep an eye on valuables. And finally, a tip for the boys: if there's nobody about, the women's toilets are always cleaner than the men's.

TOURIST INFORMATION

Tibet is officially a province of China and does not have tourist offices as such. Similarly, the Tibetan government-in-exile does not provide information specifically relating to travel in Tibet. Several of the pro-Tibetan organisations abroad offer travel advice; see p13.

Tibet Tourism Bureau

The main function of the state-sponsored **Tibet Tourism Bureau** (TTB; www.tibet-tour.com; Shanghai ☎ 021-6321 1729; Beijing ☎ 010-6410 5822; Chengdu ☎ 028-333 3988; Kathmandu ☎ 977-01-119787) is to direct travellers into group tours in Tibet. It issues the permits necessary to enter Tibet (see p304), although very few travellers deal with it directly.

VISAS

Visas for individual travel in China are easy to get from most Chinese embassies. China will even issue a visa to individuals from countries that do not have diplomatic relations with the People's Republic of China (PRC). The Chinese government has been known to stop issuing individual visas in summer or the run-up to sensitive political events, as a control on tourist numbers.

Most Chinese embassies and consulates will issue a standard 30-day, single-entry tourist (an 'L' category) visa in three to five working days. The 'L' means *luxing* (travel). Fees vary according to how much your country charges Chinese citizens for a visa. At the time of writing, a standard 30-day visa cost A$30 in Australia, €30.50 in France, UK£25 in the UK and US$30 in the USA. Fees must be paid in cash at the time of application and you'll need two passport-sized photos. It's best to get an application form in person at the embassy or consulate, although it is possible to obtain one online at embassy websites. Some Chinese embassies (not the US) offer a postal service for a fee but this takes around three weeks. Express services cost double the normal fee. Your application must be written in English, and you are advised to have one entire blank page in your passport for the visa.

The visa application form asks you a lot of questions (your entry and exit points, travel itinerary, means of transport etc), but once in China you can deviate from this as much as you like. Regulations state that you should have a ticket out of the country but this is rarely enforced. Whatever you do, however, *do not* let on that you plan to visit Tibet when you fill in this section. When listing your itinerary, pick the obvious contenders: Beijing, Shanghai and so on. Don't list your occupation as journalist and don't mention bicycles (otherwise you may be told erroneously that you have to take a tour to travel by bike).

Visas valid for more than 30 days can be difficult to obtain anywhere other than Hong Kong, although some embassies abroad (in the US and UK, for example) may give you 60 or even 90 days out of high season if you ask nicely. This saves you the considerable hassle of getting a visa extension in Tibet. Most agencies in Hong Kong should be able to arrange a 90-day visa.

A standard single-entry visa is activated on the date you enter China, and must be used within three months from the date of issue. There is some confusion over the validity of Chinese visas. Most Chinese officials look at the 'valid until' date, but on most 30-day visas this is actually the date by which you must have *entered* the country, not the visa's expiry date. Longer-stay visas are often activated on the day of issue, not the day you enter the country, so there's no point in getting one too far in advance of your planned entry date. Check with the embassy if you are unsure.

If you want more flexibility to enter and leave China several times, most Chinese embassies will issue a double-entry visa.

Recent changes mean that it is now possible to travel in Tibet with any visa type, including a resident or business visa. This means you could get a six-month business visa (easily obtained in Hong Kong) and stay in Tibet for most of that time!

Hong Kong

In Hong Kong, the cheapest 30-day visas (HK$100 for next-day service, HK$250 for same-day service) can be obtained from the **visa office** (☎ 2827 1881; Ministry of Foreign Affairs of the PRC, 5th fl, Low Block, China Resources Bldg, 26 Harbour Rd, Wanchai; 9am-12.30pm & 2-5pm Mon-Fri, 9am-12.30pm Sat). US citizens (unless of Chinese descent) face an additional surcharge of HK$160. You'll have to queue but you'll save a few dollars. From Tsimshatsui on the Kowloon side, the cheapest and easiest way to get there is to take the Star Ferry to Wanchai Pier (not to Central), one block away from the China Resources Building.

China Travel Service (CTS; ☎ 2315 7188; 1st fl, Alpha House, 27-33 Nathan Rd, Tsimshatsui, enter from Peking Rd) is a more convenient and popular place to get a visa. Tourist visas of up to 90 days cost HK$580 for same-day service (hand your passport in before noon, pick up at 6.30pm), HK$410 for next-day service and HK$210 for two-day service. Passport photos are available here for HK$30.

Kathmandu

Regulations at the Chinese embassy in Kathmandu change frequently. At the time of writing the embassy was not issuing visas to individual travellers, only to those travellers booked on a tour (see p314) and even then only group visas. If you turn up with a Chinese visa already in your passport it will be cancelled.

A group visa is a separate sheet of paper with all the names and passport numbers of the group members. Try to get your own

individual 'group' visa, as otherwise, come the end of your tour in Lhasa, you will either have to exit China with the group or split from this group visa. (At the time of writing at least two people had to be on a group visa but the policy changes frequently.) Splitting from a group visa costs up to US$40 and can only officially be done by the Chinese partner of the Nepali travel agency that arranged your travel into Tibet. It is a *real* pain to be avoided at all costs. Group visas are generally issued for a maximum of 25 days. It is possible to extend a group visa but only outside Tibet.

At other times, the embassy has allowed travellers to travel on their existing individual visas, so you'll just have to try to find out the current situation in advance.

Visa Extensions

The foreign affairs section of the local PSB handles visa extensions. Extensions are very rarely given in Lhasa. It is far easier to extend your visa in Chengdu, Leshan, Zhongdian, Xining or Xi'an, where a 30-day extension is commonplace. The best place to get a visa extension inside Tibet is in Ali or Chamdo, the latter only if you are on a legitimate tour. You'll generally only get an extension within a few days of your visa expiring so it's a bit of a gamble. Fees vary according to your nationality but generally cost around Y160.

Travel agencies should be able to arrange a visa extension for as long as you are on one of their tours.

WOMEN TRAVELLERS

Sexual harassment is extremely rare in Tibet and foreign women seem to be able to travel here with few problems. Naturally, it's worth noticing what local women are wearing and how they are behaving, and making a bit of an effort to fit in, as you would in any other foreign country. Probably because of the harsh climate, Tibetan women dress in bulky layers of clothing that mask their femininity. It would be wise to follow their example and dress modestly, especially when visiting a monastery. Several women have written of the favourable reactions they have received from Tibetan women when wearing Tibetan dress.

Women may be not be permitted to enter the *gönkhang* (protector chapel) of some monasteries.

Transport

TRANSPORT

> **THINGS CHANGE...**
>
> The information in this chapter is particularly vulnerable to change. In particular, Chinese visa and permit requirements change like the wind. Check directly with the airline or a travel agent to make sure you understand how a fare (and ticket you may buy) works and be aware of the security requirements for international travel. Shop carefully. The details given in this chapter should be regarded as pointers and are not a substitute for your own careful, up-to-date research.

Tibet is not the most accessible of destinations, but then getting there is half the fun. For most international travellers, getting to Tibet will involve at least two legs: the first to the gateways of Kathmandu (Nepal) or Chengdu (China) and the second from these cities into Tibet. The first section of this chapter details long-haul options to China and Nepal, while the second section details the practicalities of actually getting into and around Tibet. The Gateway Cities chapter (p77) offers basic information for travellers transiting through Kathmandu or Chengdu.

Once you are within the region, direct air access to Lhasa is basically limited to flights from Kathmandu, Chengdu or Zhongdian. There are also connections from Chongqing, Xining, Xi'an, Beijing and Guangzhou, but these tend to involve considerably more bureaucratic hassle.

Overland routes into Tibet involve days of gruelling travel from either Nepal or China. The only officially sanctioned overland routes into Tibet are via the Qinghai–Tibet Hwy, which runs between Lhasa and Golmud, or the Friendship Hwy, which runs from Kathmandu to Lhasa.

At the time of writing, bureaucratic obstacles to entering Tibet (a potentially more insurmountable barrier than even the Himalaya) had loosened enough to make entry

relatively easy, though there is a cost involved. Travellers heading from Golmud or flying from elsewhere in China still have to join a nominal 'tour' in order to get into Lhasa but after that you can break off on your own. The situation from Nepal is trickier because of ever-changing visa requirements.

Political events, both domestic and international, heavily affect regulations for entry into Tibet. It would be wise to check on the latest developments in Tibet before setting out.

GETTING THERE & AWAY – GATEWAY CITIES

ENTERING THE COUNTRY
Passports

Chinese embassies will not issue a visa if your passport has less than six months of validity remaining.

Hong Kong residents have reported problems entering Nepal on a British National Overseas (BNO) passport after exiting China on their brown Huixiangzhen (used for travelling in China), as the BNO passport then lacks a Chinese exit stamp. If you are travelling this way, try to get an exit stamp put in your BNO passport.

Permits are very rarely checked on arrival at Lhasa's Gongkar Airport, though they are checked when checking in for your flight to Lhasa.

AIR

Air travel is complicated because there are no direct long-haul flights to Tibet. You will probably have to stop over in Kathmandu, Beijing or Hong Kong if you are making a beeline for Lhasa.

Generally, flights to Kathmandu are not all that cheap as there are now a limited number of carriers operating out of the Nepali capital. Depending on where you are coming from, it may be cheaper to fly to Delhi and make your way overland from there.

To China, you generally have the choice of flying first to Beijing or Hong Kong, although there are a small number of flights direct to Chengdu or Kunming from Southeast Asia. Hong Kong has traditionally enjoyed the cheapest flights but these days this is not always the case. If there's little difference in the fares, then it's just a choice of which city you would prefer to visit. It costs more to fly to Chengdu from Hong Kong than from Beijing, but fares even up if you fly from Shenzhen, just over the Guangdong border from Hong Kong. Hong Kong is the easiest place to get a Chinese visa of longer than 30 days.

If you are heading straight to Chengdu you could fly to Bangkok or Singapore and then take a direct flight from there to Chengdu.

Full-fare flights to/from Chengdu to other Chinese cities include Beijing (Y1440), Shanghai (Y1660), Guangzhou (Y1300), Kunming (Y700) and Hong Kong (Y2204), though discounted fares are often sold.

Tickets

If you want to get to Tibet as quickly as possible (perhaps to get the maximum use from your visa) consider buying a domestic Air China ticket to Chengdu as part of your international ticket to, say, Beijing. Some Air China offices will give you a discount of up to 50% on the domestic leg if you buy the long-haul leg through them.

Another ticket worth looking into is an open-jaw ticket. This options might involve,

---

for example, flying into Hong Kong and then flying out of Kathmandu, allowing you to travel overland across Tibet.

Australia & New Zealand

Check major newspapers such as the *Age,* the *Sydney Morning Herald* and the *Australian* for information on long-haul travel agencies.

The cheapest flights from Australia to China generally go via one of the Southeast Asian capitals, such as Kuala Lumpur, Bangkok or Manila. The cheapest one-way (low-season) tickets from Australia to Hong Kong cost around A$840; return tickets will cost at least A$1100. Flights from New Zealand cost around NZ$990/1345 for a one-way/return fare.

Return fares to Kathmandu from the east coast of Australia range from around A$1300 to A$1500, depending on the season. A one-way ticket costs around A$1100 with Singapore Airlines or Thai Airways. Return flights from New Zealand cost from around NZ$1820 to NZ$2170.

STA Travel (www.statravel.com; Australia ☎ 1300 733 035; New Zealand ☎ 0508 782 872)

Flight Centre (www.flightcentre.com; Australia ☎ 133 133; New Zealand ☎ 0800 24 35 44)

Trailfinders (☎ 1300 780 212; www.trailfinders.com.au) In Australia only.

Continental Europe

Air fares to the Indian subcontinent and China are generally cheaper in the UK than they are in the rest of Europe.

STA Travel (www.statravel.com; Paris ☎ 01 43 59 23 69; Frankfurt ☎ 69-430 1910) has dozens of offices across Europe.

Hong Kong

Hong Kong is the main port of entry for China and is now formally part of the People's Republic of China. Most nationalities don't need a visa for a visit to Hong Kong. Most travellers make their way from Hong Kong into China by train or ferry, but there are also daily direct flights from Hong Kong to Chengdu with Dragonair and China Southwest Airlines for around HK$2330/3710 one way/return.

It is considerably cheaper to fly from Shenzhen or Guangzhou to Chengdu than from Hong Kong. From Shenzhen it costs around HK$1250 (for a ticket bought in Hong Kong),

---

DEPARTURE TAX

The domestic/international departure tax from China is currently Y50/90, generally paid at check-in. There are plans to include this fee directly into the airfare so check when purchasing your ticket.

or as low as Y900 (bought in Chengdu); it costs about HK$1170 from Guangzhou. The Shenzhen airport is just a Turbojet hydrofoil ride (HK$189) from Hong Kong's Tsim Sha Tsui district. As a comparison, the 40-hour train ride from Guangzhou to Chengdu costs around Y500/800 for a hard/soft sleeper.

China Travel Service (CTS; ☎ 2315 7188; www .ctshk.com; 1F, Alpha House, 27-33 Nathan Rd, Tsimshatsui) can book all these tickets and also offers a discount deal on hydrofoil tickets booked in conjunction with a flight out of Shenzhen.

A flight from Hong Kong to Kathmandu costs around US$320 one way.

Phoenix Services Agency (☎ 2722 7378; phoe nix1@netvigator.com; Rm A, 7th fl, Milton Mansion, 98 Nathan Rd, Tsimshatsui) is a recommended travel agency.

Southeast Asia

There are direct flights from Bangkok and Singapore to Chengdu and from Bangkok, Chiang Mai, Yangon (Rangoon), Vientiane and Singapore to Kunming.

Bangkok is a popular place to pick up air tickets, and prices are generally very competitive. The best place to shop around is the Bangkok backpacker ghetto of Khao San Rd. Flights with China Southwest Airlines from Bangkok to Chengdu/Kunming cost around US$255/180 one way. Singapore is slightly more. It's also possible to fly direct three times a week from Chiang Mai to Kunming for around US$100 (Y1450 in Kunming). Flights to Kathmandu can be picked up for around US$300.

STA Travel (www.sta.com) operates branches in Singapore, Bangkok and Kuala Lumpur.

UK

There are some very good deals available in London's bucket shops for flights to Beijing, Hong Kong and major Indian cities, mainly Delhi. Check the travel sections of newspapers, and magazines like *Time Out*.

Those looking at travelling via the Indian subcontinent and shaving costs wherever possible will find it cheapest to fly to Delhi and then travel overland to Nepal. Fares to India generally start from UK£400 return. The cheapest high-season return fares to Kathmandu are around UK£650 with Gulf Air. The cheapest one-way fares from Kathmandu to London cost around US$400, also with Gulf Air.

Several specialist agencies in London can book both international and Chinese domestic tickets, including **China Travel Service and Information Centre** (☎ 020-7388 8838; www .chinatravel.co.uk; 124 Euston Rd, London NW1 2AL).

Summer peak-season fares to Beijing cost around UK£300 one way and UK£500 return, although low-season return flights can be as little as UK£340. Virgin Atlantic offers excellent fares to Shanghai for around UK£400 return, from where it's about US$150 to get to Chengdu. Cheap flights (often with Middle Eastern Airlines) to Hong Kong cost around the same price.

Most British travel agencies are registered with the Association of British Travel Agencies (ABTA). If you have paid for your flight with an ABTA-registered agency that then goes out of business, the ABTA will then provide you with either a refund or an alternative.

Bridge the World (☎ 0870-814 4400; www.bridgethe world.com)

Flight Bookers (☎ 020-7757 2444, www.flightbookers .co.uk)

STA (☎ 0870-160 0599; www.statravel.co.uk)

Trailfinders (☎ 020-7938 3366, 7938 3939; www.trail finders.com)

USA & Canada

It is far cheaper to fly to Hong Kong or Beijing from the USA or Canada than it is to fly to India. This might work out quite well if your ultimate destination is India. Overland travel from Hong Kong to Nepal and India through Tibet is reasonably time-consuming – but what a trip!

Coming from the west coast, the cheapest one-way/return fares to Hong Kong start at around US$385/750. To Beijing return fares begin at US$860. From New York to Hong Kong, one-way/return fares start at around US$410/900. Fares are likely to be higher at the peak of summer.

A useful website with information about international and domestic airfares in China is www.flychina.com.

Tickets from the west coast cost around US$1350 return to Delhi or Mumbai (Bombay), and US$1500 return to Kathmandu. From the east coast you are looking at around US$1000 return to Delhi. From Kathmandu, a one-way ticket with Northwest or Thai International to the west coast costs US$673.

The cheapest tickets to Hong Kong are offered by bucket shops run by ethnic Chinese in San Francisco, Los Angeles and New York.

Reliable, long-running agencies:

Gateway Travel (☎ 800-441 1183, 214-960 2000)

Overseas Tours (☎ 800-323 8777, 650-692 4892; www.overseastours.com)

STA Travel (☎ 24-hours 800-781 4040; www.sta.com)

China Travel Service (www.chinatravelservice.com; San Francisco ☎ 1-800-899 8618, 415-398 6627; 575 Sutter St; Los Angeles ☎ 1-800-890 8818; 119 S Atlantic Blvd, Suite 303, Monterey Park) Offers flights and independent tours.

Canadian prices are similar to those available in the USA. Try **Travel Cuts** (☎ 1-866-416 2887; www.travelcuts.com) for excellent deals on tickets to Asia. Canadian Airlines and Korean Air have the cheapest flights to Hong Kong.

LAND

There are countless ways to cross overland into China.

The Karakoram Hwy, in particular, provides travellers with the opportunity to do a subcontinental circuit through Tibet, Nepal, India and Pakistan and back into China (in any order you like).

GETTING THERE & AWAY – TIBET

This section details how to get into Tibet from Nepal or China.

AIR

The only airline that flies into Tibet is currently Air China, though it is reported that a new airline called Air Tibet will be created to operate flights in and out of Lhasa. Royal Nepal Airlines also has plans to fly the Kathmandu–Lhasa leg.

Flights to and from Lhasa are frequently cancelled or delayed in the winter months, so if you are flying at this time give yourself a couple of days' leeway in Chengdu if you have a connecting flight.

There are flight connections to Lhasa from half a dozen Chinese cities but 99% of travellers fly from Chengdu or Zhongdian, because arranging a permit is so much easier from there.

Nepal

Flights between Kathmandu and Lhasa are twice weekly in the low season (departing Tuesday and Saturday) and three times a week in the high season.

Individual travellers can't buy air tickets from the Air China office without a TTB permit. Purchase a three- to eight-day package tour through a travel agency.

At the time of research, the cheapest package was a three-day tour for around US$360. This included the flight ticket (US$273), airport transfer to Kathmandu and Lhasa, TTB permits and dormitory accommodation for three nights in Lhasa. For a list of travel companies in Kathmandu see p78.

The Chinese embassy in Kathmandu is currently not giving Chinese visas to individual travellers and will even cancel any existing Chinese visa you have. See p309 for more on visa headaches in Kathmandu.

At the slightest whiff of trouble in Lhasa or in Kathmandu, flights between the two cities may be cancelled and they may also be shut down during the winter months.

Chengdu

Flights between Chengdu and Lhasa cost Y1270, but you'll be very lucky if this is all you end up paying for the flight. Both in Chengdu and other cities, Air China will not sell you a ticket to Lhasa unless you already have a TTB permit.

To get around this, many travel agencies, especially those close to the Traffic Hotel in Chengdu, will sell you a 'tour' that allows them to arrange a ticket for you. What the tour consists of depends largely upon the political climate in Lhasa. Out of the high tourist season (July to September) you can normally get away with booking only a ticket and airport transfers. However, at the height of summer, agencies may have to book your transport from Gongkar airport to Lhasa, three nights' dormitory accommodation and a tour in Lhasa.

In May 2004 the cheapest Tibet package, consisting of one airport transfer and a one-way flight, cost Y1700. In other years three-day packages have reached Y2400. Packages are generally cheaper in March and April and start rising by May, reaching a peak in August. Travellers sometimes have to travel in groups of five, although the agencies can normally rustle up enough individual

REGIONAL AIR ROUTES

All of the following flights operate in both directions. Fares given are one way.

From	To	Flights per Week	Fare (Yuan)
Lhasa	Beijing (via Chengdu)	2	2040
Lhasa	Chamdo	1	700
Lhasa	Chengdu	21	1270
Lhasa	Chongqing	1	1400
Lhasa	Guangzhou (via Zhongdian)	1	2500
Lhasa	Kathmandu	3	1830-2290
Lhasa	Kunming	1	1380
Lhasa	Shanghai (via Xining)	2	2880
Lhasa	Xi'an	4	1420
Lhasa	Xining	4	1390
Lhasa	Zhongdian	1	1250
Chamdo	Chengdu	3	750
Zhongdian	Kunming	7	560
Kunming	Lijiang	7	520
Xining	Chengdu	7	900
Xining	Golmud	2	840

travellers to form a small group. Everyone goes their own way once in Lhasa. Agencies normally need 24 hours to process the mythical TTB permit. This is still the most cost-effective way to enter Tibet.

Whether you actually see your TTB permit is unlikely, although your travel agency may wave it at check-in to allow you through.

On a clear day the views from the plane are stupendous so try to get a window seat. In general the best views are from the left side of the plane from Chengdu to Lhasa and on the right side from Lhasa to Chengdu.

Zhongdian & Kunming

Air China/China Southern operate a useful flight from Kunming to Lhasa via Zhongdian in northwest Yunnan. The flight costs Y1670 from Kunming and Y1250 from Zhongdian, but as with other flights to Lhasa, foreigners need to sign up on a tour to get a ticket.

The cheapest tour package means you start in Zhongdian; the package costs around Y2250 (including the air ticket, TTB permit, airport transfers and three nights' worth of dormitory accommodation in Lhasa). You must arrange the TTB permit and pick it up in Kunming, although the flight ticket can be picked up in either Zhongdian or Kunming. Flight packages from Kunming start at about Y2600

LAND

Many individual travellers make their way to Tibet as part of a grand overland trip through China, Nepal, India and onwards. In many ways, land travel to Tibet is the best way to go, not only for the scenery en route but also because it can help spread the altitude gain over a few days.

In theory there are several land routes into Tibet. In practice, most travellers only use one of two officially sanctioned routes: Kathmandu to Lhasa via the Friendship Hwy or Golmud to Lhasa via the Qinghai–Tibet Hwy. Other possible routes (for now officially closed) are the Sichuan–Tibet Hwy, the Yunnan–Tibet Hwy and the Xinjiang–Tibet Hwy. Of these the Yunnan–Tibet Hwy is the 'most closed' (ie very few travellers are getting through to Tibet this way); the 'least closed' is the Xinjiang–Tibet Hwy.

By 2007 there should be a daily rail link between Golmud and Lhasa. See Mission Impossible (p44) for details.

Friendship Highway (Nepal to Tibet)

The 865km stretch of road between Kathmandu and Lhasa is known as the Friendship Hwy. The journey is without a doubt one of the most spectacular in the world.

From Kathmandu (elevation 1300m) the road travels gently up to Kodari (1873m), before leaving Nepal to make a steep switchback ascent to Zhangmu (2300m), the Tibetan border town, and then Nyalam (3750m), where most people spend their first night. The road then climbs to the top of the Tong-la (5120m), continuing to Tingri (4390m) for the second night.

It is essential to watch out for the effects of altitude sickness during the early stages of this trip (see p329). Try to slip in a rest day at Tingri or Nyalam if you are heading up to Everest Base Camp (5200m). See the Tsang chapter (p160) for details of sights and landmarks en route.

This highway is very well travelled nowadays and is a pleasant journey, except for one major problem – the Chinese authorities will not let individual travellers enter Tibet without a TTB permit and tour.

Because of this, several of Kathmandu's travel agencies (p78) offer 'budget' tours of Tibet to get you into Lhasa. At the time of research the cheapest of these tours cost around US$120 per person for a basic five-day minibus trip to Lhasa, stopping in Nyalam, Lhatse, Shigatse, Gyantse and Lhasa. A similar trip with three more days in Lhasa will cost US$230 to US$270. Land Cruiser trips cost a little more. A seven-day trip via Everest Base Camp and Sakya Monastery, amongst others, costs US$440 per person but these are harder to find. Prices normally include transport, permits, basic dormitory accommodation, a fairly useless guide and (usually) admission fees. Trips normally depart on Saturday and Tuesday. Agencies may pool clients so you could find yourself travelling in a larger group than expected and perhaps a bus instead of the promised Land Cruiser. Other potential inconsistencies may include having to share a room when you were told you would be given a single, or paying a double room supplement and ending up in a dorm. We do get a fair number of complaints about the service of some of these tours; it's best just to view it as the cheapest way to get to Tibet.

For more information about the potential visa snags involved in a trip from Kathmandu see p309.

From Lhasa it is often possible to get a ride direct to the Nepali border (with an overnight stop in Shigatse) on minibuses heading down to pick up groups arriving from Kathmandu – see p116.

A private Land Cruiser tour from Lhasa to the Nepali border will cost around Y2800 to Y3500 for a four- or five-day trip, which works out around US$100 per person.

Political instability in Nepal means that the Nepali/Chinese border is occasionally closed. Strikes and blockades on the Nepali side can make onward transport a problem so try to find out in advance if any strikes are planned.

See p196 for details of the border crossing to Nepal. China is 2¼ hours ahead of Nepali time.

Qinghai–Tibet Highway

The 1115km journey between Golmud and Lhasa is the subject of an ancient Chinese curse: 'May you travel by Chinese bus from Golmud to Lhasa'. Actually, we made that one up – but it deserves to be.

Golmud (elevation 2800m, pop 200,000), the drab little Chinese town where the long journey begins, is normally approached from Xining by rail (15 hours, from Y117 hard sleeper), though there are also twice weekly flights (Y840). If Golmud were not one of the most utterly depressing places in China, it would probably serve as a good place to hang out for a few days and acclimatise to the altitude. But it *is* one of the most utterly depressing places in China and consequently most people jump on a Lhasa-bound bus quicker than a CITS official can say 'give us your cash'.

If Golmud did not exist, CITS would have to invent it. It is a perfect bottleneck to capture Lhasa-bound individual travellers and screw them for every yuan possible. CITS officials make it their job to form welcoming parties for all incoming buses and trains.

CITS-approved buses for Lhasa depart from the Tibet bus station on Jinfen Lu at around 3pm daily. Foreigners are required to buy their tickets from **CITS** (☎ 0979-413 003; 2nd fl, Golmud Hotel; ✆ 8.30am-noon & 2.30-6pm Mon-Fri) or at the Tibet bus station, at a massive mark-up.

Current regulations require that foreigners buy a four-day tour package, which includes accommodation and a TTB permit. The cheapest package currently costs Y1700, which includes the return bus fare to Golmud and accommodation at the Kirey Hotel in Lhasa. For almost the same

TRANSPORT

TRANSPORT

price you can fly to Lhasa from Chengdu! Once you arrive, you're free to stick with the 'tour' or strike off on your own. Note that CITS won't issue permits on weekends.

The other option is to hang around the regular bus station (across from the train station) and make a deal with one of the drivers. They generally ask for about Y600 (bus) or Y800 (jeep); it's understood that this price includes a bribe for the PSB. There is no way to guarantee that you will get to Lhasa or that you won't be fined and sent back. The main check post lies 25km south of Golmud but some travellers have been sent back from Nagchu, about three-quarters of the way to Lhasa! You shouldn't hand over any money until you actually have a seat in a vehicle, and ideally the bulk of the payment should be made only once you've arrived.

The official policy changes often, and the railway to Lhasa is expected to further revolutionise the whole permit system. Lonely Planet's Thorn Tree (http://thorntree.lonely planet.com/) is a good way to stay on top of the latest rules and regulations.

In contrast, travellers making their way from Lhasa to Golmud by bus can just buy a ticket from Lhasa bus station (Y210 to Y250). Double check in advance whether you are booked on a sleeper bus or normal bus – for a trip which is up to 40 hours, a sleeper bus has reclining seats that make beds and allows you to sleep.

The Qinghai–Tibet Hwy is cold, bleak and almost devoid of interesting sights. Before setting off you should stock up on munchies and drinks and, if you have not already done so, buy some warm clothing – toasty-warm People's Liberation Army (PLA) overcoats are available for around

Y75. Some travellers buy oxygen canisters (Y30) from the CITS office to help with the altitude sickness.

The trip itself takes around 24 hours, longer if there is a breakdown. Even in summer it can get bitterly cold, especially up on the high passes, the highest of which is Tangu-la (5180m). It is one of those once-in-a-lifetime trips.

Sichuan–Tibet Highway

The road between Chengdu and Lhasa is around 2400km or 2100km, depending on whether you take the northern or southern route.

The Sichuan section of the Sichuan–Tibet Hwy is now open to foreigners as far as the Tibetan border. Beyond this, the road is closed to individual travellers, although the occasional tour group and renegade explorer passes along it. Be prepared for a difficult trip that might end with a fine and an abrupt return.

There is very little in the way of public transport on this route. Truck drivers face fines of up to Y2000 and the loss of their licence for taking foreigners in their trucks, and it is a dangerous trip – a number of accidents have occurred along it. Perhaps your best chance is to hook up with a truck that is itself slightly illegal and therefore inclined to drive through the check posts at night. Apart from the check posts the likeliest place to be caught is at a hotel.

Food and accommodation is of a better standard and more widely available than on the Qinghai–Tibet Hwy (where there is basically nothing) or in western Tibet. For coverage of the sights along the route see the Roads to Tibet (p249) and Eastern Tibet (p224) chapters. For an overview of routes see p18. There are public buses as far as Derge on the northern branch and Batang on the southern branch.

The 780km stretch of road between Markham and Bayi is likely to be the biggest hurdle for travellers making their way to Lhasa. There are PSB offices in most towns, particularly Pomi, Lunang and Nyingtri. Markham is where the Yunnan–Tibet Hwy joins the Sichuan–Tibet Hwy and so the local PSB is particularly scrupulous about making sure that no travellers continue on to Lhasa. If you make it as far as Bayi, you will have to deal with the Bayi PSB. Many

TIBETAN TASTERS

If you are heading to Golmud overland there are several worthwhile detours you can make to give you an idea of what you are in for. **Labrang Monastery**, around 100km south of Lanzhou in Gansu, is one of the six major monasteries of the Gelugpa Buddhist order and is well worth a visit. Another of the six is **Kumbum Monastery** (Ta'er Si), 26km southeast of Xining. Both are easily visited on the way from Xi'an to Golmud.

OVERLAND TRAVEL AGENCIES IN CHINA

A few Chinese adventure travel agencies specialise in travel in western Sichuan and northwest Yunnan, including organised overland trips to Lhasa through remote Kham.

- **China Golden Bridge Travel Service** (☎ 28-8662 6052; www.plateautour.com; Chengdu) Offers a 15-day Chengdu–Lhasa overland tour for US$400 per person.
- **China Minority Travel** (www.china-travel.nl) Dutch-Chinese operation based in Dali; runs a nine-day overland trip from Zhongdian to Lhasa for US$630 to US$690 per person.
- **Dreams Travel** (☎ 28-8515 7151; www.dreams-travel.com/english; No 9, 1 Huan Lu Nan 4 Duan, Shenzhou Travel Mansion, Chengdu) Tours to and around Tibet.
- **Forbidden Frontier** (☎ 21-6471 8222; www.forbiddenfrontier.com; No 40, 1487 Huaihai Zhonglu, Shanghai) Trips throughout Kham.
- **Gyaltang Travel** (☎ 887-822 3646; www.coloursofsangana.com/gyalthang) Upper-end tours; based in the stylish Gyalthang Dzong Hotel, Zhongdian. Contact Uttara Crees.
- **Haiwei Trails** (www.haiweitrails.com; Lijiang ☎ 888-512-4540; Zhongdian ☎ 887-687-8737) US-British company that operates out of Lijiang and runs jeep trips and charters into central and eastern Tibet.
- **Khampa Caravan** (☎ 887-828 8648; www.khampacaravan.com; Beimen Jie, Zhongdian) Overland trips from Zhongdian to Lhasa, with an emphasis on sustainable tourism and local communities. Contact Dakpa or Yeshi.
- **Wild China** (☎ 10 6465 6602; www.wildchina.com; Rm 801, Oriental Place, 9 Dongtang Donglu, North Dongsanhuan Rd, Chaoyang District, Beijing) Professionally run trips in Yunnan and Sichuan regions of Kham.

travellers have had problems with this PSB, and the best advice is to tell them you have come from Lhasa and let them have the pleasure of sending you back. Be patient and try not to be belligerent.

Yunnan–Tibet Highway

The Yunnan–Tibet Hwy would be a wonderful way to approach Tibet if it were ever to open. From lovely Lijiang a road heads up to the Tibetan towns and monasteries of Zhongdian (Gyeltang) and Deqin (Jol), from where there are public buses north across the Tibetan border (and checkpost) 112km to Yanjing. From here it's 111km to Markham, where the road joins the Sichuan southern route (see p257). The road from Deqin to Markham is currently being upgraded. For details on the Tibetan areas of northwest Yunnan see Lonely Planet's *China*.

The Yunnan route is officially closed to individual travellers but increasing numbers of people are getting through. Markham is the place where most permitless travellers get caught and sent back. A few travel companies are starting to organise nine- or 10-day overland tours on this route, including

the excellent Khampa Caravan in Zhongdian (see p317). TTB permits take around five days to arrange so contact these agencies in advance.

The Zhongdian **TTB office** (☎ 887-822 9028; yunnantibettour@yahoo.com.cn; Rm 2206, Shangbala Hotel, Chengzheng Lu) can organise eight-to 10-day overland trips to Lhasa for about US$625 per person in a group of four and is also open to budget packages.

The owner of Dukezhong Guesthouse in Zhongdian, **Zhi Shi Pei Chu** (kangbaren@hotmail .com) claims he can arrange 4X4s to Lhasa for around US$100 per day. Travellers can get the permit process rolling in advance through the **MCA Guesthouse** (☎ 0872-267 3666; mcahouse@hotmail.com; Wenxian Lu) in Dali, before travelling on to Zhongdian.

FIT in Lhasa (see p91) charges around Y15,000 for a Lhasa–Bayi–Pomi–Pomda–Markham–Deqin Land Cruiser trip, which also works out at about US$500 per person.

Xinjiang–Tibet Highway

The Xinjiang–Tibet Hwy is officially off limits, but interestingly, at the time of research, there were quite a number of travellers who were managing to get through, even on bicycles. Approximately 1350km of road separates Kashgar from Ali in western Tibet and for the adventurous this can form an extension to a trip along the Karakoram Hwy.

With at least two passes over 5400m, the Xinjiang–Tibet Hwy is the highest road in the world. It can be bitterly cold and closes down for the winter months from December to February. The whole trip takes at least four days of travel, depending on how lucky you are with lifts. There are truck stops along the way, about a day's travel apart, but it's wise to bring food and a sleeping bag. A tent can be useful in emergencies. Coming from Kashgar, you have to be particularly careful about altitude sickness as the initial rate of altitude gain is dramatic.

There are buses every half hour from Kashgar to Yecheng (Karghilik; Y23, five hours), and a bus makes the journey between Yecheng and Ali (Y280, 30 hours) when road conditions allow. If you're hitching from Yecheng to Ali, the truck stop 4km southeast of Yecheng is the best place to sniff out a lift. Accommodation is available here and trucks depart in the early morning. Expect to pay Y150 to Y500 for a lift, depending on the road conditions.

FIT in Lhasa was offering a three-week Mt Everest–Kailash–Guge-Kingdom–Yecheng–Kashgar Land Cruiser trip for about Y25,000, which works out at around US$780 per person for four sharing.

THE ROUTE
Leaving Yecheng, there's a checkpoint south of town, but it's possible to drive around it. The road climbs two passes (3150m and 4800m), then follows a narrow gorge to the truck stop and checkpost at **Kudi**. Around 270km from Yecheng, K2 is visible across the Pakistan border. About 150km later you'll reach **Mazar** (3700m), which has some shops and restaurants. The road turns east from here and climbs over a couple of passes, fanning out across barren plains in between. Road conditions improve around 60km before you reach the depressing little town of **Dahongliutan** (4200m), which offers basic food and a guesthouse.

From here the road turns south, and around 23km beyond Dahongliutan you climb out of the Xinjiang plains to the Jitai Daban pass (5050m), which marks the beginning of the remote region of Aksai Chin. For the next 170km road conditions are very bad and progress is slow. The construction of the road here, through a triangle of territory that India claimed as part of Ladakh, was a principal cause of the border war between India and China in 1962. The fact that the Chinese managed to build this road without India even realising that it was under construction is an indication of the utter isolation of the region. Finally you come to the edge of Aksai Chin and climb up to the Jieshan Daban pass (5200m), which has stunning views and which takes you over the border into Tibet. From here, Ali is around 420km away.

Road conditions don't get any better over the border. For the next 30km the road is muddy, rutted and desolate, though the route is currently being upgraded. The road climbs a 5050m pass where conditions do improve, before heading down to the small town of **Sumzhi**, which has basic accommodation and a restaurant. After crossing the last major pass (5250m) the road descends to the town of **Dormar** (4350m), 80km away, which has a few restaurants. It then skirts around the eastern end of **Palgon-tso** (4170m) and, soon afterwards, the road arrives at **Rutok Xian** (p220). From here it is 130km south to Ali.

Other Routes into Tibet

Since 1994 another route into Tibet has been open, to tour groups only, passing through Purang (Nepali: Taklakot). Special visas are required for this trip. Trekkers start by travelling by road or flying from Kathmandu to Nepalganj, then flying from there to Simikot in the far west of Nepal. From Simikot it's a five- or six-day walk to the Tibetan border, crossing the Humla Karnali. You can then drive the 28km to Purang and 107km on to the Mt Kailash area via Manasarovar. For details on the route from the Nepali border to Mt Kailash see p221.

The border between Nepal and China is sometimes closed to foreigners, especially when tensions are high between the authorities and the Maoist rebels based in western Nepal. At the time of writing the rebels were charging some trekkers a US$60 'fee' to walk through the territory they held. See Lonely Planet's *Trekking in Nepal* for more information.

Indian travellers can cross into Tibet from Gangtok in Sikkim via the Natu-la and the

Jelep-la, along the former trading routes between Lhasa and Kalimpong. Other foreign travellers are not yet allowed on this route. There is talk of opening two other crossings at the Kerung-la and Nangpa-la but, again, for locals only.

GETTING AROUND

Tibet's transport infrastructure is poorly developed and, with the exception of the Friendship Hwy and the Qinghai–Tibet Hwy, most of the roads are in rough condition. Some work is being undertaken to improve this situation – a vital aspect of Chinese plans to develop Tibet – but it is unlikely that travel in Tibet will become comfortable or easy in the near future.

The main problem for travellers short on time is the scarcity of public transport. There are no internal flights (except to Chamdo, a closed area) and only a handful of buses and minibuses plying the roads between Lhasa and other major Tibetan towns such as Shigatse and Tsetang.

Many travellers band together to hire a Land Cruiser to get around Tibet but this isn't absolutely necessary. Minibuses run to most monasteries around Lhasa, and to Shigatse, Gyantse, Sakya and Lhatse. If you can get a travel permit (see p304) and you have time, hitching isn't a bad idea. You will still have to pay, but only a fraction of the amount for a Land Cruiser. You'll need to be more self-sufficient and prepared to wait perhaps for hours for a ride. Hitching in Tibet can be the best way to get around but it can also be very frustrating.

Those with more time can, of course, trek or cycle their way around the high plateau. A combination of hiking and hitching is the best way to get to many off-the-beaten-track destinations.

BICYCLE

Long-distance cyclists are again appearing on the roads of Tibet. Most pack their bikes onto their tour to Lhasa and then cycle back along the Friendship Hwy. Others buy mountain bikes in China and bring them up to Lhasa; some even buy their bikes in Lhasa. Any of these options is currently feasible, and local authorities appear to be turning a blind eye to the phenomenon.

You can rent a clunky locally made bike in Lhasa for around Y20 per day, which are fine for getting around town but no further. Test the brakes and tyres before taking the bike out onto the streets. An extra padlock might be a good idea, as there is a problem with bicycle theft in the capital.

Nowadays it is possible to buy a Chinese-made or (better) Taiwanese-made mountain bike in Lhasa for about Y500, or a good quality Thai bike for around Y2000. Standards aren't all that bad, although you should check the gears in particular. Do not expect the quality of such bikes to be equal to those you might buy at home – bring plenty of spare parts. Bikes have a relatively high resale value in Kathmandu and you might even make a profit if the bike is in good shape (which is unlikely after a trip across Tibet!).

Touring

Most PSB officials have no idea whether foreigners are allowed to cycle around Tibet, which means that most will leave you alone as long as you have a valid Chinese visa and a travel permit (see p304).

Despite the official ambivalence, Tibet still poses unique challenges to individual cyclists. The roads are generally very bad. Even though there's not much traffic, wind squalls and dust storms can make your work particularly arduous, the warm summer months can bring flash flooding, and then there is the question of your fitness. Tibet's high-altitude mountainous terrain is sure to test the determination of all cyclists who set out on its roads.

You will need to be prepared to do your own repairs. A full bicycle-repair kit, several spare inner tubes, and a spare tyre and chain are essential. Preferably bring an extra rim and some spare spokes. Extra brake wire and brake pads are useful (you'll be descending 3000m from Lhasa to Kathmandu!). Other useful equipment includes reflective clothing, a helmet, a dust mask, goggles, gloves and padded trousers.

You will also need to be prepared with supplies such as food, water-purifying tablets and camping equipment, just as if you were trekking. Most long-distance cyclists will probably find formal accommodation and restaurants only available at two- or three-day intervals. It may be possible to stay with

TRANSPORT

TRANSPORT

road repair camps (known as *daoban* in Chinese) in remote places.

The Trailblazer guide *Tibet Overland: A Route and Planning Guide for Mountain Bikers and Other Overlanders* by Kym McConnell has some useful route plans and gradient charts aimed at bikers.

Obviously you need to be in good physical condition to undertake road touring in Tibet. Spend some time acclimatising to the altitude and taking leisurely rides around Lhasa (for example) before setting off on a long trip.

On the plus side, while Tibet has some of the highest-altitude roads in the world, gradients are usually quite manageable. The Tibetan roads are designed for low-powered Chinese trucks, and tackle the many high passes of the region with its low-gradient switchback roads.

Touring Routes

The most popular touring route at present is Lhasa–Kathmandu, along the Friendship Hwy. It is an ideal route in that it takes in most of Tibet's main sights, offers superb scenery and (for those leaving from Lhasa) features a spectacular roller-coaster ride down from high La Lung-la into the Kathmandu Valley. The trip will take a minimum of two weeks, although to do it justice and include stopovers at Gyantse, Shigatse and Sakya, this will expand to 20 days. The entire trip is just over 940km, although most people start from Shigatse. Watch for the kilometre markers, as these can be a very useful way of knowing exactly how far you have gone and how far you still have to go. For detailed information on the route, see p180 and p146.

Keen cyclists with good mountain bikes might want to consider the detour to Everest Base Camp as a side trip on the Lhasa–Kathmandu route. The trip would have to be tackled from the Shegar turn-off, and it would take around two days to Rongphu Monastery.

Other possibilities are endless. Tsurphu and Ganden Monasteries are relatively easy (although uphill) trips. Drigung Til also makes a good destination. Cycling in the Yarlung Valley region would be a wonderful option if it were not for permit problems. Some cyclists even tackle the trip to Namtso, although the nomads' dogs can be a real problem here.

Hazards

Cycling in Tibet is not to be taken lightly. Traffic on Tibetan roads is relatively light, but cyclists do have to be prepared for some very erratic driving. Some cyclists have also complained of deliberate offensive driving by Chinese troop convoys, for whom forcing a couple of foreign cyclists off the road is a brief escape from the tedium of soldiering up on the high plateau. It would be wise to pull off the road and wait for such convoys to pass.

Dirt roads prevail in Tibet, and these present particular problems. Cyclists who pick up too much speed on downhill stretches run the grave risk of slipping on gravel. Wear a cycling helmet and lightweight leather gloves and, weather permitting, try to keep as much of your body covered with protective clothing as possible. It goes without saying that cyclists should also be prepared with a comprehensive medical kit (see p325).

Dogs are a major problem for cyclists in Tibet, especially in more remote areas. You may have to pedal like mad to outpace them. Children have been known to throw stones at cyclists.

BUS

Bus travel in Tibet is slow and patchy but you can get to most places in this book by bus or minibus, with time and a little effort. Most services originate in Lhasa or Shigatse and run to most towns that have a sizeable Chinese presence. Smaller towns may have just one daily bus that runs to Lhasa in the morning and returns in the afternoon.

Sometimes bus stations will not sell bus tickets to foreigners. The local authorities occasionally fine private minibus services, notably between Lhasa and Shigatse, because they don't have government permission (and insurance) to take foreigners. Consequently, some minibus drivers are cautious of taking foreigners. Accidents do sometimes happen: in 2003, five foreign tourists died when their minibus overturned en route to the Kambala near Yamdrok-tso. Outside of the bus station most drivers will take foreigners but often try to charge double the local price. Some buses run to places off limits to foreigners, such as Yatung or Bayi, and you'd be lucky to be allowed to board.

When travelling by bus, try to avoid sitting in the back of the bus. You will probably be required to stow your baggage on the roof if you have a bulky backpack. If possible, check that it is tied down properly (bus drivers normally do a good job of checking such details), lock your pack as a precaution against theft and make sure you have all you might need for the trip (food, water, warm clothes etc). Try to see what everyone else is paying for the fare before you hand over your cash. You can expect to spend a lot of time sitting around waiting for minibuses to fill up.

CAR

Renting a Land Cruiser (plus driver) and splitting the cost amongst a band of travellers has become the most popular way of getting around in Tibet. Tourists are not yet permitted to drive rental vehicles in China.

Prices depend largely on the kilometres driven (roughly Y3.50 per kilometre) not the time taken, meaning that you can often add an extra day to your itinerary for the same cost. If you are not returning with your vehicle (from Lhasa to the Nepali border,

---

ORGANISING A LAND CRUISER TRIP *Andre Ticheler*

When dealing with an agency to rent a vehicle, you need to establish a few ground rules. First, work out a detailed itinerary for your trip. This will allow the agency to give you a firm quote based on distance covered and number of days on the road.

You'll need to fix the rate for any extra days that may need to be tacked onto an itinerary. For delays caused by bad weather, blocked passes, swollen river crossings and so on, there should be no extra charge for jeep hire. At the very least the cost for extra days should be split 50% between your group and the agency. For delays caused by vehicle breakdowns, driver illness etc then the agency should cover 100% of the costs and provide a backup vehicle if necessary.

Second, ask the agency about its policy on refunds for an uncompleted trip. Some agencies refuse any kind of refund, others are more open to negotiation.

Third, clarify whether the price you agree on covers all permit costs, and establish which costs are not covered in the price (for example, the Y400 vehicle fee to drive to Everest Base Camp).

Finally, be aware that the vehicle you receive has probably been subcontracted from outside the agency. You should ensure that the vehicle and driver have the necessary permits and insurance required to carry foreigners. Also, and more importantly, you should verify that the agency will take responsibility in the event of a vehicle breakdown. Some reputable agencies will calmly refuse to take any role in disputes between you and the owner of the vehicle. Find out where you stand in advance.

Once you are sorted with the agency it's a good idea to organise a meeting between your group and the driver(s) and guide a day or two before departure. Make sure the drivers are aware of your itinerary (it may be the first time they have seen it!). Ensure that the guide speaks fluent Tibetan, good Chinese and useable English. Strong personality clashes would suggest a change of personnel.

Unless you are qualified mechanic, inspecting the soundness of the vehicle may prove to be difficult, but you should carry out the following basic checks. First make sure that the 4WD can at least be engaged (not just that the stick moves!) and that the 'diff lock' can be locked and unlocked (this is usually done via tabs on the front wheel hubs). For longer trips, make sure that at least one shovel and a long steel tow cable (rope cables are useless) are supplied. Tyres and spares should be in reasonable condition (by Tibetan standards). Check that fuel cans don't leak and that there's rope to tie baggage to the roof rack.

The only other predeparture issues to consider for long trips are warm clothing, a good sleeping bag, plenty of food and perhaps a small stove. A tent is an excellent backup. A few plastic barrels or sacks (available in most markets) are useful to protect your gear and food from the dust and general thrashing it will get in the back of the truck. Some travellers invest in a decent piece of foam mattress to save their backside from the worst punishments of the road (a square big enough to sit on costs Y10). Jerry cans to carry water (and even *chang*, or Tibetan barley beer!) are always a good idea.

TRANSPORT

for example) you can expect to pay an extra 50% of the one-way hire rate for the vehicle to return empty. Prices are higher on trips where a permit and both guide and driver are needed. Guide fees are normally calculated at Y150 per day.

Land Cruisers have room for six people and their luggage, although five is more comfortable. For longer trips where a guide is required it's worth limiting the number of passengers in a Land Cruiser to four (plus the guide) as any more than that is a real grind. The guides provided on budget tours are almost invariably useless.

The best place to hire vehicles is Lhasa. Before organising a vehicle, check the notice boards at the main budget hotels. There are usually dozens of notices advertising seats on trips to all quarters of Tibet. The most popular destinations are the Nepali border, Nam-tso, Drigung Til and Mt Kailash, and there will probably be a few notices about more-obscure destinations. The availability of vehicles has increased recently, but in the peak summer months of August and September there can still be a squeeze and prices can rise. For a rundown of prices see p117.

Hiring a vehicle is subject to all kinds of pitfalls (see Organising a Land Cruiser Trip, p321, for some guidelines). If possible, it is a good idea to reach an agreement that payment be delivered in two instalments: one before setting off and one on successful completion of the trip. This gives you more leverage in negotiating a refund if your trip was unsuccessful (one reason why agencies are loathe to do this).

Drawing up a contract in English as well as Tibetan or Chinese can be a good idea. List your exact itinerary, the price and method of payment. Above all, get together with the driver before the trip and go through the main points of the agreement verbally. You are likely to have far fewer problems if you can reach friendly terms with your driver by treating him with respect – giving him some cigarettes or some kind of small gift – rather than waving a contract in his face.

HITCHING

Hitching is never entirely safe in any country in the world, and we don't necessarily recommend it. Travellers who decide to hitch should understand that they are taking a small but potentially serious risk. However,

in Tibet, hitching is often the only alternative to hiring an expensive Land Cruiser and so has become a fairly established practice for getting around.

With the exception of travellers hitching out to western Tibet and the very small number making their way illegally from Chengdu to Lhasa, few foreigners travel long distances by truck these days. The main reason is that the authorities impose heavy fines on truck drivers caught transporting foreign travellers and may even confiscate their licence. There seems to be little stopping truck drivers from picking up travellers off the main highways, however, especially if there are no check posts en route. Sometimes you can get a lift on a pilgrim truck or an organised passenger truck.

If you hitch by truck in Tibet, be prepared to share the hardships of a trucker's life. You will probably end up helping to drag the vehicle out of rivers and sand drifts, and assisting in repairs. If you are headed out to fairly remote destinations you should be equipped to camp out for the night if you don't get a ride. One guy we heard of waited so long for a lift to Mt Kailash that he built a chörten from stones out of boredom. By the time he got a ride it was over 1m tall!

Trucks aren't the only transport on the roads. There are also plenty of half-empty Land Cruisers heading down the Friendship Hwy to pick up a group, or returning after having dropped one off. It's a wonderful feeling to finally get a lift in an empty Land Cruiser after being rejected all day by a stream of dilapidated trucks travelling at 30km/h!

Normally you will be expected to pay for your lift. The amount is entirely negotiable, but in areas where traffic is minimal, drivers will often demand quite large sums.

It's a good idea to start hitching a few kilometres out of town because then you know that traffic is going in your direction and is not about to turn off after 400m. This is especially important if there is a check post nearby. It's best to walk through the check post yourself and wait for a lift a couple of kilometres on the other side.

The most common hitching gesture is to stick out one or two fingers towards the ground and wave them up or down.

LOCAL TRANSPORT

Local city transport only operates in Lhasa and Shigatse. Minibuses run on set routes around Lhasa and Shigatse and they charge a fixed fare of Y2.

Pedicabs (pedal-operated tricycles transporting passengers) are available in Lhasa, Gyantse, Shigatse and Bayi, but are quite slow and require serious haggling.

A couple of towns in eastern Tibet have motorised three-wheeler rickshaws that take passengers around town or to destinations (eg monasteries) just outside of town. Negotiate the fare before you set off.

One result of China's economic infusion into Tibet is the large number of taxis now available in most towns, even Ali in western Tibet. Taxis in Lhasa, Shigatse and Ali charge a standard Y10 to anywhere in the city; for longer trips negotiate a fare. Fixed-route passenger taxis (which you can pay for by the seat) also run between Lhasa, Gongkar airport and Tsetang.

Tractors can be an option for short trips in rural areas, especially in the Yarlung Valley. For a few yuan, drivers are normally quite happy to have some passengers in the back. Rides of anything over 10 minutes quickly become excruciatingly painful unless on a tarmac road.

TOURS

Nominally, any organised tours must be arranged before you enter Tibet. Moreover, to get into Tibet from Kathmandu (and also occasionally Chengdu) or you have to book a so-called 'tour' of three days which usually includes transport, accommodation, transfers and a guide (although most travellers skip the 'tour' section once they've arrived in Lhasa).

However, if you hire a Land Cruiser, with a driver and often a guide, you have effectively arranged a kind of do-it-yourself tour within Tibet. For detailed information on 'do-it-yourself' tours, see p321 and p117.

TRANSPORT

Health

CONTENTS

Tibet poses particular risks to your health, although for the large part these are associated with the high average altitude of the plateau.

There is no need to be overly worried; very few travellers are adversely affected by the altitude for very long, and greater risks are present in the form of road accidents and dog bites. Insect-borne and infectious diseases are quite rare because of the high altitude.

Sensible travellers will rely on their own medical knowledge and supplies when travelling throughout Tibet. It is a very isolated place, and outside the city of Lhasa there is not much in the way of expert medical care available.

BEFORE YOU GO

INSURANCE

Keep in mind that Tibet is a remote location, and if you become seriously injured or very sick, you may need to be evacuated by air. Under these circumstances, you don't want to be without adequate health insurance. Be sure your policy covers evacuation.

RECOMMENDED VACCINATIONS

China doesn't officially require any immunisations for entry into the country, however the further off the beaten track you go, the more necessary it is to take all precautions. The World Health Organization (WHO) requires travellers who have come from an area infected with yellow fever to be vaccinated before entering the country. Record all vaccinations on an International Health Certificate, available from a doctor or government health department.

Plan well ahead and schedule your vaccinations because some require more than one injection, while others should not be given together. Note that some vaccinations should not be given during pregnancy or to people with allergies.

It is recommended that you seek medical advice at least six weeks before travel. Note that there is a greater risk of all kinds of disease with children and during pregnancy.

Discuss your requirements with your doctor, but vaccinations you should consider for this trip include the following:

Diphtheria & Tetanus Vaccinations for these two diseases are usually combined and are recommended for everyone. After an initial course of three injections (usually given in childhood), boosters are necessary every 10 years.

Hepatitis A The vaccine for Hepatitis A (eg Avaxim, Havrix 1440 or VAQTA) provides long-term immunity (possibly more than 10 years) after an initial injection and a booster at six to 12 months. Alternatively, an injection of gamma globulin can provide short-term protection against hepatitis A – two to six months, depending on the dose given. It is not a vaccine, but is ready-made antibody collected from blood donations. It is reasonably effective and, unlike the vaccine, it is protective immediately, but because it is a blood product, there are concerns about its long-term safety. Hepatitis A vaccine is also available in a combined form, Twinrix, with hepatitis B vaccine. Three injections over a six-month period are required, the first two providing substantial protection against hepatitis A.

Hepatitis B China (although not so much Tibet) is one of the world's great reservoirs of hepatitis B infection, a disease spread by contact with blood or by sexual activity. Vaccination involves three injections, the quickest course being over three weeks with a booster at 12 months.

Polio This serious, easily transmitted disease is still prevalent in many developing countries, including Tibet. Everyone should keep up-to-date with this vaccination, which is normally given in childhood. A booster every 10 years maintains immunity.

Rabies Officially there is no rabies in Tibet. All the same, there are a lot of rabid-looking dogs about. Recent surveys by the Chinese indicate that instances of rabies may have occurred in Qinghai, which borders Tibet. Vaccination should be considered if you are spending a month or longer in Tibet, especially if you are cycling, handling animals, caving or travelling to remote areas, and for children (who may not report a bite). Pretravel rabies vaccination involves three injections over 21 to 28 days. The vaccine will not give you 100% immunity, but will extend the time you have for seeking treatment. If someone who has been vaccinated is bitten or scratched by an animal they will require two vaccine booster injections, while those not vaccinated will require more.

Tuberculosis The risk of tuberculosis (TB) to travellers is usually very low, unless you'll be living with or closely associated with local people in high-risk areas. As most healthy adults don't develop symptoms, a skin test before and after travel to determine whether exposure has occurred may be considered. A vaccination (BCG) is recommended for children and young adults living in these areas for three months or more.

Typhoid This is an important vaccination to have in Tibet where hygiene standards are low. It is available either as an injection or oral capsules. A combined hepatitis A-typhoid vaccine was launched recently but its availability is still limited – check with your doctor to find out its status in your country.

Yellow Fever This disease is not endemic in China or Tibet and a vaccine for yellow fever is required only if you are coming from an infected area.

MEDICAL CHECKLIST

Following is a list of items you should consider including in your medical kit for travelling – consult your pharmacist for brands available in your country.

- Antibiotics – include these if you're travelling well off the beaten track; see your doctor, as antibiotics must be prescribed, and carry the prescription with you
- Antifungal cream or powder – for fungal skin infections and thrush
- Antihistamine – for allergies, eg hay fever; to ease the itch from insect bites or stings; and to prevent motion sickness
- Antiseptic (such as povidone-iodine) – for cuts and grazes
- Aspirin or paracetamol (acetaminophen in the USA) – for pain or fever
- Bandages, Band-Aids (plasters) and other wound dressings
- Calamine lotion, sting-relief spray or aloe vera – to ease irritation from sunburn and insect bites or stings

- Cold and flu tablets, throat lozenges and nasal decongestant
- Homeopathic medicines – useful homeopathic medicines include gentiana for altitude sickness, echinacea, and tea-tree oil for cuts and scrapes
- Insect repellent, sunscreen, lip balm and eye drops
- Loperamide or diphenoxylate – 'blockers' for diarrhoea
- Multivitamins – for long trips, when dietary vitamin intake may be inadequate
- Prochlorperazine or metaclopramide – for nausea and vomiting
- Rehydration mixture – to prevent dehydration, which may occur, for example, during bouts of diarrhoea; particularly important when travelling with children
- Scissors, tweezers and a thermometer – note that mercury thermometers are prohibited by airlines
- Sterile kit – in case you need injections in a country with medical hygiene problems; discuss with your doctor
- Water purification tablets or iodine

INTERNET RESOURCES

There are a number of excellent travel-health sites on the Internet. From the Lonely Planet website (www.lonelyplanet.com) there are links to the WHO and the US Centers for Disease Control & Prevention.

FURTHER READING

Lonely Planet's *Healthy Travel Asia & India* is a handy pocket size and is packed with useful information including pretrip planning, emergency first aid, immunization and disease information, and what to do if you get sick on the road. *Travel with Children* from Lonely Planet also includes advice on travel health for younger children.

Other detailed health guides that you may find useful:

Complete Guide to Healthy Travel Recommendations for international travel from the US Centers for Disease Control & Prevention.

Staying Healthy in Asia, Africa & Latin America by Dirk Schroeder. A detailed and well- organized guide.

Travellers' Health by Dr Richard Dawood. This is comprehensive, easy to read, authoritative and highly recommended, although it's rather large to lug around.

Where There Is No Doctor by David Werner. A very detailed guide intended for people going to work in a developing country.

OTHER PREPARATIONS

Make sure you're healthy before you start travelling. If you are going on a long trip make sure your teeth are OK. If you wear glasses, take a spare pair and your prescription.

If you require a particular medication take a good supply, as it may not be available in Tibet. Take along part of the packaging showing the generic name rather than the brand, which will make getting replacements easier. To avoid problems, it's a good idea to have a legible prescription or letter from your doctor to show that you legally use the medication.

IN TRANSIT

DEEP VEIN THROMBOSIS (DVT)

Deep vein thrombosis (DVT) occurs when blood clots form in the legs during plane flights, chiefly because of prolonged immobility. Although most of these blood clots are reabsorbed uneventfully, some of them may break off and travel through the blood vessels to the lungs, where they may cause life-threatening complications.

The chief symptom of DVT is swelling or pain of the foot, ankle or calf, usually but not always on just one side. When a blood clot travels to the lungs, it may cause chest pain and difficulty in breathing. Travellers with any of these symptoms should immediately seek medical attention.

To prevent the development of DVT on long flights you should walk about the cabin, perform isometric compressions of the leg muscles (ie contract the leg muscles while sitting), drink plenty of fluids, and avoid alcohol and tobacco.

MOTION SICKNESS

Eating lightly before and during a trip will reduce the chances of motion sickness. If you are prone to motion sickness try to find a place that minimises movement – near the wing on aircraft, near the centre on buses. Fresh air usually helps; reading and cigarette smoke don't.

Commercial preparations for motion sickness, which can cause drowsiness, have to be taken before the trip commences. Ginger (available in capsule form) and peppermint (including mint-flavoured sweets) are natural preventatives.

IN TIBET

AVAILABILITY & COST OF HEALTH CARE

Self-diagnosis and treatment can be risky, so you should always seek medical help. Although we do give drug dosages in this section, they are for emergency use only. Correct diagnosis is vital.

In Tibet the top-end hotels can usually recommend a good place to go for advice. In most places in Tibet standards of medical attention are so low that for some ailments the best advice is to go straight to Lhasa and in extreme cases get on a plane to Chengdu or Kathmandu.

Global Doctor (Map p82; ☎ 028-678 6746; www .eglobaldoctor.com; Holiday Inn Crowne Plaza, 31 Zongfu Lu, Chengdu) offers pre-Tibet medical examinations and a Tibet Travellers Assist Package that can be useful if you are worried about an existing medical condition. See the website for details.

Antibiotics should ideally only be administered under medical supervision. Take only the recommended dose at the prescribed intervals and use the whole course, even if the illness seems to be cured before the medication is finished. Stop immediately if there are any serious reactions and don't use the antibiotic at all if you are unsure that you have the correct one. Some people are allergic to commonly prescribed antibiotics such as penicillin; carry this information (eg on a bracelet) when travelling.

EVERYDAY HEALTH

Normal body temperature is up to 37°C (98.6°F); more than 2°C (4°F) higher indicates a high fever. The normal adult pulse rate is 60 to 100 per minute (children 80 to 100 and babies 100 to 140). As a general rule the pulse increases about 20 beats per minute for each 1°C (2°F) rise in fever.

Respiration (breathing) rate is also an indicator of illness. Count the number of breaths per minute: between 12 and 20 is normal for adults and older children (up to 30 for younger children and 40 for babies). People with a high fever or serious respiratory illness breathe more quickly than normal. More than 40 shallow breaths a minute may indicate pneumonia.

INFECTIOUS DISEASES
Hepatitis
A general term for inflammation of the liver, hepatitis is a common disease worldwide. There are several different viruses that cause hepatitis, and they differ in the way that they are transmitted. The symptoms are similar in all forms of the illness and include fever, chills, headache, fatigue, feelings of weakness and aches and pains, followed by loss of appetite, nausea, vomiting, abdominal pain, dark urine, light-coloured faeces, jaundiced (yellow) skin and yellowing of the whites of the eyes. People who have had hepatitis should avoid alcohol for some time after the illness, as the liver needs quite some time to recover.

Hepatitis A is transmitted by contaminated food and drinking water. You should seek medical advice, but there is not much you can do apart from resting, drinking lots of fluids, eating lightly and avoiding fatty foods.

Hepatitis A is most often spread in China and Tibet as a result of the custom of sharing food from a single dish rather than using separate plates and a serving spoon. It is wise to use the disposable chopsticks now freely available in most restaurants in Tibet, or else buy your own chopsticks and spoon. Hepatitis E is transmitted in the same way as hepatitis A; it can be particularly serious in pregnant women.

There are almost 300 million chronic carriers of hepatitis B in the world, and China has more cases than any other country – almost 20% of the population are believed to be carriers. It is spread through contact with infected blood, blood products or body fluids, for example through sexual contact, unsterilised needles and blood transfusions, or contact with blood via small breaks in the skin. Other risk situations include having a shave, tattoo or body piercing with contaminated equipment. The symptoms of hepatitis B may be more severe than those for type A and the disease can lead to long-term problems such as chronic liver damage, liver cancer or a long-term carrier state. Hepatitis C and D are spread in the same way as hepatitis B and can also lead to long-term complications.

There are vaccines against hepatitis A and B, but there are currently no vaccines against the other types of hepatitis. Following the basic rules about food and water (hepatitis A and E) and avoiding risk situations (hepatitis B, C and D) are important preventative measures.

HIV & AIDS
Infection with human immunodeficiency virus (HIV) may lead to acquired immune deficiency syndrome (AIDS), which is a fatal disease. Any exposure to blood, blood products or body fluids may put the individual at risk. The disease is often transmitted by sexual contact or dirty needles – vaccination, acupuncture, tattooing and body piercing can be potentially as dangerous as intravenous drug use. HIV/AIDS can also be spread through infected blood transfusions; some developing countries cannot afford to screen blood used for transfusions.

HIV is not thought to be a major problem in Tibet, although anyone who intends to work or study in Tibet for longer than 12 months is required by the Chinese authorities to undergo an AIDS test.

If you do need an injection, ask to see the syringe unwrapped in front of you, or take a needle and syringe pack with you when travelling. Fear of HIV infection should never preclude treatment for serious medical conditions.

Rabies
This fatal viral infection is found in many countries. While officially there is no rabies in Tibet, it would be foolish not to get treatment if you are bitten. Many animals can be infected (such as dogs, cats, bats and monkeys) and it is their saliva that is infectious. Any bite, scratch or even lick from an animal should be cleaned immediately and thoroughly. Scrub with soap and running water, and then apply alcohol or iodine solution. Prompt medical help should be sought to receive a course of injections to prevent the onset of symptoms and death.

At the time of writing, no treatment for rabies was available anywhere in Tibet and it was necessary to fly to Kathmandu or Chengdu. If you think you've been infected, get to Lhasa as quickly as you can and seek medical advice.

Respiratory Infections
Upper respiratory tract infections (like the common cold) are common ailments all over

HEALTH

China, including Tibet. Why are they such a serious problem in China? Respiratory infections are aggravated by the high altitude, the cold weather, air pollution, chain smoking and overcrowded conditions, all of which increase the opportunity for infection. But the main reason is that Chinese people spit a lot, thereby spreading the disease. It is a vicious circle: they are sick because they spit and they spit because they are sick.

Some of the symptoms of influenza include a sore throat, fever and weakness. Any upper-respiratory-tract infection, including influenza, can lead to complications such as bronchitis and pneumonia, which may need to be treated with antibiotics. Seek medical help in this situation.

The Chinese treat bronchitis, which can be a complication of flu, with a powder made from the gall bladder of snakes – a treatment of questionable value, but there is no harm in trying it.

No vaccine offers complete protection, but there are vaccines against influenza and pneumococcal pneumonia that might help. The influenza vaccine is good for no more than a year.

Sexually Transmitted Infections

While HIV/AIDS and hepatitis B can be transmitted through sexual contact, other sexually transmitted infections (STIs) include gonorrhoea, herpes and syphilis. Sores, blisters or rashes around the genitals and discharges or pain when urinating are common symptoms. In some STIs, such as wart virus or chlamydia, symptoms may be less marked or not observed at all, especially in women. Syphilis symptoms eventually disappear completely but the disease continues and can cause severe problems in later years. Although abstinence from sexual contact is the only 100% effective prevention, using condoms is also effective. Gonorrhoea and syphilis are treated with antibiotics. The different STIs each require specific antibiotics. There is no cure for herpes or AIDS.

Condoms are available in China – the word is *baotao*, which translates literally as 'insurance glove'.

TRAVELLER'S DIARRHOEA

Simple things like a change of water, food or climate can all cause a mild bout of diarrhoea (*la duzi* – spicy stomach – in Chinese),

but a few rushed toilet trips with no other symptoms are not indicative of a major problem. Even Marco Polo got the runs.

Dehydration is the main danger with any diarrhoea, particularly in children or the elderly as it can occur quite quickly. Under all circumstances *fluid replacement* (at least equal to the volume being lost) is the most important thing to remember. Weak black tea with a little sugar, soda water, or soft drinks allowed to go flat and diluted 50% with clean water are all good. With severe diarrhoea a rehydrating solution is preferable to replace lost minerals and salts. Commercially available oral rehydration salts (ORS) are very useful; add them to boiled or bottled water. In an emergency you can make up a solution of six teaspoons of sugar and half a teaspoon of salt to a litre of boiled or bottled water. You need to drink at least the same volume of fluid that you are losing in bowel movements and vomiting. Urine is the best guide to the adequacy of replacement – if you have small amounts of concentrated urine, you need to drink more. Keep drinking small amounts often. Stick to a bland diet as you recover.

Loperamide or diphenoxylate can be used to bring relief from the symptoms, although they do not actually cure the problem. However, neither is available in China. A good Chinese alternative treatment is berberine hydrochloride (*huang lian su*). Only use these drugs if you do not have access to toilets, eg if you *must* travel. For children under 12 years these drugs are not recommended. Do not use these drugs if you have a high fever or are severely dehydrated.

In certain situations antibiotics may be required: diarrhoea with blood or mucus (dysentery), any diarrhoea with fever, profuse watery diarrhoea, persistent diarrhoea not improving after 48 hours and severe diarrhoea. These suggest a more serious cause, in which case gut-paralysing drugs should be avoided.

In these situations, a stool test may be necessary to diagnose what bug is causing your diarrhoea, so you should seek medical help urgently. Where this is not possible the recommended drugs for bacterial diarrhoea (the most likely cause of severe diarrhoea in travellers) are norfloxacin 400mg twice daily for three days or ciprofloxacin 500mg twice daily for five days. These are not recommended for children or pregnant women. The drug of choice for children would be co-trimoxazole (Bactrim, Septrin or Resprim) with dosage dependent on weight. A five-day course is given. Ampicillin or amoxycillin may be given in pregnancy, but medical care is necessary.

Two other causes of persistent diarrhoea in travellers are giardiasis and amoebic dysentery.

Amoebic Dysentery

Caused by the protozoan *Entamoeba histolytica,* amoebic dysentery is characterised by a gradual onset of low-grade diarrhoea, often with blood and mucus. Cramping abdominal pain and vomiting are less likely than in other types of diarrhoea, and fever may not be present. It will persist until treated and can recur and cause other health problems.

You should seek medical advice if you think you have giardiasis or amoebic dysentery, but where this is not possible, tindazole or metronidazole are the recommended drugs. Treatment is a 2g single dose of tindazole or 250mg of metronidazole three times daily for five to 10 days.

Metronidazole is not easily obtained in Tibet, although equivalent drugs are available in Lhasa. If you are going to be travelling in high mountain areas, it might be a good idea to keep your own stock of metronidazole with you.

Cholera

This is the worst of the watery diarrhoeas. Outbreaks of cholera are generally widely reported, so you can avoid such problem areas. *Fluid replacement is the most vital treatment* – the risk of dehydration is severe as you may lose up to 20L a day. If there is a delay in getting to hospital, then begin taking tetracycline. The adult dose is 250mg four times daily. It is not recommended for children under nine years or for pregnant women. Tetracycline may help shorten the illness, but adequate fluids are required to save lives. Seek medical advice if you think you may have this disease.

Giardiasis

Known as giardia, giardiasis is a type of diarrhoea that is relatively common in Tibet and is caused by a parasite, *Giardia lamblia.* Mountaineers often suffer from this problem. The parasite causing this intestinal disorder is present in contaminated water. Many kinds of mammals harbour the parasite, so you can get it easily from drinking 'pure mountain water' unless the area is devoid of animals. Simply brushing your teeth using contaminated water is sufficient to get giardiasis, or any other gut bug. Symptoms include stomach cramps, nausea, a bloated stomach, a watery, foul-smelling diarrhoea and frequent gas. Giardiasis can appear several weeks after you have been exposed to the parasite. The symptoms may disappear for a few days and then return; this can go on for several weeks.

ENVIRONMENTAL HAZARDS
Acute Mountain Sickness

On average, one tourist a year dies in Tibet from altitude sickness – make sure that it is not you. Any traveller who flies or buses into Lhasa, where the elevation is just over 3600m, is likely to experience some symptoms of AMS. Take care to acclimatise slowly and take things easy for the first couple of days. Lack of oxygen at high altitudes (over 2500m) affects most people to some extent. The effect may be mild or severe and it occurs because less oxygen reaches the muscles and the brain at high altitude, requiring the heart and lungs to compensate by working harder. Acute mountain sickness (AMS) – altitude sickness – is common at high elevations; relevant factors are the rate of ascent and individual susceptibility. The major risk factor in AMS is the speed with which you make your ascent.

AMS is a notoriously fickle affliction and can also affect trekkers and walkers accustomed to walking at high altitudes. AMS has been fatal at 3000m, although 3500m to 4500m is the usual range.

ACCLIMATISATION

AMS is linked to low atmospheric pressure. Those who travel up to Everest Base Camp, for instance, reach an altitude where atmospheric pressure is about half of that at sea level.

With an increase in altitude, the human body needs time to develop physiological mechanisms to cope with the decreased oxygen. This process of acclimatisation is still not fully understood, but is known to involve modifications in breathing patterns

HEALTH

and heart rate induced by the autonomic nervous system, and an increase in the blood's oxygen-carrying capabilities. These compensatory mechanisms usually take about one to three days to develop at a particular altitude. Once you are acclimatised to a given height you are unlikely to get AMS at that height, but you can still get ill when you travel higher. If the ascent is too high and too fast, these compensatory reactions may not kick into gear fast enough.

SYMPTOMS

Mild symptoms of AMS are very common in travellers visiting high altitudes, and usually develop during the first 24 hours at altitude. Most visitors to Tibet will suffer from some symptoms; these will generally disappear through acclimatisation in several hours to several days.

Symptoms tend to be worse at night and include headache, dizziness, lethargy, loss of appetite, nausea, breathlessness and irritability. Difficulty sleeping is another common symptom, and many travellers have trouble sleeping for the first few days after arriving in Lhasa.

AMS may become more serious without warning and can be fatal. Symptoms are caused by the accumulation of fluid in the lungs and brain, and include breathlessness at rest, a dry irritative cough (which may progress to the production of pink, frothy sputum), severe headache, lack of coordination (typically leading to a 'drunken walk'), confusion, irrational behaviour, vomiting and eventually unconsciousness.

The symptoms of AMS, however mild, are a warning – be sure to take them seriously! Trekkers should keep an eye on each other as those experiencing symptoms, especially severe symptoms, may not be in a position to recognise them. One thing to note is that while the symptoms of mild AMS often precede those of severe AMS, this is not always the case. Severe AMS can strike with little or no warning.

PREVENTION

If you are driving up from Kathmandu you will experience rapid altitude gain. An itinerary that takes you straight up to Everest Base Camp is unwise; plan to see it on your way back if possible. The best way to prevent AMS is to avoid rapid ascents to high altitudes. If you fly or bus into Lhasa, take it easy for at least three days – for most travellers this is enough to get over any initial ill-effects. At this point you might step up your programme by visiting a few sights around town. Within a week you should be ready for something a bit more adventurous, but do not push yourself to do anything that you are not comfortable with.

To prevent acute mountain sickness:

- Ascend slowly. Have frequent rest days, spending two to three nights at each rise of 1000m. If you reach a high altitude by trekking, acclimatisation takes place gradually and you are less likely to be affected than if you fly directly to high altitude.
- Trekkers should bear in mind the climber's adage of 'Climb high, sleep low'. It is always wise to sleep at a lower altitude than the greatest height that's reached during the day. High day climbs followed by a descent back to lower altitudes for the night are very good preparation for high-altitude trekking. Also, once above 3000m, care should be taken not to increase the sleeping altitude by more than 400m per day. If the terrain won't allow for less than 400m of elevation gain, be ready to take an extra day off before tackling the climb.
- Drink extra fluids. Tibet's mountain air is cold and dry, and moisture is lost as you breathe. Evaporation of sweat may occur unnoticed and result in dehydration.
- Eat light, high-carbohydrate meals to keep up energy.
- Avoid alcohol as it may increase the risk of dehydration, and don't smoke.
- Avoid sedatives.
- When trekking, take a day off to rest and acclimatize if feeling over-tired. If you or anyone else in your party is having a tough time make allowances for unscheduled stops.
- Don't push yourself when climbing up to passes; rather, take plenty of breaks. You can usually get over the pass as easily tomorrow as you can today. Try to plan your itinerary so that long ascents can be divided into two or more days. Given the complexity and unknown variables involved with AMS and acclimatization, trekkers should always err on the side of caution and ascend mountains slowly.

TREATMENT

Treat mild symptoms by resting at the same altitude until recovery, usually a day or two. Take paracetamol or aspirin for headaches. If symptoms persist or become worse, however, *immediate descent* is necessary – even 500m can help.

The most effective treatment for severe AMS is to get down to a lower altitude as quickly as possible. In less severe cases the victim will be able to stagger down with some support; in other cases they may need to be carried down. Whatever the case, do not delay, as any delay could be fatal.

AMS victims may need to be flown out of Tibet as quickly as possible – make sure you have adequate travel insurance.

The drugs acetazolamide (Diamox) and dexamethasone are recommended by some doctors for the prevention of AMS. However, you should be aware that their use is controversial. They can reduce the symptoms, but they may also mask warning signs; severe and fatal AMS has occurred in people taking these drugs. Drug treatments should never be used to avoid descent or to enable further ascent.

Several hotels in Lhasa sell a Tibetan herbal medicine recommended by locals for easing the symptoms of mild altitude sickness. The medicine is known as *solomano* in Tibetan and *hongjingtian* in Chinese. A box of vials costs around Y25.

Cuts, Bites & Stings

CUTS & SCRATCHES

Wash any cut well and treat it with an antiseptic such as povidone-iodine. Where possible avoid bandages and Band-Aids, which can keep wounds wet.

BEDBUGS & LICE

Bedbugs live in various places, but particularly in dirty mattresses and bedding, evidenced by spots of blood on bedclothes or on the wall. Bedbugs leave itchy bites in neat rows. Calamine lotion or a sting-relief spray may help.

All lice cause itching and discomfort. They make themselves at home in your hair (head lice), in your clothing (body lice) or in your pubic hair (crabs). You catch lice through direct contact with infected people or by sharing combs, clothing and the like. Powder or shampoo treatment will kill the lice. Infected clothing should then be washed in very hot, soapy water and left in the sun to dry.

BITES & STINGS

Bee and wasp stings are usually painful rather than dangerous. However, people who are allergic to them may have severe breathing difficulties and require urgent medical care. Calamine lotion or a sting-relief spray will give relief and ice packs will reduce the pain and swelling.

LEECHES

In the damper, low-lying areas of eastern Tibet, leeches may be present; they attach themselves to your skin to suck your blood. Trekkers often get them on their legs or in their boots. Salt or a lighted cigarette end will make them fall off. Do not pull them off, as the bite is then more likely to become infected. Clean and apply pressure if the point of attachment is bleeding. An insect repellent may help keep them away.

Food

There is an old colonial adage that says 'If you can cook it, boil it or peel it you can eat it … otherwise forget it'. Vegetables and fruit should be washed with purified or bottled water or peeled where possible. Beware of ice cream that is sold in the street or anywhere it might have been melted and refrozen; if there's any doubt (eg a power cut in the last day or two) steer well clear. Undercooked meat should be avoided.

If a place looks clean and well run and the vendor also looks clean and healthy, then the food is probably safe. In general, places that are packed with travellers or locals will be fine, while empty restaurants are questionable. Chinese food in particular is cooked over a high heat, which kills most germs.

Frostbite

This is the freezing of extremities, including fingers, toes and nose. Signs and symptoms of frostbite include a whitish or waxy cast to the skin, or even crystals on the surface, plus itching, numbness and pain. Warm the affected areas by immersing them in warm (not hot) water or with blankets or clothes, only until the skin becomes flushed. Frostbitten parts should not be rubbed. Pain and swelling are inevitable. Blisters should not be broken. Get medical attention right away.

HEALTH

Heat Exhaustion

Dehydration and salt deficiency can cause heat exhaustion. Take time to acclimatise to high temperatures, be sure to drink sufficient liquids and do not do anything too physically demanding.

Salt deficiency is characterised by fatigue, lethargy, headaches, giddiness and muscle cramps; salt tablets may help, but adding extra salt to your food is better.

Hypothermia

Winter in Tibet is not to be taken lightly. Even in mid-summer, passes and high areas around northern Tibet and the Changtang can be hit without warning by sudden snow storms. You should always be prepared for cold, wet or windy conditions, especially if you're out walking, hitching or trekking at high altitudes or even taking a long bus trip over mountains (particularly at night).

Hypothermia occurs when the body loses heat faster than it can produce it and the core temperature of the body falls. It is surprisingly easy to progress from very cold to dangerously cold through a combination of wind, wet clothing, fatigue and hunger, even if the air temperature is above freezing.

It is best to dress in layers; silk, wool and some of the new artificial fibres are all good insulating materials. A hat is important, as a lot of heat is lost through the head. A strong, waterproof outer layer and a 'space' blanket for emergencies are essential. Carry basic supplies, including food that contains simple sugars to generate heat quickly, and fluid to drink.

Symptoms of hypothermia are exhaustion, numb skin (particularly toes and fingers), shivering, slurred speech, irrational or violent behaviour, lethargy, stumbling, dizzy spells, muscle cramps and violent bursts of energy. Irrationality may take the form of sufferers claiming they are warm and trying to take off their clothes.

To treat mild hypothermia, first get the person out of the wind and rain, remove their clothing if it's wet and replace it with dry, warm clothing. Give them hot liquids (not alcohol) and some high-energy, easily digestible food. Do not rub victims; instead, allow them to slowly warm themselves. This should be enough to treat the early stages of hypothermia. The early recognition and treatment of mild hypothermia is the only way to prevent severe hypothermia, which is a critical condition.

Sunburn

It's very easy to get sunburnt in Tibet's high altitudes. Sunburn is more than just being uncomfortable. Among undesirable effects are premature skin ageing and possible skin cancer in later years. Sunscreen with a high sun protection factor (SPF), sunglasses and a wide-brimmed hat are good means of protection. Calamine lotion is good for treating mild sunburn.

Those with fair complexions should bring reflective sunscreen (containing zinc oxide or titanium oxide) with them. Apply the sunscreen to your nose and lips (and especially the tops of your ears if you are not wearing a hat).

Water

The number-one rule is *be careful of the water* and especially ice. If you don't know for certain that the water is safe assume the worst. In urban centres Tibetans, like the Chinese, boil their drinking water making it safe to drink hot or cooled. In the country you should boil your own water or treat it with water-purification tablets. Milk should be treated with suspicion as it will be unpasteurised in the countryside, although boiled milk is fine if it is kept hygienically. Soft drinks and beer are always available wherever there is a shop, and these are always safe to drink, as is tea. Locally brewed beer, *chang,* is another matter. It is often made with contaminated well water and there is always some risk in drinking it.

WATER PURIFICATION

The simplest way to purify water is to boil it thoroughly. At Tibet's high altitude water boils at a lower temperature and germs are less likely to be killed, so make sure you boil water for at least 10 minutes.

Consider purchasing a water filter for a long trip. There are two main kinds of filters. Total filters take out all parasites, bacteria and viruses, and make water safe to drink. They are often expensive, but can be more cost effective than buying bottled water. Simple filters (which can even be a nylon mesh bag) take out dirt and larger foreign bodies from the water so that chemical solutions work much more effectively;

if water is dirty, chemical solutions may not work at all. It's very important when buying a filter to read the specifications, so that you know exactly what it removes from the water and what it doesn't. Simple filtering will not remove all dangerous organisms, so if you cannot boil water it should be treated chemically.

Chlorine tablets (eg Puritabs or Steritabs) will kill many pathogens, but not giardia and amoebic cysts. Iodine is more effective for purifying water and is available in tablet form (eg Potable Aqua). Follow the directions carefully and remember that too much iodine can be harmful.

WOMEN'S HEALTH
Gynaecological Problems
Antibiotic use, synthetic underwear, sweating and contraceptive pills can all lead to fungal vaginal infections, especially when travelling in hot climates. Fungal infections are characterised by a rash, itch and discharge. Nystatin, miconazole or clotrimazole pessaries or vaginal cream are the usual treatments, but some people use a more traditional remedy involving vinegar or lemon-juice douches, or yogurt. Maintaining good personal hygiene and wearing loose-fitting clothes and cotton underwear may help prevent these infections.

Sexually transmitted infections are one major cause of vaginal problems. Symptoms include a smelly discharge, painful intercourse and sometimes a burning sensation when urinating. Medical attention should be sought and sexual partners must also be treated. For more information on STIs, see p328. Besides abstinence, the best thing is to practise safe sex using condoms.

Pregnancy
It is not advisable to travel to some places while pregnant as some vaccinations normally used to prevent serious diseases are not advisable during pregnancy (eg yellow fever). In addition, some diseases are much more serious for the mother (and may increase the risk of a stillborn child) in pregnancy.

Most miscarriages occur during the first three months of pregnancy. Miscarriage is not uncommon and can occasionally lead to severe bleeding. The last three months should also be spent within reasonable distance of good medical care. A baby born as

early as 24 weeks stands a chance of survival, but only in a good modern hospital. Pregnant women should avoid all unnecessary medication, although vaccinations should still be taken where needed. Additional care should be taken to prevent illness and particular attention should be paid to diet and nutrition. Alcohol and nicotine, for example, should be avoided.

TIBETAN MEDICINE
The basic teachings of Tibetan medicine share much with those of other Asian medical traditions, which according to some scholars made their way to the East via India from ancient Greece. While the Western medical tradition treats symptoms that indicate a known medical condition (measles or mumps, say), the Eastern medical tradition looks at symptoms as indications of an imbalance in the body and seeks to restore that balance.

It is not correct to assume, however, that Tibetan medicine was practised by trained doctors in clinics scattered across the land. The Tibetan medical tradition is largely textual, derives from Indian sources and was studied in some monasteries in much the same way that Buddhist scriptures were studied. When Tibetans needed medical help they usually went to a local 'apothecary' who sold concoctions of herbs; equally, help was sought in prayers and good-luck charms.

The theory of Tibetan medicine is based on an extremely complex system of checks and balances between what can be broadly described as three 'humours' (related to state of mind), seven 'bodily sustainers' (related to the digestive tract) and three 'eliminators' (related to the elimination of bodily wastes). And if the relationship between bodily functions and the three humours of desire, egoism and ignorance were not complex enough, there is the influence of harmful spirits to consider. There are 360 harmful female influences, 360 harmful male influences, 360 malevolent *naga* influences (*naga* being water spirits) and finally 360 influences stemming from past karma. All these combine to produce 404 basic disorders and 84,000 illnesses!

How does a Tibetan doctor assess the condition of a patient? The most important skill is pulse diagnosis. A Tibetan doctor is attuned to 360 'subtle channels' of energy

HEALTH

that run through the body's skin and muscle, internal organs, and bone and marrow. The condition of these channels can be ascertained through six of the doctor's fingers (the first three fingers of each hand). Tibetan medicine also relies on urine analysis as an important diagnostic tool.

If Tibetan diagnostic theory is mainly Indian in influence, the treatment owes as much to Chinese medicine as to Indian practices. Herbal concoctions, moxibustion and acupuncture are all used to restore balance to the body. Surgery was practised in the early days of Tibetan medicine, but was outlawed in the 9th century when a king's mother died during an operation.

For more on Tibetan medicine see the website www.tibetan-medicine.org.

Yuthok Yongten Gonpo, the physician of King Trisong Detsen, who was born near Ralung Monastery, is credited as the founder of the Tibetan medical system

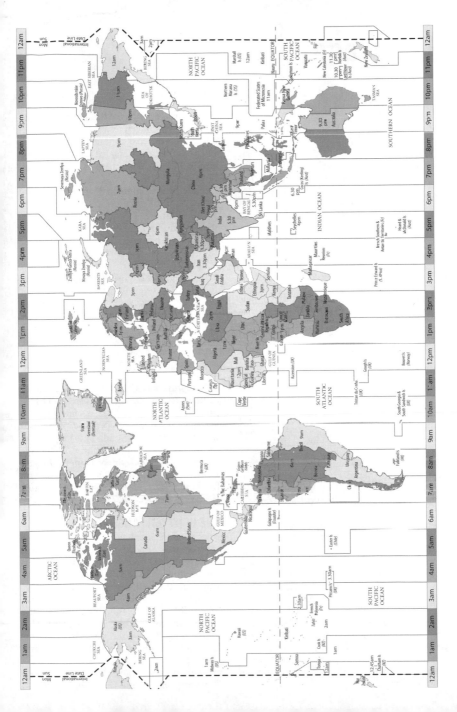

Language

CONTENTS

The two principal languages of Tibet are Tibetan and (Mandarin) Chinese. The importance of Chinese is an unfortunate reality in Tibet, and all Tibetans undertaking higher studies do so in Chinese. In urban Tibet (the countryside is another matter) almost all Tibetans speak Chinese. Nevertheless, even if you have studied or picked up some Chinese in China, it's worth trying to get a few phrases of Tibetan together. It will be much appreciated by the Tibetans you encounter on your travels.

Linguistically, Chinese and Tibetan have very little in common. They use different sentence structures, and the tonal element is far less crucial in Tibetan than in Chinese. Also, unlike the dialects of China, Tibetan has never used Chinese characters for its written language.

TIBETAN

Tibetan is a member of the Tibeto-Burman family of languages, and is spoken in Tibet and within exiled communities of Tibetans. Lhasa dialect, the standard form of Tibetan, employs a system of rising and falling tones, but the differences are subtle and meaning is made clear by context. Beginners need not worry about them.

Like Chinese, Tibetan has no articles (a, the) and doesn't use plurals. Here the similarity ends, however. Tibetan differs from European and Chinese languages, as it has a subject-object-verb sentence structure. Thus, where in English we would say 'I see John' (subject-verb-object), in Tibetan the sentence is *nga John thong gi duk*, ('I John see', subject-object-verb). In another marked difference from Chinese, Tibetan has tenses and conjugates its verbs with particles. There's also a fairly complicated system of prepositions (words like 'in' and 'on').

If all this makes Tibetan sound extremely difficult to pick up on the road, don't fret; providing you relax a little, it's fairly easy to get together a basic repertoire of phrases that will win you friends and help to get things done. For information on language courses, see p298. Lonely Planet's *Tibetan Phrasebook*, which includes sections on trekking, visiting temples and handicrafts, is also recommended.

THE WRITTEN LANGUAGE

The Tibetan script was developed during the reign of Songtsen Gampo in the 7th century. It was founded on Indian models and comprises 30 basic letters including the vowel 'a', and four extra vowel signs for 'e', 'i', 'o' and 'u'. Each letter can be written in three different styles, depending on the context in which a text is to be used. This 7th-century Tibetan script was based on the language spoken in Tibet at the time, and spellings have never been revised since. As a result of significant changes in spoken Tibetan over the last 12 centuries, written

Tibetan and spoken Tibetan are very different, and the development of a transliteration system for use by speakers of European languages is a formidable task.

In this book we've generally chosen the most commonly used spelling of each term. In cases where there is wide disagreement, we have chosen the spelling that's easiest to pronounce.

PRONUNCIATION
Tibetan has some tricky sounds for English speakers – there are quite a few consonant clusters, and, like Korean and Thai, Tibetan makes an important distinction between aspirated and non-aspirated consonants.

Vowels
The following pronunciation guide is based on standard British pronunciation.

a	as in 'father'
ay	as in 'play'
e	as in 'met'
ee	as in 'meet'
I	as in 'begin'
o	as in 'go'
oo	as in 'soon'
ö	similar to the 'u' in 'put'
u	as in 'rude'
ü	similar to the 'u' in 'flute'

Consonants
With the exception of the examples listed below, Tibetan consonants should be pronounced as in English. Where a consonant is followed by an **h**, it means that the consonant is aspirated (accompanied by a puff of air). An English example of this might be 'kettle', where the 'k' is aspirated and the 'tt' is non-aspirated. The distinction is fairly important, but in simple Tibetan the context should make it clear what you are talking about.

ky	as the 'kie' in 'Kiev'
ng	as the 'ng' in 'sing'
r	like a slightly trilled 'r'
ts	as the 'ts' in 'bits'

ACCOMMODATION
Where's a ...?	... kaba du?	... གང་པར་འདུག
guesthouse	dhön khang	མགྲོན་ཁང
hotel	dru-khang	འགྲུལ་ཁང

Do you have a room available?
kang mi yöpe?
ཁང་མི་ཡོད་པས

How much is it for one night?
tsen chik la katsö ray?
མཚན་གཅིག་ལ་ག་ཚོད་རེད

I'd like to stay with a Tibetan family.
nga phöbe mi-tsang nyamdo dendö yö
ང་བོད་པའི་མི་ཚང་མཉམ་དུ་བསྡད་འདོད་ཡོད

I need some hot water.
nga la chu tsapo go
ང་ལ་ཆུ་ཚ་པོ་དགོས

CONVERSATION & ESSENTIALS
Hello.	tashi dele	བཀྲ་ཤིས་བདེ་ལེགས
Goodbye. (when staying)	kale phe	ག་ལེ་ཕེབས
Goodbye. (when leaving)	kale shoo	ག་ལེ་བཞུགས
Thank you.	thoo jaychay	ཐུགས་རྗེ་ཆེ
Sorry.	gonda	དགོངས་དག
I want ...	nga la ... go	ང་ལ་ ... དགོས

What's your name?
kerang gi ming la karey zer gi yö?
ཁྱེད་རང་གི་མིང་ལ་ག་རེ་ཟེར་གྱི་ཡོད

My name is ... – and yours?
ngai ming-la ... sa, a- ni kerang-gi ming-la karey zer gi yö?
ངའི་མིང་ལ ... ས། ཨ་ནི་ཁྱེད་རང་གི་མིང་ལ་ག་རེ་ཟེར་གྱི་ཡོད

Is it OK to take a photo?
par gyabna digiy-rebay?
པར་བརྒྱབ་ན་འགྲིག་གི་རེད་པས

Where are you from?
kerang lung-pa ka-ne yin?
ཁྱེད་རང་ལུང་པ་ག་ནས་ཡིན

I'm from ...	nga ... ne yin	ང་ ... སྐུ་ནས་ཡིན
Australia	ausitaliya	ཨོ་སི་ཏ་ལི་ཡ
Canada	canada	ཀེ་ན་ཌ
France	farensi	ཕ་རན་སི
Germany	jarman	འཇར་མན
New Zealand	shinshilen	ནིའུ་ཛི་ལནྡ
UK	injee lungpa	དབྱིན་ཇི་ལུང་པ
USA	amerika	ཨ་མེ་རི་ཀ

Yes & No
There are no words in Tibetan that are the direct equivalents of English 'yes' and 'no'. Although it won't always be correct, you'll be understood if you use *la ong* for 'yes' and *la men* for 'no'.

HEALTH
hospital	menkang	སྨན་ཁང
diarrhoea	troko shewa	གྲོད་ཁོག་བཤལ་བ
fever	tsawa	ཚ་བ

EMERGENCIES – TIBETAN

Help!
rog nangda! རོགས་གནང་དང་།
Fire!
may bahgi! མེ་འབར་གྱིས།
Thief!
kuma du! རྐུ་མ་འདུག
Go away!
phah gyuk! ཕར་རྒྱུགས།
I'm ill.
nga nagidu ང་ན་གི་འདུག
It's an emergency.
za dagpo ray! ཛ་དྲག་པོ་རེད།
Call a doctor!
amchi kay tongda! ཨེམ་ཆི་སྐད་གཏོང་དང་།
Call the police!
korsung-wa kay tongda! སྐོར་སྲུང་བ་སྐད་གཏོང་དང་།
I'm lost.
nga lamga lasha ང་ལམ་ག་ལ་བཟུགས་ལ་ཤག
Where are the toilets?
sangchö kabah yöray? གསང་སྤྱོད་ག་བར་ཡོད་རེད།

LANGUAGE DIFFICULTIES

Do you speak English?
injeeke shing gi yö pe? དབྱིན་ཇི་སྐད་ཤེས་ཀྱི་ཡོད་པས
I don't understand.
ha ko ma song ཧ་གོ་མ་སོང་
I understand.
ha ko song ཧ་གོ་སོང་

NUMBERS

1	chik	གཅིག
2	nyi	གཉིས
3	sum	གསུམ
4	shi	བཞི
5	nga	ལྔ
6	dug	དྲུག
7	dün	བདུན
8	gye	བརྒྱད
9	gu	དགུ
10	chu	བཅུ
11	chu chik	བཅུ་གཅིག
12	chu nyi	བཅུ་གཉིས
13	chok sum	བཅུ་གསུམ
14	chub shi	བཅུ་བཞི
15	chö nga	བཅོ་ལྔ
16	chu dug	བཅུ་དྲུག
17	chu dun	བཅུ་བདུན
18	chö gye	བཅོ་བརྒྱད
19	chu gu	བཅུ་དགུ
20	nyi shu	ཉི་ཤུ་
21	nyi shu tsa chik	ཉི་ཤུ་རྩ་གཅིག
30	sum chu	སུམ་བཅུ་

40	shib chu	བཞི་བཅུ་
50	nga chu	ལྔ་བཅུ་
60	dug chu	དྲུག་བཅུ་
70	dün chu	བདུན་བཅུ་
80	gye chu	བརྒྱད་བཅུ་
90	gub chu	དགུ་བཅུ་
100	gya	གཅིག་བརྒྱ
1000	chik tong	ཆིག་སྟོང་

SHOPPING & SERVICES

How much is it?
ka tsö ray? ག་ཚོད་རེད
It's expensive.
gong chenpo ray གོང་ཆེན་པོ་རེད

TIME & DATES

What's the time?
chutsö katsö ray? ཆུ་ཚོད་ག་ཚོད་རེད།
... hour ... minute
... chutsö ... karma ... ཆུ་ཚོད་ ... སྐར་མ

When?	kadü?	ག་དུས
now	thanda	ད་ལྟ
today	thiring	དེ་རིང
tomorrow	sangnyi	སང་ཉིན
yesterday	kesa	ཁ་སང
morning	shogay	ཞོགས་སྐད
afternoon	nying gung gyab la	ཉིན་གུང་ཕྱི་དྲོ་རྒྱབ་ལ
evening/night	gonta	དགོང་དག

TRANSPORT

I want to go to ...
nga ... la drondö yö
ང ...ལ་འགྲོ་འདོད་ཡོད
Can I get there on foot?
phagay gompa gyab-nay leb thub-kiy rebay?
ཕ་གིར་གོམ་པ་བརྒྱབ་ནས་སླེབ་ཐུབ་ཀྱི་རེད་པས
Where is the bus going?
mota diy kaba drugiy ray
མོ་ཊ་འདི་ག་པར་འགྲོ་གི་རེད
Is this bus going to (Ganden Monastery)?
mota di (ganden gompa) drugiy rebay?
མོ་ཊ་འདི་ (དགའ་ལྡན་དགོན་པ) འགྲོ་གི་རེད་པས
What time do we leave?
ngatso chutsö katsö la dro-gi yin?
ང་ཚོ་ཆུ་ཚོད་ག་ཚོད་ལ་འགྲོ་གི་ཡིན
What time do we arrive?
ngatso chutsö katsö la lep-gi ray?
ང་ཚོ་ཆུ་ཚོད་ག་ཚོད་ལ་སླེབ་ཀྱི་རེད
Where can I hire a bicycle?
kanggari kaba ragi ray?
ཀང་སྒ་རི་ག་པར་ལ་ག་པར་ལ་ཡོད་རེད
How much per day?
nyima chik-la gong katsö ray?
ཉི་མ་གཅིག་ལ་གོང་ག་ཚོད་རེད

SIGNS – TIBETAN

ཉེན་ཁ།	nyen-ka	Danger
འཛུལ་ས།	zu-sa	Entrance
དོན་ས།	donsa	Exit
ཁ་བཀག	kah kag	Stop
སྒོ་ཕྱེ།	ko-chay	Open
སྒོ་བརྒྱབ།	ko-gyab	Closed
པར་བརྒྱབ་མི་ཆོག	pa gyab michok	No Photographs
ཐ་མག་འཐེན་མི་ཆོག	tama ten michok	No Smoking
གསང་སྤྱོད།	sang cho	Toilets

What time is the ... bus?

mota ... chutsö katsay-la drogiy ray?

མོ་ཊ ... ཆུ་ཚོད་ག་ཚོད་ལ་འགྲོ་གི་རེད

next	jema-te	རྗེས་མ་དེ
first	tanqpo-te	དང་པོ་དེ
last	thama-te	མཐའ་མ་དེ

airport	nam-tang	གནམ་ཐང་
bicycle	kanggari	ཀང་སྒ་རི་ལ
bus	basay/mota/ lamkhor	འབབ་ས་/མོ་ཊ/ ལམ་འཁོར་
pack animals	kel semchen/ kelma	ཁལ་སེམས་ཅན་/ ཁལ་མ
porter	dopo khur khen	དོ་པོ་ཁུར་མཁན་
yak	ya	གཡག

Directions

Where is the ...?
... kaba yo ray?

... ག་པར་ཡོད་རེད

I'm looking for ...
... ka-bah yö-may

... ག་པར་ཡོད་མེད་ང་ཚུག་གི་ཡོད།

right	yeba	གཡས་པ་
left	yönba	གཡོན་པ་
straight ahead	shar gya	ཤར་རྒྱག
north	chang	བྱང་
south	lo	ལྷོ་
east	shar	ཤར་
west	nub	ནུབ་

Geographical Terms

road/trail	lam	ལམ་
mountain	ri	རི་
cave	puk/trapoo	ཕུག་སྤུག་
pass	la	ལ
river	chu/tsangpo	ཆུ་/གཙང་པོ་
valley	loong shon	ལུང་གཤོང་
lake	tso	མཚོ་
hot spring	chu-tsen	ཆུ་ཚན་

MANDARIN

Travellers going from China into Tibet or from Tibet onwards into China are well advised to pick up a Chinese phrasebook such as Lonely Planet's *Mandarin Phrasebook*. It should help you through most of your travel needs, in both Tibet and China.

PRONUNCIATION

The dialects of China are tonal, which means that variations in vocal pitch within words are used to determine their meaning. When learning Mandarin Chinese, the standard example given to demonstrate the principle of its four tones is *ma*:

high tone: *ma* – 'mother'
rising tone: *má* – 'hemp' or 'numb'
falling-rising tone: *mǎ* – 'horse'
falling tone: *mà* – 'scold' or 'swear'

Pinyin

The standard form of Romanisation for Mandarin adopted by China is known as Pinyin. It means literally 'spell the sounds', and once you get used to the idiosyncrasies of its spellings it is an accurate way of representing the sounds of Mandarin. The pronunciation of Pinyin spellings are by no means obvious to speakers of European languages, however, and need to be memorised. There's no way of knowing, for example, that a Pinyin **x** is pronounced like an English 's' or that **zh** is pronounced like a 'j'.

Vowels

Pronunciation of Mandarin vowels can be fairly tricky for English speakers. In some instances they change depending on the consonant that precedes them, and in others they're sounds that aren't used in English.

The following examples of vowel sounds follow standard British pronunciation.

a	as in 'father'
ai	as in 'aisle'
ao	as the 'ow' in 'cow'
e	as in 'her'
ei	as in 'rein'
i	as in 'police' when preceded by **j**, **q**, **x** or **y**
i	as in 'fir' when preceded by other consonants

ian	as in 'yen'
iao	as in the exclamation 'yow!'
ie	as in 'pier'
o	as in 'or'
ou	as the 'oa' in 'boat'
u	as in 'flute' after **j**, **q**, **x** or **y**
u	as in 'rude' when preceded by other consonants
ü	as the 'u' in 'flute'
ui	as the word 'way'
uo	as the word 'war'

Consonants

Many Mandarin consonants are pronounced differently from their English equivalents. Some pairs of consonants have the same pronunciation as each other (eg **q** and **c** sound the same), but the sound of the following vowel changes depending on which is used. Thus **ci** is pronounced 'tser', while **qi** is pronounced 'tsee'. There are three such pairs of consonants in Pinyin: **c/q**, **j/z**, and **s/x**.

c	as the 'ts' in 'bits'
ch	as the 'ch' in 'church'
j	as the 'ds' in 'suds'
h	as the guttural 'ch' in Scottish *loch*
q	as the 'ts' in 'bits'
r	between an English 'r' and the 's' in 'pleasure'
s	as in 'sock'
sh	as in 'shack'
x	as the 's' in 'sock'
z	as the 'ds' in 'suds'
zh	as the 'j' in 'judge'

ACCOMMODATION

I'm looking for a ...
Wǒyào zhǎo ... 我要找...
  guesthouse
  bīnguǎn 宾馆
  hotel
  lǚguǎn 旅馆

Do you have a room available?
Nǐmen yǒu fángjiān ma
你们有房间吗?
May I see the room?
Wǒ néng kànkan fángjiān ma
我能看看房间吗?
Where's the bathroom?
Yùshì zài nǎr?
浴室在哪儿?

Where's the toilet?
Cèsuǒ zài nǎr?
厕所在哪儿?

How much is it ...?
... duōshǎo qián? . . .多少钱?
  per night
  měitiān wǎnshàng 每天晚上
  per person
  měigerén 每个人

CONVERSATION & ESSENTIALS

Hello.	*Nín hǎo.*	您好
Goodbye.	*Zàijiàn.*	再见
Please.	*Qǐng.*	请
Thank you.	*Xièxie.*	谢谢
Many thanks.	*Duōxiè.*	多谢
You're welcome.	*Búkèqi.*	不客气
Excuse me, ...	*Qǐng wèn, ...*	请问, . . .

Yes & No

There are no words in Mandarin that specifically mean 'yes' and 'no' when used in isolation. When asked a question the verb is repeated to indicate the affirmative. A response in the negative is formed by using the word 不 *bù* (meaning 'no') before the verb. When *bù* (falling tone) occurs before another word with a falling tone, it becomes *bú* (ie with a rising tone).

Are you going to Shanghai?
Nǐ qù shànghǎi ma? 你去上海吗?
  Yes.
  Qù. (go) 去
  No.
  Bú qù. (no go) 不去

No.
  Méi yǒu. (don't have) 没有
No.
  Búshì. (not so) 不是

DIRECTIONS

Where is (the) ...?
  ... zài nǎr? . . .在哪儿?
Go straight ahead.
  Yìzhí zǒu. 一直走
Turn left.
  Zuǒ zhuǎn. 左转
Turn right.
  Yòu zhuǎn. 右转
at the next corner
  zài xià yíge guǎijiǎo 在下一个拐角
at the traffic lights
  zài hónglǜdēng 在红绿灯

Could you show me (on the map)?
Nǐ néng bunéng (zài dìtú shang) zhǐ gěi wǒ kàn?
你能不能（在地图上）指给我看？

behind	*hòubianr*	后边儿
in front of	*qiánbianr*	前边儿
near	*jìn*	近
far	*yuǎn*	远
opposite	*duìmiànr*	对面儿

EMERGENCIES – MANDARIN

Help!
Jiùmìng a!   救命啊！

emergency
jǐnjí qíngkuàng   紧急情况

There's been an accident!
Chūshìle!   出事了！

I'm lost.
Wǒ mílùle.   我迷路了

Go away!
Zǒu kāi!   走开！

Leave me alone!
Bié fán wǒ!   别烦我！

Could you help me please?
Nǐ néng bunéng bāng wǒ ge máng?
你能不能帮我个忙？

Call ...!
Qǐng jiào ...!   请叫，...！

   a doctor
   yīshēng   医生

   the police
   jǐngchá   警察

HEALTH

I'm sick.
Wǒ bìngle.
我病了

It hurts here.
Zhèr téng.
这儿疼

Is there a doctor here who speaks English?
Zhèr yǒu huì jiǎng yīngyǔ de dàifu ma?
这儿有会讲英语的大夫吗？

I'm ...
Wǒ yǒu ...   我有...

   asthmatic
   xiàochuǎnbìng   哮喘病

   diabetic
   tángniàobìng   糖尿病

   epileptic
   diānxiánbìng   癫痫病

I'm allergic to ...
Wǒ duì ... guòmǐn.   我对...过敏

   antibiotics
   kàngjùnsù   抗菌素

   aspirin
   āsīpīlín   阿司匹林

   bee stings
   mìfēng zhecì   蜜蜂蜇刺

   nuts.
   guǒrén   果仁

   penicillin
   qīngméisù   青霉素

LANGUAGE DIFFICULTIES

Do you speak English?
Nǐ huì shuō yīngyǔ ma?
你会说英语吗？

Does anyone here speak English?
Zhèr yǒu rén huì shuō yīngyǔ ma?
这儿有人会说英语吗？

I understand.
Wǒ tīngdedǒng.
我听得懂

I don't understand.
Wǒ tīngbudǒng.
我听不懂

NUMBERS

0	*líng*	零
1	*yī, yāo*	一, 幺
2	*èr, liǎng*	二, 两
3	*sān*	三
4	*sì*	四
5	*wǔ*	五
6	*liù*	六
7	*qī*	七
8	*bā*	八
9	*jiǔ*	九
10	*shí*	十
11	*shíyī*	十一
12	*shí'èr*	十二
20	*èrshí*	二十
21	*èrshíyī*	二十一
22	*èrshíèr*	二十二
30	*sānshí*	三十
40	*sìshí*	四十
50	*wǔshí*	五十
60	*liùshí*	六十
70	*qīshí*	七十
80	*bāshí*	八十
90	*jiǔshí*	九十
100	*yìbǎi*	一百
1000	*yìqiān*	一千

LANGUAGE

SIGNS – MANDARIN

入口	Rùkǒu	Entrance
出口	Chūkǒu	Exit
问讯处	Wènxùnchù	Information
开	Kāi	Open
关	Guān	Closed
禁止	Jìnzhǐ	Prohibited
有空房	Yǒu Kòngfáng	Rooms Available
客满	Kèmǎn	No Vacancies
警察局	Jǐngchájú	Police Station
厕所	Cèsuǒ	Toilets
男	Nán	Men
女	Nǚ	Women

PAPERWORK

name	xìngmíng	姓名
nationality	guójí	国籍
date of birth	chūshēng rìqī	出生日期
place of birth	chūshēng dìdiǎn	出生地点
sex (gender)	xìngbié	性别
passport	hùzhào	护照
visa	qiānzhèng	签证
visa extension	yáncháng qiānzhèng	延长签证
Public Security Bureau (PSB)	gōng'ānjú	公安局
Foreign Affairs Branch	wàishíkē	外事科

TIME & DATES

What's the time?
Jǐ diǎn? 几点?
... hour ... minute(s)
... diǎn ... fēn ...点...分

When?	Shénme shíhòu?	什么时候?
now	xiànzài	现在
today	jīntiān	今天
tomorrow	míngtiān	明天
yesterday	zuótiān	昨天

TRANSPORT

I want to go to ...
Wǒ yào qù ...
我要去...
I'd like to hire a bicycle.
Wǒ yào zū yíliàng zìxíngchē?
我要租一辆自行车

What time does ... leave/arrive?
... jǐdiǎn kāi/dào?
...几点开/到?

intercity bus/coach
chángtú qìchē 长途汽车
microbus taxi
miànbāochē, miàndī 面包车, 面的
the plane
fēijī 飞机

When's the ... bus?
... bānchē shénme shíhou lái?
... 班车什么时候来?
first	tóu	头
last	mò	末
next	xià	下

I'd like a ...
Wǒ yào yíge ...
我要一个...
one way ticket	dānchéng piào	单程票
return ticket	láihuí piào	来回票

SHOPPING & SERVICES

I'd like to buy ...
Wǒ xiǎng mǎi ... 我想买...
How much is it?
Duōshǎo qián? 多少钱?
I don't like it.
Wǒ bù xǐhuan. 我不喜欢
That's too expensive.
Tài guìle. 太贵了
I'll take it.
Wǒ jiù mǎi zhèige. 我就买这个

GAZETTEER

Ali	狮泉
Chamdo	昌都
Chongye	阴结
Chushul	曲水
Damxung	当雄
Drepung Monastery	哲蚌寺
Everest, Mt (Qomolangma)	珠峰
Ganden Monastery	甘丹寺
Gegye	革吉
Gertse	改则
Golmud	格尔木
Gongkar	贡嘎
Gongkar Airport	贡嘎机场
Gyantse	江孜

Gyatsa	加查	Potala, the	布达拉宫
Hor Qu	霍尔区	Purang	普兰
Jokhang, the	大昭寺	Rongphu Monastery	绒布寺
Kailash, Mt	神山	Sakya	萨迦
Kangding	康定	Samding Monastery	桑顶寺
Kashgar	喀什	Samye Monastery	桑耶寺
Lhasa	拉萨	Sangsang	桑桑
Lhatse	拉孜	Sera Monastery	色拉寺
Lhundrub	林周	Shegar	新定日
Litang	理塘	Shigatse	日喀则
Manasarovar, Lake	圣湖(马旁雍错)	Tingri	定日
Markam	芒康	Trandruk Monastery	昌珠寺
Medro Gungkar	墨竹工卡	Tsaparang	札达
Mindroling Monastery	敏珠林寺	Tsetang	泽当
Nam-tso	纳木错	Tsochen	措勤
Nangartse	浪卡子	Tsomei	指美
Naqu	那曲	Tsona	错那
Norbulingka	罗布林卡	Yamdrok-tso	羊卓雍错
Nyalam	聂拉木	Yatung	亚东
Nyingchi	林芝	Yumbulagang	雍布拉康
Paryang	帕羊	Zhangmu	樟木
Pongba	雄巴	Zhongba	仲巴

LANGUAGE

Glossary

For ease of reference, this glossary is divided into two sections. The first section, 'Who's Who', provides succinct descriptions of some of the deities, historical figures and other people mentioned in this book. The second section covers general terms used.

WHO'S WHO

Many of the terms in this section are of Sanskrit origin. Entries in parentheses indicate the Sanskrit equivalent of each Tibetan term. An exception is Sakyamuni (Sakya Thukpa), in which case the Sanskrit 'Sakyamuni' is commonly used in Tibet. For more information on who's who in Tibet, see p62.

Akshobhya – see *Mikyöba*
Amitabha – see *Öpagme*
Amitayus – see *Tsepame*
Atisha (Jowo-je) – Buddhist scholar from contemporary Bengal. His arrival in Tibet at the invitation of the king of Guge, in western Tibet, was a catalyst in the 11th-century revival of Buddhism on the high plateau.
Avalokiteshvara – see *Chenresig*

Bhrikuti – the Nepali consort of King Songtsen Gampo, an early Tibetan king
Büton Rinchen Drup – compiler of the Tibetan Buddhist canon; established a sub-school of Tibetan Buddhism, based in Shalu Monastery

Chana Dorje (Vajrapani) – the wrathful Bodhisattva of Energy whose name means 'thunderbolt in hand'
Chenresig (Avalokiteshvara) – an embodiment of compassionate bodhisattvahood and the patron saint of Tibet. The *Dalai Lamas* are considered to be manifestations of this deity.
Chögyel (Dharmaraja) – *Gelugpa* protector deity; blue, with the head of a bull
Chökyong (Lokpalas) – the Four Guardian Kings
Citipati – dancing skeletons, often seen in protector chapels

Dakini – see *Khadroma*
Dalai Lamas – the 14 (so far) manifestations of *Chenresig* (Avalokiteshvara), who, as spiritual heads of the *Gelugpa* order, ruled over Tibet from 1642 until 1959. It is an honorific title that means 'ocean of wisdom' and was bestowed by the Mongolian Altyn Khan. The present (14th) Dalai Lama resides in Dharamsala, India.

Dharmaraja – see *Chögyel*
Dorje Chang (Vajradhara) – one of the five Dhyani *buddhas*, recognisable by his crossed arms holding a bell and thunderbolt
Dorje Jigje (Yamantaka) – a meditational deity who comes in various aspects. The Red and Black aspects are probably the most common.
Dorje Lekpa – *Dzogchen* deity, recognisable by his round green hat
Drölma (Tara) – a female meditational deity who is a manifestation of the enlightened mind of all *buddhas*. She is sometimes referred to as the mother of all *buddhas*, and has many aspects, but is most often seen as Green Tara or as Drölkar (White Tara).
Dromtönpa – 11th-century disciple of *Atisha* (Jowo-je) who founded the *Kadampa* order and Reting Monastery

Ekajati (Tsechigma) – deity with one eye, one tooth and one breast, associated with the *Dzogchen* movement

Gesar – a legendary king and also the name of an epic concerning his fabulous exploits. The king's empire is known as Ling, and thus the stories, which are usually sung and told by professional bards, are known as the *Stories of Ling*.
Guru Rinpoche – credited with having suppressed demons and other malevolent forces in order to introduce Buddhism into Tibet during the 8th century. In the *Nyingmapa* order he is revered as the Second Buddha.

Hayagriva – see *Tamdrin*

Jamchen Chöde – disciple of *Tsongkhapa* and founder of Sera Monastery; also known as Sakya Yeshe
Jampa (Maitreya) – the Buddha of Loving Kindness; also the Future Buddha, the fifth of the 1000 *buddhas* who will descend to earth (*Sakyamuni* or Sakya Thukpa was the fourth)
Jampelyang (Manjushri) – the Bodhisattva of Insight. He is usually depicted holding a sword, which symbolises discriminative awareness, in one hand, and a book, which symbolises his mastery of all knowledge, in the other.
Jamyang Chöje – founder of Drepung Monastery
Je Rinpoche – an honorific title used for *Tsongkhapa*, founder of the *Gelugpa* order
Jowo-je – see *Atisha*
Jowo Sakyamuni – the most revered image of *Sakyamuni* (Sakya Thukpa) in Tibet. It depicts the Historical Buddha at the age of 12 and is kept in the *Jokhang* in Lhasa.

Karmapa – a lineage of spiritual leaders of the *Karma Kagyupa*. They are also known as the *Black Hats,* and there have been 17 so far.
Khadroma (Dakini) – literally 'sky dancer'; a fierce, lower-ranking *Tantric* goddess, often depicted as red

Langdharma – the 9th-century Tibetan king accused of having persecuted Buddhists
Lokpalos – see *Chökyong*

Maitreya – see *Jampa*
Manjushri – see *Jampelyang*
Marpa – an ascetic of the 11th century whose disciple, *Milarepa,* founded the *Kagyupa* order
Mikyöba (Akshobhya) – the Buddha of the State of Perfected Consciousness, or Perfect Cognition; literally 'unchanging', 'the immutable one'
Milarepa – (1040–1123) disciple of *Marpa* and founder of the *Kagyupa* order; renowned for his songs

Namri Songtsen – 6th-century Tibetan king, father of *Songtsen Gampo*
Namse (Vairocana) – Buddha of Enlightened Consciousness
Namtöse (Vaishravana) – the Guardian of the North, one of the Lokpalas or Four Guardian Kings
Nechung – protector deity of Tibet and the *Dalai Lamas.* Nechung is manifested in the State Oracle, who is traditionally installed at Nechung Monastery, near Drepung, Lhasa.
Nyentri Tsenpo – legendary first king of Tibet

Öpagme (Amitabha) – the Buddha of Perfected Perception; literally 'boundless light'

Palden Lhamo (Shri Devi) – special protector of Lhasa, the *Dalai Lama* and the *Gelugpa* order; the female counterpart of Nagpo Chenpo (Mahakala)
Panchen Lama – literally 'guru and great teacher'. The Panchen Lama lineage is associated with Tashilhunpo Monastery, Shigatse, and goes back to the 17th century. The Panchen Lama is a manifestation of *Öpagme* (Amitabha).
Pehar – oracle and protector of the Buddhist state, depicted with six arms, wearing a round hat and riding a snow lion

Rahulla – *Dzogchen* deity with nine heads, eyes all over his body, a mouth in his belly and the lower half of a serpent (coiled on the dead body of ego)
Ralpachen – 9th-century king whose assassination marked the end of the Yarlung Valley dynasty

Sakya Pandita – literally 'scholar from Sakya'; former abbot of Sakya Monastery who established the priest-patron system with the Mongols; also known as Kunga Gyaltsen
Sakyamuni – literally the 'sage of Sakya'; the founder of Buddhism, the Historical Buddha; known in Tibetan as Sakya Thukpa; see also *Siddhartha Gautama* and *buddha*

Samvara – a wrathful manifestation of *Sakyamuni* (Sakya Thukpa)
Shantarakshita – Indian scholar of the 8th century and first abbot of Samye Monastery
Shenrab – mythical founder of the *Bön* faith
Shiromo – *Bönpo* name for *Sakyamuni* (Sakya Thukpa)
Shri Devi – see *Palden Lhamo*
Siddhartha Gautama – the personal name of the Historical Buddha; see also *Sakyamuni* (Sakya Thukpa)
Songtsen Gampo – the 7th-century king associated with the introduction of Buddhism to Tibet

Tamdrin (Hayagriva) – literally 'horse necked'; a wrathful meditational deity and manifestation of *Avalokiteshvara*, usually associated with the *Nyingmapa* order
Tara – see *Drölma*
Tenzin Gyatso – the 14th and current *Dalai Lama*
Terdak Lingpa – founder of Mindroling Monastery
Trisong Detsen – 8th-century Tibetan king; founder of Samye Monastery
Tsechigma – see *Ekajati*
Tsepame (Amitayus) – a meditational deity associated with longevity; literally 'limitless life'. Tsepame is often featured in a trinity with *Drölma* (Tara) and Vijaya.
Tseringma – protector goddess of Mt Everest, depicted riding a snow lion
Tsongkhapa – 14th-century founder of the *Gelugpa* order and Ganden Monastery

Vairocana – see *Namse*
Vaishravana – see *Namtöse*
Vajradhara – see *Dorje Chang*
Vajrapani – see *Chana Dorje*

Wencheng Chinese consort of King *Songtsen Gampo*

Yama – Lord of Death, who resides in *sky burial* sites
Yamantaka – see *Dorje Jigje*
Yeshe Tsogyel – female consort of *Guru Rinpoche* and one-time wife of King *Trisong Detsen*

GENERAL TERMS

Ambans – Chinese representatives of the Manchu Qing dynasty posted in Lhasa from the early 19th century until the Chinese republican overthrow of the Qing in 1911
Amdo – a traditional province of Tibet, now Qinghai province
AMS – acute mountain sickness; often referred to as altitude sickness
ani – Tibetan for 'nun', as in 'ani gompa' (nunnery)
arhat – literally 'worthy one'. The arhat is neither a *buddha* nor a *bodhisattva*, but one who has become free of the *Wheel of Life* and is free of hatred and all delusions.

Bardo – as detailed in the *Tibetan Book of the Dead*, this term refers to the intermediate stages between death and rebirth

Barkhor – an intermediate circumambulation circuit, or *kora*, but most often specifically the intermediate circuit around the *Jokhang* temple of Lhasa

binguan – Chinese term for guesthouse or hotel

Black Hat – strictly speaking, this refers to the black hat embellished with gold that was presented to the second *Karmapa* of the *Karma Kagyupa* order of Tsurphu Monastery by a Mongol prince, and worn ceremoniously by all subsequent incarnations of the Karmapa. By extension the black hat represents the Karma Kagyupa order.

Bö – Tibetans' name for their own land, sometimes written 'Bod' or 'Po'

Bodhgaya – the place in contemporary Bihar, India, where *Sakyamuni* (Sakya Thukpa), the Historical Buddha, attained enlightenment

bodhisattva – literally 'enlightenment hero'. The bodhisattva voluntarily does not take the step to *nirvana*, being motivated to stay within the *Wheel of Life* by compassion for all sentient beings.

Bön – the indigenous religion of Tibet and the Himalayan borderlands. In its ancient form its main components were royal burial rites, the cult of indigenous deities and magical practices. In the 11th century, Bön was systematised along Buddhist lines and it is this form that survives today.

Bönpo – a practitioner of *Bön*

buddha – literally 'awakened one'; a being who through spiritual training has broken free of all illusion and karmic consequences and is 'enlightened'; most often specifically the Historical Buddha, *Sakyamuni* (Sakya Thukpa)

Büton – suborder of Tibetan Buddhism based on the teachings of Büton Rinchen Drup, the 14th-century compiler of the major Buddhist texts; associated with Shalu Monastery, near Shigatse

CAAC – Civil Aviation Authority of China

cairn – a mound of stones erected as a marker

chakje – handprint

chaktsal – Tibetan for the ritual of prostration

chaktsal gang – prostration point

cham – a ritual dance carried out by monks and *lamas*, usually at festivals. All participants except the central *lama* are masked.

chang – Tibetan barley beer

Changtang – vast plains of north Tibet extending into Xinjiang and Qinghai; the world's largest and highest plateau

chö – see *dharma*

chömay – butter lamp

chörten – Tibetan for 'stupa'; usually used as reliquary for the cremated remains of important *lamas*

chu – river, stream, brook etc

chuba – long-sleeved sheepskin cloak

CITS – China International Travel Service

CTS – China Travel Service

darchok – string of prayer flags

dharma – 'chö' in Tibetan, and sometimes translated as 'law', this very broad term covers the truths expounded by *Sakyamuni* (Sakya Thukpa), the Buddhist teachings, the Buddhist path, and the Buddhist goal of *nirvana*. In effect it is the 'law' that must be understood, followed and achieved in order for one to be a Buddhist.

dorje – literally 'diamond' or 'thunderbolt'; a metaphor for the indestructible, indivisible nature of buddhahood; also a *Tantric* hand-held sceptre symbolising 'skilful means'

drokpa – Tibetan for 'nomad'

dukhang – Tibetan for 'assembly hall'

dukkha – *Sanskrit* for 'suffering', the essential condition of all life

dürtro – sky-burial site; see also *sky burial*

dzo – domesticated cross between a bull and a female yak

Dzogchen – the Great Perfection teachings associated with the *Nyingmapa* order

dzong – fort

Eightfold Path – one of the *Four Noble Truths* taught by *Sakyamuni* (Sakya Thukpa); the path that must be taken to achieve enlightenment and liberation from the *Wheel of Life*

FIT office – Family (or Foreign) and Independent Traveller office

Four Noble Truths – as stated in the first speech given by *Sakyamuni* (Sakya Thukpa) after he achieved enlightenment, the Four Noble Truths are the truth that all life is suffering; the truth that suffering originates in desire; the truth that desire may be extinguished; and the truth that there is a path to this end

Ganden – the *pure land* of *Jampa* (Maitreya), and the seat of the *Gelugpa* order; 'Tushita' in *Sanskrit*

Garuda – mythological bird associated with Hinduism. In Tibetan *Tantric* Buddhism it is seen as a wrathful force that transforms malevolent influences.

gau – an amulet or 'portable shrine' worn around the neck, containing the image of an important spiritual figure, usually the *Dalai Lama*

Gelugpa – major order of Tibetan Buddhism, associated with the *Dalai Lamas*, the *Panchen Lamas* and Drepung, Sera, Ganden and Tashilhunpo Monasteries. The order was founded by *Tsongkhapa* in the 14th century, and is sometimes known as the Yellow Hats.

geshe – title awarded on completion of the highest level of study (something like a doctorate) that monks may undertake after completing their full indoctrinal vows; usually associated with the *Gelugpa* order

gompa – Tibetan for 'monastery'

gönkhang – protector chapel

Guge – a 9th-century kingdom of western Tibet

guru – *Sanskrit* term for 'spiritual teacher', literally 'heavy'. The Tibetan equivalent is *lama*.

Hinayana – also called Theravada, this is a major school of Buddhism. It follows the original teachings of the Historical Buddha, *Sakyamuni* (Sakya Thukpa), and places less importance on the compassionate *bodhisattva* ideal and more on individual enlightenment. See also *Mahayana*.

Jokhang – situated in Lhasa, this is the most sacred and one of the most ancient of Tibet's temples. It is also known as the *Tsuglhakhang*.

Kadampa – order of Tibetan Buddhism based on the teachings of the Indian scholar *Atisha* (Jowo-je). The school was a major influence on the *Gelugpa* order.
Kagyupa – order of Tibetan Buddhism that traces its lineage back through *Milarepa* and *Marpa* and eventually to the Indian *mahasiddhas*. It is divided into numerous sub-orders, the most famous of which is the *Karma Kagyupa*, or the *Karmapa*.
kangtsang – monastic residential quarters
Kangyur – the Tibetan Buddhist canon. The complement of the Kangyur is the *Tengyur*.
karma – action and its consequences, the psychic 'imprint' that action leaves on the mind and that continues into further rebirths. The term is found in both Hinduism and Buddhism, and may be likened to the law of cause and effect.
Karma Kagyupa – suborder of the *Kagyupa* order, established by Gampopa and Dusum Khyenpa in the 12th century
Kashag – Tibetan for the cabinet of the *Gelugpa* lamaist government
kathak – prayer scarf; used as a ritual offering or as a gift
Kham – traditional eastern Tibetan province; much of it is now part of western Sichuan and northwestern Yunnan
Khampa – a person from *Kham*
Khangjung – Land of Snows
khenpo – Tibetan term for 'abbot'
kora – ritual circumambulation circuit; pilgrimage circuit
kumbum – literally '100,000 images', this is a *chörten* that contains statuary and paintings. The most famous in Tibet is the Gyantse Kumbum in *Tsang*.

la – Tibetan for 'mountain pass'
lama – literally 'unsurpassed'; Tibetan equivalent of *guru*; a title bestowed on monks of particularly high spiritual attainment
lamaism – term used by early Western writers on the subject of Tibet to describe Tibetan Buddhism; also used by the Chinese in the term 'lamajiao', literally 'lama religion'
lamrim – the stages on the path to enlightenment; a graduated approach to enlightenment as expounded by *Tsongkhapa*. Lamrim is associated with the *Gelugpa* order.
lapse – see *cairn*
lha – Tibetan term for 'life spirit'. It may also be present in inanimate objects such as lakes, mountains and trees.

lhakhang – Tibetan term for 'chapel'
ling – Tibetan term usually associated with lesser, outlying temples
lingkhor – an outer pilgrimage circuit; famously, the outer pilgrimage of Lhasa
Losar – Tibetan New Year
lu – 'road' in Chinese; see also *naga*
lungta – prayer flag

mahasiddha – literally 'of great spiritual accomplishment'. A mahasiddha is a *Tantric* practitioner who has reached a high level of awareness; there are 84 famous mahasiddhas. The Tibetan term is 'drubchen'.
Mahayana – the other major school of Buddhism along with *Hinayana*. Mahayana emphasises compassion and the altruism of the *bodhisattva* who remains on the *Wheel of Life* for the sake of all sentient beings.
mandala – a circular representation of the three-dimensional world of a meditational deity; used as a meditational device. The Tibetan term is 'kyilkhor'.
mani – prayer
mani lhakhang – small chapel housing a single large prayer wheel
mani stone – a stone with the mantra *'om mani padme hum'* ('hail to the jewel in the lotus') carved on it
mani wall – a wall made with *mani stones*
mantra – literally 'protection of the mind'. This is one of the *Tantric* devices used to achieve identity with a meditational deity and break through the world of illusion; a series of syllables recited as the pure sound made by an enlightened being.
meditational deity – a deified manifestation of the enlightened mind with which, according to *Tantric* ritual, the adept seeks union and thus experience of enlightenment
momo – Tibetan dumpling
Mönlam – a major Lhasa festival established by *Tsongkhapa*
Mt Meru – the sacred mountain at the centre of the universe; also known as *Sumeru*

naga – water spirits that may take the form of serpents or semi-humans. The latter can be seen in images of the naga kings. The Tibetan term is 'lu'.
nangkhor – inner circumambulation circuit, usually within the interior of a temple or monastic assembly hall, and taking in various chapels en route
Newari – the people of the Nepali Buddhist kingdoms in the Kathmandu Valley
Ngari – ancient name for the province of western Tibet; later incorporated into *Ütsang*
nirvana – literally 'beyond sorrow'. Nirvana is an end to desire and suffering, and an end to the cycle of rebirth.
Norbulingka – the summer palace of the *Dalai Lamas* in Lhasa
Nyingmapa – the earliest order of Tibetan Buddhism, based largely on the Buddhism brought to Tibet by *Guru Rinpoche*

'om mani padme hum' – this mantra means 'hail to the jewel in the lotus' and is associated with *Chenresig* (Avalokiteshvara), patron deity of Tibet

oracle – in Tibetan Buddhism an oracle serves as a medium for protective deities, as in the State Oracle of Nechung Monastery near Drepung, Lhasa. The State Oracle was consulted on all important matters of state.

Pandita – a title conferred on great scholars of Buddhism, as in the Sakya Pandita

parikrama – the Hindu equivalent of a *kora*

PLA – People's Liberation Army (Chinese army)

PRC – People's Republic of China

protector deities – (chojung in Tibetan) deities who can manifest themselves in either male or female forms and serve to protect Buddhist teachings and followers. They may be either wrathful aspects of enlightened beings or worldly powers who have been tamed by *Tantric* masters.

PSB – Public Security Bureau. The Chinese term is 'gonganju'.

puk – Tibetan for 'cave'

pure lands – otherworldly realms that are the domains of *buddhas*. They are realms completely free of suffering, and in the popular Buddhist imagination are probably something like the Christian heaven.

Qiang – proto-Tibetan tribes that troubled the borders of the Chinese empire

Qomolangma – Tibetan name for Mt Everest as transliterated by the Chinese; also spelt 'Chomolangma'

Qu – Chinese term for the administrative district Shannan Qu (around Tsetang)

ranjung – self-manifesting or self-arising. For example, a rock spire could be a ranjung *chörten*.

rebirth – a condition of the *Wheel of Life*; all beings experience limitless rebirths until they achieve enlightenment

regent – a representative of an incarnate *lama* who presides over a monastic community during the *lama's* minority. Regents came to play an important political role in the *Gelugpa* lamaist government.

ri – Tibetan for 'mountain'

Rigsum Gonpo – trinity of *bodhisattvas* consisting of *Chenresig* (Avalokiteshvara), *Jampelyang* (Manjushri) and *Chana Dorje* (Vajrapani)

Rinpoche – literally 'high in esteem', a title bestowed on highly revered *lamas*. Such *lamas* are usually incarnate but need not be.

ritrö – hermitage

RMB – acronym for Renminbi or 'people's money', the currency of China

rogyapas – the 'body-breakers' who prepare bodies for *sky burial*

sadhu – an Indian ascetic who has renounced all attachments

Saga Dawa – festival held at the full moon of the fourth lunar month to celebrate the enlightenment of *Sakyamuni* (Sakya Thukpa)

Sakyapa – Tibetan Buddhist order associated with Sakya Monastery and founded in the 11th century; also known as the Red Hats

samsara – 'kyor dumi' in Tibetan; the cycle of birth, death and *rebirth*

Samye – the first Buddhist monastery in Tibet, founded by King *Trisong Detsen* in the 8th century

sang – incense

Sangha – community of Buddhist monks or nuns

sangkang – pot-bellied incense burners

Sanskrit – ancient language of India, with a complex grammar and rich vocabulary; a classical mode of expression with the status that Latin had in earlier Western society

self-arising – thought to have been created naturally by itself (ie not by humans); often applied to rock carvings; see also *ranjung*

shabje – footprint

Shambhala – the mythical great northern paradise, near the Kunlun mountains. The modern era consists of 32 kings of Shambhala. We are in the reign of the 29th king at present. There will be a terrible war in the reign of the 32nd king, followed by a great period of peace and enlightenment.

Shangshung – ancient kingdom of western Tibet and place of origin of the *Bön* faith

shedra – Buddhist college

sky burial – Tibetan funerary practice of chopping up the corpses of the dead in designated high places (dürtro) and leaving them for the birds

stupa – see *chörten*

sutra – Buddhist scriptures that record the teachings of the Historical Buddha, *Sakyamuni* (Sakya Thukpa)

Tantra – scriptures and oral lineages associated with *Tantric* Buddhism

Tantric – of Tantric Buddhism, a movement combining mysticism with Buddhist scripture

TAR – Tibetan Autonomous Region

Tengyur – a Tibetan Buddhist canonical text that collects together commentaries on the teachings of *Sakyamuni* (Sakya Thukpa)

terma – 'discovered' or 'revealed' teachings; teachings that have been hidden until the world is ready to receive them

terton – discoverer of *terma*

thamzing – 'struggle sessions', a misconceived Chinese tool for changing the ideological orientation of individuals; ultimately a coercive tool that encouraged deceit under the threat of torture

thangka – a Tibetan religious painting usually framed by a silk brocade

Theravada – see *Hinayana*

thugpa – traditional Tibetan noodle dish

torana – halo-like garland that surrounds Buddhist statues
torma – offerings of sculptured *tsampa* cakes
trapa – Tibetan for 'monk'
tratsang – monastic college
Tripa – the post of abbot at Ganden Monastery; head of the *Gelugpa* order
trulku – incarnate *lama*
tsampa – roasted-barley flour, traditional staple of the Tibetan people
Tsang – traditional province to the west of *Ü*, with Shigatse as its capital
tsangpo – large river
tso – Tibetan for 'lake'
tsuglhakhang – literally 'grand temple', but often specifically the *Jokhang* of Lhasa
TTB – Tibetan Tourism Bureau

Ü – traditional province to the east of *Tsang*, with Lhasa as its capital
Ütsang – the area comprising the provinces of *Ü* and *Tsang*, also incorporating *Ngari*, or western Tibet; effectively central Tibet, the political, historical and agricultural heartland of Tibet

Vajrayana – literally the 'diamond vehicle', a branch of *Mahayana* Buddhism that finds a more direct route to bodhisattvahood through identification with meditational deities

Wheel of Life – this term refers to the cyclical nature of existence and the six realms where *rebirth* take place. The Wheel of Life is often depicted in monasteries.

yabyum – *Tantric* sexual union, symbolising the mental union of female insight and male compassion. Fierce deities are often depicted in yabyum with their consorts.
yidam – see *meditational deity*; may also have the function of being a personal protector deity that looks over an individual or family
yogin – 'yoga' in *Sanskrit* refers to a 'union' with the fundamental nature of reality. For Tibetan Buddhists this can be achieved through meditative techniques and through identification with a meditational deity. A yogin is an adept of such techniques.
yuan – unit of Chinese currency

zhaodaisuo – Chinese for 'guesthouse', usually a basic hostel

Behind the Scenes

THIS BOOK

For this 6th edition of *Tibet* Michael Kohn updated the Ü and Eastern Tibet (Kham) chapters. Bradley Mayhew, who has worked on the last three editions of Tibet, coordinated this edition. Bradley researched the Lhasa, Western Tibet (Ngari), Tsang, Roads to Tibet and Gateway Cities chapters, and updated the rest of the book. The Trekking chapter was written by John Bellezza.

THANKS from the Authors

Bradley Mayhew Many thanks to Chris Walker and his team for generating the Tibetan script for the majority of the headings in this book. Best wishes to Amy Frey and Matt McGarvey from the Tibet Poverty Alleviation Fund (TPAF); all the best with your excellent projects in Tibet. Thanks also to Sonam as always, our great driver Dawa and the ever-grinning Namse for a fine trip out to Kailash.

Thanks also to Eva Gerlach for keeping me up to date with events in Lhasa and to Katherine Thornton for hotel updates. Cheers to Cheyney 'Hughass' Steininger for info on his vagabonding overlanding trips through all places forbidden and thanks to David Jennings for joining me on a frozen trip out to Yading Nature Reserve.

In Kathmandu my thanks as always to Rajeev Shrestra of Wayfarers and *namaste* to Rajan Simkhada and Ramchandra from the company Earthbound Expeditions.

At Lonely Planet my thanks to Katja Gaskell for updated information from parts of western Sichuan.

Michael Kohn Thanks to Janine Eberle for packing me off on another great assignment and fellow writer Bradley Mayhew for advice, camaraderie and shared beers in Lhasa. Thanks also in the Melbourne office to Shahara Ahmed, Will Gourlay and Danielle North.

On the road, Brad Stevens made a fine travel partner in Chengdu and Nam-tso. Paul Voller, David Duggett, Karl Lenz and Stijn Urkens shared the ride out to Samye and back, and survived the trip despite being danced upon by the demons of Mindroling Monastery! Sarah Chung and Brett Voegele were great drinking companions in Lhasa. A big thanks to Gary Poon for help all over Eastern Tibet and for coping with numerous misadventures on mountainsides and in remote river valleys.

Thanks also to Lhasa long-timers, especially Matt McGarvey and Sienna Craig. Tashi Tsering lent much insight into Tibetan culture. Chris Walker helped with the script. Thanks also to local tourism experts Dorjee Gyaltsen, Lhakhpa and Baasan. In California, thanks to Susan and Stephen Kohn, Norm, and most of all, to Baigalmaa.

CREDITS

This title was commissioned and developed in Lonely Planet's Melbourne office by Janine Eberle. Cartography for this guide was developed by Shahara Ahmed. Will Gourlay and Stefanie DiTrocchio assessed the manuscript.

Coordinating editor Danielle North was assisted by Andrew Bain, Yvonne Byron, Laura Gibb, Margedd Heliosz, Piers Kelly and Kate McLeod. Coordinating cartographer Malisa Plesa was assisted by

---

THE LONELY PLANET STORY

The story begins with a classic travel adventure: Tony and Maureen Wheeler's 1972 journey across Europe and Asia to Australia. There was no useful information about the overland trail then, so Tony and Maureen published the first Lonely Planet guidebook to meet a growing need.

From a kitchen table, Lonely Planet has grown to become the largest independent travel publisher in the world, with offices in Melbourne (Australia), Oakland (USA) and London (UK). Today Lonely Planet guidebooks cover the globe. There is an ever-growing list of books and information in a variety of media. Some things haven't changed. The main aim is still to make it possible for adventurous travellers to get out there – to explore and better understand the world.

At Lonely Planet we believe travellers can make a positive contribution to the countries they visit – if they respect their host communities and spend their money wisely. Every year 5% of company profit is donated to charities around the world.

Laurie Mikkelsen. The book was laid out by Yvonne Bischofberger (coordinator) and Pablo Gastar; Yvonne also created the colour pages. Laura Gibb and Vicki Beale assisted in layout. Tibetan script was checked by Sandup Tsering. Tamsin Wilson designed the cover. Sonya Brooke did the cover artwork and Wayne Murphy designed the back-cover map. Project manager Chris Love kept an eye on the whole project.

Thanks to Jodie Martire and Quentin Frayne for the language chapter, to Mark Germanchis and Lachlan Ross for technical support, and to Nicholas Stebbing for his advice on the Tibetan language and Rebecca Lalor for help with Chinese. Thanks also to the managers involved: Kerryn Burgess (editorial), Shahara Ahmed (cartography), and Adriana Mamnarella and Sally Darmody (layout).

THANKS from Lonely Planet
Many thanks to the travellers who used the last edition and wrote to us with helpful hints, useful advice and interesting anecdotes:

A Claudine Alberti, Victoria Almiroty, Frida Andrae, Muneeza Aumir **B** Wolfgang Bayer, Marie-Nathalie Beaudoin, Inger-Anne Becker Wold, Rachel Beit-Arie, Illla Bekel, Carmen Belmonte, Oran Bertelsen, Juergen Birnkammer, Hugo Bouman, Bernhard Bouzek, Titus Brand, Marek Brejl, Anthony Brown, Majella Butler **C** Paul Cammaert, Andy Carn, Marq Chapman, Dean Clarke, Neil Cloake, Robyn Cook, Alistair Cunningham **D** Dom Davey, Howard Davies, Rimli & Sushil Dawka, Paul di Stefano, Annemarie Dijk, T R Discombe, Steffi Doering, Anna Dowdall, Filip Dvoracek **E** Amy Fisner, Karsten Eller **F** Daren Fawkes, Elinor Feldman, Michel Findhammer, Taryn Firkser, Julie French **G** Sean Geiger, Mark Griffiths, Karen Groves **H** Paul Haddock, Eyal Harel, Cecilia Harlitz, Manfred Hartmann, Jon Hartsel, Koe Kok Hau, Nicole Havranek, Jianhui He, Kerry Hennigan, Bengt Hildebrand, Thea Hill, Chris Holmes, Polly Holmes, Jeff Homme, Susanne Hoorn, Jenny Hu, Adam Hughes **J** Steven James, Amanda Justice **K** Patricia Kelly, Wouter Kers, C Kim, Paul Koetsawang, Pamela Krone-Davis, Tessie & Dennis Kuiper **L** Robert Leitz, Angela Li, Mei Jiun Liu, Martin Lundgren, Jason Lynn **M** Christine Maier, Martin Maranus, Bronwyn McEwen, Robert McKelleher, John McKirdy, Daniel Meier-Behrmann, Arjan Meijer, Marieke Meijer, Matteo Miele, Sarah Mihailovich, Ariane Minnaar, Dennis Mogerman, Kira Moriah, Kathryn Morris **N** Jorand Nadege, Ciska Nijland, Alex Nikolic **O** Andreas Osterbye **P** Tom Partridge, Carlo & Emanuela Paschetto, Mario Pavesi, Bridget Phelps, Elisabetta Piormarta **R** Anita Rau, Fitzcarl Reid, Peter Reimann, Angela Claire Roberts, Jay Ruchamkin **S** Sebastian Schwertner, Girish Shahane, Anneke Sips, Jeroen Slikker, Frans Spijkers, Viktor Streicher, Joanne Sugiono **T** Peter A Tanner, Myrtha Sukristina Tirtadihardja, Scott Tuurie **V** Paul van Mechelen, Peter van Nes, Alan van Raalte, Richard Verbeek, Clem Vetters **W** Reto Wagner, Jim & Jill Waits, Marci Welton, Frank Wheby, Camilla White, Rogier Wilms, Jan Winning, Aleksandra & Georg Winterberger, Lori Woods **Y** Ryan Young, Nitzan Yudan **Z** Su Zhang, Wierd Zijlstra

SEND US YOUR FEEDBACK

We love to hear from travellers – your comments keep us on our toes and help make our books better. Our well-travelled team reads every word on what you loved or loathed about this book. Although we cannot reply individually to postal submissions, we always guarantee that your feedback goes straight to the appropriate authors, in time for the next edition. Each person who sends us information is thanked in the next edition – and the most useful submissions are rewarded with a free book.

To send us your updates – and find out about Lonely Planet events, newsletters and travel news – visit our award-winning web site: **www.lonelyplanet.com/feedback**

Note: We may edit, reproduce and incorporate your comments in Lonely Planet products such as guidebooks, websites and digital products, so let us know if you don't want your comments reproduced or your name acknowledged. For a copy of our privacy policy visit www.lonelyplanet.com/privacy

ACKNOWLEDGMENTS
Many thanks to the following for the use of their content:

Globe on back cover © Mountain High Maps 1993 Digital Wisdom, Inc.

Index

INDEX

000 Map pages
000 Location of colour photographs

INDEX

360

MAP LEGEND

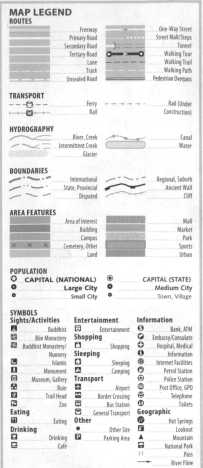

ROUTES

- Freeway
- Primary Road
- Secondary Road
- Tertiary Road
- Lane
- Track
- Unsealed Road
- One-Way Street
- Street Mall/Steps
- Tunnel
- Walking Tour
- Walking Trail
- Walking Path
- Pedestrian Overpass

TRANSPORT

- Ferry
- Rail
- Rail (Under Construction)

HYDROGRAPHY

- River, Creek
- Intermittent Creek
- Glacier
- Canal
- Water

BOUNDARIES

- International
- State, Provincial
- Disputed
- Regional, Suburb
- Ancient Wall
- Cliff

AREA FEATURES

- Area of Interest
- Building
- Campus
- Cemetery, Other
- Land
- Mall
- Market
- Park
- Sports
- Urban

POPULATION

- ◎ CAPITAL (NATIONAL)
- ● Large City
- ● Small City
- ◉ CAPITAL (STATE)
- ◉ Medium City
- ◉ Town, Village

SYMBOLS

Sights/Activities
- Buddhist
- Bön Monastery
- Buddhist Monastery/Nunnery
- Islamic
- Monument
- Museum, Gallery
- Ruin
- Trail Head
- Zoo

Eating
- Eating

Drinking
- Drinking
- Café

Entertainment
- Entertainment

Shopping
- Shopping

Sleeping
- Sleeping
- Camping

Transport
- Airport
- Border Crossing
- Bus Station
- General Transport

Other
- Other Site
- Parking Area

Information
- Bank, ATM
- Embassy/Consulate
- Hospital, Medical
- Information
- Internet Facilities
- Petrol Station
- Police Station
- Post Office, GPO
- Telephone
- Toilets

Geographic
- Hot Springs
- Lookout
- Mountain
- National Park
- Pass
- River Flow

LONELY PLANET OFFICES

Australia
Head Office
Locked Bag 1, Footscray, Victoria 3011
☎ 03 8379 8000, fax 03 8379 8111
talk2us@lonelyplanet.com.au

USA
150 Linden St, Oakland, CA 94607
☎ 510 893 8555, toll free 800 275 8555
fax 510 893 8572, info@lonelyplanet.com

UK
72-82 Rosebery Ave,
Clerkenwell, London EC1R 4RW
☎ 020 7841 9000, fax 020 7841 9001
go@lonelyplanet.co.uk

Published by Lonely Planet Publications Pty Ltd
ABN 36 005 607 983

© Lonely Planet 2005

© photographers as indicated 2005

Cover photographs: Buddhist monks of the Gelugpa (Yellow Hat) order, Jeremy Hunter/Impact Photos (front); Gyantse Kumbum and Pelkor Chöde Monastery, Chris Beall/LPI (back). Many of the images in this guide are available for licensing from Lonely Planet Images: www.lonelyplanetimages.com

Printed through Colorcraft Ltd, Hong Kong.
Printed in China